THE TWO HORIZONS

THE TWO HORIZONS

*New Testament Hermeneutics
and Philosophical Description
with Special Reference to
Heidegger, Bultmann, Gadamer,
and Wittgenstein*

by

ANTHONY C. THISELTON

With a Foreword by Professor J. B. Torrance

THE PATERNOSTER PRESS
CARLISLE

WILLIAM B. EERDMANS PUBLISHING COMPANY
GRAND RAPIDS, MICHIGAN

First published 1980 by The Paternoster Press
PO Box 300, Carlisle, Cumbria CA3 0QS.
First American edition published through special
arrangement with Paternoster by
Wm. B. Eerdmans Publishing Co.
255 Jefferson Ave. S.E.
Grand Rapids, Michigan 49503.

Reprinted April 1993

Printed in the United States of America

British Library Cataloguing in Publication Data

Thiselton, Anthony C.
  The two horizons.
  1. Bible. New Testament — Hermeneutics
  I. Title
  225.6'3'0904   BS2331

  ISBN 0 85364 557 4

Library of Congress Cataloging in Publication Data

Thiselton, Anthony C.
  The two horizons.

  Bibliography: p. 447.
  Includes indexes.
  1. Bible. N. T. — Hermeneutics. 2. Hermeneutics.
3. Heidegger, Martin, 1889-1976. 4. Bultmann, Rudolf
Karl, 1884-1976. 5. Gadamer, Hans Georg, 1900-
6. Wittgenstein, Ludwig, 1889-1951. I. Title.
BS476.T46   1979   225.6'01   79-14387

  ISBN 0-8028-0006-8

Contents

Foreword

One of the central concerns in contemporary theology and biblical studies has been the interest in linguistics and hermeneutics. It is impossible to do genuine scientific biblical study today without raising questions of hermeneutics—the science of interpretation—and we cannot raise the question of interpretation without raising questions about the nature of knowledge, the use of language, and the scientific and ontological presuppositions operative in the mind of the exegete. This book not only gives an excellent survey of the field but examines with great thoroughness the contribution of philosophy to the debate, to ask how far philosophy can provide us with tools (a) to elucidate the hermeneutical task, (b) to unfold the meaning of parts of the New Testament, and (c) to lead us beyond semantics and traditional linguistics by enlarging the interpreter's prior understanding and conceptual capacities.

The pioneer work of Schleiermacher in hermeneutics arising out of his study of literary texts, followed by the application of this by Dilthey to the human studies in general (history, sociology, art, and religion), and by Rudolf Bultmann to the New Testament, highlighted the fact that the problem of hermeneutics is twofold, relating to the interpreter as well as to the text. This raises three main issues: the problem of historical distance between ourselves and the biblical writers; questions about the role of theology in interpretation; and the relation of hermeneutics to language. In the light of these concerns, Dr. Thiselton in a masterly way examines the work of Bultmann, Gadamer, Heidegger, and Wittgenstein, comparing and contrasting the last two philosophers, each in the light of their earlier and later work.

The book shows thorough familiarity with the many authors examined and a first-hand acquaintance with the work of writers in linguistics, New Testament language and literature, and contemporary philosophy (Continental, British, and American). Dr. Thiselton has a remarkable gift of clear exposition and a dialectical ability which with his critical insight gives this most important work a remarkable unity.

I had the privilege of acting as one of the external examiners for Dr. Thiselton when he presented his work on the above subject as a Ph.D. thesis and regard it as one of the most competent dissertations I have ever read. I am convinced that it will prove invaluable for students and scholars of different disciplines as a first-class account of some of the major areas in modern theology. It provides an admirable survey in depth of these important subjects. The English-speaking world desperately needs just such a study.

J. B. TORRANCE
Professor of Systematic Theology
University of Aberdeen

Acknowledgments

The substance of the present work, which has since been revised, was submitted as a Ph.D. thesis to the University of Sheffield. I should like first of all to express my thanks to my two external examiners, Professor John Macquarrie of the University of Oxford and Professor James Torrance of the University of Aberdeen, for their encouragement in the work of preparing this study for publication. In particular I am grateful to Professor Torrance for writing such a generous Foreword to the book, and to both of them for their very kind and constructive comments on my work. My warm thanks are also due to my friend and former colleague Professor Colin Brown of Fuller Theological Seminary, California, for going carefully through the whole manuscript and making a number of valuable suggestions, which I have adopted.

I am deeply grateful to my wife Rosemary for her constant and ready support and encouragement throughout this whole endeavor. She has spent considerable time and effort in typing various parts of the manuscript, in checking through material, and in helping with the compilation of the indices. Both she and our three children have had to put up with my spending long hours at my desk which might well have been spent with them. I should also like to acknowledge the part played by the very congenial and happy atmosphere in the Department of Biblical Studies in the University of Sheffield, where I have received much stimulus from the researches of my colleagues and many hours of constructive theological discussion with them. I owe much to the kindness of our Department Head, Professor James Atkinson.

I should also like to express my heartfelt gratitude to the Directors of Paternoster Press Ltd., Exeter, and of Wm. B. Eerdmans, Grand Rapids, Michigan, for undertaking to publish a volume of this size and level of technicality. In particular Mr. Jeremy Mudditt, Managing Director of Paternoster Press, and Mr. Peter Cousins, Editorial Director, have shown me every kindness in constantly giving me their help, advice, and encouragement at all stages of preparing this manuscript for the press.

At three or four points the argument of these chapters overlaps with works which I have already published elsewhere. I am grateful for permission to use some of the arguments and, here and there, even some of the sentences which occur in my two essays in *New Testament Interpretation*, edited by I. Howard Marshall (Paternoster Press, Exeter, and Eerdmans, Grand Rapids, Mich., 1977, pp. 75-104 and 308-33). At one point my argument also overlaps with part of my earlier article "The Semantics of Biblical Language as an Aspect of Hermeneutics," published in *Faith and Thought* CIII (1976), 108-20. Originally my material on justification by faith in Paul overlapped significantly with a paper delivered at the Fifth International Congress on Biblical Studies (1973) entitled "On the Logical Grammar of Justification in Paul," which is still forthcoming in *Studia Evangelica*, published by the Berlin Academy. However, this material has been thoroughly revised, expanded, and rewritten in the form in which it appears in the present study.

ANTHONY C. THISELTON
Department of Biblical Studies
University of Sheffield

Abbreviations

An.	*Analysis*
A.T.R.	*Anglican Theological Review*
B.B.	L. Wittgenstein, *The Blue and Brown Books. Preliminary Studies for the Philosophical Investigations.* Blackwell, Oxford, ²1969
B.J.R.L.	*Bulletin of the Journal of the John Rylands Library*
B.Q.T.	W. Pannenberg, *Basic Questions in Theology.* 3 vols. Eng. S.C.M., London, 1970, 1971, and 1973
B.T.	M. Heidegger, *Being and Time.* Eng. Blackwell, Oxford, 1962
B.T.B.	*Biblical Theology Bulletin*
C.B.Q.	*Catholic Biblical Quarterly*
Cert.	L. Wittgenstein, *On Certainty.* Germ. and Eng. Blackwell, Oxford, 1969
C.J.T.	*Canadian Journal of Theology*
E.B.	M. Heidegger, *Existence and Being.* Eng. Vision Press, London, ³1968
E.F.	R. Bultmann, *Existence and Faith,* Fontana edn., Collins, London, 1964
E.P.T.	R. Bultmann, *Essays Philosophical and Theological.* S.C.M., London, 1955
Exp.T.	*Expository Times*
F.U.	R. Bultmann, *Faith and Understanding* I. Eng. S.C.M., London, 1969
G.u.V.	R. Bultmann, *Glauben und Verstehen. Gesammelte Aufsätze.* 4 vols. Mohr, Tübingen, 1964-65
Holz.	M. Heidegger, *Holzwege.* Klostermann, Frankfurt, 1950
Herm.	E. Fuchs, *Hermeneutik.* Mohr, Tübingen, ⁴1970
H.T.R.	*Harvard Theological Review*
I.M.	M. Heidegger, *An Introduction to Metaphysics.* Eng. Yale University Press, New Haven, 1959
Int.	*Interpretation*
I.P.Q.	*International Philosophical Quarterly*
I.T.T.L.	G. Ebeling, *Introduction to a Theological Theory of Language.* Eng. Collins, London, 1973

J.B.L.	*Journal of Biblical Literature*
J.B.S.P.	*Journal of the British Society for Phenomenology*
J.H.I.	*Journal of the History of Ideas*
J.H.P.	*Journal of the History of Philosophy*
J.Ph.	*Journal of Philosophy*
J.R.	*Journal of Religion*
J.T.C.	*Journal for Theology and the Church*
J.T.S.	*Journal of Theological Studies*
K.M.	H.-W. Bartsch (ed.), *Kerygma und Myth.* 2 vols. S.P.C.K., London, ²1964 and 1962
K.u.M.	H.-W. Bartsch (ed.), *Kerygma und Mythos, Ein theologisches Gespräch.* 6 vols. Reich & Heidrich, Evangelischer Verlag, Hamburg, 1948 onwards
L.C.A.P.R.	L. Wittgenstein, *Lectures and Conversations on Aesthetics, Psychology and Religious Belief.* Blackwell, Oxford, 1966
M.W.	*Man and World*
N.H.	James M. Robinson and J. B. Cobb, Jr. (eds.), *New Frontiers in Theology: II, The New Hermeneutic.* Harper & Row, New York, 1964
N.	L. Wittgenstein, *Notebooks 1914-16.* Eng. Blackwell, Oxford, 1961
N.T.S.	*New Testament Studies*
O.W.L.	M. Heidegger, *On the Way to Language.* Eng. Harper & Row, New York, 1971
P.A.S.S.	*Proceedings of the Aristotelian Society Supplement*
P.B.	L. Wittgenstein, *Philosophische Bemerkungen.* Blackwell, Oxford, 1964
P.G.	L. Wittgenstein, *Philosophical Grammar.* Blackwell, Oxford, 1974
P.H.	H.-G. Gadamer, *Philosophical Hermeneutics.* Eng. University of California Press, Berkeley, 1976
P.I.	L. Wittgenstein, *Philosophical Investigations.* Germ. and Eng. Blackwell, Oxford, ³1967
P.L.T.	M. Heidegger, *Poetry, Language, and Thought.* Harper & Row, New York, 1971
Ph.R.	*Philosophical Review*
Ph.T.	*Philosophy Today*
R.E.	*Review and Expositor*
R.F.M.	L. Wittgenstein, *Remarks on the Foundations of Mathematics.* Germ. and Eng. Blackwell, Oxford, 1956
R.M.	*Review of Metaphysics*
R.St.	*Religious Studies*
S.H.J.	E. Fuchs, *Studies of the Historical Jesus.* Eng. S.C.M., London, 1964
S.J.T.	*Scottish Journal of Theology*
T.	L. Wittgenstein, *Tractatus Logico-Philosophicus.* Germ. and Eng. Routledge & Kegan Paul, London, 1961

Th.T.	*Theology Today*
T.B.	*Tyndale Bulletin*
T.M.	H.-G. Gadamer, *Truth and Method*. Eng. Sheed & Ward, London, 1975 (Eng. trans. of *W.M.*)
T.N.T.	R. Bultmann, *Theology of the New Testament*. 2 vols. Eng. S.C.M., London, 1952 and 1955
T.R.B.	C. W. Kegley (ed.), *The Theology of Rudolf Bultmann*. S.C.M., London, 1966
U.A.B.	D. E. Nineham, *The Use and Abuse of the Bible. A Study of the Bible in an Age of Rapid Cultural Change*. Macmillan, London, 1976
U.S.	M. Heidegger, *Unterwegs zur Sprache*. Neske, Pfullingen, ²1960
U.S.Q.R.	*Union Seminary Quarterly Review*
V.u.A.	M. Heidegger, *Vorträge und Aufsätze*. Neske, Pfullingen, 1954
W.F.	G. Ebeling, *Word and Faith*. Eng. S.C.M., London, 1963
W.M.	H.-G. Gadamer, *Wahrheit und Methode. Grundzüge einer philosophischen Hermeneutik*. Mohr, Tübingen, ²1965
W.W.	M. Heidegger, *Vom Wesen der Wahrheit*. Klostermann, Frankfurt, 1954
Z.	L. Wittgenstein, *Zettel*. Germ. and Eng. Blackwell, Oxford, 1967
Z.N.W.	*Zeitschrift für die neutestamentliche Wissenschaft*
Z.Th.K.	*Zeitschrift für Theologie und Kirche*

Introduction

The nature and purpose of the present study has already been described in the very generous Foreword provided by Professor J. B. Torrance. There are only three specific points which require further explanation.

First of all, a comment must be made about the title *The Two Horizons*. The reason for this choice of title will emerge in section two of the first chapter, and still more explicitly in the chapter on Gadamer. Although the word has now become a technical term in hermeneutical theory, even in popular parlance "horizon" is used metaphorically to denote the limits of thought dictated by a given viewpoint or perspective. The goal of biblical hermeneutics is to bring about an active and meaningful engagement between the interpreter and text, in such a way that the interpreter's own horizon is re-shaped and enlarged. In one sense it is possible to speak, with Gadamer, of the goal of hermeneutics as a "fusion" of horizons. In practice, because the interpreter cannot leap out of the historical tradition to which he belongs, the two horizons can never become totally identical; at best they remain separate but close. Nevertheless the problem of historical distance and tradition should not give rise to undue pessimism. Even if the problems of hermeneutics are not trivial, neither are they insoluble, and there is always progress *towards* a fusion of horizons. The Bible can and does speak today, in such a way as to correct, reshape, and enlarge the interpreter's own horizons.

Secondly, a word of explanation is needed about the scope of this book, and the degree of originality (or lack of it) claimed for its various parts. As Professor Torrance stresses in his Foreword, the three chapters on hermeneutics and history, hermeneutics and theology, and hermeneutics and language do not constitute a digression from our main task. For no serious hermeneutical discussion can be complete without a consideration of these fundamental issues. At the same time, the most distinctive contribution of this book concerns the work of Heidegger, Bultmann, Gadamer, and especially Wittgenstein. I have tried to offer some original comments on the work of Heidegger, Bultmann, and Gadamer. But it is in the chapter on Wittgenstein that I believe my most distinctive work is to be found, partly in my comments on the significance of Wittgenstein for hermeneutical theory, and partly in my use of his writings to clarify conceptual problems in the New Testament itself.

Thirdly, our aim is certainly not to impose certain philosophical categories onto the biblical text. Indeed the point is precisely the reverse. A full awareness of the problems of hermeneutics provides a *defense against* the interpreter's so reading the text that he merely hears back echoes of his own attitudes or pre-judgments. As Ebeling reminds us, "According to Luther, the word of God always comes as *adversarius noster*, our adversary. It does not simply confirm and strengthen us in what we think we are and as what we wish to be taken for" *(I.T.T.L.,* p. 17).

Some fifteen years ago, Dennis Nineham wrote, "What I plead for is that we should have some biblical scholars . . . whose expertise is, if I may put it so, in the modern end of the problem. . . . What they might produce . . . would be of inestimable value to all serious students of the Bible" *(The Church's Use of the Bible,* S.P.C.K., London, 1963, p. 168). But it would be a pity if the only writers to respond to this kind of plea were those who felt deep pessimism about the capacity of the Bible to speak to men today. Far from making the hermeneutical task seem unimportant, the belief that God speaks through the Bible today makes hermeneutics all the more urgent a study. For viewed from this theological perspective, the Bible is seen neither as the mere past record of the religious beliefs and aspirations of men in the ancient world, nor as a trigger designed to spark off premature "applications" of men's own devising. To hear the Bible speak in its own right and with its due authority, the distinctive horizon of the text must be respected and differentiated in the first place from the horizon of the interpreter. This is not only a theological point. As we shall see from the writings of Gadamer, it also arises from general hermeneutical theory.

Why, then, is our study concerned with philosophy? Professor Torrance has answered this question briefly in the first paragraph of the Foreword. But we now turn to consider it more fully in the first two chapters of our study.

PART ONE

Introductory Questions

CHAPTER I

The Nature and Scope of the Subject

1. *Why Philosophical Description?*

Why should the interpreter of the New Testament concern himself with philosophy? Two objections come to mind immediately. First of all, interdisciplinary studies have become fashionable. Their increasing importance in biblical studies can be seen, for example, in the founding of the journal *Semeia* in 1974. Does the present study, therefore, represent only one more attempt to cash in on a current trend of fashion in a way which is artificially contrived?

Secondly, suspicions have been voiced in Christian theology from Tertullian onward that the use of philosophical concepts and categories corrupts an otherwise "pure" understanding of the biblical writings. Tertullian believed that the interpretation of Christian truth in philosophical terms could lead only to heresy. In our own day Helmut Thielicke has charged Rudolf Bultmann with this kind of error. He writes, "Whenever a non-Biblical principle derived from contemporary secular thought is applied to the interpretation of the Bible, the Bible's *facultas se ipsum interpretandi* is violated with fatal results. This is what happened in Kant's philosophy, and again in theological idealism. It is happening in Bultmann too."[1]

How strong are these two objections? To begin with, in practice the first is largely answered by the second. The very fact that Thielicke can make his accusation against Bultmann shows that the subject is a live issue. Quite apart from the work of earlier thinkers, it is simply a fact that Rudolf Bultmann and the exponents of the new hermeneutic have drawn

1. H. Thielicke, "The Restatement of New Testament Mythology" in *K.M.* I, 149. Cf. pp. 150-57 and, for a more recent discussion, *The Evangelical Faith* (Eng. Eerdmans, Grand Rapids, Michigan, 1974) I, 38-114.

on philosophical categories in their work on the New Testament. We cannot ignore this work and attempt to turn back the clock, even if we wished to do so. Bultmann himself readily admits how closely his New Testament studies are bound up with his interest in philosophy. It is not merely his opponents who stress this fact. He writes, "Heidegger's analysis of existence has become for me fruitful for hermeneutics, that is for the interpretation of the New Testament."[2] He adds, "I learned from him [Heidegger] not *what* theology has to say, but *how* it has to say it."[3]

With regard to the second objection, it is difficult to see how its validity can be assessed in practice unless the biblical interpreter is free to examine the philosophical categories which are in question. How can we assess whether Thielicke's view of Bultmann is correct unless we actually examine for ourselves the nature and extent of his indebtedness to Heidegger? But we cannot discover this unless we first inquire what it is that Bultmann has borrowed from Heidegger. Only then can we assess how his use of philosophy has influenced his New Testament interpretation. Purely exegetical study might suggest concrete instances of points at which Bultmann is right or wrong, but the underlying considerations which led him to his conclusions would not have been assessed. In any case, the need to examine the distinctively philosophical background emerges still more clearly when we see the need to disentangle what Bultmann owes to Heidegger from what he owes to the philosophy of Marburg Neo-Kantianism. This latter factor affects his attitude towards objectification and his proposals about demythologizing the New Testament.

Secondly, concepts drawn from philosophy also facilitate the description and critical appraisal of the hermeneutical task. This can be seen from the writings of the New Testament scholar Ernst Fuchs, the systematic theologian Gerhard Ebeling, and especially the philosopher Hans-Georg Gadamer. Fuchs, for example, makes much of the category of *Einverständnis,* variously rendered by different translators as "common understanding," "mutual understanding," and "empathy."[4] Ebeling, for his part, goes as far as to say: "Hermeneutics now takes the place of the classical epistemological theory. . . . For theology the hermeneutic problem is therefore today becoming the place of meeting with philosophy."[5]

2. R. Bultmann, "Reply to John Macquarrie, 'Philosophy and Theology in Bultmann's Thought' " in *T.R.B.,* p. 275.
3. R. Bultmann, "Reply to Götz Harbsmeier, 'The Theology of Rudolf Bultmann and its Relation to Philosophy' " in *ibid.,* p. 276.
4. E. Fuchs, *Herm.,* p. 136; and "The Hermeneutical Problem" in J. M. Robinson (ed.), *The Future of Our Religious Past: Essays in Honour of Rudolf Bultmann* (S.C.M., London, 1971), p. 270 (Germ. E. Dinkler, ed., *Zeit und Geschichte Dankesgabe an Rudolf Bultmann zum 80 Geburtstag,* Mohr, Tübingen, 1964, p. 360).
5. G. Ebeling, *W.F.,* p. 317.

Hans-Georg Gadamer's magisterial work *Wahrheit und Methode* has recently been translated into English, but without its German subtitle. The German editions carry the explanatory phrase *Grundzüge einer philosophischen Hermeneutik*. For Gadamer stresses that today we can no longer talk innocently about understanding an ancient text, or a past tradition, in isolation from a responsible consideration of the philosophical problems that have emerged with the rise of historical consciousness. Just as in New Testament studies we cannot ignore the work of Bultmann on hermeneutics, so in hermeneutics we cannot ignore the work of Wilhelm Dilthey and his philosophical successors on the nature of historical understanding. Gadamer re-examines the notion of *Verstehen* as a technical concept in philosophy and hermeneutics, and asks questions about the way in which both the interpreter and the text stand in given historical traditions.

While Dilthey represents a key point in the history of hermeneutics by underlining the historical aspect of the problem of understanding, an earlier turning point had been reached in the work of Friedrich Schleiermacher. The particular importance of Schleiermacher for hermeneutics has been demonstrated above all by Heinz Kimmerle, who is himself a former pupil of Gadamer. Kimmerle undertook some important original research on Schleiermacher's unpublished papers and expounded them in such a way as to lead to a reappraisal of his work. He writes, "The work of Schleiermacher constitutes a turning-point in the history of hermeneutics. Till then, hermeneutics was supposed to support, secure, and clarify an already accepted understanding. . . . In the thinking of Schleiermacher hermeneutics achieves the qualitatively different function of first of all making understanding possible, and deliberately initiating understanding in each individual case."[6]

Under the older view, hermeneutics was concerned with the formulation of "rules" to insure that a particular understanding of a text was an accurate one. But Schleiermacher showed that this presupposed a particular answer to the wider question of how any understanding, even a preliminary one, was possible. A man might possess all the linguistic and historical knowledge required in order to interpret a text, but still not be able to understand the text in question. Hence there is a wider and more philosophical dimension to the problem than the mere accumulation of linguistic and historical data, and the application of scientific rules of interpretation.

It is not surprising, then, that Ernst Fuchs, writing as a New Testament specialist, cites the philosophical writings of Heidegger and Gadamer, as well as works by Bultmann, Ebeling, and himself, when he

---

6. H. Kimmerle, "Hermeneutical Theory or Ontological Hermeneutics" in *J.T.C.* IV (ed. by R. Funk), 107; cf. pp. 108-21.

sets out the main literature on modern hermeneutics.[7] The same point emerges from the title of Richard Palmer's book: *Hermeneutics. Interpretation Theory in Schleiermacher, Dilthey, Heidegger and Gadamer.*[8] Philosophical concepts cannot be left out of account when we are attempting to formulate the tasks and problems of New Testament hermeneutics.

Philosophical description, thirdly, also enters the picture for a different reason. In addition to facilitating the description of hermeneutical tasks, philosophical categories may also be of service in the actual interpretation of New Testament texts. One of the best-known examples of this is Bultmann's use of existentialist categories in order to interpret Paul's view of man. For example, drawing partly on Heidegger's contrast between *existentialia* and "categories," Bultmann refuses to interpret σῶμα in substantival terms, when Paul clearly uses it to characterize *human* existence. Hence Bultmann concludes that σῶμα in Paul represents a way of being rather than a substance or a thing: "Man does not *have* a *soma;* he *is soma.*"[9]

Bultmann is not alone, however, in using existentialist categories to interpret specific New Testament passages. We may cite the work of two particular authors on the parables of Jesus. Geraint Vaughan Jones interprets the Parable of the Prodigal Son in this way (Luke 15:11-32).[10] The characters, Jones argues, come out of "the same pool of existence as our own experience."[11] Several key themes of existentialist philosophy emerge from the parable. The younger son undergoes experiences of estrangement, of longing, and of not-belonging. Character is indelibly marked by decision; for "the new self living in destitution and abandonment is in a sense different from the confident defiant self at the moment of departure."[12] Life becomes meaningless and empty without personal relations. The elder brother treats the prodigal son as a "type" to be dealt with by a standardized approach. Jones draws on a number of existentialist themes to bring the New Testament text to life.

A second author who calls for attention in this connection is Dan Otto Via. Via draws on existentialist themes to expound various parables, including that of the talents (Matt. 25:14-30).[13] The one-talent man, he points out, acted to preserve his own safety. Because he was paralyzed by

7. E. Fuchs, "The Hermeneutical Problem," *The Future of Our Religious Past*, pp. 269-70.
8. R. E. Palmer, *Hermeneutics. Interpretation Theory in Schleiermacher, Dilthey, Heidegger and Gadamer* (Northwestern University Press, Evanston, 1969) (Studies in Phenomenology and Existential Philosophy).
9. R. Bultmann, *T.N.T.* I, 194; cf. pp. 192-203.
10. G. V. Jones, *The Art and Truth of the Parables* (S.P.C.K., London, 1964), pp. 167-205.
11. *Ibid.*, p. 167.
12. *Ibid.*, p. 175.
13. D. O. Via, Jr., *The Parables. Their Literary and Existential Dimension* (Fortress Press, Philadelphia, 1967), pp. 113-22.

anxiety, he would not risk stepping into the unknown and trying to fulfil his own possibilities. He represses his own sense of guilt, and projects it onto his employer. He views the whole universe as inimical to human enterprise, and he chooses to understand himself as one of life's victims. Because he refuses to accept responsibility, responsibility is denied him, and his one talent is taken away. "We see the following connected movement: *from* the refusal to take a risk, *through* repressed guilt which is projected onto someone else, *to* the loss of opportunity for meaningful existence."[14] Via concludes, "The refusal to risk and the concomitant inability to hold oneself responsible become unfaith. The man who retreats from risking his life wants to provide his own security."[15]

We are not suggesting that Via could not have expounded the parable in this way without drawing on existentialist categories of thought. Indeed, if this were the case, such categories would presumably falsify its original meaning, by imposing a distinctively modern interpretation onto the parable. Nevertheless, philosophy, as Wittgenstein expresses it, often affects "the way we look at things."[16] It sheds light on "facts which no one has doubted, and which have only gone unremarked because they are always before our eyes."[17] This seems to have occurred in Via's exposition. There can be little question that through the work of such writers as Bultmann, Jones, and Via, we notice features of the biblical text which, although they were always there, may otherwise have escaped our attention, and therefore not been fully grasped. Later in this present study I shall attempt to show how certain concepts in Wittgenstein's philosophy shed fresh light on the Pauline doctrine of justification by grace through faith, in such a way that the same material can be seen from a fresh angle.

Fourthly, light is shed on the biblical text not only by the study of particular languages, such as Hebrew and Greek, but also by inquiries about the nature of language as such. Admittedly questions about the nature of language arise in linguistics no less than in philosophy. But these questions are not exactly the same as those raised by philosophers. I have discussed some of them in other studies.[18] Meanwhile, philosophers ask penetrating questions about the nature of language. One of Heidegger's essays explicitly bears the title "The Nature of Language," and in his later writings Wittgenstein is largely concerned with particular relations between language and life.[19] Forms of life, Wittgenstein observes, condi-

14. *Ibid.*, p. 119.
15. *Ibid.*, p. 120.
16. L. Wittgenstein, *P.I.*, sect. 122.
17. L. Wittgenstein, *R.F.M.* I, sect. 141.
18. A. C. Thiselton, "The Supposed Power of Words in the Biblical Writings" in *J.T.S.* N.S. XXV (1974), 283-99; and "Semantics and the New Testament" in I. H. Marshall (ed.), *New Testament Interpretation* (Paternoster Press, Exeter, and Eerdmans, Grand Rapids, Mich, 1977).
19. M. Heidegger, "The Nature of Language" in *O.W.L.*, pp. 57-108.

tion the ways in which language functions within the settings to which
these forms of life give rise.

The relevance to biblical studies of philosophical inquiries about
language is noted both from the side of New Testament studies and from
the side of philosophy. In the first introductory number of *Semeia* Amos
Wilder takes pains to explain why the biblical scholar should concern
himself with fields as diverse as structuralism, social anthropology,
folklore studies, and linguistics, and asserts that the one common denominator in all these varied studies is "the new concern . . . with a better
understanding of language in all its aspects."[20] This is why they all
concern the biblical specialist. He also notes that many of the earlier
pioneers of biblical studies, including Herder, Gunkel, and Norden, were
more interested than many of their successors in "how language
works."[21] Hence, Wilder concludes, the New Testament scholar today
has ample precedent for returning to these broader but basic concerns,
and need not feel that he is merely pursuing novelty for its own sake. The
Roman Catholic biblical scholar Roger Lapointe similarly insists, "The
hermeneutic question is interdisciplinary. It is correlated to philosophy,
theology, exegesis, literary criticism, the human sciences in general."[22]

From the side of philosophy Paul Ricoeur stresses the necessary
connections between hermeneutics, philosophy, and the study of the
nature of language. He writes, "In what way do these exegetic debates
concern philosophy? In this way: that exegesis implies an entire theory of
signs and significations." He adds, "Hermeneutics . . . relates the technical problems of textual exegesis to the more general problems of meaning
and language."[23]

We return, fifthly, to the problem which we outlined first, namely that
of suspicions about the danger of distorting the meaning of the biblical
text by imposing philosophical categories onto it from outside. James Barr
discusses this kind of problem in his book *Old and New in Interpretation*.[24] He compares the "purist" or "internalist" approach with the
"externalist" one, and argues that there are more dangers in the former
than in the latter. He comments, "The fundamental error in purist thinking is the supposition that by taking an 'internal' stance we somehow
guard against error."[25] One such example of error, in Barr's judgment,

20. A. M. Wilder, "An Experimental Journal for Biblical Criticism. An Introduction" in
Semeia I (1974), 3.
21. *Ibid.*, p. 4.
22. R. Lapointe, "Hermeneutics Today" in *B.T.B.* II (1972), 107.
23. P. Ricoeur, *The Conflict of Interpretations, Essays in Hermeneutics,* ed. by D. Ihde
(Northwestern University Press, Evanston, 1974), p. 4.
24. J. Barr, *Old and New in Interpretation. A Study of the Two Testaments* (S.C.M.,
London, 1966), pp. 171-92.
25. *Ibid.*, p. 173.

even within the purist or internal approach, is that of exaggerating the supposed distinctiveness of Hebraic thought, and of contrasting it with Greek perspectives in ways which cannot be supported. "The idealization of the Hebraic," he urges, "is a complacent self-projection of the purist consciousness."[26] On the other hand, from the other side it can be argued that "the use of concepts and categories taken from 'without' the Bible is both natural and necessary."[27]

As Barr himself is very quick to assert, this point should not be reduced to the level of the loaded and inaccurate slogan that presuppositions are the key to all that is done in the handling of a text. We are not simply arguing that since everyone has his presuppositions, these might as well be philosophical ones. We are following Barr in his claim that categories which come from outside the Bible are not necessarily wrong or inappropriate. The critic might as well argue that it would have been inappropriate to describe the speech of Molière's Monsieur Jourdain as "prose" before Monsieur Jourdain himself had been informed that it was prose he was speaking. Categories of grammar, such as "aorist middle," or categories of philosophy, such as "open-textured concept," do not depend for their applicability on whether the speaker or writer is aware that he is using them. They may still be "external" to the text, but this use clarifies rather than distorts the meaning.

There is one particular theological school, namely that of the conservative American writer Cornelius Van Til, which may well view with disfavor any attempt to utilize insights from philosophies that are not distinctively Christian.[28] It would take us too far beyond the confines of the present study to attempt to respond in detail to Van Til's position. We agree with his emphasis on the central importance of Christian revelation for all aspects of life and thought. Nevertheless, we must first repeat our earlier point that criticisms about the use of philosophy in New Testament interpretation cannot be adequately assessed without considering the philosophical categories in question. Many of the standard criticisms brought against Bultmann, for example, turn out to be not arguments against his use of philosophy, but arguments against the use of a particular philosophy, such as that of Heidegger or Neo-Kantianism. Secondly, where we have attempted to draw more positively and constructively on philosophical categories, as is the case especially in our use of Wittgenstein, our concern is only to borrow from this thinker certain conceptual tools for the various tasks which we shall undertake in formulating hermeneutical theory and in expounding the text of the New Testament. To

26. *Ibid.*
27. *Ibid.*, p. 172.
28. Cf. C. Van Til, *The Defense of the Faith* (Presbyterian and Reformed Publishing Company, Philadelphia, 1955).

make constructive use of a particular philosopher's conceptual tools is not necessarily to subscribe to his view of the world. Even the New Testament writers themselves were willing to borrow *concepts* from the Graeco-Roman world around them in order to expound their distinctively Christian message.

2. *The Underlying Problem in Hermeneutics: The Two Horizons*

The term "hermeneutics" is in disfavor in some quarters, partly perhaps on the ground that it is no more than theological jargon for "interpretation." Admittedly the two terms are often interchangeable. Ebeling, for example, asserts, "The words 'interpretation' and 'hermeneutics' at bottom mean the same"; and C. F. Evans declares that " 'hermeneutics' . . . is only another word for exegesis or interpretation."[29] P. J. Achtemeier attempts to distinguish between exegesis, interpretation, and hermeneutics. He argues that while exegesis denotes inquiry into the meaning which a text had for its own author and its original readers, interpretation concerns its present meaning for today, and hermeneutics formulates "rules and methods to get from exegesis to interpretation."[30] Many writers, however, use "interpretation" and "hermeneutics" differently from the ways indicated by Achtemeier. Sometimes "interpretation" simply denotes the whole range of historical-textual and literary methods employed in biblical studies, as in the title of Stephen Neill's book *The Interpretation of the New Testament.* Often the term denotes the historical study of the text, without any special reference to the situation of the modern reader or interpreter. This occurs in E. C. Blackman's *Biblical Interpretation* and in J. D. Wood's *The Interpretation of the Bible;* while James Smart's modern study *The Interpretation of Scripture* hardly deals with hermeneutics in the most recent sense of the term.

By contrast, in recent years the term "hermeneutics" has undergone a definite expansion and revision of its traditional meaning. In addition to the titles of books or essays by Bultmann, Fuchs, and Ebeling, the kinds of issues with which we are most concerned in the present study are discussed under such titles as *Introduction to Hermeneutics* by René Marlé, *Language, Hermeneutic and Word of God* by Robert Funk, and *Hermeneutics* by Richard Palmer.

In what does this revision and expansion of the term "hermeneutics"

29. G. Ebeling, *W.F.,* p. 321; and C. F. Evans, *Is 'Holy Scripture' Christian?* (S.C.M., London, 1971), p. 33.
30. P. J. Achtemeier, *An Introduction to the New Hermeneutic* (Westminster Press, Philadelphia, 1969), pp. 13-14.

consist? Traditionally hermeneutics entailed the formulation of rules for the understanding of an ancient text, especially in linguistic and historical terms. The interpreter was urged to begin with the language of the text, including its grammar, vocabulary, and style. He examined its linguistic, literary, and historical context. In other words, traditional hermeneutics began with the recognition that a text was conditioned by a given historical context. However, hermeneutics in the more recent sense of the term begins with the recognition that historical conditioning is two-sided: *the modern interpreter, no less than the text, stands in a given historical context and tradition.*

Before we illustrate the point at issue with reference to a particular text, we should also note that a second contrast is bound up with the first. Traditionally it was often supposed, or implied, that the understanding of an ancient text could be achieved by the observance of hermeneutical rules. However, we have already noted Kimmerle's new interpretation of Schleiermacher to the effect that a modern reader might have access to all necessary linguistic and historical information, and even apply this information scientifically to the text, and yet lack the creative insight to understand it. Gerhard Ebeling underlines the crucial importance of this point both negatively and positively when he asserts that nowadays hermeneutics must not be "reduced to a collection of rules," but on the contrary must "serve the understanding."[31] He asks, "Can the event of the Word of God be served at all by scientific methods?"[32] By way of reply he does not question the role of critical historical methods as such, but he nevertheless stresses that biblical criticism can take us only part of the way towards understanding the ancient text.[33]

James Robinson and John Cobb have tried to pinpoint this double contrast between older and newer understandings of the scope of hermeneutics by drawing a contrast between "hermeneutics" (plural), denoting the traditional approach, and "hermeneutic" (singular), denoting more recent perspectives. They discuss its linguistic justification on the basis of an analogy with the singular form *Hermeneutik,* and several other writers have taken up this suggestion as a new convention.[34] Carl Braaten, however, sharply criticizes the proposal in his article "How New is the New Hermeneutic?" He attacks the broadening of the term, and argues that the use of the singular noun is "too artificial to be taken seriously."[35] We agree with Braaten that it seems artificial to mark these

31. G. Ebeling, *W.F.,* p. 313.
32. *Ibid.,* p. 314.
33. Cf. also Ebeling's essay "The Significance of the Critical Historical Method for Church and Theology in Protestantism" in *W.F.,* pp. 17-61.
34. J. M. Robinson and J. B. Cobb, Jr. (eds.), *N.H.,* pp. ix-x.
35. C. E. Braaten, "How New is the New Hermeneutic?" in *Th.T.* XXII (1965), 220 (cf. pp. 218ff.).

basic contrasts by using the singular rather than the plural form (except in the actual phrase "new hermeneutic," since this has already become virtually a technical term). However, we agree with Robinson that the change in meaning is fundamental. The nature of the hermeneutical problem cannot be discussed today without reference to the two sets of contrasts which we have just described.

Robinson himself in his essay "Hermeneutic Since Barth" comments on this change of perspective in a striking way, by going so far as to describe traditional hermeneutics as "superficial." He asserts, "One can say that the new hermeneutic began to emerge in a recognition of the superficiality of hermeneutics."[36]

Theologians who have been trained in the traditions of German philosophy find little problem in taking seriously the double-sided nature of historicality, or historical conditionedness, on the part of *both* the ancient text *and* the modern interpreter. However, a number of British and American scholars seem to view the problem as a merely theoretical one which is only of peripheral concern to the New Testament interpreter. It is perhaps necessary, therefore, to offer a concrete example of the problem which will illustrate its importance at a commonsense level. Only then can we escape the suspicion that the problem before us is merely a product of devious Germanic minds, which would never have been formulated without the aid of Dilthey and Heidegger.

In Luke 18:9-14 Jesus tells the Parable of the Pharisee and the Tax-Collector. The historical particularities of the text are fruitfully discussed and expounded by such writers as Jülicher, Dodd, Jeremias, and Linnemann. The following points shed light on the historical context of the parable and its linguistic features.

(1) Klostermann and Jeremias interpret σταθεὶς πρὸς ἑαυτὸν ταῦτα προσηύχετο (v. 11) to mean "he took up a prominent position and uttered this prayer." Πρὸς ἑαυτόν "renders an Aramaic reflexive (*leh*) which lays a definite emphasis on the action."[37] However, following the manuscript reading ταῦτα πρὸς ἑαυτὸν προσηύχετο, Jülicher interprets it to mean "prayed with himself." This might convey either the idea of "an inaudible prayer uttered in the heart," or of a prayer "spoken in an undertone, not intelligible to the bystanders, as the Jewish rule was (cf. Berakoth V.1.31a)."[38]

(2) The piety of the Pharisee is partly expressed in the words νηστεύω δὶς τοῦ σαββάτου, ἀποδεκατῶ πάντα ὅσα κτῶμαι (v. 12). These are voluntary deeds, involving personal sacrifice. The Law laid on every Jew one

36. J. M. Robinson, "Hermeneutic Since Barth" in *N.H.*, p. 21.
37. J. Jeremias, *The Parables of Jesus* (Eng. S.C.M., London, rev. edn. 1963), p. 140.
38. E. Linnemann, *The Parables of Jesus. Introduction and Exposition* (Eng. S.P.C.K., London, 1966), p. 143 n. 2.

fast a year as a day of repentance, but the Pharisee fasted not only on the Day of Atonement but on Mondays and Thursdays. As Linnemann comments, "To do this he has to give up not only food but also drink completely from sunrise to sunset, which in the heat of the East is a great act of self denial."[39] The fasting was not simply a self-centered work of merit, but was regarded as an act of intercession or even vicarious atonement for the sins of his people. Strack and Billerbeck elucidate this background.[40] On the matter of tithing, the Pharisee made sure that he used nothing that had not been tithed, even though corn, new wine, and oil should have been already tithed by the producer. This extra voluntary tithe would have involved considerable economic sacrifice.[41]

(3) Jesus' hearers would not have interpreted the Pharisee's prayer as one of arrogance or hypocrisy, but as a genuine prayer of thankfulness that God had given him the opportunity and inclination to carry out this practical piety. Prayers of this kind were not exceptional. A very similar one has been handed down in the Talmud, and another comes from the time of Qumran.[42]

(4) While taxes such as poll-tax and land-tax were collected by state officials, the customs of a district could be farmed out for collection by a τελώνης who would bid for this right. Although tariffs were probably fixed by the state, the collectors had no lack of devices for defrauding the public. "In the general estimation they stood on a level with robbers; they possessed no civil rights; and were shunned by all respectable persons."[43] Or, as another writer expresses it, the tax-collector "not only collaborated with the Roman occupation powers, who oppressed the people of God, and continually hindered it in the fulfilment of its religious duties, but he belonged to a profession that as a whole was regarded as being no better or worse than swindlers."[44]

(5) The phrase ἔτυπτεν τὸ στῆθος αὐτοῦ (v. 13) admittedly expressed deep contrition according to the conventions of the day. Nevertheless, when the tax-collector stands "afar off," in the view of Jesus' audience this is the only place where he naturally belongs.

(6) Jesus' verdict that the tax-collector went home δεδικαιωμένος παρ' ἐκεῖνον (v. 14) is interpreted by Jeremias in an exclusive rather than comparative sense. He cites several examples of where the Hebrew

39. *Ibid.*, p. 59; cf. J. Jeremias, *The Parables of Jesus*, p. 140.
40. H. L. Strack and P. Billerbeck, *Kommentar zum Neuen Testament aus Talmud und Midrasch* (6 vols.; Beck, Munich, 1922 onward) II, 243-44.
41. J. Jeremias, *The Parables of Jesus*, pp. 140-41; and E. Linnemann, *The Parables of Jesus*, p. 59.
42. E.g. b. Ber. 28b; cf. J. Jeremias, *ibid.*, E. Linnemann, *ibid.*, and J. D. Crossan, *In Parables. The Challenge of the Historical Jesus* (Harper and Row, New York, 1973), p. 69.
43. J. Jeremias, *The Parables of Jesus*, p. 41.
44. E. Linnemann, *The Parables of Jesus*, p. 60.

comparative *min* is used to convey the idea of "one, not the other," rather than "more one than the other" (e.g. 2 Sam. 19:44 and Ps. 45:8).[45] It is the tax-collector, not the Pharisee, who is declared righteous.

These six points help to explain how the meaning of the parable is conditioned by various historical, sociological, and linguistic factors which relate directly to its setting in first-century Palestine. These are precisely the kind of questions which concern New Testament scholars like Jeremias.

However, with the dawn of discussions about hermeneutics in the sense of "understanding," John D. Crossan and Walter Wink have drawn attention to a further dimension of the problem of interpreting this parable. Because he expresses the point so strongly, it is worth quoting Wink's words in full. He begins: "The scholar, having finished his work lays down his pen, oblivious to the way in which he has *falsified the text* in accordance with unconscious tendencies; so much so that he has maimed its original intent until it has actually turned into its opposite."[46]

Wink explains: "Any *modern* reader at all familiar with the text knows that (1) 'Pharisees' are hypocrites, and (2) Jesus praises the publican. The unreflective tendency of every reader is to identify with the more positive figures in an account. Consequently, modern readers will almost invariably identify with the *publican*. By that inversion of identification, the paradox of the justification of the *ungodly* is lost. . . . The story is then deformed into teaching cheap grace for rapacious toll collectors."[47] Wink concludes: "All this because the exegete hid behind his descriptive task without examining the recoil of the parable upon contemporary self-understanding. I know of no more powerful way to underline the inadequacy of a simply descriptive or phenomenological approach which fails to enter into a phenomenology of the exegete."[48]

We may admit that in one or two respects Walter Wink probably overstates the case. It is not the biblical scholar who "falsifies" the text. Indeed a careful examination of how Pharisees and tax-collectors were regarded in ancient Palestinian Judaism takes us a considerable way forward in the task of interpreting the parable for modern man. Simply as a piece of scholarly research into the historical context it is possible to see, as Wink admits, that the original hearer "would at first identify with the Pharisee as the bearer of religious and social status, and then suffer shock and consternation at the wholly unexpected justification of the publican."[49] However, Wink is correct to point out that in terms of the

45. J. Jeremias, *The Parables of Jesus*, pp. 141-42.
46. W. Wink, *The Bible in Human Transformation. Toward a New Paradigm for Biblical Study* (Fortress Press, Philadelphia, 1973), p. 42 (Wink's italics).
47. *Ibid.*, pp. 42-43 (Wink's italics).
48. *Ibid.*, p. 43 (Wink's italics).
49. *Ibid.*, p. 42.

horizons of hearers who already stand at the end of a long Christian tradition, the impact of the parable is quite different from what it was in its original setting. Pharisaism is nowadays so nearly synonymous with self-righteousness and hypocrisy that, far from suffering a sense of shock at the verdict of Jesus, the modern audience expects it.

John D. Crossan underlines the importance of this point almost as emphatically as Walter Wink. Again, it is perhaps worth quoting several lines in full. He writes, "There is an immediate problem. Parables are supposed to overturn one's structure of expectation and therein and thereby to threaten the security of one's man-made world. Such terms as 'Pharisee' and 'Publican' (or toll collector) evoke no immediate visual reaction or expectation from a modern reader. In fact . . . the former have become almost stereotyped villains rather than the revered moral leaders they were at the time of Jesus. So our structure of expectation is not that of the original hearer of the parable."[50] Hermeneutically, Crossan concludes, this raises a serious difficulty. In one sense the parable can be "explained"; but "a parable which has to be explained is, like a joke in similar circumstances, a parable which has been ruined as parable."[51]

The comments of Crossan and Wink illustrate exactly the two-sidedness of the hermeneutical problem. To pay attention to the historical particularities and historical conditionedness of the text remains of paramount importance, and the use of works such as Jeremias's remains indispensable for interpreting the ancient text. However, the modern reader is also conditioned by his own place in history and tradition. Hence the hermeneutical problem assumes new dimensions. No one today wishes to be cast in the role of a Pharisee. Hence in our example from Luke 18 the parable is usually "understood" as a reassuring moral tale which condemns the kind of Pharsaism that everyone already wishes to avoid. A parable which originally had the function of unsettling the hearer and overturning his values now serves to confirm him in the values which he already has. This situation illustrates one of the major aspects of the problem of hermeneutics.

Even if, for the moment, we leave out of account the modern reader's *historical* conditionedness, we are still faced with the undeniable fact that if a text is to be *understood* there must occur an engagement between two sets of horizons (to use Gadamer's phrase), namely those of the ancient text and those of the modern reader or hearer. The hearer must be able to relate his own horizons to those of the text. Gadamer compares the analogy of the "understanding" which occurs in a conversation. ". . . In a conversation, when we have discovered the standpoint and horizon of

50. J. D. Crossan, *The Dark Interval. Towards a Theology of Story* (Argus Communications, Niles, Illinois, 1975), pp. 101-02.
51. *Ibid.*, p. 102 (Crossan's italics); cf. *In Parables*, pp. 68-69.

the other person, his ideas become intelligible, without our necessarily having to agree with him."[52] Nevertheless, Gadamer goes on to argue that in hermeneutics the modern interpreter must also try to become aware of the distinctiveness of his own horizons, as against those of the text. On the one hand, "every encounter with tradition that takes place within historical consciousness involves the experience of the tensions between the text and the present. The hermeneutic task consists of not covering up this tension by attempting a naive assimilation but consciously bringing it out."[53] On the other hand, Gadamer adds, for understanding to take place there must also occur what he calls a "fusion of horizons" (*Horizontverschmelzung*).[54] We will try to make clear how these two apparently contradictory principles can be held together when we discuss Gadamer's philosophy. Meanwhile, we may note that his simile has been taken up by several writers, including Moltmann and Pannenberg.[55]

Richard Palmer also makes much of the concept of a fusion of horizons. Meaning, he argues, depends on "a relationship to the listener's own projects and intentions. . . . An object does not have significance outside of a relationship to someone."[56] He continues, "To speak of an object apart from a perceiving subject is a conceptual error caused by an inadequate realistic concept of perception and the world."[57] Hence: "Explanatory interpretation makes us aware that explanation is contextual, is 'horizonal'. It must be made within a horizon of already granted meanings and intentions. In hermeneutics, this area of assumed understanding is called pre-understanding."[58] Understanding takes place when the interpreter's horizons engage with those of the text. "This merging of two horizons must be considered a basic element in all explanatory interpretation."[59]

The problem, then, which Wink and Crossan have illustrated with reference to a particular text, is formulated in more general terms by Gadamer and Palmer. The nature of the hermeneutical problem is shaped by the fact that both the text and the interpreter are conditioned by their given place in history. For understanding to take place, two sets of variables must be brought into relation with each other. Gadamer's image of a fusion of horizons provides one possible way of describing the main problem and task of hermeneutics. So important for hermeneutics is the issue behind Gadamer's formulation that we have used the phrase *The*

52. H.-G. Gadamer, *T.M.*, p. 270.
53. *Ibid.*, p. 273.
54. *Ibid.* For the German term, cf. *W.M.*, pp. 286-90.
55. E.g. W. Pannenberg, *B.Q.T.* I, pp. 117-28.
56. R. E. Palmer, *Hermeneutics*, p. 24.
57. *Ibid.*
58. *Ibid.*
59. *Ibid.*, p. 25.

Two Horizons as the main title of the present study. A preliminary word of explanation about this title was given in the introduction.

3. *Some Issues Which Arise from the Hermeneutical Problem*

It has sometimes been suggested that to formulate the hermeneutical problem as a two-sided one moves the center of gravity entirely from the past to the present in the task of interpretation. Everything becomes dominated, it is argued, by the interpreter's own pre-understanding and the ancient text becomes merely a projection of his own ideas or preconceptions.

This issue can be illustrated with reference to two suggestions put forward by Palmer and by Smart. We have seen that Palmer follows Gadamer in viewing understanding in terms of a relation between two horizons. He claims to find a precedent for this view of hermeneutics in Luke 24:25-27, in which Christ interprets the Old Testament in terms of his own messiahship. Luke writes, "Beginning with Moses and all the prophets, he interpreted (διερμήνευσεν) to them in all the Scriptures the things concerning himself." This "interpretation," Palmer argues, does not entail a mere repetition of the ancient texts, nor even an examination of them in the context to which they already belong. It involves *placing the Old Testament texts in the context of the present events of Jesus' messiahship, and at the same time expounding his own sufferings in the context of the Old Testament passages.* Meaning depends on context. More specifically it involves establishing a relationship between *two* horizons. The disciples "understood" the texts when this subject-matter could be viewed within their own frame of reference.

Such a perspective, however, at once raises the issue, to which we have alluded, of whether the present becomes a wholly dominating factor in understanding the past. Cannot the past somehow be understood on its own terms? Is it not a fatal flaw in Palmer's formulation of the hermeneutical problem that his approach seems to imply that Christian disciples were the very first to "understand" the Old Testament passages in question?

James D. Smart also seems to come near to such a position in his discussion of the interpretation of certain parts of Isaiah. Second Isaiah, he urges, "seems fairly knocking on the door of the Christian gospel, and yet it was five hundred years and more before he was heard in such a way that the content of his words shaped the life of a people. . . . He had to wait centuries to be understood.''[60] Smart himself believes that, in the fullest sense of the word "understanding," certain parts of the Bible, including the Old Testament, can be understood only from within a Christian frame of reference. He asserts, "Something more was needed than philosophical, historical, and literary expertness combined with religious and ethical earnestness. A key to its meaning was missing.''[61]

Bultmann, Fuchs, and Ebeling would agree that a text cannot be understood without an appropriate pre-understanding; but all of them would deny that its pre-understanding need be distinctively Christian. Bultmann declares, "The interpretation of the Biblical writings is not subject to conditions different from those applying to all other kinds of literature.''[62] Fuchs puts the matter more theologically. How can we claim, he argues, that the biblical writings can *create* Christian faith, if we also insist that an understanding of them *presupposes* faith?[63]

Before we follow this debate further, we may also compare the approach of Palmer and Smart with the claims put forward by Prosper Grech in an article published in 1973 under the title "The 'Testimonia' and Modern Hermeneutics.''[64] The New Testament writers, Grech argues, interpreted Old Testament texts "within the framework of a tradition and of contemporary events." The context of a work of Scripture was *"no longer the original context in which it was written but the context of their own Kerygma* based on the recent crucifixion and resurrection of Jesus of Nazareth.''[65] They were "not interested," he declares, "in the objective scientific interpretation of scripture. No one even dreamt of interpreting Pss. ii and cx, for example, as coronation psalms addressed to the king by a court poet. The scriptures speak to the Church now.''[66]

However, Grech considers that "this does not mean that their exegesis was arbitrary or out of context." It means simply that "Scripture was read with a pre-understanding *(Vorverständnis).*''[67] "The words of Scripture were interpreted within a double context: that of God's salvific action in the past and that of contemporary happenings.''[68] Grech concludes, "The New Testament authors make no attempt to give an objective, detached, explanation of the texts in question. Their vision is a subjective one, but it is not arbitrary, it is hermeneutical. . . . They begin

---

60. J. D. Smart, *The Interpretation of Scripture* (S.C.M., London, 1961), p. 14.
61. *Ibid.,* p. 16.
62. R. Bultmann, "The Problem of Hermeneutics" in *E.P.T.,* p. 256.
63. E. Fuchs, *Zum hermeneutischen Problem in der Theologie* (Mohr, Tübingen, 1959; Gesammelte Aufsätze I), pp. 9-10; and *S.H.J.,* p. 30.
64. P. Grech, "The 'Testimonia' and Modern Hermeneutics" in *N.T.S.* XIX (1973), 318-24.
65. *Ibid.,* p. 319 (my italics).
66. *Ibid.*
67. *Ibid.,* p. 320.
68. *Ibid.*

with a pre-understanding."[69]

Although he also calls attention to the belief of the New Testament writers concerning a continuity in the work of the Holy Spirit in inspiring both the Old Testament and the saving events of the apostolic age, Grech believes that in terms of relating two sets of contexts the hermeneutic which is presupposed is similar to that expounded by Heidegger and especially Gadamer.[70] The New Testament authors, he declares, come to terms with the hermeneutic gap which otherwise existed between the Old Testament writers and their own day.

Questions about the primitive Christian interpretation and understanding of the Old Testament throw this issue into very sharp relief. However, it should not be assumed that the problem is entirely peculiar to primitive Christianity, or to those who follow Gadamer or Bultmann in their views about pre-understanding. Daniel Patte has shown how the same issue arises, even if admittedly in a less radical form, within Jewish hermeneutics.[71] In his recent work *Early Jewish Hermeneutic in Palestine* he carefully discusses the use of Scripture in classical and sectarian Judaism, and concludes that in all strands of Judaism there is a dialectic of emphasis, now on the past, now on the present. One pole stresses the Torah, and the anchorage of Judaism in the "salient history" of the past. Here Scripture is used to preserve Jewish self-identity by maintaining continuity with the past. The other pole stresses "the history of the cultural changes" which invites re-interpretation of the ancient texts in the light of new experiences and situations.[72] Here Scripture is orientated towards the present. The degree of emphasis may vary, for example, between the Sadducees, the Pharisees, or the Qumran community. But the tension between the two poles was never entirely absent. Midrash, or "inquiring of God" was done "either by scrutinizing scripture in the light of the new cultural situation, or by scrutinizing Tradition in the light of scripture."[73] In either case, two horizons are brought together in the hermeneutical process.

The conclusions of Grech and Patte demonstrate that the two-sided nature of the underlying problem of hermeneutics is more than a novel creation of Bultmann, Gadamer, and the exponents of the new hermeneutic. In this sense, they serve to confirm that the problem which we have outlined is a genuine one. However, far from solving the problem about whether the center of gravity lies in the past or the present, in certain

69. *Ibid.*, p. 321.
70. *Ibid.*, pp. 321-24.
71. D. Patte, *Early Jewish Hermeneutic in Palestine* (S.B.L. Dissertation Series 22, Scholars Press, University of Montana, 1975).
72. *Ibid.*, pp. 120-27 *et passim*.
73. *Ibid.*, p. 124.

respects they further aggravate it. For neither primitive Christian hermeneutics nor Jewish hermeneutics entailed the use of critical historical inquiry. How does the use of historical criticism affect the questions we are asking?

No modern scholar denies that critical historical inquiry remains indispensable in the interpretation of ancient texts. Even James Smart, in spite of a theological position which at times reflects affinities with Barth, fully endorses the need for such criticism. Although in some ways (as will become clear) his actual formulation of the principle begs a key question in hermeneutics, we may accept his principle provisionally when he states, "All interpretation must have as its first step the hearing of the text with exactly the shade of meaning that it had when it was first spoken or written."[74] To return to Smart's own example of Second Isaiah, we cannot short-circuit the painstaking inquiries of scholars such as C. R. North by appealing directly and uncritically to a christological interpretation of the figure of the servant. To put the matter crudely, if an "understanding" of Isaiah depends entirely on the possession of a Christian frame of reference, Isaiah himself must have lacked an understanding of what he wrote, since he lived in pre-Christian times.

Some theologians would reply that a text may well transcend the conscious horizons of an author on the basis of a theological doctrine of *sensus plenior*. This question will be left over for the present, but we may note, further, that even from a purely philosophical viewpoint, Gadamer insists that in the case of any historical text we cannot simply restrict its meaning to what was in the mind of the original author. As a *philosophical* and *hermeneutical* principle Gadamer declares, "Every age has to understand a transmitted text in its own way. . . . The real meaning of a text, as it speaks to the interpreter, does not depend on the contingencies of the author and whom he originally wrote for."[75] Gadamer continues, "An author does not need to know the real meaning of what he has written, and hence the interpreter can, and must, often understand more than he. But this is of fundamental importance. *Not occasionally only, but always, the meaning of a text goes beyond its author.* That is why understanding is not merely a reproduction, but always a productive attitude as well."[76] In due course we shall attempt to assess whether Gadamer goes too far in making such assertions. However, our present purpose is to demonstrate that neither a theological hermeneutic such as Smart's, nor a philosophical hermeneutic such as Gadamer's, with all their emphasis on the present and on developing tradition, excludes the place of historical criticism as a starting-point. The issue is not *whether* historical criticism has a neces-

74. J. D. Smart, *The Interpretation of Scripture*, p. 33.
75. H.-G. Gadamer, *T.M.*, p. 263.
76. *Ibid.*, p. 264 (my italics).

THE NATURE AND SCOPE OF THE SUBJECT 21

sary place; but what that place should be. To invoke a doctrine of *sensus plenior* in order to exclude historical criticism would certainly be, as Grech remarks, to try to establish a hermeneutic based on an unjustifiable appeal to a theology of *deus ex machina*.[77]

Gerhard Ebeling considers the role of historical criticism in hermeneutics at great length. He stresses both its necessity and its limitations. Uncompromisingly he states, "Literal historical exegesis . . . is the foundation of the church's exposition of scripture."[78] Only when he has firmly established this principle does he admit: "Nevertheless the possibilities of conflict between the literal meaning and the requirements arising from the application to the present are not entirely excluded."[79] Even Bultmann adopts a similar starting-point, although (like Ebeling) he stresses the importance of pre-understanding and indeed is criticized by Ebeling (as well as by other writers) for going too far in separating historical-critical inquiry from Christian faith.[80] Bultmann writes, "The old hermeneutic rules of grammatical interpretation, formal analysis, and explanation of the basis of the conditions of the historical period are indisputably valid."[81]

Ernst Fuchs and Walter Wink also acknowledge the necessity for historical criticism, but equally stress its limitations. Fuchs writes, "There is no objection to the historical method"; for "the historical method may establish what things were once like."[82] Nevertheless, as "an important point" it must also be said that "every *analysis* of the text *must* in the first instance 'strike the text dead'."[83] This constitutes a necessary stage in the hermeneutical process, even though it can hardly be said to represent the most creative moment in the whole enterprise. Once again, whether Fuchs may be overstating the case is left open for future discussion.

If Fuchs' simile is striking, Wink's comments are still more emphatic. He declares, "The historical critical method has reduced the Bible to a dead letter. Our obeisance to technique has left the Bible sterile and ourselves empty."[84] The biblical writers, he argues, addressed concrete situations in life; but the biblical scholar who adopts the methods of

77. P. Grech, *N.T.S.* XIX, 324.
78. G. Ebeling, "The Significance of the Critical Historical Method for Church and Theology in Protestantism" in *W.F.*, p. 32.
79. *Ibid.*
80. G. Ebeling, *Theology and Proclamation. A Discussion with Rudolf Bultmann* (Eng. Collins, London, 1966), pp. 32-81 *et passim*.
81. R. Bultmann, "The Problem of Hermeneutics" in *E.P.T.*, p. 256.
82. E. Fuchs, "The Reflection which is Imposed in Theology by the Historical-Critical Method" in *S.H.J.*, pp. 42-43; cf. pp. 32-47.
83. E. Fuchs, *S.H.J.*, p. 194 (his italics). Cf. also "Die historisch-kritische Methode" in *Herm.*, pp. 159-66; and *Marburger Hermeneutik* (Mohr, Tübingen, 1968), pp. 95-134.
84. W. Wink, *The Bible in Human Transformation*, p. 4.

historical criticism suppresses the very questions which are most fruitful to ask in order to arrive at an understanding of the text. Wink states, "The outcome of biblical studies in the academy is a trained incapacity to deal with the real problems of actual living persons in their daily lives."[85] Critical inquiry, he concludes, too often asks questions that are acceptable only to "the guild of biblical scholars" rather than ones which the text itself demands.[86]

In spite of the manner of his approach, it would be a mistake to assume that Wink leaves no room for critical historical inquiry. Such inquiry performs, in his judgment, the key function of insuring a necessary measure of objectivity in hermeneutics. This is associated with the process which he describes as "distancing," which is probably inspired by closely parallel ideas in Gadamer. Wink observes, "Though objectivism has been exposed as a false consciousness, objectivity cannot be surrendered as a goal. . . . So the scholar distances the Bible from the church, from the history of theology, from creed and dogma, and seeks to hear it on its own terms."[87] Indeed in discussions of specific New Testament passages in which he illustrates his own hermeneutical procedure, Wink consistently begins with the kinds of questions which can only be answered with reference to critical historical research undertaken by biblical scholars.[88] "Critical procedure," he urges, is indispensable as a matter of principle.[89]

Why, then, does Wink attack the use of standard methods and methodologies in biblical studies? His reservations about critical methods are twofold. First of all, they do not complete the whole hermeneutical process. They begin it, but they do not end it, and we must not mistake the part for the whole. Secondly, while the questions posed by critical historical research are admittedly necessary, they are not always the questions which best allow the text to "speak" to man today. The texts of the Bible, he insists, speak to more practical issues about life, especially life within communities. These are not always the same as the questions which win a hearing from the scholarly guild.

We must now try to draw together some of the threads of this section. We first identified the underlying problem of hermeneutics as a two-sided one, involving the historical conditionedness both of the ancient text and of the modern interpreter. We have now seen that at least four specific issues arise from this. (i) The horizons of the modern interpreter, or any interpreter standing in a tradition subsequent to the ancient text, mark out

85. *Ibid.*, p. 6.
86. *Ibid.*, pp. 2-15.
87. *Ibid.*, p. 24 (Wink's italics).
88. *Ibid.*, pp. 52-55, on Matthew 9:1-8 and parallels.
89. *Ibid.*, p. 53.

the area of his pre-understanding. How is this category of pre-understanding to be described, and what are its implications for the tasks of hermeneutics? (ii) Once we allow the importance of questions about pre-understanding and the interpreter's own horizons, need this mean that the center of gravity now shifts from the past entirely to the present? We shall argue in the third chapter that while the problem should not be exaggerated, nevertheless the difficulty raised by the pastness of the past in hermeneutics cannot be side-stepped. Further in the course of our discussions of Bultmann and Wittgenstein, we shall argue that in neglecting to give adequate place to the Old Testament as a history of publicly accessible tradition, Bultmann has made the hermeneutical problem more difficult. For if the hermeneutical question is reduced to a wholly present question about meaning "for me," it becomes almost impossible to heed Wittgenstein's warnings about private language. (iii) If the New Testament writers approached the Old Testament in the light of a pre-understanding that was theologically informed (for example, by Christology), does this not mean that in order to be true to the tradition of the New Testament itself the interpreter will consciously approach the text from a particular theological angle? This raises very far-reaching questions about the relationship between exegesis and systematic theology, and about historical and theological objectivity. We shall touch on these issues in the third and fourth chapters, but our main consideration of them will come in chapter eleven, when we examine the hermeneutical implications of Gadamer's philosophy. (iv) The question which is never far in the background is to what extent, if at all, philosophical description can help us to find answers to these and to other similar questions. In the next chapter we shall try to show why in particular we have selected Heidegger, Bultmann, Gadamer, and Wittgenstein as our four major representatives of philosophical or hermeneutical thought and inquiry. We shall then examine three broader issues, hermeneutics and history, hermeneutics and theology, and hermeneutics and language, before returning to Heidegger, Bultmann, Gadamer, and Wittgenstein.

CHAPTER II

Further Introductory Questions: Heidegger, Bultmann, Gadamer, and Wittgenstein

4. *Heidegger, Bultmann, Gadamer, and Wittgenstein: Three General Points*

Why have we selected these four particular thinkers for the major part of our study? An adequate answer to this question can be given only at the end of this study, when our specific arguments and conclusions about these four figures have emerged. However, by way of introduction to their thought, we shall put forward five points which may serve to indicate something of their importance for the present inquiry in a preliminary way.

(1) In the first place, with the possible exception of Gadamer, each of these thinkers stands as a towering figure in his own right, who has had an immense influence on twentieth-century thought. Thus J. Macquarrie begins his book on Heidegger with the words, "By any standard Martin Heidegger must be reckoned among the greatest and most creative philosophers of the twentieth century."[1] Similarly, Marjorie Grene, who is far from being uncritical of him, asserts, "Heidegger occupies a unique place in the intellectual history of our time."[2] Indeed so far-reaching has been his influence in Europe that in an oral comment to me in 1969 Wolfhart Pannenberg expressed the view that it was regrettable that any one thinker had had such a dominating influence on the ground that a greater diversity of approaches in philosophy was more desirable.

Rudolf Bultmann, for his part, is widely considered to be the most significant and influential New Testament scholar of this century. How-

1. J. Macquarrie, *Martin Heidegger* (Lutterworth Press, London, 1968), p. 1.
2. M. Grene, *Martin Heidegger* (Bowes & Bowes, London, 1957), p. 12.

24

ever negative may be many of the historical conclusions reached in his *History of the Synoptic Tradition*, Bultmann expressed his agreement with Karl Barth in their common concern that the message of the New Testament should be heard as the word of God.[3] It is Bultmann's refusal to abandon this perspective of a "theology of the Word" that calls forth Dennis Nineham's disparaging comment: "In the last resort Bultmann too is a biblicist."[4] Above all, Bultmann is concerned with the problem of hermeneutics. In his celebrated comment at the end of his *Theology of the New Testament*, Bultmann declares that historical research and reconstruction is not simply an end in itself, but "stands in the service of the interpretation of the New Testament writings under the presupposition that they have something to say to the present."[5] We admit that there are very grave problems about Bultmann's program of demythologizing, and we shall consider these in detail in due course. However, his hermeneutics as a whole also relate to broader issues, and however we finally assess it, it is impossible to ignore his contribution to the hermeneutical debate. Not least, we must ask: how successful or otherwise is Bultmann's attempt to use philosophical description in the service of New Testament hermeneutics?

Gadamer's influence in twentieth-century intellectual thought may be less than that of Heidegger, Bultmann, or Wittgenstein. Nevertheless he stands as a key figure in the area of hermeneutics. As examples of scholarly estimates of his importance we may cite first the verdict of a sympathetic commentator and then the response of one of his severest critics. Roger Lapointe writes, "Gadamer . . . is without doubt at present the most important theoretician of philosophical hermeneutics."[6] And even his critic E. D. Hirsch declares, "Hans-Georg Gadamer has published the most substantial treatise on hermeneutic theory that has come from Germany this century."[7] Gadamer shares certain fundamental assumptions with Heidegger, but he is more systematic and less elusive in articulating them. Thus Theodore Kisiel offers an illuminating comparison between the two thinkers. Heidegger, he observes, is profound but also frustratingly elusive. He continues: "An antidote to this frustrating obfuscation is to be found in the work of Hans-Georg Gadamer, which locates itself between Heidegger's comprehensive and radical hermeneutic and the more customary problems of textual interpretation, thereby providing a specific context and concreteness to the profound and elusive

---

3. Cf. W. G. Kümmel, *The New Testament. The History of the Investigation of its Problems* (Eng. S.C.M., London, 1973), pp. 369 and 372.
4. D. Nineham, *U.A.B.*, p. 221.
5. R. Bultmann, *T.N.T.* II, 251.
6. R. Lapointe, "Hermeneutics Today," *B.T.B.* II (1972), 111.
7. E. D. Hirsch, Jr., *Validity in Interpretation* (Yale University Press, New Haven, 1967), p. 245.

issues involved here, like the filter glasses used to peer into white-hot furnaces."[8]

No New Testament scholar, as far as I know, has attempted to take up Ludwig Wittgenstein's insights and to apply them to problems of New Testament hermeneutics. It might at first sight appear to be arbitrary, therefore, to select this particular thinker to stand alongside Heidegger, Bultmann, and Gadamer in the present study. Once again, whether this procedure is justified depends on the outcome of the study itself. We shall argue most emphatically for the relevance of Wittgenstein's thought both to hermeneutical theory in general and to the interpretation of the New Testament. At this stage our point is only the introductory one of underlining his immense stature as one of the most creative and influential thinkers of this century. One of today's most respected philosophers, P. F. Strawson, is by no means uncritical of Wittgenstein; yet he has described him as "a philosopher of genius" and even as "the first philosopher of the age."[9] Wittgenstein's powerful influence on twentieth-century philosophy, together with his own stature as a thinker, has been the subject of too many remarks by too many writers to require further comment in the same vein. Wittgenstein is above all a creative *thinker,* and those who have wrestled with his many writings will never see any problem in quite the same way as if they had never encountered his thought.

(2) The second main point to be made is that all four writers are concerned with philosophy as philosophical *description.* The sense in which philosophy remains descriptive, however, is not exactly the same in all four writers. In Heidegger's case the descriptive status of philosophy is connected with his use of the phenomenological method. It is noteworthy that Heidegger dedicated *Being and Time* to Husserl, the founder of modern phenomenology, "in friendship and admiration."[10] The slogan of phenomenology, as Heidegger himself recalls, was *Zu den Sachen selbst.*[14] The inquirer, in theory, refrains from projecting a prior understanding onto the facts, but "lets things appear as they are." In Heidegger's more complex language, the aim is "to let that which shows itself be seen from itself in the very way in which it shows itself from itself."[12]

At first sight this may look like almost a parody of naive objectivism. Anyone familiar with the problems of post-Kantian philosophy will in-

8. T. Kisiel, "The Happening of Tradition: The Hermeneutics of Gadamer and Heidegger" in *M.W.* II, no. 3 (1969), 359; cf. pp. 358-85.
9. P. F. Strawson, "Critical Notice of Wittgenstein's *Philosophical Investigations*" in H. Morick (ed.), *Wittgenstein and the Problem of Other Minds* (McGraw-Hill, New York, 1967), pp. 3 and 14 (cf. pp. 3-42).
10. M. Heidegger, *B.T.,* p. 5.
11. *Ibid.,* p. 50; German, p. 28.
12. *Ibid.,* p. 58; German, p. 34.

evitably ask: how can we let things appear "as they are"? Indeed, although we have quoted Heidegger's actual words, this whole approach seems to be the very opposite of what we should expect from one who is so fully aware of the problem of historicality, or historical conditionedness. This is one reason why Heidegger is so important for hermeneutics. On the one hand, he states that his aim is that of philosophical description. On the other hand, he also recognizes that man can only interpret the world as he sees it from within his given situation in life. Both sides belong to Heidegger's thought.

This pinpoints precisely one of the most persistent problems of New Testament hermeneutics. On the one hand the exegete wants to arrive at "what the New Testament actually says." We return to James Smart's comment, "All interpretation must have as its first step the hearing of the text with exactly the shade of meaning that it had when it was first spoken or written."[13] Nevertheless Smart himself, as a biblical scholar, recognizes the problem involved in articulation, an ideal of "pure" description. He also writes, "The claim of absolute scientific objectivity in interpreting scripture involves the interpreter in an illusion about himself that inhibits objectivity."[14] The biblical scholar therefore needs the help of someone who has made it his life's work to wrestle with the problem of how these two sides of the situation can be held together, without either being lost to view.

Heidegger has paid closer attention to the two-sidedness of this problem than perhaps any other thinker. He stands in the philosophical tradition that goes back through Kierkegaard to Kant in his recognition that we cannot leap outside the confines of our finite or "historic" existence. In his characteristic style Kierkegaard declared, "I am only a poor existing human being, not competent to contemplate the eternal either eternally or theocentrically, but compelled to content myself with existing."[15] Heidegger takes up this perspective in his analysis of "Dasein," rather than simply "man." He can investigate Being (Sein) only if he begins with Dasein, the concrete, human "I." Dasein does not have a viewpoint outside history. Hence Heidegger asserts, "The phenomenology of Dasein is a hermeneutic."[16] My understanding of Being is bound up with, and conditioned by, my understanding of my own concrete existence. Heidegger insists, "An interpretation (Auslegung) is never a presuppositionless apprehending of something presented to us (eines Vorgegebenen)."[17]

13. J. D. Smart, The Interpretation of Scripture, p. 33.
14. Ibid., p. 29.
15. S. Kierkegaard, Concluding Unscientific Postscript to the Philosophical Fragments (Eng. Princeton University Press, 1941), p. 190.
16. M. Heidegger, B.T., p. 62 (German, p. 37; his italics).
17. Ibid., pp. 191-92 (German, p. 150).

The attempt on Heidegger's part to do justice to both sides of the problem is very well expressed by Michael Gelven. He writes, "Heidegger and other hermeneutic thinkers want to be true to both terms of their descriptive methodology: to let the facts speak for themselves; and at the same time to claim that there are no such things as uninterpreted facts—at least not in those cases where the hermeneutic method applies."[18] Even if, in the end, we conclude with A. de Waelhens and David Cairns that Heidegger's philosophy is not, after all, genuinely descriptive, nevertheless his attempt to grapple with the two-sidedness of the problem remains instructive and relevant to all other attempts to formulate the nature of the hermeneutical problem.

Rudolf Bultmann also claims that the role of philosophy in his own hermeneutical program remains purely descriptive. Looking back from a point in later life, Bultmann observes concerning his use of Heidegger's philosophy, "I learned from him not *what* theology has to say but *how* it has to say it."[19] Elsewhere he writes approvingly of Gogarten's *Demythologizing and History* on the ground that it "makes it clear that we do not necessarily subscribe to Heidegger's philosophical theories when we learn something from his existentialist analysis."[20] In the second of our three chapters on Bultmann we shall discuss especially Bultmann's replies on this subject to Kuhlmann, when he argues that philosophy provides for theological hermeneutics not a theory of reality but a conceptual scheme. In more technical terms, theology is ontic and *existentiell;* philosophy is ontological and existential.

Gadamer's insistence that his philosophy is purely descriptive occurs in the context of the same kind of debate as we have noted in connection with Heidegger. His assertions to this effect emerge not only in his work as a whole, but in his explicit assertion to this effect in correspondence with his critic Emilio Betti, which has been published as part of the first supplement to *Truth and Method*. Gadamer writes, "Fundamentally, I am not proposing a method, but I am describing *what is the case (ich beschreibe,* was ist). That it is as I describe it cannot, I think, be seriously questioned. . . . I consider the only scientific thing is *to recognize what it is* (anzuerkennen, was ist), instead of starting from what ought to be or could be."[21]

If Gadamer's claim is correct, it is clear that the use of philosophical categories derived from his work cannot be said to lead to distortion in interpreting the New Testament. However, Betti is not satisfied with

18. M. Gelven, *A Commentary on Heidegger's 'Being and Time'* (Harper and Row, New York, 1970), pp. 34-35.
19. R. Bultmann, "Reply," in *T.R.B.*, p. 276; cf. pp. 273-78.
20. *K.M.* II, p. 182.
21. H.-G. Gadamer, *T.M.*, pp. 465-66; German, pp. 483-84 (his italics).

Gadamer's reply. Palmer sums up the debate with the words, "For Betti, Gadamer is lost in a standardless existential subjectivity."[22] But far from being an argument against the relevance of Gadamer for New Testament hermeneutics, this makes it all the more urgent to explore what he has to say. For the issue between Gadamer and Betti turns precisely on what "description" might be said to entail. Is it possible to distinguish between "the meaning of a text" and "the meaning of a text as I understand it from my place in a historical tradition"? Gadamer does not try to avoid the genuine issue which is raised by such a question, but he denies that it can be answered from outside a given tradition and without reference to the phenomenon of historical conditionedness. This is part of the very "description" of the hermeneutical situation that he gives. Thus Kisiel observes, "Gadamer focusses on the 'fact' that the actual situation in which human understanding takes place is always an understanding through *language* within a tradition, both of which have always been manifest considerations in hermeneutical thinking."[23]

In Wittgenstein's work the descriptive status of his philosophy is even clearer and more explicit. It is precisely because this principle applies in the claims of all four thinkers that we have used the phrase "philosophical description" in the subtitle of the present work. Wittgenstein makes this point clear in many places, but especially in a part of the *Zettel* which concerns the nature of philosophy. Wittgenstein writes, "Disquiet in philosophy might be said to arise from looking at philosophy wrongly. . . . We want to replace wild conjectures and explanations by quiet weighing of linguistic facts *(sprachlicher Tatsachen)*. . . . Philosophy unties knots in our thinking. . . . The philosopher is not a citizen of any community of ideas. That is what makes him into a philosopher."[24] Philosophical investigations are "conceptual investigations."[25]

This verdict is not confined to the *Zettel*. Even in the *Tractatus* Wittgenstein declared, "Philosophy is not a body of doctrine but an activity. . . . Philosophy does not result in 'philosophical propositions', but rather in the clarification of propositions."[26] As far back as 1913 in his very early "Notes on Logic" he wrote, "Philosophy . . . is purely description."[27] In the *Philosophical Investigations* he declares, "We must do away with all *explanation* and description alone *(nur Beschreibung)*

22. R. E. Palmer, *Hermeneutics,* p. 59.
23. T. Kisiel, "The Happening of Tradition: The Hermeneutics of Gadamer and Heidegger" in *M.W.* II, 359 (his italics).
24. L. Wittgenstein, *L.,* sects. 447, 452, and 455; cf. sects. 448-67.
25. *Ibid.,* sect. 458.
26. L. Wittgenstein, *T.,* 4.112; cf. 4.111-4.115, 6.53, and 6.54.
27. L. Wittgenstein "Notes on Logic" in *N.,* p. 93.

must take its place."[28] He adds, "Philosophy simply puts everything before us. . . . The work of the philosopher consists in assembling reminders for a particular purpose."[29]

It would be a grave mistake, however, to infer that because his philosophy is descriptive, Wittgenstein's work is in any way shallow or trivial. Characteristically he once remarked in a letter to Norman Malcolm, "You can't think decently if you don't want to hurt yourself."[30] Malcolm recalls his "extreme seriousness, absorption, and force of intellect . . . his passionate love of truth . . . his ruthless integrity which did not spare himself or anyone else."[31] In the *Zettel* Wittgenstein gives a warning about philosophers for whom "no deep problems seem to exist any more; the world becomes broad and flat and loses all depth, and what they write, becomes immeasurably shallow and trivial."[32] Even though he himself is content to describe and to remind, he does it in such a way that, as he puts it, "I have changed your way of seeing (*Anschauungsweise*)."[33] The same word is used in the *Philosophical Investigations* as in the *Zettel*.[34]

(3) The third main point emerges naturally from the second. We have already seen that for Heidegger and for Gadamer the problem of philosophical description is rooted in the question of the givenness of the "world" (Heidegger) or the tradition (Gadamer) to which I already belong.

We shall consider Heidegger's notion of worldhood in detail in a subsequent chapter. We may note provisionally, however, that the notion of worldhood is inseparable from three considerations. First of all, the "world" of *Dasein* is embraced by the horizons of its *practical concerns and tasks*. It is bound up with Heidegger's distinction, which is discussed in our chapter on the subject, between the ready-to-hand (*zuhanden*) and the present-at-hand (*vorhanden*). For example, in the world of the carpenter "wood" or "timber" is never "mere" wood or timber, as a neutral object of scrutiny, but acquires a given meaning from a given world. This means that, secondly, "world" has hermeneutical significance in providing and sustaining a given *horizon of meaning*. Because "mountain," for example, is not merely viewed as an object (as something present-at-hand), but in the context of the concerns of *Dasein*, it means something different in the world of the climber from what it means in the world of the

28. L. Wittgenstein, *P.I.*, sect. 109 (his italics).
29. *Ibid.*, sects. 126-27.
30. N. Malcolm and G. H. von Wright, *Ludwig Wittgenstein. A Memoir* (Oxford University Press, London, 1958), p. 40.
31. *Ibid.*, pp. 26-27.
32. L. Wittgenstein, *Z.*, sect. 456.
33. *Ibid.*, sect. 461.
34. L. Wittgenstein, *P.I.*, sect. 144.

cartographer. Hence Magda King observes, "The world of our own existence is the horizons in which our everyday understanding moves, so that from it and in reference to it the things we come across are intelligible as . . . things that can be useful for some purpose. The horizon of our world is primarily 'meaning-giving'."[35] Thirdly, worldhood, in Heidegger's view, is "given" as part of our existence, *prior to* our raising questions about meaning. This "givenness," we shall see in chapter six, is articulated in Heidegger's notion of facticity. Thus he writes, " 'World' can be understood . . . as that *'wherein'* a factical *Dasein* as such can be said to 'live'. 'World' has here a pre-ontological existentiell significance."[36] As Richard Palmer puts it, and as we shall set out in greater detail later, it is prior to conceptualizing and even to the contrast between subjectivity and objectivity.[37]

These three features of worldhood lead to three consequences for hermeneutics. First of all, they suggest that understanding and meaning operate at the level of practical concern, and not merely theoretical observation. If this is so, these considerations lend weight to the claims of Walter Wink and others (noted above) about the limitations of a hermeneutical "objectivism" which is not in practice a genuine "objectivity." Some may claim that, on this basis, the meanings of New Testament texts may be seen differently from the standpoint of the worlds of the scholarly exegete, the systematic theologian, and so on. Some of the questions which this suggestion raises are discussed in the chapter on hermeneutics and theology. Secondly, at a much deeper level Ernst Fuchs has shown the relevance of the notion of worldhood for the hermeneutics of the parables of Jesus. By entering his hearers' world, he established a "common understanding" *(Einverständnis)* with them. But Jesus then extends and transforms the horizons of the world in such a way that reality is grasped differently. The reality is understood differently because the world has become a new world.[38] Thirdly, Fuchs, followed by Funk, Crossan, and others, believes that this operates at a pre-conceptual, pre-cognitive level. This is because "world" and "understanding" are *a priori* existentialia, which are prior to cognition and the subject-object model of knowledge.

Rudolf Bultmann also pays close attention to the pre-judgments or pre-understanding of the interpreter. Pre-understanding, for Bultmann, is "not a prejudice, but a way of raising questions."[39] The interpreter need

35. M. King, *Heidegger's Philosophy. A Guide to his Basic Thought* (Blackwell, Oxford, 1964), p. 7 (his italics).
36. M. Heidegger, *B.T.*, p. 93 (German, p. 65; his italics).
37. R. E. Palmer, *Hermeneutics*, p. 132.
38. E. Fuchs, *Herm.*, pp. 62-72 and 211-30; *Marburger Hermeneutik*, pp. 171-81 and 208-13; and *S.H.J.*, pp. 84-103.
39. R. Bultmann, *E.F.*, p. 346.

not and must not suppress his questions. Moreover, like the early Barth, Bultmann attacks what he regards as a naive objectivism in hermeneutics and theology. We see how far he is prepared to go in this direction when we recall André Malet's comment that in Bultmann's view "The truly 'objective' Christ is not Christ *in se*, but the Christ of the *beneficia*."[40] We shall look more closely at these issues in Bultmann in due course.

Gadamer shows an extremely strong awareness of the part played by historical tradition, and also by language, in shaping understanding. We noted the point in a preliminary way in our example of the Parable of the Pharisee and the Publican. Twentieth-century Western man already has an understanding of "Pharisee" which has to be corrected if the parable is to be understood in a way likely to have been the case for a first-century Palestinian audience. Yet even this way of formulating the problem is open to question. Is there some "correct" interpretation to which other interpretations must correspond? Is this supposedly "correct" meaning itself free from cultural or historical relativity? We may recall in this connection a comment made by John Dillenberger. He writes, "The problem of interpretation is that of analogically translating from one universe of discourse or configuration to another. But there is never simply an 'in between' stage; nor is there the possibility of peeling off layers until the essence has been laid bare. . . . The problem of interpretation . . . of the New Testament is not that of the kernel and the husks."[41]

Perhaps surprisingly Dillenberger accuses not only Bultmann but also exponents of the new hermeneutic of failing to see this problem. However, Gadamer himself seems to be fully alive to the issue. He writes, "Understanding is not to be thought of so much as the action of one's subjectivity, but as the placing of oneself within a process (strictly happening or occurrence) of tradition *(ein Überlieferungsgeschehen)*, in which past and present are constantly fused (almost "adjusted", *vermitteln*). This is what must be expressed in hermeneutical theory."[42] In the view of many of Gadamer's critics, he fails to solve this problem in an "objective" way. To Gadamer himself, however, such criticisms merely try to cut the knot which is itself a given fact of life. The way of actually living with the problem is to accept the part played by language and tradition, but to explore the positive possibilities of the hermeneutical situation. Gadamer attempts to do this by showing the positive potential of such phenomena as "temporal distance" *(Zeitabstand)*, "prejudgment" or "prejudice" *(Vorurteil)*, and "world" *(Welt)*.[43] He takes up all these categories, which at first sight seem only to aggravate the

40. A. Malet, *The Thought of Rudolf Bultmann* (Eng. Doubleday, New York, 1971), p. 20.
41. J. Dillenberger, "On Broadening the New Hermeneutic" in *N.H.*, p. 154.
42. H.-G. Gadamer, *T.M.*, p. 258; German, pp. 274-75 (the German is in italics).
43. *Ibid.*, pp. 235-74; German, pp. 250-90; and pp. 397-414 (cf. 91-99); German, pp. 415-32 (cf. 97-105).

hermeneutic problem, and shows how they may perform a fruitful role in facilitating understanding, especially the interpreter's understanding of texts written in the past.

Whether it may also be said that Wittgenstein takes adequate account of the givenness of man's place within the world and his inherited tradition remains a matter of controversy. I myself have no doubt that his emphasis on "training," "forms of life," and the kinds of considerations about "the scaffolding of our thought" which he puts forward in his book *On Certainty* prove beyond doubt that Wittgenstein is fully aware of the problem. The point cannot be proved, however, before we have examined his writings in detail and observed the irreducible nature of the language-game in Wittgenstein's thought. However, we shall pursue this question further in a preliminary way as part of the next of our five considerations about these four thinkers.

5. *The Relation of Wittgenstein to Heidegger, Gadamer, and Bultmann*

One of the major conclusions of the present study will be that in the context of the problem of hermeneutics Wittgenstein's notion of "language-game" has striking parallels with Heidegger's understanding of "world" and even with Gadamer's notion of the interpreter's horizons. This brings us to our fourth main point about Heidegger, Bultmann, Gadamer, and Wittgenstein.

What kind of relationship, if any, exists between the thought of Wittgenstein and those who stand in the tradition of existentialist or hermeneutical philosophy? I am aware that many British philosophers would regard Wittgenstein and Heidegger as representing two totally incompatible traditions of philosophical thought and method, and that from this point of view some would doubtless argue that their questions and contexts of thought are so radically different as to be incapable of fruitful comparison. But powerful pleas have also been made to the effect that a fruitful comparison between these two approaches is long overdue. Paul van Buren, for example, writing as a theologian who is sympathetic with Anglo-American linguistic philosophy in Wittgenstein's tradition, expresses regret that linguistic philosophers have simply ignored Heidegger's approach. He asserts, "What bothers me . . . is that the really competent analysts of language seem to have made no serious effort to enter into conversation with Heidegger."[44] Carl Braaten directs a criticism of the same type more specifically to the exponents of the new hermeneutic. He writes, "It is unfortunate that this continental linguistic

44. P. M. van Buren, *Theological Explorations* (S.C.M., London, 1968), p. 82.

hermeneutic makes no attempt to escape its confinement within Heidegger's mystagogical speculations about language."[45] Braaten wonders "what kind of little ones a wedding between the later-Wittgenstein and the later-Heidegger would produce," and concludes: "To the by-stander it is distressing to see two such schools ignore each other, especially when each seems to need what the other has."[46]

In point of fact, since the time of Braaten's plea in 1965 a number of studies have appeared which do attempt to compare the approaches of Wittgenstein and Heidegger, or at the least the philosophical traditions to which each belongs. This comparison constitutes one of the special interests of Karl-Otto Apel, who has published a variety of writings on the subject including articles entitled "Wittgenstein und Heidegger" and "Wittgenstein und das Problem des hermeneutischen Verstehens," and his book *Analytic Philosophy of Language and the Geisteswissenschaften*.[47] Taking Apel's work as her point of departure, Blanche I. Premo has argued that affinities between Heidegger and Wittgenstein are not to be confined only to Wittgenstein's later writings.[48] She concludes, "If the late work is hermeneutic, if Wittgenstein truly shared the vision that language is disclosure of world, then the early work must be included in this category as well."[49] Another major book which bears directly on the subject is Anton Grabner-Haider's study *Semiotik und Theologie,* to which he gives the explanatory subtitle *Religiöse Rede zwischen analytischer und hermeneutischer Philosophie.*[50]

From a very different viewpoint P. McCormick, E. Schaper, and J. Heaton have published three articles under the general heading "Symposium on Saying and Showing in Heidegger and Wittgenstein."[51] G. Ebeling expresses concern about the subject in the course of his *Introduction to a Theological Theory of Language.*[52] Franz Mayr is yet another writer who speaks of "parallels" between Heidegger and Wittgenstein in

45. C. E. Braaten, "How New is the New Hermeneutic?" in *Th.T* XXII (1965), 229-30 (cf. 218-35).

46. *Ibid.,* p. 230.

47. K.-O. Apel, *Analytic Philosophy of Language and the Geisteswissenschaften* (Foundations of Language Supplement Series Vol. IV; Reidel, Dordrecht, 1967); "Wittgenstein und das Problem des hermeneutischen Verstehens" in *Z.Th.K.* LXIII (1966), 49-88; "Wittgenstein und Heidegger" in *Philosophisches Jahrbuch* LXXV (1967), 56-94; and "Heideggers philosophische Radikalisierung der Hermeneutik und die Frage nach dem Sinnkriterium der Sprache" in O. Loretz and W. Strolze (eds.), *Die hermeneutische Frage in der Theologie* (Herder, Freiburg, 1968), pp. 86-152.

48. B. I. Premo, "The Early Wittgenstein and Hermeneutics" in *Ph.T.* XVI (1972), 42-65.

49. *Ibid.,* p. 59.

50. A. Grabner-Haider, *Semiotik und Theologie. Religiöse Rede zwischen analytischer und hermeneutischer Philosophie* (Kosel-Verlag, Munich, 1973).

51. P. McCormick, E. Schaper, and J. Heaton, "Symposium on Saying and Showing in Heidegger and Wittgenstein" in *J.B.S.P.* III (1972), 27-35, 36-41, and 42-45.

52. G. Ebeling, *I.T.T.L.,* pp. 153-58, beginning with the section entitled "Hermeneutics and Linguistic Analysis."

their apppoach to language, especially in terms of a common belief that uses of language reflect a prior "understanding."[53] Even before Braaten's comments in 1965, Ingvar Horby had compared the relation between language and "world" in Wittgenstein and Heidegger in an article entitled "The Double Awareness in Heidegger and Wittgenstein."[54] One of the clearest accounts of similarities as well as differences between Wittgenstein and Heidegger appears in 1965 in an article by F. Kerr entitled "Language as Hermeneutic in the Later Wittgenstein."[55] One of the sections of his article explicitly bears the heading "Wittgenstein and Heidegger: The Same Programme."[56] Karsten Harries also argues that Wittgenstein and Heidegger share the same point of departure and travel in the same direction in their work on language.[57] One writer, J. D. Caputo, even claims, "There is a growing sense of a kinship between Heidegger and Wittgenstein, and an increasing number of efforts to link continental and Anglo-American thought more closely together."[58]

In addition to these studies, a further stimulus to the present approach comes from approaches to Wittgenstein's writings which attempt to see them (or at least certain themes in them) less in the context of British philosophy than in the context of Continental thought. Allan Janik and Stephen Toulmin, for example, approach Wittgenstein not as a British philosopher in the tradition of Russell and Moore, but as "a Viennese thinker whose intellectual problems and personal attitudes alike had been formed in the neo-Kantian environment."[59] This kind of approach to the *Tractatus* is certainly suggested by Paul Engelmann's *Letters from Ludwig Wittgenstein*.[60] In addition to this, two articles by Stanley Cavell view Wittgenstein in an almost Kierkegaardian perspective.[61]

This is not to pre-judge whether the whole of Wittgenstein's thought

53. F. Mayr, "Language" in K. Rahner (ed.), *Sacramentum Mundi. An Encyclopedia of Theology* III (Burns and Oates, New York and London, 1969), 272; cf. pp. 268-74.
54. I. Horby, "The Double Awareness in Heidegger and Wittgenstein" in *Inquiry* II (1959), 235-64.
55. F. Kerr, "Language as Hermeneutic in the Later Wittgenstein" in *Tijdskrift voor Filosophie* XXVII (1965), 491-520.
56. *Ibid.*, pp. 500-504.
57. K. Harries, "Wittgenstein and Heidegger: The Relationship of the Philosopher to Language" in *The Journal of Value Inquiry* II (1968), 281-91.
58. J. D. Caputo, "Review of M. Heidegger, *On the Way to Language*" in *R.M.* XXV (1971), 353.
59. A. Janik and S. Toulmin, *Wittgenstein's Vienna* (Wiedenfeld & Nicholson, London, 1973), p. 22.
60. P. Engelmann, *Letters from Ludwig Wittgenstein. With a Memoir* (Blackwell, Oxford, 1967).
61. S. Cavell, "Existentialism and Analytical Philosophy" in *Daedalus* XCIII (1964), 946-74; and "The Availability of Wittgenstein's Later Philosophy" in G. Pitcher (ed.), *Wittgenstein: The Philosophical Investigations* (Macmillan, London, 1968), pp. 151-85. The latter is reprinted in S. Cavell, *Must We Mean What We Say?* (Cambridge University Press, Cambridge, 1976), pp. 44-72.

can be adequately viewed in this way. Nor does it necessarily open the door to an entirely pluralistic and relativistic interpretation of "language-games" as seems to be hinted at by Peter Winch and Paul van Buren.[62] It suggests, however, that Wittgenstein's philosophy is to be seen in a more radical, if not "hermeneutical" way than that which some Anglo-American interpretations of Wittgenstein might suggest. Such an approach is represented, for example, by George Pitcher, who in spite of the value of much of his work has also received sharp criticism from Rush Rhees.[63]

There are two other contributions to this part of the debate which must also be considered. It was only after I had completed my own study that I came across George F. Sefler's book *Language and the World,* to which he gave the subtitle: *A Methodological Synthesis Within the Writings of Martin Heidegger and Ludwig Wittgenstein.*[64] Sefler concludes, "Both men, although belonging to different philosophical traditions, share in common several definite views, structurally speaking, about language, its cognitive limitations, its relation to the world, and even philosophy in general. The two men's writings are indeed methodologically congruent in many respects; their thoughts are upon many topics structurally complementary rather than contradictory."[65] Certainly, as Sefler reminds us, in December 1929 Wittgenstein "brushed aside as over-intellectualist the moral philosphy of G. E. Moore . . . and spoke with genuine respect of Heidegger."[66] Both thinkers, Sefler continues, view the method of philosophy as purely descriptive; both believe that meaning is contextually determined; both are dissatisfied with the traditional "property" theory of meaning; both believe that the language of philosophy is not representational; and finally both, according to Sefler, believe that "the logical structure of the language of metaphysics, or ontology, is akin to that of poetry."[67] He writes, "For both Heidegger and Wittgenstein it is language which demonstrates and structures the things of one's world. . . . 'Only where there is language is there world'. . . . Things as differentiated entities do not just exist and then language tags them with a

62. Cf. the criticisms made by W. D. Hudson in "Some Remarks on Wittgenstein's Account of Religious Belief" in *Royal Institute of Philosophy Lectures, Vol. 2: Talk of God* (Macmillan, London, 1969), pp. 45-49; cf. 36-51. Cf. also P. van Buren, *Theological Explorations,* pp. 18-19.
63. G. Pitcher, *The Philosophy of Wittgenstein* (Prentice Hall, Englewood, Cliffs, N.J., 1964; and R. Rhees, *Discussions of Wittgenstein* (Routledge and Kegan Paul, London, 1970), pp. 37-54.
64. G. F. Sefler, *Language and the World. A Methodological Synthesis Within the Writings of Martin Heidegger and Ludwig Wittgenstein* (Humanities Press, Atlantic Highlands, N.J., 1974).
65. *Ibid.,* p. 195.
66. *Ibid.,* p. 198.
67. *Ibid.,* p. 200.

name."[68] It is possible that Sefler reads out of Wittgenstein a greater significance for poetry than Wittgenstein in fact would have claimed. Nevertheless he is basically correct in seeing some kind of parallel between Heidegger's deep concern about the creative power of language and Wittgenstein's concern about conceptual grammar and the power of pictures or metaphors.

The other comment on Wittgenstein comes from Gadamer himself. Gadamer declares, "Something like a convergence is occuring between Wittgenstein's critique of Anglo-Saxon semantics on the one hand, and the criticism of the ahistorical art of phenomenological description that is made by . . . hermeneutical consciousness on the other."[69] In his introduction to Gadamer's *Philosophical Hermeneutics*, David E. Linge writes, "Wittgenstein's idea of the language-game is thus in certain respects similar to Gadamer's own concept of prejudice structures. . . . What Gadamer and Wittgenstein share in common . . . is the affirmation of the unity of linguisticality and institutionalized, intersubjectively valid ways of seeing. . . . Both of them stress that the rules of language-game are discovered only by observing its concrete use in interpersonal communication."[70] We dissent from Linge's interpretation of Wittgenstein only insofar as he tends to overstress the relativity and pluralism of Wittgenstein's approach, as if to imply that his language-games were virtually self-contained and autonomous. As we shall see, the matter is more complex and subtle than this.

In his later writings Wittgenstein stressed that the formation of concepts depends on judgments, and that judgments are themselves bound up with language-games and therefore with "forms of life."[71] The functions of definitions and propositions depend on some *prior context in life*. P. M. S. Hacker and more recently especially John T. E. Richardson have argued that in this respect Wittgenstein was greatly influenced by a paper delivered in March 1928 by L. E. J. Brouwer.[72] Brouwer argued that mathematics, science, and language should all be viewed as human activities belonging to a social and historical context. Certainly throughout his later thought Wittgenstein stresses that they are bound up with the problem of historical conditionedness. However, the parallel is perhaps close enough at this point to allow us to see an element of truth in a striking statement of F. Kerr. He declares, "The programme carried

68. *Ibid.*, p. 188.
69. H.-G. Gadamer, *P.H.*, p. 127.
70. *Ibid.*, p. XXXV.
71. L. Wittgenstein, *P.I.*, sects. 19, 23, and 241-42; cf. *Z.*, sect. 173 with *Z.*, sects. 227-28.
72. J. T. E. Richardson, *The Grammar of Justification. An Interpretation of Wittgenstein's Philosophy of Language* (Sussex University Press, London, 1976), pp. 11-44; and P. M. S. Hacker, *Insight and Illusion: Wittgenstein on Philosophy and the Metaphysics of Experience* (Oxford University Press, London, 1972), esp. pp. 100-102.

through in *Sein und Zeit* is, on the one level, exactly the same as that in the *Investigations:* that is to say, the surmounting of a post-Cartesian philosophy of this isolated worldless 'I' by means of a thoroughgoing retrieval of a philosophy in which the human subject is always the participant in a community *prior to all objectification and subjectivism.*"[73] Thus, for Wittgenstein, all language-uses, all meanings, are embedded in concrete situations. But because language is bound up with judgments and forms of life, Wittgenstein believed that (in the words of David Pears) "our language determines our view of reality."[74] Wittgenstein's own remarks on the question are too complex to be summarized here, and must be considered later. However, we may note one of his key remarks: "Only in the stream of thought and life do words have meaning."[75]

One final comment, which is important for New Testament hermeneutics, should be made before we leave this particular consideration. If Wittgenstein's approach to language does in fact possess affinities with that of Heidegger, have we not proved too much in order to establish Wittgenstein's relevance to the present subject? How can it still be worthwhile to examine Wittgenstein's philosophy, if his significance for New Testament hermeneutics is similar to that of Heidegger? The answer is clear when we consider two points. First of all, it would be overstating the case to claim that these two approaches to language are *similar.* We are suggesting only that there is a certain *overlapping* of perspectives, especially on the relationship between language and understanding. In other areas this approach is quite different. Secondly, British and American critics of Bultmann and the new hermeneutic often argue that Heidegger's philosophy provides too narrow a basis for theories of hermeneutics. A study of Wittgenstein will either confirm that Bultmann and other Continental theologians have left certain important considerations out of account, or else it will demonstrate that the same conclusions about language and understanding can be reached by a quite different route from that taken by Heidegger. In practice, these are not totally exclusive alternatives. Our examination of Wittgenstein's philosophy will serve to confirm certain aspects of Heidegger's approach to language. But in other respects it will call in question certain assumptions about language which feature in the new hermeneutic and especially in Bultmann.

We turn, indeed, at this point to the relationship between Wittgenstein and Bultmann. Perhaps surprisingly, Wittgenstein's philosophy is relevant to claims made by Bultmann in two basic directions. The first concerns Bultmann's dualism; the second concerns his claim that theolog-

---

73. F. Kerr, "Language as Hermeneutic in the Later Wittgenstein," *Tijdskrift voor Filosophie* XXVII, 502 (my italics).
74. D. Pears, *Wittgenstein* (Fontana/Collins, London, 1971), p. 13.
75. L. Wittgenstein, *Z.,* sect. 173.

ical statements are best understood in terms of anthropology, or through what the New Testament says about man.

Bultmann, we shall argue, has absorbed a philosophical dualism from Marburg Neo-Kantianism, which he carries over into his view of language. Everywhere in his theology this dualism is apparent, since the Kantian dualism between fact and the Beyond mediated through Marburg (!) philosophy is linked with a Lutheran dualism between grace and law. Bultmann draws a sharp line between fact and value, between myth and kerygma, between *Historie* and *Geschichte*, between history and eschatology, between indicative and imperative, and between law and gospel. We shall discuss this dualism in chapter nine, especially section 34. So eager is Bultmann to emphasize the second term of each pair that the first tends to become lost from view.

Wittgenstein also began from a sharp dualism between fact and value which is reflected in the outlook of the *Tractatus*. "Facts" *(Tatsachen)* could be stated in terms of a propositional calculus; but "values" belonged to the realm which, though they might be "shown" or might "make themselves manifest" *(dies zeigt sich),* nevertheless "cannot be put into words" *(es gibt allerdings Unaussprechliches).*[76] However, Wittgenstein abandoned this dualism in his later work. He saw, for example, that a sharp dualism between indicative and imperative, or between description and command, simply fails to do justice to the complexity of (!) human life as it is. The "given" is no longer the *a priori* dualism of Kant or of Neo-Kantianism; it is human life in all its variety and complexity.[77] In this respect it may be claimed that Wittgenstein's later writings provide a necessary corrective to some of Bultmann's philosophical assumptions.

In spite of his dualism, however, Bultmann also insists that "in speaking of God, theology must *at the same time speak of man.*"[78] Similarly, "Every assertion about God is *simultaneously an assertion about man* and vice versa."[79] This brings us to the second point. I shall attempt to assess the significance and validity of this claim in due course in the light of Wittgenstein's remarks about public criteria of meaning. Wittgenstein's work shows, I believe, that there is a sense in which Bultmann is right, and a sense in which he is wrong.

If Wittgenstein is correct about public criteria of meaning (and I believe that he is), this seems to confirm Bultmann's assumption that speech about God must entail speech about man if it is to acquire and retain an adequate currency of meaning. For example, the cash-value of the confession that "Christ is Lord" is seen in terms of the disciple's

76. L. Wittgenstein, *T.* 1-2.063 as against 6.522; cf. 6.41-47.
77. Cf. L. Wittgenstein, *P.I.,* sects. 108, 217, and 325.
78. R. Bultmann, *F.U.* I, 148 (my italics).
79. R. Bultmann, *T.N.T.* I, 191 (German, p. 188; my italics).

public obedience to Christ as Lord. Wittgenstein and Bultmann would agree, in effect, that language about the lordship of Christ is self-involving. All the same, can language about God be reduced to language about man *exhaustively and without remainder?* Does the statement "God will judge you" mean only "you must live responsibly"? Sometimes Bultmann seems to come very close to saying so. Wittgenstein can shed light on this issue because he is always at pains to distinguish conceptual investigations from those which concern ontology. In his well-known discussion about pain-language and pain-behavior, he exclaims, "We have only rejected the grammar which tries to force itself on us here."[80] This is why he can insist that he is not "a behaviourist in disguise."[81] But is Bultmann as successful as Wittgenstein in distinguishing between conditions which operate at the level of *intelligibility* and those which concern *reality?* Wittgenstein provides us with a finer set of tools for conceptual and linguistic inquiries than those which Bultmann has at his disposal, and we shall argue that in practice Bultmann fails to meet the standards of intelligibility that Wittgenstein shows must be met. This is not unconnected with Bultmann's devaluation of the Old Testament, which provides a public tradition and linguistic training from the framework of which certain religious concepts draw their cash-value.

6. *Heidegger, Bultmann, Gadamer, and Wittgenstein and the New Testament*

We have already argued in the previous chapter that certain perspectives and conceptual schemes which have been drawn from philosophy may serve in certain circumstances to illuminate the text of the New Testament itself. We referred in particular to Bultmann's work on σῶμα, to the work of G. V. Jones on the Parable of the Prodigal Son, and to D. O. Via's approach to the Parable of the Talents. The relationship between Heidegger's thought and the text of the New Testament has been viewed in a variety of ways. In due course we shall look closely at Bultmann's use of Heidegger's categories for the interpretation of the New Testament. Meanwhile, we may note that a number of writers apart from Bultmann argue that there are close affinities between Heidegger's view of human existence and the New Testament portraits of man. The New Testament scholar Erich Dinkler writes: "When Heidegger criticizes man as enslaved by the pseudo-security of concrete objects . . . when he analyzes idle talk and gossip as an attempt to escape from ultimate anxiety towards death—then he says nothing else than what Paul has said charac-

80. L. Wittgenstein, *P.I.*, sect. 304.
81. *Ibid.*, sect. 307; cf. sects. 293-309.

terizing man according to the flesh. In fact Heidegger's portrait of the
thrown and fallen man is very similar to what Paul with the Greek term
καυχᾶσθαι says about self-glorification and boasting."[82] In particular
Dinkler considers that Heidegger's view of the human tension between
fate and freedom comes close to the New Testament description of man.
He continues, "As a New Testament student I cannot refrain from saying
that it is just this interrelation and correlation of freedom *and* predestina-
tion explained by Paul . . . which we re-discover here in philosophical
terms."[83]

The same kind of point is made by other theologians, in spite of some
dissenting voices whose criticisms we shall discuss in due course. G.
Miegge comments, "It is not necessary to spill much ink in order to
demonstrate the affinity which exists between the formulating of problems
current in existentialist philosophy . . . and that to be found in the New
Testament."[84] This affinity is not restricted to Paul. J. Macquarrie writes,
"It may fairly be claimed that there is some affinity between existentialism and the teaching of Jesus."[85] Macquarrie contrasts, on the one
hand, the concreteness and particularity both of the New Testament and
of Heidegger's thought with the more abstract categories of Greek
philosophy.

It would be a mistake, however, to limit Heidegger's relevance to
New Testament interpretation to the so-called "existentialism" of *Being
and Time.* The detailed work of Ernst Fuchs on the text of the New
Testament also owes much to the stimulus of Heidegger's later thought. In
chapter twelve, therefore, we examine Heidegger's thought after the
"turn" *(Kehre,* sometimes translated "reversal") which occurred around
1935.

Admittedly Fuchs himself seems hesitant to allow that he has been
influenced by the distinctively later thought of Heidegger. However,
James Robinson, who is perhaps the leading chronicler of the new hermeneutic of Fuchs and Ebeling, writes: "It was Ernst Fuchs who first
translated the hermeneutical discussion from the categories of inauthentic
and authentic existence derived from *Being and Time* into the later
Heidegger's analogous distinction between everyday language of the
subject-object dilemma and the uncorrupted language of being."[86] Similarly, after describing the main thrust of Heidegger's later thought, Paul
Achtemeier comments, "Such is the kind of thought in which the new

82. E. Dinkler, "Martin Heidegger" in Carl Michaelson (ed.), *Christianity and the Existentialists* (Scribner, New York, 1956), p. 117; cf. pp. 97-127.
83. *Ibid.,* pp. 118-19.
84. G. Miegge, *Gospel and Myth in the Thought of Rudolf Bultmann* (Eng. Lutterworth
Press, London, 1960), p. 62.
85. J. Macquarrie, *An Existentialist Theology,* p. 21.
86. J. M. Robinson and J. B. Cobb, *N.H.,* p. 49.

hermeneutic is anchored, and in terms of which it seems to carry out its theological task."[87] Indeed so convincing is the case that it might seem strange that there should be any controversy about it.

The particular way in which Fuchs himself has commented on this issue has perhaps been the cause of what controversy there is about it. In the *Ergänzungsheft* of the second and third editions of his book *Hermeneutik* he explicitly rejects the idea that his own view of language is tied to Heidegger's later thought.[88] However, what Fuchs wishes to deny is not the existence of close affinities between Heidegger's later thought and his own, but the suggestion that all credit for originality should be given to Heidegger. He himself, he claims, sensed the direction in which *Being and Time* might be thought to point, and reached a similar perspective to Heidegger's independently of his later thought, although admittedly by doing so from Heidegger's earlier starting-point. In point of fact we have only to compare certain themes in Fuchs' hermeneutics with Heidegger's later writings to be aware of striking similarities. Thus it may perhaps be not entirely without significance that the fourth edition of *Hermeneutik* (1970), which comes from a different publisher, omits the four-page preface to the second and third editions, including the comments that can so easily lead to misunderstanding.

The twenty or so writings of Heidegger that span the years 1935 to 1960 reflect a pessimistic assessment of the capacity of the language of the Western language-tradition to convey anything other than the day-to-day practicalia of technology and idle talk. Because man has, in Heidegger's view, fallen out of Being, his language has become trivialized and atomized. In *An Introduction to Metaphysics* Heidegger writes, "Man . . . is always thrown back on the paths that he himself has laid out: he becomes mired in his paths, caught in the beaten track. . . . He excludes himself from Being. He turns round and round in his own circle."[89] It is illuminating to compare Heidegger's view of the atomizing and degeneration of language with that of Gerhard Ebeling. Ebeling writes, "The atoms of speech, all that remain in language, the empty words, now produce not understanding but . . . take hold of you like a whirlpool and carry you off into the void."[90] Where this happens, there occurs "a complete collapse of language."[91] Today, Ebeling concludes, "We threaten to die of language poisoning."[92]

87. P. J. Achtemeier, *An Introduction to the New Hermeneutic* (Westminster Press, Philadelphia, 1969), p. 54.
88. E. Fuchs, "Ergänzungsheft" to *Hermeneutik* (Müllerchön, Bad Canstatt, ³1963), p. 5 (not in *Hermeneutik*, Mohr, Tübingen, ⁴1970, which is the edition normally cited).
89. M. Heidegger, *I.M.*, pp. 157-58 (Anchor edn. p. 132).
90. G. Ebeling, *I.T.T.L.*, p. 71.
91. *Ibid.*, p. 76.
92. G. Ebeling, *God and Word* (Eng. Fortress Press, Philadelphia, 1967), p. 2; cf. p. 17.

By contrast, both Heidegger and the exponents of the new hermeneutic look, positively, for a new "coming-to-speech." Heidegger waits for the disclosure of Being in an authentic event of language. In the writings of Fuchs, the message of Jesus "strikes home" *(treffen)* in language-event *(Sprachereignis)*.[93] Robert Funk and J. D. Crossan adopt a closely related approach to the parables of Jesus. In the parables, they urge, the conventional "world" that holds man in bondage to everyday values is shattered, and the way is opened up for a new vision of reality. Funk sees metaphor as opening up such a process in the parables. He writes, "Metaphor shatters the conventions of predication in the interests of a new vision . . . a fresh experience of reality."[94] Where Heidegger invokes the creative power of the poet, Funk calls attention to the creative power of metaphor in the language of Jesus.[95]

We have already made the point that the interpretation of the New Testament texts themselves remains the prime concern of Rudolf Bultmann in all his writings. The point is too obvious to require further elaboration. But it is otherwise with the work of Hans-Georg Gadamer. We have already argued that Gadamer's writings are of the utmost importance in relation to any attempt to formulate a theory of hermeneutics. But does his work have any more immediate relevance to the interpretation of the text of the New Testament itself?

There are at least three ways in which Gadamer's work relates directly to New Testament interpretation. First of all, in chapter ten we shall illustrate the problem of fusion and distance in Gadamer's hermeneutics with reference to the relation between systematic theology and biblical exegesis. We take up these issues especially in the light of the claims of Diem and Ott (sections 45 and 46), and it is unnecessary to anticipate this discussion here. Secondly, Gadamer raises questions about the relation of language and understanding to experience *(Erfahrung)*. He is concerned with "modes of experience *(Erfahrungsweisen)* in which a truth is communicated that cannot be verified by the methodological means proper to science."[96] This includes the kind of experience which is generated by a work of art. Clearly this is relevant to questions about the communication of a content through biblical texts which are approached not simply as discursive propositions, but as imaginative narrative, art-forms, and so on. Gadamer traces connections between experience and

93. E. Fuchs, *S.H.J.*, pp. 196-98 and 202 (German, pp. 411-14 and 418).
94. R. W. Funk, *Language, Hermeneutic and Word of God. The Problem of Language in the New Testament and Contemporary Theology* (Harper and Row, New York, 1966), p. 139.
95. *Ibid.*, pp. 133-222; cf. also *Jesus as Precursor* (S.B.L. *Semeia* Supplement No. 2, Scholars Press, Missoula, 1975) and M. Heidegger, "Hölderlin and the Essence of Poetry" in *E.B.*, pp. 291-316.
96. *Ibid.*, p. xii; German, p. xxvi.

truth in the history of Western philosophy. All this relates closely, once again, to the kind of approaches to New Testament hermeneutics which we have briefly noted in connection with such varied writers as Fuchs, Funk, and Crossan. These writers share the perspective of Heidegger and Gadamer that language is bound up with "world," and that the conveying of information and descriptive concepts is not necessarily the most important function of language. We may note Crossan's aphorism, to which we shall return later: "Myth establishes world. Apologue defends world. Action investigates world. Satire attacks world. Parable subverts world."[97]

Thirdly, we may note that one writer, Franz Mussner, has already taken Gadamer as his point of departure in interpreting a particular text of the New Testament. Mussner is concerned with the problem of the historical Jesus and the kerygmatic Christ in relation to the language and theology of the Fourth Gospel. He writes, "The 'Johannine problem' is chiefly a hermeneutical one. Considerable light and help can be had from the discussions and results of modern hermeneutics, as these have been pursued and achieved in particular by Martin Heidegger . . . in the footsteps of W. Dilthey, and in succession to both by Hans-Georg Gadamer in his important work *Wahrheit und Methode*."[98] Mussner adds that it was *"only his acquaintance with Gadamer's work* that gave him courage to examine" this key problem of the Johannine writings.[99]

Taking up Gadamer's concepts of historical tradition, temporal distance, and the merging of horizons, Mussner expounds Johannine thought as moving between two poles. On the one hand there is the "past" pole of the historical Jesus and historical testimony. On the other hand there is the "present" pole of the church of John's day, and his use of "Johannine" language. John is faithful to the historical apostolic witness, but he also creatively interprets it for his own time. He can do justice to both sides at once, because in Mussner's view (following Gadamer), "Understanding is more than the reproduction of past events."[100]

Johannine language is necessarily bound up with Johannine understanding. But neither John's language nor his understanding is merely arbitrary. "'Understanding' of Jesus was for John primarily an *historical knowledge.*"[101] At the same time, "Retrospection is not a mechanical reproduction of the history of Jesus, and in the act of vision there occurs the exposition effected by the Spirit, and so the historical Jesus becomes

---

97. J. D. Crossan, *The Dark Interval. Towards a Theology of Story*, p. 59.
98. F. Mussner, *The Historical Jesus in the Gospel of St. John* (Eng. Herder, Freiburg, and Burns and Oates, London, 1967), p. 8.
99. *Ibid.* (my italics).
100. *Ibid.*, p. 13.
101. *Ibid.*, p. 17 (Mussner's italics).

the Christ of the kerygma."[102] This is because, in Gadamer's sense, "history" becomes "history as operative influence."[103] Drawing also on his category of temporal distance, Mussner quotes with approval Gadamer's statement that "the time-interval . . . alone brings out fully the true meaning that something involves."[104]

This is not to suggest that verdicts about John's relation to historical tradition can be arrived at with reference to Gadamer rather than in the light of Johannine studies. Gadamer's significance for Johannine interpretation must not be exaggerated. Indeed Mussner himself seems not to be entirely consistent in whether or not he sees John as a historical witness to the earthly life of Jesus, in the usual sense in which this is understood. However, Mussner does provide us with an example of how a student of the New Testament draws on the work of a philosopher for categories and perspectives which, at least in his own view, help him towards a better understanding of the New Testament itself.

We have already noted that no New Testament scholar has as yet sought to draw on the insights of Wittgenstein in order to enrich or deepen his understanding of the New Testament. We can appeal to no precedent. Nevertheless while in chapter thirteen I shall try to show the relevance of Wittgenstein to hermeneutical theory in general, in chapter fourteen I shall endeavor to draw on some of Wittgenstein's categories and methods in order to shed further light on the text of the New Testament itself. First of all, I shall explore his notion of analytical or "grammatical" utterances, and try to show how this type of language serves to perform certain functions in the Pauline epistles. This will entail a form-critical inquiry about the settings of such utterances. More especially, however, I shall draw on Wittgenstein's notion of language-games, together with his work on "seeing as." Armed with these three concepts, I shall undertake a completely fresh exploration of Paul's doctrine of justification by faith. I shall take up three standard problems in Pauline interpretation. First of all, how can man be both righteous and yet a sinner? Secondly, how can justification be both present and yet only future? Thirdly, how can faith constitute a "means" of justification without thereby becoming a special kind of "work"? I shall argue that none of these pairs of contrasts involves a contradiction or "paradox," and also that neither side of the contrasts in question is to be softened at the expense of the other. The picture presented by Paul is a coherent and logically satisfying one, provided that it is seen in the appropriate perspective. We shall also look at the concept of faith in the Epistle of James, in the light of Wittgenstein's remarks about belief.

102. *Ibid.,* p. 47.
103. *Ibid.*
104. *Ibid.,* p. 78.

We may note, in passing, that to "use" Wittgenstein in this way is by no means to do violence to the intention of his own writings. Wittgenstein never viewed his own work as a statement of philosophical "results," but rather as a way (or as many ways) of thinking. In his Preface to the *Investigations* he explicitly states, "I should not like my writing to spare other people the trouble of thinking. But, if possible, *to stimulate some-one to thoughts of his own.*"[105] Commenting on this aspect of Wittgenstein's work, Dallas M. High concludes, "There is clear propriety for 'using' rather than commenting upon the writings, working through some of his thoughts and puzzles rather than summarizing them, applying his insights rather than grouping, categorizing, or classifying them."[106]

We have tried to set out reasons to show why it is by no means arbitrary to draw on the work of Heidegger, Bultmann, Gadamer, and Wittgenstein in order to explore issues in New Testament hermeneutics. Our concern with philosophy is by no means restricted to the work of these thinkers. We shall refer, for example, not only to Marburg Neo-Kantianism, but also, from time to time, to the work of Paul Ricoeur. We shall also glance briefly at the use made by certain Latin-American theologians of Marxist philosophy in their approach to the problem of pre-understanding in hermeneutics. Nor can we avoid raising wider questions about historical understanding which involve considerations of the philosophy of such thinkers as W. Dilthey. However, we must draw a line somewhere, and after we have critically examined issues in hermeneutics that concern history, theology, and language, we shall return to look more closely at the work of Heidegger, Bultmann, Gadamer, and Wittgenstein.

It will have become clear by now that we are drawing on philosophical description only in order to shed light on the hermeneutics of the New Testament. Our approach to the subject is different, therefore, from that of Nels F. S. Ferré in his essay "Biblical Faith and Philosophic Truth," or from that of Georges Van Riet in his paper "Exégèse et Réflexion Philosophique."[107] Ferré allows that whereas biblical truth is historical, concerned, personal, and concrete, philosophical truth is general, universal, objective, and rational. However, he concludes that "the two kinds of truth at heart are one. . . . Biblical faith and philosophic truth, while

---

105. L. Wittgenstein, *P.I.*, p. x (my italics).
106. D. M. High, *Language, Persons and Belief. Studies in Wittgenstein's 'Philosophical Investigations' and Religious Uses of Language* (Oxford University Press, New York, 1967), p. 20.
107. N. F. S. Ferré, "Biblical Faith and Philosophic Truth," in L. S. Rouner (ed.), *Philosophy, Religion and the Coming World Civilization. Essays in Honour of William Ernest Hocking* (Nijhoff, The Hague, 1966), pp. 198-212; and G. Van Riet, "Exégèse et Réflexion Philosophique" in G. Thils and R. E. Brown (eds.), *Donum Naticalicum Iosepho Coppens, Vol. III: Exégèse et Theologie. Les saintes Ecritures et leur interpretation theologique* (Bibliotheca Ephemeridum Theologicarum Lovaniensum xxvi; Duculot, Gembloux, 1968), pp. 1-16.

different roads to reality, converge towards the same centre."[108] The theologian, he argues, needs the philosopher's capacity for methodological objectivity; the philosopher needs to recognize that "concerned truth alone can fulfill interested truth. . . . Truth in the service of life is truly truth for truth's sake."[109] Van Riet also argues that exegesis and philosophy "coincide at least partially," inasmuch as each represents an aspect of the search for truth.[110]

In our own inquiries we have consistently tried to avoid making any grandiose metaphysical claim about the status of particular philosophies as theories of *truth*. We nowhere claim that Heidegger, Gadamer, or Wittgenstein either substantiates or undermines the *truth* of the New Testament. We claim only that this philosophical description provides us with tools which may help us both to elucidate the nature of the *hermeneutical* task which confronts the New Testament interpreter and also to unfold the *meaning* of certain parts of the New Testament itself. There are admittedly some traditions of philosophical theology, for example that of the conservative writer Cornelius Van Til, in which these claims may well be taken with a measure of scepticism.[111] To those who stand in this tradition I only make the request that they patiently suspend any unfavorable *a priori* judgment until they have followed through the arguments of the present study in detail. Only at the end of our study will the reader be in a position to judge finally whether, for example, our use of Wittgenstein has clouded or clarified some of the issues under discussion.

108. N. F. S. Ferré, in *Philosophy, Religion and the Coming World Civilization*, p. 199.
109. *Ibid.*, p. 211.
110. G. van Riet, in *Donum Naticalicum Iosepho Coppens, Vol. III*, p. 16.
111. Cf. C. Van Til, *The Defense of the Faith*, and "Introduction" to B. B. Warfield, *Inspiration and Authority of the Bible* (Presbyterian and Reformed Publishing Company, Philadelphia, 1948), pp. 3-68.

subject of hermeneutics and history when we discuss the work of Hans-Georg Gadamer, since he devotes more than a third of *Truth and Method* to this subject.

7. *The Pastness of the Past*

Although the next chapter more strictly concerns hermeneutics and theology, it is impossible to isolate questions about hermeneutics and history from all theological considerations. D. E. Nineham's broad perspective, at least in his writings to date, invites close comparison with the orientation of Ernst Troeltsch. Yet it will become clear that while Troeltsch aimed at a strict historical objectivity which was independent of religious or theological dogma, from the point of view of the perspective advocated by Wolfhart Pannenberg Troeltsch's historical criteria are simply "anthropocentric."[8] Nineham rightly warns us that we must not *pre-judge* questions about the relevance of the past simply on the basis of theology. But neither must we *pre-judge* questions about the relevance of theology simply on the basis of prevailing cultural assumptions which belong to the present. It is precisely in order to guard against this latter temptation that we conclude this chapter with a comparison between the claims of Troeltsch and Pannenberg.

Nineham's first essay on the present subject, written in 1963, is less polemical than his subsequent writings. Certainly he gives expression to the theme which comes to dominate all his more recent thought, and speaks of "the deep gulf between its context (i.e. that of the ancient text) and our situation."[9] Nevertheless, like Dilthey and Bultmann he still emphasizes that the hermeneutical problem has some positive solution in that "after all, we share the basic humanity of the biblical men and women."[10] Hence we may "try to discover a way of approaching the Bible that is likely to discover its message for our day with the least likelihood of distortion."[11] Nineham broadly approves of Bultmann's hermeneutical aims, though he rejects his "absolutizing" of a particular philosophy as a means of reaching them. He writes, "What I plead for is that we should have some Biblical scholars who come to this study from a background of professional philosophy and other 'modern' studies, and whose expertise is, if I may put it so, in the modern end of the problem. Perhaps in the light of their studies they might do for us what Bultmann

---

8. W. Pannenberg, *B.Q.T.* I, 39-50. See section 10 of the present chapter.
9. D. E. Nineham, "The Lessons of the Past for the Present" in *The Church's Use of the Bible Past and Present* (S.P.C.K., London, 1963), p. 166; cf. pp. 145-69.
10. *Ibid.*, p. 166.
11. *Ibid.*, p. 167.

has tried to do, more systematically and at the same time more tentatively and empirically."[12]

In his second essay on this subject, published in 1969 under the title "The Use of the Bible in Modern Theology," Dennis Nineham attacks the assumption that we can necessarily move on from questions about "what the New Testament *meant*" to questions about "what it *means.*"[13] He insists, "Many statements in ancient texts have no meaning today in any normal sense of the word 'meaning'."[14] In particular he rightly attacks the uncritical use of certain passages in such a way as to force them to speak on such distinctively modern issues as the ecumenical movement or the ordination of women.[15]

The third and fourth essays appeared in 1976, one as an untitled contribution to the report *Christian Believing,* the other under the title *New Testament Interpretation in an Historical Age.* In the first of these two essays he calls attention to the difference of perspective by which the same phenomenon might be described as demon possession in the New Testament and psychic disturbance today. He infers from this difference of perspective: "We cannot interpret Jesus exactly in the way they did. . . . Our range of knowledge and the absolute presuppositions integrity compels us to share are so different from those of the early Christians that we naturally find ourselves asking: if men of their cultural background and presuppositions interpreted the facts like that, how should we, with our quite different cultural background, have interpreted them?"[16]

In the fourth essay, *New Testament Interpretation in an Historical Age,* Nineham begins by repeating the warning which he made in his article of 1969 against assumptions about "the present meaning" of the New Testament.[17] However, he also makes much more of the rise of historical consciousness. He observes, "Modern man is aware in a way that his predecessors have not been, of the historically conditioned character of all human experience, speech, and institutions."[18] What one culture or historical era accepts as axiomatic is by no means necessarily shared by another culture or era. Interpretations of all religious phenomena, Nineham urges, including the New Testament itself, must take this principle into account. It is the failure to come to terms with it which vitiated the attempts of nineteenth-century Liberal Protestant writers to provide a "life" of Jesus of Nazareth. Nineham approves

---

12. *Ibid.,* p. 168.
13. D. E. Nineham, "The Use of the Bible in Modern Theology" in *B.J.R.L.* LII (1969).
14. *Ibid.,* p. 181 (Nineham's italics).
15. *Ibid.,* pp. 191-92.
16. D. E. Nineham, untitled essay in *Christian Believing,* p. 81; cf. pp. 75-88.
17. D. E. Nineham, *New Testament Interpretation in an Historical Age* (Athlone Press, London, 1976), pp. 3-4.
18. *Ibid.,* p. 5.

Schweitzer's statement: "Jesus of Nazareth will not suffer himself to be modernized. As an historic figure he refuses to be detached from his own time. . . . The historic Jesus and the (modern) Germanic spirit cannot be brought together except by an act of historic violence which in the end injures both religion and history."[19] "Jesus has no answer to the question, 'Tell us Thy name in our speech and for our day'."[20] Nineham attacks both C. H. Dodd's realized eschatology and Bultmann's so-called existentialism as producing "woefully hybrid figures, precisely the products of reading an ancient text through modern spectacles."[21]

We come finally to Nineham's most recent publication on this subject, the volume entitled *The Use and Abuse of the Bible*.[22] In some respects this book shows even greater pessimism about biblical hermeneutics than the four previous essays; in other respects (for example in his commendations of Troeltsch) he is concerned to add caveats which almost nullify the force of his main arguments.[23] The Bible, Nineham constantly stresses, was written in an age which is emphatically not ours. But, quoting Lionel Trilling, Nineham writes: "To suppose that we can think like men of another age is as much of an illusion as to suppose that we can think in a wholly different way. . . . It ought to be for us a real question whether, and in what way, human nature is always the same."[24] Nineham seems to have abandoned his belief in 1963 that "after all, we share the basic humanity of the biblical men and women."[25] At least, he describes this principle as "a compound of truths, half-truths, and untruths."[26] The biblical writers lived within a context which Troeltsch described as a *Totalität*, which constitutes a meaning-system into which modern man cannot necessarily enter. If this meaning-system included the belief that God regularly intervened in human affairs in a miraculous way, then to believe in a miracle is something different from what it would be to hold that belief today. Thus: "to believe now in the halting of the sun, or for that matter in the raising of Lazarus, is to hold a quite different belief from that which was held by the biblical writers."[27] Nineham argues that in the context of a belief that illness, for example, is caused by demons, the very *experience* of illness and healing would amount to something different from the *experience* of parallel events today. Necessarily this means a lack of hermeneutical continuity with the past, which

19. *Ibid.*, p. 14; cf. A. Schweitzer, *The Quest of the Historical Jesus* (Eng. Black, London, 1910), pp. 310-11.
20. *Ibid.*
21. *Ibid.*
22. D. E. Nineham, *U.A.B.*
23. *Ibid.*, e.g., cf. p. 34 with pp. 35-36, and the whole argument of the book with p. 265.
24. *Ibid.*, p. 39.
25. D. E. Nineham, *The Church's Use of the Bible*, p. 166.
26. D. E. Nineham, *U.A.B.*, p. 2.
27. *Ibid.*, p. 33.

cannot be overcome by appeals to continuity in human nature or to the use of sympathetic imagination.

Nineham firmly rejects the traditional view of the Bible according to which, he claims, there is a dualism between the natural and supernatural, and each biblical passage is believed necessarily to have something to say to the present. In particular he attacks what he regards as the inadequacies of three approaches. First of all, he rejects the outlook of pre-critical orthodoxy which failed to be aware of the problem of historical relativism and which failed to regard "authorities" with sufficient criticism. Secondly, he identifies what he regards as a simplistic strain in nineteenth-century Liberalism, according to which the biblical writers were seen merely as "simple-minded and ill-educated primitives, and at worst . . . distorters of the truth."[28] Thirdly, Nineham attacks the "biblical theology" approach of Barth and Richardson. Barth is mistaken, he argues, in his claim that he works only with "biblical" categories, while the whole salvation-history school, including Richardson and Cullmann, is guilty of giving a privileged status to what amounts to a tiny segment of events when viewed against the backcloth of world-history. By contrast, "for the New Testament writers, God has been active . . . throughout the world's history from creation day to Doomsday."[29]

The rest of the book is devoted to defending a fourth approach. Above all, this approach takes full account of the revolution in historical consciousness that dominated the eighteenth and nineteenth centuries. These chapters develop themes which we have already noted in Nineham's writings, although in the course of the argument he also makes much of the theological pluralism of the New Testament, and draws on Maurice Wiles' well-known remarks on history and story.[30] He exclaims concerning the whole problem of biblical hermeneutics, "What a relief then to be able to acknowledge its [the Bible's] pastness frankly!"[31] Even Bultmann does not go far enough here, for "in the last resort Bultmann too is a biblicist."[32] The New Testament is basically the *story* of what an ancient experience meant to ancient men. What the same story means to us today may well be something quite different. In this sense, the Bible is no longer a "sacred book."[33]

We return now to Nineham's five writings as a whole. In the first place, we may admit that some of his arguments about historical particularity and distance can at once be supported on the basis of purely *historical* considerations. James Smart, who would by no means share

28. *Ibid.*, p. 71.
29. *Ibid.*, p. 92.
30. *Ibid.*, pp. 174-97.
31. *Ibid.*, p. 192.
32. *Ibid.*, p. 221.
33. *Ibid.*, p. 229.

Cadbury begins by reminding us of some of the more obvious ways in which the interpreter can become guilty of anachronism in thinking about Jesus. For example, phrases such as "the kingdom of God" have been used to describe modern humanitarian ideals of creating a better world. These are then understood in this way when they are heard from the lips of Jesus. Some of the actual examples of modern biographies of Jesus cited by Cadbury almost defy belief. For example, in a book called *The Man Nobody Knows* Bruce Barton interpreted Jesus from "the viewpoint of the advertising expert." "Jesus exemplifies all the principles of modern salesmanship. He was, of course, a good mixer; he made contacts easily and was quick to get en rapport with his 'prospect'. He appreciated the values of news, and so called his message 'good news'. His habit of early rising was indicative of the high pressure of the 'go-getter' so necessary for a successful career."[45] His life was one of business: "Wist ye not that I must be about my Father's *business?*"[46] Cadbury multiplies such examples from a variety of authors. The Parable of the Pounds, one writer argues, gives us "as clear and definite a justification of interest as is contained in any text-book on economics. The episode of the barren fig-tree is a clear lesson in the conservation of land. . . ."[47]

By contrast, Cadbury discusses what he calls the Jewishness of Jesus, his place in the ancient world, the limitations of his social teaching, and his purposes and aims. He writes, "We are only too prone to criticize the past generations for making Jesus in their own image. The tendency to do so we cannot escape ourselves, but the twentieth century is not so justified in representing Jesus as a sociological expert as the sixth century was in painting him as an ascetic or monk. We at least pride ourselves on an honest effort at historical perspective."[48] We may agree with Nineham that one of the practical lessons of Albert Schweitzer's book *The Quest of the Historical Jesus* was to show how readily biographers from Reimarus to Wrede had read their own philosophical and theological convictions into the figure of Jesus.

James Smart, once again, diagnoses the problem clearly. He writes, "We unconsciously modernize the patriarchs, the prophets, Jesus and Paul, in our reading of scripture, letting the elements fall away that are peculiar to their age and strange to ours, and focussing our attention upon those more universally human features which seem to convey readily the meaning of the ancient story."[49] Thus too often Jesus "ceases to be a Jew living in the milieu of the Judaism of the first century A.D. and becomes a

---

45. H. J. Cadbury, *The Peril of Modernizing Jesus*, p. 11.
46. *Ibid.*
47. *Ibid.*, p. 13.
48. *Ibid.*, p. 90.
49. J. D. Smart, *The Interpretation of Scripture*, p. 37.

high minded citizen of some modern culture."[50]

Must we then reluctantly accept Schweitzer's verdict that Jesus can only remain "to our time a stranger and an enigma"? Whatever the merits and difficulties of the book in other respects, J. A. T. Robinson's study *The Human Face of God* represents an attempt *both* to be faithful to the portrait of Jesus conveyed by the ancient text *and* to let this portrait speak to modern man. We cannot, he insists, jump out of the confines of our own horizons, *at least as a starting-point*. Hence we must "genuinely . . . ask *our* questions."[51] But we must also question our own presuppositions in the light of the New Testament itself. We must "constantly be prepared to go freshly, and deeply, into the New Testament witness, if we are to get beneath the presuppositions with which over the centuries we have come to read it."[52] Bishop Robinson's concern is "with *how today* one can truthfully and meaningfully say . . . 'Jesus is Lord'."[53] We must go beyond "ways of speaking about the Christ, or of Jesus as the Christ, which today are unreal or remote—or merely not ours."[54] Nevertheless, Robinson is well aware, as a New Testament scholar, of the problem of the pastness of the past. He writes, "The danger, of course, is that each generation simply sees its own Christ. . . . The safeguard lies in the rigour of our historical criticism, so that we do not 'modernize Jesus' at the cost of taking him out of his age. . . . There is a real difference between making Christ in our own image and allowing the best, critically controlled, scholarly picture to speak to our century."[55]

Our concern here is not to discuss the success of Robinson's specific program. It is possible that he is not entirely successful in his attempt to exchange a christological dualism of natural and supernatural for something else. However, the illuminating point is his attempt both to retain historical rigor and to allow the New Testament to speak to our day. In concrete terms, for example, he attempts to rescue the New Testament portrait of the humanity of Jesus from beneath a historical and cultural tradition which portrayed him as "the complete man of renaissance humanism," or "an average level-headed man, such as parents of a daughter would welcome as a son-in-law."[56] The "perfection" presented in the New Testament is not "the static perfection of flawless porcelain."[57] Robinson rejects "both the static and the sexless Jesus," which constitute "powerful versions today of the cardboard Christ."[58] Robinson

50. *Ibid.*
51. J. A. T. Robinson, *The Human Face of God*, p. x.
52. *Ibid.*
53. *Ibid.*, p. xi.
54. *Ibid.*, p. 12.
55. *Ibid.*, p. 15.
56. *Ibid.*, p. 70.
57. *Ibid.*, p. 77.
58. *Ibid.*, p. 80.

attempts to recapture the Jesus of the past in such a way that he speaks to the present. He accepts Cadbury's warnings, but rejects Schweitzer's conclusions.

The problem of the pastness of the New Testament, then, should neither be ignored nor exaggerated. In order to try to gain a more systematic view of the issues raised by this problem, we shall now turn to the work of historians and philosophers of history.

8. *The Emergence of Historical Consciousness*

From the Middle Ages to the eighteenth century history was viewed very differently from the conception of history held by most modern historians. Alan Richardson underlines the profound consequences which followed from viewing history under the dual headings of "history sacred and profane."[59] Sacred history was valued highly as a source of knowledge on the basis of divine revelation, and its traditions accepted uncritically. Secular history was valued as a source of knowledge only by a small minority. In the Enlightenment itself it was widely considered that history was vitiated by the credulity of historians who failed to examine their traditions critically enough. Indeed from a later vantage-point Troeltsch argued that prior to this time "there is not the slightest trace of a desire for real knowledge or of a critical spirit."[60]

Descartes and Hobbes were typical of their day in their dismissal of history as a source of knowledge. It must be noted, however, that the reason for this attitude had little to do with any awareness of the problem of the pastness of the past, which emerged as a real difficulty only in nineteenth- and twentieth-century thought. The difficulty was not that of *understanding* the past. If history was ignored, this was mainly for two reasons. First of all, the *truth* of given traditions from the past was felt to be uncertain, especially in contrast to purely logical or rational inquiry. Secondly, as far as moral or religious lessons from the past were concerned, this was already adequately provided through the medium of the "sacred history" of the Bible. This "sacred history" was felt to avoid the first difficulty over truth, since it spoke to the present with divine authority.

Even those who were themselves historians rather than philosophers

59. A. Richardson, *History Sacred and Profane* (Bampton Lectures for 1962) (S.C.M., London, 1964), pp. 23-29.
60. E. Troeltsch "Historiography," reprinted from J. Hastings (ed.), *Encyclopedia of Religion and Ethics* VI (1913), 716-23 in J. Macquarrie (ed.), *Contemporary Religious Thinkers* (S.C.M., London, 1968), pp. 77-78; cf. 76-97.

shared this negative attitude towards history. To cite Richardson's verdict again, "Even the antiquarians of the period . . . loved the past for its own sake, not for the sake of the present; and to this extent . . . they were something less than historians in the full contemporary sense."[61] The intellectual who no longer viewed the Bible with the uncritical eyes of the Middle Ages turned to arguments from nature, rather than from history, for inferences about God and religion. When isolated figures from this period did turn to history for knowledge of the present, its relevance was based entirely on the universal principles belonging to human nature which *cut across* the pastness of the past. Thus David Hume wrote in his *Enquiry Concerning Human Understanding,* "Mankind are so much the same, in all times and places, that history informs us of nothing new or strange in this particular. Its chief use is only to discover the constant and universal principles of human nature."[62]

This outlook of the eighteenth century is perhaps most widely known today in terms of the well-known dictum of G. E. Lessing (1729-81). Lessing writes, "If no historical truth can be demonstrated, then nothing can be demonstrated by means of historical truths. That is: accidental truths of history can never become the proof of necessary truths of reason."[63] Recently David Pailin has argued forcefully that Lessing's dictum is still as relevant as it ever was. He comments, "The logical type-jump he refers to is that between claims about what was the case . . . and claims about how reality is to be 'understood' and life to be lived. . . ."[64]

If we express the matter in Pailin's terms, it is clear that Lessing's dualism has close connection with the perspective of the Kantian tradition, including the Marburg Neo-Kantianism that lies behind Bultmann's thought, and even the ethical dualism of Wittgenstein's *Tractatus.* Thus Wittgenstein writes, "If there is any value that does have value, it must lie outside the whole sphere of what happens and is the case. For all that happens and is the case is accidental."[65] Every theologian and philosopher who stands in the Kantian tradition, especially Rudolf Bultmann, is influenced by this perspective, and it has profound repercussions for their views of hermeneutics and history, where these are

61. A. Richardson, *History Sacred and Profane,* p. 26; cf. also his book *The Bible in the Age of Science* (S.C.M., London, 1961), pp. 32-51.
62. D. Hume, *An Enquiry Concerning Human Understanding* (Oxford University Press, 1961), sect. VIII, part 1; cf. also C. E. Braaten, *History and Hermeneutics* (New Directions in Theology Today, Vol. II) (Lutterworth Press, London, 1968), pp. 34-36.
63. G. E. Lessing, "On the Proof of the Spirit and of Power" in H. Chadwick (ed.), *Lessing's Theological Writings* (Black, London, 1956), p. 53; cf. pp. 51-56.
64. D. Pailin, "Lessing's Ditch Revisited: The Problem of Faith and History" in R. H. Preston (ed.), *Theology and Change. Essays in Memory of Alan Richardson* (S.C.M., London, 1975), p. 86; cf. pp. 78-103.
65. L. Wittgenstein, *T.* 6-41; cf. 6-42 to 6-54.

expressed.

However, it is also possible to approach Lessing's dictum from the other side. It is not merely that Lessing's view leads to a devaluation of "facts" in contrast to values. From the other side, it can be seen that Lessing had a theological purpose in his stress on human reason. This aspect has been noted by Helmut Thielicke.[66] Lessing was concerned, Thielicke argues, with the autonomy of the inquirer's rationality, as over against the authoritarianism inherent in the notion of accepting a received tradition. From Lessing's viewpoint, man may believe the truths of the Christian faith not because the apostles or the church claim that certain events took place, but because he himself can endorse the rationality of these truths. In Thielicke's words, "Since I am a rational being . . . any truth-claim that reaches me can be received and appropriated by me only if it contains rational truth. . . . I thus have my own autonomous access to truth."[67] Thielicke concludes, "Lessing adopts the Cartesian approach in so far as he examines the structure of the conditions of absolute certainty in the consciousness."[68] Thus in effect, if not in intention, Lessing has brought us to the place where the nature and value of historical inquiry is judged in terms of *its relation to the interpreter's present horizons.* Lessing urges the limitations of historical inquiry not because history cannot speak to these horizons, but because it cannot provide the kind of truth that rationally compels assent.

If Thielicke's interpretation is correct, the problem of history has already begun to assume hermeneutical significance, even if at this stage only negatively. The truths of reason, Lessing assumes, may more readily be appropriated within the horizons of the interpreter than "reports" about facts of history. We are still far from R. G. Collingwood's almost equally famous dictum that "The past . . . is not a dead past. By understanding it historically we incorporate it into our present thought and enable ourselves . . . to use that heritage for our own advancement."[69]

It is often argued that the first stirrings of modern historical consciousness began to occur with Johann G. Herder. This is the view of Alan Richardson, for example, both in his detailed study *History Sacred and Profane* and in his smaller book *The Bible in the Age of Science.*[70] The point is complicated by different understandings of the phrase "historical consciousness." If it means simply a suspicion that events were really other than has been commonly believed together with the attempt

66. For Thielicke's work on Lessing as a whole, cf. H. Thielicke, *Offenbarung, Vernunft, und Existenz, Studien zur Religions-Philosophie Lessings* (Gutersloher Verlagshaus,[4] 1957).
67. H. Thielicke, *The Evanglical Faith: Vol. I, The Relation of Theology to Modern Thought-Forms* (Eerdmans, Grand Rapids, 1974), p. 42.
68. *Ibid.*, pp. 42-43.
69. R. G. Collingwood, *The Idea of History* (Clarendon Press, Oxford, [2]1946), p. 230.
70. A. Richardson, *History Sacred and Profane*, p. 289.

to demonstrate that this is the case, the rise of historical consciousness may be dated with the English Deists and Spinoza. However, if the term is used to describe theorizing about the meaning and direction of history, independently of received views, then this activity must be attributed to a number of eighteenth-century thinkers (including Lessing), of whom Herder was the most articulate. At all events, Alan Richardson writes, "A revolution in the sphere of history, comparable to that which had taken place in the sphere of natural science in the seventeenth century, did not occur until the nineteenth century. . . . As with the seventeenth century revolution in man's way of looking at nature, so in the nineteenth century the revolution in man's way of looking at history involved a complete break with tradition. . . . The nineteenth century attained the conception of real change in history."[71] Following the work of Herder, Hegel, and Ranke, it came to be felt that "the secret of human existence and destiny is somehow locked away not in the inexorable rhythms of atoms in motion but in the self-understanding of man in his history."[72]

Herder's contribution to historical understanding, or to the philosophy of history, is also underlined by Karl Barth. Barth writes, "It was just those aspects of history which made it particularly suspect, and even an object of hatred, to the Enlightenment . . . that Herder emphasized with love and care. . . . History, for him, is nothing else but living experience."[73] For Herder, history was both "living experience," and events of the past which were to be studied in terms of their own times. This is at least partly because, in Collingwood's words, "Herder, as far as I know, was the first thinker to recognize in a systematic way that . . . human nature is not uniform but diversified. Human nature was not a datum but a problem."[74]

The nature of historical understanding was further explored by G. W. F. Hegel (1770-1831). To quote Collingwood again, "The culmination of the historical movement which began in 1784 with Herder came with Hegel."[75] Hegel's lectures on the philosophy of history were first delivered in 1822-23. In these lectures "history is not merely *ascertained* as so much fact, but *understood* by apprehending the reasons why the facts happened as they did."[76] Hegel's view of history certainly involves a conception of universal history, or history-as-a-whole. This is the story of the development of consciousness, and this process takes the form of cosmic unfolding of self-consciousness or spirit. Kierkegaard vigorously

71. A. Richardson, *The Bible in the Age of Science*, pp. 41 and 46.
72. A. Richardson, *History Sacred and Profane*, p. 290.
73. K. Barth, *From Rousseau to Ritschl* (Eng. S.C.M., London, 1959), pp. 209 and 211; cf. pp. 209-13.
74. R. G. Collingwood, *The Idea of History*, pp. 90-91.
75. *Ibid.*, p. 113.
76. *Ibid.*, pp. 113-14 (Collingwood's italics).

attacked this universalistic, systematic, speculative dimension in Hegel's philosophy. Nevertheless Hegel also stressed that, unlike nature, history does not repeat itself.

In spite of his speculations about the absolute, Hegel recognized the relativity and finitude of particular historical events. This particularly gives rise to novelty in history. If individual phases in the historical process seem to contradict each other, this seeming antithesis gives rise to a new creative synthesis. Thus individual aspects of history can be understood only in this context, and this context, in turn, can be understood only in the light of the whole. To paraphrase Hegel fairly closely but perhaps more clearly: "experience" occurs when that which is new emerges to consciousness in the dialectical process. This experience, in turn, "comprehends in itself nothing less than the whole system of consciousness."[77] The implications of Hegel's double emphasis for Christian theology are discussed by W. Pannenberg.[78]

In Hegel's concept of history there begin to emerge at least two points of connection with hermeneutics, both of which are stressed by Gadamer. First of all, in Gadamer's words, Hegel believes that "the essential nature of the historical spirit does not consist in the restoration of the past, but in thoughtful mediation with contemporary life."[79] The present horizons of the historian or philosopher are at issue. Secondly, Hegel's emphasis on universal history leads to a perspective which can be traced through Ranke and Dilthey to Gadamer himself, and which also has affinities with Schleiermacher's understanding of the hermeneutical circle, according to which the parts must be viewed in terms of the whole. Pannenberg observes, "In fact the theory of understanding as a fusion of horizons has its home on the ground of the Hegelian dialectic."[80]

It is hardly necessary for our purposes to examine Kierkegaard's approach to historical understanding. His notion of paradox has little to do with the problems of hermeneutics as such, even though his remarks about the relationship between truth and subjectivity as well as his work on indirect communication remain deeply relevant to hermeneutics considered apart from its relation to history. We may note in passing, however, that in his book entitled *Repetition* Kierkegaard proposes to use this term to replace the more traditional category of recollection. "Repetition," however, means not the mere repeating of an experience, but the re-creation of it in a way that brings it to life. He compares this process with the fulfilment of the promise "Behold, I make all things new." While

77. G. W. F. Hegel, *The Phenomenology of Mind* (Eng. Allen & Unwin, London, ²1964), "Introduction," sects. 14 and 16.
78. W. Pannenberg, "The Significance of Christianity in the Philosophy of Hegel" in *B.Q.T.* III, 144-77; cf. I, p. 121 n. 55.
79. H.-G. Gadamer, *T.M.*, p. 150.
80. W. Pannenberg, *B.Q.T.* I, p. 121 n. 55.

this is in no way a formal theory of historical understanding, it is suggestive for the relation between hermeneutical experience and the past.

It is often said that with the great historian Leopold von Ranke (1795-1886) there emerged a genuinely scientific concern for the facts of the past in their own right and for their own sake. Ranke's famous statement about historical method occurs in the preface of his *History of Latin and Teutonic Nations 1494-1514*, first published in 1824. Ranke wrote, "To history has been assigned the office of judging the past, of instructing the present for the benefit of future ages. To such high office this work does not aspire: it wants only to show what actually happened *(Wie es eigentlich gewesen)*."[81] Some writers have perhaps exaggerated the extent to which Ranke required the historian to suppress his own subjectivity. Thus Van Harvey warns us, "When Ranke . . . called for rigorous objectivity on the part of the historian he did not mean that the historian should not be interested or open; he meant, rather, that the historian should have a respect for the past as it really was and not as the historian wished it might have been, and that he should refrain from the rhetoric of praise and blame."[82] Indeed Ranke himself wrote, "The historian must keep his eye on the universal aspect of things. He will have no preconceived ideas as does the philosopher; rather, while he reflects on the particular, the development of the world in general will become apparent to him."[83]

This is not the language of a man who believed that the pastness of the past prevented history from speaking to the present, even though it is the language of a historian who begins to recognize the particularities of the past. Scholars seem to be firmly agreed that there are two distinct sides to Ranke's work. On the one side, "Detachment is the cardinal virtue of the historian. Facts were to be rescued from the conflict of opinion."[84] But there is another side to Ranke. As Alan Richardson writes, "The paradox has become apparent that Ranke, who has been the Newton of modern scientific history, is now discovered to have been the foremost myth-maker of the Bismarckian National State." Ranke brought to his historical inquiry a particular theology of history in which the progress of mankind was seen to be bound up with the development of sovereign national states. Ranke came to see in Bismarck's successes on behalf of his own native Prussia "the regular, continued, development of world-history." If Bismarck had been defeated, "world-history in the

---

81. L. von Ranke, "Preface to the History of the Latin and Teutonic Nations," translated in F. Stern (ed.), *The Varieties of History* (Macmillan, London, ²1970), p. 57; cf. pp. 55-62.
82. Van A. Harvey, *The Historian and the Believer: The Morality of Historical Knowledge and Christian Belief* (S.C.M., London, 1967), p. 183.
83. L. Von Ranke in *The Varieties of History*, p. 59.
84. A. Richardson, *History Sacred and Profane*, p. 173.

objective sense would have been impossible."[85]

There are perhaps two morals to be drawn from Ranke's historiography. First of all, his recognition of the particularity of the past and the need for objectivity on the part of the historian made him no less ready than any other thinker to conceive of past history as speaking to the present. Secondly, although in theory he advocated a degree of detachment in the past of the historian, his work demonstrates that past history "spoke to" his own situation on the basis of what in hermeneutics we should call his pre-understanding. He came to history with questions of his own, and the past spoke back to those questions.

9. Historical Method in Ernst Troeltsch

A comprehensive discussion of hermeneutics and history would be expected to include a consideration of Dilthey, who comes chronologically before Troeltsch. The present study does indeed include a later discussion of Wilhelm Dilthey. But so close is the connection between Dilthey's work and Bultmann's view of history and hermeneutics that it will be more convenient to allow a direct comparison between these two thinkers by reserving our section on Dilthey (together with Collingwood) until our consideration of Bultmann. The connections between Dilthey and Bultmann turn not only on their common concerns about "life," but also on their relationship to Kant, their concern about the present significance of history, and their assumption that throughout history, as H. N. Tuttle expresses it, "all men think, feel, will as we ourselves would in a like situation."[86] This last verdict, as we shall see, is very different from that which would be expressed by Troeltsch, who insisted that the problem of historical distance cannot be solved so easily.

Ernst Troeltsch (1865-1929) believed that the rise in the nineteenth century of critical historical consciousness and rigorous historical method had profound and far-reaching effects for traditional Christian belief. Christian origins, he argued, must no longer be viewed in terms of unique supernatural divine acts in history, but as a historical phenomenon viewed in the context of its own times. In his attitude towards the New Testament, Troeltsch stood on the opposite side of the gulf from Albrecht Ritschl and Martin Kähler. Ritschl had insisted that while judgments of fact concern the scientist, judgments of value concern the theologian. The New Testament and especially the message of Jesus fall under the cate-

85. *Ibid.*, p. 176.
86. H. N. Tuttle, *Wilhelm Dilthey's Philosophy of Historical Understanding. A Critical Analysis* (Brill, Leiden, 1969), p. 11.

gory of value. Similarly Martin Kähler asserted that the faith of the Christian cannot be said to depend on the conclusions of historical scholars.[87] Ernst Troeltsch declared, however, that "it is merely a figure of speech when one says that simple faith cannot be made dependent upon scholars and professors."[88] If Jesus is a historical fact, he is, like all historical facts, inescapably subject to the methods of historical research, and faith waits upon the results of historical science. Such a position, Braaten comments, is as clearly opposed to Kähler's as it is possible to conceive.[89] Borrowing Pannenberg's kind of language, we might say that Troeltsch refuses to place Jesus in a ghetto of salvation-history, but places him on the stage of universal religious and historical consciousness. In this respect Troeltsch embodies the outlook of the History of Religions School at the turn of the century.

In the opening section of this chapter, on "the pastness of the past," we claimed that D. E. Nineham's approach to the historical interpretation of the New Testament very accurately reflected Troeltsch's perspective. We suggest that this similarity becomes evident at three distinct points.

First of all, Troeltsch believed that the rise of the historical-critical method constituted one of the great advances of human thought, and entailed a revolution in the consciousness of Western man. The historian's attention to "facts," together with his awareness of the problem of context and historical relativity, meant that man's intellectual life could never be the same again. In his article on historiography, he notes that primitive man was content with the recollections of his family and clan, and that "the beginnings of history are found in religious traditions, legends, myths and tales" in which "recollection is embedded in a vast romanticism."[90] "At this stage there is not the slightest trace of a desire for real knowledge or of a critical spirit."[91] The Greeks were ready to move beyond this stage, but, according to Troeltsch, Christianity kept the clock back for fifteen hundred years, by its attempt to view all history within the framework of a supernaturalist theology. Hints of a new spirit came with the Renaissance; and then more fully with the Enlightenment, until eventually "modern historical reflection" emerged in the nineteenth century.[92]

It is not to criticize or to undervalue Troeltsch's approach to point out

---

87. Cf. M. Kähler, *The So-Called Historical Jesus and the Historic Biblical Christ* (Eng. ed. by C. E. Braaten, Fortress Press, Philadelphia, 1964).
88. E. Troeltsch, *Die Bedeutung der Geschichtlichkeit Jesus für den Glauben* (Mohr, Tübingen, 1929), p. 34.
89. C. E. Braaten, "Introduction" in M. Kähler, *The So-Called Historical Jesus*, p. 27.
90. E. Troeltsch, "Historiography" in *Contemporary Religious Thinkers*, p. 77 (cf. pp. 76-97).
91. *Ibid.*, pp. 77-78.
92. *Ibid.*, pp. 80-81.

that this very attitude towards history is itself a product of its times, thereby demonstrating the inescapability of historical relativity. For, as Herbert Butterfield points out, the end of the nineteenth century and the beginning of the twentieth stand "on the crest of what might be called a great wave of historical thinking." He adds, "Perhaps it is not going too far to say that the wave has been receding ever since."[93] Thus at this particular point in time, near the turn of the century, Lord Acton was arguing in many different ways that "the historical revolution of the nineteenth century was a bigger event, a bigger change in the character of human thought, than that 'revival of learning' which we associate with the Renaissance."[94] D. E. Nineham's claims may be a little less sweeping than those of Troeltsch or Lord Acton, but he insists that there is "an important element of novelty in the task of the New Testament interpreter today, 'because he is doing his work in an historical age.' "[95] "It is like what I think Nietzsche meant when he said that in the nineteenth century mankind developed, or recognized, a sixth sense, the historical sense."[96] To talk about historical consciousness as a sixth sense is to make a far-reaching claim.

Secondly, Troeltsch believed that the application of rigorous historical method to Christian faith and Christian origins was in conflict with a supernaturalistic Christian theology as a matter of basic principle. Van A. Harvey makes the point clearly. He writes, "The problem was not, as so many theologians then believed, that the Biblical critics emerged from their libraries with results disturbing to believers, but that the method itself . . . was based on assumptions quite irreconcilable with traditional belief. If the theologian regards the Scriptures as supernaturally inspired, the historian must assume that the Bible is intelligible only in terms of its historical context and is subject to the same principles of interpretation and criticism that are applied to other writings. If the theologian believes that the events of the Bible are the results of the supernatural intervention of God, the historian regards such an explanation as a hindrance to true historical understanding."[97]

There is a sense in which this is axiomatic for all biblical criticism. Questions about the language and literary character of the New Testament can only be answered in terms of Troeltsch's principle that the historian's task "is to explain every movement, process, state and nexus of things by reference to the web of its causal relations."[98] However, Troeltsch insists

93. H. Butterfield, *Man on his Past. The Study of the History of Historical Scholarship* (Cambridge University Press, 1955), p. 97.
94. *Ibid.*
95. D. E. Nineham, *New Testament Interpretation in an Historical Age*, p. 5.
96. *Ibid.*
97. V. A. Harvey, *The Historian and the Believer*, p. 5.
98. E. Troeltsch, "Historiography" in *Contemporary Religious Thinkers*, p. 83.

that even the theological subject-matter within the New Testament that claims to be unique or to represent an intervention of God must be interpreted exclusively in terms of "the web of its causal relations." For Troeltsch himself it was a matter of principle that "once the historical method is applied to Biblical science . . . it is a leaven that alters everything. . . . Whoever lends it a finger must give it a hand."[99] It is an all-or-nothing affair, which must be applied not only to sources, theories of development, and the dating of documents, but to questions about miracles, Christology, and revelation.

It is indeed important for Troeltsch's philosophy of history that the historian of religion excludes the possibility of any explanation in terms of divine interventions or unique events. The causal nexus that surrounds an event is, in Troeltsch's view, part of a wider, universal network of cause and effect. Christianity and Christian origins must be seen in the wider cultural context of religion in the ancient world. In this repect we have already noted that Troeltsch stands with the pioneers of the History of Religions School. We cannot make any absolute and final claim on behalf of Christianity, Troeltsch urges, precisely because neither we nor the Christian faith can be extracted from a particular context in culture and history.

Once again, D. E. Nineham adopts the same kind of perspective in his fourth essay. He alludes to the questioning of belief in a unique incarnation voiced by such scholars as Don Cupitt, Maurice F. Wiles, and Harry Williams, and comments, "What I should like to see would be New Testament scholars subjecting it to like questioning in their own sphere. . . . I should not be altogether surprised if those who adopted such an approach concluded that, while the events of Jesus' career were such as to demand interpretation in terms of a unique—indeed literally final—divine intervention given the presuppositions of certain circles in first-century Jewish culture, they might not have seemed to demand such interpretations given different cultural assumptions."[100] The key to this approach is a historical methodology which approaches its subject matter on the assumption "that all past events form a single interconnected web and that no event occurs without this-worldly causation of some sort."[101] These sentences could well have been written by Troeltsch.

Thirdly, Troeltsch formulates a theory of historical probability in terms of a principle of analogy with the historian's present experience. Troeltsch writes, "On the analogy of the events known to us we seek by conjecture and sympathetic understanding to explain and reconstruct the past. From this point, again, we advance to the criticism of extant tradi-

99. E. Troeltsch, *Gesammelte Schriften* (Mohr, Tübingen, 1913), II, 730 and 734.
100. D. E. Nineham, *New Testament Interpretation,* pp. 18 and 20 (his italics).
101. *Ibid.,* p. 18.

a special problem of the modern era is "the task of achieving an understanding that spans the historical distance between primitive Christianity
and the present time."[112] In addition to this, Pannenberg stands nearer to
Troeltsch than to Kähler and Bultmann in his firm insistence that faith is
not independent of historical research. He sees the perspective of Kähler
and Bultmann as resting on an untenable dualism between fact and value,
or between event and interpretation. He comments, "Under the influence
of positivism and of neo-Kantianism, scholars have come to distinguish
more sharply between the facts, on the one hand, and their evaluation or
significance on the other hand. Most radically of all, Rudolf Bultmann
carries out this distinction by relegating the early Christian Easter message totally to the significance side, describing it as the interpretation of
Jesus' cross."[113] He adds, "Against this we must reinstate today the
original unity of facts and their meaning."[114]

The key example of the relevance of history to faith, in Pannenberg's
theology, concerns the event of the resurrection of Jesus Christ. In
Jesus—God and Man he argues that it has simply not been shown why
historiography should not in principle be able to speak of the event of the
resurrection as "the explanation that is best established" of the account
of the disciples' experience of Christ's appearance and even of the discovery of the empty tomb.[115] Pannenberg concludes, "If, however, historical study declares itself unable to establish what 'really' happened on
Easter, then all the more, faith is not able to do so. For faith cannot
ascertain anything certain about events of the past that would perhaps be
inaccessible to the historian."[116]

If Pannenberg seems to agree with Troeltsch on the points which we
have mentioned, how is it that in practice their approaches to theology are
so different, and that Pannenberg attacks some of Troeltsch's most
cherished assumptions? The difference emerges clearly when we notice
the sentence which precedes the quotation which we have just cited.
Pannenberg writes, *"As long as historiography does not begin dogmati-
cally with a narrow concept of reality according to which 'dead men do
not rise,'* . . . it is not clear why historiography should not in principle be
able to speak about Jesus' resurrection as the explanation . . . of such
events as the disciples' experience of the appearance and the discovery of
the empty tomb" (my italics). What Troeltsch would see as firmly established on the basis of analogy with the historian's own experience of life,

112. *Ibid.*, p. 97.
113. W. Pannenberg, "The Revelation of God in Jesus of Nazareth" in J. M. Robinson and
J. B. Cobb, Jr. (eds.), *New Frontiers in Theology: 3, Theology as History* (Harper and Row,
New York, 1967), p. 126; cf. pp. 101-33.
114. *Ibid.*, p. 127.
115. W. Pannenberg, *Jesus—God and Man* (Eng. S.C.M., London, 1968), p. 109.
116. *Ibid.*

Pannenberg sees as a "narrow concept of reality," in that it allows for something less than is already demanded as an explanation for the events described in the New Testament. What Troeltsch regards as a necessary outlook of modern culture, Pannenberg characterizes as historical and philosophical positivism. It is simply empiricism under the guise of historiography in the same way that logical positivism is empiricism under the guise of language.[117] The fact that this positivism is disguised as a theory of history or of language does not alter the basic fact that underneath it is still a brand of positivism.

Pannenberg develops criticisms of the approach in several essays in *Basic Questions in Theology,* including the one entitled "Redemptive Event and History."[118] Indeed he is so sharply critical of positivist presuppositions in historical inquiry that, as E. F. Tupper points out, he would rather stand in the end, if this were the choice, with Martin Kähler and even Bultmann than with Troeltsch and the positivist school. Tupper comments, "Since the reigning historiography (as defined by Troeltsch and others) bypassed the intention of the Biblical texts to witness to the acts of God . . . , Kähler and, subsequently, kerygmatic theology strongly protested. Pannenberg speaks positively of this protest."[119] In Pannenberg's words, "When they (i.e. Biblical writings) are read *merely as documents of secular events and human religiosity,* their genuine content, which is precisely their witness to the deeds of God, remains untapped. Kerygma theology, in discovering this, was perfectly correct over against the historical practice and methodology of its time."[120] Pannenberg's criticism of the kind of approach adopted by kerygmatic theologians is that they allowed themselves to accept a false alternative in the first place. They thought themselves compelled to "accept all too uncritically the neo-Kantian distinction between being and value."[121] But this dualism was already vitiated by a positivistic notion of "fact." "Both neo-Kantianism and the philosophy-of-life school have accepted historical positivism as one of their presuppositions, and have merely supplemented it by an 'evaluating' contemplation or by the interpretation of the facts according to their expressive value."[122]

We find Pannenberg's account of these approaches completely con-

117. Cf. H. J. Paton, *The Modern Predicament* (Allen and Unwin, London, 1955), pp. 32-46. Paton writes, "There is a risk that a purely linguistic approach may conceal from us what we are doing. . . . If we choose to confine our beliefs within the limits of common sense it is not easy to see why it becomes a more serious argument simply because it appears in a linguistic dress" (*ibid.,* p. 42).
118. W. Pannenberg, *B.Q.T.* I, 15-80; cf. pp. 81-181 and 13-15 and 45-79.
119. E. F. Tupper, *The Theology of Wolfhart Pannenberg* (S.C.M., London, 1974), p. 38.
120. W. Pannenberg, *B.Q.T.* I, 85 (my italics).
121. *Ibid.,* p. 86.
122. W. Pannenberg, "The Revelation of God in Jesus of Nazareth" in *New Frontiers in Theology: 3,* p. 127.

vincing. However, he has a number of more specific criticisms to make of Troeltsch's position. First and foremost, Pannenberg argues that Troeltsch's historical method is *anthropocentric*.[123] He observes, "A fundamental antithesis between the world-views of historical method and the biblical history of God can be found in the anthropocentricity of the historical-critical procedure, which seems apt to exclude all transcendent reality as a matter of course."[124] Vico provided the philosophical basis of this approach to history, Pannenberg continues, but he asks: "Were not the anti-Christian implications of this methodological anthropocentrism obvious by the time of Voltaire, at the latest?"[125] He then explicitly questions Troeltsch's assumptions that "Analogy with what happens before our eyes . . . is the key to criticism. . . ."[126]

It is important, however, to note that there are certain aspects of Troeltsch's approach which Pannenberg does *not* criticize. He agrees with Troeltsch, as we have seen, that the history of what Christians see as acts of God is to be seen "within the universal correlative connections of human history, and not in a ghetto of redemptive history."[127] Still more to the point he agrees that "the basic thesis of the universal correspondence of all historical phenomena does not have a primarily anthropocentric structure."[128] The principle of analogy does indeed have a necessary place in historical understanding. For example, Israel's testimonies of faith, understood as historical documents, must be viewed against the background of the ancient Near Eastern world, just as the New Testament writings need to be understood in connection with phenomena in Judaism and Hellenism. Pannenberg does not merely concede this point reluctantly, but insists on it as a major theme in his own theology. For it is only by strongly asserting this principle that it can be seen why biblical history, even the history of biblical faith, belongs not to salvation-history (*Heilsgeschichte*)—which is different in kind from world-history—but is itself part of universal history.

However, Troeltsch means more than this when he speaks of analogy. Pannenberg distinguishes between "historical correlation," which involves the use of analogy in the sense just defined, and analogy in the narrower sense in which "something difficult to understand . . . is to be conceived and understood by the investigator in terms of *what lies closer to him*."[129] Taking up Troeltsch's statement that the criterion of historical probability is "agreement with normal, ordinary, repeated modes of oc-

123. W. Pannenberg, *B.Q.T.* I, 39-50.
124. *Ibid.*, p. 39.
125. *Ibid.*, pp. 39-40 (my italics).
126. *Ibid.*, pp. 43-44.
127. *Ibid.*, p. 41.
128. *Ibid.*, p. 40.
129. *Ibid.*, p. 43 (my italics).

currence and conditions as we know them," Pannenberg comments: "There is obviously an anthropocentric structure in the way in which analogizing deliberations proceed from what lies closest to the investigator's current state of knowledge."[130] He is not arguing that *all* use of historical analogy is out of place. Historical events may partly be explained in terms of other events. But historical method becomes anthropocentric when the interpreter's own experience of life becomes the test of all historical truth.

In the second place, Pannenberg now takes this criticism a stage further. This whole approach which we have described in Troeltsch entails "a biassed world view."[131] When he postulated the basic homogeneity *(Gleichartigkeit)* of all reality, including the experience of the interpreter, Troeltsch turns historical theory into an explicit metaphysic, in this case of a positivistic kind. By taking "this step beyond the purely methodological anthropocentrism of the historical conclusion from analogy," Troeltsch brings about "a constriction of the historical question itself."[132] In other words, he begins with what Pannenberg elsewhere calls a narrow conception of reality, whereby certain possibilities are excluded on an *a priori* basis. This conception is by no means value-neutral. It arises, like the historian's own experience of life which in effect provides its basis, from "an already given world of expressions in which the historian is at home, and never from a value-free sense experience."[133] In this respect, Pannenberg concludes, Troeltsch's philosophy represents a retrograde step back beyond Dilthey, for the latter had seen that the historian's use of analogy or life-experience could not be merely value-neutral.

It is perhaps illuminating at this point to compare Ludwig Wittgenstein's criticisms of Sir James Frazer's approach in *The Golden Bough.*[134] Wittgenstein complains that Frazer's "explanations" of the beliefs and practices of other cultures and religions relate exclusively to "men who think in a similar way to himself."[135] Thus, on the basis of a positivist *a priori* or of his own experience of life, practices such as the killing of the priest-king "are finally presented, so to speak, as *stupidities*. It will never be plausible, however, that men do all that out of pure stupidity. . . . One can only describe *(nur beschreiben)* here and say: human life is like that *(so ist das menschliche Leben)."*[136] Wittgenstein concludes: "What nar-

130. *Ibid.,* p. 44.
131. *Ibid.,* p. 45.
132. *Ibid.,* p. 46.
133. *Ibid.,* pp. 44-45.
134. L. Wittgenstein, "Bemerkungen über Frazers *The Golden Bough"* in *Synthese* XVII (1967), 233-53.
135. *Ibid.,* p. 235.
136. *Ibid.,* pp. 235-36.

rowness of spiritual life we find in Frazer! And as a result: How impossible for him to conceive of a different way of life from the English one of his time. Frazer cannot imagine a priest who is not basically an English parson of our times with all his stupidity and feebleness."[137] The result is that, far from being "historical," Frazer's explanations of primitive practices "are much cruder than the meaning of these practices themselves."[138] Wittgenstein sees, unlike Frazer and perhaps Troeltsch, that any world-view that excludes in advance certain ways of seeing the world, is in fact not neutrally *descriptive* at all.

Pannenberg's third explicit criticism constitutes a further extension of the second. Clearly, if we begin with Troeltsch's world-view, we have already excluded in advance the possibility of events which are new or unique. Admittedly Troeltsch followed Dilthey in giving some attention to the particularity of human life in contrast to nature. But this must be the kind of particularity which the modern historian encounters day by day. By contrast, Pannenberg asserts, "If the historian keeps his eye on the nonexchangeable individuality and contingency of an event, then he will see that he is dealing with non-homogeneous things, which cannot be continued without remainder in any analogy."[139] We are reminded of A. Boyce Gibson's striking comment in his book *Theism and Empiricism* that on the basis of a Humean epistemology or a thoroughly empiricist worldview "anything that happens for the first time is to be discredited."[140]

In Pannenberg's view, such a straightjacket leaves impossible consequences for Christian theology. "Theology must take a burning interest in this side of historical work. It is characteristic of the activity of the transcendent God . . . that it constantly gives rise to something new in reality, something never before present. For this reason, theology is interested primarily in the individual, particular, and contingent. In the revelatory history, the theological stress falls not least upon the new, upon that which is peculiar to the particular event within the contexts of the history and the promises in which it belongs."[141] The example of novelty which looms large in Pannenberg's theology is of course the resurrection of Jesus Christ. By contrast, Pannenberg alludes critically to the mood of the History of Religions School around the turn of the century, in which the tendency was to emphasize the common factor between the Hebrew-Christian tradition and Hellenistic, agnostic, or other Near Eastern religions, at the expense of noting what was particular, distinctive, or even unique. This is not, however, to criticize a History

---

137. *Ibid.*, pp. 237 and 238.
138. *Ibid.*, p. 241.
139. W. Pannenberg, *B.Q.T.* I, 46.
140. A. B. Gibson, *Theism and Empiricism* (S.C.M., London, 1970), p. 268.
141. W. Pannenberg, *B.Q.T.* I, 48.

of Religions approach as such *in principle*. Even when the historian discovers peculiarities in the Hebrew-Christian tradition, "this peculiarity . . . must be understood against the background of the general phenomena of religious experience, and in connection with the history of religions, especially those of the Ancient Near East."[142]

As a fourth point of divergence between Pannenberg and Troeltsch we must call attention to the part placed by the transmission of traditions in Pannenberg's thought. Because of the context of his own times, it is understandable that for Troeltsch tradition was, in effect, a bad word; tradition was to be viewed always with suspicion. This is because for Troeltsch the great breakthrough in historical thinking was the new critical spirit of nineteenth-century historiography, which saw that traditions can never be accepted at their face value. Pannenberg, of course, also recognizes this, but the notion of tradition also has the utmost positive significance for him. In *Revelation as History* he writes that the events involved in the history of a given people "have no meaning apart from the connection with the traditions and expectations in which men live. The events of history speak their own language, the language of facts; however, this language is understandable only in the context of the traditions and the expectations in which the given events occur."[143]

Once again, this is where Pannenberg attacks *both* the positivist notion of "brute facts" in abstraction from interpretation *and* the Neo-Kantian dualism taken over by Bultmann which turns on a sharp distinction between fact and interpretation and assigns theological value to the side of interpretation. It is not the case that certain bare facts occurred, to which Israel or the primitive church then attached "religious" interpretations. Facts are always experienced in a context in which they have significance.[144] This "context" is formed not only by the *thoughts* or *theology* or even (as Nineham would have it) *cultural outlook* of Israel or the New Testament church, but also *by the historical events which surround it*. The tradition is not just one of thought and culture, but constitutes, in Pannenberg's words, "an intertwining both of . . . words and events."[145] In the context of prophetic promise, for example, "time and time again *the course of events surpassed the words* giving them new meaning and a new reference."[146]

This has radical implications for historical understanding. It means,

142. W. Pannenberg, "The Revelation of God in Jesus of Nazareth" in *New Frontiers in Theology: 3*, p. 105.
143. W. Pannenberg (ed.), *Revelation as History* (Eng. Sheed and Ward, London, 1969), pp. 152-53.
144. Cf. A. D. Galloway, *Wolfhart Pannenberg* (Allen and Unwin, London, 1973) pp. 35-59.
145. W. Pannenberg, "The Revelation of God in Jesus of Nazareth" in *New Frontiers in Theology: 3*, p. 120.
146. *Ibid.* (my italics).

for example, that the resurrection of Jesus Christ is to be viewed and understood not simply in terms of analogies with the day-to-day experience of the modern interpreter or historian, but in the setting of the apocalyptic tradition which constitutes its historical context. A. D. Galloway shows how this principle relates to the previous point that we considered, about historical novelty. The transcendence of God, in Pannenberg's view, consists in his power to bring forth what is new in the course of human affairs. However, as Galloway puts it, *"Significant novelty is not a mere bolt from the blue but something positively related to what has gone before and what comes after. It shows the past in a new light and opens new questions for the future."*[147] "History itself thus forms the tradition which supplies the context in which each new event is experienced."[148]

There is, therefore, in this sense, something more objective about the traditions of past history than is allowed for by the preoccupation of writers such as Troeltsch with the problem of cultural relativity. Tradition is not a mere disposable cultural wrapping which disguises the "proper" way to see historical facts. To suggest this is to imply that meaning is detachable from the events, or that bare events or brute facts can be abstracted from the tradition and then re-interpreted. The tradition is itself shaped by events as well as by thoughts. Like Wittgenstein's language-games, it constitutes a "whole consisting of language and the actions into which it is woven."[149] Pannenberg refuses to accept a dualism from which (with Troeltsch) we abstract facts for the historian but relativize the meaning; or from which (with Kähler and Bultmann) we abstract meaning for the theologian but relativize, as it were, the facts. Pannenberg refuses to allow the wholeness of the tradition to be torn apart, and either the facts or the interpretation to be evaporated.

Fifthly, Pannenberg rejects the assumption that beliefs such as the acceptance of divine interventions in the world are merely culture-relative rather than matters of religion and theology. In the course of his long essay on myth in biblical and Christian tradition he asserts that belief in divine intervention in this-worldly events "is fundamental to every religious understanding of the world, including one which is not mythical in the sense in which comparative religion uses the term."[150] Such belief, he adds, is by no means in conflict with modern attitudes and concerns about natural laws in the physical universe. Whereas Troeltsch begins from the standpoint of cultural and historical relativity and then advances towards a relativistic view of Jesus as the Christ, Pannenberg's approach is al-

147. A. D. Galloway, *Wolfhart Pannenberg*, p. 55 (his italics).
148. *Ibid.*, p. 57.
149. L. Wittgenstein, *P.I.*, sect. 7.
150. W. Pannenberg, *B.Q.T.* III, 14.

together different: "What is historically unique is as far as anything possibly can be from myth. . . . The theme of the incarnation prevented Christian theology from becoming identified entirely with myth."[151] We postpone further consideration of this point at present, since we must return to it when we discuss Bultmann's program of demythologizing.

Sixthly and finally, there is a sense in which Pannenberg accepts the relativity of both history and the historian in the way stressed by Dilthey and Troeltsch; but he also gives the issue a special turn by relating the concept of history-as-a-whole to Christian eschatology. Pannenberg cites Dilthey's statement that "The last step to the liberation of man is the historical consciousness of the finiteness of every historical appearance and every human or social condition, and of the relativity of every sort of faith."[152] But if meaning could not in some way be related to wholeness, hermeneutics and historical understanding would be impossible. "For the individual human being," Pannenberg writes, "receives the meaning that constitutes his wholeness only in relation to an encompassing whole."[153] The apocalyptic tradition, he believes, established an expectation that knowledge of God's divinity would come "no longer . . . from single events, but from one final occurrence which could gather together all earlier single events into one single history." This would be "the last, the eschatological event which binds history into a whole."[154] According to the New Testament writers, the revelation of God in Jesus Christ is an event of the end, even though it is so only proleptically and provisionally. Because this revelation is an event of the end only in a provisional sense, it does not short-circuit the problem of historical relativity. But it does provide a basis for hermeneutics. Thus, on the one hand, "The anticipated coming of the end of history in the midst of history, far from doing away with history, actually forms the basis from which history as a whole becomes understandable."[155] On the other hand, "This does not make possible, however, an oversight over the drama of world history as from a stage box. Second Corinthians 5.7 applies here: 'we walk by faith and not by sight.' "[156]

In spite of his admiration for Hegel, Pannenberg accepts the view that Hegel overlooked the provisional nature of his own attempt to view history, as it were, from the standpoint of the end. Hegel's philosophy, in this respect, involves an attempt to foreclose the future. Troeltsch was nearer the mark when he recognized that all historical knowledge can be

151. *Ibid.*, pp. 71 and 73.
152. W. Pannenberg, *B.Q.T.* I, 34.
153. *Ibid.*, p. 164.
154. W. Pannenberg, "The Revelation of God in Jesus of Nazareth" in *New Frontiers in Theology: 3*, p. 122.
155. W. Pannenberg, *B.Q.T.* I, 36-37 (my italics).
156. *Ibid.*, p. 37.

called into question by fresh discoveries. Thus in his essay entitled "What is Truth?" Pannenberg asserts, "The proleptic character of the dealing of Jesus is the basis for the openness of the future for us, despite the fact that Jesus is the ultimate revelation of the God of Israel as the God of all men. . . . The openness of the future belongs constitutively to our reality—against Hegel."[157] Nevertheless, Pannenberg draws his understanding of the nature of hermeneutics from Hegel. For in the same essay he writes, "Hegel's thesis that the truth of the whole will be visible only at the end of history approximates the biblical understanding of truth in two respects. It does so, firstly, by the fact that the truth as such is understood not as timelessly unchangeable. . . . Secondly, it does so by asserting that the unity of the process, which is full of contradictions while it is under way, will become visible *along with the true meaning of every individual moment in it, only from the standpoint of its end.*"[158] Hegel's philosophy of history, Pannenberg believes, is basically correct, but his attempt actually to stand at the end of history is "the one earth-shaking objection that has to be raised against Hegel."[159]

All this leads Pannenberg to the conclusion that the hermeneutics of Schleiermacher and Dilthey, no less than the historical positivism of Troeltsch, will fall into relativism without an adequate concept of universal history, which itself calls for some reference to the deed of God in Jesus Christ. Understanding of the parts presupposes understanding of the whole because "only knowledge of the whole can make clear what sigificance the parts really deserve. Thus, insight into the inaccessibility of the whole of history leads to the impasse of relativism."[160] Pannenberg therefore reaches the conclusion that in this respect "philosophical reflection constantly presupposes a religious basis."[161] However, this must not be taken to imply that historical research is to be short-circuited by an act of Christian faith. On this point, we noted, Pannenberg stands nearer to Troeltsch than to Kähler, given an adequate understanding of the nature of historical research. A. D. Galloway sets out Pannenberg's view clearly in four short sentences. He observes, "Merely probable knowledge is psychologically compatible with the trustful certainty of faith. . . . There is nothing illogical or unreasonable in the combination of such trust with merely probable knowledge. . . . This does not make faith independent of knowledge. Trust where there were no rational grounds for belief would be sheer irresponsibility."[162]

157. W. Pannenberg, *B.Q.T.* II, 25.
158. *Ibid.,* p. 22 (my italics).
159. *Ibid.*
160. W. Pannenberg, *B.Q.T.* I, 164.
161. *Ibid.,* p. 174.
162. A. D. Galloway, *Wolfhart Pannenberg,* p. 48.

Pannenberg, then, is not involving some religious *a priori* as a means of escaping from the rigor of historical research. It is rather the reverse. Because God is the God of all the world, and not just God of Israel and the church, faith relates to world-history and not just to salvation-history. However, in the end, he does not attempt to provide an answer to the problem of hermeneutics and history without reference to theology. He concludes, "It is possible to find in the history of Jesus an answer to the question of how 'the whole' of reality and its meaning can be conceived without compromising the provisionality and historical relativity of all thought, as well as openness to the future on the part of the thinker who knows himself to be only on the way and not yet at the goal."[163]

It is doubtful whether Troeltsch or Nineham would feel that their problems about the pastness of the past are genuinely answered by Pannenberg. Nevertheless, although Pannenberg believes that in the end questions about hermeneutics and history cannot be adequately answered without reference to theology, this is not because he begins with an *a priori* derived only from Christian faith. After examining the work of Dilthey and Troeltsch as systems of philosophy or historical understanding in their own right, Pannenberg is convinced that the questions they raise actually *demand* theological answers, as well as answers on the level of philosophy and historiography. In this respect there is, it seems, a parallel with the direction of his method in *Jesus—God and Man,* where he reaches a full Christology "from below."[164]

The work of Pannenberg has three main points of significance for the present study. First of all, he shows that Troeltsch's approach is not in the end theologically neutral, since it indirectly implies a positivist metaphysic which is smuggled through under the guise of being a "modern" understanding of history. Secondly, he also rejects the Neo-Kantian dualism between fact and value which lies behind Rudolf Bultmann's hermeneutics and much kerygmatic theology. We shall return to this point when we examine Bultmann's approach. Thirdly, Pannenberg has called in question the assumption that issues about history and hermeneutics can be discussed without full reference to theological considerations. We shall turn to this subject in subsequent chapters.

163. W. Pannenberg, *B.Q.T.* I, 181.
164. W. Pannenberg, *Jesus—God and Man,* pp. 33-37.

the act of God" even though "the event of the Word of God is not continuation, but the end of all other events that we know."[19] Not only does the event of the Word of God stand in discontinuity with all human thought and experiences, it also stands altogether apart from them. Thus: "The presence of the Word of God is not an experience, precisely because and as it is the divine decision concerning us."[20]

Barth's starting-point is in accord with the outlook of Pauline and Johannine theology. The Holy Spirit is active in interpreting the word of God to men. However, Barth's opposition to the emphasis of Schleiermacher and Ritschl on religious experience, together with his stress on the sovereign transcendence of God, has led him beyond this starting-point, so that at times it seems to be implied that the Spirit's communication of the Word of God is somehow independent of all ordinary processes of human understanding. It is not surprising, therefore, to find a head-on collision between Barth and Bultmann in the former's well-known essay "Rudolf Bultmann—An Attempt to Understand Him."[21] Barth declares, "This Word of God can only confront and illuminate man as truth and reality if it is seen to run *counter to his whole natural capacity to understand*."[22] He himself, Barth claims, tried to emancipate the Bible from its Egyptian bondage to "one philosophy after another," which tried to "teach us what the Holy Spirit was allowed to say as the Word of God." But: "Bultmann has forsaken our road and gone back to the old one again."[23]

Although we used the phrase "head-on collision," in point of fact it is doubtful whether Barth and Bultmann are actually addressing themselves to the same issue. H.-W. Bartsch helpfully pinpoints G. Gloege's verdict that the misunderstanding which lies at the center of Barth's criticisms against Bultmann "arises from the confusion between the ontic and noetic approaches, and the respective points of view they imply."[24] The point that Gloege is making is so important that his words may be quoted in full. He writes, "There is no question that Bultmann is right: the problem of understanding (i.e. hermeneutics), the question of knowledge, comes before the question of the object known. That, however, does not rule out, in fact it assumes, that the question of the object known provides the basis and structures of the question of knowledge."[25] We sympathize with the theological values which Barth is seeking to preserve; but he has paid an unnecessary price to do this. Many scholars, including some who are

19. *Ibid.*, pp. 527 and 528.
20. *Ibid.*, p. 532.
21. K. Barth, "Rudolf Bultmann—An Attempt to Understand Him" in *K.M.* II, 83-132.
22. *Ibid.*, p. 123 (my italics).
23. *Ibid.*, p. 127.
24. H. W. Bartsch, *K.M.* II, 31.
25. *Ibid.*, quoted from G. Gloege, *Mythologie und Luthertum*, p. 89.

otherwise supporters of Barth's own general position, see that it in no way diminishes the crucial importance of the role of the Holy Spirit to say that the Spirit works *through* the normal processes of human understanding, and neither independently of them nor contrary to them.

John Macquarrie looks carefully at this particular theological criticism of hermeneutics with reference not only to Barth, but also to Helmut Thielicke.[26] This kind of thinking about the role of the Holy Spirit, Macquarrie urges, tends to make the Spirit into a mysterious *tertium quid* which stands over against both God and man. However, "the Holy Spirit is the God who addresses us, not an intermediary between us."[27] When the biblical writers or Christian theologians speak of the testimony of the Spirit, this is not to invoke some *additional* means of communicating the word of God, but is to claim that a message which is communicated in human language to human understanding addresses man *as* the word of God.[28] It would not invalidate Macquarrie's argument to point out that in Pauline theology the Spirit is sometimes portrayed as standing over against God, as, for example, when the Spirit calls forth from the Christian the response of "Abba, Father" (Rom. 8:15, 16). For this has nothing to do with any suggestion that, as Prosper Grech expresses it, in the context of hermeneutics the Spirit operates on the principle of *deus ex machina*.[29]

Heinrich Ott and Wolfhart Pannenberg also reject this view of the work of the Holy Spirit. Ott examines the objection that "one should not concern oneself so much about the problem of understanding, since the Holy Spirit surely sees to it that the message is understood. This 'pious' objection, designed to make light of the hermeneutical problem, is quite popular."[30] The objection, Ott replies, rests on a kind of "inferior orthodoxy" that fails to see the issue: "One should not degrade God to a *deus ex machina*. Actually . . . the witness of the Spirit is taken fully into account in the concept of understanding, when the concept is itself correctly understood."[31]

Wolfhart Pannenberg makes a similar point about a doctrine of the Holy Spirit in the context of wider questions about truth and the role of argument. He writes, "An otherwise unconvincing message cannot attain the power to convince simply by appealing to the Holy Spirit."[32] "Argument and the operation of the Spirit are not in competition with each

26. J. Macquarrie, *The Scope of Demythologizing*, pp. 48-53.
27. *Ibid.*, p. 50.
28. *Ibid.*
29. P. Grech, "The 'Testimonia' and Modern Hermeneutics" in *N.T.S.* XIX, 324.
30. H. Ott, "What is Systematic Theology?" in J. M. Robinson and J. B. Cobb, Jr. (eds.), *New Frontiers in Theology: I, The Later Heidegger and Theology*, p. 81.
31. *Ibid.*
32. W. Pannenberg, *B.Q.T.* II, 34.

other. In trusting in the Spirit, Paul in no way spared himself thinking and arguing."[33] In other words, the Spirit is conceived of as working *through* these means, not independently of them.

In addition to these arguments about the role of a doctrine of the Holy Spirit, we may note that in practice many authors who do take the hermeneutical problem seriously also have a doctrine of the Spirit. Gerhard Ebeling, for example, warns us against short-circuiting hermeneutics by a premature appeal to the Spirit, but he also states that "the Holy Spirit, which is the Spirit of the Word, is concerned with everything which has to do with the word-event."[34] Conversely, Helmut Thielicke, who repeats in *The Evangelical Faith* his earlier criticism that "the final secret or difficulty of Bultmann's theology is that he has no doctrine of the Spirit," devotes considerable attention to hermeneutics as the problem of understanding in this same volume.[35]

The argument that the Holy Spirit works *through* human understanding, and does not therefore short-circuit the problem of hermeneutics, may be confirmed still more clearly with reference to two chapters in T. F. Torrance's book *God and Rationality.* The two chapters are entitled "The Word of God and the Response of Man" and "The Epistemological Relevance of the Spirit," and both come under the general heading of "Word and Spirit."[36] Torrance points out that to speak of the epistemological relevance of the Spirit does not mean that the problem of knowledge becomes Spirit-centered in the more obvious and superficial sense of the term. "By His very mode of being as Spirit He hides Himself from us so that we do not know Him directly in His own hypostasis, and in His mode of activity as transparent Light He effaces Himself that the one Triune God may shine through Him to us."[37] This reminds us of John Macquarrie's warnings against theologies which make the Spirit a *tertium quid.* This means also that the Holy Spirit does not bypass human rationality, or make questions about the nature of human language irrelevant.[38] The parables of Jesus, Torrance points out, illustrate the interaction between the word of God and methods of communication through con-

---

33. *Ibid.,* p. 35; cf. p. 43.
34. G. Ebeling, *Theology and Proclamation. A Discussion with Rudolf Bultmann* (Eng. Collins, London, 1966), p. 102; cf. p. 42.
35. H. Thielicke, *The Evangelical Faith: Vol. I, The Relation of Theology to Modern Thought-Forms* (Eng. Eerdmans, Grand Rapids, Mich., 1974), p. 60; cf. also "Reflections on Bultmann's Hermeneutic" in *Exp.T.* LXVII (1956), 157 (cf. pp. 154-57), where he uses the phrase "final embarrassment."
36. T. F. Torrance, *God and Rationality* (Oxford University Press, London, 1971), pp. 137-92.
37. *Ibid.,* p. 167.
38. *Ibid.,* pp. 146-51 and 183-92.

crete human language.[39] Because man is still man in his ordinary humanity, it is still relevant to take account of "this sign-world which God has
appointed and uses."[40] The epistemological relevance of the Holy Spirit
lies not in some esoteric gnostic route to knowledge, but "in the dynamic
and transformal aspects of this knowledge."[41]

We may conclude, then, that the Holy Spirit may be said to work
through human understanding, and not usually, if ever, through processes
which bypass the considerations discussed under the heading of hermeneutics. Indeed from the point of view of Christian theology, the more
concerned the New Testament interpreter is about a doctrine of the word
of God and the work of the Spirit, the more concerned he should be to
approach hermeneutical issues seriously and responsibly as problems
which require thought but are nevertheless capable of some solution.
Moreover, an emphasis on the Holy Spirit is by no means incompatible
with Schleiermacher's insight that understanding constitutes an art rather
than a mechanistic science, since the Spirit is thought of in Christian
theology as acting in and through men creatively. This emphasis also
harmonizes well with the hermeneutical conclusions of Fuchs and Funk
that the interpreter does not simply pass judgment on the Word, but also
places himself under the judgment of the Word. To pronounce judgment
on man is an activity of the Spirit. In the end, then, far from suggesting
that the problem of hermeneutics can be bypassed, considerations about
the Holy Spirit serve to underline the legitimacy and importance of this
subject.

12. *Faith, "Timeless Truth," Time, and the Word*

The second theological argument against the legitimacy of hermeneutics concerns the role of faith. It is sometimes argued that since, without
faith, the New Testament will necessarily remain a closed book, considerations about hermeneutics will fail to solve the problem of understanding. Conversely, it is argued, if an interpreter already has faith the New
Testament is *already* intelligible, and hence hermeneutics remains
unnecessary.

To some extent the standard passages cited in the New Testament for
supposed support for this outlook raise the very same issues as those
outlined in the previous section about the Holy Spirit. We have seen, for
example, that Barth's appeal to such passages as 1 Corinthians 2:6-16 fails

39. *Ibid.,* p. 150.
40. *Ibid.,* p. 184.
41. *Ibid.,* p. 166.

and twisting biblical passages in order to defend their heterodox opinions. In this context Irenaeus and many of the Church Fathers insisted on two principles: first of all, that Scripture is to be interpreted in the light of its own witness as a whole; secondly, that valid interpretation depends on Christian faith, in the sense of accepting the tradition accepted by the believing community. This particular point in no way invalidates the task of hermeneutics, however. Indeed the reverse is the case, since it raises precisely the questions about the relation between exegesis and systematic theology that we discuss at length in chapter eleven.

This positive point may also be expressed in broader and more general terms. R. P. C. Hanson rightly asserts, "The Bible . . . was written from faith to faith. It was intended for the use of a worshipping community, and outside the context of a worshipping community it is inevitably . . . misapplied. It is intended for the use of a living Church. . . ."[52] This claim cannot be said to contradict what we have already said about the Bible's capacity to *create* faith, for both principles are equally true to the experience of the Christian community down the centuries. The point in question in no way challenges the legitimacy or necessity of hermeneutics, even though it may well call in question some of the claims for a purely "historical" approach, as over against a "faith" interpretation (e.g. of the causes of the Exile) which we have noted in D. E. Nineham's writings.

We come now to a third objection to the relevance of hermeneutics which is often put forward on supposedly theological grounds. We shall see that the issues it raises point in the end rather to the validity and relevance of hermeneutical discussions. However, it is sometimes argued that the truth of God conveyed through the New Testament is changeless, and therefore "timeless." Hence questions about understanding the Bible cannot be said to vary from generation to generation. It is perhaps implied that the truth of the New Testament, because it is the truth of God, stands apart from historical and cultural change in much the same way as may be claimed for the truth of mathematics. The angles of a triangle add up to 180° independently of what particular triangles a mathematician actually draws. In the language of philosophical logic, such truths are said to be necessary truths rather than contingent truths.

If this is what is meant by claiming that the Bible conveys "timeless" truth, quite clearly this would not be the view of the biblical writers themselves. Such a view of truth can be described as theological only if Christianity is built on Platonist metaphysics. In practice, this point need not detain us, for it is generally accepted today that this view of truth is drawn from Greek philosophy, and not from the Bible, and that, in any

---

52. R. P. C. Hanson, *The Bible as a Norm of Faith* (Durham University Press, 1963), p. 11.

case, a God of "necessary" truth would be unrelated to human life and experience. The point is expressed admirably by Wolfhart Pannenberg in his essay "What is Truth?" He writes, "For Greek thought . . . truth excluded all change. . . . It belongs to the essence of truth to be unchangeable and, thus, to be one and the same, without beginning or end."[53] *Necessary* truth depends not on the actual occurrence of particular events, but on whether a proposition is true by definition; on whether, for example, it is part of the very concept of triangularity that the sum of the angles of a triangle should amount to 180°. By contrast, contingent truth depends on circumstances which may change from time to time, such as in the case of the statement "it is raining." Pannenberg insists that in the Bible truth is contingent rather than necessary because it is related to historical events. It is "not the result of logical necessity. . . . The truth of God must prove itself anew."[54] "The Greek dualism between true being and changing sense-appearance is superseded in the biblical understanding of truth. Here, true being is thought of not as timeless, but instead as historical, and it proves its stability through a history whose future is always open."[55]

Quite clearly statements such as "God was in Christ reconciling the world to himself" (2 Cor. 5:19) or "Christ died for our sins according to the scriptures" (1 Cor. 15:3) would have been false if uttered before a certain date in history. In this sense they are not timeless. But are there not other types of statements which occur in the New Testament, of which this cannot be said?

The wide range of meanings which might be conveyed by the term "timeless truth" has been discussed from a philosophical point of view by Friedrich Waismann, and more recently by Paul Helm.[56] Waismann, for example, considers such questions as "Is a statement about the future true now?", and indeed "What is *meant* by saying that a statement about the future is true now?" The statement *"p is true,"* he argues, is *not a description of "p,"* which can be completed by adding a time-specification. To say that truth is timeless is only to say that it is logically confusing and inappropriate to add a time-specification to the words "It is true that. . . ." It would be logically puzzling, for example, to say: "It is true at 4 o'clock on Tuesday that God is good." To quote Waismann's own words, "One is misled by the external form of the expression. It seems as if the adjective 'true' stands for a quality of propositions of which it can be asked: 'When does *p* have this quality?' It is quite right to say, 'Truth is

53. W. Pannenberg, *B.Q.T.* II, 19; cf. pp. 1-27.
54. *Ibid.*, p. 8.
55. *Ibid.*, p. 9.
56. F. Waismann, *The Principles of Linguistic Philosophy* (Macmillan, London, 1965), pp. 27-34; and P. Helm, "Revealed Propositions and Timeless Truths" in *R.St.* VIII (1972), 127-36.

theology is fundamentally no other than the history of its various attempts at address."[64] Thielicke concludes that it is not necessarily to "accommodate" theological truth to attempt to "actualize" it through re-address and re-interpretation from generation to generation.[65]

The part played by nearly two thousand years of intervening tradition and history also affects the nature of the discussion. Pannenberg, Fuchs, and especially Gerhard Ebeling strongly emphasize this point. Each of these three writers argues that on the basis of this historical situation merely to abstract certain words from the New Testament and to repeat them mechanically would be *un*faithful to the intention of the New Testament writers. Pannenberg asserts, "In a changed situation the traditional phrases, even when recited literally, do not mean what they did at the time of their original formulation."[66] He adds, "An external assimilating of Christian language to the thoughts and manner of speaking of the biblical writings is always an infallible sign that theology has sidestepped its own present problems, and thus has failed to accomplish what Paul or John, or, in his own way, even Luther, each accomplished for his own time."[67] Theology, Pannenberg concludes, comes closest to agreement with the biblical witnesses when it seriously engages with the problems and thought-forms of its own time. At this point in his argument he explicitly appeals to the contribution of modern hermeneutics, making special reference to Gadamer's concept of a fusion of horizons.

In his essay "Time and Word" Gerhard Ebeling also asserts, "The same word can be said to another time only by being said differently."[68] In addition to the discussions in *Word and Faith* to which we have already referred, the issue emerges, as perhaps the titles suggest, in Ebeling's books *The Word of God and Tradition* and *The Problem of Historicity*. In this last work Ebeling considers concrete examples where the text of the Bible seems already to speak, as it were, timelessly, without any expository interpretation from the Christian preacher. For instance, he recalls how at the end of the war, when he heard of Hitler's death, he read to his fellow-soldiers Isaiah 14, the song of triumph at the overthrow of the king of Babylon. The impact of the passage was effective in its own right, after many centuries of historical change. However, Ebeling argues, "it would not be right to want to adduce such an example as evidence for the opinion that in certain cases proclamation may consist in mere repetition of the word of the Scriptures and need not have the structure of interpre-

64. *Ibid.*
65. *Ibid.*, pp. 27-29.
66. W. Pannenberg, *B.Q.T.* I, 9.
67. *Ibid.*
68. G. Ebeling, "Time and Word" in J. M. Robinson (ed.), *The Future of Our Religious Past*, p. 265.

tation, or that this might even be the ideal way to test the Scriptures."[69] This is because, he claims, something like interpretation did indeed take place. Everything hinged on a parallel in the mind of the hearers between the historical situation behind the text and that of the hearers themselves. Ebeling adds, "However, no situation is identical with another. Therefore every interpretation of the scriptural word which rests its case on the similarity of the past and present situations already rests on a translation (*Übertragung*) and thus on a fully unconscious exegetical operation which, on reflection, is seen to touch upon difficult hermeneutical questions."[70] Every understanding, he concludes, even if it is not explicitly arrived at by a conscious process of hermeneutics, still tacitly includes interpretation.

Ebeling turns at this point to consider the theological question of whether Luther and the Reformers do not in fact draw a sharp contrast between "interpretation" as the changing word of man and "Scripture" as the word of God. He concludes: "Luther is concerned with setting forth and affirming the necessity of an interpretation which is always carried through anew in repeated listening to the word of Scripture, as opposed to a persistence in a normative interpretation previously established and now placed above the Scriptures."[71] The recognition of the necessary place of interpretation, Ebeling argues, accords with Luther's conviction that Scripture is not merely a written word belonging to the past, but a *viva vox evangelii*, a word of God which encounters us here and now. In accordance with this understanding of Luther's thought, Ebeling declares, "Interpretation does not jeopardize but actually establishes the claim of the Scriptures to be the Word of God."[72]

Ebeling brings us back, in the end, to the considerations which we outlined in the first chapter of this study. The history of interpretation, he argues, begins in the Bible itself, for example when the Old Testament is expressed through the medium of the Septuagint. Even the supposedly straightforward matter of Bible translation, he points out, involves interpretation, and this cannot be done "timelessly," but is achieved in different ways from age to age and culture to culture. Indeed most of the many arguments about the need for interpretation put forward by Ebeling and Fuchs appeal, at some point, to the dual activities of Bible translation and Christian preaching. If the New Testament does not need to be articulated anew, why do we need translations which "speak to" a given

---

69. G. Ebeling, *The Problem of Historicity in the Church and its Proclamation* (Fortress Press, Philadelphia, 1967), p. 11.
70. *Ibid.*
71. *Ibid.*, p. 14.
72. *Ibid.*, p. 15.
73. *Ibid.*, p. 16.

language, culture, and community? If the New Testament already speaks in a "timeless" way, why do we believe that sermons are still necessary as means of expounding the meaning of Scripture for today? Fuchs declares, "Although preaching may say the same thing as the text, it in no case says the identical thing."[74] The task of the preacher, he urges, is so to "translate" the text that it speaks anew to his own time.[75] In one of Fuchs' typically aphoristic utterances he writes, "God's revelation consisted simply in God's letting men state *God's own problems in their language.*"[76]

What began as a consideration of a theological objection to hermeneutics on the basis of language about "timeless truth" has become, instead, the exposition of an argument for the urgency of hermeneutics on the ground of considerations about time and temporal change. We shall see in due course that Fuchs and Ebeling are admittedly influenced by Heidegger's thought about the relation between time and being. However, the validity of the comments about interpretation which we have noted are by no means dependent on any particular philosophical theory about time.

The fourth theological objection to the relevance of hermeneutical inquiry is based on the theory that, according to the outlook of many of the biblical writers, the word of God encounters man with utterly compelling force. Appeals are made, for example, to such passages as Hebrews 4:12-13: "The word of God is living and active, sharper than any two-edged sword, piercing to the division of soul and spirit, of joints and marrow, and discerning the intentions of the heart." The word of God is spoken of as "the power of God" for believers (1 Cor. 1:18) and as the sword of the Spirit (Eph. 6:17). Old Testament passages are cited still more frequently in this connection. The word of God is as efficacious as the snow and rain which nourish the earth: "it shall not return to me empty" (Isa. 55:10, 11). The word of God has power to pluck up and to break down and is like a hammer that breaks in pieces, or like a fire (Jer. 1:9, 10; 5:14; 23:29). If the word of God is said to be like this, can there (from an admittedly *theological* viewpoint) be any room or need for hermemeneutics?

This question need not detain us long at this point, for we shall return to consider this view, put forward as a theory of *language*, in the next chapter. In an article entitled "The Supposed Power of Words in the Biblical Writings" I have considered the issue in detail, and conclude that allusions to the power of the word of God in the Old and New Testaments

---

74. E. Fuchs, *Zum Hermeneutischen Problem in der Theologie*, p. 95.
75. E. Fuchs, *Herm.*, pp. 249-56; and *Marburger Hermeneutik*, pp. 2-4.
76. E. Fuchs, "The New Testament and the Hermeneutical Problem" in *N.H.*, pp. 135-36.

depend not on a particular supposedly ancient or "Hebraic" view of language, but on the fact that the word in question is spoken with the authority of *God*.[77] Once this point is accepted, however, it only remains to ask what *kind* of authority or power God is said to exert in the communication of the word. If this is conceived of quasi-physically or mechanically, it would certainly short-circuit discussions about hermeneutics. However, most traditions in Christian theology conceive of this "power" as being exercised in moral and above all personal terms. If this is the case, the points which we made in our discussion about the work of the Holy Spirit provide an adequate answer already to the question under consideration.

It is noteworthy that Helmut Thielicke finds no incompatibility between stressing, on the one hand, the creative power of the word of God and the Holy Spirit to give birth to new capacities and orientations in man, and stressing, on the other hand, that God respects the personhood of the addressee in such a way that he does not impose upon him an external heteronomy. On the one hand he writes, "The creative Spirit of God . . . cannot be integrated into the structure of the 'old' existence. . . . Who God is and what he does to me cuts right across my theories about him."[78] The communication of the word of God, Thielicke urges, involves new creation by the Spirit.[79] Nevertheless, he also writes, on the other hand, "As Kant pointed out, God's dignity is also at stake. For God does not want to force us as a heteronomous tyrant. He does not want servile obedience. He wants filial obedience. He wants us to turn to him spontaneously. We can do this, however, only if we are vanquished or inwardly persuaded by the claim of the message. . . . It is unavoidable, then, that the *autos* should become a theme of theological importance, that the anthropological question should be given a new stress. The question is now relevant what points of contact the message finds in our prior understanding . . . what concepts, e.g. in contemporary philosophy, are at our disposal in putting the message into another schema."[80] This perspective, Thielicke allows, although he believes that it contains many dangers, "does not have to be an enemy of theological tradition. . . . The question of understanding thus becomes more and more central until finally hermeneutics becomes a theological discipline of its own."[81]

Theological considerations about the creative power of the word of God, then, no more call hermeneutics in question than parallel consid-

77. A. C. Thiselton, "The Supposed Power of Words in the Biblical Writings" in *J.T.S.* N.S. XXV (1974), 283-99.
78. H. Thielicke, *The Evangelical Faith* I, 145.
79. *Ibid.*, pp. 138-211.
80. *Ibid.*, pp. 38-39; cf. also p. 51.
81. *Ibid.*, p. 39.

erations about the work of the Holy Spirit, the need for faith, or claims about so-called timeless truth. On the contrary, each of these four sets of considerations serve in the end only to underline the importance of the hermeneutical task. We must now turn, however, to a broader issue, namely the questions raised by the problem of pre-understanding.

13. *Understanding and Pre-understanding: Schleiermacher*

Before we can try to evaluate the force of theological criticisms brought against the notion of pre-understanding, we must first outline what it is that is often under attack. We have already argued that theological considerations do not short-circuit the relevance of hermeneutics as the problem of human understanding. Further, in the first chapter we argued that understanding takes place when two sets of horizons are brought into relation to each other, namely those of the text and those of the interpreter. On this basis understanding presupposes a shared area of common perspectives, concepts, or even judgments. Fuchs describes this as the phenomenon of "common understanding" *(Einverständnis)*. But if understanding, as it were, presupposes understanding, how can it begin?

Friedrich Schleiermacher was one of the first major thinkers to wrestle with this problem. His early aphorisms on hermeneutics in 1805 and 1806 were sparked off by his critical dialogue with Friedrich Ast (1778-1841) and Friedrich August Wolf (1759-1824). Schleiermacher frequently alludes to these two writers, especially in his comments on their approach written in August 1829.[82] Schleiermacher saw that what is to be understood must, in a sense, be already known. If this seems to involve a circularity or even a contradiction, it can only be said that this very account of understanding is true to the facts of everyday experience. Schleiermacher drew attention to this when he wrote, "Every child arrives at the meaning of a word only through hermeneutics *(Jedes Kind kommt nur durch Hermeneutik zur Wortbedeutung)*."[83] On the one side, the child attempts to relate a new word to what he already knows. If he cannot achieve this, the new word remains meaningless. On the other side (as Gadamer phrases it in his comment on Schleiermacher's aphorism), the child has to assimilate "something alien, universal, which always signifies a resistance for the original vitality. To that extent it is an accomplishment of hermeneutic."[84] Schleiermacher adds that since un-

82. F. D. E. Schleiermacher, *Hermeneutik*, pp. 123, 125-26, 128-29, 133, and 152-55.
83. *Ibid.*, p. 40.
84. H.-G. Gadamer, "The Problem of Language in Schleiermacher's Hermeneutic" in *J.T.C.* VII (1970), 72; cf. pp. 68-95.

derstanding new subject-matter still depends on a positive relation to the interpreter's own horizons, "lack of understanding is never wholly removed."[85] It constitutes a progressive experience or process, not simply an act that can be definitively completed.

Richard Palmer defends Schleiermacher's approach. He writes, "Is it not vain to speak of love to one who has not known love, or of the joys of learning to those who reject it? One must already have, in some measure, a knowledge of the matter being discussed. This may be termed the minimal pre-knowledge necessary for understanding, without which one cannot leap into the hermeneutical circle."[86]

Although it has now become a fixed and unalterable technical term in hermeneutics, the phrase "hermeneutical circle" is in one respect an unfortunate one. For although the center of gravity moves back and forth between the two poles of the interpreter and the text, there is also an ongoing movement and progressive understanding which might have been better conveyed by some such image as that of the spiral. There is also the additional problem that the phrase "hermeneutical circle" is used in two distinct ways. Often, as in other parts of this present study, it is used in connection with the process of putting questions to the text, which are in turn reshaped by the text itself. Here, however, we are concerned with the principle that understanding a whole stretch of language or literature depends on an understanding of its component parts, while an understanding of these smaller units depends, in turn, on an understanding of the total import of the whole. For example, in attempting to grapple with the meaning of a difficult philosophical text such as Heidegger's *Being and Time*, we understand paragraphs and sentences only if we understand individual words within them. Yet the words cannot be understood by looking up their separate meanings in a dictionary. They depend for this meaning on their role within the sentence, paragraph, or chapter. Even the use of a technical glossary to explain individual terms depends on the understanding of the work as a whole arrived at in this case vicariously through the compiler of the glossary. In principle, the truth of the hermeneutical circle holds good. This is why a really difficult text which deals with new or seemingly strange subject-matter may require a second or even a third reading if satisfactory understanding is to be achieved. This way of describing the issue, of course, only scratches the surface of Schleiermacher's hermeneutics, and we shall return to his approach again.

Meanwhile, in effect we have been exploring the category of pre-understanding *(Vorverständnis)*. John Macquarrie helpfully expounds this

85. F. D. E. Schleiermacher, *Hermeneutik*, p. 141.
86. R. E. Palmer, *Hermeneutics*, pp. 87-88.

tention to these problems in his article "Interpretation and Understanding in Schleiermacher's Theology: Some Critical Questions."[98] Schleiermacher shares with romanticism the emphasis on feeling and subjective experience. But when he turns to questions about Christian faith, does he not go too near to translating Christian doctrine into descriptions of human states? J. B. Torrance allows that Schleiermacher does not reduce all theological content to human consciousness without qualification, but questions whether he pays adequate attention to "the 'objective' 'factual' reference of theological statements."[99] The weakness of this type of approach from the standpoint of Christian theology is that "it becomes so pre-occupied with the self-understanding of the human subject, that it fails to yield any positive affirmation about the Being of God as He is in Himself."[100] This is a recurring difficulty in the application of hermeneutics to theological texts. While as a hermeneutical starting-point Bultmann rightly begins with the problem of pre-understanding, many writers have argued that in the end he reduces theology to anthropology. Whether this criticism is justified with reference to Bultmann we must postpone until a later chapter. However, we may note that the problem itself begins to emerge with Schleiermacher, as soon as we have a sensitive awareness of the problem of pre-understanding.

Thirdly, we may also note that Schleiermacher's recognition of the importance of understanding the whole as well as the parts, together with his emphasis on the role of sympathetic imagination, finds further expression in his notion of "divination." Divination entails a "leap" into fresh understanding. Schleiermacher writes, "The divinatory is that in which one transforms oneself into the other person in order to grasp his individuality directly."[101] Once again, this is connected with the hermeneutical circle. For Schleiermacher states that one must have an understanding of man himself in order to understand what he speaks, and yet one comes to know what man is from his speech.[102] Thus, understanding, once again, is not merely a matter of scientific "rules," but is a creative act.

14. Pre-understanding and Theology

We shall postpone until the middle of the three chapters on Bultmann's hermeneutics our fuller discussions of Bultmann's use of the

98. J. B. Torrance, "Interpretation and Understanding in Schleiermacher's Theology: Some Critical Questions" in *S.J.T.* XXI, 268-82.
99. *Ibid.*, p. 272; cf. p. 274.
100. *Ibid.*, p. 278.
101. F. D. E. Schleiermacher, *Hermeneutik*, p. 109.
102. *Ibid.*, p. 44.

category of pre-understanding. However, one or two preliminary comments may be made, since it is most frequently in the context of Bultmann's thought that the concept of pre-understanding is attacked. We shall see that Bultmann is heavily indebted to Dilthey for the belief that understanding of a text depends on a prior relation to "life." Thus Bultmann writes, "Can one understand economic history without having a concept of what economy and society in general mean? Can one understand the history of religion and philosophy without knowing what religion and philosophy are? . . . One cannot understand the Communist Manifesto of 1848 without understanding the principles of capitalism and socialism."[103] Bultmann concludes, "A specific understanding of the subject-matter of the text, on the basis of a 'life-relation' to it, is always presupposed by exegesis."[104]

Two elements in Bultmann's hermeneutics are attacked on the basis of their alleged dependence on his view of pre-understanding. First of all, he is attacked for laying down for the principle that, in his own words, "The interpretation of the biblical writings is not subject to conditions different from those applying to all other kinds of literature."[105] Secondly, Bultmann also insists that for the interpreter to begin with questions about his own existence *(Existenz)* is thereby to ask questions about God. In *Jesus Christ and Mythology,* for example, he asks: What is the "life-relation" which the interpreter already has in advance to the theological subject-matter of the New Testament? He is moved, he answers, "by the question about his personal existence." He then adds: "The question of God and the question of myself are identical."[106] Similarly, in his essay on hermeneutics Bultmann writes, "In human existence an *existentiell* knowledge about God is alive in the form of the inquiry about 'happiness', 'salvation', the meaning of the world, and . . . the real nature of each person's particular 'being'."[107]

In our later discussion of Bultmann's hermeneutics we shall attempt to show how these two principles relate to his wider thought. For instance, it would be unwise to jump to conclusions about any supposed naturalism or immanentism implied by the second principle until we have first noted how strongly Bultmann is influenced by dialectical theology and by a recognition of the limitations of theological liberalism. His thought on this subject is complex, not least because he is attempting to do justice to a variety of theological perspectives, not all of which are

103. R. Bultmann, "Is Exegesis Without Presuppositions Possible?" in *E.F.,* p. 347; cf. pp. 342-51.
104. *Ibid.*
105. R. Bultmann, *E.P.T.,* p. 256.
106. R. Bultmann, *Jesus Christ and Mythology* (S.C.M., London, 1960), p. 53; cf. pp. 52-56.
107. R. Bultmann, *E.P.T.,* p. 257.

clearly compatible with one another. However, our immediate purpose is simply to note that a number of writers, including Karl Barth, James Smart, and Carl Braaten, among others, explain these principles on the basis of Bultmann's view of pre-understanding.[108] Carl Braaten writes, "The Achilles' heel of Bultmann's hermeneutical proposal is his narrow conception of the pre-understanding appropriate in Biblical interpretation."[109]

In practice, however, other theologians invoke the category of pre-understanding without accepting the two principles which are so often attacked in Bultmann's hermeneutics, and certainly without accepting an existentialist analysis of human existence. We shall illustrate this point by selecting for consideration the hermeneutics of some theologians who write from the standpoint of very different theological traditions. We shall refer briefly to some statements made by two Catholic theologians, Edward Schillebeeckx and Bernard Lonergan. We shall then compare the approach to New Testament hermeneutics represented by Latin-American theologians such as Gustavo Gutiérrez and José Porfirio Miranda. After this we shall turn, finally, to the work of the philosopher Paul Ricoeur, in order to show that the category of pre-understanding is fruitfully employed by a thinker who cannot be accused of having any particular theological axe to grind.

We begin with a brief reference to the hermeneutics of Edward Schillebeeckx and Bernard Lonergan. Both stress that the truth of the New Testament is communicated through ordinary human language and appropriated by the normal processes of human understanding. In his wide-ranging book *The Understanding of Faith* Schillebeeckx gives more than adequate weight to distinctively theological considerations about faith.[110] However, he also emphatically asserts, a relationship with "lived experience" is an indispensable criterion for the meaning of theological interpretation.[111] He writes, "Language only communicates meaning when it expresses an experience that is shared."[112] That is to say, he advocates what he calls "hermeneutics of experience."[113] He points out that he is not claiming that it is possible to deduce from ordinary human experiences the meaning of, say, the resurrection of Jesus Christ. He goes on: "What I am saying, however, is that the Christian meaning of the

108. K. Barth, "Rudolf Bultmann—An Attempt to Understand Him" in *K.M.* II, 83-132; J. D. Smart, *The Interpretation of Scripture*, p. 48; and C. E. Braaten, *New Directions in Theology Today: 2, History and Hermeneutics*, p. 135.
109. C. E. Braaten, *ibid.*
110. E. Schillebeeckx, *The Understanding of Faith. Interpretation and Criticism* (Eng. Sheed and Ward, London, 1974), e.g. pp. 5-19 and 135-55.
111. *Ibid.*, pp. 14-17.
112. *Ibid.*, p. 15.
113. *Ibid.*, p. 16.

resurrection . . . will be *a priori* unintelligible to us . . . if the universally intelligible content of this concept does not include human experience."[114] The criterion of intelligibility is "the relationship with lived human experience."[115] In effect this is a defense of the category of pre-understanding as a necessary hermeneutical tool and as grounded in human life.

Bernard Lonergan also argues for the importance of pre-understanding, simply as a given fact of life by virtue of the nature of language and understanding. We cannot claim to find meaning in a biblical text, he argues, if we approach it on the basis of "the principle of the empty head."[116] This approach is merely "naive." We see that it is naive, he argues, as soon as we pause to think what the "empty head" will in practice see. "There is·just a series of signs. Anything over and above a re-issue of the same signs in the same order will be mediated by the experience, intelligence and judgment of the interpreter. The less that experience, the less cultivated that intelligence, the less formed that judgment, the greater will be the likelihood that the interpreter will impute to the author an opinion that the author never entertained."[117]

This conclusion, which Lonergan states in his book *Method in Theology,* also echoes his more general comments in his earlier work *Insight. A Study of Human Understanding.* In this earlier work he writes, "If a correct interpretation is possible, it has to be possible . . . for interpreters to proceed from their own experience, understanding, and judgment, to the range of possible meanings of documents."[118] Lonergan does not seem to suggest in his later book on theology that when the subject-matter to be understood is theological, more general theories of understanding become irrelevant.

Hermeneutics and especially theological questions about the significance of pre-understanding have been given a new turn in the last few years by the emergence of the theology of liberation in Latin America. In a survey-article about this movement, published in 1976, José Miguez Bonino of Buenos Aires writes that biblical studies constitute a challenge for the theology of liberation not least because "we have, in the first place, the question of hermeneutics: Is it legitimate to start Biblical interpretation from a contemporary historical interpretation? . . . How can the freedom of the text be maintained?"[119] Bonino gives a fuller

114. *Ibid.,* p. 17.
115. *Ibid.*
116. B. J. F. Lonergan, *Method in Theology* (Darton, Longman and Todd, London, 1972), p. 157.
117. *Ibid.* Cf. pp. 153-266.
118. B. J. F. Lonergan, *Insight. A Study of Human Understanding* (Longmans, Green and Co., London, ²1958), p. 578.
119. J. Miguez Bonino, "Theology and Theologians of the New World: II. Latin America" in *Exp.T.* LXXXVII (1976), 199; cf. pp. 196-200.

description of the hermeneutics of the movement in his book *Revolution-ary Theology Comes of Age,* and the hermeneutics can be seen in action in such works as José Porfirio Miranda's *Marx and the Bible.*[120] The hermeneutics of the movement is also critically discussed in a recent doctoral thesis by J. Andrew Kirk.[121]

These writers, together with others such as Gustavo Gutiérrez, Juan Luis Segundo, and Hugo Assmann, stress that biblical hermeneutics turns on a pre-understanding which is shaped, in turn, by *praxis.* Theoretical knowledge, it is argued, especially the philosophical values associated with the Western bourgeoisie, distort the message of the Bible and obscure the rights of the text. There is no such thing as purely neutral knowledge. Bonino asserts, "The sociology of knowledge makes abundantly clear that we think out of a definite context . . . , *out of a given praxis.* What Bultmann has so convincingly argued concerning a *pre-understanding* which every man brings to his interpretation of the text *must be deepened and made more concrete."*[122] Pre-understanding, Bonino continues, relates to such concrete considerations as a man's social class and nationhood. Freud and Marx, he argues, were correct in their suspicions about hidden factors which control man's conscious accounts of life and literature. The Latin-American theologians are especially suspicious of approaches to the Bible undertaken from bourgeois or non-Marxist perspectives. "Why is it, for instance, that the obvious political motifs and undertones in the life of Jesus have remained so hidden to liberal interpreters until very recently?"[123] Juan Luis Segundo argues that theologians have managed to draw from the Bible and Christian tradition the image of a timeless and impersonal God only because their interpretations were shaped by a prior view of life in which God was relegated to an "inner" or "private" zone. "Hermeneutics in this new context means also an identification of the ideological framework of interpretation implicit in a given religious praxis."[124]

Many of the Latin-American theologians themselves quite explicitly and consciously interpret the New Testament in terms of a pre-

120. J. P. Miranda, *Marx and the Bible. A Critique of the Philosophy of Oppression* (Eng. Orbis Books, Maryknoll, New York, 1974); G. Gutiérrez, *A Theology of Liberation* (Eng. Orbis Books, Maryknoll, New York, 1973); and other writers discussed in J. Míguez Bonino, *Revolutionary Theology Comes of Age* (Eng. S.P.C.K., London, 1975), especially the selection "Hermeneutics, Truth, and Praxis," pp. 86-105.
121. J. A. Kirk, *The Theology of Liberation in the Latin American Roman Catholic Church Since 1965: An Examination of its Biblical Basis* (unpublished Ph.D. thesis, University of London, 1975). Part II concerns especially pre-understanding and hermeneutics. Cf. also J. A. Kirk, *Liberation Theology. An Evangelical View from the Third World* (Marshall, Morgan and Scott, London, 1979).
122. J. Míguez Bonino, *Revolutionary Theology Comes of Age,* p. 90.
123. *Ibid.,* p. 91.
124. *Ibid.,* p. 94.

understanding oriented towards Marxist perspectives. Thus Bonino asks, "Is it altogether absurd to re-read the resurrection today as a death of the monopolies, the liberation from hunger, or a solidary form of owner-ship?"[125] José Porfirio Miranda's *Marx and the Bible* provides a more detailed example. Too often, he complains, the biblical interpreter has approached the text with a pre-understanding of man as an abstraction, "a Platonic essence valid *semper et pro semper,* not real flesh-and-blood humanity, a humanity of blood and tears and slavery and humiliations and jail and hunger and untold sufferings."[126] Miranda also stresses that pre-understanding must be oriented to *praxis.* Otherwise the interpreter becomes sidetracked into merely dealing in "concepts" *about* God. The God of the Bible, he declares, is the one "to objectify whom is to break off the imperative relationship."[127]

Yet Miranda and Bonino do not wish to open the door to subjectivism (as against subjectivity). Miranda asserts, "I am not reducing the Bible to Marx. . . . I only wish to understand what the Bible says. . . . We want to take the Bible seriously."[128] Indeed, he argues that his own approach is motivated by an attempt to read the Bible on its own terms. It is precisely *not* simply all "a matter of the mind of the interpreter." It is only the defeatist and cynical belief that "Scripture has various 'meanings' " that (in Miranda's view) allows conservative theologians of the West "to prevent the Bible from revealing *its* own subversive message. Without a recourse to this belief, how could the West, a civilization of injustice, continue to say that the Bible is its sacred book? Once we have estab-lished the possibility of different 'meanings' each as acceptable as any other, then Scripture cannot challenge the West."[129] Bonino also insists that critical appraisal must take place to insure that "reading" the New Testament does not become a matter of "only arbitrary inventions."[130] Andrew Kirk sums up the perspective as follows: "The Marxist interpre-tation provides an ideological mechanism which is capable of exposing the intentions of any exegesis seeking, through the employment of pre-understanding tied to conservative philosophical systems, to use the Biblical text . . . to defend the status-quo of a pre-revolutionary situa-tion."[131]

The effect of this approach is first of all to stress the importance of questions about pre-understanding, and secondly to show that the use of

125. *Ibid.,* p. 101.
126. J. P. Miranda, *Marx and the Bible,* p. 31.
127. *Ibid.,* p. 41.
128. *Ibid.,* pp. 35 and 36.
129. *Ibid.,* p. 36.
130. J. Miguez Bonino, *Revolutionary Theology Comes of Age,* p. 100.
131. J. A. Kirk, *The Theology of Liberation,* Part II, sect. 2-1.

this category in New Testament hermeneutics does not belong exclusively to those who start from the standpoint of Heidegger and existentialist philosophy, nor even from the philosophical tradition of Schleiermacher and Dilthey. But thereby they provide two warnings which we must heed when we look at Bultmann's thought more closely. First of all, the fact that Marxist interpreters do in fact tend to arrive at Marxist interpretations of the Bible even when they are aware of their own pre-understanding sharpens the problem of objectivity in biblical hermeneutics. A mere awareness of the problem of pre-understanding is not enough to solve the problems to which this phenomenon gives rise. We have arrived at the point where the problem is less "the pastness of the past" than that of evaporating past meaning in the horizons of the present. Secondly, if such different pre-understandings seem to lead on to such different ways of interpreting the New Testament, we must beware of the claim of any one New Testament interpreter to start from the "right" pre-understanding. This is sometimes urged as a criticism of Bultmann, and we shall see in due course that it is not entirely without some truth. On the one hand, Bultmann sets too high a value on the *one* starting-point of the earlier Heidegger's view of existence; but on the other hand he does also stress that any pre-understanding is provisional and open to later correction.

As a final comment on the subject of pre-understanding in general we may also note that the debate, in effect, is even more wide-ranging than we have yet seen. The philosopher Paul Ricoeur (as well as others, including for example Peter Homans) shows how hermeneutics is affected by considerations which emerge not only from Marx but also from Sigmund Freud.[132] One of the most startling features of Ricoeur's discussion from the point of view of the present study is that it serves in effect to demonstrate that conclusions about the importance of pre-understanding can be arrived at from *two radically opposing philosophical traditions*. We have seen that in the tradition of Schleiermacher hermeneutical principles are formulated from the point of view of an emphasis on human consciousness. Freud (together with Nietzsche and Marx) approaches the problem of meaning on the basis of a *rejection* of the category of human consciousness as the key starting-point. Because of the complexity of the human mind, Freud argues that meaning is not always synonymous with *consciousness of* meaning. Ricoeur comments, "These three exegetes of modern man (Freud, Nietzsche and Marx) . . . all attack the same illusion, that illusion which bears the hallowed name of self-consciousness. . . . These three masters of suspicion, however, are not three masters of

132. P. Ricoeur, *The Conflict of Interpretations*, pp. 99-208, especially "The Place of Freudian Hermeneutics," pp. 142-50. Cf. also P. Homans, "Psychology and Hermeneutics" in *J.R.* LV (1975), 327-47.

skepticism. . . . Marx, Nietzsche and Freud triumph over their doubt about consciousness through an exegesis of meanings. For the first time comprehension is hermeneutics."[133]

However, in each individual case, these thinkers approach questions about meanings with pre-understandings which, in their view, unlock and disclose them. Freud believes that the key to meaning comes from the unconscious psyche. Hence he interprets consciousness from the standpoint of this pre-understanding. Nietzsche approaches the matter in terms of man's will to power. Marx interprets life and history with presuppositions about man as a social being. Their view of "meaning" is inseparable from their own pre-understanding. None of these three thinkers could achieve his goal by ignoring or suppressing his own pre-understanding. "Understanding" dawns in the interaction between pre-understanding and meaning.[134]

We cannot claim, then, that the importance of pre-understanding in New Testament hermeneutics depends either on special pleading in theology or on too narrow a philosophical base. The problems posed by this phenomenon cannot be avoided. In the words of the Church of England's Doctrine Communion Report *Christian Believing*, "No one expounds the Bible to himself or to anyone else without bringing to the task his own prior frame of reference, his own pattern of assumptions which derives from sources outside the Bible."[135]

---

133. *Ibid.*, pp. 148-49.
134. *Ibid.*, p. 150.
135. "The Christian and the Bible" in *Christian Believing*, p. 30.

CHAPTER V

Hermeneutics and Language

Questions about hermeneutics and language discussed in the present chapter still come under the heading of broader issues in hermeneutics. More specialized issues about language will emerge when we explore the work of Heidegger, Gadamer, and especially Wittgenstein. A systematic consideration of issues in hermeneutics, however, raises certain questions about language which do not arise directly from the work of these three philosophers.

In the history of New Testament interpretation from earliest times there have been three periods in which the importance of linguistic inquiries for hermeneutics has been stressed. In the first place, the school of Antioch, including especially Theodore of Mopsuestia and John Chrysostom, called attention to the value of language study as a means of arriving at the "literal" meaning of the text, in contrast to the allegorizing of the Alexandrian school. The term "literal," however, can be misleading. It does not exclude metaphorical or symbolic meaning when this plainly accords with the intention of the author, but demands that meaning be understood in the customarily acknowledged sense that it would normally bear in its proper linguistic context. In other words, the New Testament is approached as stretches of human language, to which normal linguistic procedures apply, rather than as a reservoir of oracles charged with additional meanings not ordinarily conveyed by the language itself and its context. Theodore of Mopsuestia quite explicitly attempted to pay attention to the particularities of linguistic context, refusing, Farrar puts it, "to read the latest revelations into the earliest utterances."[1]

The second period is that of the Reformation, and owes much in this respect to Martin Luther. Luther goes out of his way to stress that the

---

1. F. W. Farrar, *History of Interpretation*, p. 217.

study of *language as such* makes a positive contribution to biblical hermeneutics. One striking example comes from his letter to Eobanus Hessus, written to compliment him on the writing of a poem. The man of God, Luther urges, does not despise linguistic or literary skill: "I myself am convinced that without knowledge of (Humanistic) studies (Latin, *literae)* pure theology can by no means exist. . . . There has never been a great revolution of God's Word, unless God had first prepared the way by the rise and flourishing of languages and learning. . . . I realize that through these studies . . . people are wonderfully equipped for grasping the sacred truths, as well as for handling them skillfully and successfully."[2]

Various writers, including Ebeling and Moeller, stress that for Luther "there is only one genuine meaning of scripture, and this is the literal sense, which as such is spiritual."[3] But Luther's interest in language-studies was not motivated simply by a hostility towards allegory. Not least because of his work in translating the Bible, Luther was concerned about the relation of the language of the text to his own world. He spent long hours over a word or phrase, on at least one occasion spending four days over three lines from Job. He was also aware of how experience of life contributed to the understanding of language. Thus, for example, he went to the slaughterhouse to see how animals were killed in order the better to understand language about sacrifice.

The third period when the study of language as such was seen as a necessary hermeneutical tool began in the eighteenth century (if not even earlier with Spinoza), and continued and developed with the rise of biblical criticism. Robert Lowth's work on Hebrew poetry, in 1753, provides one example of how the study of language *as language* had decisive importance for biblical interpretation.[4] From this time onward, until Bultmann and the new hermeneutic, the story of New Testament hermeneutics becomes virtually synonymous with the progress of New Testament criticism, although scholars like Norden and perhaps Deissmann are especially noteworthy for their interest in language *qua* language. The development of these studies is too well known to require

2. M. Luther, "Letter to Eobanus Hessus" (March 29th, 1523) in *Luther's Works, Vol. 49: Letters, II,* ed. by Gottfried G. Krodel (general editor, Helmut T. Lehmann, Fortress Press, Philadelphia, 1972), p. 34. The editor argues (n. 12) that the Latin *Literae* means humanistic studies, because it is a recognized abbreviation for *bonae literae.* The translation "literature" would be possible, but the context probably favors the broader reference to Renaissance studies. Luther assures Hessus that Germans are not barbarians, who cannot appreciate poetry, and that he himself sees the value of such learning for theology.
3. G. Ebeling, *Luther. An Introduction to his Thought* (Eng. Collins, London, 1972), p. 107; cf. B. Moeller, "Scripture, Tradition and Sacrament in the Middle Ages and in Luther" in F. F. Bruce and E. G. Rupp (eds.), *Holy Book and Holy Tradition* (Manchester University Press, 1968), p. 130.
4. Lowth showed that in Hebrew poetic parallelism the language of the second line expressed the same meaning as the language of the first.

further comment, and is set out in such standard works as that of W. G. Kümmel.[5] More recently, in 1966, Luis Alonso Schökel wrote on the subject of "Scripture in the Light of Language and Literature," but while there is value in his work it breaks little new ground.[6] The most important recent developments have been from the standpoint of general linguistics and the relevance to biblical studies of linguistics and semantics. Here we may mention the work of James Barr and John Sawyer in Britain; R. Kieffer and especially E. Güttgemanns in Continental Europe; and the contributions to *Semeia* in America.[7]

15. *The Restricted Hermeneutical Role of Linguistic and Semantic Investigations: Distance, Fusion, and Reference*

From the standpoint of hermeneutics, traditional approaches to language usually carry with them an inbuilt limitation, namely that they concentrate attention on the language of the ancient text, and do not attempt to bring about a fusion of horizons between the world of the text and that of the interpreter. In effect, they tend to ignore the problem of pre-understanding (although in practice we reject the claim of D. O. Via, discussed later in this chapter, that James Barr's work carries with it a repudiation of the genuineness of this problem).[8] This is neither to criticize this approach, nor indeed to claim that it has no positive role to play in hermeneutics. We shall see that semantic inquiries perform a positive role in distancing the interpreter from the text. Nevertheless, because these investigations concern only the world of the text, their role in hermeneutics remains a restricted one. As Ebeling insists, it is possible to understand all the individual words of a text, but still not to understand its message.[9]

John Sawyer's work illustrates the principle in question. Even before he introduces his methodology concerning semantic fields, he argues that

---

5. W. G. Kümmel, *The New Testament. The History of the Interpretation of its Problems*, pp. 108-19 *et passim*.
6. L. Alonso Schökel, *The Inspired Word. Scripture in the Light of Language and Literature* (Eng. Burns and Oates, London, 1967).
7. J. Barr, *The Semantics of Biblical Language* (Oxford University Press, 1961); J. F. A. Sawyer, *Semantics in Biblical Research. New Methods of Defining Hebrew Words for Salvation* (S.C.M., London, 1972); R. Kieffer, *Essais de méthodologie néotestamentaire* (Gleerup, Lund, 1972); and E. Güttgemanns, *Studia Linguistica Neotestamentica. Gessammelte Aufsätze zur linguistischen Grundlage einer Neutestamentlichen Theologie* (Beiträge zur evangelischen Theologie Bd. 60; Kaiser, Munich, 1971). Cf. also the journal edited by Güttgemanns entitled *Linguistica Biblica: Interdisziplinäre Zeitschrift für Theologie und Linguistik*.
8. Cf. D. O. Via, *The Parables*, pp. 48-49.
9. G. Ebeling, *The Nature of Faith* (Eng. Collins, London, 1961), p. 16.

semantic ambiguity can be avoided "by substituting for the question 'What *does* it mean?' the questions 'What *did* it mean in its original context?' or 'What *did* it mean in Babylon in the sixth century BC?' or 'What *did* it mean in Alexandria in the third century BC?' and so on."[10] Here we are solely in the world of the text, in which "maximum objectivity is . . . the aim."[11] Distinctions are rightly drawn between what a text meant to its original author, what it meant to an early editor, and what it meant to the later Masoretes. As an example of this issue, Sawyer cites the problem of the meaning of the phrase *weĥêlîlû šîrôṭ hêḵāl* in Amos 8:3. Did *hêḵāl* mean "palace" (N.E.B.) or "temple" (R.S.V.)? Did Amos speak of "singing women" (N.E.B., presupposing *šārôṭ)* or "songs" (RSV, presupposing *šîrôṭ*)? Amos himself, Sawyer points out, was addressing a judgment oracle to the high-living royal establishment at Samaria. Hence he says, "The palace singing-girls will wail." But in the Masoretic tradition *hêḵāl* becomes the Jerusalem temple; and since the temple had "songs" but not "singing-girls," *šārôṭ* becomes *šîrôṭ*. "For masoretic tradition, followed by AV and RSV, the *original meaning* of these words, as they were understood in Samaria in the eighth century BC, would have been of purely academic interest, whereas the words as they stand are addressed to Jerusalem and foretell the destruction of the temple in 587 BC . . . *Hekal* . . . denoted 'palace' in Samaria, but 'temple' after the oracle had been applied to Jerusalem."[12] What it means *today,* Sawyer concludes, rests on a purely arbitrary decision about whether our interest lies with Amos's Samaria or with the editor's Jerusalem.

Sawyer points out that this principle operates in the case of many of the psalms. Gunkel's work, he argues, has been invaluable in pointing to an original *Sitz im Leben,* but this original setting "is not the only situational context. . . . Timeless compositions like the psalms have been contextualized in many situations."[13] Similar comments have been made about the meaning of passages in the Synoptic Gospels. Dodd and Jeremias have argued, for example, that what the parables of crisis *meant* in the situation in which Jesus addressed his Jewish audience was not necessarily synonymous with what they meant for the evangelists or the early church.[14]

In one sense, Sawyer's comments represent a hermeneutical standpoint, in that they underline the point that the biblical writers them-

---

10. J. F. A. Sawyer, *Semantics in Biblical Research,* p. 10 (my italics).
11. *Ibid.,* p. 2.
12. *Ibid.,* p. 5 (Sawyer's italics).
13. *Ibid.,* p. 7.
14. C. H. Dodd, *The Parables of the Kingdom* (Nisbet, London, 1936), pp. 111-74; and J. Jeremias, *The Parables of Jesus,* pp. 33-114.

selves are concerned to hear earlier texts in a way that speaks to their own
world. He also helps the interpreter to distance himself from the text, and
to pay attention to the particularity of each context of situation, rather
than imposing on the text his own prior judgment about levels of meaning.
However, for the most part Sawyer is concerned only with the horizons of
the ancient texts themselves, and not with the standpoint or world of the
modern interpreter.

This becomes especially clear when we move on from considerations
about context of situation to Sawyer's more distinctive contribution in the
area of field semantics. The major figure in the pioneering of field semantics was J. Trier, who first formulated field theory explicitly in 1931. Trier
asserted that a word has meaning not independently of its linguistic
context, but "only as part of a whole" *(nur als Teil des Ganzen);* "only
within a field" *(im Feld).*[15] The principle first emerged, however, in
embryonic form in the work of Ferdinand de Saussure (1857-1913), who is
generally regarded as the founder of modern linguistics. Saussure's work
is largely founded on three principles: first of all, on the principle that
language operates on the basis of human convention; secondly, on the
contrast between synchronic and diachronic linguistics; and thirdly, on
the nature of language as a structured system. We shall look more closely
at the first two principles in other parts of this present chapter, but we are
concerned at this particular point with the third. I have also undertaken a
more detailed discussion of Saussure and his significance for New Testament studies in a separate essay.[16]

Saussure writes, "Language is a system of interdependent terms *(les
termes sont solidaires)* in which the value *(la valeur)* of each term results
solely from the simultaneous presence of the others. . . . All words used
to express related ideas limit each other reciprocally."[17] A standard
example of this principle in general linguistics is that of color-words.
Where is the cut-off point between "red" and "yellow"? The answer
depends on whether "orange" is part of the field of color-words. If so,
"red" will be defined more narrowly than otherwise. Thus what "red"
means depends on what other terms exist within the same field, and how
they contribute to that field. Saussure himself illustrated the principle
with reference to a field of fear-words. The semantic value of *craindre,* to

15. J. Trier, *Der Deutsche Wortschatz im Sinnbezirk des Verstandes* (Winter, Heidelberg,
1931), p. 6.
16. A. C. Thiselton, "Semantics and New Testament Interpretation" in I. H. Marshall
(ed.), *New Testament Interpretation* (Paternoster Press, Exeter, and Eerdmans, Grand
Rapids, 1977), pp. 75-104.
17. F. de Saussure, *Cours de linguistique générale* (édition critique par R. Engler, Harrasowitz, Wiesbaden, 1967, 3 fascicles), fasc, 2, pp. 259 and 261-62; and *Course in General
Linguistics* (Eng. Owen, London, 1960, ed. by C. Bally et al.), pp. 114 and 166. (Baskin's
English translation has not been without criticism.)

fear, and *avoir peur*, to be afraid, is conditioned by whether or not *redouter*, to dread, also contributes to the field.[18]

John Sawyer examines the semantic field of words which relate to salvation in the Old Testament. Thus he compares the distinctive roles played within this field by various Hebrew words. Sometimes their distinctive roles are sufficiently close to parallel lexical distinctions in English to allow a rough correlation of the idea which they express with a corresponding difference between English words. For example, we may distinguish broadly between *'āzar*, to protect or help, and *pāraq*, to rescue. But for the most part the whole purpose of the operation is to see how these distinctions operate within Hebrew itself. Thus in a statement which is of key importance for our present argument, Sawyer asserts: "Instead of defining a word L in terms of another language, it can be defined as associated with A, B, C (in the same language), opposed to D, influenced semantically by G because of frequency collocation with it in idiom I, and so on. This is the most reliable method of describing meaning, *and must precede translation, not follow it.*"[19]

Sawyer's conclusion firmly underlines the point that semantic inquiries, by their very nature, can only assist with one half of the hermeneutical task, namely with elucidating the meaning of the text in terms of its horizons in the ancient world. This is an invaluable aid in *distancing* the text from the interpreter. For example, Sawyer's work reminds the interpreter that he cannot simply assimilate the meanings of Hebrew words to the meaning of their nearest English equivalents. However, it is important to call attention to the restricted scope of semantic investigations, at least from the point of view of hermeneutics, for a more general reason. From a supposedly "common-sense" standpoint it may be suggested (1) that hermeneutics is elucidating the meaning of a text; (2) that semantics concerns the meanings of words and sentences; and hence (3) that the scope of hermeneutics and the scope of semantic investigations are one and the same. To reach such a conclusion, however, would be a disastrous mistake.

If we seem to be perhaps laboring a fairly obvious point, it is worth noting that the philosopher Paul Ricoeur devotes an essay of some seventeen pages to this subject.[20] But his point of emphasis is slightly different. We ourselves have been at pains to point out that whereas linguistics (or semantics) concerns only the horizons of the text, hermeneutics concerns both those of the text and those of the interpreter. Ricoeur's parallel

18. F. de Saussure, *Cours de linguistique générale* (édition critique), p. 261; *Course in General Linguistics*, p. 116.
19. J. F. A. Sawyer, *Semantics in Biblical Research*, p. 32 (my italics).
20. P. Ricoeur, "The Problem of Double Meaning as Hermeneutic Problem and as Semantic Problem" in *The Conflict of Interpretations. Essays in Hermeneutics*, pp. 62-78.

problems about the theory of reference which are outlined by Wittgenstein.

First of all, Wittgenstein notes that the problem of *communication* or *intelligibility* cannot be solved by referential theories. It is often suggested that young children do in practice learn the meaning of words through the method of ostensive definition. The mother points to a metal object and says "spoon," and it is supposed that this is how the child learns the meaning of the word in question. If this were correct, it would be of importance for hermeneutics, for we have already observed how Schleiermacher stressed the parallel between hermeneutics and how a child learns the meaning of language. But Wittgenstein shows that this account of the matter is open to question. If I hold up a pencil and say, "this is *tove*," the ostensive definition may itself be understood in various ways. It *might* mean "this is a pencil"; but it might equally well mean "this is wood," or "this is hard," or "this is round," or even "this is one."[30] Wittgenstein writes, "Point to a piece of paper—And now point to its shape—Now to its colour—Now to its number. . . . How did you do it?"[31]

The second problem about both theories of reference and ostensive definition is that they only work when we are thinking of certain types of words. Wittgenstein writes, "If you describe the learning of language in this way, you are, I believe, thinking primarily of nouns like 'table', 'chair', 'bread', and of people's names, and only secondarily of the names of certain actions and properties, and of the remaining kinds of word as something that will take care of itself."[32] The unbeliever does not learn the meaning of such words as "God," "love," or "salvation," by being shown observable objects to which these words refer. They draw their meaning *in the first place* from the role which these words play in the lives of Christian believers, even if this does not completely exhaust their meaning for the believer himself. As Paul van Buren puts it, "To examine the word (i.e. "God") in isolation from its context in the life of religious people is to pursue an abstraction."[33]

Once again, this is not to deny that theories of reference may sometimes come into their own when we are testing the *truth* of language. We have already seen how Frege found it necessary to distinguish between meaning and truth in his essay on sense and reference. This is why it is not inconsistent to allow Wittgenstein's account of meaning, largely in functional terms, to pass without criticism, but at the same time to criticize

30. L. Wittgenstein, *B.B.*, pp. 2-4; cf. *P.I.*, sects. 26-37.
31. L. Wittgenstein, *P.I.*, sect. 33.
32. *Ibid.*, sect. 1.
33. P. M. van Buren, *The Edges of Language* (S.C.M., London, 1972), p. 71.

Rudolf Bultmann for basing his interpretation of the language of the New Testament on a functional account of meaning. For Wittgenstein does not attempt to construct a theory of reality, whereas the writers of the New Testament literature are making truth-claims which go beyond merely functional considerations. Our own view is that the functional approach is the most fruitful one for hermeneutics, provided that we do not reduce the total subject-matter of theology to the narrower area of what we have established as *criteria of meaning*. In practical, concrete terms: public human behavior provides the currency of meaning for many theological assertions; but this is not to say that these theological statements can be translated into statements about man without remainder. We cannot invoke a referential theory of meaning *as a basis for hermeneutics*. But we are entitled to ask whether the language of the New Testament carries a referential dimension of meaning. Indeed two recent studies in particular make this an urgent issue.[34] Hans Frei has made much of the distinction between history itself, which has ostensive *reference* to events in the world, and history-*likeness* which does not, although it characterizes the "world" of the narrative. More recently Norman R. Petersen has taken up Frei's distinction, to conclude that Luke-Acts constructs a narrative world, but does not possess the referential dimension of true history. We cannot examine his argument here (except to say that it is too brief to sustain such a conclusion). But it serves to underline the point that questions about reference remain an important part, even if not the major part, of hermeneutical inquiries.

16. *Respecting the Particularity of the Text; Word and Context; Hermeneutics as Translation*

We have not yet concluded our discussion of Ferdinand de Saussure. We have said that in addition to stressing the role of human convention in language, he also viewed language as a structural system and drew a clear-cut contrast between synchronic and diachronic linguistics. James Barr and Eugene Nida have shown how the second and third of these principles, especially when taken together, underline the decisive importance of context in biblical interpretation in a way which guarantees that we pay due attention to rights of the text as a linguistic particularity. Whereas in the previous chapter we argued that the meaning of a text could not be uncritically assimilated to the dictates of systematic theology on *theological* grounds, our purpose is now to argue for the rights of the

---

34. Above, note 28.

word-studies; it demands only that the semantic contribution made by each word-in-context is considered separately and given due weight, without uncritical assimilation into meanings conveyed by the same word in different contexts. Indeed it is possible to overstress the modern reaction against the autonomy of words. Stephen Ullman remarks, "There is usually in each word a hard core of meaning which is relatively stable and can only be modified by the context within certain limits."[51] G. Stern goes further, and argues that "single words have more or less permanent meanings. . . . They actually do refer to certain referents and not to others."[52] However, dictionary definitions are at best provisional generalizations about the meanings of words in standard contexts. Like the hermeneutical circle, they constitute starting-points from which we arrive at the meanings of words-in-context; not definitive semantic descriptions which are autonomous in the sense of being context-free.

We arrive at the conclusion, then, that the word alone, in isolation from its context, is not the primary bearer of meaning, but a stretch of language which many linguists and philosophers call a speech-act. Commenting on the limitations of traditional approaches to language, Max Black remarks that too often the traditional approach stressed the communication of thought to the neglect of feelings and attitudes and "emphasized words rather than speech-acts in context."[53] Before we look at one particular consequence of this perspective for hermeneutics, it is worth observing how the relevance of this issue to New Testament studies has been brought out not only by Barr, but by a very different type of study undertaken by Samuel Laeuchli. In his book *The Language of Faith* he compares Christian uses of language in the New Testament and the Fathers with Gnostic uses of the same or similar terms. He writes, "The Gnostic terminology, such as 'gnosis', 'cosmos', 'aeon', 'pleroma', can be found in various books of the New Testament. The terminology of the Gospel of Thomas does not differ radically from the terminology of the Synoptic Gospels. If terminology alone had to furnish the criterion between Gnostic and biblical material we would be confronted with a most chaotic situation. It is not the concept itself which can furnish the answer, but only the relation in which it stands to other concepts."[54] For example, the Naassene fragment quoted by Hippolytus repeats the Pauline phrases of 1 Corinthians 2:13-14 and 2 Corinthians 12:24, but changes their mean-

51. S. Ullmann, *Semantics. An Introduction to the Science of Meaning* (Blackwell, Oxford, 1962), p. 49.
52. G. Stern, *Meaning and Change of Meaning* (Göteborgs Högskolas Arsskrift 38; Gothenburg, 1931), p. 85.
53. M. Black, *The Labyrinth of Language* (Pall Mall Press, London, 1968), p. 9.
54. S. Laeuchli, *The Language of Faith. An Introduction to the Semantic Dilemma of the Early Church* (Epworth Press, London, 1965), pp. 15-16.

ing by placing them within the frame of Gnostic cosmology.[55]

It is against the background of considerations about words and speech-acts, or language and *uses* of language, that we must consider a particular argument about the nature of hermeneutics which has been put forward very recently by David H. Kelsey in his book *The Uses of Scripture in Recent Theology*.[56] Kelsey challenges the long-established assumption in theology that theological formulations which have the purpose of articulating the message of the New Testament in the language of a later age constitute "translations" of this message.

Kelsey admits that this way of looking at hermeneutics is so widespread that it deserves to be called "the standard picture." He remarks, "It trades on 'translation' as a metaphor. Scripture is regularly represented as related to theological proposal as the Hebrew and Greek originals, say, are to the New English Bible. The metaphor seems to have been accepted at every point on the spectrum of theological opinion."[57] Thus he admits that the term "translation" is used in this way by writers as diverse as Barth, Bultmann, Kenneth Hamilton, James Robinson, and Carl Braaten. However, Kelsey concludes that "This standard picture, despite its impressive theological validation, must be set aside as radically misleading."[58]

The grounds on which Kelsey rejects this view is that there can be no "conceptual continuity" between what the New Testament says and what the theological proposals which attempt to "translate" it say. The reason which Kelsey gives for this conclusion is simply that all the arguments concerned rest on an "overextended use of 'translation' as a metaphor."[59] In "real" translation, as it were, "when one translates . . . a poem from German words, say, into English words . . . one hopes to preserve the same concepts."[60]

If Kelsey were correct, his argument would be a serious blow against a widespread view of hermeneutics. We admit that in hermeneutics "translation" is used in an extended or perhaps even metaphorical way. But while we accept that there is a difference *in degree* between strictly linguistic translation and hermeneutical translation, we cannot accept that there is a difference *in kind*. What gives the game away is Kelsey's

55. *Ibid.*, p. 20; Hippolytus, *Refutatio omnium haeresium* vii.25-26.
56. D. H. Kelsey, *The Uses of Scripture in Recent Theology* (S.C.M., London, 1975), pp. 185-92.
57. *Ibid.*, p. 185.
58. *Ibid.*, p. 186.
59. *Ibid.*, p. 188.
60. *Ibid.*

language about *words* and *concepts*. He presupposes that linguistic translation is largely a matter of replacing one set of *words* for another, in the course of which conceptual continuity is preserved. As soon as we alter the structure or content of the language, however, Kelsey seems to assume that conceptual continuity has been lost. But, to take up his own allusion to the New English Bible, into which category do we place the "translation" of the New English Bible when it renders ταῦτα ἔγραψα ὑμῖν in 1 John 2:26 as "*So much for* those who would mislead you?" Strictly, it is not a linguistic translation at all, but in practice it admirably "translates" words based on a literary convention according to which "I have written to you" indicates a change of topic.

It is axiomatic in modern translation theory that we cannot draw a sharp dividing-line between translation and interpretation. Thus in their work *The Theory and Practice of Translation* Nida and Taber insist: "The extent to which the forms must be changed in order to preserve the meaning will depend upon the linguistic *and cultural* distance between languages."[61] Indeed, whereas the Authorized Version, the Revised Version, and the Revised Standard Version attempt to preserve the actual structure of the Greek New Testament as far as possible, the New English Bible and Today's English Version deliberately re-structure passages precisely "in order to preserve the meaning of the original."[62]

Nida and Taber do distinguish between linguistic and cultural translation, but they allow that the line between them is a fluid one, and certainly do not hesitate to speak of cultural *translation*. What is to be said about J. B. Phillips' "translation" of Luke 13:11 ("a woman . . . who had an evil spirit in her") by "ill from some psychological disease"? He "translates" Luke 22:3 ("Satan went into Judas") as "a diabolical plan came into the mind of Judas." Some might well feel that Phillips has gone beyond the scope of purely linguistic translation, and indeed Nida and Taber consider that these examples show the introduction of cultural ideas which are "at least absent, if not foreign to the culture of the text."[63] But we cannot claim, on the other hand, that there is no conceptual continuity between the two translations. For what has to be translated, as Dennis Nineham insists, is not a wooden repetition of certain phrases, but a nexus of words-in-context, whose total context spreads out from its immediate linguistic syntagm into the wider field of the historical and cultural situation in which the language is embedded. As Nida and Taber

61. E. A. Nida and C. R. Taber, *The Theory and Practice of Translation* (Brill, Leiden, 1969), p. 5 (my italics).
62. *Ibid.*, p. 9.
63. *Ibid.*, p. 134.

remind us, "The translation must strive for equivalence rather than identity."[64]

Numerous concrete problems in translation underline the fact that translation inevitably merges into interpretation. Should "gird up the loins of your mind" (1 Pet. 1:13) become "stripped for action" (N.E.B.)? Any responsible consideration of the function of metaphor will suggest that *only* by cultural transference can the metaphor be kept alive, and thus "translated" as effective *metaphor*. But how this is best achieved is a matter of interpretative judgment, and not of translation in the narrowest merely mechanical sense. Sometimes a translator has to decide whether he prefers power or clarity in the translation of a metaphor. Thus in the sentence παρένεγκε τοῦτο τὸ ποτήριον ἀπ' ἐμοῦ (Luke 22:42) the Spanish *Version Popular* loses power but ensures clarity by rendering it "Free me from having to suffer this trial." But is this translation or interpretation; or a mixture of both? A clear-cut dividing-line cannot be drawn between them. This becomes clearest of all when many popular versions rely on the technique of transforming the Greek surface-structure to deep structure, and then proceeding from kernel sentences by back-transformation to what is most idiomatic in the receptor language. For example, the phrase "light of the world" (Matt. 5:14) is reduced to "he lights the world," and is then translated in Today's English Version "light *for* the world." But on the basis of the same principle, under which transformation is said to draw out the speaker's intention, the same version translates καὶ ἰδὼν ὁ 'Ιησοῦς τὴν πίστιν αὐτῶν (Mark 2:5) as "Jesus saw *how much* faith they had." Whether this constitutes a translation or an interpretation is not self-evident, but is a matter of judgment, since the one merges into the other.

In point of fact I have reservations about the extent to which the techniques of transformational grammar, as developed by N. Chomsky and others, are to be used in Bible translation, and I have expressed these reservations in another study.[65] However, these techniques have two merits in relation to Kelsey's criticism of the notion of hermeneutics as translation. First of all, they show how artificial is the matter of a correspondence of surface-structure between two languages, which is what Kelsey seems to mean by a correspondence between "concepts." The use of the word "concept" here begs the entire question. Secondly, Nida and Taber and other linguists remind us that the criterion of a "correct" translation depends on whether the intended *reader* can *understand* it. But understanding may not be possible, in some cases, without what

---

64. *Ibid.*, p. 12.
65. A. C. Thiselton, "Semantics and New Testament Interpretation" in *New Testament Interpretation*, pp. 75-104.

tionality of language at the same time. He continues: "We cut nature up, organize it into concepts, and ascribe significances as we do, largely because we are parties to an agreement to organize it in this way. . . . We cannot talk at all except by subscribing to the organization and classification of data which the agreement decrees."[77] Color-words are cited as an example which may perhaps support this approach. Eskimo people are said to have several distinct words denoting different shades of whiteness which are used often in connection with snow. Because of this, it is often urged, they "see" snow differently from other peoples.

Whorf's own researches were among the Hopi and on American-Indian languages. But Max Black, who has paid careful attention to questions about thought and language, together with other writers, urges caution about accepting Whorf's conclusions concerning the alleged relation between the Hopi world-view and language.[78] Does language *shape* culture, or does it *serve* cultural outlooks which have already arisen through the community's activities? John Lyons observes, "Each [language] is adapted to the characteristic pursuits of its users."[79]

But can the point not also be put the other way around? Once a language is "adapted to the characteristic pursuits of its users," it hands on an inherited tradition which then makes it easier or more difficult for a later generation to raise certain questions, or to notice certain aspects of life. This is part of the problem of language that occupied the attention both of Heidegger and Wittgenstein in their later thought. Both of these thinkers, each in his own distinctive way, underline the close relationship of language to human life, and the force of *habit* which given uses of language exemplify and hand on. Both see the element of truth which Georg Christoph Lichtenberg expressed when he said that our false philosophy is incorporated in the whole of language. This is why Wittgenstein also stresses, both in the *Investigations* and *On Certainty,* the linguistic significance of "training." He observes, "One thinks that one is tracing the outline of the thing's nature . . . and one is merely tracing round the frame through which we look at it. A *picture* held us captive. And we could not get outside it, for it lay in our language and language seemed to repeat it to us inexorably."[80] Fresh vision can come only when we are able to reverse certain habits of thinking which are perpetuated by the ways in which we use language. For the later Heidegger, this fresh vision comes only by waiting; for Wittgenstein it comes

77. B. L. Whorf, in J. B. Carroll (ed.), *Language, Thought and Reality: Selected Writings of Benjamin Lee Whorf* (M.I.T. Press, Cambridge, Mass., 1956), pp. 212-14.
78. M. Black, *The Labyrinth of Language,* pp. 63-90, especially pp. 71-75; and his article "Linguistic Relativity. The Views of Benjamin Lee Whorf" in *Ph.R.* LXVIII (1959), 228-38. Cf. also S. Ullmann, *Language and Style* (Blackwell, Oxford, 1964), pp. 212-28.
79. J. Lyons, *Introduction to Theoretical Linguistics,* p. 45.
80. L. Wittgenstein, *P.I.,* sects. 114-15.

only through strenuous thought.

The classification achieved by Wittgenstein, however, is to show that the influence of language on thought is not merely a matter of vocabulary-stock and surface-grammar, but of how language is *used*. The arguments of Boman, Whorf, and others, that accidents of lexicology and surface-grammar condition thought, remains entirely open to question and doubt. We can now see why it is possible to claim that, on the one hand, Barr is right and Boman is wrong about the role of vocabulary in shaping thought; but that, on the other hand, Barr has not said the last word about the relationship between thought and language. To return to Via's comments which we noted at the beginning of this section, Barr's approach does not in fact "oppose" theories about a relation between language and pre-understanding, although it does oppose their resting on arguments about vocabulary-stocks and grammar. To investigate this issue further, we need to inquire not about "grammar" in the morphological sense of surface-grammar, but about "grammar" in the conceptual or logical sense employed by Wittgenstein. This is one of our tasks in our chapters on Wittgenstein. Wittgenstein remarks, "When language-games change, then there is a change in concepts *(die Begriffe)*, and with the concepts the meanings of words change."[81]

We have by no means exhausted all that could be said about the relation between hermeneutics and language, even excluding what will be said in our chapters on Heidegger, Gadamer, and Wittgenstein. In particular, it might have been useful to demonstrate how semantic inquiries help us to view questions about language from an angle insufficiently explored in biblical studies to date. These inquiries ask questions about types of opposition between words, about synonymy and substitution, about hyponymy and types and degrees of vagueness. However, I have discussed the importance of these categories for New Testament interpretation in some detail in an essay entitled "Semantics and New Testament Interpretation," and much more briefly in an article called "The Semantics of Biblical Language as an Aspect of Hermeneutics."[82] I have also discussed questions about opposition and specificity in my study "The Meaning of Σάρξ in 1 Corinthians 5.5: A Fresh Approach in the Light of Logical and Semantic Factors."[83] These issues, however, perhaps more strictly concern exegesis than hermeneutics in the broader sense under discussion. Their value for hermeneutics is, first, that they help to pre-

---

81. L. Wittgenstein, *Cert.*, sect. 65.
82. A. C. Thiselton, "Semantics and New Testament Interpretation" in *New Testament Interpretation*, pp. 75-104, and "The Semantics of Biblical Language as an Aspect of Hermeneutics" in *Faith and Thought* CIII (1976), 108-20.
83. A. C. Thiselton, "The Meaning of Σάρξ in 1 Corinthians 5.5: A Fresh Approach in the Light of Logical and Semantic Factors" in *S.J.T.* XXVI (1973), 204-28.

serve the linguistic and semantic particularity of the text before us, thereby distancing the interpreter objectively from the passage; secondly, by helping the interpreter to see old problems from a fresh angle, they help him, in Wittgenstein's words, to *notice* what was always before his eyes. In the present chapter, however, we have restricted our attention to those particular questions about language and language-study that constitute issues in hermeneutics.

meaning of Being must already be available to us in some way."[19] We seem to be in a dilemma. If we do not know what Being is, how do we know what it is that we are asking? But if we do know what Being is, why should we need to ask what it means? Michael Gelven reminds us that both the problem and Heidegger's answer to it are not dissimilar from Plato's formulation in the *Meno*.[20] Socrates is asked how it is possible to inquire at all, since if we know what to inquire about there is no need for inquiry; whereas if we do not know, inquiry becomes impossible, since we should not know what we were looking for. Heidegger, rather like Plato, answers that our initial understanding of Being is preliminary, provisional, and "still veiled in darkness." We begin with a "vague, average understanding of Being."[21] However, this initial understanding must be clarified and deepened. "What we seek when we inquire into Being is not something entirely unfamiliar, even if proximally (*zunächst*; in the first instance?) we cannot grasp it at all."[22]

It is noteworthy that already we find something like a formulation of the hermeneutical circle in Heidegger, not in connection with a theory of hermeneutics, but as a necessary way of describing how his fundamental inquiry proceeds. He explicitly writes, "Is there not, however, a manifest circularity in such an understanding? . . . In working out our question have we not 'presupposed' something which only the answer can bring?"[23] Significantly, Heidegger dismisses the charge of circular argument on the ground that it is "sterile." What is important is what enables us to "penetrate into the field of study."

Heidegger now grasps the third set of issues about the inquiry into Being. Everything turns here on the fundamental contrast between ontological and ontic inquiry. Ontological inquiry concerns Being (*Sein*); ontic inquiries concern "entities" or "existents" (*das Seiende*). Magda King expresses the contrast aphoristically: "ontic" characterizes beings, not their being.[24] Albert Chapelle underlines the same contrast by distinguishing, on the one hand, the connection between "ontologique" and "Être" or "l'Être," and on the other hand the connection between "ontique" and "étant" or "l'étant."[25] This key distinction leads on in the closing section of Heidegger's first introduction to the entry of the term *Dasein*. *Dasein* denotes "the manner of Being which . . . man himself

19. *Ibid.*, p. 25.
20. M. Gelven, *A Commentary on Heidegger's 'Being and Time,'* p. 22.
21. M. Heidegger, *B.T.*, pp. 23 and 25.
22. *Ibid.*, p. 25 (German, p. 6). J. Macquarrie and E. Robinson discuss whether *zunächst* may sometimes be rendered "in the first instance," rather than more technically as "proximally" (p. 25 n. 1).
23. *Ibid.*, p. 27.
24. M. King, *Heidegger's Philosophy*, p. 64.
25. A. Chapelle, *L'ontologie phénoménologique de Heidegger. Un commentaire de "Sein und Zeit"* (Editions universitaires, Paris, 1962), p. 12.

possesses."[26] "*Dasein* itself has a special distinctiveness as compared with other entities. . . . It is ontically distinguished by the fact that, in its very Being, that Being (*Sein*) is an issue for it."[27] The conclusion of the first introduction is that "*fundamental ontology*, from which alone all other ontologies can take their rise, must be sought in the *existential analytic of Dasein*."[28]

In attempting now to elucidate what Heidegger means by Dasein we automatically proceed to the second of his two introductions. The first of these examined the question of Being; the second outlines the procedure of his inquiry, which consists first and foremost of providing an analysis of Dasein, although this leads on to further considerations in due course.

Some writers attempt to translate *Dasein* as either "being-there" or "being-here." J. Macquarrie and E. Robinson leave it untranslated, since the term is used as a technical one the meaning of which is best conveyed by observing its use itself rather by any single translation. From one point of view, *Dasein* means almost "human being," since it characterizes *human* existence in contrast to that of objects in the world such as tables and chairs, or stones and mountains. In attempting to answer the question of Being from the standpoint of Dasein, Heidegger is firmly rejecting the tendency in Western philosophy to interpret Being, or even man's being, from the being of *things*. He reverses this procedure. But Dasein does not allow the philosopher even to view *man* as a mere "object" or thing. Man, as Dasein, is certainly not the psychologist's "object of inquiry." Heidegger is concerned with what Kant or Kierkegaard would have called man in his subjectivity. Yet for Heidegger Dasein is even more than this, for it is prior to the separation of subject from object. From an ontic point of view, he urges, "Dasein is not only close to us . . . we *are* it, each of us, we ourselves."[29] We can go further than this and say that Dasein is to be understood in terms of possibility rather than actuality, and also in terms of that individuality whereby "my" existence is always mine (*Jemeinig-keit*). However, this would be to go beyond the scope of Heidegger's introductions.

The initial points which Heidegger wishes to make are, first, that Dasein can wonder about itself as existing; and secondly, that to begin inquiring about Being from the standpoint of Dasein means at once that this question will be seen in fresh terms. The traditional approach asks questions about being-ness (*das Seiende*) as an entity, from an ontic perspective, and makes observations in terms of "categories," namely

26. M. Heidegger, *B.T.* p. 32.
27. *Ibid.* (Heidegger's italics).
28. *Ibid.*, p. 34 (Heidegger's italics).
29. *Ibid.*, p. 36.

qualities that are fitted to describe "objects." Heidegger believes that his own approach from the standpoint of Dasein asks the question of Being (*Sein*) from an ontological perspective, and makes observations in terms of "existentialia" that are fitted to this mode of inquiry.

19. *Dasein, Hermeneutics, and Existenz*

Heidegger also introduces very briefly three other themes that relate to Dasein before he goes on to other matters in his second introduction. Each is touched on briefly, and then later developed in the manner of an overture. First of all, Dasein is understood in terms of its "world." We shall discuss this point further in the next section. Secondly, it is viewed "proximally and for the most part in its average *everydayness* (*in seiner durchschnittlichen Alltäglichkeit*)."[30] Heidegger reserves explanation of this term to a later section in *Being and Time*, but it seems that here the emphasis lies on the descriptive status of the analysis of Dasein. In accordance with the method of phenomenology, which he discusses shortly, he wishes to avoid any pre-judgment about the nature of Dasein which belongs to a particular world-view or philosophical tradition.[31] Thirdly, Heidegger now introduces his fundamental conviction that the question of Being, formulated from the standpoint of Dasein, must be asked from within the horizon of time. Time is the horizon which makes it possible for us to understand the meaning of being. Heidegger asserts, "*Time* needs to be *explicated primordially as the horizon for the understanding of Being, and in terms of temporality as the Being of Dasein, which understands Being*."[32] "Being cannot be grasped except by taking time into consideration."[33]

Heidegger's use of the phrase "horizon for understanding" raises a second consideration about hermeneutics. Everything, in Heidegger's view, is seen and understood from within a particular horizon. Meaning is that *from* which something is understandable as the thing it is. To use Magda King's example, a theatre is understandable from the viewpoint of writing, producing, and appreciating plays. It is this "for the sake of which" we have things like theatres.[34] The world of our own existence is the horizon in which our everyday understanding moves, "so that from it and in reference to it the things we come across are intelligible to us *as*

30. *Ibid.*, p. 38.
31. We have already noted that this procedure would not be "phenomenological" in Husserl's sense of the term.
32. M. Heidegger, *B.T.*, p. 39 (his italics).
33. *Ibid.*, p. 40.
34. M. King, *Heidegger's Philosophy*, pp. 6 and 7.

theatres, *as* buses, *as* knives and forks, in one word, *as* things that can be useful for some purpose."[35] If we suddenly view the same range of objects from the standpoint, for example, of theoretical physics, at one stroke what they are to use, their meaning, becomes radically different. In this sense, the horizon which is appropriate and fruitful for an understanding of Being is time. Within this horizon we can speak meaningfully of Being, of Dasein, of existentialia, and of ontological structure or possibility. If this world is shattered, we are left only with being-ness, with things, with categories, and with ontic structure or mere entities. In his later section on understanding and interpretation Heidegger relates this consideration about horizons to a statement about pre-understanding. He writes, "*Meaning is the 'upon-which' of a projection in terms of which something becomes intelligible as something, it gets its structure from a fore-having, a fore-sight and a fore-conception.*"[36] Hermeneutics then appears a second time already in Heidegger's thought, once again at a point which is of crucial importance in the development of his argument.

Heidegger has three further sections in his second introduction on method and procedure. The first of these clarifies his attitude towards philosophical tradition. Heidegger writes, "If the question of Being is to have its own history made transparent, then this hardened tradition must be loosened up, and the concealments which it has brought about must be dissolved. . . . By taking the question of Being as our clue, we are to destroy the traditional content of ancient ontology until we arrive at those primordial experiences in which we achieved our first way of determining the nature of Being."[37] Tradition otherwise "blocks our access" to primordial sources, especially in pre-Socratic thought, which point more genuinely to Being. In his urge to reach back to before the time of Platonism and of Christianity, Heidegger reminds us of Nietzsche. As A. de Waelhens suggests, there is more than a hint of the myth of the eternal return.[38] But even here Heidegger insists that his aim is positive rather than negative. His aim is to enter into dialogue with philosophers of the past—not to explain what they say to their own time, but to make them speak to his own question about Being. For example, Heidegger believes that it sheds light on the question of Being to show that Kant's concern about the subjectivity of the subject was side-tracked because he allowed himself to fall too uncritically under the influence of Descartes.

Here, therefore, we find a third point of connection between Heidegger and hermeneutics. His concern is to "loosen up" the encrusted layers of tradition under which lesser minds, by their repetitions and interpreta-

---

35. *Ibid.*, p. 7.
36. M. Heidegger, *B.T.* p. 193 (his italics).
37. *Ibid.*, p. 44.
38. A. de Waelhens, *La Philosophie de Martin Heidegger*, pp. 354-55.

tions, have buried creative and seminal thinkers. Temporal distance must be overcome so that these genuinely creative minds may speak anew to Heidegger's own question. As we shall see, Heidegger did not carry this work through in the way that he originally planned, but he has left a number of works on historical philosophers, including Plato, Kant, Hegel, and Nietzsche, which exemplify his approach to the great texts of Western philosophy.[39] With regard to the pre-Socratic philosophers, Heidegger comes near to the standpoint once expressed concerning music by Bartok, especially in his later writings. Bartok observes, "I came to believe that only from the entirely old could come the entirely new."

We need not delay over Heidegger's remarks on phenomenology, since we have already discussed his similarities to, and differences from, Husserl. However, we may note how these remarks bear on Heidegger's own distinctive views of truth. Heidegger repeatedly urges that we must avoid anything which suggests a correspondence theory of truth. Falsity is a matter of deceiving in the sense of covering something up; truth is a matter of "letting-something-be-seen."[40] In this sense "phenomenology" conveys truth, for it means "to let that which shows itself be seen from itself in the very way in which it shows itself from itself."[41] However, even here, yet once again, as we saw in our second chapter, we return to hermeneutics. "The phenomenology of Dasein is a *hermeneutic* in the primordial significance of this word, where it designates this business of interpreting."[42]

The last section of the introduction outlines the strategy and plan of Heidegger's work. Part One of his projected work was to be the interpretation of Dasein in terms of temporality, and the explication of time as the horizon for the question of Being. *Being and Time*, as it stands, represents in its entirety only the first two of three divisions which were to make up Part One. Division One of *Being and Time* represents Heidegger's analysis of Dasein; Division Two represents his treatment of Dasein and temporality. Part of the task described as belonging to Division Three is attempted in Heidegger's lecture "Time and Being," delivered at Freiburg in January 1962, some thirty-five years after the publication of *Being and Time*. But the text of this lecture amounts to no more than about twenty-five pages, and it is not intended to be understood as Division Three of *Being and Time*. In 1953, in the preface to the seventh edition of *Being and Time*, Heidegger explicitly stated that the second

39. M. Heidegger, *Kant and the Problem of Metaphysics* (Eng. Indiana Unviersity Press, Bloomington and London, 1962); *Hegel's Concept of Experience* (Eng. Harper and Row, New York, 1970, originally in *Holz.*; and *Nietzsche* (2 vols.; Neske, Pfullingen, 1961).
40. M. Heidegger, *B.T.*, p. 56.
41. *Ibid.*, p. 58.
42. *Ibid.*, p. 62 (Heidegger's italics).

main half of his work, namely the destruction of the history of ontology, could not now be attempted. We have only hints of how Heidegger would have gone about this work in such writings as his *Kant and the Problem of Metaphysics*.

Even if, as J. G. Gray claims, Heidegger's interest moves "from human existence to nature" as his later writings proceed, the plan of the projected work begun in *Being and Time* nevertheless confirms that Heidegger remains at all times concerned with the question of Being.[43] In reviewing the two introductions of *Being and Time*, however, we have seen that he approaches this question in a distinctive way, in terms of Dasein. Moreover, we have also noted that at no less than four specific points he raises issues which concern hermeneutics. The inquiry about Being brings into view the hermeneutical circle; everything must be understood in terms of a given horizon or meaning in the light of which we see something *as* something; tradition is made to speak afresh to the present; and even the phenomenological method of "letting something be seen" involves interpretation or hermeneutics.

Before he turns to the key theme of worldhood, Heidegger begins the main part of his work with a consideration of Dasein as "existence" (*Existenz*). But he warns us that he is not using this term in a way comparable with the traditional understanding of *existentia*. The traditional meaning of "existence" carries the idea of "occurring in the universe." (This is one of the reasons why Paul Tillich, for example, refuses to say that God "exists.") However, in Heidegger's own thought *Existenz* applies only to Dasein. Only Dasein can have "*Ek-sistenz*" in the sense that only Dasein can "stand out" (ἐκ-στασις) from itself to inquire about, and observe, its own being.[44] "Things," such as mountains, stones, or trees, have only *existentia*, or the character of being "present-at-hand" (*vorhanden*). They are simply "there," and cannot ask questions about their own being. Heidegger draws a basic contrast here: "We shall always use the . . . expression *'presence-at-hand' (Vorhandenheit)* for the term *'existentia'*, while the term 'existence' (*Existenz*), as a designation of Being (*Sein*), will be allotted solely to Dasein."[45] Thus, as Chapelle remarks, Dasein is synonymous with *Existenz* "by definition."[46]

This background is important not only for Heidegger's thought as a whole, but also for understanding his statement "*The essence of Dasein lies in its existence.*"[47] Magda King and others have rightly attacked the

---

43. J. G. Gray, "Heidegger's Course: From Human Existence to Nature" in *J.Ph.* LIV (1957), 197-207.
44. Heidegger uses the hyphenated form "Ek-sistenz" particularly in his later writings, utilizing an accident of etymology, as he frequently does.
45. M. Heidegger, *B.T.*, p. 67 (German, p. 42).
46. A. Chapelle, *L'ontologie phénoménologique de Heidegger*, p. 14.
47. M. Heidegger, *B.T.*, p. 67 (his italics).

way in which this statement is often misinterpreted in a wholly "existen-tialist" sense. She writes: "The well-known sentence . . . does not mean, as some interpretations would have it, that man first of all 'really exists' (really occurs) and then proceeds to produce his own essence, i.e. to make himself into who he is by exercising his freedom of choice, but means: Understanding himself in his own ability-to-be enables man to be a man in the most essential respect, namely in respect of his self."[48] Heidegger himself goes on to explain that since Dasein is *Existenz*, its characteristics are "not 'properties' present-at-hand . . .; they are in each case possible ways for it to be. . . . When we designate this entity with the term 'Dasein', we are expressing not its 'what' (as if it were a table, house, or tree) but its Being."[49] Heidegger reinforces this stress on the distinctiveness of Dasein by repeating the point that "Dasein has in each case mineness" (*Jemeinigkeit*).[50] It therefore invites the use of the personal pronoun, "I" or "you"; and it is characterized not by "having properties," but by *possibility*.

J. Macquarrie underlines the importance of these three aspects for Bultmann's interpretation of man in the New Testament, and especially in Paul.[51] First of all, "the body, as Saint Paul uses the term, is a way of being—not a substance or a thing."[52] Secondly, man in his being has a relation to himself. In Bultmann's words, *"Man is called sōma in respect to his being able to make himself the object of his own action. . . . He can be called sōma, that is, as having a relationship to himself*—as being able in a certain sense to distinguish himself from himself."[53] Thirdly, man's being is seen in terms of his possibilities. "Man has two fundamental possibilities: he can be at one with himself or he can be estranged from himself."[54] Paul's view of man is not merely ontic, but also ontological.[55]

Heidegger presses home his insistence on the distinctive character of Dasein by drawing a contrast between "categories" and "existentialia." Objects which are merely present-at-hand may be described in terms of categories; Dasein is to be characterized in terms of existentialia. Later in his work he describes these existentialia as including "state-of-mind" (*Befindlichkeit*), understanding, and speech. Heidegger also stresses that his analysis of Dasein transcends the view of man implied by anthropology, psychology, and biology. In all of these approaches his genuine personhood, what Kierkegaard would call his subjectivity, can be lost

48. M. King, *Heidegger's Philosophy*, p. 46.
49. M. Heidegger, *B.T.*, p. 67.
50. *Ibid.*, p. 68 (German, p. 42).
51. J. Macquarrie, *An Existentialist Theology*, pp. 30-34 in relation to pp. 40-45.
52. *Ibid.*, p. 40.
53. R. Bultmann, *T.N.T.* I, 195-96. (his italics).
54. J. Macquarrie, *An Existentialist Theology*, p. 41.
55. *Ibid.*, p. 30.

from view: "The person in not a Thing, not a substance, not an object (*Gegenstand*)." Here Heidegger appeals to the work of Max Scheler. To Scheler the person is "the unity of living-through (*Er-lebens*) which is immediately experienced in and with our experience (*Erlebnis*)—not a Thing merely thought of behind and outside what is immediately experienced."[56] Heidegger adds: "Any physical Objectification of acts . . . is tantamount to depersonalization."[57]

We shall see when we turn to Bultmann's hermeneutics that the problem of objectification constitutes one of the key issues in assessing the validity of his thought. We may note in this connection that in this section in *Being and Time* Heidegger explicitly attacks "an orientation thoroughly coloured by the anthropology of Christianity and the ancient world" for leading the basic question of Dasein's Being off the track.[58] In spite of the recognition of Christianity that man reaches beyond himself, its ancient ontology tended to encourage the view of man and even God as a "something" endowed with intelligence. We are left too easily with Aristotle's notion of man as an animal with reason, or Descartes' view of him as a "something" which thinks. Bultmann was doubtless sensitive about Heidegger's strictures against Christian theology. At the same time, however, we need not accept all that Heidegger claims about Dasein uncritically. To recognize the value of the perspective brought into focus by this term is not necessarily to accord it an exclusively privileged position in a theory of knowledge or in a theory of reality. We shall reserve our critical comments, however, until the second half of the next chapter.

20. *World and Worldhood*

Heidegger now moves on to consider "world" and "worldhood." World does not mean for Heidegger the totality of the things or occurrences of nature, nor does it mean the environment of man or of Dasein considered from an objective or merely ontic viewpoint. It is a whole in which man finds himself already immersed. Heidegger does not begin, like Descartes, with an isolated ego, nor does he seek to discover, like Husserl, a standpoint of pure consciousness. "World" is not, therefore, *ontic*, in the sense that we can begin first with an individual, and then proceed to the idea of "world" as that which emerges from his experience or is construed by his mind. Heidegger insists that world is *ontological*, or

56. M. Heidegger, *B.T.*, p. 73.
57. *Ibid.*
58. *Ibid.*, p. 74.

world, and that the view which we often think of as that of "scientific objectivity" occurs only at a secondary level of abstraction. Descartes, he urges, held that the *one and only* way of access to beings in the world "lies in knowing, *intellectio*, in the sense of knowledge (*Erkenntnis*) we get in mathematics and physics. Mathematical knowledge is regarded by Descartes as the one manner of apprehending entities which can always give assurance that their Being has been securely grasped."[74] Like the later Wittgenstein, Heidegger regarded "certainty" as something more primitive than scientific knowledge and anchored more firmly to human attitudes and practices in life. One way in which he stressed the diversity of possible ways of "seeing" the world was to distinguish between *Umsicht*, "circumspection," when Dasein looks at the world as environment; *Rücksicht*, "considerateness" or "regard," when it looks at the world of other Daseins; and *Durchsichtigkeit*, "transparency," when it looks "through" at itself. To make the Cartesian model of knowledge the *only* one is, in Heidegger's view, not only narrow but also arbitrary.

It is noteworthy that today many scientists themselves adopt an approach to knowledge which is very different from that of Descartes, and from that which is implied by the era of Newtonian physics. The biologist Jacob Bronowski makes this point in his popular series of talks *The Ascent of Man*. He writes, "Science is a very human form of knowledge. . . . Every judgment in science stands on the edge of error, and is personal."[75] One achievement of physics in the twentieth century has been to show that "to give an exact picture of the material world . . . is unattainable. . . . There is no absolute knowledge."[76] Bronowski appeals to the findings of quantum physics, to W. Heisenberg's Principle of Uncertainty, and even to the early work of J. C. Maxwell and Heinrich Hertz on light and electromagnetic waves. He writes, "Max Born meant that the new ideas in physics *amount to a different view of reality*. The world is not a fixed, solid array of objects, out there, for it cannot be fully separated from our perception of it. . . . *It interacts with us*, and the knowledge that it yields *has to be interpreted by us*. There is no way of exchanging information that does not demand an act of judgment."[77] Bronowski then cites the classic example of whether the electron "is" a particle or a wave. It "behaves" like a particle in the Bohr atom; but in 1924 de Broglie successfully made a wave model. Born thought of a train of electrons as collectively constituting a wave of probability. What an electron *is* is not a matter of "objectivity" in the traditional sense. To view

74. M. Heidegger, *B.T.*, p. 128.
75. J. Bronowski, *The Ascent of Man* (Book Club Associates and B.B.C., London, 1976), p. 374.
76. *Ibid.*, p. 353.
77. *Ibid.*, p. 364 (my italics); cf. pp. 353-74, entitled "Knowledge or Certainty."

an electron "objectively" can only mean to view it in the way that does justice to the nature of the particular inquiry that is in progress at a given time. We are not obliged to depend on Bronowski for this perspective. Among the numerous writers to whom reference might be made, we shall refer later (in sect. 30) especially to Karl Heim and to T. F. Torrance.

Heidegger's notion of worldhood leaves ample room for this more recent perspective of science. Indeed the whole point of Bronowski's passionate argument in his long chapter on knowledge and certainty is that modern physics in incompatible with a naive objectivism that postulates certain knowledge independently of the standpoint of the subject. *How* we observe affects *what* we observe. But this principle concerns human life and not only physical science. The contrast between the "how" and the "what" plays an important part in Kierkegaard's notion of subjectivity. He writes, "Truth becomes untruth in this or that person's mouth. . . . The objective accent falls on *what* is said, the subjective accent on *how* it is said. . . . Subjectivity becomes the truth."[78] Heidegger's view of worldhood is different from the outlook of either Kierkegaard or the modern physicist; but all three agree in rejecting the implications of a naive "commonsense" type of objectivism. They reject the popular outlook which tends, as James Brown puts it, to identify truth with objectivity and error with subjectivity, without more ado.[79] For Heidegger, the very notion of "objectivity" in *this* sense presupposes the definitive finality of a Kantian way of seeing the world, which Heidegger himself seeks to get behind and beyond. He would agree with James Brown's verdict that far from being a "commonsense" perspective, it is in fact a distinctively "modern" way of seeing the world, since it is parasitic on Kant's way of formulating the problem of knowledge.[80]

We shall see in due course that Heidegger's perspective, together with his notion of "world," bears a close relationship to the work of Funk, Via, and Crossan, as well as that of Fuchs, on the parables of Jesus. These writers claim that we must go beyond the Cartesian model of epistemology if we are to understand the hermeneutics of the parables. Parables found or destroy "worlds"; and they operate at a pre-cognitive or pre-conceptual level. A parable, Funk writes, may "induce a vision of that which cannot be conveyed by prosaic or discursive speech. . . . Metaphor shatters the conventions of predication in the interests of a new vision, one which grasps the 'thing' in relation to a new 'field', and thus in

78. S. Kierkegaard, *Concluding Unscientific Postscript to the Philosophical Fragments* (Eng. Princeton University Press, 1941), p. 181 (his italics).
79. J. Brown, *Subject and Object in Modern Theology* (S.C.M., London, 1955), p. 13.
80. *Ibid.*, p. 19. Brown traces the different ways in which the terms "subject" and "object" have been understood in the history of philosophy, in the first chapter of his book.

relation to a fresh experience of reality."[81]

21. State-of-mind, Understanding, and Discourse

In some respects it would be convenient to consider Heidegger's discussion of understanding, interpretation, language, and discourse in a separate section exclusively devoted to these linguistic and hermeneutical subjects. But it is of the utmost importance to see how Heidegger's conceptions of understanding and language are rooted in his approach to Dasein and its world. It is precisely not a separate "subject" in Heidegger's thought. This must be underlined not only in the interests of accuracy in describing Heidegger's philosophy, but also in the interests of doing justice to the part played by understanding and self-understanding in Bultmann's theology. To achieve this, it is necessary to observe how closely "understanding" is bound up with the notion of Dasein's *possibilities of existence*.

In order to make this point, we have singled out as our section-heading the three terms which Heidegger describes as constituting together the fundamental *existentialia* of the Being of the "there." He writes: "The fundamental *existentialia* which constitute the Being of the "there", the disclosedness of Being-in-the-world, are states-of-mind and understanding. . . . Discourse is existentially equiprimordial with state-of-mind and understanding."[82]

(1) We begin with an examination of Heidegger's notion of "state-of-mind" (*Befindlichkeit*). As Macquarrie and Robinson point out, the term more literally means "the state in which one may be found."[83] Some interpreters of Heidegger, including Werner Brock, stress the aspect of "being found," or, as Brock puts it, "placed" in life and in the world.[84] We shall see shortly that there is indeed an important connection between *Befindlichkeit* and the sense of being "placed" in the world. But Macquarrie and Robinson add the English words "state-of-mind" partly on the basis of the term's connection in Heidegger with the notion of "mood," and partly because of its connection with the German phrase "Wie befinden Sie sich?", "How are you?", or "How are you feeling?" Heidegger writes, "What we indicate *ontologically* by the term 'state-of-mind' is *ontically* the most familiar and everyday sort of thing; our mood, our Being-attuned (*die Stimmung, das Gestimmtsein*). Prior to all

81. R. W. Funk, *Language, Hermeneutic and Word of God*, pp. 136 and 139.
82. M. Heidegger, *B.T.*, p. 203 (his italics).
83. *Ibid.*, p. 172 n. 2.
84. W. Brock, "An Account of 'Being and Time' " in M. Heidegger, *E.B.*, p. 47.

psychology of moods . . . it is necessary to see this phenomenon as a fundamental *existentiale*."[85]

Heidegger has indeed suggested that our moods convey a disclosure (*Erschlossenheit*) of what characterizes our existence, although he does not say that they disclose the full meaning of that existence. Moods are "by no means nothing ontologically. . . . A mood makes manifest 'how one is, and how one is faring'."[86] What Heidegger calls a "pallid" mood may disclose that Being has become a burden, just as a mood of elation may alleviate this sense of burden. Most characteristically Heidegger stresses that it discloses "the 'thrownness' (*Geworfenheit*) of this entity into its 'there'; indeed it is thrown in such a way that, as Being-in-the-world, it is the 'there'. The expression 'thrownness' is meant to suggest the *Facticity of its being delivered over*."[87] Marjorie Grene comments, "*Facticity* means that human being is always one being among others—not in the sense of being one pebble on the beach or even one fish in the sea—but in the sense that at one and the same time it finds at its disposal things it can handle and finds itself determined by the things it must suffer. Human being is being always already in a world: a world in which, beyond its willing, it has been cast (*geworfen*)."[88] Facticity (*Faktizität*) is more than factuality. In Heidegger's words, "*Facticity is not the factuality of the factum brutum of something present-at-hand, but characteristic of Dasein's Being. . . .*"[89]

Moods, then, direct our attention to what is inevitable in life. Moods can do this, not least, because they may turn attention *away* from the *possible*, thereby emphasizing the actual or the given. They are not *mere* feelings which invite a purely psychological account, feelings *of* something. John Macquarrie has emphasized this point in his essay "Feeling and Understanding" in *Studies in Christian Existentialism*. He warns us against accepting the presupposition of the positivist criticism that feeling is "mere feeling," a subjective emotion divorced from any cognitive function.[90] "The correct procedure is not to fall over backward in an attempt to get away from feeling, but to show that the opposition between feeling and understanding, on which the emotive theory's denial of meaning to religious statements rests, is false and misleading. We have to look anew at feeling in religion and its relation to understanding."[91] Macquarrie discusses this principle with reference to Schleiermacher's notion of feeling in religion, Rudolf Otto's concept of creaturely feeling and the

85. M.Heidegger, *B.T.*, pp. 172-73 (German, p. 134).
86. *Ibid.*, p. 173.
87. *Ibid.*, p. 174 (Heidegger's italics).
88. M. Grene, *Martin Heidegger*, p. 20.
89. M. Heidegger, *B.T.*, p. 174 (his italics).
90. J. Macquarrie, *Studies in Christian Existentialism* (S.C.M., London, 1966), pp. 30-42.
91. *Ibid.*, p. 33.

numinous, and Paul Tillich's notion of ultimate concern, as well as to Heidegger's belief that feeling-states "disclose" something to us. This principle also relates closely, once again, to Robert Funk's claim that in New Testament hermeneutics understanding is not tied exclusively to cognition, or to discursive and conceptual language. The "mood" conveyed, for example, by a narrative or by a parable, may confront the reader more effectively with the facticity of his own existence, or with his own finitude, "thrownness," or creatureliness, than a highly sophisticated abstract presentation of certain concepts.

Heidegger next illustrates one of the ways in which Dasein relates to the givenness of its world by a brief discussion of fear. Fear is a particular mode of Dasein's *Befindlichkeit*. He first looks at *what* is feared *(das Wovor der Furcht)*. This is something within one's world, whether something present-at-hand, or ready-to-hand, or the Dasein of others. It is something threatening or harmful. Next, Heidegger looks at the fearing itself *(das Furchten)*. This exhibits concern and perhaps envisages the object of fear explicitly. Thirdly, he considers "on behalf of what" the fear fears *(das Worum der Furcht)*. This discloses the endangered state of Dasein and its dependence on itself. Thus Heidegger shows that a specific mode of *Befindlichkeit* necessarily "discloses" something by virtue of what it is and its relation to Dasein and its world. (It will be seen later that fear is not equated in Heidegger with anxiety or dread.)

(2) We turn next to Heidegger's discussion of understanding *(Verstehen)*. Not only is this section important for hermeneutics; Michael Gelven argues that it is one of the most important sections of the whole book.[92] First of all, because understanding is an existential, in Heidegger's view it is *a priori*, and prior to cognition. This is partly because understanding is rooted in possibility, in Dasein's ability-to-be or "potentiality-for-Being" *(Seinkönnen)*. Dasein *has* possibilities before it *knows* possibilities. Heidegger distinguishes the existential "Being-possible" which "is essential for Dasein" both from logical possibility and "from the contingency of something present-at-hand." "Possibility as an *existantiale* is the most primordial and ultimate positive way in which Dasein is characterized ontologically."[93]

The key to the relationship between understanding and existential possibility lies, secondly, in Heidegger's notion of projection *(Entwurf)*. Heidegger's language becomes more complex even than usual at this point, perhaps mainly because he presupposes what he has said earlier about worldhood and "for-the-sake-of": "Understanding projects Dasein's Being both upon its 'for-the-sake-of-which' and upon significance,

92. M. Gelven, *A Commentary on Heidegger's 'Being and Time,'* p. 83; cf. pp. 84-91.
93. M. Heidegger, *B.T.*, p. 183.

as the worldhood of its current world."[94] Heidegger's words may be elucidated with reference to what he has already said about involvement, significance, and concern. First of all, "significance" depends on relating something to one's universe of concern. Thomas Langan compares the relative lack of significance held by rocks or weeds for a hungry man, with that held by a bush bearing edible fruit.[95] The bush is "for" fruit; the fruit is "for" eating. A blackberry is significant in terms of one's *projected* eating; a doorlatch is significant in terms of one's *projected* opening of the door. Secondly, at its deepest level understanding discloses to Dasein "for the sake of what" (*Worumwillen*) it exists. Werner Brock comments, "Things and persons and the whole of one's 'Being-in-the-world' gain their 'significance' (*Bedeutsamkeit*) from the dominant purpose or aim for the sake of which man understands himself to 'exist'."[96] Hence "understanding" involves not seeking actual objects or situations so much as seeing their *possible* uses, *possible* contexts, *possible* ways of service. We return to the notion of "potentiality-for-Being" (*Seinkönnen*).

Michael Gelven has a striking way of expounding this aspect of Heidegger's thought; a way which reminds us of Wittgenstein's approach to the relation between logic, language, and life. Heidegger argues, he says, that the purely cognitive functions of understanding are generated from existential awareness of possibilities, and that this awareness itself is based on being able to exist in various ways. It is not that "logic" is prior to understanding and determines its limits, but that life determines understanding and logic. We know that "the wall is blue" is a contingent statement, because we can think of it as being of another color. "I am capable of thinking in a way that is *not* determined by what *is* the case. On the other hand, I may say that a circle necessarily has 360 degrees because I *cannot* think of a circle in any other way except that it has so many degrees. *The limits of what I can do determine the laws of logic.*"[97] In this sense, Gelven concludes, understanding, which is an *a priori* existentiale of Dasein, or *human life*, is prior to cognition. Wittgenstein would not have expressed the point in this way. As we shall see, he prefers to speak of necessary propositions as grammatical utterances. However, in Wittgenstein's later thought one cannot go deeper than "life" and "forms of life." It is life which determines logical grammar, and not the other way around. We are reminded of Wittgenstein's notion of "understanding" in terms of "Now I know how to go on," which is itself tantamount to "a glad start."[98] "If I have exhausted the justifications . . . I am inclined to

94. *Ibid.*, p. 185.
95. T. Langan, *The Meaning of Heidegger*, p. 22.
96. W. Brock, in *E.B.*, p. 49 (my italics).
97. M. Gelven, *A Commentary on Heidegger's 'Being and Time,'* pp. 87-88 (my italics).
98. L. Wittgenstein, *P.I.*, sects. 151 and 323.

say: 'This is simply what I do'."[99]

(3) Heidegger's view of understanding is not yet complete, for in his next section he discusses the relationship between *understanding and interpretation* (*Auslegung*). In this section Heidegger makes at least five distinct points.

First of all, interpretation, Heidegger states, is not "the acquiring of information about what is understood; it is rather the working out of possibilities projected in understanding."[100] The interpretative function of understanding is not some "additional something" which is different from understanding itself, but is rather an *explication* or elucidation of it. Understanding operates through a projection of possibilities; interpretation constitutes a *working out* of this projection, which makes explicit what was already given through human awareness.

Secondly, what is explicitly understood "has the structure of *something as something*." We "see" something "as a table, a door, a carriage, or a bridge."[101] This relates closely to what has been said earlier about "in order to" (*Um-zu*) or "for the sake of what" (*Worumwillen*). We see a bush *as* a bush that bears fruit for eating; or see a doorlatch in terms of its in-order-to-open-a-door. Conversely, "when we merely stare at something, our just-having-it-before-us lies before us as *a failure to understand it any more.*"[102] This is connected with the fact that meaning is not something which we "stick" onto some naked object which is present-at-hand. It is not a property attached to objects, but is grounded in human life and attitudes. We are reminded of Wittgenstein's words, "Only in the stream of thought and life do words have meaning."[103] "Every sign *by itself* seems dead. . . . In use it is *alive.*"[104]

Thirdly, Heidegger writes: "Interpretation is grounded in *something we have in advance—in a fore-having* (*Vorhabe*). . . . In every case interpretation is grounded *in something we see in advance—in a fore-sight* (*Vorsicht*). . . . It is grounded in *something we grasp in advance—in a fore-conception* (*Vorgriff*)."[105] "An interpretation is never a presuppositionless apprehending of something presented to us."[106] This corresponds to the role of pre-understanding in theories of theological hermeneutics, as we have discussed above. We come to an object with prior attitudes and prior questions by virtue of which we can interpret it as something, and thereby understand it.

99. *Ibid.*, sect. 217.
100. M. Heidegger, *B.T.*, pp. 188-89.
101. *Ibid.*, p. 189 (Heidegger's italics).
102. *Ibid.*, p. 190 (Heidegger's italics).
103. L. Wittgenstein, *Z.*, sect. 173.
104. L. Wittgenstein, *P.I.*, sect. 432.
105. M. Heidegger, *B.T.*, p. 191 (German, p. 150).
106. *Ibid.*, pp. 191-92.

When, fourthly, this as-structure becomes explicit, the object in question has become meaningful for us. Thus Heidegger declares, *"Meaning is the 'upon-which' of a projection in terms of which something becomes intelligible as something.* . . . Meaning is an *existentiale* of Dasein, not a property attaching to entities. . . . Hence only Dasein can be meaningful or meaningless."[107] In other words, for something to have meaning its meaning must be made explicit in terms of its relationship to the *concerns* of Dasein. This is why partly for Bultmann but radically for Ernst Fuchs, for example, a parable can *mean* something to the hearer only when it *grasps* him; it is not that he sees its meaning, as it were, from a distance, and then subsequently decides whether it has any relevance to him. This does explain why the principle in question is not a matter of *theology* for Fuchs, even though it certainly has theological implications. Being grasped by the parable and understanding it are one and the same language-event, which does not depend on prior cognition.[108]

This brings us, fifthly, to the hermeneutical circle. In Heidegger's words, "Any interpretation which is to contribute understanding, must already have understood what is to be interpreted." He admits that this entails moving in a circle. But he adds: *"If we see this circle as a vicious one and look out for ways of avoiding it* . . . *then the act of understanding has been misunderstood from the ground up.* . . . The 'circle' in understanding belongs to the structure of meaning."[109] We have already discussed the principle involved in the hermeneutical circle with reference to Schleiermacher, Dilthey, and others. We have seen that this principle underlines the fact that interpretation is a *process* and not a once-for-all event. We discuss this with special reference to Heinrich Ott, who himself draws on Heidegger's thought. We have also seen that prior questions shape our preliminary approach to a text. We place ourselves in the posture that we believe is appropriate to the understanding of the text, even if our subsequent understanding of it in its wholeness serves to correct both our preliminary posture and questions, and our preliminary understanding of its "parts." Heidegger's work further underlines the general point that, as Richard Palmer puts it, understanding "is not in some context outside time and space . . . but rather in a particular time and place."[110] Heidegger underlines the point that we cannot ignore the horizons of the interpreter in hermeneutics.

(4) In his next section Heidegger explicitly discusses the hermeneutical significance of propositions or assertions *(die Aussage)*. Assertions, he admits, have been regarded from ancient times as the locus of truth.

107. *Ibid.*, p. 193.
108. Cf. E. Fuchs, *S.H.J.*, pp. 32-38, 84-103; *Herm.*, pp. 126-34; and the discussion below.
109. M. Heidegger, *B.T.*, pp. 194-95 (his italics).
110. R. E. Palmer, *Hermeneutics*, p. 136.

Logic is usually a logic of propositions. Heidegger himself believes that assertions function in three ways. They achieve a "pointing out" *(Aufzeigen)*, and not mere "representation" *(Vorstellung)*. When I assert something about a hammer, it is not an assertion about the concept of a hammer, but the entity itself *(das Seiende selbst)*, as I use it. This point is perhaps especially worth noting in view of Gilbert Ryle's criticism that Heidegger's account of meaning is dominated, through Husserl, by Brentano's theory of "ideas" *(Vorstellungen)*. A meaning, Ryle insists, is "just the intentional 'accusative' of an act of 'having an idea'. . . . Meanings must be the contribution of acts of consciousness."[111] The second function of an assertion, Heidegger states, is that of predication. It gives the subject a definite character *(bestimmt)* by the predicate. This emphasis on "definiteness" is in fact open to serious question, and in an article on the subject of the hermeneutics of the parables I have taken up Wittgenstein's view that assertions can be open-ended.[112] The third function of assertions is that of communication *(Mitteilung)*. This aspect draws attention to the existential context in which assertions operate. Even assertions are not merely abstract but achieve their purpose in the setting of human life.

This last point is the one that is most important for Heidegger. A statement such as "the hammer is too heavy" is not merely a theoretical statement. It may serve to say, "Hand me the other hammer." Heidegger adds, "Interpretation is carried out primordially not in a theoretical statement but in an action of circumspective concern—laying aside the unsuitable tool, or exchanging it 'without wasting words'. From the fact that words are absent, it may not be concluded that interpretation is absent."[113]

In this sense, Heidegger views assertions as a *derivative* mode of interpretation. The statement "the hammer is heavy" derives from a prior understanding that the tool is unsuitable for the job in hand. Thus Heidegger contrasts "the primordial 'as' " of *hermeneutical* experience with "the *apophantical* 'as' of the assertion."[114] Gelven comments, "The hermeneutical 'as' occurs, for example, when I 'see' or 'interpret' the hammer *as* something to drive a nail into wood. The apophantical 'as' is to 'see' or 'interpret' the hammer *as* an object that is simply there in the world, with certain 'characteristics' that can be attributed to it. The danger lies in the fact that when judgments or propositions are analysed

111. G. Ryle, "Heidegger's 'Sein und Zeit' " in *Collected Writings* (Hutchinson, London, 1971) I, 213; cf. pp. 197-214.
112. A. C. Thiselton, "The Parables as Language-Event. Some Comments on Fuchs's Hermeneutics in the Light of Linguistic Philosophy" in *S.J.T.* XXIII (1970), 437-68.
113. M. Heidegger, *B.T.*, p. 200.
114. *Ibid.*, p. 201.

they are often treated solely in terms of the apophantical 'as'."[115] In due course we shall criticize this claim in Heidegger. For his own example demonstrates the point made again and again by Wittgenstein, that assertions do not always *function* merely descriptively. If I say "This is poison," it may function as a warning: "Look out! Don't drink this"; or as a plea: "Avenge me!"; or as an imperative: "Quick! Fetch a doctor"; or as a reproach: "You put sugar in my tea."[116]

(5) Heidegger believes that these considerations lead us directly into a discussion of language and "discourse" *(Rede)*. *"Discourse* (Rede) is existentially equiprimordial with state-of-mind and understanding."[117] The important point here is that Heidegger grounds all language not in words themselves or in abstract considerations about propositional logic, but in *the sharing of communication between human persons*. "Talk" *(Rede)* is Heidegger's term for how human beings interrelate. To view language as something "broken up into word-Things" is to adopt a standpoint which sees speech as merely "present-at-hand." Genuine *hearing*, Heidegger insists, is not a matter of scrutinizing a series of individual words. Children, for example, can "hear" speech without knowing how each sentence is split up (like the small child who responded to a question by writing "Goodnessnose" as his answer). Heidegger declares, "Communication is never anything like a conveying of experiences, such as opinions or wishes, from the interior of one subject into the interior of another. Dasein-with is already essentially manifest in a co-state-of-mind and a co-understanding. In discourse Being-with becomes 'explicitly' *shared*; that is to say, it *is* already, but it is unshared as something that has not been taken hold of and appropriated."[118]

Once again, this is of the utmost importance for New Testament hermeneutics. Understanding is not simply a matter of looking up individual words in a grammar and dictionary, but of communication between two sets of horizons. One of the writers who most frequently and emphatically repeats this point is Gerhard Ebeling. He writes, "We need not emphasize that the problem lies too deep to be tackled by cheap borrowing of transient modern jargon for the preacher's stock of words. *It is not a matter of understanding single words, but of understanding the word itself*, not a matter of new means of speech, but of a new coming to speech."[119]

115. M. Gelven, *A Commentary on Heidegger's 'Being and Time,'* p. 101.
116. I have used this example and discussed the point further in A. C. Thiselton, *Language, Liturgy and Meaning* (Grove Liturgical Studies, Nottingham, 1975), pp. 10-16.
117. M. Heidegger, *B.T.*, p. 203 (German, p. 161).
118. *Ibid.*, p. 205.
119. G. Ebeling, *The Nature of Faith*, p. 16.

CHAPTER VII

Further Themes in Heidegger's Earlier Thought

22. *The Falling of Dasein: Dasein's Being as Care; Reality and Truth*

In an earlier section of *Being and Time* Heidegger briefly introduced the notion of "everydayness" (*Alltäglichkeit*) and its application as a description of the Being of Dasein. He writes: "Distantiality, averageness and levelling down, as ways of Being for the 'they', constitute what we know as 'publicness' (*die Offentlichkeit*). . . . By publicness everything gets obscured, and what has thus been covered up gets passed off as something familiar and accessible to everyone".[1] He adds, "*The 'they' is an existentiale; and as a primordial phenomenon, it belongs to Dasein's positive constitution.*"[2] Together with this notion of "levelling down" and the impersonal "they," Heidegger also introduces the phenomenon of "Being-with" others (*Mitdasein*). However, these ideas are more fully and explicitly explored when Heidegger turns, after his discussions of feeling-state, understanding, and discourse, to the "falling" of Dasein and to the Being of Dasein as care.

"Fallenness" is a general characteristic which is manifested in specific terms by idle talk (*Gerede*), curiosity (*Neugier*), and ambiguity (*Zweideutigkeit*). In these three "definite existential characteristics," Heidegger remarks, "there is revealed a basic kind of Being which belongs to everydayness; we call this the 'falling' (*Verfallen*) of Dasein."[3] Heidegger is quick to add that this notion of "falling" does not carry with it any overtones of ethical or theological judgment: "The term does not express any negative evaluation, but is used to signify that Dasein is

1. M. Heidegger, *B.T.*, p. 165.
2. *Ibid.*, p. 167.
3. *Ibid.*, p. 219.

proximally and for the most part *alongside* the 'world' of its concern. This 'absorption in . . .' (*Aufgehen bei . . .*) has mostly the character of Being-lost in the publicness of the "they'."⁴ The fallenness of Dasein is not "a 'fall' from a purer and higher 'primal status'."⁵ Nevertheless it is a mode of being in which the awareness of what it means to be is lost or obscured. Heidegger characterizes it as "inauthentic" (*uneigentlich*) not because of any ethical defect, but because it is "fascinated by the 'world' and by the Dasein-with of Others in the 'they'."⁶ Part of Heidegger's meaning is lost in English translation, in which it is impossible to retain the connection in the German between "authentic" (*eigentlich*) and "own" (*eigen*). We have already seen that for Heidegger it is an important feature of Dasein that it is "in each case mine" (*die Jemeinigkeit*). By contrast, Dasein can, as it were, lose itself in the inauthentic, impersonal, everyday world of the "they." This mode of being is seen in more specific terms, to begin with, in idle talk, curiosity, and ambiguity.

Even idle talk (*Gerede*), Heidegger warns us, is "not to be used here in a 'disparaging' signification."⁷ "Idle talk is the possibility of understanding everything without previously making the thing one's own."⁸ It "releases one from the task of genuinely understanding."⁹ Idle talk discourages any new inquiry and inhibits any fresh angle of vision, because "the 'they' prescribes one's state-of-mind, and determines what and how one 'sees'."¹⁰ This short section is highly significant both in relation to the hermeneutics of Bultmann, and also the work of Fuchs, Funk, and Crossan on the parables of Jesus. Language which merely perpetuates conventional and generally accepted perspectives cannot generate creative understanding and response. The point is reinforced in Heidegger's other two short sections on curiosity and ambiguity. Curiosity seeks the kind of supposed novelty that catches the imagination of the crowd, and which follows fashions, or, as Heidegger puts it, "what one 'must' have read or seen."¹¹ This attitude invites the experience of ambiguity, in which it seems as if one has understood everything, while at bottom understanding has not genuinely taken place. Heidegger develops this theme in his section on "Falling and Thrownness." He writes, "This downward plunge into and within the groundlessness of the inauthentic Being of the 'they' . . . constantly tears the understanding away from the projecting of authentic possibilities."¹²

4. *Ibid.*, p. 220.
5. *Ibid.*
6. *Ibid.*
7. *Ibid.*, p. 211.
8. *Ibid.*, p. 213.
9. *Ibid.*
10. *Ibid.*
11. *Ibid.*, p. 217.
12. *Ibid.*, p. 223.

Heidegger has now reached a crucial stage in his argument. Up to this point in *Being and Time* he has examined the phenomenon of Being-in-the-world in its various constitutive aspects. He now attempts to view it as a unitary structural whole. The Being of Dasein is now viewed in its wholeness as care (*Sorge*). Care unifies all the existentials of Dasein into a single structure. Heidegger believes that what brings to light this unifying significance of care is the phenomenon of dread or anxiety (*Angst*). He first explains this methodological procedure in the section entitled "The Question of the Primordial Totality of Dasein's Structural Whole," and then turns to examine dread or anxiety "as a distinctive way in which Dasein is disclosed."[13]

Like Kierkegaard, Heidegger sharply distinguishes between anxiety or dread (*Angst*) and fear (*Furcht*). Fear is always fear of something specifiable and definite. We have already discussed Heidegger's analysis of fear in our section on state-of-mind. We saw that, in his view, fear carries with it the distinction between what is feared, the fearing itself, and the endangered state of Dasein.[14] By contrast, dread or anxiety is aroused not by some entity within the world, but by Dasein's own existence. It is the experience of turning away from all that is involved in the responsibility of existence itself. Thus: "*The turning-away of falling is grounded rather in anxiety, which in turn is what makes fear possible. . . . That in the face of which one has anxiety* (das Wovor der Angst) *is Being-in-the-world as such.*"[15] Heidegger continues: "Anxiety does not 'see' any definite 'here' or 'yonder' from which it comes. That in the face of which one has anxiety is characterized by the fact that what threatens is *nowhere.*"[16]

Heidegger now relates dread or anxiety to the phenomenon of authentic existence. Marjorie Grene sums up the point: "There is one mood which is unique, which does recall human beings from self-betrayal to self-knowledge; and that mood is dread. . . . It is a sense of the loss of objects, of nothingness—a sense of nothingness which lays hold of me when I face, not this or that thing or person, but the whole structure of being-on-the-world itself."[17] In Heidegger's own words, "Anxiety brings Dasein face to face with its *Being-free for (propensio in* . . . [Freisein für . . .]) the authenticity of its Being, and for this authenticity as a possibility which it always is."[18] Heidegger adds at once, by way of further explanation of the point he wishes to make: "In anxiety one feels '*uncanny*' (*In*

13. *Ibid.*, sect. 39-40, pp. 225-35.
14. Above, sect. 21, towards the end of (1).
15. M. Heidegger, *B.T.*, p. 230 (his italics).
16. *Ibid.*, p. 231 (Heidegger's italics).
17. M. Grene, *Martin Heidegger*, pp. 29-30.
18. M. Heidegger, *B.T.*, p. 232.

der Angst ist einem 'unheimlich').''[19] This "uncanniness" means "not-being-at-home (*das Nicht-zuhause-sein*).''[20] Therefore, Heidegger concludes, anxiety brings back Dasein out of its absorption in the world of everyday. "Everyday familiarity collapses. Dasein has been individualized, but individualized *as* Being-in-the-world.''[21] He repeats: "Anxiety individualizes. This individualization brings Dasein back from its falling.''[22]

At this point in *Being and Time* Heidegger comes close to Kierkegaard and to other existentialist thinkers such as Jaspers and Sartre. The limitations of the unexamined and comfortable conventions of the anonymous "they" are set over against the individualizing significance of such experiences as faith, decision, limit-situation, or dread, according to which existentialist thinker is under consideration. We shall comment briefly on Heidegger's relation to Kierkegaard, Jaspers and Sartre when we offer some assessments of his thought as a whole. Heidegger shares with these thinkers, however, the notion that through the dominance of the impersonal and anonymous "they" Dasein may fall away from its own responsibility and freedom by accepting the tranquilizing path of retreat from anxiety and decision.

All that has so far emerged in *Being and Time* is now summed up in Heidegger's description of Dasein under the unitary and unifying term "care" (*Sorge*). Heidegger reiterates that "the fundamental ontological characteristics of this entity are existentiality, facticity, and Being-fallen . . . woven together . . . in a primordial context which makes up the totality of the structural whole.''[23] In his attempt to characterize this wholeness of Dasein as care, Heidegger finds himself forced to frame the clumsy-sounding sentence: "The Being of Dasein means ahead-of-itself-Being-already-in (the world) as Being alongside (entities encountered within the world).''[24] We have seen that these notions are implied by existentiality, facticity, and being-fallen. Existentiality, or "making my own" in appropriation, calls attention to Dasein's mode of being as anticipation of its own possibilities, as existence "ahead-of-itself." Facticity calls attention to Dasein's thrownness as "Being-already-in-the-world." Fallenness calls attention to the capacity of Dasein to be distracted by the cares of the everyday; it arises from "Being-alongside" entities encountered within the world. It involves life with others (*Mitsein, Mitdasein*).

19. *Ibid.*, p. 233 (German, p. 188).
20. *Ibid.*
21. *Ibid.*
22. *Ibid.*, p. 235.
23. *Ibid.*, pp. 235-36.
24. *Ibid.*, p. 237.

In the context of his discussion of Being as care, Heidegger distinguishes between Being-alongside objects which are ready-to-hand as "concern" (*Besorgen*) and Being-alongside other Daseins as "solicitude" (*Fürsorge*). Gelven suggests that we retain the connection of these two terms with care (*Sorge*) in English translation by rendering concern as "caring *about*" and solicitude as "caring *for*."[25] We shall follow the translation of Macquarrie and Robinson, but Gelven's suggestion helps to remind us that Heidegger's all-embracing term for "Being-ahead-of-itself-already-in (the world) as Being-alongside" is care.

J. Macquarrie suggests that it is not entirely by accident that Heidegger turns at this point to the language of myth for support, or perhaps illustration, of the claim that what it means for man to be is care.[26] At all events, Heidegger shows that this view is not a new one. The Latin fable tells how Care (*cura*) shaped a piece of clay into the form of man, and asked Jupiter to give it spirit. Jupiter does this, but then Jupiter, earth, and Care dispute with one another over the right to name man. Saturn decrees that since each has a part in man, man shall be called *homo*, because he is made out of *humus*; his life shall be marked by care while he lives; and at death his spirit shall return to Jupiter. Heidegger interprets this myth as meaning that on the one hand man, as spirit, may transcend his own past and present in possibility; while on the other hand he is limited by his earthly facticity. His being is temporal, and is marked by care. However, this "double meaning" of care does not signify two "parts" of man, but "a single basic state in its essentially twofold structure of thrown projection."[27] As we should expect, in Bultmann's thought this has close connections with the argument that in the New Testament Paul does not conceive of body and spirit as two "parts" of man, but rather as modes of his one being.

Heidegger concludes this division of *Being and Time* by setting out the implications of his analysis for a view of reality and truth, and comparing it with that of other philosophers and traditional Western thought. He pays particular attention to points of similarity to, and difference from, Kant, and also alludes to the approach of Descartes. In spite of his claim that he presents us with a phenomenology and with ontological questions rather than an epistemological theory, Heidegger and Kant both believe that the nature and capacities of human reason (Kant) or of Dasein (Heidegger) must be examined before we consider the world about which we reason. Nevertheless, Heidegger attacks what he regards as Kant's persistent fault, carried over from Descartes, of still regarding "reality" as something present-at-hand (*vorhanden*). "'Consciousness of my Da-

25. M. Gelven, *A Commentary of Heidegger's 'Being and Time,'* p. 122; cf. M. Heidegger, *B.T.*, p. 237.
26. J. Macquarrie, *An Existentialist Theology*, p. 107.
27. M. Heidegger, *B.T.*, p. 243; cf. sect. 42, pp. 241-44.

sein' means for Kant a consciousness of my Being-present-at-hand in the sense of Descartes."[28]

Heidegger cites Kant's verdict that the absence of a convincing proof of the reality of the external world is a "scandal of philosophy." But this only shows, Heidegger insists, that Kant has not been fully successful in liberating himself from the terms of the problem set by Descartes. He comments, "If Dasein is understood correctly, it defies such proofs, because, in its Being, it already *is* what subsequent proofs deem necessary to demonstrate for it."[29] We may compare Heidegger's reaction to this issue with Wittgenstein's reaction to G. E. Moore's "Proof of an External World" in his notes *On Certainty*. Wittgenstein believes that Moore's argument misuses the expression "I know. . . ." Such propositions as "the external world exists" are not suppositions for which we should look for grounds or evidence. They belong "to our frame of reference."[30] "Doubt comes *after* belief."[31] Such propositions belong "to the *scaffolding* of our thoughts."[32] Or we might equally approach the problem from the other end and say, with Peter Geach, that the Cartesian "I" is "derivative from, parasitic upon, its use in talking to others; when there are no others, 'I' is redundant and has no special reference."[33] In Heidegger's terms, Dasein is already in a "world" prior to the separation of epistemological subject and object. In this respect, Heidegger claims to have carried out Kant's program more consistently and effectively than Kant himself. Heidegger's broader account of his relation to Kant in respect of other philosophical questions is given in his book *Kant and the Problem of Metaphysics*.[34]

This approach to the question of "reality" naturally leads on to Heidegger's rejection of a correspondence view of truth. He writes, "Representations (*Vorstellungen*) do not get compared, either among themselves or in relation to the Real Thing. What is to be demonstrated is not an agreement of knowing with its object . . . but neither is it an agreement between 'contents of consciousness' among themselves. What is to be demonstrated is solely the Being-uncovered (*Entdeckt-sein*) of the entity itself. . . . '*Confirmation*' signifies *the entity's showing itself in its*

28. *Ibid.*, p. 247.
29. *Ibid.*, p. 249.
30. L. Wittgenstein, *Cert.*, sect. 83.
31. *Ibid.*, sect. 160 (Wittgenstein's italics).
32. *Ibid.*, sect. 211 (Wittgenstein's italics).
33. P. Geach, "The Fallacy of 'Cogito Ergo Sum'," reprinted from *Mental Acts* (Routledge and Kegan Paul, London, 1957) in H. Morick (ed.), *Wittgenstein and the Problem of Other Minds* (McGraw-Hill, New York, 1967), p. 213; cf. pp. 211-14.
34. Two brief critical accounts of Heidegger's attitude towards Kant in this book are offered by M. Grene, *Martin Heidegger*, pp. 62-74, and T. Langan, *The Meaning of Heidegger. A Critical Study of an Existentialist Phenomenology* (Routledge and Kegan Paul, London, 1959), pp. 69-85.

selfsameness. . . . The *Being-true* (truth) of the assertion must be understood as *Being-uncovering.*"[35]

Heidegger develops this approach further in his small work *Vom Wesen der Wahrheit*, first published 1943, although basically sketched out in 1930. As if corroborating the position of Heidegger's section on truth in *Being and Time*, Thomas Langan goes so far as to describe this short work as "the summit and conclusion of the existential analysis of Dasein."[36] The first two sections concern the conventional or traditional concept of truth, and especially what is entailed in the notion of agreement or correspondence.[37] If we accept what Heidegger also calls this "metaphysical" conception of truth as correspondence between the intellect and the thing, we make truth reside in human judgment. This is a matter of propositional truth (*die Satzwahrheit*). However, "truth does not possess its original seat in the proposition."[38] The "original" or "ultimate" ground of truth is not human judgment, but that which makes it possible that such a judgment can occur. Heidegger describes this as the "standing-open" of Dasein's attitude or comportment (*Offenständigkeit des Verhaltens*).[39]

In the next two sections of *Vom Wesen der Wahrheit* Heidegger argues that the essence of truth is, therefore, freedom. Freedom makes possible the "letting-be" of things-that-are (*das Seinlassen von Seiendem*).[40] The notion of truth as letting-be or even as revelation (*Unverborgenheit*) goes hand in hand with the very possibility of asking about what-is (*Seiendes*), and Heidegger sees the dawning both of the concept and the question as a key moment in Western historical destiny (*Geschichte*).[41] Truth is historical in two ways. First of all, it is continually being created, and is not some "timeless" property attaching to propositions or to logic. Secondly, because of the finitude of Dasein's freedom, any unveiling or letting-be leaves aspects which are still veiled. Untruth is not simply the result of human miscalculation or mistakes, but is bound up with Dasein's finitude and relation to history. At the same time, this is not to deny the point that Heidegger makes in his seventh section, that man's "erring" (*das Irren*) occurs when he misses the mystery (*Geheimnis*) because he is always moving on from one practicality (*Gangbaren*) to the next.[42] The point is, rather, that this moving to and fro from disclosure to

---

35. M. Heidegger, *B.T.*, p. 261 (his italics; German, p. 218).
36. T. Langan, *The Meaning of Heidegger*, p. 130.
37. M. Heidegger, *W.W.*, pp. 5-12. Also in M. Heidegger, *Wegmarken* (Klostermann, Frankfurt am Main, 1967), pp. 73-97.
38. M. Heidegger, *W.W.*, p. 12 (*Wegmarken*, p. 81).
39. *Ibid.* (*Wegmarken*, p. 80).
40. M. Heidegger, *W.W.*, p. 14 (*Wegmarken*, p. 83).
41. M. Heidegger, *W.W.*, p. 16 (*Wegmarken*, p. 85).
42. M. Heidegger, *W.W.*, p. 22 (*Wegmarken*, p. 92).

practicality is itself conditioned by man's situation in history.

This brings us out of the area of *Being and Time* into the realm of Heidegger's later thought. For in his closing section he observes that in place of man's hurried concern with practicalities, what is needed is *Gelassenheit der Milde*, that attitude of quiet composure or yieldedness in which the thinker may listen for the quiet voice of Being.[43] We shall return to this aspect of Heidegger's thought in a later chapter. Meanwhile, we may underline the point that in *Being and Time* Heidegger is concerned mainly to show the limitations of a correspondence view of truth, and to argue that the truth of propositions is only derivative from the prior phenomenon of truth as disclosure or letting-be. Truth, he argues, refers not to objects but to Dasein. Truth emerges as Dasein becomes aware of itself in terms of its own possibilities and limitations.

This point is not unrelated to the way in which in New Testament studies Bultmann and Fuchs lay so much emphasis on man and on human self-understanding. Heidegger has urged that truth itself is always a matter of self-understanding or appropriation. Propositions *about* entities or realities which do not stem from Dasein's self-disclosure are true only in a derivative sense. Hence, if they accept Heidegger's view of truth, it is less surprising than it would otherwise seem to find Bultmann and Fuchs laying such stress on man, on human decision, and on self-understanding. Such a perspective becomes inadequate only on the basis of a view of truth which Heidegger rejects. We shall look more closely at this problem in due course. However, we have yet to explore some further themes in *Being and Time*, as well as Heidegger's later thought, especially on language. We shall postpone our assessments of Heidegger's thought as a whole until later.

23. *Being-towards-Death and Authentic Existence*

Death is significant for Heidegger's argument in *Being and Time* for two reasons. First of all, Dasein's awareness of its future death may serve to bring it face to face with its own being as a totality. "Dasein reaches its wholeness in death. . . . In Dasein there is undeniably a constant 'lack of totality' which finds an end with death."[44] " 'Ending', as dying, is constitutive for Dasein's totality."[45] Secondly, death isolates a man from the

---

43. M. Heidegger, *W.W.*, p. 24 (*Wegmarken*, p. 94). Cf. also M. Heidegger, *Gelassenheit* (Neske, Pfullingen, 1959), translated into English in *Discourse on Thinking* (Harper and Row, New York, 1966). On the term *Gelassenheit*, see *Discourse in Thinking*, p. 54 n. 4.
44. M. Heidegger, *B.T.*, pp. 281 and 286.
45. *Ibid.*, p. 284.

crowd, from the anonymous "they." Dying is the one thing a man has to do for himself. *"No one can take the Other's dying away from him. . . . Dying is something that every Dasein itself must take upon itself at the time. By its very essence, death is in every case mine."*[46] "Death is Dasein's *ownmost (eigenste)* possibility."[47]

Heidegger is not speaking of present death, however, as an event of actual experience of life, for, in Wittgenstein's words, "Death is not an event of life: we do not live to experience death."[48] Nor is he speaking of the impact of the death of others. For when someone has died, Heidegger argues, he becomes present-at-hand as "the deceased": "The *end* of the entity *qua* Dasein is the beginning of the same entity *qua* something present-at-hand."[49] What concerns Heidegger is the existential phenomenon of the imminence, or futurity, of our own death. Even so, however, this is not necessarily or even primarily the impact of immediate imminent death in the sense described by Dostoevski or Sartre, or in Jaspers' notion of limit-situations. It is not a matter of "Being-at-an-end" *(Zu-Ende-Sein)* but of "Being-towards-the-end" *(Sein zum Ende)*, or of "Being-towards-death" *(Sein zum Tode)*. Once again, this does not necessarily imply a morbid brooding over the likelihood of death, for the emphasis is not upon the psychological aspect of the phenomenon. "The existential analysis of death is distinguished from other possible interpretations of this phenomenon."[50] According to this existential perspective, death, as something unavoidable, *"is something that stands before us—something impending* (Bevorstand)."[51]

In order to underline the point that death is "my own" Heidegger also describes it as "nonrelational" *(unbezügliche)*. Similarly, in order to underline his other point that death cannot be avoided, he describes it as "not to be outstripped" *(unüberholbare)*.[52] When it exists inauthentically, however, Dasein attempts to obscure these two aspects of death. Heidegger comments, "The expression 'one dies' spreads abroad the opinion that what gets reached, as it were, by death, is the 'they'. . . . 'Dying' is levelled off to an occurrence which reaches Dasein, to be sure, but belongs to nobody in particular."[53] Thus: *"The 'they' does not permit us the courage for anxiety* (Angst) *in the face of death."*[54] "Thinking about

46. *Ibid.*
47. *Ibid.*, p. 307 (Heidegger's italics).
48. L. Wittgenstein, *T.*, 6.4311.
49. M. Heidegger, *B.T.*, p. 281 (his italics).
50. *Ibid.*, p. 290 (part of the title of sect. 49).
51. *Ibid.*, p. 294 (German, p. 250). On *Bevorstand* cf. the note by Macquarrie and Robinson, *ibid.*, n. 1.
52. *Ibid.*
53. *Ibid.*, p. 297.
54. *Ibid.*, p. 298 (Heidegger's italics).

death" is regarded by common consent as cowardly, morbid, or otherwise out of place. Heidegger concludes: "Our everyday falling evasion *in
the face of* death is an *inauthentic* Being-*towards*-death."[55] It is not that in
its inauthentic mode Dasein actually believes that death can be avoided,
but that its way of approaching death robs it of its full existential-
ontological significance.

Just as he earlier distinguished between fear and dread or anxiety,
Heidegger now draws a contrast between "expecting" death (*erwarfen*)
and "anticipating" it (*vorlaufen*). The difference between these two
terms, in Heidegger's use of them, has to do with the contrast between
viewing death as an actuality and viewing it as a possibility. We must
note, however, what "anticipation" does *not* mean. In a note on their
translation of the term Macquarrie and Robinson observe, "The kind of
'anticipation' which is involved in Being-towards-death does not consist
in 'waiting for' death or 'dwelling upon it' or 'actualizing' it before it
normally comes; nor does 'running ahead into it' in this sense mean that
we 'rush headlong into it'."[56] The emphasis in authentic existence is upon
possibility. Thus Heidegger asserts, *"The closest closeness which one
may have in Being towards death as a possibility is as far as possible from
anything actual."* He adds, "The more unveiledly this possibility gets
understood, the more purely does the understanding penetrate into it *as
the possibility of the impossibility of any existence at all."*[57] Hence: "The
non-relational character of death, as understood in anticipation, individualizes Dasein down to itself. This individualizing is a way in which the
'there' is disclosed for existence. It makes manifest that all Being-
alongside the things with which we concern ourselves, and all Being-with
Others, will fail us when our ownmost potentiality-for-Being is the issue.
Dasein can be authentically itself only if it makes this possible for itself of
its own accord."[58]

We are now in a position to see why this perspective should come to
occupy such a prominent place in Rudolf Bultmann's hermeneutics of the
New Testament. Bultmann sees a very deep affinity between Heidegger's
analysis and the Pauline-Lutheran emphasis on the laying aside of all
earthly and even "religious" securities. Two more quotations from
Heidegger will clarify this point. He writes, "Anticipation discloses to
existence that its uttermost possibility lies *in giving itself up*, and thus it
shatters all one's tenaciousness to whatever existence one has
reached."[59] "In this state-of-mind, Dasein finds itself face to face with the

55. *Ibid.*, p. 303 (Heidegger's italics).
56. *Ibid.*, p. 306 n. 3.
57. *Ibid.*, pp. 306-07 (Heidegger's italics).
58. *Ibid.*, p. 308.
59. *Ibid.* (my italics).

'nothing' of the possible impossiblity of its existence. . . . *Anticipation reveals to Dasein its lostness in the they-self, and brings it face to face with the possibility of being itself . . . in freedom towards death—a freedom which has been released from the Illusions of the 'they' . . . .*"⁶⁰

At this point Heidegger introduces his notion of the call of conscience, which leads on to a consideration of guilt and "resoluteness" as characterizing authentic existence. We shall see in due course that this is closely related to certain themes in the work of Bultmann, who lays great stress on "decision" in his theology. An authentic self is willing to be open to the call of conscience. Dasein's authentic "potentiality-for-Being . . . is attested by that which, in Dasein's everyday interpretation of itself, is familiar to us as the '*voice of conscience*' (Stimme des Gewissens)."⁶¹ Heidegger's central aim in calling attention to conscience, however, is to introduce the basic phenomenon of "resoluteness" (*Entschlossenheit*). In the whole phenomenon of being open to the call of conscience and hearing it "lies that existentiell choosing which . . . we call '*resoluteness*'."⁶²

Heidegger stresses that the notion of conscience as "call" is no mere picture or metaphor, like the Kantian representation of the conscience as a court of justice. In and through its calling, "Conscience summons Dasein's Self from its lostness in the 'they'."⁶³ However, Heidegger does not make conscience into some reified abstraction. Conscience is an aspect of the self; but it is an aspect of the self which has lost the comfortable feeling of sheltering as part of the crowd, or the "they." In this sense, Dasein both does the calling, and also listens to the calling. The phenomenon of conscience thus brings to Dasein's awareness the distinction between the self who does the calling, the self which is called, and that *to which* the self is called.

Several points are thus brought together. First of all, "*In conscience Dasein calls itself.*"⁶⁴ Secondly, however, "The call is precisely something which *we ourselves* have neither planned nor prepared for, nor voluntarily performed. . . . 'It' calls ('*es*' *ruft*) against our expectations and even against our will. . . . The call comes from me and yet *from beyond* me. . . . The caller is unfamiliar to the everyday they-self; it is something like an *alien* voice. . . . Conscience manifests itself as the call of care . . . anxious about its potentiality-for-Being."⁶⁵ Thirdly, while it "gives no information about events," nevertheless the call of conscience "points forward to Dasein's potentiality-for-Being" as a call which comes

60. *Ibid.*, pp. 310 and 311 (Heidegger's italics).
61. *Ibid.*, p. 313.
62. *Ibid.*, p. 314.
63. *Ibid.*, p. 319.
64. *Ibid.*, p. 320 (Heidegger's italics).
65. *Ibid.*, pp. 320, 321, and 322 (Heidegger's italics).

"from uncanniness" (aus *der Unheimlichkeit,* where it is not "at home").[66] This introduces us to the phenomena of guilt and responsibility. Conscience and guilt thus disclose to Dasein its authentic selfhood by individualizing the self out of the anonymous "they" on the basis of responsibility and freedom.

Three warnings must now be added against possible misunderstandings, all of which are underlined by Heidegger himself. First of all, the isolation or individualization of Dasein effected by the call of conscience does not remove it from its world of Being with others. Heidegger states: "Resoluteness, as *authentic Being-one's-Self,* does not detach Dasein from its world, nor does it isolate it so that it becomes a free-floating 'I'."[67] Indeed, in view of the individualism that Bultmann seems to derive partly from Heidegger it is worth noting that Heidegger goes further. He exclaims: "Resoluteness brings the Self right into its current concernful Being-alongside what is ready-to-hand, and pushes it into solicitous Being with Others."[68] While resoluteness signifies "letting oneself be summoned out of one's lostness in the 'they'," nevertheless "even resolutions remain dependent upon the 'they' and its world."[69] Heidegger spells out this point by introducing the term "situation."[70] This calls attention to the "involvement-character" of the circumstances in which Dasein, through resoluteness, manifests care and concern.

Secondly, earlier in his argument Heidegger is at pains to say that his analysis of conscience and its call is not concerned with a theory of ethics as such. Here we come against the far-reaching theme which has connections with Kant, Schopenhauer, Kierkegaard, Bultmann, and the earlier thought of Wittgenstein, that ethics cannot be based on intellectual foundations, or on propositions which give information about the world.[71] Heidegger argues that Dasein which is open to the call of conscience receives a disclosure which is constituted by discourse, state-of-mind, and understanding. But the "discourse" of conscience is silent, and neither state-of-mind nor understanding is an intellectual mode of apprehending truth. In language that reminds us of the closing section of Wittgenstein's *Tractatus,* Heidegger insists, "This calling is therefore a keeping-silent. The discourse of conscience never comes to utterance. Only in keeping silent does the conscience call; that is to say, the call comes from the soundlessness of uncanniness, and the Dasein which it summons is called back into the stillness of itself, and called back as

66. *Ibid.,* p. 325.
67. *Ibid.,* p. 344 (Heidegger's italics).
68. *Ibid.*
69. *Ibid.,* pp. 345-46.
70. *Ibid.,* pp. 346-48.
71. Cf. the comments in A. Janik and S. Toulmin, *Wittgenstein's Vienna,* pp. 194 *et passim.*

something that is to become still."[72] With this we may compare the earlier Wittgenstein's remark, "It is clear that ethics cannot be put into words."[73] As Janik and Toulmin have so convincingly shown, this is an expression of a perspective that ran deep in European thought at the turn of the century.[74] Already in *Being and Time*, then, and not only in Heidegger's later thought, there arises the contrast between the "idle talk" of inauthentic existence and the silence or "reticence" (*Verschwiegenheit*) that characterize authentic existence. "They," he declares, "hear and understand nothing but loud idle talk," and hence cannot hear the call of conscience.[75] By contrast, authentic existence is characterized by resoluteness, or, in Bultmann's terms, by decision.

Thirdly, Heidegger warns us that his notion of guilt (*Schuld*) is not to be confused with a theological conception of sin. Nevertheless the phenomenon of conscience takes up the tension which we have already noted in Heidegger's characterization of Dasein both as facticity and possibility. Marjorie Grene underlines the nature of this tension: "It challenges human being to escape from enslavement into freedom, and by the same act to transform historical necessity into resolution." But: "I never escape forfeiture; facticity is inalienably the alien ground of my existence. . . . The self owes to itself a debt it cannot discharge."[76] This tension is taken up in the theology of Rudolf Bultmann. Bultmann stresses not only the role of decision and the contrast between authentic existence and mere "information," but also the tension between freedom and human facticity. For both Heidegger and Bultmann, however, this tension can be fully described only in terms of time. Freedom is a matter of openness towards the future.

24. *Time, Temporality, and History*

Heidegger approaches the subject of time and temporality in two ways. In the third chapter of Division Two of *Being and Time*, temporality (*Zeitlichkeit*) first arises in the course of his attempt to bring together anticipation and resoluteness and then in his discussion of care. In the fourth chapter of this Division (sections 67-71) all the essential findings of Heidegger's preparatory analysis of Dasein are once more analyzed and interpreted in terms of temporality. Temporality, however, for Heidegger

72. M. Heidegger, *B.T.*, pp. 342-43.
73. L. Wittgenstein, *T.* 6.421.
74. See n. 28.
75. M. Heidegger, *B.T.*, p. 343.
76. M. Grene, *Martin Heidegger*, p. 33.

is not the same as time. Temporality refers to Dasein; time relates to objects within the world. Temporality is, moreover, the ground *on the basis of which* Dasein's existence, facticity, and falling may be disclosed as temporal phenomena. In existential-ontological terms, as Gelven puts it, *"Dasein's temporality is the basis for time."*[77] Temporality is the basis of Dasein's experience in time, and not simply of the existence of objects in time.

Heidegger begins by making the point that "Temporality gets experienced in a phenomenally primordial way in Dasein's authentic Being-a-whole, in the phenomenon of anticipating resoluteness."[78] For this phenomenon is experienced, or attested, "in an existentiell way."[79] This section (62) is perhaps more obscure than most, but Macquarrie and Robinson comment in a footnote, "The idea seems to be that authentic resoluteness keeps reiterating itself in the face of a constant awareness that it may have to be retracted or taken back at any time."[80] Thus Heidegger speaks of *"authentic resoluteness which resolves to keep repeating itself."*[81] Once again, this has close connections with Bultmann's notion of decision in relation to faith. Such a decision is never, either for Heidegger or for Bultmann, once-for-all. Dasein is free and responsible as long as it lives and can never put the tension involved in this situation behind it. In this sense, it can never escape its existential relation to the past, present, and especially the future.

This brings Heidegger to the relation between temporality and care. But he first pauses to reiterate his earlier comments about the circular character of hermeneutics. An existential analysis of Dasein carried out in a preliminary way is a necessary starting-point for the understanding of existence, even if it is carried out in terms of inauthentic everyday existence. But such an interpretation cannot be complete or final. Its very possibility, even as a provisional interpretation, depends on the "fore-having" of a perspective of wholeness, which in turn relates to authentic existence and to temporality. Thus, while we begin with everyday existence, a more authentic understanding has the character of "doing violence" to our preliminary interpretation, even though no other starting-point was possible.[82] Thus Heidegger's view of hermeneutics (discussed in the previous chapter) and his work in *Being and Time* shed further light on each other. Once again this is also related to Bultmann's view of pre-understanding.

Heidegger contrasts his own view of Dasein as care with Kant's view

77. M. Gelven, *A Commentary on Heidegger's 'Being and Time,'* p. 221 (his italics).
78. M. Heidegger, *B.T.*, p. 351.
79. *Ibid.*, p. 357.
80. *Ibid.*, p. 355 n. 3.
81. *Ibid.*, p. 355.
82. *Ibid.*, p. 359.

of the self. The self of rationalism is merely a "subject"; the self of empiricism is merely an "object." Kant saw that Descartes was wrong in interpreting the self in substantival terms, but in the end he could not break away from seeing the self only as subject. Moreover, Kant insisted that time belonged only to phenomena, and was not a characteristic of the noumenal world. By contrast, Heidegger asserts that what it means to be a self is disclosed by Dasein's relation to the future, or by "the primordial phenomenon of the *future as coming towards* (*das ursprüngliche Phäno-men der Zu-kunft*)."[83] What it means to be a Dasein is authentically disclosed in Being-towards-death; but "Being-towards-death is possible only as something futural (*als zukünftiges*)."[84]

We must now recall what was said in the previous chapter about viewing human existence in terms of possibility. The very ability of Dasein to have possible ways of being means that futurity acquires the utmost significance. Thus Heidegger writes, "The primary phenomenon of primordial and authentic temporality is the future."[85] However, futurity does not mean, in this connection, some abstract or metaphysical series of not-yet points in time. The future is the ground of Dasein's possibility or existentiality, just as its facticity is grounded in the past and its fallenness is related to the present.

It is often said in criticism of Heidegger that he is guilty of reifying abstractions, especially, for example, nothingness and time. Both in the *Blue Book* and in the *Philosophical Investigations* Wittgenstein warns us against the seductive character of such questions as "What is Time?", and the consequent temptation to reify the concept in terms of some such picture as that of a moving band or a flowing river.[86] However, Heidegger asks not "What is Time?"; but "What does it mean to be in time?" Gelven urges, "What Heidegger has scrupulously avoided is precisely such a formulation of 'metaphysical time' as would treat time as some sort of entity or substance. . . . Time and temporality *are* in so far as a human being *is*; but this is not to suggest a subjectivism, because it has nothing to do with the problem of knowledge. . . . Temporality is exposed as the necessary ontological condition for the ways in which we exist."[87] It is an irony that Bultmann and Fuchs are accused of reducing the kerygma of the New Testament to "timeless truth," when they agree with Heidegger about the temporality of human existence. However, their determination to follow Heidegger, interpreting the present and future existentially rather than (for example, in contrast to Cullmann) in terms of a series of linear-temporal "points," is partly responsible for this confusion.

83. *Ibid.*, p. 372.
84. *Ibid.*, p. 373.
85. *Ibid.*, p. 378.
86. L. Wittgenstein, *B.B.*, pp. 26-27, and *P.I.*, sects. 89, 90 and 607-08.
87. Cf. M. Gelven, *A Commentary of Heidegger's 'Being and Time,'* pp. 188-89.

Heidegger now proceeds to show how certain specific characteristics of Dasein as care, namely understanding, state-of-mind, fallenness, and discourse, are grounded in temporality. Understanding, we have already seen, involves "projection." Heidegger declares, "Projection is basically futural. . . . Understanding, as existing in the potentiality-for-Being . . . is *primarily* futural."[88] However, understanding, especially in its inauthentic mode, is "determined with equal primordiality by having been and by the present."[89] For inauthentic understanding becomes caught up in the concerns of everyday business. By contrast, "One's state-of-mind . . . temporalizes itself primarily in *having been (Gewesenheit)*."[90] Falling relates to the present, since the present becomes the center of preoccupation and concern. This is another feature of Heidegger's thought which is taken up by Bultmann. Finally, discourse is not related especially to any one of the three "ecstases" of time. In general terms, however, "discourse in itself is temporal."[91]

Heidegger has some further comments to make about time at the very end of his work. However, at this point he introduces his last major theme, namely that of history, historicality, and destiny. His key point is that history is what it is by virtue of the historicality (*Geschichtlichkeit*) of Dasein, rather than because of the mere pastness of historical events and objects. Hence the focus of the history lies not in the past but *in the present*. Once again, this is an aspect of Heidegger's thought which has close connections with Rudolf Bultmann's interpretation of the New Testament.

It would be tempting, Heidegger suggests, to view the historical nature of Dasein as consisting in its "filling up" an allotted stretch of time "between" its moments of birth and death. It is not that birth is merely a moment in the past: "Factical Dasein exists *as born*; and as born, it is *already dying*, in the sense of being-towards-death."[92] The historical locus of birth and death is the *present*: "As long as Dasein factically exists both the 'ends' of their 'between' *are*."[93] Heidegger urges, "Dasein . . . *is not 'temporal' because it 'stands in history' . . . . On the contrary it exists historically . . . only because it is temporal in the very basis of its Being*."[94] The main point throughout this analysis is the difference between the historical character of objects present-at-hand, which are "historical" only in a secondary sense, and the historical character of Dasein. This contrast is brought out in a comment made by T. Langan. He writes,

88. M. Heidegger, *B.T.*, pp. 385 and 387.
89. *Ibid.*, p. 387.
90. *Ibid.*, p. 390.
91. *Ibid.*, p. 400.
92. M. Heidegger, *B.T.*, p. 426 (my italics).
93. *Ibid.* (Heidegger's italics).
94. *Ibid.*, p. 428 (Heidegger's italics).

"Because the Dasein knows the course it is taking and resolutely wills it, the historical motion is not a passive undergoing, such as the material living thing experiences, but an active 'letting itself happen', the free shouldering of a destiny. For this reason Heidegger terms the motion of the Dasein's self-extension *Geschehen*—a 'happening', from which of course he would derive the word Geschichte (*historical destiny*)."[95]

Heidegger next distinguishes between four different ways in which the word "history" can be used. For example, antiquities preserved in museums are said to be "historical." But on what basis are they described in this way? Since these objects still exist in the present it is not their own pastness which makes them "historical," but their relation to a world of a past Dasein: "The historical character of the antiquities that are still preserved is grounded in the 'past' of that Dasein to whose world they belonged."[96] At this point in his argument, however, Heidegger recalls that Dasein cannot itself be viewed merely as an object present-at-hand. Hence, he concludes, "Dasein can never be past . . . because it essentially can never be present-at-hand."[97] We may observe, in passing, that logically Heidegger's conclusion depends on whether "Dasein," rather than "human being," is strictly necessary in his statement about the historical nature of antiquities. Our own opinion is that at *this* point the term "Dasein" covers a sleight of hand, and we shall develop this criticism in due course. It has repercussions, it need hardly be said, for the view of history held by Bultmann and Fuchs.

Heidegger has emphasized the present locus of history, then, by considering the "world" of Dasein. His next task is to make the same point by considering the phenomenon of historical heritage and what he calls "fate." Historical heritage is bound up with Dasein's facticity. It is part of the givenness of life into which man is "thrown," and underlines man's historical conditionedness. However, authentic existence, Heidegger has already argued, involves "resoluteness" that is significant in relation to the future. In the context of history this introduces us to Heidegger's distinctive use of the term "fate." Fate entails Dasein's awareness both of its own limited possibilities which are conditioned by historical heritage and also of the significance of its decisions for the present and the future. Resoluteness entails appropriating a historical heritage in a way that is fateful, or significant for the present and future.

The actual sentences in which Heidegger expresses these ideas are complex and at times obscure. He writes, "The resoluteness in which Dasein comes back to itself discloses current factical possibilities of

95. T. Langan, *The Meaning of Heidegger*, p. 57.
96. M. Heidegger, *B.T.*, p. 432.
97. *Ibid*. (Heidegger's italics).

authentic existing, and discloses them *in terms of heritage* which that resoluteness, as thrown, takes over."[98] When it is fully aware of its heritage and yet authentically open to the future in decision, Dasein can *"take over its own thrownness and be in the moment of vision for 'its time'. Only authentic temporality which is at the same time finite, makes possible something like fate—that is to say, authentic historicality."*[99]

In his section entitled "Dasein's Historicality and World-History" Heidegger now draws a contrast between history as it is viewed inauthentically and authentic historicality. In inauthentic existence the "they" tries to build history only on the occurrence of "facts" or "events" of the past. History is *about* that which happened in the past. Facts concerning buildings, battlefields, occurrences of nature, and so on, are described by Heidegger as "the world-historical." By contrast, authentic historicality involves Dasein's existential awareness *of itself* through which it understands itself as Being in history, and related in resoluteness and in fate to its own historical heritage. Hence, we reach the conclusion, which is once again closely relevant to Bultmann's thought, that the "inauthentic" view of history is that in which history is viewed in terms of past facts, whereas the "authentic" view relates to Dasein and its world. Heidegger writes concerning the inauthentic perspective of the they-self: "The 'they' evades choice. Blind for possibilities, it cannot repeat what has been, but only retains and receives the 'actual' that is left over, the world-historical that has been the leavings, *and the information about them that is present-at-hand.*"[100] On the other hand, "When historicality is authentic it understands history as the 'recurrence' of the possible, and knows that a possibility will recur only if existence is open for it fatefully, in a moment of vision, in resolute repetition."[101]

The importance of the possible, rather than the actual, is underlined in Heidegger's section on historiology, or the study of history. To start with facts and with questions about whether certain historical facts *as facts* can be repeated or are "once-for-all" is to start, he believes, at the wrong end. Authentic historiology "is necessarily a critique of the 'Present'."[102] Gelven's paraphrase of Heidegger's main point reveals its connection with the outlooks of Bultmann and Fuchs in their interpretation of the New Testament. Gelven comments, "Again, it is not the mere fact of something actually occurring that makes it historical, but its *significance* as part of human existing."[103]

Heidegger acknowledges that his own approach to history and histor-

98. *Ibid.*, p. 435.
99. *Ibid.*, p. 437 (Heidegger's italics).
100. *Ibid.*, p. 443 (my italics).
101. *Ibid.*, p. 444.
102. *Ibid.*, p. 449.
103. M. Gelven *A Commentary on Heidegger's 'Being and Time,'* p. 217 (his italics).

ined."[117] Objectivity, Bultmann declares, can only mean "a knowledge appropriate to the subject."[118] Hence a truly "objective" interpretation of a text has nothing to do with the objectivism of the Cartesian standpoint: "It is valid in the investigation of a text to allow oneself to be examined by the text, and to hear the claim it makes."[119]

It is important for the hermeneutics of Ernst Fuchs, and also Robert Funk, that there is no one "standard" way of seeing the world. The interpreter's view of reality is bound up with the "world" in which he already stands. Fuchs makes much of the point that in the parables Jesus stands alongside the hearer *in the world of the hearer.* He therefore begins not with "concepts" or "information" but by entering into the *everyday attitudes* of the audience. In our chapter on the new hermeneutic we shall illustrate this point with reference to the example of the Parable of the Labourers in the Vineyard (Matt. 20:1-6).[120] Jesus begins by entering the world of his audience by taking up and apparently sharing their own attitudes to questions about employment and wages. Only from *within* this world does he then proceed to transform it, even to overturn it. On this basis Fuchs claims that the word of Jesus grasps his hearer "deep down"; in other words, at a level prior to that of mere "concepts" and of the subject-object relation.

(2) Heidegger's attempt to overcome the distinction between subject and object relates not only to his view of worldhood, but also to the part played in his thought by *states-of-mind.* States-of-mind are said to disclose truth, and must not be interpreted merely as feelings to be explained psychologically. Oddly enough, Heidegger is sometimes compared *unfavorably* in this connection with Kierkegaard, Nietzsche, or Sartre. Whereas they actually *underwent* experiences of dread or anxiety (*Angst*), it is said that Heidegger only philosophizes *about* such experiences at arm's length. If dread or anxiety discloses truth, must not Heidegger, some of his critics claim, need to undergo extreme psychological experiences of the kind that we associate with Kierkegaard's battles of faith and doubt, or with Sartre's experiences in the Resistance? However, is Heidegger's conception of "state-of-mind" (*Befindlichkeit*), or even more specifically of "anxiety" (*Angst*) or "Being-towards-death" (*Sein zum Tode*), really the same kind of thing as Jasper's notion of limit-situations or boundary-situations (*Grenzsituationen*)?

Heidegger is concerned not with the psychological or *existentiell* significance of these states-of-mind as such, but with their ontological or

117. R. Bultmann, *E.P.T.*, pp. 254-55.
118. *Ibid.*, p. 255.
119. *Ibid.*, p. 254; cf. pp. 252-56.
120. Cf. E. Fuchs, *S.H.J.*, pp. 32-38 and 154-56.

existential-ontological significance. In other words, he asks, how are such states-of-mind *possible*? Understanding is rooted in Dasein's ability-to-be (*Seinkönnen*). Possibility is not experienced, in the sense that what is experienced is the ontic, actual, or *existentiell*. Thus we saw, for example, that it is not the "experience" of dying or Being-at-an-end (*Zu-Ende-sein*) that discloses Dasein's finitude, but Being-*towards*-death, or Being-*towards*-the-end (*Sein zum Ende*).[121] This is not to deny that the ontic or *existentiell* has an important place in Heidegger's thought, but it leads on to existential questions about possibility and hence to ontology. In his article "Heidegger's Concern for the Lived-World in his Dasein-Analysis," John McGinley observes "Life is for Dilthey . . . what Dasein is for Heidegger. . . . It was the 'lived experience' quality of human subjectivity which was determinative for Heidegger's conception of Dasein."[122] This reference to Dilthey's notion of "life" serves also to underline a further point of connection with Bultmann's hermeneutics.

State-of-mind, then, is not pure feeling. Paul Tillich makes this point not only in connection with his defense of Schleiermacher, but also in a way which relates it illuminatingly to our previous point. He writes: "The thinking of the Existential thinker . . . is rooted in an interpretation of Being or Reality which does *not* identify Reality with 'objective being'. But it would be equally misleading to say that it identifies Reality with 'subjective being', with 'consciousness' or feeling. Such a view would still leave the meaning of 'subjective' determined by its contrast with that of 'objective'. . . . It is trying to find a level on which the contrast between 'subject' and 'object' has not arisen."[123]

On this basis Tillich makes two points. First of all, he insists that the language of Heidegger and others about states-of-mind is not only psychological but also ontological. Secondly, however, he agrees with Heidegger's critics that the latter has not been entirely successful in fully explaining the difference between their psychological and ontological meaning.[124] Significantly, because of its importance both for Heidegger and for Bultmann, Tillich claims that this ambiguity applies to the ontological use of the psychological conception of "will." He compares Schelling's early view of the will as "*Ur-Sein*" with attempts on the part of Nietzsche, Bergson, and Schopenhauer to reach a "creative source" behind the subject-object distinction. Tillich also underlines the importance of will for Duns Scotus and for Luther. It need hardly be recalled that Heidegger's *Habilitation* in 1916 was on Duns Scotus, and that Bultmann's indebtedness to Luther is difficult to exaggerate.

121. See above, sect. 23.
122. J. McGinley, in *Ph.T.* XVI, 98-99.
123. P. Tillich, "Existential Philosophy" in *J.H.I.* V (1944), 55-56; cf. pp. 44-68.
124. *Ibid.*, p. 58.

It is perhaps particularly significant that Tillich concedes the existence of some ambiguity between the psychological and ontological aspects of states-of-mind when he himself bases so much on this approach in his *Systematic Theology*. It is of pivotal importance for his own theology that he can claim: "The ultimate of the act of faith and the ultimate in the act of faith are one and the same."[125] In other words, he is so convinced of the ontological significance of states-of-mind that he can use the term "ultimate concern" to refer both to a human attitude and to the reality of which it constitutes an awareness. God, for Tillich, is beyond the "god" of human concepts. He is "that which is unconditionally beyond the conceptual sphere" and who therefore transcends the realm of awareness "that is split into subjectivity and objectivity."[126] Tillich's own approach, therefore, calls attention to both the strength and the weakness of Heidegger's position. On the one hand, both thinkers insist that an awareness of truth is more than a merely cognitive or cerebral matter. "State-of-mind" is not merely a purely subjective feeling. On the other hand, there remains an ambiguity in attempts to explain the relationship between the psychological and the ontological, and even Tillich himself concedes this in spite of its centrality in his own theology.[127] (This criticism is connected with a parallel difficulty which we shall note, shortly, about Heidegger's use of the term "primordial.")

125. P. Tillich, *Dynamics of Faith*, p. 11.
126. P. Tillich, "The Religious Symbol" in S. Hooke (ed.), *Religious Experience and Truth* (Oliver and Boyd, Edinburgh, 1962), p. 303.
127. Tillich describes his own early experience of the numinous, connected with the Gothic church building of which his father was pastor, as "the foundation of all my religious and theological work." He adds, "When I first read Rudolf Otto's *Idea of the Holy* I understood it immediately in the light of these early experiences" ("Autobiographical Reflections" in C. W. Kegley and R. W. Bretall, eds., *The Theology of Paul Tillich*, p. 6). The positive direction towards which all this leads is a repudiation of a merely theoretical account of theology. Thus Tillich writes, "*Only those statements are theological which deal with this subject in so far as it can become a matter of being or non-being for us*" (*Systematic Theology* I, 17; his italics). "*The object of theology is what concerns us ultimately*" (*ibid.*, p. 15; his italics). Tillich sees that both God and human life transcend what can be expressed in cognitive propositions. He instances, by way of illustrating the principle, a Rubens landscape, and comments: "What this mediates to you cannot be expressed in any other way than through the painting itself" (*Theology of Culture*, Galaxy Books, New York, 1964, p. 57). At the same time, serious difficulties also emerge from Tillich's approach, which, we shall argue, also apply to Heidegger. There is an element of ambiguity and even circularity in his comments about *criteria of truth*. For example, on "ultimate concern" Tillich writes, "This does not mean that first there is a being called God and then the demand that men should be ultimately concerned about him. It means that *whatever* concerns a man ultimately becomes god for him" (*Systematic Theology* I, 234; my italics). Sometimes in Tillich's writings, including his more popular ones, ultimate concern seems to represent *any* concern which so grasps hold of man that it unites all his energies and aspirations in one all-embracing serious goal. But *need* such a goal *always* have a positive relation to truth and ontology? I have tried to develop both the positive values and the difficulties of this position in A. C. Thiselton, "The Theology of Paul Tillich," in *The Churchman* LXXXVIII (1974), 86-107.

The general effect of this perspective for New Testament hermeneutics, however, is seen in a variety of ways. We have already noted the connection of this perspective with a philosophical emphasis on "will" or, in Heidegger's language, "resoluteness." In Bultmann this becomes an emphasis on "decision," which has affinities both with Kierkegaard and with the New Testament itself. Fuchs also stresses the inadequacy of an approach to truth which remains only on the level of concepts, cognition, and propositions. More broadly, however, this also has connections with the approach to the parables adopted by Robert Funk and Dan Otto Via. Both writers stress the role of pre-cognitive states-of-mind for an understanding of the language of Jesus. Via insists that the parables are to be regarded not as the communication of concepts which give information, but as works of art. He compares their function to that of a novel. He writes, "A novel is the pre-philosophical living-through of an experience within an horizon, or the giving of a new configuration to pre-conceptual existential forces. This pre-articulate element must be something of what Frye has in mind when he speaks of the 'dumbness' of literature which calls for interpretation or criticism."[128] In aesthetic experience, Via urges, the emphasis is on life itself, or "happening existence." In interpretation, focal attention shifts to the secondary level of concepts, and thereby "the strictly aesthetic posture is abandoned." The parables, however, must not be understood in this way. Via and Funk both urge that, in spite of the insights of New Testament scholarship, the "one point" approach to the parables from Jülicher to Jeremias has resulted in a narrowly ideational understanding of their significance.[129] Their own approach, therefore, is much nearer to Heidegger's emphasis on "world" and on "state-of-mind" than the Cartesian objectivism. We explore the strengths and weaknesses of this approach in a later chapter.

26. Further Comments on Heidegger's Thought

(3) Our third comment concerns Heidegger's view of language and hermeneutics. We have seen that he does not merely theorize about the hermeneutical circle, but actually puts the principle into operation in his own work. His discussion of world and worldhood, moreover, underlines the fact that considerations about the horizons of the interpreter cannot be

---

128. D. O. Via, *The Parables. Their Literary and Existential Dimension* (Fortress Press, Philadelphia, 1967), p. 83. Cf. N. Frye, *Anatomy of Criticism* (Princeton University Press, 1957), pp. 45-46, 27-28, and 86.
129. D. O. Via, *The Parables*, pp. 21-24 and 94; and R. W. Funk, *Language, Hermeneutic and Word of God*, p. 149.

avoided, while his emphasis on facticity reminds us that these horizons are, in the first place, given rather than chosen. Language cannot be understood without reference to these horizons of meaning. Like the later Wittgenstein, for all their differences, Heidegger stresses that language is *grounded in human life*, indeed in particular contexts in human life, whether we call these language-games grounded on forms of life, or "worlds" grounded on the worldhood of Dasein. Language is to be understood as communication or "discourse." J. Macquarrie comments, "The later Wittgenstein seems to have moved in the direction of Heidegger's concreteness when he insisted on setting language in its living context and when indeed he went so far as to call language 'a form of life'."[130] The close relationship between language and world (parallel to Wittgenstein's relation between language-game and form of life) emerges with reference to Heidegger's view of idle talk as characterizing inauthentic existence. In the world of the "they-self," language assumes the function of communicating the trivia or even more serious "information" which is called forth by what Heidegger terms "curiosity." In our chapter on Heidegger's later thought, we shall trace the full development of this perspective on language.

Meanwhile, two other points about language and hermeneutics have special relevance for the present study. First of all, Heidegger rightly recognizes that effective language does not merely *describe*. Like the later Wittgenstein, Heidegger sees that this follows as soon as language is properly viewed as a human activity grounded in life. Nevertheless, Heidegger is less successful than Wittgenstein about guarding against the opposite error. He rightly sees that description or assertion does not occupy a privileged status over against other linguistic activities. However, he tends perhaps to go too far in actually devaluing the role of assertion. This is because it is always, he insists, a derivative mode of speech, since it presupposes an act of cognition and the use of concepts which depend on the subject-object distinction. This devaluing of assertions, against which Pannenberg protests so strongly, is found in Bultmann, Fuchs, Ebeling, and Gadamer. In Bultmann it is further aggravated because he is influenced by the Kantian tradition which accords privileged status to the imperative. Once again, when we look at Heidegger's use of the term "primordial," we shall consider the correlative term "derivative."

Heidegger belongs to the tradition in the philosophy of language which moves from Herder through Wilhelm von Humboldt to Cassirer. This tradition protests against the kind of standpoint found in Locke, to the effect that language serves to articulate concepts which are already

---

130. J. Macquarrie, *Martin Heidegger*, p. 54.

formulated independently of language itself. By contrast, Ernst Cassirer insists that "All theoretical cognition takes its departure from a world already preformed by language."[131] Herder began by relating language not to the formulation of concepts, but to the expression of pre-cognitive emotions and urges, and R. L. Brown traces the development of this tradition in the philosophy of language from Herder, through Wilhelm von Humboldt, Hermann Steinthal, Franz Boas, and E. Sapir, to Benjamin Lee Whorf, whose views on language were discussed in chapter five (sect. 17).[132] However, one major problem which is shared both by Herder and by the quite different tradition represented by Carnap and by Ogden and Richards is that, in the words of W. M. Urban, they rest too heavily on the assumption that "some uses of language are *wholly* indicative and some *wholly* emotive and evocative."[133] The same difficulty is expressed by Luis Alonso Schökel in his criticism of Karl Bühler's work on language. Bühler sharply distinguishes between language as statement (*Darstellung*), language as expression (*Kundgabe* or *Ausdruck*), and language as address (*Auslösung* or *Appell*). But Alonso Schökel rightly comments, "Rarely do we find in language as it actually exists any of these three functions in a pure state: language is not the juxtaposition of clinical statements, pure interjections, and simple commands. In reality these functions are operative conjointly, mutually affecting one another."[134]

I have already argued this point in an article on the hermeneutics of Ernst Fuchs with special reference to the function of assertions at the close of parables.[135] Assertions may overlap with other types of language especially for two reasons: they may be open-ended, and they may be self-involving. Heidegger, we believe, has gone too far in his devaluation of assertions and in his hints that "information" is necessarily related to the "curiosity" of inauthentic existence. In New Testament hermeneutics this has serious consequences when Bultmann takes this still further, and it makes its mark, with negative effects, on the work of Fuchs, Ebeling, and Gadamer.

We return, secondly, to Heidegger's view of hermeneutics and in particular the hermeneutical circle. We have seen that he appeals to this principle not only in his section on hermeneutics, but at several strategic points in *Being and Time*. It is sometimes claimed by conservative theologians that the hermeneutical circle enforces an anthropocentric perspec-

---

131. E. Cassirer, *Language and Myth* (Eng. Harper, New York, 1946), p. 28; cf. pp. 23-43, on "language and conception."
132. R. L. Brown, *Wilhelm von Humboldt's Conception of Linguistic Relativity* (Mouton, The Hague, 1967), pp. 13-17.
133. W. M. Urban, *Language and Reality. The Philosophy of Language and the Principles of Symbolism* (Allen and Unwin, London, 1939), pp. 68-69 (my italics).
134. L. Alonso Schökel, *The Inspired Word*, pp. 134-35.
135. A. C. Thiselton, "The Parables of Language-Event" in *S.J.T.* XXIII, 437-68.

tive on all interpretation, because it makes human experience the measure of truth.[136] However, in Heidegger's case it is possible that the reverse is true. To be sure, he begins with Dasein, and insists that the disclosure of truth comes through self-understanding, even through one's own resoluteness. Truth is a matter of Dasein's awareness of itself. Heidegger is too well aware of the Copernican revolution in philosophy brough about by Kant and perhaps furthered by Nietzsche to abandon such a standpoint. Dasein or, as Tillich paraphrases it, "self-relatedness," is "the only door to Being itself."[137] But each provisional view of the past is revised in the light of a fuller view of the whole, and Dasein's view of itself is consequently revised. Thus the preparatory analysis of Dasein is repeated once again in the light of considerations which arise about time and temporality. If Heidegger's view is anthropocentric (and from a theological viewpoint it is in *some* measure unavoidably so) this is not *because* of the hermeneutical circle, but *in spite of* its operation. For only on this basis can anything approaching an understanding of Being be achieved.

The hermeneutical circle, we might say, allows Heidegger's philosophy to embody not only truth *about* Dasein, but truth which has been disclosed *through* Dasein's self-awareness and decision. Admittedly this distinction is a very fine one. When we look more closely at Heidegger's influence on Bultmann, Fuchs, and Ebeling, we must ask: have these writers reduced theology to mere truth *about* man, even if this is truth disclosed in a preconceptual experience of self-understanding and decision? Or have they simply made much of the *hermeneutical* insight that truth can be understood only *in relation to* man? If the hermeneutical circle is allowed to call for adequate revisions of provisional starting-points, in principle it should only *begin* with truth *about* Dasein, although it will always concern only truth which can be viewed *in relation to* Dasein. In this sense Ebeling declares, "The primary phenomenon in the realm of understanding is not understanding *of* language, but understanding *through* language."[138]

We may note that in this sense it is difficult either to accept or to reject the charge of A. de Waelhens and David Cairns that Heidegger's philosophy is not genuinely descriptive. Heidegger would perhaps say that it is descriptive insofar as it is possible for such a treatise to be so; with the proviso that from the point of view of the hermeneutical circle such a description can never be definitive or "once-for-all," as if there were some independent vantage-point from which a supposedly objective view of the whole could be achieved.

---

136. The most emphatic statement comes from J. W. Montgomery, "An Exhortation to Exhorters" in *Christianity Today* XVII (1973), 606.
137. P. Tillich, "Existential Philosophy" in *J.H.I.* V, 57.
138. G. Ebeling, *W.F.*, p. 318.

(4) We may now consider Heidegger's use of the "primordial" and the difficulty which seems to attach to it. In what precise sense does Heidegger speak of the "primordial" as against the secondary or "derivative"? Since he explicitly declares that his concern is not with epistemology but with ontology, this presumably does not refer to priority in knowledge. It is likely that Heidegger means "logically primitive" in the sense of "irreducible." But at this point we have some sympathy with one of the main points made by Gilbert Ryle in his criticisms of *Being and Time*. He writes, "Heidegger seems to be confusing what is anthropologically primitive with what is logically primitive."[139] Ryle explains, "It is perhaps a fact of human nature that I begin by being interested in things for what I can or can't do with them, and only later do I want to know as a scientist what they are. But the former attitude involves equally with the latter the knowledge of things as having attributes and relations, though in infancy I restrict my interest to a few of those attributes and relations, namely those which bear on my business."[140]

It might perhaps be argued, by way of reply, that other philosophers have appealed to what is logically primitive, and the validity of their appeal is accepted. For example, Peter Strawson argues in his book *Individuals* for "the logical primitiveness of the concept of person."[141] But Strawson is not making the same kind of point as Heidegger. His whole analysis is about concepts. Given the use of certain concepts of material bodies, and given certain concepts about personal agency, he asks, how do these relate together? What conceptual conditions prevail when we describe or identify ourselves as persons? Strawson argues that we do not arrive at the idea of personality from dubious notions about "mind," nor about mind and body; we begin with a logically prior concept of the whole person.[142] Heidegger's inquiry operates at a different level. We have already noted the point, conceded by Tillich, that the distinction between the ontological and merely psychological is not always clear. Here we seem to encounter a further application of the same general point. But this time there are overtones of value-judgment. Because states-of-mind are experienced *prior* to cognition and conceptualizing, it is sometimes assumed that they are somehow more reliable or more comprehensive. Neither aspect, however, *can* be "comprehensive" if the

---

139. G. Ryle, in *Collected Writings* I, 208.
140. *Ibid.*
141. P. F. Strawson, *Individuals. An Essay in Descriptive Metaphysics* (Methuen, London, 1959), pp. 103-04.
142. *Ibid.*, pp. 90-116. Strawson argues that predicates which can be applied to material bodies (M-predicates) cannot stand in for those applicable to persons (P-predicates). But persons are not described in terms of two unrelated conceptual schemes which have to do with mind on the one hand, and body on the other hand. There is an area of logical overlap which is distinctive of persons.

other is down-graded as merely "derivative" or "secondary."

It might seem as if this criticism is so far-reaching that to accept it is necessarily to reject Heidegger's whole perspective. This is not the case. We do not reject the fact that *at the level of human experience* the relation between Dasein and its world is indeed prior to the subject-object distinction. We accept the point that the role of states-of-mind in the disclosure of truth has too often been overlooked in theology and philosophy. We accept Robert Funk's claim, when he draws on this perspective for his hermeneutics, that poetry, narrative, or the feeling-state induced by story or parable may convey "a vision of that which cannot be conveyed by prosaic or discursive speech."[143] As James Brown expresses it, "Elimination of the subjective may be a virtue in natural science: would it be a virtue in poetry?"[144] It is not necessary to catalogue the many points at which we consider Heidegger's philosophy to be fruitful and constructive. However, this does not prevent us from voicing the suspicion that along with the use of "primordial" as an existential description goes its use as a value-judgment carrying more implications for ontology than are strictly required. Admittedly "concepts" or descriptive assertions do not always reach through to disclose truth when states-of-mind or even resoluteness are at issue. But this does not mean that concepts are "mere" concepts, or that concepts and assertions have no part to play, especially in the testing of truth. Nor are they simply limited to the area of natural science.

(5) We spent some time examining Heidegger's view of truth, not only in *Being and Time* but also in *Vom Wesen der Wahrheit*. His account of truth shows perhaps more clearly than any other aspect of his thought how keenly he is aware of the philosophical problems raised by Kant and by Nietzsche. He sees that the clock can never be turned back to before Kant. Hence he can never be satisfied with a correspondence view of truth which locates truth in terms of a relationship between concepts "in the mind" and "reality out there." Kant showed decisively that far from testing truth, such a criterion merely begged the question it was intended to answer. To borrow a simile used by Wittgenstein in a different context, as a criterion of truth it is like buying several copies of the same newspaper in order to check whether what the paper said was true.

Does it follow, however, that Heidegger's own notion of truth as the "letting be of things-that-are" (*das Seinlassen von Seiendem*) answers the problem more adequately? Furthermore, does this view of truth *necessarily* carry with it the negative implication that propositional truth (*die Satzwahrheit*) is only of derivative or secondary value? Heidegger has

143. R. W. Funk, *Language, Hermeneutic and Word of God*, p. 136.
144. J. Brown, *Subject and Object in Modern Theology*, p. 13.

taken us into deep waters, and the answer is not easy to fathom. However, two considerations seem to suggest that we cannot remain content with the position reached in Heidegger's earlier thought.

First of all, Heidegger's recognition of the problems exposed by Kant has led him to the view that truth, as Gelven puts it, "refers not to objects but to Dasein."[145] But this brings us back to a difficulty which we have already outlined. Is truth to be seen only *in relation to* Dasein or is all truth only truth *about* Dasein? This issue reappears, we have argued, in Bultmann's theology. In his later writings Heidegger himself, however, moves away from a philosophy which is oriented wholly around Dasein to one which gives the primacy to Being. Has Bultmann been persuaded to remain at a point from which Heidegger himself has advanced because he has seen its inadequacy?

Secondly, Heidegger's correct recognition that cognitive judgments are *relative* does not mean that they are worthless or relevant only to the day-to-day concerns of inauthentic existence. In accordance with Heidegger's own formulation of the hermeneutical circle, the repetition of each disclosure of truth reaches Dasein at a new place of vision, carrying it forward towards an increasing wholeness of self-understanding. But each advance calls for *both* openness to truth *and* critical testing, even if the relativity of that testing is acknowledged. To take up the newspaper simile, it is less like trying to check on a report by reading another copy of the same paper than reading the next day's paper, even if it comes from the same reporters and editor. A recognition of the relativity and circularity of the correspondence view of truth does not entail the conclusion that propositional truth and cognitive critical judgment should be accorded a place that is entirely secondary. It should take its place alongside Heidegger's notion of truth as unveiling, for truth needs to be tested as well as communicated. Heidegger's insistence that he is concerned with ontology rather than espitemology does not seem to weaken the force of these two criticisms.

(6) We must also ask whether Heidegger's philosophy is unduly individualistic. At first sight, admittedly, such a criticism seems wide of the mark, for Heidegger is at pains to say that the "Dasein-with of others" is part of being in the world. He explores the contrast between "circumspection" (*Umsicht*) and "considerateness" (*Rücksicht*) or looking at the world of other Daseins. He states that life with others (*Mitdasein*) calls for "solicitude" (*Fürsorge*) as against mere "concern" about objects (*Besorgen*). Nor are we criticizing his valid insight that Dasein, which constitutes an "I," is not to be made into a mere object. When Dasein is understood only as "human being," its distinctive subjectivity (in Kier-

---

145. M. Gelven, *A Commentary on Heidegger's 'Being and Time,'* p. 132.

kegaard's sense) is lost from view. As Heidegger expresses it, Dasein has "in each case mineness" (*Jemeinigkeit*).

Nevertheless, Heidegger's philosophy is individualistic in two particular ways. First of all, although he rejects Descartes' starting-point of the *cogito*, Heidegger rejects not so much beginning with the individual self, but beginning with a self which is isolated from its world as the epistemological subject in an act of cognition. Dasein is more than a thinking subject, but it remains an "I am." This is the theme of Paul Ricoeur's essay entitled "Heidegger and the Question of the Subject."[146] Ricoeur writes, "The kind of ontology developed by Heidegger gives ground to what I shall call a *hermeneutics of the 'I am'*, which is a repetition of the *cogito* conceived of as a simple epistemological principle."[147] The objection voiced by Heidegger against the starting-point of Descartes is not that it began with the "I am," but that it starts with "a previous model of certitude." Indeed, "a retrieval of the *cogito* is possible only as a regressive movement beginning with the whole phenomenon of 'being-in-the-world' and turned towards the question of the *who* of that being-in-the-world."[148] Although he recognizes the centrality of Being and language in Heidegger's later writings, Ricoeur concludes that even in this later period the "hermeneutics of the 'I am' " is not entirely abandoned, since the role of "resolve" and freedom in the face of death in *Being and Time* is taken over by "primordial poetizing" (*Urdichtung*) "as the answer to the problem of the who and to the problem of the authenticity of the who."[149]

In some respects this perspective is of great value, quite apart from questions about its philosophical necessity. Heidegger's conceptual scheme helps us to avoid reducing the "I" to a mere object in hermeneutics, and prevents us from losing sight of the importance of self-understanding. We shall see how Bultmann attempts to develop this perspective constructively. Nevertheless, when we come to questions about language, a perspective provided by individual Dasein contrasts unfavorably with Gadamer's starting-point in life and tradition, or still more with Wittgenstein's emphasis on the community. Language is rooted in convention and in the life of human societies, and no amount of philosophizing about authenticity can alter this fact. Hence no account of language can be adequate which fails to take full account of community and tradition. Equally, Heidegger's individualistic perspective is inadequate when we come to the subject of history. Marjorie Grene rightly calls attention to this problem. She writes, "Heidegger does distinguish

146. P. Ricoeur, *The Conflict of Interpretations*, pp. 223-35.
147. *Ibid.*, p. 223 (Ricoeur's italics).
148. *Ibid.*, p. 231.
149. *Ibid.*, p. 234.

between *Schicksal*, individual destiny, and *Geschick*, a collective destiny of some sort. . . . Yet he does nothing, so far as I can see, with the latter concept. Any substantive conception of the rootedness of the single person among and along with his contemporaries is quite wanting."¹⁵⁰ For this we have to turn, once again, to Heidegger's one-time pupil, Gadamer.

The second way in which Heidegger's individualistic perspective reveals itself is in his language about authentic existence, resoluteness, and being-towards-death. Once again, this analysis provides both positive insights and difficulties. Both aspects can be seen in the writings of Kierkegaard, Nietzsche, Jaspers, and Sartre. Kierkegaard believes that he encountered truth when he decided to live as himself, to accept responsibility for his own future, rather than passively to accept the role suggested by convention and by society. But unlike the secular existentialists he regarded these decisions as moments of truth before God. Self-discovery and authenticity meant, for Kiekegaard, the disclosure of sin and the call to repentance and faith. His individualism comes in the content of Christian faith. Thus he writes, "The most ruinous evasion of all is to be hidden in the crowd in an attempt to escape God's supervision . . . in an attempt to get away from hearing God's voice as an individual. . . . Each one shall render account to God as an individual."¹⁵¹ Kierkegaard was concerned not with questions about Being, but with what is entailed in genuine Christian discipleship. However, even Kierkegaard's approach invites certain difficulties, which I tried to set out elsewhere.¹⁵²

Perhaps partly in the light of Kierkegaard's approach, it is sometimes suggested that Heidegger's notion of individual resoluteness amounts to a Christian philosophy of existence. We have only to compare the thought of Jean-Paul Sartre in his *Being and Nothingness* to see that Heidegger's kind of individualism is equally compatible with atheism. Not only does Sartre take up Heidegger's basic contrast between *Vorhandenheit* and *Existenz*, which he develops in terms of *être-en-soi* and *être-pour-soi*; he also discusses the relation between individuality, self-knowledge, and death. Most of all, for the individual to lose himself in the crowd of the "they" is to suffer a fate "like that of the wasp which sinks into the jam and drowns in it . . . as ink is absorbed by the blotter."¹⁵³ But, as Marjorie Grene expresses it, "The Sartrean hero tragically seeking his own act . . . never achieves his own act; he can only die absurdly."¹⁵⁴

150. M. Grene, *Martin Heidegger*, pp. 39-40.
151. S. Kierkegaard, *Purity of Heart is to Will One Thing* (Eng. Fontana, Collins, London, 1961), p. 163.
152. A. C. Thiselton, "Kierkegaard and the Nature of Truth" in *The Churchman* LXXXIX (1975), 85-107.
153. J. P. Sartre, *Being and Nothingness* (Eng. Methuen, London, 1957), pp. 609-10.
154. M. Grene, *Martin Heidegger*, p. 54.

The comparison with Kierkegaard and Sartre underlines the double-sidedness of the issue. Marjorie Grene expresses both equally clearly. On the one hand, "Through the isolation of the individual in Heidegger's analysis we can come to see . . . the ethical importance of the concept of personal integrity or authenticity. . . . Authenticity is a kind of honesty or a kind of courage."[155] But there is also a problem here. Heidegger has stated that he is not concerned with theology or ethics in his contrast between authentic and inauthentic existence. A. de Waelhens underlines this point with reference to his view of conscience.[156] This is not "conscience," he argues, in the usual Christian or ethical sense. Does "authentic" (*eigentlich*), then, mean *nothing more than* "one's very own"? Marjorie Grene implies that the term has little positive content. Heidegger's notion of responsibility, she insists, "is not, in the last analysis, responsibility for anything or in any setting beyond the given situation of the individual himself. Human being facing its own non-being alone and in dread is human being emptied of substance. . . . Heidegger's man of resolve is wanting in all sense of community with his fellow beings. *Mitdasein*, being-together, occurs only on the level of forfeiture (i.e. fallenness). The authentic individual knows no friend or fellow. . . . To view the existence of others only as a means to my freedom is worse than not good enough—it is positively evil. . . . It is a doubly self-centred philosophy: a philosophy of the individual, centred in his own responsibility to become himself."[157]

These criticisms probably go too far, in that they seem to presuppose that the notion of authentic existence has an ethical overtone which Heidegger explicitly warns us is not his intention. However, they serve to remind us that there is both a positive and a negative side to Heidegger's individualism which should make us cautious in exploring his philosophy in the service of New Testament hermeneutics other than eclectically. Whether Bultmann has succeeded in escaping an undue individualism will be discussed in due course. We do not consider, however, that Heidegger's individualism vitiates his whole philosophy as our discussion of other aspects of his thought will have shown.

(7) We return, finally, to the one remaining point about Heidegger which we raised in chapter two. How relevant are Heidegger's concepts to the hermeneutical task of actually elucidating the contents of the New Testament? Heidegger, we have seen, distinguishes human existence from the brute existence of objects or physical entities. He describes man not in terms of substances or of "parts," but in terms of his possibilities. Man's

155. *Ibid.*, pp. 45 and 47.
156. A. de Waelhens, *La Philosophie de Martin Heidegger*, pp. 152-68.
157. M. Grene, *Martin Heidegger*, pp. 53 and 55.

situation in the world is "given" to him. His understanding is bound up with his own attitudes, as well as his own thoughts, and these attitudes include his attitude towards himself. He experiences not only fears, but also anxiety, which discloses to him that he is not altogether "at home" in the world. He is bound, yet he is summoned to freedom. He is called to abandon any false sense of security which is achieved by evading his finitude or by hiding in the crown. He is summoned to accept responsibility in decision. Death assumes an existential role in life, and is more than a merely biological phenomenon. Finally, history does not primarily concern facts of the past, but the present possibilities of human existence.

At first sight, most, or perhaps even all, of these ways of viewing man have close connections with outlooks expressed in the New Testament writings, especially by Paul. To explore the nature and significance of these connections, however, is thereby to examine the hermeneutics and theology of Rudolf Bultmann. A discussion of this seventh and final point, therefore, now converges with the task of considering Bultmann's thought. Moreover, the further relevance of Heidegger's writings to the New Testament itself will be seen when we turn in chapter twelve to the nature of his later thought and its influence on the new hermeneutic.

CHAPTER VIII

The Ingredients of Bultmann's Hermeneutical Concerns Prior to Heidegger's Philosophy

27. *Bultmann's Relation to Liberal Theology and to Neo-Kantian Philosophy: Modern Man and Objectifying Thinking*

It is not our purpose to try to offer a comprehensive account of Bultmann's thought. However, discussions of certain aspects of Bultmann's work, especially his proposals about demythologizing, have invited the criticism that they miss or distort important points because they fail to view the issues in question in the wider context of his thought as a whole. Thus Walter Schmithals, for example, expresses surprise at the sharp reactions to Bultmann's essay on myth in 1941 when his program of demythologizing "merely sums up in a systematic way what Bultmann had been teaching and publishing for twenty years. *All* his work had been 'demythologizing', even when this term did not occur."[1] Precisely the same point is made by Schubert Ogden, who speaks of the "complete agreement between Bultmann's book *Jesus*, first published in 1926, and his *Jesus Christ and Mythology*, published in 1958."[2]

We accept this verdict, but we must go still further. Even Bultmann's main concerns can be more readily understood and appreciated when they are viewed against the background of what became, in effect, their sources. This is not to suggest that Bultmann's thought is entirely an amalgam of the thought of others. It is, however, to claim that Bultmann addresses himself primarily to questions and problems that have been posed by others, and that he accepts and uses conceptual schemes which

---

1. W. Schmithals, *An Introduction to the Theology of Rudolf Bultmann* (Eng. S.C.M., London, 1968), p. 250.
2. S. M. Ogden, "Introduction" to R. Bultmann, *E.F.*, p. 11.

have been formulated by others. Bultmann's thought is more closely related to some seven or eight distinct movements in theology and philosophy than is generally recognized.

Many distinct influences make themselves felt in Bultmann's thought. It is unnecessary to resort to any speculative theory to support this claim. Quite apart from other considerations, Bultmann has clearly expressed his indebtedness to three main directions of thought in his "Autobiographical Reflections," and these three contain all the more specific elements to which we have referred.[3] Bultmann expresses his indebtedness, first, to his own theological teachers, who include Hermann Gunkel, Adolf Harnack, Adolf Jülicher, Johannes Weiss, and Wilhelm Herrmann. Bultmann's years as a student extended from 1903 to 1912. Secondly, he speaks of his dialogue with philosophers, especially with Martin Heidegger when they were colleagues at Marburg from 1923 to 1928. Thirdly, he describes the influence of dialectical theology, especially through Barth, Gogarten, and Thurneysen in the period from about 1920 to 1927.[4]

One major influence on Bultmann's thought was theological liberalism. The most influential theological teacher during the first decade of the century, when Bultmann was a student, was Adolf von Harnack (1851-1930). In 1900 Harnack gave the semi-popular lectures which later reached an enormous readership, in German as *The Essence of Christianity*, and then in English under the title *What is Christianity*? Bultmann was influenced by Harnack and the liberal movement in three ways. First of all, Harnack was concerned to show the relevance of Jesus to the men of his own day, while taking account of their distinctive outlooks as men of the modern world. Secondly, Harnack drew a sharp distinction between the message of Jesus and the emergence of dogmatic theology, which developed, he believed, largely under the influence of Greek thought. This negative attitude towards dogma looks back to Albrecht Ritschl as well as forward to Bultmann himself. Thirdly, Harnack offered to his pupils a model of scholarly integrity.

Bultmann takes up the last two of these three characteristics in his essay "Liberal Theology and the Latest Theological Movement," written in 1924. Whatever criticisms may be levelled against liberalism, he urges, nothing can call in question its concern for "freedom and veracity . . . the earnest search for radical truth."[5] In this respect he comments, "We can never forget our debt of graditude to G. Krüger for that often cited article

3. R. Bultmann, "Autobiographical Reflections" in *E.F.*, pp. 335-41 (also reprinted in C. W. Kegley, ed., *T.R.B.*, pp. xix-xxv, with one additional paragraph).
4. *Ibid.*, pp. 336, 339, and 340.
5. R. Bultmann, *F.U.* I (Eng. S.C.M., London, 1969), 29-30; cf. pp. 28-52; and *G.u.V.* I, 1-25.

of his on 'unchurchly theology'. For he saw the task of theology to be to imperil souls, to lead men into doubt, to shatter all naïve credulity. Here, we felt, was the atmosphere of truth in which alone we could breathe."[6] Inevitably this attitude is related to the desire to be free from the shackles, real or supposed, of church doctrine. Critical research, it was argued, would free men from the burden of dogmatics.

Bultmann derived this liberal perspective not only from Harnack, his teacher at Berlin, but also from Wilhelm Herrmann (1846-1922), his teacher at Marburg. Herrmann not only stressed that Christian faith could never be mere assent to orthodox doctrine; he also urged that science and technology had made Christian faith more difficult in the modern world. This constitutes a further theme in Bultmann's hermeneutics, as well as a major characteristic of liberalism. In his introduction to Herrmann's book *The Communion of the Christian with God*, Robert Voelkel discusses the impact of Marx, Darwin, and Nietzsche on the intellectual world of Herrmann's day, together with its preoccupations with the methods and outlooks of science. He declares, "Coming to terms with this scientific world was what Wilhelm Herrmann's whole career was about. . . . It infected his personality and his teaching style as well."[7]

There are, however, many more points of affinity between Herrmann and Bultmann than this. We have mentioned Herrmann's theological belief that mere "ideas" cannot make a man a Christian. Faith involves trust, rather than merely intellectual assent. Herrmann also emphasizes that faith is for him never something "completed," but something which is ever renewed again and again. Like Bultmann, he sees the locus of faith not simply or perhaps even primarily in an objective event in the past, but in a present "event" (*Ereignis*) in the believer's own life. He writes, "All Christian faith is thus really a confidence in an event which has taken place in the Christian's own life. No discussions concerning the credibility of a report or inquiries into the truth of a doctrine can supply faith with its real object, at least not that faith which regards itself as an experience of divine help, and not as simply the work of man."[8] In his recent study of Herrmann, Michael Beintker has shown with special clarity that Bultmann's teacher Herrmann prepared the way for a number of themes in Bultmann's own thought, not least for his understanding of history and even his use of Heidegger's analysis of Dasein. Beintker cites a remark made by Bultmann in 1964 that "Through Wilhelm Herrmann the problem of history and historicality (*Geschichtlichkeit*) became significant for me. Thereby I was prepared beforehand for my relation to existentialist

6. *Ibid.*, p. 30.
7. W. Herrmann, *The Communion of the Christian with God Described on the Basis of Luther's Statements* (Eng. S.C.M., London, 1972), p. xix.
8. *Ibid.*, pp. 225-26.

philosophy."[9] In 1958 the *Expository Times* invited Bultmann to contribute to a series entitled "Milestones in Books." Bultmann listed six as being of primary significance to him, and these included Barth's *Romans*, Heidegger's *Being and Time*, and Herrmann's *Ethik*. Of Herrmann's book he wrote, "This opened out to me a truer understanding of history than was contained in the so-called *Historismus*."[10]

There are many other affinities between Bultmann's thought and that of Herrmann his teacher. For example, both stress that the experience of faith means freedom, especially freedom from legalism and from any authoritarian system of doctrine. One of my doctoral students, Clive Garrett, is at present engaged on working out these points of affinity and influence in greater detail. He also criticizes part of the work of Roger Johnson for failing to differentiate adequately between Bultmann's particular debt to Herrmann, and what he owes to the Neo-Kantian philosophers Cohen and Natorp.[11] Johnson tends to group all three figures together, whereas Garrett traces an important development of thought between Herrmann's earlier and later writings. Nevertheless, in broad terms Johnson is utterly right in his insistence on the extent of the influence of Neo-Kantian thought on Bultmann, and we must now turn to consider this second basic influence.

Hermann Cohen (1842-1918) and Paul Natorp (1854-1924) took Kant's philosophy as their point of departure, but sought to move beyond him in a way which was basically consistent with his own principles. We have already discussed Heidegger's attempt to do this. Heidegger and the Marburg Neo-Kantian thinkers share the view that Kant failed to follow through radically enough the implications of his own philosophy. Kant had stressed, firmly enough, the activity of the mind in shaping and conceptualizing the phenomena placed before it. Cohen and Natorp agreed with Kant that we cannot speak of an object (*Objekt*) as if it preceded thought or could be described or apprehended independently of thought. We know an object (*der Gegenstand*) only insofar as it is already an object of thought. However, Cohen challenged Kant's assumption that it was necessary to postulate the prior "givenness" of sensations (*Empfindung*) to thought: "Sensation finally can be nothing else but a question mark."[12] Kant's position, Cohen argued, confused consciousness in the psychological sense (*Bewusstheit*) with consciousness as the ground of knowledge in a purely logical sense (*Bewusstsein*). Thus he writes,

9. Cited in M. Beintker, *Die Gottesfrage in der Theologie Wilhelm Herrmanns* (Evangelische Verlagsanstalt, Berlin, 1976) p. 182 n. 51, from a letter of 11 March, 1964.
10. R. Bultmann, "Milestones in Books," *Exp.T.* LXX (1959), 125.
11. R. A. Johnson, *The Origins of Demythologizing. Philosophy and Historiography in the Theology of Rudolf Bultmann* (Brill, Leiden, 1974). Cf. especially pp. 32 and 39.
12. H. Cohen, *Logik der reinen Erkenntniss* (B. Cassirer, Berlin, 1902), p. 389.

"Whoever takes sensation as independent data for thought confuses *Bewusstheit* with *Bewusstsein*."[13]

Part of Cohen's purpose in extending Kant's approach in this way was to bring epistemology into relationship with current developments in science and mathematics, especially mathematical physics. Three of the most significant scientific thinkers in this connection were Hermann von Helmholtz, Heinrich Hertz, and Ludwig Boltzmann. Helmholtz, viewed in his lifetime as perhaps Germany's greatest scientist, argued for the subjectivity of sensory qualities, regarding these as signs of unknown objects interacting with our sense organs.[14] Indeed he went so far as to argue that space itself depends on man's bodily constitution, and that therefore "there could be alternative spaces and geometrics, each appropriate to a particular kind of nervous apparatus and necessary to the thing so constituted."[15] Helmholtz believed that this theory was faithful to Kant's philosophy, while admittedly in certain respects going beyond it, and that it was also in keeping with current work in physics and mathematics. The impact of Hertz and Boltzmann on German and Austrian thought at the turn of the century is set out clearly by Allan Janik in Janik and Toulmin's book *Wittgenstein's Vienna*.[16] Heinrich Hertz, as a student of Helmholtz, brought Kant's theory of knowledge into relation with theoretical physics. The central idea in Hertz's approach was the role played by "models" or "representations" (*Bilder* and *Darstellungen*). These are not, however, "ideas" in the empiricist or psychological sense, for which the term *Vorstellungen* was more frequently used. "*Darstellungen* are consciously *constructed* schemes for knowing."[17] Ludwig Boltzmann further eliminated any subjective reference to sensations by his work on statistical method, leaving only a short step, Janik argues, to the early Wittgenstein's notion of a *Bild* as representing "a possible situation in logical space," and to the role performed by truth-tables.[18]

In the work of Cohen and Natorp, the notion of "objects" now reappears not as the initial referent of thought, but "as the stated goal or end of thought. In its new status, the object, as the product of thought, replaces the Kantian 'thing'."[19] Natorp writes, "Objects are not 'given'; consciousness forms them. . . . All objectifying (is) the creative deed of

13. *Ibid.*, p. 392. For a discussion of the distinction cf. R. A. Johnson, *The Origins of Demythologizing*, pp. 44-50.
14. Cf. L. W. Beck, "Neo-Kantianism" in P. Edwards (ed.), *The Encyclopedia of Philosophy* (8 vols.; Macmillian and Free Press, New York, 1967) V, 468-73, especially p. 469.
15. *Ibid.*, p. 469.
16. A. Janik and S. Toulmin, *Wittgenstein's Vienna* (Wiedenfeld and Nicolson, London, 1973), especially pp. 132-48.
17. *Ibid.*, p. 140.
18. *Ibid.*, p. 144.
19. R. A. Johnson, *The Origins of Demythologizing*, p. 47.

210   HEIDEGGER, BULTMANN, GADAMER, AND WITTGENSTEIN

consciousness."[20] Thinking is therefore "objectifying" (objektivieren). This is not to suggest that such thinking is merely subjective in the sense of individualistic. Thinking, Cohen believes, apprehends Being (Sein). For thought constructs objects on the basis of universal laws. Indeed, "any assertion gains its status as true solely by virtue of its systematic position in a body of universal laws that, in turn, require each other on methodological grounds."[21] The result is that, as Johnson expresses it, "the principle of law has replaced sensory data as evidence for the objective validity of any cognitive judgement. . . . To know is to objectify in accordance with the principle of law."[22]

We are now in a position to see how this approach relates to Bultmann's theology. It must be admitted that very few commentators on Bultmann, with the notable exception of Roger Johnson, make more than an odd passing reference to Bultmann's indebtedness to Neo-Kantian thought. It is puzzling, and indeed in view of our own conclusions even disquieting, that in no other major discussion of the problem of objectification in Bultmann is any serious reference made to this aspect of the subject. Rosenthal, Jørgensen, and Malet all discuss his approach to the question of objectivity and objectification without reference to Neo-Kantian thought as such, although admittedly with passing references to Herrmann.[23] When Maurice Boutin discusses Bultmann's relation to philosophy, he examines the extent of his indebtedness only to Dilthey and to Heidegger.[24] Even Heinrich Ott's penetrating critique of Bultmann's dualism fails to take account of Neo-Kantian influences, even though he does refer to the influence of Herrmann.[25] We are convinced, however, by the case put forward by Johnson, and find it corroborated in writings of Bultmann above and beyond the passages which Johnson himself cites.

The key point made by Johnson is that Neo-Kantian philosophy does not influence Bultmann's thought in isolation from the Lutheranism which he also inherits. In Bultmann's theology, Johnson asserts, we find "not only Marburg Neo-Kantianism and Lutheran anthropology, but a particular fusion of the two. In Bultmann's theology one never encounters the

20. Quoted by R. A. Johnson, ibid., from P. Natorp, Religion innerhalb der Grenzen der Humanität (Mohr, Leipzig, 1894), p. 39.
21. L. W. Beck, in The Encyclopedia of Philosophy V, 471.
22. R. A. Johnson, The Origins of Demythologizing, pp. 49 and 50 (my italics).
23. K. Rosenthal, Die Überwindung des Subjekt-Objekt-Denkens als philosophisches und theologisches Problem, pp. 102-12; P. H. Jørgensen, Die Bedeutung des Subjekt-Objektverhältnisses für die Theologie, pp. 83-112; and A. Malet, The Thought of Rudolf Bultmann, pp. 5-21 et passim.
24. M. Boutin, Relationalität als Verstehensprinzip bei Rudolf Bultmann (Beiträge zur evangelischen Theologie 67; Kaiser, Munich, 1974); cf. pp. 181-90 and 511-67.
25. H. Ott, Geschichte und Heilsgeschichte in der Theologie Rudolf Bultmanns (Beiträge zur historischen Theologie 19; Mohr, Tübingen, 1955), pp. 1-57.

one apart from the other, but *always as present in and through the other.* . . . Bultmann's Lutheranism is inseparably bound up with the presuppositions of his Neo-Kantian philosophy."[26] How this occurs will not become fully apparent until we have examined Bultmann's indebtedness to nineteenth-century Lutheranism. However, at this stage the point may be made that objectification in accordance with the principle of law is seen not only as an epistemological principle, but as an attempt to extend the frontiers of human knowledge in a way which, so to speak, places that knowledge at man's disposal. "Knowledge" in this sense characterizes the realm of the human and the realm of "works" and of law. By contrast, God is encountered not in the objectified realm of knowing, but as the "Thou" of address and event.

In his essay of 1925, "What Does it Mean to Speak of God?" Bultmann rejects any attempt to make the affirmation of the existence of God "a general truth with its place in a system of cognitions (*Erkenntnissen*), universal truths (*allgemeinen Wahrheiten*) in a self-supporting system. . . . For God would be objectively given (*Da wäre Gott eine Gegebenheit*), and knowledge of that *given object* would be accessible to us and could be achieved at will."[27] On the one hand, "The work of God cannot be seen as a universal process, as an activity which we can observe (as we observe the workings of the laws of nature) apart from our own existence." On the other hand, "Nobody considers the living relationships by which he is bound to others in love, gratitude, and reverence to be functions of law—at least not when he is truly living in them."[28] The same contrast appears in Bultmann's well-known essay on myth some sixteen years later. To believe in the cross of Christ, he writes, "does not mean to concern ourselves . . . with an objective event (*ein objektiv anschaubares Ereignis*) . . . but rather to make the cross of Christ our own, to undergo crucifixion with him."[29]

The kind of dualism suggested to Bultmann, then, by the conjunction of Neo-Kantian epistemology and Lutheran theology is in one sense even more radical than Kant's own dualism of fact and value. Kant himself located an awareness of God, freedom, and immortality in the realm of practical reason. Even though these realities could not be apprehended by pure reason, they nevertheless related to man's moral experience. The theologian Albrecht Ritschl (1822-89), from whom Herrmann derived much of his thought, still stood in this Kantian tradition, locating the essence of Christianity in the realm of ethics, or of value, in contrast to

26. R. A. Johnson, *The Origins of Demythologizing*, p. 34 (my italics).
27. R. Bultmann, *F.U.* I, 60 (German, p. 32).
28. *Ibid.*, p. 59.
29. R. Bultmann, "New Testament and Mythology" in H.-W. Bartsch (ed.), *K.M.* I, 36; German *K.u.M.* I, 46.

the realm of facts. Under the Neo-Kantian revision of Kant's philosophy, however, Wilhelm Herrmann delimited the sphere of religion not only from the realm of pure reason, or science, but also from that of moral experience.[30] Morality, Herrmann stressed, always means independence, whereas in religion man feels himself in the power of a Being to whom he surrenders himself.[31] This is not to deny the place of the good within Christian faith. Herrmann writes, "The Christian can commune with God only when he desires what is good. . . . But . . . simply to desire the good cannot of itself be counted communion with God."[32]

In Herrmann and in Bultmann this becomes part and parcel of the theme that neither morality nor knowledge in accordance with law can be other than "works" in the Lutheran sense. Indeed, Bultmann points out that in this respect "Barth and Gogarten state the conclusions which are actually inherent in liberal theology. For who has emphasised more forcibly than W. Herrmann that there is no specifically Christian ethic?"[33] Bultmann argues that Herrmann's often-repeated theme "the laws of nature hide God as much as they reveal him" is to be interpreted comprehensively as "the equivalent of the constantly repeated assertion of Barth and Gogarten: 'There is no direct knowledge of God (*keine direkte Gotteserkenntnis*). God is not a given entity (*keine Gegebenheit*)."[34]

We shall see shortly that there is one particular way in which Bultmann believes Herrmann failed to carry through the full implications of his own insights. In spite of his rejection of the claims of pure reason, moral experience, or religious mysticism to absolute truth, Herrmann spoke of a "portrait of Jesus which he (i.e. the Chrisitan believer) carries within him as absolute truth."[35] In Bultmann's view, this makes faith dependent on knowledge of facts about the historical Jesus, and thereby upsets the whole of what Herrmann is trying to say. In order to acquire a more accurate picture of the point at issue, however, we must now consider Bultmann's indebtedness to nineteenth-century Lutheranism.

28. *Bultmann's Fusion of Neo-Kantian Epistemology with Nineteenth-Century Lutheranism: Objectification in Accordance with Law*

We have already noted Johnson's warning that Bultmann is not simply indebted to Lutheranism alone, but to a peculiar fusion in which it

30. W. Herrmann, *Die Religion im Verhältnis zum Welterkennen und zur Sittlichkeit* (Niemeyer, Halle, 1879).
31. W. Herrmann, *Systematic Theology* (Eng. Allen and Unwin, London, 1927), p. 31.
32. W. Herrmann, *The Communion of the Christian with God*, p. 298.
33. R. Bultmann, *F.U.* I, 45.
34. *Ibid.*, p. 33 (German, p. 6).
35. W. Herrmann, *The Communion of the Christian with God*, p. 77.

is inextricably bound up with Neo-Kantian epistemology. Johnson also provides a second valuable warning about the nature of Bultmann's Lutheranism. We must not confuse the Lutheranism of the nineteenth century, he urges, with Luther's own thought. He writes, "It is hermeneutical folly to attempt to specify the structure of Bultmann's thought by reference to the sixteenth-century theological concepts of Luther. . . . The Luther he knows is always mediated to him through the specific traditions of nineteenth-century Lutheranism."[36] In particular, "In Bultmann's version of Lutheran anthropology, the twentieth-century insecurity of the ego before a threatening world has replaced the sixteenth-century insecurity of the conscience before a judging God."[37]

While Johnson is one of the very few writers to discuss the influence of Neo-Kantian philosophy on Bultmann, most commentators on his theology allude to his connections with Lutheranism. Walter Schmithals, for example, reminds us of the "moderate Lutheranism" of Arthur Bultmann, his father, who was a pastor of the Evangelical-Lutheran Church, although his father was also beginnning to turn to liberal theology by the time Rudolf Bultmann was a student.[38] Bultmann himself explicitly asserts, "Our radical attempt to demythologize the New Testament is in fact a perfect parallel to St. Paul's and Luther's doctrine of justification by faith alone apart from the works of the Law. Or rather, it carries this doctrine to its logical conclusion in the field of epistemology. Like the doctrine of justification it destroys every false security. . . . Security can be found only by abandoning all security."[39]

Robert Funk takes up this point when he declares, "The fundamental question for Bultmann concerns the proper ground of faith, without which faith would no longer be faith."[40] Bultmann's conclusion, in essence, is that "faith must not aspire to an objective basis in dogma or in history on pain of losing its character as faith."[41] This means, in turn, that Bultmann is free "to pursue his study of Christian origins ruthlessly, since only false conceptions of the ground of faith are at stake."[42] We have already noted that it was at this one crucial point that he parted company from Herrmann. Herrmann believed that he was avoiding grounding faith either in mysticism, theoretical reason, or moral experience, in grounding it in the personality of Jesus of Nazareth. For Herrmann this was not merely a matter of "historical facts." Rather, the Christian believer is "set free by

36. R. A. Johnson, *The Origins of Demythologizing*, p. 33.
37. *Ibid.*, p. 34.
38. W. Schmithals, *An Introduction to the Theology of Rudolf Bultmann*, p. 3.
39. R. Bultmann, "Bultmann Replies to his Critics" in *K.M.* I, 210-11.
40. R. Bultmann, *F.U.* I, 14.
41. *Ibid.*, p. 15.
42. *Ibid.*

the significance which the inner life of the man Jesus has for him. . . . We start, indeed, from the records, but we do not grasp the fact they bring us until the enrichment of our own inner life makes us aware that we have touched the Living One. . . . The picture of a personality becomes visible to us. . . . The inner life of Jesus becomes part of our own sphere of reality."[43] Bultmann, however, insists that to build faith upon such a foundation is to try to base it upon "objective" facts; in effect, to base it upon "Christ after the flesh," rather than the Christ of believing faith.

For this very reason Bultmann is not concerned if the fires of historical criticism destroy much of our portrait of Jesus of Nazareth. In face of these fires, he writes, "I often have the impression that my conservative New Testament colleagues feel very uncomfortable, for I see them perpetually engaged in salvage operations. *I calmly let the fire burn*, for I see that what is consumed is only the fanciful portraits of Life-of-Jesus theology, and that means nothing other than 'Christ after the flesh'. . . . But the 'Christ after the flesh' is no concern of ours. How things looked in the heart of Jesus I do not know *and do not want to know*."[44]

Even this view, however, is not entirely original to Bultmann. The relationship between Lutheranism and a negative assessment of the value of historical inquiry for Christian faith appears first in the important writings of Martin Kähler (1835-1912). Kähler's concern for the centrality of justification by faith appears in his volume on systematic theology entitled *Die Wissenschaft der christlichen Lehre*, first published in 1883. This work is organized into three parts which concern, respectively, apologetics, dogmatics, and ethics. But in practice apologetics is set forth as the presupposition of justification by faith, dogmatics constitutes the content of justification by faith, and ethics concerns the relation between justification and moral responsibility. Paul Tillich sums up the work of his own teacher in the words: "Kähler . . . developed his ideas under the principle of the Reformers—'justification through faith by grace'."[45] Karl Barth, Braaten reminds us, saw Kähler as the first to dare to organize dogmatics around justification as a center.[46] However, it is probably as the author of *Der sogenannte historische Jesus und der geschichtliche, biblische Christus* that Kähler is most widely known today. In this work he sets forth his thesis that the "real" Christ is not the Jesus of Nazareth whose career can be reconstructed only by historical research. *"This real Christ is the Christ who is preached."*[47]

43. W. Herrmann, *The Communion of the Christian with God*, p. 74.
44. R. Bultmann, *F.U.* I, 132 (my italics; German, p. 101).
45. P. Tillich, "Foreword" in M. Kähler, *The So-Called Historical Jesus and the Historic, Biblical Christ* (Eng. Fortress Press, Philadelphia, 1964), p. xi.
46. C. E. Braaten, "Revelation, History, and Faith in Martin Kähler" in Kähler, *ibid.*, p. 8.
47. M. Kähler, *ibid.*, p. 66 (his italics).

Kähler argued that on the basis of Reformation theology the most learned theologian must be no better off and no worse off than the simplest Christian. Otherwise it would amount to the possibility of being justified on the basis of "works" of scholarly research. The Reformers, he argued, did not deliver men from the Pope in order to sell them back into the hands of scholars. But "historical research . . . requires the mastery of a sophisticated technique. . . . In this field no lay judgement is possible."[48] Kähler therefore concludes: "The historical Jesus of modern authors conceals from us the living Christ. . . . I regard the entire Life-of-Jesus movement as a blind alley."[49]

In this way Kähler brings us very close to Bultmann's own attitude towards historical research on the Gospels, especially in terms of its relationship to the Lutheran emphasis on justification through faith. It is worth noting that, in so doing, Kähler provides Bultmann with his radical contrast between objective past-history (*Historie*) and history which is significant for the present (*Geschichte*). However, it would be a mistake to conclude that Bultmann follows Kähler in regarding the "so-called" historical Jesus of Nazareth as only a pseudo-problem even for faith. On this particular matter, Ebeling warns us, there is a "very deep difference between their positions." He adds, "Bultmann faces the problem of the historical Jesus while Kähler attempts to unmask the 'so-called historical Jesus' as a pseudo-problem."[50]

Bultmann's concern to allow faith to be founded on nothing externally objective or "given" is thus more radical even than Herrmann's. However, we must not underestimate Herrmann's indebtedness to Lutheran perspectives. The particular interest which this holds for a study of Bultmann's thought is not only to underline the extent to which Bultmann drew Lutheran perspectives from Herrmann, but also to call attention to one point of connection between Lutheranism, as it was held by Herrmann, and liberalism. Herrmann insists that "we must first do away with the claim that faith, like every other means whereby men seek to come to God, is a human work."[51] But he then goes on to argue that the notion of faith as assent to doctrine is also thereby to regard it as a human work. He writes, "Luther knew a kind of faith which a man himself begets by bringing himself to assent to doctrines of some sort. Luther calls such a faith worthless, because it gives us nothing. The same holds good of acceptance of narratives of sacred scripture as true. This also is to Luther a 'natural work without grace'; even Turks and heathens may accomplish

48. *Ibid.*, p. 62.
49. *Ibid.*, pp. 43 and 46.
50. G. Ebeling, *Theology and Proclamation. A Discussion with Rudolf Bultmann* (Collins, London, 1966), p. 149 n. 3.
51. W. Herrmann, *The Communion of the Christian with God*, pp. 214-15.

it."[52] Herrmann then quotes Luther's words: "The true faith of which we speak cannot be made by our thoughts, but is purely a work of God in us."[53]

This has close connections not only with Bultmann's insistence that genuine faith is always faith in the bare word of God as address, but also with the observations made in his essay "Points of Contact and Conflict," published in 1946.[54] Bultmann declares, "God's action with man through his Word naturally has *no point of contact in man* (keinen Anknüpfungspunkt in Menschen) or in human intellectual life, to which God must accommodate himself. God's action in the first place brings to nothing the man that it seems to make alive. *God's action conflicts with man* (Gottes Handeln ist Widerspruch gegen den Menschen), and with man in his religion at that, in which he seeks to safeguard himself and to assert himself over against the world which oppresses him . . . just as for Paul Jewish service of the law is simply a means of achieving one's own glory. God's grace . . . can only be conceived of as grace by those who surrender their whole existence and let themselves fall into the unfathomable, dizzy depths without seeking for something to hold on to."[55]

Such statements, admittedly, have connections with Bultmann's debt to Barth and dialectical theology, as well as to nineteenth-century Lutheranism, and we shall consider this point briefly in our next section. The reference to man as seeking "to safeguard himself" also calls to mind our examination of Heidegger's notion of inauthentic existence, discussed in the previous two chapters. However, this is only to say that various elements in Bultmann's theology serve to strengthen and to support one another, shaping a firmly built system of thought. Bultmann's Lutheranism is never far from view, even if, as Johnson rightly warns us, it takes a form peculiar to nineteenth- and twentieth-century outlooks. Characteristically Bultmann writes in his *Theology of the New Testament*: "In his 'confession' of faith, the believer turns away from himself, confessing that all he is and has, he is and has through that which God has done. Faith does not appeal to whatever it itself may be as act or attitude, but to God's prevenient deed of grace."[56] In Bultmann's view such an outlook is not peculiar to Paul. To trace his many references to it would be beyond the scope of this study, but it is perhaps worth noting that even on a passage at first sight as unlikely as that of the Vine Discourse in John 15:1-11,

52. *Ibid.*, p. 215.
53. *Ibid.*, p. 216.
54. R. Bultmann, *E.P.T.*, pp. 133-50, and *G.u.V.* II, 117-32.
55. *Ibid.* (English, pp. 135-36; German, pp. 119-20).
56. R. Bultmann, *T.N.T.* I, 319.

Bultmann makes parallel comments.[57]

We have already stressed that Bultmann's Lutheranism is not that of the sixteenth century. He is concerned less with the problem of sin and guilt as such than with the more general question of whether man seeks to gain security by means of his own strength. It is now possible to see how this outlook relates both to Neo-Kantian philosophy and to the philosophy of Heidegger. On the one hand, man cannot reach God by objectifying thought which is in accordance with law. On the other hand, the attempt to do so is related closely to the attitude characterized as inauthentic existence or, more theologically, as justification by works. On the one hand, as Johnson expresses it, "Herrmann established the fundamental connection between an epistemology of objectification in accordance with law and the idea of work; Herrmann also bound together the idea of work with the theological meaning of justification by works . . . (and) established the meaning of justification by faith through the paradigm of the interpersonal relationships of friendship, love, and trust."[58] Bultmann fully appropriates this perspective. On the other hand, having already adopted this perspective, presumably before 1923, during the period from 1923 to 1927, when he was Heidegger's colleague, he drew from Heidegger a conceptuality which not only entailed the contrast between authentic and inauthentic existence, but also elucidated a conceptuality appropriate to the personal mode of relation in address and encounter.

Already, therefore, at least three sets of factors prepare the way for Bultmann's dualism. Justification by works stands in contrast to justification by faith; nature stands in contrast to grace; the indicative, and the realm of facts, stand in contrast to the imperative, and the realm of will; information is set over against address; objectification is set over against encounter. Other aspects of this dualism are yet to emerge, including Bultmann's use of Heidegger's contrasts between *Vorhandenheit* and *Existenz*, and between inauthentic and authentic existence; and the well-known contrast between *Historie* and *Geschichte*. However, before we comment further on this dualism, we must first consider other contributory factors to Bultmann's thought.

57. For example, on John 15:2 he writes, "Nobody can rest content in the knowledge of having borne fruit; no-one can rely on what he has achieved." On v. 4 he comments, "Faith is the unconditional decision to base oneself on the act of God, at the cost of giving up one's own ability . . . of allowing oneself to receive." Cf. R. Bultmann, *The Gospel of John. A Commentary* (Eng. Blackwell, Oxford, 1971), pp. 533 and 535.
58. R. A. Johnson, *The Origins of Demythologizing*, p. 197.

29. Bultmann's Indebtedness to the History of Religions School and to Current Biblical Scholarship: Kerygma and Myth

In his "Autobiographical Reflections" Bultmann refers to his theological teachers as including Harnack and Herrmann. But he also mentions Hermann Gunkel and Johannes Weiss, and in other writings he expresses his admiration for Wilhelm Bousset.[59] This group of scholars, together with perhaps Troeltsch, constitute a fourth major influence on Bultmann's thinking, namely the History of Religions School.

There are two ways in which the *religionsgeschichtliche Schule* decisively affected Bultmann's thought, both of which profoundly concern his hermeneutics. The first point is the emphasis which this approach brought with it on the strangeness of the New Testament figures, underlining their historical distance from modern man. We have noted that Bultmann shared the liberal concern of Harnack and others that the New Testament should be seen to be relevant to modern man. Yet the History of Religions School opened up the problem of a hermeneutical gulf which, from the point of view of liberalism, had to be bridged.

Norman Perrin expresses this point clearly. Commenting on Bultmann's relation to the History of Religions School, he observes: "He is heir therefore to the movement which . . . established the strange and foreign nature of the New Testament to the modern world. After several generations of thinking in terms of moral principles and ethical teaching which united the New Testament with the modern world, Jesus was suddenly seen as an apocalyptic visionary, and the New Testament in general was seen as saturated by mythical thinking and by the expectation of the miraculous. A great gulf opened up between the New Testament and modern man. Bultmann was enormously aware of this gulf . . . and his hermeneutics are ultimately an attempt to bridge it."[60] We have already discussed certain aspects of the problem of historical distance in our third chapter.

The second point arising from the History of Religions School is most clearly expressed by Bultmann himself in his programmatic essay on myth. The History of Religions School, he has just pointed out, "were the first to discover the extent to which the New Testament is permeated by mythology." However, he adds: "The importance of the New Testament, they saw, lay not in its teaching about religion and ethics but *in its actual religion and piety*. In comparison with that, all the dogma it contains, and therefore *all the mythological imagery (Vorstellungen) with its apparent objectivity, was of secondary importance or completely negligible*. The

59. R. Bultmann, "Autobiographical Reflections" in *E.F.*, pp. 335-36; and *F.U.* I, 270-74.
60. N. Perrin, *Jesus and the Language of the Kingdom. Symbol and Metaphor in New Testament Interpretation* (S.C.M., London, 1976), p. 10.

essence of the New Testament lay in the religious life it portrayed."[61] Admittedly in the same passage Bultmann criticizes the History of Religions School for failing to see that early Christian piety was eschatological rather than mystical. Indeed, in their own interpretation of the New Testament "the Kerygma has once more ceased to be kerygma. Like the liberals, they are silent about a decisive act of God in Christ proclaimed as the event of redemption."[62] However, they rightly define the primitive church "exclusively as a worshipping community, and this represents a great advance on the older liberalism."[63] Once we see, Bultmann argues, that what is important in the New Testament is religious devotion rather than "teaching," it is only a short step to seeing that what is important about its mythology is not the forms of the myth itself as teaching, but the religious attitude which it expresses and invites. Indeed in his discussion of the work of Wrede and Bousset at the end of his *Theology of the New Testament* Bultmann asserts that in "the intention of the history-of-religions school" religion is "an existential attitude."[64] Thus already, without reference to Heidegger and to later ideas, the foundations are well laid for the view that the New Testament itself invites the *interpretation* of myth in terms of human attitudes, even existential attitudes.

Only one more piece of the jigsaw needs to be added before we arrive at all the ingredients for Bultmann's form-critical work, embodied in *The History of the Synoptic Tradition*. Some writers seem to imply that Bultmann's form-criticism owes something to existentialism, and even to Heidegger. To invoke any allusion to Heidegger is a historical anachronism. Bultmann's *Geschichte der synoptischen Tradition* appeared in 1921, and he tells us that he was working on it when he was in Breslau between 1916 and 1920.[65] He did not return to Marburg until the Autumn of 1921, after a short period at Giessen. Heidegger did not arrive at Marburg until 1923. Up to that time he had written only his 1914 dissertation, *Die Lehre vom Urteil im Psychologismus*, and his work of 1916 on Duns Scotus. He began writing *Being and Time* only after his arrival at Marburg, and it was published in 1927. *The History of the Synoptic Tradition*, then, owes nothing to Heidegger, and probably virtually nothing to the impact of dialectical theology, which began to be significant for Bultmann from 1920 onwards.

The fifth piece of the puzzle, which served to shape Bultmann's thought, is the technical state of New Testament studies to date, including especially the work of William Wrede on the messianic secret and Albert

61. R. Bultmann, "New Testament and Mythology" in *K.M.*, p. 14 (my italics; German, p. 26).
62. *Ibid.*, p. 15.
63. *Ibid.*
64. R. Bultmann, *T.N.T.* II, 247.
65. R. Bultmann, *E.F.*, p. 337.

Schweitzer's devastating work *Von Reimarus zu Wrede*. We have already discussed the impact of Martin Kähler's thought on Bultmann's attitude to the relation between history and faith. His earlier work on form criticism also received further stimulus from the work of K. L. Schmidt, just as Gunkel's work on form criticism in Old Testament studies had provided a point of departure.

Wrede published his book *Das Messiasgeheimnis in den Evangelien* in 1901. He argued that the concept of the messianic secret, so basic for Mark, was part of the primitive church's own theology, read back into the life of Jesus. It was a matter of theology rather than history as such. Bultmann calls attention to the pivotal importance which Wrede's work held for him, on the very first page of *The History of the Synoptic Tradition*. He adds, "Mark is the work of an author who is steeped in the theology of the early Church, and who ordered and arranged the traditional material that he received in the light of the faith of the early Church."[66]

Schweitzer's survey of lives of Jesus from Reimarus to Wrede appeared in 1906, and served further to discredit the value of attempts to write lives of Jesus of Nazareth. In the light of the historical reconstructions proposed by such writers as Renan and D. F. Strauss, Schweitzer concluded that "historical research" had served only to remove those aspects of the life of Jesus which did not accord with the outlooks of nineteenth-century liberalism. Whereas Kähler had argued that the quest of the historical Jesus held only minimal value for faith, Schweitzer argued that the whole enterprise in itself was fraught with extreme difficulty. Bultmann's reaction to Schweitzer's conclusions is well expressed in his book *Jesus*, first published in 1926. He writes, "No attempt is here made to render Jesus a historical phenomenon psychologically explicable, and nothing really biographical . . . is included. . . . This book lacks all the phraseology which speaks of Jesus as a great man, genius, or hero; he appears neither as inspired nor inspiring. . . . *Interest in the personality of Jesus* is excluded. . . . We can now know almost nothing concerning the life and personality of Jesus, since the early Christian sources show no interest in either, are moreover fragmentary and often legendary; and other sources about Jesus do not exist."[67] Bultmann then alludes to the lack of value of the nineteenth-century lives of Jesus, and concludes, "Whoever reads Albert Schweitzer's brilliantly written *Quest of the Historical Jesus* must vividly realize this."[68]

66. R. Bultmann, *The History of the Synoptic Tradition* (Eng. Blackwell, Oxford, ²1968), p. 1.
67. R. Bultmann, *Jesus* (Mohr, Tübingen, ³1951); English, *Jesus and the Word* (Fontana, Collins, London, 1958), pp. 13 and 14 (his italics).
68. *Ibid.*, p. 14.

We earlier recalled Ebeling's warning that Bultmann's view was not to be equated with Kähler's, even though there are close connections between their two approaches. In his lecture on the historical Jesus and the Christian kerygma, given in 1960, he declares, "It is . . . obvious that the Kerygma presupposes the historical Jesus, however much it may have mythologized him. Without him there would be no Kerygma."[69] However, in his essay on the significance of the historical Jesus for Paul, written in 1929, he asserts, "*Any 'evaluation' of the 'personality' of Jesus* (Jede "Würdigung" der "Persönlichkeit" Jesu) *is wrong* and must be wrong, for it would be only a 'knowing after the flesh'."[70] His explanation of the meaning of "Christ after the flesh" recalls our discussion of Bultmann's relation to Neo-Kantianism. For it means, first, seeing Christ only "as a world phenomenon" (*als ein vorfindliches Weltphänomen*); and secondly, undertaking "a mere reckoning with the objects of the world" (*ein blosses Rechnen mit Weltlich-Vorfindlichen wäre*).[71] Hence for Paul it is not the "what" (*das Was*) of the historical Jesus that is important, but the mere "that" (*das Dass*) of his earthly career.[72]

All this harmonizes with what has emerged from the work of W. Wrede, K. L. Schmidt, and others, that the Gospels themselves served not to provide biographical information about the past life of the earthly Jesus, but to proclaim what he meant for the life of the church in the present. K. L. Schmidt, for example, concluded in his book *Der Rahmen der Geschichte Jesu*, published in 1919, that the earliest stratum of the Gospels consisted of small, isolated units which were only later woven into a continuous narrative. Hence at this stage there could be no question of portraying a life of Jesus in the sense of an evolving biography, while the more urgent issue was to discover the settings of the gospel pericopae.[73] In *The History of the Synoptic Tradition* Bultmann therefore endorses the verdict of Martin Dibelius that form criticism is not simply "a process of description and classification," but an attempt to establish (to use Gunkel's term) the *Sitz im Leben* of individual pericopae in relation to the preaching and worship of the primitive church.[74]

It might seem that we have digressed in describing an aspect of Bultmann's thought which has nothing to do with his hermeneutics.

69. R. Bultmann, "The Primitive Christian Kerygma and the Historical Jesus" in C. E. Braaten and R. A. Harrisville (eds.), *The Historical Jesus and the Kerygmatic Christ. Essays on the New Quest of the Historical Jesus* (Abingdon Press, New York, 1964), p. 18; pp. 15-42.
70. R. Bultmann, *F.U.* I, 239 (German, p. 207; his italics).
71. *Ibid.*
72. *Ibid.* (English, p. 238; German, p. 205).
73. Cf. W. G. Kümmel, *The New Testament. The History of the Investigation of its Problems*, pp. 327-30 for a convenient summary of Schmidt's claims.
74. R. Bultmann, *The History of the Synoptic Tradition*, pp. 3-4.

However, this is far from being the case. The issue is expressed clearly by Giovanni Miegge in an excellent discussion of the inner coherence of Bultmann's thought. He comments, "This interpretation of the origins of our canonical Gospels already contains within it the two poles of the problem. . . . On the one side is the *Kerygma*. . . . Form criticism, taking the primitive Christian *preaching* as the centre of its enquiry, laid stress on the idea that the Gospel is above all else proclamation, message. . . . The 'Christ-myth' is the centre of attraction around which the traditional elements of the *Kerygma* came to be organized; the 'myth' provides the 'framework' for the Gospel of Mark, and still more plainly that for the Gospel of John, in which the Jesus of history is entirely hidden behind the Christ of myth. . . . So then, from the earliest beginnings of the . . . work of Bultmann, we find clearly identified the two terms of our problem, the *Kerygma* and the myth."[75]

This approach is developed in the light of conclusions suggested by the History of Religions School about parallels with Judaism, Hellenism, and Gnostic religion. Jesus himself proclaims the Kerygma of the reign of God, although, as Bultmann later writes in his *Theology of the New Testament*, "the message of Jesus is a presupposition for the theology of the New Testament rather than a part of that theology itself."[76] What is new, as over against Judaism, is the message: "Now the time is come! God's reign is breaking in! The end is here!"(cf. Luke 10, 23, 24; Mark 2, 18, 19; Luke 10, 18).[77] However, the proclamation of Jesus as Messiah, Bultmann believes, is the work of the Palestinian Christian community. It expresses its own religious attitude by placing the figure of Jesus in the setting of mythology drawn mainly from Jewish apocalyptic. The Hellenistic Christian communities drew not on apocalyptic, but first of all on the language of the kyrios cult and the mystery religions, and secondly on the mythology of Gnosticism.

By the time Bultmann explicitly formulated his proposals about demythologizing, he had come to believe not only that the kerygma could not be eliminated, but also that mythology itself should be interpreted rather than simply dispensed with. One very important factor which led him to this conclusion was the work of Hans Jonas on Gnostic mythology. We shall refer later to the contribution of Jonas in greater detail. For the present, however, we may note that Jonas saw the myths of Gnosticism not simply as descriptions of heavenly entities or events, but as means of expressing a particular self-understanding. Such a view of myth suggested in advance of Bultmann's program, before 1934, that the interpretation of

---

75. G. Miegge, *Gospel and Myth in the Thought of Rudolf Bultmann* (Eng. Lutterworth Press, London, 1960), pp. 19-20.
76. R. Bultmann, *T.N.T.*, p. 3.
77. *Ibid.*, p. 6.

myth in existential terms was demanded by the very nature of myth itself.

Apart from this additional factor suggested by the work of Jonas, however, Bultmann's work can be seen as already implying the two poles of kerygma and myth well before Heidegger's philosophy enters the picture. The kerygma can on no account be eliminated; myth is a means whereby Christian communities expressed varying responses to the kerygma in their own faith and worship, and may take the form of a succession of interpretations and re-interpretations. Bultmann's relation to dialectical theology and to Heidegger's philosophy allows him to *develop* his emphasis on kerygma and myth in a particular direction, but it does not account for the *origins* of this basic contrast and perspective.

30. *Bultmann's Indebtedness to Dialectical Theology: The Final Setting of the Terms of the Hermeneutical Problem*

The criticism most frequently levelled against Bultmann is that he has reduced Christian theology to a theology of man. It is therefore essential to underline the fact that, whatever the final *effects* of his hermeneutical program, this has never been Bultmann's intention. This is clear from an important statement in which he expresses his acceptance of the central insight of dialectical theology. He declares, "The subject of theology is *God*, and the chief charge to be brought against liberal theology is that it has dealt not with God but with men. God represents the radical negation and sublimation of man. Theology whose subject is God can therefore have as its content only the 'word of the cross'. . . . But that word is a 'stumbling-block' to men. Hence the charge against liberal theology is that it has sought to remove this stumbling-block or to minimize it."[78] Bultmann writes, "The one essential is . . . to listen to the 'stumbling block' of God's Word, the Word which declares that the world exists in sin and that man in the world can do nothing which can sustain the character of service to God. . . . *God represents the total annulment of man, his negation, calling him in question, indeed judging him.*"[79]

It is worth noting, once again, how this outlook is connected, in Bultmann's approach, with Lutheranism and Neo-Kantianism. "The world which faith wills (*will*) to grasp is absolutely unattainable by means of scientific research (*mit der Hilfe der wissenschaftlichen Erkenntnis*)."[80] Nothing can claim "absolute value" (*absolute Geltung*) which stands within the nexus of "entities which exist only within an

78. R. Bultmann, *F.U.* I, 29 (his italics).
79. *Ibid.*, pp. 42 and 46 (Bultmann's italics).
80. *Ibid.* (English, p. 31; German, p. 4).

immense inter-related complex" (*Grössen innerhalb eines grossen Relationszusammenhangs*).[81] Christianity is not simply "a phenomenon of this world, subject to the laws of social psychology . . . not if *God* is the subject of theology."[82] "At every point—against both pantheism of nature and pantheism of history—the polemic of Barth and Gogarten is valid. . . . It is a protest against every kind of direct knowledge of God."[83] Ritschlian theology "mistakenly places the origin of faith . . . in man, in man's sense of value." But the basis of faith cannot be "here in this world"; for "God is wholly 'Beyond'." "Justification . . . is never present except in the 'Beyond', in God's judgement."[84]

At this point it may well seem that we have travelled furthest away from any point of contact between Bultmann and Heidegger. If God "represents the total annulment of man," how can Heidegger's analysis of Dasein have any relevance to Bultmann's theology and hermeneutics?

This question can perhaps best be answered with reference to Bultmann's essay of 1925 entitled "What Does It Mean to Speak of God?"[85] In this essay he tries to hold together two sets of principles which he admits appear at first sight to be incompatible with each other. On the one hand, he urges, theology obliges us to speak of God. On the other hand, "speaking about God becomes sin. And *sin* it remains, even when it arises from a sincere quest for God."[86] His solution to this apparent paradox is to insist that what is "not legitimate" is "to speak about God in general statements, in universal truths—which are valid without reference to the concrete existential (*existentielle*) position of the speaker."[87] The "sin" is to try to speak *about* God. Bultmann takes up Luther's comment on Genesis 3:1-2 that Adam's sin was not so much the eating of the forbidden fruit as arguing *about* God (*disputare de deo*), thereby making God's claim (*Anspruch*) on him "a debatable question."[88] But this very point suggests a second apparent contradiction. If talk of God can only take place with reference to "the concrete existential position of the speaker," Bultmann asserts: "It is clear that if a man will speak of God, he must evidently *speak of himself (von sich selbst renden).*" However, as Bultmann himself asks, "If I speak of myself, am I not speaking of man? And is it not essential to the concept of God that God is the 'Wholly Other', the annulment of man?"[89]

81. *Ibid.*
82. *Ibid.*, p. 32.
83. *Ibid.*, p. 35.
84. *Ibid.*, pp. 36, 40, 41, and 51.
85. R. Bultmann, *F.U.* I, 53-65 (German, pp. 26-37).
86. *Ibid.*, p. 55 (German, p. 28).
87. *Ibid.*, p. 53 (German, p. 26).
88. *Ibid.*, p. 54 (German, p. 27).
89. *Ibid.*, p. 55 (German, p. 28).

Bultmann tries to answer this difficulty, first, by making the negative point that he does not mean, by man's speaking of himself, his speaking of his religious experience. It does not mean "talk of experience and of the inner life" (*Reden von Erleben und innerem Leben*).[90] At this very point, however, we find that Bultmann is intertwining a theological theme from Lutheranism and dialectical theology with a philosophical theme from Neo-Kantianism. On the one hand, what he is rejecting is man's setting before himself "*our* inner life, *our* experience, *on the basis of which* we trust in God . . ." (Bultmann's italics). On the other hand, what he is rejecting is taking the "self on which I rely" as "something objective," which is "a phantom without existential reality (*das ich als das Gegegebene nehme, ist ein Phantom ohne existentielle Wirklichkeit*)."[91] It is not simply that this "I" has a stance of reliance on the self, which is to be excluded on theological grounds; it is also that this "I" has thereby objectified (*objektivieren*) itself.

The only way, then, in which theology, as talk of God, is possible at all is if some means can be found whereby the "I" may talk about itself in a way which avoids the objectification of the self. It is precisely at this point, we shall see, that Heidegger's conceptuality becomes most relevant to Bultmann's concerns.

Only on this basis is it possible to explain how what Bultmann says in an essay such as his "Points of Contact and Conflict" of 1946 can be consistent with what he is saying in other writings of similar date. In this 1946 essay he writes, "God's action with man through his Word naturally has *no point of contact* (keinen Anknüpfungspunkt) *in man* . . . to which God must accommodate himself. God's action in the first place brings to nothing the man it seeks to make alive. *God's action conflicts with man* (Gottes Handeln ist Widerspruch gegen den Menschen), and with man in his religion at that."[92] We have already noted Bultmann's use of these phrases in connection with his Lutheranism. Here, however, our point is different. The question is how such emphatic and clear-cut expressions of dialectical theology can be reconciled with statements which seem at first sight to imply almost a naturalistic "point of contact" in the setting of hermeneutics.

In the same essay Bultmann certainly allows that "man's language is the point of contact for the Word of God spoken by the human preacher."[93] In terms of the actual communication of concepts, he reminds us, in the New Testament Paul makes contact with the natural theology of the Stoics in such passages as Romans 1:18, 19. It is, he

90. *Ibid.*, p. 56 (German, p. 29).
91. *Ibid.*
92. R. Bultmann, *E.P.T.*, p. 135; cf. pp. 133-50; *G.u.V.* II, 119; cf. pp. 117-32.
93. *Ibid.*, p. 137.

writes, "paradoxically enough in the very conflict that the point of contact is created, or rather, revealed."[94] Conflict can exist only where a relationship is already presupposed. For example, a man cannot "contradict" a stone; only God or another man with whom he already stands in a certain relationship. Although Barth himself might not go quite this far, Emil Brunner's approach to the problem is little different from what Bultmann has said up to this point. But in other writings he appears to go much further than this. Thus, as we observed in our discussion about pre-understanding in chapter four, in his essay on hermeneutics which appeared in 1950 Bultmann writes, "In human existence an *existentiell* knowledge about God is alive in the form of the inquiry about 'happiness' . . . the meaning of the world, and . . . the nature of each person's particular 'being'."[95] In *Jesus Christ and Mythology*, he declares, "The question of God and the question of myself are identical."[96]

It is sometimes claimed by critics of Bultmann that he has borrowed such a view from Heidegger's philosophy or, rather, from a Christianized version of it. But we have seen that Bultmann's belief that to speak of God is necessarily to speak of man *originates* in a quite different context of ideas. Ironically, it is his very desire to do justice to the insights of dialectical theology that leads him to look for a solution to the hermeneutical problem in the direction of Heidegger's non-objectifying language about man. The disclosure of God is seen *through* the *self*-understanding of Dasein. But Bultmann turns to Heidegger only because he has first accepted the Neo-Kantian assumption that knowledge which objectifies in accordance with law is a knowledge in which *man* does the shaping and seizes the mastery. Therefore, in the light of his Lutheranism and his dialectical theology, talk of God cannot take this form. *Heidegger in no way sets the terms of the problem.* Other considerations have dictated the terms of the problem; Bultmann now turns to Heidegger to help him towards a solution of it.

94. *Ibid.*, p. 141.
95. *Ibid.*, p. 257.
96. R. Bultmann, *Jesus Christ and Mythology*, p. 53; cf. pp. 52-55.

CHAPTER IX

Further Philosophical Ingredients in Bultmann's Hermeneutics

31. *Differing Roles of Heidegger's Philosophy in Relation to Bultmann's Hermeneutics*

Three points need to be made, initially, about the role of Heidegger's thought in relation to Bultmann's hermeneutics. Two of these points emerge in Bultmann's important essay "Die Geschichtlichkeit des Daseins und der Glaube," in which he carefully replies to criticisms brought against his use of Heidegger's philosophy in an essay written by Gerhardt Kuhlmann in 1929.[1] In his own essay Kuhlmann argues that because of his dependence on Heidegger's secular philosophy Bultmann's theology can never be more than an analysis of the situation of the "natural" man. Bultmann agrees that at the level of ontic or *existentiell* decision, encounter, or experience, Christian theology says something distinctive over and above the scope of philosophy. "Theology . . . speaks of a specific 'how'—yet not by jumping into a hole that has been left open by philosophy in the totality of what is knowable or in the system of the sciences. . . . Philosophy . . . points out that the 'that' of a particular concrete 'how' is essential to man, without ever actually speaking of a concrete 'how'. Its real theme is not existence but existentiality, not the factual, but factuality."[2] In other words, philosophical analysis remains relevant at the level of ontology, even if philosophers and theologians part company at the ontic level.

---

1. G. Kuhlmann, "Zum theologischen Problem der Existenz: Fragen an Rudolf Bultmann" in *Z.Th.K.* N.F. X (1929), 28-57; and R. Bultmann, "Die Geschichtlichkeit des Daseins und der Glaube: Antwort an Gerhardt Kuhlmann, *Z.Th.K.* N.F. XI (1930), 339-64; Eng. in *E.F.*, pp. 107-29.
2. R. Bultmann, *E.F.*, p. 109.

Bultmann also expresses this less technically. He writes, "The *man of faith* is in any case a *man*."[3] Hence in a formal or ontological sense the theologian may draw on philosophical perspectives which clarify *conceptually* questions about human existence. Bultmann rightly asserts, "*Every* theology is dependent *for the clarification of its concepts* upon a *pretheological understanding of man that, as a rule, is determined by some philosophical tradition.*"[4] But this is no way compromises theology itself. (Indeed, we may add, this recognition of the situation simply makes theology all the more critically self-conscious of its own problems and tasks.) Bultmann suggests an analogy. A friendless person, he argues, knows something of what friendship is. Otherwise he could not even wish for friendship. But the "event" of friendship operates on a different level. "In knowing my friend in the *event* of friendship, the events of my life become new—'new' in the sense that is valid only for me. . . . However well I can know in advance and in general what a friend is, and also know how that friendship must surely make my life new, the one thing I can never know in advance and in general is what my friend is to me. And so it is indeed that the 'word' of proclamation tells me 'nothing more than what I already knew . . . in my profane self-understanding.' . . . What 'more' then does the man of faith know? This—that revelation has actually encountered him, that he really lives, that he is in fact graced. . . . He knows that through the *event* of revelation the events of his life become new—'new' in a sense that is valid only for the man of faith."[5]

This brings us to the second of our three points. It is precisely *because* God is "wholly Other" and outside the whole system of human knowledge that Bultmann believes himself to be secure against the possibility of compromising the truth of revelation by drawing on concepts borrowed from philosophy. In accordance with the outlook of dialectical theology, revelation itself is strictly an event, an address, an encounter, which lies outside the sphere of "this-worldly" ontological description. Faith, too, is the gift of God, and not a matter either of human endeavor, or even of the contents of human consciousness. By contrast, theology is a descriptive activity which remains in the realm of thought and human concepts. This is by no means to decry the role of reason or thought. Bultmann writes, "It is impossible to think highly enough of reason. Precisely when reason has followed its road to the end, the point of crisis is reached and man is brought to the great question mark over his own existence."[6] Nevertheless, theology as such, in Bultmann's view, cannot be exactly equated with revelation or faith. The former moves in the realm

3. *Ibid.*, p. 110 (Bultmann's italics).
4. *Ibid.*, p. 114 (italics first Bultmann's then mine).
5. *Ibid.*, pp. 116-17 (Bultmann's italics).
6. R. Bultmann, *F.U.* I, 46.

of description and the indicative mood; the latter moves in the realm of address, event, and the imperative. In *this* sense, the more rigorously critics of Bultmann charge him with compromising Christian revelation by drawing on philosophical concepts, the more firmly Bultmann can insist that, as well as missing the mark, such criticisms merely serve to establish the self-consistency of his own position. For "God is wholly 'Beyond' (*Gott ist der schlechthin Jenseitige*)."[7]

Thirdly, there is in any case one positive point of connection between the actual subject-matter of Heidegger's philosophy and the distinctive outlook of dialectical theology. In his essay "Adam, Where art Thou?" Bultmann forcefully brings out this emphasis on individual responsibility and decision. He writes, "In his decision (*Entscheidung*) at a given moment . . . lies the attainment or the loss of his real being (*seines eigentlichen Seins*). For it is here in decision, and not in the upward flight of his thoughtful contemplation towards the timeless world of the divine, that he stands before God. For it is in the concrete, historical event that God is to be met with, as the One who makes demands and judges and pardons."[8]

The same emphasis occurs seventeen years earlier in Bultmann's essay on the significance of dialectical theology for New Testament studies, written in 1928. In language reminiscent of Heidegger, Bultmann speaks of the importance of "decisions in which man does not choose something for himself but chooses himself as his possibility (*sich als seine Möglichkeit wählt*)."[9] This is what Bultmann understands by "the historical nature of man's being" (*die Geschichtlichkeit des menschlichen Seins*) and his being as "a potentiality to be" (*ein Sein-Können*).[10] But the insight into the historical nature of man's being, Bultmann asserts, is "the meaning of the slogan 'dialectical theology'."[11] He then proceeds to draw an inference about the message of dialectical theology for "the scientific study of the New Testament." If what is at issue is nothing other than the historical nature of man's being, Bultmann concludes: "We shall therefore achieve a final understanding of the text only when we reach final clarity on the possibilities of human existence (*die Möglichkeiten menschlicher Existenz*). But since as human possibilities these are at the same time our possibilities . . . *they can be understood only so far as we comprehend our own existence*."[12]

7. *Ibid.*, p. 41 (German, p. 14). Bultmann's formulation is more radical than R. Otto's "Wholly Other," since while he stressed that God transcended the merely moral and rational, Otto still located God within the realm of creaturely feeling; cf. *F.U.* I, 49-50.
8. R. Bultmann, *E.P.T.*, p. 125; and *G.u.V.* II, 111.
9. R. Bultmann, *F.U.* I, 149 (German, p. 118).
10. *Ibid.*
11. *Ibid.*
12. *Ibid.*, p. 150 (German, p. 119; my italics).

We have returned, then, to the key point which we reached at the end of the previous chapter. Dialectical theology, in conjunction with Bultmann's peculiar fusion of Lutheran theology and Neo-Kantian epistemology, had already set the terms of the hermeneutical question: how can man talk of the God who is "Beyond" except through language about *Dasein* which avoids objectification? Bultmann expresses his hostility towards objectifying language precisely in the essay on talk of God.[13] The subject-object perspective, he argues, has dominated philosophy from the age of Greece to the Enlightenment. In this tradition, whether the dominant philosophy happens to have been idealism or materialism "in both views the picture of the world is conceived without reference to our own existence (*unserer eigenen Existenz*). We ourselves are observed as an object among other objects (*als ein Objekt unter andern Objekten*)."[14]

This perspective, Bultmann argues, is always attractive to man. He desires the traditional perspective of a "world-view" (*Weltanschauung*) so that he can "dismiss the problem of his existence (*Existenz*) from his mind, when his existence becomes shattered and precarious. He need not take the moment of crisis seriously, for he can understand it simply as a special case of a general class (*als einen Fall des Allgemeinen*), fit it into a context (*einen Zusammenhang*), objectify it (*objektivieren*) and so find a way out of it."[15] However, in practice "the distinction between subject and object must be kept separate from the question of our own existence."[16] Existence, Bultmann insists, is "*your* business" at an *existentielle* level: *tua res agitur*. On any other basis we are in a double dilemma: "We cannot talk about our existence since we cannot talk about God. And we cannot talk about God since we cannot talk about our existence."[17] The only answer to the problem, in Bultmann's words, is that we should talk not *about* but *from* God (*aus Gott*); and that we should talk not *about* our own existence, but from within it.[18] Bultmann illustrates the consequences of this change of viewpoint. He writes, "We cannot say, for example, that because God rules reality, he is also my Lord. Only when man knows himself in his own existence to be claimed by God, has he reason to speak of God as the Lord of reality."[19] Talk which ignores the element in which alone we can have reality, namely talk which ignores our own existence, is, Bultmann claims, self-deceit.

In this way we reach a conclusion which, unless we trace its basis in Bultmann's thought, would easily be open to misunderstanding. Walter

13. R. Bultmann, *F.U.* I, 53-65 (German, pp. 26-37).
14. *Ibid.*, p. 58 (German, p. 31).
15. *Ibid.*, p. 59 (German, p. 31).
16. *Ibid.* (German, p. 32).
17. *Ibid.*, p. 60 (German, p. 33).
18. *Ibid.*, pp. 56 and 60 (German, pp. 29 and 33).
19. *Ibid.*, p. 60 (German, p. 33).

Schmithals sums up Bultmann's conclusion with the sentence: "Theology as talk of God on the basis of his revelation is possible only if in talking of God it does not talk *about* God but *of man.*"[20] Although we have cited Bultmann's essay "What Does It Mean to Speak of God?" as our primary source on this issue, this approach of course permeates the whole of Bultmann's theology and hermeneutics. In *Jesus Christ and Mythology* he sets this principle in the context of the problem of pre-understanding, and concludes, "The question of God and the question of myself are identical."[21] More significantly and more specifically Bultmann writes in his *Theology of the New Testament* that Paul's theology "deals with God not as He is in Himself but only with God as He is significant for man, for man's responsibility and man's salvation. Correspondingly, it does not deal with the world and men as they are in themselves, but constantly sees the world and man in their relation to God. *Every assertion about God is simultaneously an assertion about man, and vice versa.* . . . Therefore Paul's theology can best be treated as his doctrine of man."[22]

We must reiterate, however, that there are two different ways of speaking of man, and two different ways of speaking of God. When Bultmann asserts in his essay "The Problem of 'Natural Theology' " that "even the natural man can speak of God, because in his existence he knows about God," this is still knowledge *about* God, in the sense of asking the *question* of God.[23] A. Malet comments, "All he attains to is the *idea* of God. Working from nature and history we shall never find God, because God is neither in nature nor in history."[24] On the other hand, Bultmann writes in the same essay on natural theology that there is another way of talking which is "based only on the specific moment. It cannot be theoretical speculation about an idea in a system of thought; it must be only a specific act of faith in obedience to the demand of a specific situation."[25]

Schubert Ogden argues that Bultmann's acceptance of the principle of dialectical theology concerning what Kierkegaard called the "infinite qualitative difference" between God and man represents the pivotal point of his whole thought.[26] He then goes on to argue that "there can be no doubt that the relation of God to the world . . . is significantly illumined by the analogous relation that exists between the self and its world."[27] This relation, he adds, is clarified by existentialist philosophy. Taken as a

20. W. Schmithals, *An Introduction to the Theology of Rudolf Bultmann*, p. 37.
21. R. Bultmann, *Jesus Christ and Mythology* (S.C.M., London, 1958), p. 53.
22. R. Bultmann, *T.N.T.* I, 190-91 (my italics).
23. R. Bultmann, *F.U.* I, 324.
24. A. Malet, *The Thought of Rudolf Bultmann*, p. 90 (his italics).
25. R. Bultmann, *F.U.* I, 331.
26. S. Ogden, "Introduction" in R. Bultmann, *E.F.*, pp. 14-23.
27. *Ibid.*, p. 16.

very general summarizing statement, this is true. But it must not be understood to mean simply that Bultmann applied Heidegger's view of Dasein to God by analogy. The precise *role* played by Heidegger's philosophy in Bultmann's thought is more complex. First of all, his continuity with liberal thought insures his concern about the relevance of theology to modern man. Secondly, his relation to Lutheranism and to Neo-Kantianism places God outside the realm of thought which objectifies in accordance with general laws. Next, he draws from the History of Religions School the belief that the reality of God was actualized for the primitive communities in faith, in worship, and in their response to the kerygma, rather than in the acceptance of certain *ideas* about God. In the light of all these varied approaches, it seemed that a contrast between kerygma and myth was important for the understanding of the New Testament. Dialectical theology now seems to underline and confirm the seriousness of the problem of objectification in relation to talk of God.

Neither the terms of the problem nor how Bultmann wishes to solve it has been dictated by Heidegger. Heidegger's role is to offer a conceptuality which seems almost to have been designed to achieve the very task with which Bultmann was already grappling. It is not simply a matter of Heidegger's providing a vocabulary which is supposedly more intelligible to modern man than that of the New Testament itself. By his analysis of Dasein, Heidegger offers a way of talking about the self which apparently avoids the problem of objectifying it, and which promises to disclose truth beyond the self *through* self-understanding. Just as for Bultmann the disclosure of God is bound up with the disclosure of myself, so Heidegger believes that Being can be disclosed only through self-understanding. Moreover, self-understanding is not merely a matter of human "consciousness," which would bring us back again to the problem of self-understanding. It involves the whole of Dasein as care, and in particular individuates Dasein in resoluteness. Heidegger's philosophy does more than provide a descriptive model for God's relation to man and the world, and does more than provide a hermeneutical vocabulary. It *is* Bultmann's hermeneutic, in the sense that it makes talk of God possible; not merely that it makes such talk intelligible to modern man.

At the same time, when all this has been said, it must be added that the role of Heidegger's thought in relation to Bultmann's hermeneutics may be construed in more ways than one. To anyone who does not begin where Bultmann begins, with the epistemological presuppositions shaped by his relation to Lutheranism, Neo-Kantianism, and dialectical theology, the significance of Heidegger for hermeneutics takes a different form. Heidegger's philosophy may be seen, for example, as providing a corrective to the domination of New Testament hermeneutics by the perspective of idealist or Cartesian philosophy. Seen in this light, the main role of

Heidegger's philosophy is to provide a conceptuality whereby man in the New Testament can be viewed in terms of his possibilities rather than as spirit and substance. Heidegger provides a vocabulary which makes such an interpretation possible and meaningful.

Our own evaluation of Heidegger's role in relation to Bultmann's hermeneutics takes a middle course between these two alternatives. On the one hand, we do not accept Bultmann's own view of the radical nature of Heidegger's role in relation to New Testament hermeneutics, because we do not start by accepting the terms of the problem laid down by the peculiar relationship in Bultmann's thought between Lutheranism, dialectical theology, and Neo-Kantian philosophy. This transforms justification by faith into an *epistemological* principle, and thereby makes hermeneutics hang on the problem of objectification. This is not to deny Bultmann's valid distinction between talking *about* God and talking *from* God, nor to call in question John Calvin's belief that knowledge of God and knowledge of the self are bound up with each other. However, as H. P. Owen puts it, " 'Believing in' is impossible without some measure of 'believing that'."[28] On the other hand, however, Heidegger's attempt to reach through behind the subject-object contrast does more than simply provide a "personalist" vocabulary for New Testament interpretation. In our conclusions to a previous chapter we argued that Heidegger made an important contribution in this respect, which had profound consequences for biblical hermeneutics, not least for parable-interpretation, especially in encouraging the interpreter to see the New Testament as bringing the reader face to face with a reality which transcended the merely cognitive and discursive.

It is possible, then, to view Heidegger's role in relation to Bultmann's hermeneutics in at least three ways, which are not necessarily incompatible with one another. We shall return to this point again later. Meanwhile, Bultmann's preoccupation with the problem of objectification in the context of hermeneutics raises another related question. If the biblical writings actually presupposed a non-objectifying view of man, the problem of the *intelligibility* of this language would have been acute. Public criteria of meaning are established by the emergence of a historical tradition in the life of Israel and the primitive church in the light of which certain utterances about the saving activity of God become meaningful. What redemption *is*, for example, becomes meaningful in the light of a tradition of occurrences *in the world* which begin with the Exodus and continue through Israel's judges. To be sure, Bultmann rightly rejects criticisms that he has relegated acts of God to the "inner" life of man. Barth's

28. H. P. Owen, "Revelation" in *T.R.B.*, p. 47.

criticism here is wide of the mark.[29] Nevertheless, we have already seen that for Bultmann, as Malet puts it, "God is neither in nature nor in history." We shall compare this approach in due course, however, with Wittgenstein's analogy: "Everyone says he knows what a beetle is only by looking at *his* beetle.—Here it would be quite possible for everyone to have something different in his box. . . . One can 'divide through' by the thing in the box; it cancels out, whatever it is."[30]

Most probably Bultmann would respond by pointing out that Wittgenstein is concerned only with human life and human language. But in his whole approach to hermeneutics Bultmann stresses that the Christian man is still a *man*, and that theological language is still *language*. If his discussion of "talk of God" takes us, apparently, out of the realm of objectifying thought, he nevertheless begins with "life" in his approach to the problem of hermeneutics. How far this discussion takes us back into the realm of "ordinary" language is uncertain. For in his essay on talk of God Bultmann says, puzzlingly, "One cannot speak *about* love (über *Liebe*) at all, unless the speaking about it is itself an act of love."[31] And yet, as we have seen in his essay "Die Geschichtlichkeit des Daseins und der Glaube," written only five years later, he argues on the basis of the assumption that a friendless person knows full well what friendship is. "If such a person succeeds in finding a friend, what 'more' does he then know than he already knew in his friendless self-understanding?"[32] We must therefore look more closely at Bultmann's approach to the problem of "life" and pre-understanding in hermeneutics. Because this is bound up with his relation to Dilthey, it is not easily separable from his approach to questions about history.

32. *Bultmann's Hermeneutics and the Philosophy of Wilhelm Dilthey*

At first sight it may seem surprising that Bultmann looks to Wilhelm Dilthey and to R. G. Collingwood for support for his own views on hermeneutics and history. In his essay "The Problem of Hermeneutics," which appeared in 1950, he appeals to Dilthey's work explicitly more than a dozen times in little more than two dozen pages.[33] In his Gifford Lectures of 1957, entitled *History and Eschatology*, he declares, "The best that is said about the problems of history is, in my view, contained in

29. R. Bultmann, *E.P.T.*, pp. 259-60, where he attacks Barth's statements in *Church Dogmatics* III/2.
30. L. Wittgenstein, *P.I.*, sect. 293.
31. R. Bultmann, *F.U.* I, 53 (German, p. 26).
32. R. Bultmann, *E.F.*, p. 116.
33. R. Bultmann, *E.P.T.*, pp. 234, 235, 238, 239, 240, 243, 247, 248, 250, 251; cf. pp. 234-61.

the book of R. G. Collingwood, *The Idea of History* (1946, 1949)."[34] Yet Dilthey, in effect, tries to solve the hermeneutical problem on the basis of a view of human nature as constant throughout history, and one of the central ideas in Collingwood is that of the re-enactment of "thought." William Dray actually classifies both Dilthey and Collingwood, together with Croce and Hegel, as the main idealist philosophers of history.[35] It is worth noting in passing that in spite of their common Kantian inheritance, sharp divergences appear between Dilthey and Neo-Kantian philosophy. These divergences have been outlined and discussed by Rudolf A. Makkreel.[36] However, Bultmann draws on Dilthey's thought selectively, and does not endorse his philosophy as a whole. He is more open to criticism in his use of Collingwood's work, and such criticisms have very forcefully put forward in an article by Jasper Hopkins on this subject.[37]

Wilhelm Dilthey (1833-1911) saw that historical understanding is not a matter of "explanation" in terms of general laws which are relevant to the sciences. The methods and laws of the *Naturwissenschaften* are to be distinguished from those of the *Geisteswissenschaften*. The latter concern the particularities of human life (*das Leben*) and understanding (*Verstehen*). What Dilthey called the "Critique of Historical Reason" was, to use the words of H. A. Hodges, "an appreciative understanding of the meaning and value of the unique individual," rather than "an explanation of events and processes through general laws."[38] However, Dilthey also insisted that the methods of historical understanding were not for this reason unscientific. This approach, he argued, has universal validity (*Allgemeingültigkeit*).

Life, for Dilthey, included man's thinking, feeling, and willing, and constitutes the subject-matter of history. Hence, as Alan Richardson puts it, "The historian, because he is himself a historical being, can project himself into the experience of others and thus enlarge his own present experience through the understanding of the past. Historical understanding means to re-live (*nacherleben*) the past experience of others and so to make it one's own."[39] In Dilthey's own well-known words, "Understanding is a rediscovery of the I in the Thou. . . . This identity of mind in the I, in the Thou, in every subject within a community, in every system of culture . . . and of world history, makes possible the joint result of the

34. R. Bultmann, *History and Eschatology* (Edinburgh University Press, 1957, rpt. 1975), p. 130.
35. H. Dray, *Philosophy of History* (Prentice-Hall, Englewood Cliffs, N.J., 1964), p. 3.
36. R. A. Makkreel, "Wilhelm Dilthey and the Neo-Kantians" in *J.H.P.* VII (1969), 423-40.
37. J. Hopkins, "Bultmann on Collingwood's Philosophy of History" in *H.T.R.* LVIII (1965), 227-33.
38. H. A. Hodges, *The Philosophy of Wilhelm Dilthey* (Routledge & Kegan Paul, London, 1952), pp. xiv-xv.
39. A. Richardson, *History Sacred and Profane*, p. 163.

various operations performed in the human studies. The subject is here one with its object."⁴⁰

Dilthey argues that not only does the interpreter understand history through himself; he *understands himself* through history. This is one of the key points which accords most readily with Bultmann's own outlook. Thus Dilthey writes, "Not through intropection but only through history do we come to know ourselves."⁴¹ "What man is, only history can tell him."⁴² The basis of hermeneutics, however, remains that of a common human nature: "We understand individuals by virtue of their affinities with one another, the common factor which they share."⁴³ Dilthey, as is well known, draws on Schleiermacher's hermeneutics, especially on his later writings. Thus Howard N. Tuttle comments concerning Dilthey's hermeneutical conclusions, "The 'inner' life of others—past or present—is of the same 'human stuff' as our own life, and therefore understandable with all the force of one's self-knowledge."⁴⁴

If we turn now from Dilthey to Bultmann, we can see that Dilthey's outlook leads on to four points of emphasis in Bultmann's thought. These occur not only in his essay of 1950 on hermeneutics, but in such studies as "Is Exegesis without Presuppositions Possible?", in certain chapters of his *History and Eschatology*, and in various essays.⁴⁵

First of all, Bultmann takes up Dilthey's question: is it possible for our understanding of the individual, especially an individual in past history, to be "a generally valid, objective understanding (*allgemeingültigem objektiven Verständnis*)"?⁴⁶ Such an understanding, Bultmann replies, "cannot be attained simply by the observance of hermeneutical rules," as Schleiermacher clearly saw.⁴⁷ Dilthey saw that, in his own words (quoted by Bultmann), "Exegesis is a work of personal art (*der persönlichen Kunst*) . . . conditioned by the mental make-up of the exegete; and so it rests on an *affinity* (*Verwandtschaft*) intensified by a thoroughgoing communion with the author. . . ."⁴⁸ However, this in no way calls in question the validity of hermeneutics and its claim to "objectivity." The " 'most subjective' (*subjektivste*) interpretation is . . . the 'most objective' (*objektivste*), that is, only those who are stirred by the

40. W. Dilthey, *Gesammelte Schriften* (Teubner, Stuttgart, 1962 edn.) VII, 191; translated in the selections of passages in H. A. Hodges, *Wilhelm Dilthey. An Introduction* (Kegan Paul, Trench & Trubner, London, 1944), p. 114.
41. W. Dilthey, *Gesammelte Schriften* VII, 279.
42. *Ibid.* VIII, 224.
43. *Ibid.* VII, 212; translated by H. A. Hodges, *Wilhelm Dilthey. An Introduction*, p. 120.
44. H. N. Tuttle, *Wilhelm Dilthey's Philosophy of Historical Understanding. A Critical Analysis* (Brill, Leiden, 1969), p. 11.
45. R. Bultmann, *E.F.*, pp. 342-51; *G.u.V.* III, 142-50.
46. R. Bultmann, *E.P.T.*, p. 235; *G.u.V.* II, 211.
47. *Ibid.* (English, p. 237; German, p. 214).
48. *Ibid.* (English, p. 238; German, p. 215).

question of their own existence (*der eigenen Existenz*) can hear the claim which the text makes."[49]

This brings us to Bultmann's second point of emphasis. Understanding *begins* by my asking questions which represent a given standpoint on the part of the interpreter himself. He writes, "A comprehension . . . is *constantly orientated to a particular formulation of a question, a particular 'objective'* (einer bestimmten Fragestellung, an einem bestimmten Woraufhin) . . . or, to put it more precisely . . . it is *governed always by a prior understanding of the subject* (von einem Vorverständnis der Sache), in accordance with which it investigates the text. The formulation of a question, and an interpretation, is possible at all only on the basis of such a prior understanding."[50] We thus reach the principle, set out in the first chapter of the present study, that hermeneutics cannot proceed without taking account of the existing horizons of the interpreter. As Bultmann puts it, Dilthey saw that what is at issue in hermeneutics is the relation between the author of the text and the modern interpreter.

While it is true that the actual subject-matter of different texts may vary from case to case, Bultmann insists that "*all* texts can, in fact, be understood in accordance with Dilthey's formulation, that is, as documents of 'historical' personal life. . . . The presupposition for understanding is the interpreter's relationship in his life to the subject which is directly or indirectly expressed in the text."[51] Following Schleiermacher, as we have seen, Bultmann illustrates this principle with reference to a child's learning to speak and to understand language. This takes place "in close conjunction with his becoming familiar with his environment . . . in brief, in the context of his life."[52] In two of his essays Bultmann compares the understanding of various types of text with different aspects of life. "I only understand a text dealing with music if and in so far as I have a relation to music. . . . I only understand a mathematical text if I have a relationship to mathematics."[53] "Can one understand the history of religion and philosophy without knowing what religion and philosophy are? . . . One cannot understand the Communist Manifesto of 1848 without understanding the principles of capitalism and socialism."[54]

Bultmann's third point is that the interpretation of texts involves self-understanding. Texts which concern history, poetry, or art, "bring comprehension of the *possibilities* of *man's being*" (Möglichkeiten des menschlichen Seins).[55] He argues that Dilthey and Schleiermacher con-

49. *Ibid.* (English, p. 256; German, p. 230).
50. *Ibid.* (English, p. 239; German, p. 216; Bultmann's italics).
51. *Ibid.* (English, pp. 240 and 241; German, pp. 216 and 217).
52. *Ibid.* (English, p. 242).
53. *Ibid.*, pp. 242-43.
54. R. Bultmann, *E.F.*, p. 347.
55. R. Bultmann, *E.P.T.*, pp. 246 and 249 (German, pp. 222 and 224).

vey insights in this respect which were neglected or even suppressed by
Ranke and the historical school. In his *History and Eschatology* he finds
this emphasis also in Collingwood. In particular he cites the work of Graf
Yorck in showing that history involves "critical self-examination." "History does not become visible at all for the spectator who is not personally
involved in it."[56] Thus Bultmann himself insists, "It is valid in the
investigation of the text to allow oneself to be examined by the text, and
to hear the claim (*Anspruch*) it makes."[57] "The demand that the interpreter must silence his subjectivity and extinguish his individuality, in order
to attain to an objective knowledge, is therefore the most absurd one that
can be imagined."[58] History speaks only to the man who himself stands in
history and is involved in it. In his essay on presuppositions in exegesis he
declares, "History in its objective content can only be understood by a
subject who is *existentiell* moved and alive. For historical understanding
the schema of subject and object that has validity for natural science is
invalid."[59]

Fourthly, Bultmann explores the consequences of these three points
for biblical interpretation. The basic point to emerge is that the "sacred"
character of the biblical texts does not short-circuit the problem of hermeneutics as the problem of understanding. In *this* sense Bultmann
writes, "*The interpretation of biblical writings is not subject to conditions
different from those applying to all other kinds of literature.*"[60] This
means that the problem of pre-understanding is inescapable. The interpreter can only *begin* with his own questions, and his own experience of life.
In this particular sense "*there cannot be any such thing as presuppositionless exegsis* (voraussetzungslose Exegese kann es nicht geben). . . .
Every exegete is determined by his own individuality."[61] At the same
time Bultmann rightly adds, "This does not mean a falsification of the
historical picture, provided that the perspective that is presupposed is not
a prejudice, but a way of raising questions (wenn die vorausgesetzte
Fragestellung nicht ein Vorurteil, sondern eben eine Fragestellung ist)."[62]

Bultmann allows that this entails the consequence that exegesis can
never be definitive, in the sense of being final. Against the criticism of
Walter Klaas, Bultmann insists that we cannot cut the knot of the hermeneutical problem by contrasting biblical interpretation with what the
Bible "really" says. In the same way, he also rejects Barth's criticism that
biblical truth is thereby reduced to "propositions about the inner life of

56. *Ibid.*, p. 251.
57. *Ibid.*, p. 254 (German, p. 228).
58. *Ibid.*, p. 255.
59. R. Bultmann, *E.F.*, p. 348.
60. R. Bultmann, *E.P.T.*, p. 256.
61. R. Bultmann, *E.F.*, pp. 344-45; and *G.u.V.* III, 143 (his italics).
62. *Ibid.* (English, p. 346; German, p. 146).

man."[63] We have already argued in an earlier chapter that the problem of pre-understanding is inescapable. If Barth's criticism has any validity it is not because of Bultmann's view of pre-understanding, but because of the anthropological dimension necessitated by Bultmann's rejection of objectifying talk of God. Even so, Bultmann rightly rejects Barth's description of language that *relates* to human *existence* (*Existenz*) as *propositions about "inner* states." Self-understanding and *Existenz* concern more than knowledge and inner states.

This very point, however, brings us to Dilthey and to Collingwood. Two observations must be made about Dilthey. First of all, Barth's criticism of Bultmann is indeed more than justified as *a criticism of Dilthey*. H. A. Hodges writes, "Dilthey undertakes to show that all alleged transcendent realities are in fact projections from within experience. . . . The problem of the relation between God and the world is a reflection of the problem of the relation between the higher and lower worlds within ourselves, between our ideal aspirations and our animal nature."[64] In other words, for Dilthey himself God is indeed no more than a cipher which serves self-knowledge, and is a projection of inner experience. Thus Dilthey shows that his hermeneutics *allows* such a conclusion, even if it does not necessitate it, and thereby suggests the need for caution on the part of the Christian theologian in drawing on his thought.

Secondly, Dilthey's optimism about the sameness of human nature down the centuries seems to stand in tension with certain existentialist estimates of man. H. N. Tuttle interprets Dilthey as assuming that "all men think, feel, will, as we ourselves would in a like situation."[65] But writers such as Ernst Fuchs and Manfred Mezger reject this assumption. Mezger writes, "The short cut by which I picture myself . . . in the skin of Moses or Paul is certainly popular, but is not satisfactory, for I am neither the one nor the other."[66]

Is Bultmann's use of Dilthey's philosophy, and for that matter Collingwood's, fully compatible with his use of existentialist perspectives? Some writers, including for example Claude Geffré, have spoken of Dilthey and Collingwood as holding an "existentialistic conception of history."[67] In spite of the difficulty to which we have referred, in the broader sense of the term this description is justified. The great point in Dilthey which Bultmann so firmly endorses is that, as A. Malet puts it, the

63. R. Bultmann, *E.P.T.*, pp. 259-60.
64. H. A. Hodges, *The Philosophy of Wilhelm Dilthey*, p. 348.
65. H. N. Tuttle, *Wilhelm Dilthey's Philosophy of Historical Understanding*, p. 11.
66. M. Mezger, "Preparation for Preaching: the Route from Exegesis to Proclamation" in *J.T.C.* II (1965), 166; cf. pp. 159-79.
67. C. Geffré, "Bultmann on Kerygma and History" in F. O'Meara and D. M. Weisser (eds.), *Rudolf Bultmann in Catholic Thought* (Herder & Herder, New York, 1968), p. 175.

historian looks at history as that which reveals "man's various possibilities in the past as his own possibilities."[68] History is seen not as a physical chain of cause and effects only in the past, but as that which concerns men now. In this respect, there is a similarity with Heidegger's view of the historicity of Dasein, which we examined in a previous chapter. Indeed we saw that in *Being and Time* Heidegger quite explicitly expresses his indebtedness to Dilthey as well as Graf Yorck. Heidegger argues that the importance of "psychologizing" tendencies in Dilthey should not be exaggerated in such a way as to obscure other aspects of his work.

In our earlier discussion of pre-understanding and theology in chapter four we noted Bultmann's approach to the question: "What is the relation, the 'life-relation', which we have in advance to the theme (*Sache*) of the Bible from which our questions and conceptions arise?"[69] We saw that in his book *Jesus Christ and Mythology* Bultmann answers, "Man's life is moved by the search for God because it is always moved . . . by the question about his own personal existence. The question of God and the question of myself are identical."[70] We have argued, however, that Bultmann's view of talk of God through or as talk of man has other roots in theology and philosophy which do not invoke the thought of Wilhelm Dilthey. This "knowledge of God in advance" is nevertheless "not [knowledge] of the revelation of God." Bultmann is saying only that through his own finitude and creatureness man can *begin* asking questions about God. There is already a starting-point at the level of intelligibility. From Dilthey Bultmann draws not some naturalistic or immanental doctrine of God; but simply the recognition that the hermeneutical process requires some starting-point in "life," which the interpreter himself already experiences.

33. *Bultmann's Appeal to Collingwood's Philosophy of History*

We have already stated that in Bultmann's view Collingwood's book *The Idea of History* says "the best that is said" about the problems of history. Yet in his incisive article on the subject of Bultmann's appeal to Collingwood's philosophy of history, Jasper Hopkins claims that Bultmann offers "a *tendentious* interpretation of Collingwood by rendering his statements into the language of kerygmatic theology. . . . He views Collingwood through the eyes of existential categories." He concludes,

68. A. Malet, *The Thought of Rudolf Bultmann*, p. 77.
69. R. Bultmann, *Jesus Christ and Mythology*, p. 52.
70. *Ibid.*, p. 53.

"It is ironic that Bultmann's Gifford Lectures, dealing with questions of heremeneutic, should have erred so egregiously in their interpretation of Collingwood's philosophy of history."[71]

While we shall argue that there is a small element of truth in the claim made by Hopkins, he includes one argument which is scarcely fair to Bultmann. He suggests that Bultmann has erred by failing to take account of the full scope of Collingwood's writings.[72] Admittedly a particular writing must be viewed in the context of an author's wider thought. Nevertheless, Bultmann never claims to find the ideas to which he appeals for support outside Collingwood's book *The Idea of History*. One recent interpreter of Collingwood, Lionel Rubinoff, argues that Collingwood's thought underwent at least one decisive change, around 1936.[73] This makes the interpretation of *The Idea of History* particularly difficult, since it is based on lectures given in the first part of 1936, and subsequently revised, and also includes material from 1935. We shall examine, however, the claim that, simply in terms of the text of *The Idea of History* as it stands, Bultmann has, as it were, read Collingwood through existentialist and Heideggerian spectacles.

In *The Idea of History* R. G. Collingwood (1889-1943) argued that "the lonely and neglected genius Dilthey" did the best work done during his own period on the subject of historical understanding.[74] Together with Croce, Dilthey and to a greater extent Collingwood articulated the truth that, in Alan Richardson's words, "the experience of the present is the reality which lies behind the activity of the historian."[75] On this point, we have seen, Bultmann is also emphatic. Indeed it is one of the very key points in his hermeneutics and entire theology. At the same time, Collingwood parts company from Dilthey at a certain distance along the road. He writes, "A problem still remains, because life for Dilthey means immediate experience, as distinct from reflection or knowledge."[76] Where Dilthey speaks of "life," Collingwood himself prefers to speak of thought.

Collingwood explicitly describes this as an inconsistency in Dilthey's thought. It is clear that "something has gone wrong with Dilthey's argument," because everything depends on psychology; however, psychology

71. J. Hopkins, "Bultmann on Collingwood's Philosophy of History" in *H.T.R.* VIII (1965), 228, 232, and 233 (his italics).
72. *Ibid.*, p. 233.
73. L. Rubinoff, "Collingwood's Theory of the Relation between Philosophy and History: A New Interpretation" in *J.H.P.* VI (1968), 363-80. Cf. also the comments of the editor, T. M. Knox, in R. G. Collingwood, *The Idea of History* (Clarendon Press, Oxford, 1946), pp. v-xxiv.
74. R. G. Collingwood, *The Idea of History*, p. 171.
75. A. Richardson, *History Sacred and Profane*, p. 164.
76. R. G. Collingwood, *The Idea of History*, p. 172.

is not history but science, a science constructed on naturalistic principles." "To say that history becomes intelligible only when conceived in
terms of psychology is to say that historical knowledge is impossible."[77]
Collingwood gives substance to his point by considering the position of a
historian who is looking at the life of Julius Caesar. He argues that it is not
a matter of trying to *be* Caesar, but of reliving Caesar's experiences at the
level of *thought* in *the mind.* Collingwood writes, "The way in which I
incorporate Julius Caesar's experience in my own personality is not by
confusing myself with him, but by distinguishing myself from him and at
the same time making his experience my own. The living past of history
lives in the present; but it lives not in the immediate *experience* of the
present, but only in the *self-knowledge* of the present. This Dilthey has
overlooked."[78]

   The relative importance which Collingwood himself attaches to the
various strands of his own philosophy of history can be judged not only
from *The Idea of History* but also from his work entitled *An Autobiography.* The two chapters which are especially significant for the subject of
hermeneutics and history are entitled "Question and Answer" and "History as the Self-knowledge of Mind."[79] Collingwood here discusses his
own dictum that "all history is the history of thought."[80] Or as he writes
in *The Idea of History*, the object of historical knowledge is "not a mere
object, something outside the mind which knows it; it is an activity of
thought, which can be known only in so far as the knowing mind re-enacts
it and knows itself as so doing."[81]

   Three principles are laid down which amplify this point. First of all,
historical inquiry concerns not physical events *in themselves,* but the
thoughts of the men who were involved in those events. The historian
may of course draw inferences from objects discovered by ar-
chaeologists, but Collingwood endorses Dilthey's view that the subject-
matter of history is man and not nature. Secondly, "historical knowledge
is the re-enactment in the historian's mind of the thought whose history he
is studying."[82] For example, if a historian is studying Nelson, "understanding the words means thinking for myself what Nelson thought when
he spoke them."[83] But this leads on to a third principle. There is in
practice a difference between Nelson's thoughts and the historian's
thoughts. This difference is one of context. The context of questions and

77. *Ibid.*, p. 173.
78. *Ibid.*, p. 174 (my italics).
79. R. G. Collingwood, *An Autobiography* (Oxford University Press, 1939), pp. 29-43 and
107-19.
80. *Ibid.*, p. 110.
81. R. G. Collingwood, *The Idea of History,* p. 218.
82. R. G. Collingwood, *An Autobiography,* p. 112.
83. *Ibid.*

answers which shapes Nelson's thought is a present context to Nelson, but a past context to the historian. The historian's own context of questions and answers is different. *He* is not asking, "Shall I take off my decorations?" but, "Shall I go on reading this book?"[84] Thus, in Collingwood's words, "Historical knowledge is the re-enactment of a past thought incapsulated in a context of present thoughts, which, by contradicting it, confine it to a plane different from theirs."[85]

Thus, on the one hand Collingwood is in agreement with both Dilthey and Bultmann in claiming that the historian's knowledge of a past situation and past thoughts is "at the same time knowledge *of himself.*"[86] On the other hand, he differs from them in at least two ways. First of all, this occurs on the level of "thought" and "knowledge" rather than existential self-understanding. Secondly, Collingwood stands nearer to Gadamer than to Bultmann in his respect for the distinctiveness of the horizon of the *past*. If the present, rather than the past, occupies the center of the stage, it still does not monopolize it. This is partly because he gives more place than Dilthey to the recognition of novelty and particularity in history. He is critical, in this connection, of the view represented at one time by F. H. Bradley (and already discussed in this present study in connection with Troeltsch) that "our experience of the world teaches us that some kinds of things happen and others do not. This experience . . . is the criterion which the historian brings to bear on the statements of his authorities."[87] Part of his criticism is that this approach is tinged with empiricism; a criticism which we put forward against Troeltsch in our third chapter. Collingwood's main criticism, however, turns on the contrast between history and nature, which is so very important for Bultmann. Nature, it may be argued, is cyclic and uniform; but not history. "The historical, as distinct from the natural, conditions of man's life, differ so much at different times that no argument from analogy will hold."[88]

We may now return to Bultmann. First of all, are the criticisms of Jasper Hopkins justified? There is some truth in the rejection by Hopkins of one *criticism* which Bultmann makes of Collingwood. Bultmann argues that Collingwood's emphasis on thought is "one-sided," in that life includes actions and events as well as thought.[89] There is an irony in this criticism, since many attack Bultmann himself for appearing to restrict acts of God in history to the level of interpretation rather than event. This

84. *Ibid.*, p. 113.
85. *Ibid.*, p. 114.
86. *Ibid.* (my italics).
87. R. G. Collingwood, *The Idea of History*, p. 239.
88. *Ibid.*
89. R. Bultmann, *History and Eschatology*, pp. 136-37.

criticism is an oversimplification, but it is not without some justification. The real difficulty, however, is that Collingwood's notion of thought does not in practice exclude reference to events. We are not obliged to rely on the verdict of Hopkins. W. H. Walsh writes that the thought to which Collingwood refers is "thought in action . . . which develops out of, and in response to, a background of natural as well as human forces."[90] Collingwood's contrast between nature and history is perhaps less dualistic than Bultmann's.

Secondly, there is some truth in the claim of Hopkins that Bultmann sees Collingwood through existentialist spectacles, but the criticism is exaggerated. Bultmann rightly asserts, "For Collingwood mind is not simply reason, although there is no mind without reason. . . . Mind is something more than mere reason. Collingwood recognizes the unity of will and thinking in defining thought as . . . 'reflective effort'."[91] Bultmann can appeal to Collingwood for support for his own view that history brings disclosures of the self in the present, and that "every *now* . . . in its historical relatedness . . . has within itself a full meaning."[92] Moreover, since historical understanding involves the ever expanding horizons of the interpreter and of history itself, its work is never done. However, it is doubtful whether Collingwood would have entirely endorsed the verdict that "the relation of subject and object . . . has no value for historical science"; or that "the act of self-knowledge is . . . at the same time an act of decision."[93]

Bultmann, however, does no more than claim, in effect, that his view of history *overlaps* with that of Collingwood, and quite explicitly states that Collingwood has left certain factors out of account.[94] Bultmann's view of history was already decisively formulated before Collingwood's lectures of 1936, let alone the publication of *The Idea of History*. In the previous section we made the point that although the views of history represented by Dilthey and by Collingwood could not be described as "existentialist" in the narrower sense of the term, there was nevertheless a broader sense in which this description was justified. We alluded, in this connection, to C. Geffré and A. Malet. In his book *The Scope of Demythologizing* J. Macquarrie puts both sides of the point clearly. On the one side, he asserts, "that existentialist label is not applicable *simpliciter* to any one of them (i.e. Bultmann, Dilthey, or Collingwood), not even to

90. W. H. Walsh, *An Introduction to Philosophy of History* (Hutchinson, London, 1951), p. 53.
91. R. Bultmann, *History and Eschatology*, pp. 134-35.
92. *Ibid.*, p. 135.
93. *Ibid.*, pp. 133 and 136.
94. *Ibid.*, pp. 144-49.

Heidegger."[95] On the other hand, he cites four broad characteristics which are shared by each of these four writers' views of history, by virtue of which, in a broader sense, their outlook might be described as "the existentialist approach to history."[96] In the first place, all of these thinkers share the view that historical reflection has for its subject-matter human existence in the world. "A natural event is also a historical event only in so far as it touches on human existence."[97] Secondly, in historical reflection, the reflecting subject participates, in a sense, in the object of his reflection. The interpreter does not look upon historical events with the same degree of detachment or neutrality as might be said traditionally to characterize the outlook of natural science. Thirdly, "the function of historical reflection is to provide a self-understanding."[98] History, in Collingwood's words, means not only "knowing, first, what it is to be a man," but also "knowing what it is to be the man *you* are and nobody else is."[99] Fourthly, Macquarrie concludes, historical reflection is concerned primarily with possibility, in Heidegger's sense of the term which we have already discussed.

This last point leads Macquarrie to ask a further question. How are existential *possibilities*, he asks, related to the *facts* which are accessible to historical research? Gogarten, he warns us, "so stresses the difference between objective history and existential history that all contact between the two seems to be lost." Bultmann often accuses his critics of confusing the two, "but surely it is not just a case of confusing these two, but rather of raising the real problem of whether and how they are related."[100] We have seen that Bultmann is not to be faulted, in any really serious sense, for his appeal to Collingwood's philosophy of history. However, we must now take up this next question, to which J. Macquarrie and other writers have drawn attention.

34. *The Emergence of a Dualist Trend in Bultmann's View of History*

Bultmann's contrast between history and nature is much more radical and far-reaching than Collingwood's. The contrast occurs at the very beginning of *Jesus and the Word*, first published in 1926. Bultmann asserts, "Our relationship to history (*Geschichte*) is wholly different from

95. J. Macquarrie, *The Scope of Demythologizing*, p. 81.
96. *Ibid.* Cf. pp. 81-90.
97. *Ibid.*, p. 82.
98. *Ibid.*, p. 86.
99. R. G. Collingwood, *The Idea of History*, p. 10.
100. J. Macquarrie, *The Scope of Demythologizing*, p. 91.

our relationship to nature (*Natur*). Man, if he rightly understands himself, differentiates himself from nature. When he observes nature, he perceives there something objective (*Vorhandenes*), which is not himself. When he turns his attention to history, however, he must admit himself to be part of history; he is considering a living complex of events in which he is essentially involved. He cannot observe this complex objectively as he can observe natural phenomena (*als ein Vorhandenes betrachten wie die Natur*); for *in every word which he says about history he is saying at the same time something about himself*. Hence there cannot be impersonal observation of history (*objektive Geschichtsbetrachtung*) in the same sense that there can be impersonal observation of nature (*objektive Naturbetrachtung*)."[101]

Heinrich Ott rightly points out that this distinction between nature and history leads on to a radical dualism in Bultmann's thought about historical knowledge. The catchword (*Stichwort*) is "objective" and "objectification." This describes the "nature" side of the dualism (*Die Natur ist Objekt, Gegenstand*).[102] "Consequently," Ott writes, "there remain two modes of historical knowledge (*Geschichtserkenntnis*) side by side: the authentic primary knowledge of the real historical event (*wirkliche geschichtliche Geschehen*), and the inauthentic secondary historical knowledge, that of bare objective actual material substance (*bloss historisches Tatsachenmaterial*)."[103] He adds, "The introduction to *Jesus* covers Bultmann's 'double concept of history' (*doppelten Geschichtsbegriff*)," which turns on the terminological contrast between *Geschichte* and event (*Ereignis, Geschehen*) on the one side, and *Historie*, fact, nature, and object, on the other side.[104] Ott further traces the consequences of this duality (*Zweiheit*) in Bultmann's insistence that the resurrection of Christ is an event of Easter faith on the part of the disciples, rather than a historical fact that could be observed (*als historisches Faktum nicht in Betracht*), partly on the ground that *authentic* historical knowledge could occur only on the level of the former.[105] He then goes on to show how this relates to Bultmann's program of demythologizing.

The importance of this nature-history contrast is also underlined by Norman Young.[106] Because of Bultmann's contrast between nature and history, Young observes, "the very procedure many critics advocate as

---

101. R. Bultmann, *Jesus and the Word*, p. 11; German, *Jesus* (Mohr, Tübingen, 1951), p. 7.
102. H. Ott, *Geschichte und Heilsgeschichte in der Theologie Rudolf Bultmanns*, p. 10.
103. *Ibid.*
104. *Ibid.*, p. 12.
105. *Ibid.*, pp. 12-15.
106. N. J. Young, *History and Existential Theology. The Role of History in the Thought of Rudolf Bultmann* (Westminster Press, Philadelphia, 1969), pp. 18-38 (especially pp. 18-22) *et passim*.

necessary in order to establish the historical basis for the Christian faith is one which, for Bultmann, effectively removes the enquiry from the historical realm. Bultmann does not deny that the past event of Jesus of Nazareth is indispensable to the Christian faith. . . . Nor does he deny that objective-historical research into the life and teaching of Jesus can be fruitful. But he does deny that any such approach can establish Jesus as the Christ. . . . Much of the criticism of Bultmann's alleged weakening of the historical basis of the Christian faith fails to account for his nature-history distinction."[107] We have already discussed this particular aspect of Bultmann's view of history with special reference to his Lutheranism. We saw that, in spite of Ebeling's warning that we should not identify Bultmann's position with that of Kähler, nevertheless there are close connections between them on this subject. We also noted Bultmann's divergence from Wilhelm Herrmann on the value for faith of the historical Jesus.

The interpretation of Bultmann offered recently by Robert C. Roberts appeared only after I had already completed these chapters. But we may note that he calls attention to the same problem. He writes: "The fundamental idea shaping Bultmann's thought is a dichotomy of a peculiar sort, in which the reality of the human self is opposed to that of the 'world'. . . . Sometimes it is expressed as the division between 'nature' and 'history', or between 'state' and 'deed', between 'possession' and 'event', between 'factual knowledge' and 'historical self-understanding' . . . between 'objective observation' and 'encounter'. . . . To put it succinctly, Bultmann divides reality into two mutually exclusive kinds."[108]

Heinrich Ott's criticism is that Bultmann has elevated a methodological dualism into an ontological one. There is justice in this criticism. We have already discussed Wolfhart Pannenberg's attack on what he regards as a Neo-Kantian contrast between fact and value.[109] He alludes, in the course of his discussion, to Kähler's statement that "the historical fact (is) accompanied by a testimony to its revelatory value, which is supplementary to it and exists precisely for faith alone." He then exclaims, "The whole problem is already contained in this distinction. Is not the 'revelatory value' related to the 'fact' as something added from outside? Does not this argument accept all too uncritically the neo-Kantian distinction between being and value? Does not the meaning of an event belong to the event itself, in so far as it is to be understood within its own historical context (*Geschehenszusammenhang*)?"[110] Pannenberg

107. *Ibid.*, p. 21.
108. R. C. Roberts, *Rudolf Bultmann's Theology. A Critical Interpretation* (Eerdmans, Grand Rapids, 1977, and S.P.C.K., London, 1977), pp. 22-23.
109. In the last main section of chapter three.
110. W. Pannenberg, *B.Q.T.* I, 86.

then notes his agreement on this matter with Heinrich Ott, although he claims that Ott does not pay sufficient attention to how the unity of fact and meaning is grounded in the historical nexus of the events themselves.

In an article on the hermeneutics of Hegel and Pannenberg, Merold Westphal calls attention to Pannenberg's belief that, ironically, this kind of dualism in effect betrays history to positivism.[111] In view of Bultmann's estimate of "nature" and "science," this is irony indeed. Westphal writes, "Pannenberg is haunted by the ghost of Feuerbach; and he sees the positivistic or neo-Kantian dichotomy between fact and meaning (*Historie* and *Geschichte*, history and kerygma, history and faith) which has determined so much of post-Kantian theology as playing right into his hands. If the meaning is not there in the events to be discovered, but rather is brought to the bare events by faith, so that only for faith can they be said to have this or that meaning, then the question of content is delivered over to the individual's subjectivity and its arbitrariness. God is indeed created in the image of man."[112] This is why in other essays Pannenberg is at pains to reformulate the relation between faith and reason, as over against Bultmann's quasi-Lutheran interpretation of Neo-Kantian epistemology. Pannenberg declares, "The essence of faith must come to harm precisely if in the long run rational conviction about its basis fails to appear. Faith then is easily perverted into blind credulity toward the authority-claim of the preached message. . . . Paul speaks of the reverse, of the grounding of faith upon a knowledge (Rom. 6:8f.; 2 Cor. 4:13)."[113] Faith, Pannenberg insists, does not cease to be trust if reason is accorded its proper place.

When we return to Bultmann's own writings, we find that these fears about undue dualism are justified. The contrast between history and nature, set in the context of suspicions about objectifying knowledge, runs throughout Bultmann's work and is not confined to *Jesus and the Word*. As recently as 1966 Bultmann drew the contrast, once again, between "research in nature and history," declaring that "natural science views nature in an objectivizing way."[114] He continues, "Similarly, history can be viewed in different ways: first of all, in an objectivizing manner in so far as it presents the picture of a chain of events . . . understandable as a chain of cause and effect. . . . On the other hand, history can also be understood as the range of possibilities for human self-understanding, which range is disclosed precisely in man's decisions."[115] In spite of the fact that these words constitute a "reply" to Paul

---

111. M. Westphal, "Hegel, Pannenberg, and Hermeneutics" in *M.W.* IV (1971), 276-93.
112. *Ibid.*, p. 286.
113. W. Pannenberg, *B.Q.T.* II, 28 and 31-32; cf. pp. 28-64.
114. R. Bultmann, "Reply to the Essay of Paul S. Minear" in *T.R.B.*, p. 266.
115. *Ibid.*, pp. 266-67.

Minear, however, Minear's own appraisal is correct. He writes that Bultmann's "perception of reality . . . is dualistic in form," and comments: "The formula may change: nature versus history, being versus existence, cosmology versus anthropology, cosmologized history versus historicized cosmology. The primarily dualistic perception of reality, however, does not change."[116]

In an essay written in 1963 and published in the fourth volume of *Glauben und Verstehen*, Bultmann admittedly shows signs of wishing to overcome this dualism.[117] He discusses the relationship between objectification and the situation of modern man, speaking of "the objectifying way of viewing nature (*die objektivierende Naturbetrachtung*) as a symptom of the secularization of the world."[118] However, he concludes: "Only the idea of God which can find . . . the beyond in the here, the transcendent in the present at hand (*im Gegenwärtigen*), as possibility of encounter, is possible for modern man."[119] The bearing of this essay on the subject-object relation is discussed by Klaus Rosenthal.[120] That Bultmann *wishes* to avoid the kind of dualism which we have described is indicated by what Hans Goebel describes as "the paradoxical identity of the eschatological and historical (*historischem*) event in Jesus Christ."[121] Goebel cites, for instance, Bultmann's assertion in his essay "Revelation in the New Testament" that "Revelation consists in nothing other than the fact of Jesus Christ (*nichts anderem als in dem Faktum Jesus Christus*)."[122] Bultmann continues, "Because he was sent, life was revealed (1 John 1:2). . . . He 'was manifested in the flesh' (1 Tim. 3:16). But yet, on the other hand, his revelation is yet to take place (1 John 2:28; 1 Pet. 5:4; Luke 17:30). . . . Thus it is now a *veiled revelation*."[123]

The problem is not that Bultmann entirely dismisses the realm of the factual, as Norman Young rightly stresses. Rather, in Young's words, it is that "the vital . . . question of how these two realms are related remains unanswered."[124] Bultmann himself compares the so-called paradoxes of 2 Corinthians 6:8-10: ". . . as unknown and yet well known; as dying and behold we live; as punished, and yet not killed; as sorrowful, yet always rejoicing; as poor, yet making many rich; as having nothing and yet

116. P. S. Minear, "Bultmann's Interpretation of New Testament Eschatology" *T.R.B.*, p. 77.
117. R. Bultmann, *G.u.V.*, pp. 113-27.
118. *Ibid.*, p. 115.
119. *Ibid.*, p. 126; English "The Idea of God and Modern Man" in *J.T.C.* II (1965), 94.
120. K. Rosenthal, *Die Überwindung des Subjekt-Objekt-Denkens als philosophisches und theologisches Problem*, pp. 102-104.
121. H. Goebel, *Wort Gottes als Auftrag. Zur Theologie von Rudolf Bultmann, Gerhard Ebeling, und Wolfhart Pannenberg* (Neukirchener Verlag, Neukirchen-Vluyn, 1972), p. 15.
122. R. Bultmann, in *G.u.V.* III, 18 (English, *E.F.*, p. 87.
123. *Ibid.* (Bultmann's italics).
124. N. J. Young, *History and Existential Theology*, p. 23.

possessing everything." He also compares Paul's words, "When I am weak, then I am strong."[125] It would hardly be methodologically proper, however, to interpret a major obscurity in Bultmann's theology by means of exegetical discussions of difficult passages in Paul, where the context of thought is not identical.

We have still left one major ingredient of Bultmann's view of history out of account. We refer to Heidegger's work on the historicity (*Geschichtlichkeit*) of Dasein. We saw in the second of our two chapters on Heidegger that because only Dasein, and the world of Dasein, can be truly historical, the locus of history lies not in the past but in the present. Heidegger argues, we saw, that objects which are present-at-hand are not "historical" in the same way as Dasein. We quoted Langan's comments, "Because the Dasein knows the course it is taking and resolutely wills it, the historical motion is not a mere passive undergoing, such as the material living thing experiences, but an active 'letting itself happen', the free shouldering of a destiny. For this reason Heidegger terms the motion of the Dasein's self-extension a *Geschehen* . . . from which of course he would derive the word *Geschichte*."[126] We then noted Heidegger's view about the historical nature of antiquities, and his conclusion that "Dasein can *never* be past . . . because it essentially can never be *present-at-hand*."[127]

A circularity, however, has entered Heidegger's argument at this point. "History" can never be reduced to the status of what is merely present-at-hand; hence history can only concern Dasein in the present. But this is only to say that the kind of "history" which relates to Dasein in the present can only concern Dasein in the present. It is in practice a value judgment about the relative worth of different ways of using the word "historical." In practice, we sympathize with what Bultmann and Heidegger wish to affirm, although we have reservations about what they seem to be denying. It is true that, as Dilthey and Collingwood saw, what is important about history is its disclosure of the self in the present. However, this does not in itself give an exhaustive account of what history is. We may agree with Bultmann and Heidegger that certain aspects of history are *primary*. The question yet to be further explored is to what extent the singling out of some aspect of history as primary devalues other aspects and leads to their neglect. David Cairns goes so far as to describe Bultmann's position as "the flight from history."[128]

The purpose of this chapter has been to trace the impact of various

125. R. Bultmann, *G.u.V.* III, 18; *E.F.*, p. 87.
126. Cited above (from T. Langan, *The Meaning of Heidegger*, p. 57).
127. Cited above (from M. Heidegger, *B.T.*, p. 432; his italics).
128. D. Cairns, *A Gospel without Myth?*, pp. 136-63.

philosophical influences on Bultmann's hermeneutics. We have never left the problems set by Neo-Kantian thought, and although we have explored questions about Dilthey and Collingwood, we started out in this chapter from Heidegger and have returned to his thought once again. We shall not, however, leave these questions about history behind us. J. Macquarrie has an illuminating paragraph which relates our discussion of history to the subject of the next chapter. He writes, "The problem of demythologizing might be expressed as the problem of disentangling the primary historical from the secondary historical in the New Testament. The primary historical consists of possibilities of existence which are repeatable, present to me today as they were present to others in the past. . . . What Bultmann is trying to do is to spotlight this essential primary historical in the New Testament, to separate it from the now meaningless secondary historical, and so make it a real possibility of decision for man today. And if that be so, his work is not destructive of the historical element in the New Testament, but the reverse."[129]

129. J. Macquarrie, *An Existentialist Theology*, p. 156.

CHAPTER X

Bultmann's Hermeneutics
and the New Testament

The application of Bultmann's hermeneutical principles to the actual text
of the New Testament takes two distinct forms. One concerns his proposals about the interpretation of myth, as represented in his essay of 1941,
and constitutes one particular aspect of his wider hermeneutical program.
The other comes to expression more systematically in his *Theology of the
New Testament*, perhaps most characteristically in his formulation of
Paul's view of man. This work appeared in between 1948 and 1953. We
shall look first at Bultmann's proposals about the interpretation of myth.

35. *Bultmann's View of Myth*

Numerous interpreters and critics of Bultmann have pointed out that
he defines myth in the New Testament in two or three different ways,
which are not necessarily fully compatible with one another. First of all,
Bultmann regards myth as a way of speaking "of the other world in terms
of this world, and of the gods in terms derived from human life." He
comments, "Myth is here used in the sense popularized by the 'History of
Religions' school. Mythology is the use of imagery (*die Vorstel-
lungsweise*) to express the other worldly (*das Unweltliche*) in terms of this
world, and the divine in terms of human life. . . . For instance, divine
transcendence is expressed as spatial distance. It is a mode of expression
which makes it easy to understand the cultus as an action in which

material means are used to convey immaterial power."[1] This definition of myth comes very close to equating myth with analogy, although in some passages Bultmann is at pains to try to maintain a clear distinction between them. At all events it is certainly close to equating myth with any language about God that is anthropomorphic. For this reason, it is not surprising that Helmut Thielicke took up one of the central points of the Memorandum of the Confessing Church of Hesse that "the reason for myth lies in the nature of man, in the way he inevitably approaches religion. . . . It arises from the way we look at things. . . . We can no more abandon mythology than we can cease to think in terms of time and space."[2]

This point was made as early as in 1942 not only by Thielicke but also by J. Schniewind and other writers. On this basis Schniewind asks, "Is the human mind really capable of dispensing with myth?"[3] In 1956 G. Miegge repeated precisely the same response. He writes, "If this is true, anything whatever that is said about the divine, with the exception of a pure theology of negation, will have to be reduced to the status of mythological language. . . . It includes within this comprehensive definition of myth every form of expression which represents the divine by way of analogy, parable, or symbol."[4]

Although there is an obvious sense in which these responses are true, they do not quite engage with what is at issue here. In his own reply to Schniewind Bultmann offers two rejoinders. First of all, he draws a distinction between the uncritical use of this-worldly imagery in order to express the divine, and a more modern critical awareness that such imagery is being used metaphorically.[5] This, of course, raises the quite different question of how uncritically the New Testament writers did in practice use such imagery, and we shall return to this question later. However, it is not the issue raised by Schiewind and Miegge. Secondly, Bultmann warns us that this "mythological" use of imagery drawn from this world seduces us into substituting a *Weltanschauung* for faith.[6] This rejoinder is much more to the point. We have already seen that for Bultmann faith is not a "this-worldly" phenomenon in the sense of bringing a disclosure of God into the realm of objectifying knowledge. The problem, for Bultmann, is that in order to solve the problem of *intelligibility* man risks misunderstanding the genuine *epistemological* basis of reve-

1. R. Bultmann, "New Testament and Mythology" in *K.M.* I, 10 n. 2.; German, *K.u.M.* I, 23 n. 2.
2. H. Thielicke, "The Restatement of New Testament Mythology" in *K.M.* I, p. 141.
3. J. Schniewind, "A Reply to Bultmann" in *K.M.* I, 48.
4. G. Miegge, *Gospel and Myth in the Thought of Rudolf Bultmann*, pp. 98-99.
5. R. Bultmann, "A Reply to Theses of J. Schniewind" in *K.M.* I, 103.
6. *Ibid.*, pp. 103-04.

254 HEIDEGGER, BULTMANN, GADAMER, AND WITTGENSTEIN

lation in the New Testament. In the language of dialectical theology, it confuses revelation with mere "religion." In the language of Neo-Kantian epistemology, it seems to place the other-worldly within the realm of this-worldly objectifying knowledge. In the language of Bultmann's Lutheranism, this would be to place God within the grasp of man's own efforts. While it is perhaps going a little too far to claim with Gustaf Wingren that "everything in this essay (i.e. the famous essay of 1941) was old and familiar," it is nevertheless true that the significance of Bultmann's statements in this essay can be fully appreciated only in the light of his earlier concerns, which we have set out in the previous two chapters.[7]

This leads on naturally to Bultmann's second formulation of myth. Myth explains unusual or surprising phenomena in terms of the invasion of supernatural forces. In Bultmann's language, it is indeed bound up with a particular world-view (*Weltbild*) or cosmology. This *Weltbild* is essentially that of a pre-scientific age. Bultmann writes, "The cosmology (*das Weltbild*) of the New Testament is essentially mythical in character. The world is viewed as a three-storeyed structure, with the earth in the centre, the heaven above, and the world underneath. Heaven is the abode of God and of celestial beings. . . . The underworld is hell. . . . The earth . . . is the scene of the supernatural activity of God and his angels on the one hand, and of Satan and his demons on the other. These supernatural forces intervene in the course of nature and in all that men think and will and do. Miracles are by no means rare. Man is not in control of his own life."[8] Connected with this picture of the world is the belief that this present evil age is held in bondage to demons (1 Cor. 2:8; 2 Cor. 4:4); that at the last day "the Lord himself will descend from heaven with a cry of command" (1 Thess. 4:16); that men and women may be demon-possessed (Luke 4:33-34; 8:27-28; 9:39-40; 11:20); and that men will be raised from the dead (1 Cor. 15:35-44).

This is not exactly the same as the previous point about myth. Indeed, Ian Henderson has argued that Bultmann's objections to each are different, while Ronald Hepburn devastatingly argues that they are not merely different but actually contradictory.[9] One, he argues, concerns the *form* of mythology in principle; the other concerns questions about the *content* of particular myths. Furthermore, on the basis of Bultmann's view of this second definition of myth, it is necessarily bound up with a

---

7. G. Wingren, *Theology in Conflict: Nygren, Barth, Bultmann* (Eng. Oliver & Boyd, Edinburgh, 1958), p. 133.
8. R. Bultmann, "New Testament and Mythology" in *K.M.* I, 1 (German, p. 15).
9. I. Henderson, *Myth in the New Testament* (S.C.M., London, 1952), p. 46; R. W. Hepburn, "Demythologizing and the Problem of Validity" in A. Flew and A. MacIntyre (eds.), *New Essays in Philosophical Theology* (S.C.M., London, 1955), pp. 227-42.

primitive or pre-scientific way of looking at the world. In this respect it often, though not always, fulfils an aetiological function, seeking to provide "explanations" of surprising phenomena which cannot otherwise be accounted for. On this level it may take the form of what Schubert Ogden calls "a report or narrative of non-natural or supernatural occurrences. . . . For the mythological mind there is always a 'second' history alongside the history comprised of ordinary events. . . . The resulting complex of ideas . . . takes the form of a double history."[10] In Bultmann's words, "Other-worldly causality is introduced into the causal chain of worldly events."[11]

This particular view of myth stems from the period of the Enlightenment. It comes to expression in the writings of Bernard Fontenelle in 1724, although he uses the term "fable" rather than "myth." Fontenelle believed that the fable expressed a view of the world in which "causalities" in terms of gods, demons, or other supernatural agencies assumed the roles which, for men of reason, were performed by the phenomena described under scientific laws. C. Hartlich and W. Sachs have shown how this view of myth colored the work of R. Lowth in the eighteenth century, and C. G. Heyne in the nineteenth century, together with J. G. Eichhorn's work in Old Testament studies and that of D. F. Strauss on the New Testament.[12] On this basis Eichhorn insisted that the mentality behind the literature of the Hebrews belonged to the days of infancy of the human race, and that the only way to understand the Old Testament was to try to see events in the pre-rational way which, he believed, characterized this mythical outlook. A similar assessment of myth lies behind David Strauss's work *The Life of Jesus Critically Examined,* even though Strauss's approach is different from Bultmann's.

This view of myth persisted in the intellectual circles in which Bultmann moved. Ernst Cassirer, the Neo-Kantian philosopher who produced his main works during the 1920's, is a key exponent of this approach. Mythical outlooks characterize the earliest of three great stages of man's intellectual developments. "Mythical thinking," Cassirer writes, "comes to rest in the immediate experience; the sensible present is so great that everything else dwindles before it."[13] In other words, mythical thinking is essentially *uncritical.* "The subjective excitement becomes objectified, and confronts the mind as a god or a demon."[14] After the primitive myth-making stage comes the stage which is now logical, but

10. S. M. Ogden, *Christ Without Myth. A Study Based on the Theology of Rudolf Bultmann* (Collins, London, 1962), p. 30.
11. R. Bultmann, in *K.u.M.* II, 183.
12. C. Hartlich and W. Sachs, *Der Ursprung des Mythosbegriffes in der modernen Bibelwissenschaft* (Mohr, Tübingen, 1952), pp. 6-19, 87-90, and 148-64.
13. E. Cassirer, *Language and Myth* (Eng. Harper, New York, 1946), p. 32.
14. *Ibid.*, p. 33.

nevertheless pre-scientific. Aristotle and the Greeks characterize this stage. Finally comes the age of science, when man's conceptual awareness reaches full maturity. It is against the background of this kind of approach, as we shall see, that Bultmann draws the contrast between ancient myth and modern man.

This is a very different assessment of myth from that which is represented by Mircea Eliade, Karl Jaspers, or C. G. Jung. However, we must next note Bultmann's third definition of myth. Bultmann writes, "The real purpose of myth is not to present an objective picture of the world as it is (ein objektives Weltbild), but to express man's understanding of himself in the world in which he lives. Myth should be interpreted not cosmologically, but anthropologically, or better still, existentially."[15] He adds, "The real purpose of myth is to speak of a transcendent power which controls the world and man, but that purpose is impeded and obscured by the terms in which it is experienced."[16] We have already seen in some detail how the problem of objectification is one of the central issues in Bultmann's hermeneutics as a whole. This issue is here simply transferred into the realm of the discussion about myth. On this view, as Schubert Ogden puts it, myth " 'objectifies' the reality of which it speaks." Ogden then comments, "This notion of the 'objective' . . . is as important for Bultmann as for the entire neo-Kantian tradition . . . that provides the philosophical background of his thought."[17]

James M. Robinson, followed more recently by Roger Johnson, has stressed the importance of Bultmann's indebtedness to Hans Jonas for this understanding of the nature of myth.[18] In his book Augustin und das paulinische Freiheitsproblem, first published in 1930, Jonas described how symbolism can, in a sense, camouflage what is really being expressed through it. He writes, "Only by means of a long process of back-tracking, often an exhaustive traversal of that detour, is a demythologized (entmythologisierte) consciousness able to approach the original phenomena hidden in this camouflage also in a conceptually direct way."[19] Precisely the same understanding of myth appeared in Jonas's Marburg dissertation of 1928, entitled Der Begiff der Gnosis. This was carried out under Heidegger's supervision, and apparently read at the time by Bultmann.[20] In published form, however, it appeared only in 1954 in Volume II.1. of

15. R. Bultmann, in K.M. I, 10 (German, p. 23).
16. Ibid., p. 11.
17. S. M. Ogden, Christ Without Myth, p. 28.
18. J. M. Robinson, "The Pre-history of Demythologization" in Int. XX (1966), 65-77, which is also his translation of his Introduction to the revised edition of Hans Jonas, Augustin und das paulinische Freiheitsproblem, published in 1965. Cf. also R. A. Johnson, The Origins of Demythologizing, pp. 116-23, 170-76, and 240-54.
19. Ibid., p. 70; p. 68 of the first edition of Jonas's book.
20. Cf. J. Robinson's extended note, p. 70 n. 17.

Gnosis und spätantiker Geist. Here Jonas contrasts the "hypostasized" language of myth with "logicized" or "demythed" (*entmythisiert*) forms of language. Jonas writes, "We first turn to an anthropological, ethical sphere of concepts . . . to show how the existential basic principle we have postulated, the 'gnostic' principle . . . is here in a quite distinctive way drawn back out of the outward mythical objectification (*der äusseren mythischen Objektivation*) and transposed into inner concepts of Dasein (*in innere Daseinsbegriffe*) and into ethical practice, i.e. it appears so to speak 'resubjectivized'."[21] The first twenty pages of Jonas's introduction then discuss the relation between myth and "objectification" (*Objektivation*).

Jonas further traces his special debt to Heidegger in his epilogue to the second enlarged edition of *The Gnostic Religion*, which appeared in 1962. He writes, "The viewpoints, the optics, as it were, which I acquired in the school of Heidegger, enabled me to see aspects of gnostic thought that had been missed before."[22] For example, "For the Gnostics . . . man's alienation from the world is to be deepened and brought to a head, for the extrication of the inner self which only thus can gain self . . . the aspiration of the gnostic individual was . . . to 'exist authentically'."[23]

We are not concerned here, however, to trace Heidegger's influence on Jonas, as much as to trace that of Jonas on Bultmann. The main point is that, as James Robinson remarks, the basic notion of "demythologizing" as the de-objectification of myth "has been a factor in the public history of research since 1930." "Bultmann found in Hans Jonas's work the point of departure for his demythologization essay of 1941."[24]

We may distinguish, then, between three different views of myth which Bultmann tries to hold together. Some writers, like L. Malevez, D. Cairns, and R. W. Hepburn, distinguish between two notions of myth in Bultmann; others, like Ogden and Johnson, draw contrasts between three different aspects.[25] From Bultmann's own viewpoint, the effect of these

21. H. Jonas, *Gnosis und spätantiker Geist: II, 1, Von der Mythologie zur mystischen Philosophie* (Vandenhoeck & Ruprecht. Göttingen, 1954, F.R.L.A.N.T. 45 N.F.), pp. 3-4; cf. J. M. Robinson, in *Int.* XX, 70-71.
22. H. Jonas, "Epilogue: Gnosticism, Existentialism, and Nihilism" in *The Gnostic Religion* (Beacon Press, Boston, ²1963), p. 320; cf. pp. 320-40.
23. *Ibid.*, pp. 329-30.
24. J. M. Robinson, in *Int.* XX, 71.
25. L. Malevez, *The Christian Message and Myth. The Theology of Rudolf Bultmann* (Eng. S.C.M., London, 1958), pp. 68-70; D. Cairns, *A Gospel without Myth?* pp. 85-86; R. W. Hepburn, in *New Essays in Philosophical Theology*, pp. 227-42; S. M. Ogden, *Christ Without Myth*, pp. 28-50 (though in the end Ogden defends Bultmann's consistency, and is content to speak about three different "aspects" of myth); and R. A. Johnson, *The Origins of Demythologizing*, pp. 87-231. Much of Johnson's argument turns on the distinction between what he calls the *religionsgeschichtliche* formulation of myth, the Enlightenment formulation of myth, and the existentialist formulation of myth.

differences is not to suggest, in practice, differences between *what* may be characterized as myth in the New Testament. With the one exception of the Christ-event itself, the category of myth is almost all-embracing. Thus David Cairns writes, "When we read the list of what he considers mythical elements of belief found in the Bible, we are somewhat shaken. Among the New Testament contents which he relegates to the mythological shelf . . . are the following: the three-decker view of the universe . . . ; miracle; demon possession; the belief that God guides and inspires men; the notion that supernatural powers influence the course of history; the belief that the Son was sent in the fullness of time; the resurrection of Christ regarded as an event beyond and different from the rise of the Easter faith in the disciples; and the belief in the Holy Spirit, if that Spirit be regarded as more than 'the factual possibility of a new life realized in faith'."[26] J. Macquarrie and Schubert Ogden make a similar point, not so much by listing what is considered by Bultmann as mythological, but rather by calling attention to one single thing that is *not* so regarded. Macquarrie argues that a limit is set to the scope of the mythological "almost at the last moment," while Ogden in fact attacks Bultmann for not going to the very end of the road, and leaving only "a unique act of God in the person and destiny of Jesus of Nazareth."[27] The three different accounts of myth in Bultmann lead him not to different accounts of *what* in the New Testament is mythical; but they do lead him to different parallel accounts of *why* demythologizing is necessary.

36. Bultmann's Proposals for the Interpretation of Myth

Corresponding to his second approach to myth, which regards myth as fundamentally a pre-scientific world-view, Bultmann calls attention to the alleged incompatibility of the world-view of the New Testament with that of modern man. He writes: "Now that the forces and the laws of nature have been discovered, we can no longer believe in spirits, whether good or evil. . . . It is impossible to use electric light and the wireless and to avail ourselves of modern medical and surgical discoveries, and at the same time to believe in the New Testament world of spirits and miracles."[28] In his later book *Jesus Christ and Mythology* Bultmann adds, "To

26. D. Cairns, *A Gospel without Myth?* p. 83.
27. J. Macquarrie, *The Scope of Demythologizing*, p. 22 (cf. pp. 11-22 and 222-29); and S. M. Ogden, "Bultmann's Project of Demythologization and the Problems of Theology and Philosophy" in *J.R.* XXXVII (1957), 168; cf. pp. 156-73.
28. R. Bultmann, in *K.M.*, pp. 4-5.

demythologize is to reject not scripture . . . but the world-view of scripture, which is the world-view of a past epoch." Thereby, however, "it will eliminate a false stumbling-block and bring into sharp focus the real stumbling-block, the word of the cross."[29]

The role performed by this argument in Bultmann's hermeneutics, however, is widely misunderstood, or at least overemphasized. At first sight it seems as if Bultmann is standing squarely in the tradition of liberal theology, endeavoring to harmonize the Christian message with the outlook of the modern man. Even Walter Schmithals comes near to implying that this is the major part of Bultmann's motivation.[30] First-century man, he points out, could believe in miracles with complete intellectual integrity, whereas it may entail insincerity or schizophrenia if modern man is required to believe in such phenomena. To be sure, Bultmann inherits a *concern* about this from Herrmann and liberalism. However, it becomes part of the motivation behind his program of demythologizing only when it is seen to relate to his belief about the relation of God to the world. Schmithals is on stronger ground when he points out that in Bultmann's view the belief in miracles is not distinctively *Christian*.

An extremely important set of statements come in Bultmann's essay of 1953 entitled "The Case for Demythologizing: A Reply." Here he writes: "The purpose of demythologizing is not to make religion more acceptable to modern man by trimming the traditional Biblical texts, but to make clearer to modern man what the Christian faith is. He must be confronted with the issue of decision."[31] But this is not the way of liberalism. "Such an attempt does not aim at reassuring modern man by saying to him: 'You no longer have to believe this and that' . . .; not by showing him that the number of things to be believed is smaller than he had thought, but because it shows him that to believe at all is qualitatively different from accepting a certain number of propositions."[32] Even in his original essay of 1941 Bultmann writes, "The liberal theologians of the last century were working on the wrong lines. They threw away not only the mythology but also the kerygma itself. . . . It is characteristic of the older liberal theologians that they regarded mythology as relative and temporary. Hence they thought they could safely eliminate it altogether. . . . It will be noticed how Harnack reduces the kerygma to a few basic principles of religion and ethics."[33]

The clue to Bultmann's assessment of the hermeneutical and theolog-

29. R. Bultmann, *Jesus Christ and Mythology*, pp. 35-36.
30. W. Schmithals, *An Introduction to the Theology of Rudolf Bultmann*, pp. 255-56.
31. R. Bultmann, in *K.M.* II, 182-83.
32. *Ibid.*, p. 183.
33. R. Bultmann, in *K.M.* I, 23-33.

ical significance of the so-called scientific world-view can be found in his essay "The Question of Wonder," first published in 1933 in *Glauben und Verstehen*. The idea of scientific causality, he writes, "is not 'an interpretation of the world' . . . 'a world-view' (*Weltanschauung*). . . . *It is given in our existence in the world (er ist mit unserem Dasein in der Welt- gegeben*)."[34] It would simply not be responsible, Bultmann argues, to try to live on the assumption that God might suddenly suspend the law of gravity. "The idea of two causalities, different in kind, working concurrently (*zwei miteinander konkurrierenden Kausalitäten*) is not really conceivable."[35] On this basis "the idea of miracle (*Mirakel*) . . . must be abandoned."[36] We have already seen, however, that the real reason why Bultmann reaches this conclusion is not primarily because of any liberal concern about man, but because of his theological response to an acceptance of Neo-Kantian epistemology. God is, as it were, outside the realm of objectifying knowledge, and consequently outside the realm of "law." Thus Bultmann goes on in this same essay to speak of the hiddenness of God. We cannot speak of miracle (*Mirakel*) but we can indeed speak of wonder (*Wunder*). This is the "one wonder" of revelation, in accordance with which "to speak of wonder means to speak of my own existence."[37] Characteristically, almost predictably, Bultmann now adds, "Thus the concept of wonder radically negates the character of the world as the controllable, working world (*Arbeitswelt*), because it destroys man's understanding of himself as made secure through his work."[38]

From this perspective we are in a position to assess the relative force of claims made by Macquarrie, Cairns, Ogden, and Schmithals about Bultmann's attitude towards science and the scientific world-view. Macquarrie speaks of those Christians who do in practice seek spiritual healing today, and comments, "We perceive in Bultmann's thought not the influence of existentialism, but the hangover of a somewhat old-fashioned liberal modernism. He is still obsessed with the pseudo-scientific view of a closed universe that was popular half a century ago."[39] Cairns reaches a similar conclusion, pointing out that G. J. Warnock and other philosophers are content to allow that certain phenomena may answer to both a mechanical and a teleogical explanation, without resorting to the idea that the latter violates laws of causation.[40] It would be possible to appeal to a number of contemporary philosophers to support

34. R. Bultmann, *F.U.* I, 248 (German, p. 215).
35. *Ibid.*, p. 248 (German, p. 216).
36. *Ibid.*, p. 249 (German, p. 216).
37. *Ibid.*, p. 254.
38. *Ibid.*, p. 255 (German, p. 222).
39. J. Macquarrie, *An Existentialist Theology*, p. 158 (first edn. p. 168).
40. D. Cairns, *A Gospel without Myth?*, pp. 123-24; cf. pp. 112-35.

Cairns's statements. As A. Boyce Gibson puts the matter, it is generally agreed that natural "laws" are *descriptive generalizations* about regularities hitherto observed, not prescriptive formulations about what "must" happen. He comments, "If, as Hume supposes, laws of nature are founded on experience, there is no question of violation, because laws are only progress reports. Anything may happen later. . . ."[41] Long ago Thomas Aquinas argued that miracles were not *contra naturam* but *praeter naturam*.

Schubert Ogden, however, explicitly attacks Macquarrie's comments, and Walter Schmithals also tries to defend Bultmann against this kind of criticism.[42] Ogden simply appeals to Bultmann's own words to the effect that whatever specific conclusions scientists happen to have reached about the world, the scientific *method* of experimentation is permanently with us, although this hardly answers the kind of point made by Boyce Gibson and discussed by Macquarrie and Cairns. Schmithals, too, claims that whatever modifications have been made to nineteenth-century conclusions, "that does not alter the method of scientific thought." What demonstrates the importance of Macquarrie's language about a closed universe, however, is not debates about scientific method, but Bultmann's acceptance of Neo-Kantian epistemology as the point of departure for his own view of the sphere of revelation and faith. As we saw two chapters back, the whole point about the Neo-Kantian theory of knowledge was that, in Cohen's words, "any assertion gains its status as true solely by virtue of its *systematic position in a body of universal laws* that, in turn, require each other on methodological grounds." In his essay of 1925, "What Does It Mean to Speak of God?", we saw that Bultmann rejects any attempt to place God "in a system (*in einem System*) of general truths (*allgemeinen Wahrheiten*)."[43] Whatever may be affirmed or denied about science as a closed system, there can be no doubt that in accordance with Neo-Kantian epistemology there is a sense in which Bultmann conceives of *all* objectifying knowledge as one vast systematic calculus, *within* which God, revelation, and faith are not to be found.

Perhaps Ogden is right, then, in claiming that Bultmann's three views of myth are not all that far apart, after all. For we have now arrived at Bultmann's existentialist formulation of myth. What Bultmann has been criticizing is myth as that which conveys a world-view. That the world-view of the New Testament is incompatible, or so it is claimed, with modern science, certainly adds fuel to the fire. But this is not in itself the

41. A. B. Gibson, *Theism and Empiricism*, p. 268.
42. S. M. Ogden, *Christ Without Myth*, pp. 38-39; and W. Schmithals, *An Introduction to the Theology of Rudolf Bultmann*, pp. 253-54.
43. R. Bultmann, *F.U.* I, 60 (German, p. 32).

main reason behind the call to demythologize. The reason is a much deeper one. Bultmann's indebtedness to liberalism shows itself partly, admittedly, in his concerns about modern man and modern science. But the major impact of his liberalism can be seen, rather, in the historical scepticism which characterizes *The History of the Synoptic Tradition*, and in his suspicions of theology as orthodox dogma. The very least that can be said is to endorse Ian Henderson's verdict that the rejection of what does not harmonize with "the scientific conception of the world as a closed causal system" constitutes one of three or four parallel reasons why we are invited to demythologize the New Testament.[44]

We may see how readily this set of problems about "science" merges into the problem of objectification when we recall Bultmann's warnings about the relation between myth in the New Testament and modern man's understanding of himself. Man knows, Bultmann urges, that he bears responsibility for himself. However, in mythology he projects his sense of bondage outside himself, with the result that the New Testament speaks of being in bondage to the powers of the old aeon or the god of this world.[45] We return to Bultmann's "existentialist" formulation of myth: "The real purpose of myth is not to present an objective picture of the world as it is, but to express man's understanding of himself in the world in which he lives."[46] As Norman Perrin puts it, Bultmann tends to regard language as "essentially a vehicle for transmitting an understanding of existence."[47]

At this point many of Bultmann's critics accuse him of selling out the message of the New Testament to Heidegger's philosophy. It is crucial to Bultmann's own argument, however, to say that *the New Testament itself, by its very nature,* invites demythologization. Thus Bultmann writes, "Some critics have objected that I am borrowing Heidegger's categories and forcing them upon the New Testament. I am afraid this only shows that they are blinding their eyes to the real problem."[48] "The New Testament itself invites this kind of criticism" (i.e. criticism of its mythological language).[49] In essence, Bultmann puts forward three arguments about the New Testament material. First of all, its language is really intended to speak of human existence and to challenge man to new self-understanding. It only *appears* to describe objective events, and insofar as it does so, this obscures and impedes its intention. Secondly, various myths contradict each other, thereby demonstrating that myth is no more, as it were, than a way of speaking. Thirdly, Bultmann claims

44. I. Henderson, *Myth in the New Testament*, p. 46.
45. R. Bultmann, *K.M.* I, 5-6.
46. *Ibid.*, p. 10.
47. N. Perrin, *Jesus and the Language of the Kingdom*, p. 110.
48. R. Bultmann in *K.M.* I, 25.
49. *Ibid.*, p. 11.

that the process of demythologizing begins in the New Testament itself. Before we look at specific examples in the New Testament, one more point must first be noted. The first of these three points is bound up with the view of faith which Bultmann supposes that he draws from the New Testament and from Luther. Thus in a key statement in one of his replies to his critics he writes, "The restatement of mythology is a requirement of faith itself. For faith needs to be emancipated from its association with every world view expressed in objective terms."[50] He continues: "Our radical attempt to demythologize the New Testament is in fact *a perfect parallel to St. Paul's and Luther's doctrine of justification by faith alone* apart from the works of the Law. Or rather, *it carries this doctrine to its logical conclusion in the field of epistemology.* Like the doctrine of justification it destroys every false security. . . . The man who wishes to believe in God as his God must realize that he has nothing in his hand on which to base his faith. . . . Security can be found only by abandoning all security."[51] We have reached exactly the point which we made about Bultmann's view of history when we compared it with that of Kähler two chapters back, and we are about to encounter precisely the problems that we noted about Bultmann's view of history in the previous chapter.

We must now ask how this principle applies to the interpretation of certain specific types of material in the New Testament, including its eschatology, Christology, view of the atonement, the resurrection of Christ, and language about miracles.

37. *Specific Examples of Re-interpretation in the New Testament: A Critique of Bultmann's Claims about Eschatology and Christology*

It is not difficult to see how, on the basis of Bultmann's approach, eschatology seems to have become entangled with a particular view of the world. When the Son of Man comes, believers will "meet him in the air" (1 Thess. 4:15-17). He will come "with the clouds of heaven" (Mark 14:62). These look like descriptive statements about the future. But Bultmann asserts, "We can no longer look for the return of the Son of Man on the clouds of heaven, or hope that the faithful will meet him in the air."[52] Not only is this apparently bound up with the three-decker view of the universe, it also, in Bultmann's view, allows faith to rest on something which is said to happen objectively in the world. He therefore rejects an

50. *Ibid.*, p. 210.
51. *Ibid.*, pp. 210-11 (my italics).
52. *Ibid.*, p. 4.

interpretation which understands such passages as primarily, if at all, predicting a future event. If we wish to speculate about a future ending of the world, he argues, this can only take the form of a purely natural event. The New Testament is only drawing on the mythology of apocalyptic in order to challenge man with the urgency of present decision.

In his earlier book *Jesus* in 1926 Bultmann had already urged that the whole point of apocalyptic language about the Kingdom of God was that it forces man to decision. "The future Kingdom of God, then, is not something which is to come in the course of time. . . . It determines the present because it now compels man to decision. . . . Attention is not to be turned to the contemporary mythology in terms of which the real meaning in Jesus' teaching finds its outward expression. This mythology ends by abandoning the fundamental insight to which it gave birth, the conception of man as forced to decision through a future act of God."[53] In a sermon of June 1936, Bultmann makes a similar point about the language of Acts 17:31: "He has fixed a day on which he will judge the world. . . ." This means that man "must choose his way in responsibility and decision." "Man stands before God alone . . . in stark loneliness."[54]

This eschatological language also seems to fit in with Bultmann's second criterion of myth, namely that it involves contradiction. In *Jesus Christ and Mythology* he states, "History continues. . . . The course of history has refuted mythology. For the conception 'Kingdom of God' is mythological, as is the conception of the eschatological drama."[55] Elsewhere he writes, "The mythical eschatology is untenable for the simple reason that the parousia of Christ never took place as the New Testament expected."[56] The contradiction would be serious, if there is indeed a contradiction, if the language of eschatology functions as descriptive assertions. It is different, however, if it is only language which relates to man's understanding of himself, or to present decision.

It is in the realm of eschatology that, from Bultmann's own viewpoint, there is least difficulty in invoking his third principle, that the New Testament writers actually begin the process of demythologization themselves. Bultmann writes, "Very soon the process of demythologizing began, partially with Paul, and radically with John. The decisive step was taken when Paul declared that the turning point from the old world to the new was not a matter of the future but did take place in the coming of Jesus Christ. 'But when the time had fully come, God sent forth his Son.' (Gal. 4:4)."[57] Paul can say that death is swallowed up in victory (1 Cor.

53. R. Bultmann, *Jesus and the Word*, pp. 44 and 47.
54. R. Bultmann, *This World and Beyond. Marburg Sermons* (Lutterworth Press, London, 1960), p. 21.
55. R. Bultmann, *Jesus Christ and Mythology*, p. 14.
56. R. Bultmann, *K.M.* I, 5.
57. R. Bultmann, *Jesus Christ and Mythology*, p. 32.

15:54), and that "now" is the day of salvation (2 Cor. 6:2). "After Paul, John demythologized the eschatology in a radical manner."[58] "This is the judgement, that light has come into the world, and men loved darkness rather than light" (John 3:19). "Now is the judgement of this world; now shall the ruler of this world be cast out" (John 12:31). Bultmann claims, "For John the resurrection of Jesus, Pentecost, and the *parousia* . . . are one and the same event."[59] He even claims that the mythological figure of the Antichrist (2 Thess. 2:7-12) has been demythologized in the Johannine writings into the historical figures of false teachers.[60]

If he had not been writing as a New Testament scholar, we might have imagined that Bultmann was unaware of what other New Testament scholars have regularly called the double polarity of eschatology in the New Testament, according to which both the "now" and "not yet" have weight and importance. C. K. Barrett, G. E. Ladd, and numerous other writers have rightly underlined this feature, G. E. Ladd arguing that it even constitutes a particular point of common unity among different New Testament writers.[61] C. K. Barrett argues that future eschatology in John is an important part of his total theological perspective.[62] However, Bultmann argues that the notion of a "time-between," of an interval between the resurrection and the parousia, is bound up with the church's embarrassment at the delay of the parousia, and, worse, allows Christianity to pass "for a worldly phenomenon, namely the Christian religion."[63] Bultmann insists that even though the author of Luke-Acts conceived of Christian faith in this way, a way which accords with the New Testament interpretation of Oscar Cullmann, nevertheless Paul and John cannot conceive of history and eschatology in this way. Paul's view of history, he claims, is not cosmological but anthropological. This "is indicated by the fact that Paul can present the course of history from Adam . . . to Christ in the form of an autobiographical 'I' (Rom. 7:7-25a)."[64] Bultmann concludes, "Eschatological existence is possible only in faith; it is not yet realized in sight (2 Cor. 5:7). That is to say, *it is not a worldly phenomenon*, but is realized in the new self-understanding which faith imparts."[65]

---

58. *Ibid.*, p. 33.
59. *Ibid.*
60. *Ibid.*, p. 34.
61. C. K. Barrett, *The Gospel according to St. John* (S.P.C.K., London, 1958), pp. 56-58; and G. E. Ladd, "Eschatology and the Unity of New Testament Theology" in *Exp.T.* I.XVIII (1957), 268-73. Cf. also A. L. Moore, *The Parousia in the New Testament* (Brill, Leiden, 1966; *Supplements to Novum Testamentm* 13).
62. C. K. Barrett, *The Gospel according to St. John*, pp. 56-58.
63. R. Bultmann, "History and Eschatology in the New Testament" in *N.T.S.* I (1954), 15; cf. pp. 5-16.
64. R. Bultmann, *History and Eschatology*, p. 41.
65. R. Bultmann in *K.M.* I, 208 (my italics).

Once again, then, the specter of Bultmann's theological response to Neo-Kantian epistemology haunts his interpretation of the New Testament. It is assumed on the basis of *Sachkritik* that Paul and John *must* "really" have meant to convey an understanding of eschatology that accords with Bultmann's understanding of eschatological existence as a present reality which is not "this-worldly." It is difficult to see what, on the basis of Bultmann's assumptions, *could have counted as evidence against* his interpretation. For the retention of futurist imagery is regarded as evidence in the New Testament for the *need* to demythologize; while realized eschatology is regarded as evidence that the *process* of demythologizing has begun in the New Testament. Either way, Bultmann claims to find support for his argument, *whatever* exegetical considerations are brought into play. In three other studies, however, I have tried to argue that the perspective of a futurist eschatology is part and parcel of the outlook of Paul and other New Testament writers.[66]

We turn next to Christology. Bultmann insists that it is only Gnostic influence which suggests that Jesus Christ was "not a mere human being but a God-man." He adds, "And as for the pre-existence of Christ . . . this is not only irrational but utterly meaningless."[67] He writes, "It is beyond question that the New Testament presents the event of Jesus Christ in mythical terms. . . . Jesus Christ is certainly presented as the Son of God, a pre-existent divine being, and therefore to that extent a mythical figure."[68] However, he is also a concrete figure of history (*ein bestimmter historischer Mensch*), and to this extent we have a unique combination of history and myth (*Historisches und Mythisches sind hier eigentümlich verschlungen*).[69] The person of Christ "was mythologized from the very beginnings of earliest Christianity." The Palestinian communities used mythology relating to the figures of Messiah and Son of Man; while the Hellenistic churches drew on mythical language about the Son of God. Bultmann asserts, "It is evident that such conceptions are mythological, for they were widespread in the mythologies of Jews and Gentiles and then were transferred to the historical person of Jesus."[70]

The first two of Bultmann's three principles about myth are explicitly applied to Christology. First of all, the myth represents an attempt on the part of the primitive churches to express the *meaning* of the historical

66. A. C. Thiselton, "Realized Eschatology at Corinth" in *N.T.S.* XXIV (1978), 510-26; "The Parousia in Modern Theology: Some Questions and Comments" *T.B.* XXVII (1976), 27-54; and *Eschatology and the Holy Spirit in Paul with Special Reference to 1 Corinthians* (unpublished M.Th. Dissertation, University of London, 1964).
67. R. Bultmann, *K.M.* I, 8.
68. *Ibid.*, p. 34.
69. *Ibid.* (German, p. 44).
70. R. Bultmann, *Jesus Christ and Mythology*, pp. 16-17.

Jesus (*den Sinn . . . die Bedeutsamkeit der historischen Gestalt Jesu und seiner Geschichte*). Hence we can dispense with the objective form in which the language is cast (*ihr objektivierender Vorstellungsgehalt*).[71]

This outlook accords completely with Bultmann's approach in his lecture of 1951 on the Christological Confession of the World Council of Churches.[72] The "decisive question," Bultmann urges, is whether the titles of Jesus in the New Testament "intend to tell us something about the nature of Jesus . . . objectifying him in his being in himself (*in seinem An-sich-Sein objektivierend*), or whether and how far they speak of him in his significance for man, for faith (*in seiner Bedeutsamkeit für den Menschen*). Do they speak of his *phusis* or of the *Christus pro me*? How far is a christological pronouncement about him also a pronouncement about me? Does he help me because he is God's Son, or is he the Son of God because he helps me?"[73] On the one hand, a confession such as "we believe and are sure that thou art the Christ, the Son of the living God" (John 6:69) is a confession (*Bekenntnis*) not a dogmatic statement (*Satz*). On the other hand, in the sense of dogmatic statements, "the devils also believe and tremble" (James 2:19). The Christian confession is that Christ is the power of God *for us* (1 Cor. 1:30). Bultmann then virtually sums up his program of demythologizing when he adds, "So far . . . as such pronouncements digress into objectivizing propositions (*objektivierende Sätze*), they are to be interpreted critically."[74]

On this basis Bultmann argues that "the formula 'Christ is God' is false in every sense in which God is understood as an entity which can be objectivized, whether it is understood in an Arian, or Nicene, an Orthodox, or a Liberal sense. It is correct, if 'God' is understood here as the event of God's acting."[75] The Chalcedonian formula is "impossible for our thought" because it rests on Greek thought "with its objectivizing nature."[76] We return, then, to the statement of A. Malet, to which we alluded earlier: "The truly 'objective' Christ is not Christ *in se* but the Christ of the *beneficia*."[77]

Bultmann invokes his second principle just as explicitly, claiming that glaring contradictions occur if christological confessions are interpreted as descriptive statements. For example, in one set of passages the New Testament portrays Christ as Judge (1 Thess. 2:19; 1 Cor. 4:5); in other passages the Judge is God himself (1 Thess. 3:13; Rom. 3:5). Both

71. R. Bultmann, *K.M.* I, 35 (German, p. 44).
72. R. Bultmann, *E.P.T.*, pp. 273-90; German, *G.u.V.* II, 246-61.
73. *Ibid.*, p. 280 (German, p. 252).
74. *Ibid.*, p. 281 (German, p. 253).
75. *Ibid.*, p. 287.
76. *Ibid.*, p. 286.
77. A. Malet, *The Thought of Rudolf Bultmann*, p. 20.

ideas occur together in Acts 17:31. But this does not mean "that we have to be responsible before two tribunals or even just two persons; rather that our responsibility to Christ is identical with our responsibility to God."[78] Similarly, Bultmann argues that the statement "He emptied himself . . . being made in the likeness of man" (Phil. 2:7) contradicts the portrait of Jesus and Nazareth as "a man approved by God to you by mighty works and wonders" (Acts 2:22). Christ's pre-existence in Paul and John, he claims, is difficult to reconcile with the story of the Virgin Birth in Matthew and Luke.[79]

Bultmann cannot invoke the third principle, that of demythologizing within the New Testament, except in the obvious sense that many christological confessions are expressions of the believer's *experience* of Christ, especially in Paul. In one sense it is true that Paul's favorite title for Christ, that of Lord, expresses man's own experience of yieldedness to Christ and devotion to his sovereignty. This comes out magnificently in Bultmann's *Theology of the New Testament* where he describes how the believer lets the care of himself go, yielding himself entirely to the grace of God. Bultmann rightly cites as an outstanding example of Christian yieldedness and freedom Paul's words: "None of us lives to himself and none of us dies to himself. If we live, we live to the Lord; and if we die, we die to the Lord. So then, whether we live or whether we die, we are the Lord's" (Rom. 14:7, 8).[80] However, it is in the later Pauline passages that an increasingly cosmic perspective emerges for Christology. Even from Bultmann's viewpoint, one would be forced to admit that, far from seeing the perils of objectification, Paul seems to move increasingly from the realm of existential language to that of a world perspective.

As it stands, the material of the New Testament writings may allow different linguistic explanations from those offered by Bultmann. Contradictions, if such they are, are usually explained by New Testament scholars in terms of a series of developing Christologies, as Bultmann himself, in historical terms, views them. But the category of myth is not the only alternative to that of flat *description*. The use of imagery, metaphor, or the language of evaluation, each contributes to a total picture which in purely descriptive terms would constitute contradiction. The fact that the term "Son of God" is applied to Christ only *metaphorically* was established as long ago as the Arian controversy, when it was pointed out that the chronological implications of the term "son" were not applicable to the relation between Christ and God. Moreover, christological terms are indeed not simply flatly descriptive, in that they are

78. R. Bultmann, *E.P.T.*, p. 283.
79. R. Bultmann, *K.M.*, p. 34.
80. R. Bultmann, *T.N.T.* I, 331.

self-involving utterances.[81] To confess that Christ is my Lord carries with it the corollary that I commit myself to be his servant or slave. However, as we shall see, British philosophers, especially J. L. Austin, have demonstrated that for self-involving utterances, or performative utterances, to be effective, *some particular state of affairs must be true.*[82] If this is so, the language of Christology cannot simply be transposed into language about human attitudes. The question "Does he help me because he is God's Son, or is he the Son of God because he helps me?" presents a thoroughly false alternative. To be sure, in one sense he is the Son of God because he helps me. But how could he help me unless he was the Son of God?

38. *Further Examples: A Critique of Bultmann's Claims about the Cross and Resurrection*

Our next set of examples concerns the atonement in the New Testament. Bultmann exclaims, "What a primitive mythology it is that a divine being should become incarnate, and atone for the sins of men through his own blood!" He adds, "If the Christ who died such a death was the pre-existent Son of God, what could death mean for him? Obviously very little, if he knew that he would rise again in three days!"[83] The notion that the guilt of one person can be expiated by the death of another rests only on primitive notions of guilt and righteousness. Bultmann asserts, "To believe in the cross of Christ does not mean to concern ourselves with a mythical process wrought outside of us and our world, with an objective event (*ein objektiv anschaubares Ereignis*) turned by God to our advantage, but rather to make the cross of Christ our own, to undergo crucifixion with him."[84]

Once again, Bultmann applies the three principles which we have described to this area of theology. First of all, far from being "a mythical process wrought outside us," the cross is "an ever-present reality" and "not just an event of the past which can be contemplated."[85] The significance of the cross lies in being "crucified with Christ" (Rom. 6:6; Gal.

81. Cf. D. D. Evans, *The Logic of Self-Involvement, A Philosophical Study of Everyday Language with Special Reference to the Christian Use of Language about God as Creator* (S.C.M., London, 1963).
82. J. L. Austin, *How to Do Things with Words* (Clarendon Press, Oxford, 1962), p. 45 *et passim*.
83. R. Bultmann, *K.M.*, pp. 7 and 8.
84. *Ibid.*, p. 36 (German, p. 46).
85. *Ibid.*

6:14), and in knowing "the fellowship of his sufferings" in conformity with his death (Phil. 3:10). It is "always bearing in our body the dying of Jesus" and "always being delivered to death for Jesus' sake" (2 Cor. 4:10, 11). The cross of Christ is "a historic (*geschichtliche*) fact originating in the historical (*historische*) event which is the crucifixion of Jesus. . . . Christ is crucified 'for us', not in the sense of any theory of sacrifice or satisfaction. . . . Mythological language is only a medium for conveying the significance of the historical event (*nichts anderes als eben die Bedeutsamkeit des historischen Ereignisses zum Ausdruck bringen*)."[86] It is a matter of the hearers "appropriating this significance for themselves."

Secondly, Bultmann claims, once again, that language about the cross and atonement is contradictory. "The mythological interpretation is a mixture of sacrificial and juridical analogies, which have ceased to be tenable for us today."[87] The language of expiatory sacrifice, Bultmann believes, comes from the Jewish cult. Paul takes over this language in such passages as Romans 5:9 and Galatians 3:13, but he "is following a tradition. . . . The above passages do not contain his characteristic view."[88] But there is also a quite different approach in Paul. "Christ's death is not merely a sacrifice . . . but is also the means of release from the powers of this age: law, sin, and death."[89] Still further, Paul describes Christ's death "in analogy with the death of a divinity of the mystery religions."[90] The initiate participates in both the dying and the reviving of the divinity. This approach is even extended by Paul so that he interprets Christ's death "in the categories of the Gnostic myth," with its emphasis on humiliation and exaltation.[91] As they stand, Bultmann argues, these different approaches are "actually contradictory."[92]

Thirdly, however, Bultmann insists that all these mythologies "fail to do justice to what the New Testament is trying to say."[93] As we have just seen, they do not express "Paul's characteristic view." "Clearly Paul found none of these thought-complexes and none of these terminologies adequate to express his understanding of the salvation-occurrence."[94] The reason why he resorted to the mythology of the mystery religions and Gnosticism was that at least this language allowed the cross to be interpreted "as happening actually to and for and in man."[95] Such language

---

86. *Ibid.*, p. 37 (German, p. 47).
87. *Ibid.*, p. 35.
88. R. Bultmann, *T.N.T.* I, 296.
89. *Ibid.*, pp. 297-98.
90. *Ibid.*, p. 298.
91. *Ibid.*
92. R. Bultmann, *K.M.* I, 11.
93. *Ibid.*, pp. 35-36.
94. R. Bultmann, *T.N.T.* I, 300.
95. *Ibid.*

can be seen in its true intention only when it is integrated with the message of the resurrection. Then the whole complex of atonement-mythology can be seen to signify "the utter reversal of a man's previous understanding of himself—specifically, the radical surrender of his human 'boasting'."[96]

All the New Testament language about the atonement, then, is merely an elaborate linguistic medium which is really intended to express what amounts to a doctrine of justification by faith, and a challenge to man's old self-understanding. That a doctrine of the atonement necessarily involves this existential dimension, no New Testament scholar denies. The question that must be asked, however, is whether this existential aspect interprets all the so-called objective imagery *exhaustively and without remainder*. All the difficulties which we described in connection with Christology apply here. Joachim Jeremias, for example, comments, "By an increasing number of comparisons and images, Paul tries to make his hearers and readers understand the meaning of this 'for us'."[97] Jeremias cites the four different sets of imagery relating to sacrifice with its cultic background, punishment with its forensic background, purchase with its sociological background, and obedience with its personal and ethical background. But he does not suggest that as soon as the "for us" aspect has been understood, the rest of Paul's language is dispensable. Ian Henderson makes the same point about the interpretation of myth in more general terms.[98] There are two different kinds of interpretation, he suggests. There is the interpretation whose completion allows us to dispense with the original, as when we might, for example, decipher a code. Once the code has been deciphered the original may be discarded without loss. But there is also the kind of interpretation which can never substitute for the original. A commentary on a masterpiece of literature or another kind of art would constitute such an example. In this sense, the language of sacrifice and ransom cannot be interpreted in purely existential terms exhaustively and without remainder.

This principle becomes even more urgent in its application to Bultmann's claims about the resurrection of Christ. Once again we can see at work the three sets of considerations about myth which Bultmann usually brings into play. In the first place, the event of the resurrection is, in Bultmann's view, not to be objectified into an empirical occurrence in the world. He writes, "Faith in the resurrection is really the same thing as faith in the saving efficacy of the cross."[99] "Obviously it is not an event of

96. *Ibid.*
97. J. Jeremias, *The Central Message of the New Testament* (Eng. S.C.M., London, 1965), p. 36; cf. pp. 34-39.
98. I. Henderson, *Myth in the New Testament*, p. 31.
99. R. Bultmann, *K.M.* I, 41.

past history (*ein historisches Ereignis*) with a self-evident meaning. . . .
The resurrection cannot be a miraculous proof capable of demonstration."[100] Bultmann in fact allows that the New Testament writers often do
interpret it as a miraculous proof, as for example in Acts 17:31. He also
allows that within the New Testament itself there emerges the tradition of
the empty tomb and the appearances of Christ which presuppose the
physical reality (*Leiblichkeit*) of the risen body of Christ (Luke 24:39-43).
Nevertheless, he argues that this conflicts with the main intention and
logic of the New Testament writers, since they conceive of the resurrection as a matter of *faith*. "The difficulty is not simply the incredibility of a
mythical event like the resurrection of a dead person. . . . Nor is it merely
the impossibility of establishing the objective historicity of the resurrection (*als objektives Faktum*). . . . The real difficulty is that the resurrection is itself an article of faith (*Gegenstand der Glaubens*)."[101]

Bultmann brings together the two questions about contradiction and
demythologization within the New Testament, although he does not do
this in explicit terms. The most revealing statements in this connection
come in Bultmann's early discussion of Karl Barth's book *The Resurrection of the Dead* in 1926.[102] Contrary to Barth, Bultmann accepts that 1
Corinthians 15:1-11 does indeed constitute "an attempt to make the
resurrection of Christ credible as an objective historical fact (*ein objektives historisches Faktum*)."[103] But he then adds, "Paul is betrayed by his
apologetic into contradicting himself. For what Paul says in vv. 20-22 of
the death and resurrection of Christ cannot be said of an objective historical fact."[104]

The verses to which Bultmann appeals, however, prove his point
only if we accept his own prior assumptions about the problem of objectification and the sphere of God's revelation and saving activity. 1 Corinthians 15:20-22, to which Bultmann appeals, asserts simply that Christ
was raised from the dead as the firstfruits of the new humanity, and that
"in Christ shall all be made alive." Bultmann's presupposition is that, if
the resurrection of Christ is an act of God, it cannot be a "worldly"
phenomenon. A. Malet underlines this point: "The risen Christ is not an
earthly phenomenon. He is not an objective reality. Contrary to what
common sense assumes, . . . objectivity is the antithesis of otherness. . . .
The resurrection of Jesus cannot be a *Mirakel* which mythologizes the
divine and degrades it to the status of a 'work'. . . . A resurrection in this
world no more manifests God than does any phenomenon that we call

100. *Ibid.*, pp. 38-39 (German, pp. 47-48).
101. *Ibid.*, pp. 39-40 (German, p. 49).
102. R. Bultmann, *F.U.* I, 66-94 (German, pp. 38-64).
103. *Ibid.*, p. 83 (German, p. 54).
104. *Ibid.*, pp. 83-84.

normal."[105] The resurrection as an objective event would belong to the realm which man controls. But there is also a very different way of approaching the problem. Bultmann sees the meaning of the resurrection in terms of the believer's sharing in the experience of dying and rising with Christ. However, J. Macquarrie asks: "Does it . . . make sense to talk of 'dying and rising with Christ' without an assurance that, in some sense, Christ actually died and rose? . . . Can we be assured that a possibility is a genuine one unless we see it actually exemplified under the conditions of historical existence in the world?"[106]

Admittedly the rejoinder can be offered that to view the issue in this way is to interpret "possibility" in quasi-empirical terms, and to return to the subject-object pattern of thinking. Friedrich Gogarten writes, "Once our thinking is caught up in this subject-object pattern, the only possible way to disentangle it is to seek a philosophical means by which the pattern can be overcome. . . . Since our thinking . . . has been conducted in accordance with this pattern in the past three hundred years or so, the subject-object pattern cannot be overcome except by very considerable effort."[107] Gogarten believes that a misunderstanding and neglect of this point accounts for much of the criticism brought against Bultmann's view of history. The basis of faith, he claims, can only be the Word of God, and never an "objective" or "factual" reality.[108] But unless we begin from the starting-point of Bultmann and Gogarten, we do not have to choose between two artificial alternatives of either "fact" or "act of God." The setting up of this artificial alternative, moreover, does not spring from Bultmann's relation to Heidegger. It has much more to do with a theological response dictated by dialectical theology and Bultmann's version of Lutheranism to the epistemological problems set by Neo-Kantianism.

At this point Bultmann's dualism between the this-worldly and the other-worldly becomes even more serious than it is in his interpretation of the cross. As L. Malevez reminds us, when the theology of the atonement has been demythologized we are still left with the factual event of the crucifixion of Jesus of Nazareth under Pontius Pilate. But when the resurrection has been demythologized, there is no "event" other than the rise of the Easter faith of the primitive church. In Malevez's words, "Everything is mythical, not only the New Testament setting, but the tangible fact itself."[109] It is of course true, as Hans Conzelmann and others have argued, that the testimony to the resurrection in such passages as 1 Corinthians 15:3-8 takes the form of *confession*. Nevertheless,

---

105. A. Malet, *The Thought of Rudolf Bultmann*, pp. 155-56.
106. J. Macquarrie, "Philosophy and Theology in Bultmann's Thought" in *T.R.B.*, p. 141.
107. F. Gogarten, *Demythologizing and History* (Eng. S.C.M., London, 1955). p. 51.
108. *Ibid.*, p. 82.
109. L. Malevez, *The Christian Message and Myth*, p. 83.

as Vernon H. Neufeld has conclusively shown, we cannot drive a wedge between confession and report, as if one belonged only to the realm of faith, and the other belonged exclusively to the realm of fact. Confession, Neufeld concludes, combines the expression of a personal attitude with the declaration that a certain state of affairs has occurred.[110] The appeal to the category of "confession" cannot sustain Bultmann's dualism.

We have already noted Pannenberg's criticisms of Bultmann's dualism, both in our chapter on hermeneutics and history, and also towards the end of the previous chapter on Bultmann's hermeneutics. We saw that he not only endorsed Heinrich Ott's conclusions about this dualism in Bultmann's account of history, but that he also challenged the view of faith on which Bultmann's argument depends. On the basis of such an approach, Pannenberg insists, faith is "perverted into blind credulity towards the authority-claim of the preached message. . . . Paul speaks of the reverse, of the grounding of faith upon a knowledge (Rom. 6:8f.; 2 Cor. 4:13)."[111] Perhaps nothing indicates more sharply the radical difference between Pannenberg's concept of faith and Bultmann's than the statement in *Jesus—God and Man:* "If historical study declares itself unable to establish what 'really' happened at Easter, then all the more, faith is not able to do so. For faith cannot ascertain anything certain about the events of the past that would perhaps be inaccessible to the historian."[112] Such a criticism would not worry Bultmann because, for him, faith cannot be based on "worldly" events. But Pannenberg rightly demands to know what, in this case, faith really amounts to. *How* are the two sides of the dualism related?

It would achieve nothing to set out a detailed discussion of exegetical considerations about the resurrection of Christ in the New Testament. For one of the greatest difficulties about Bultmann's hermeneutics is his use of *Sachkritik.* He is always willing to allow that a *certain passage* in the New Testament may conflict with his own interpretation of Paul and John. But such passages, he always replies, conflict with the real intention or the inner logic of Pauline and Johannine thought. We have already noted that Paul's own arguments about the historical objectivity of the resurrection event are not denied, but are said to betray Paul into contradicting himself, because of his immediate apologetic purpose. The only criteria which can be invoked to test such a claim relate to beliefs about Paul's theology as a whole. However, that picture, in turn, is built up from concrete exegetical considerations. The interpreter or critic of Bultmann

110. V. H. Neufeld, *The Earliest Christian Confessions* (Brill, Leiden, 1963; New Testament Tools and Studies V), *passim.*
111. W. Pannenberg, *B.Q.T.* II, 28 and 31-32; cf. pp. 28-64.
112. W. Pannenberg, *Jesus—God and Man*, p. 109.

can only judge for himself whether the theological ingredients of Bultmann's thought allow him to construe Pauline or Johannine thought "as a whole" in a way which does full justice to Paul and John.

39. The Use of Heidegger's Conceptuality in New Testament Theology: Paul's View of Man

In the previous two chapters we argued that other philosophical and theological ingredients, apart from Heidegger, contributed to the *setting* of the terms of the hermeneutical problem for Bultmann. In his essay "The Case for Demythologizing" Bultmann insists that "Demythologizing involves a hermeneutic problem arising from a concrete situation . . . which is not defined by any special method of philosophizing."[113] However, we could also cite numerous comments from Bultmann to the effect that, as he put it in 1966, "Heidegger's analysis of existence has become for me fruitful for hermeneutics, that is, for the interpretation of the New Testament."[114] Although he claims that he does not subscribe to his philosophical theories as a system of metaphysics, nevertheless, "we learn something from his existentialist analysis."[115] At the same time, in this chapter so far we have observed Bultmann drawing on Heidegger's thought only in *general* terms. Partly through the work of Jonas, Bultmann sees myth as an expression of man's self-understanding, in contrast to the language of objectifying description. However, a rejection of objectifying language, as Friedrich Gogarten puts it, "does not have to be learnt from Heidegger. If one thinks one can learn it better from another source, all well and good."[116]

In terms of the demythologizing controversy, Bultmann's use of Heidegger is less concrete and specific than it is when he interprets parts of the New Testament which relate more directly to human existence. As J. Macquarrie comments, "Demythologizing is more restricted than existential interpretation. Demythologizing is directed upon those parts of the New Testament which are more or less mythical in their form. But not all of the New Testament is myth." Further, "demythologizing displays a radical scepticism towards any objective understanding of the stories which it seeks to interpret. . . . This is not a necessary concomitant of existential interpretation."[117] It is in this area in which existential in-

113. R. Bultmann, *K.M.* II, 182.
114. R. Bultmann, "Reply" in *T.R.B.*, p. 275.
115. R. Bultmann, *K.M.* II, 182.
116. F. Gogarten, *Demythologizing and History*, p. 52 n. 1.
117. J. Macquarrie, *The Scope of Demythologizing*, pp. 15 and 17.

terpretation extends beyond the more specific question about demythologizing that we see the most detailed and concrete use of Heidegger's conceptuality by Bultmann.

This area relates in particular to the New Testament portrait of man,
especially as this is expressed in Paul's anthropological vocabulary, and
also to the existence of man under faith as one who has been set free for
the future and now lives in the realm of eschatological existence. Because
of this, there is in fact not any real contradiction, as Johnson seems to
think there is, between his own recognition, which is correct, that
"Bultmann uses precisely those aspects of Heidegger's thought which fit
within the limits of his own philosophical perspective," and the arguments of J. Macquarrie and Heinrich Ott, which are also convincing,
about the extent of Bultmann's actual indebtedness to Heidegger.[118]
Johnson unnecessarily exaggerates the difference between his own approach and that of Ott and Macquarrie because he overlooks the extent to
which they are dealing with different areas of Bultmann's thought. In his
book *An Existentialist Theology*, Macquarrie is primarily concerned with
the concept of existence, with man in the world, with facticity and
fallenness, and with authentic existence, as these ideas are brought into
play both in *Being and Time* and in Bultmann's *Theology of the New
Testament*. It is precisely in this area that the latter's indebtedness to
Heidegger is most apparent. By contrast, the title of Johnson's book, *The
Origins of Demythologizing*, indicates an area where Heidegger's influence is almost perhaps minimal, except indirectly through the work of
Hans Jonas.

Were it not for Macquarrie's book *An Existentialist Theology*, we
should be obliged in this present study to go over this ground in detail.
However, even in 1969, some years after the publication of the volume in
question, Norman J. Young observes that Macquarrie has covered this
ground so thoroughly that "there is little that can be usefully added to that
discussion."[119] Our aim will be not to go over this whole area again in
detail, but to consider part of it sufficiently fully to establish three points.
First of all, we wish to underline the point that Heidegger's philosophical
perspectives can and indeed do shed light on the subject-matter of the
New Testament, partly by allowing the interpreter to step back from other
conceptual frames, such as that of idealism, and partly (to use Wittgenstein's language) by allowing him to notice what was always before his
eyes. Secondly, it is necessary to take account of more recent exegetical
discussions. Robert H. Gundry, for example, has very recently argued

118. R. A. Johnson, *The Origins of Demythologizing*, p. 28; cf. pp. 18-29, especially
p. 19 n. 1.
119. N. J. Young, *History and Existential Theology*, p. 47.

that Paul uses the term *sōma* in a consistently substantival or physical way.[120] Thirdly, it is of fundamental importance to the argument of the present study to note that although philosophical description allows the interpreter to notice certain features of New Testament thought that might otherwise be neglected, it also tempts the interpreter to emphasize only those features which are thereby brought to his attention. It encourages a selective or partial interpretation of the New Testament.

Bultmann first expounds his understanding of Paul's view of man in his long article on Paul written for the second edition of *Die Religion in Geschichte und Gegenwart* in 1930.[121] Here Bultmann declares that, in Paul, man is not an isolated being in the world, that he manifests his being in the world as care, and by resting his confidence in his own achievements and by understanding himself in terms of the transitory, "his being is not authentic."[122] "Body" and "soul," Bultmann states, "do not refer to *parts* of man . . . , but rather always mean *man as a whole*, with respect to some specific possibility of his being. . . . Paul can use almost every one of these (anthropological) concepts in the sense of 'I' (cf. e.g. 1 Cor. 6:15 with 12:27; or 1 Cor. 13:3 with 2 Cor. 1:23, 12:15). . . . Man is 'body' in his temporality and historicity."[123] That this language could equally well be Heidegger's is clear both from Macquarrie's discussion and from our two earlier chapters on Heidegger.

Bultmann expands this picture in greater detail in his *Theology of the New Testament*, some twenty years later. We may consider particularly his sections on "flesh," "flesh and sin," and "body" in Paul.[124] Bultmann allows that flesh may sometimes mean physical substance animated in the body (2 Cor. 12:7; Rom. 2:28). But he rightly points out that this use must be seen in the framework of the Old Testament rather than Hellenistic dualism. "Flesh and blood" merely means "people" or "humanity" (Gal. 1:16), and often such phrases as "my flesh" are synonymous with "I" (2 Cor. 7:5). However, a different picture emerges from a phrase such as "in the flesh" when it describes a mode of human existence. "This formula shows that according to Paul a man's nature is not determined by what he may be as to substance . . . nor by what qualities he may have . . . , but that his nature is determined by the sphere within which he moves. . . ."[125] With this we might compare Heidegger's language about man's possibilities being determined by his "world." In this sense, "those

120. R. H. Gundry, *Sōma in Biblical Theology with Emphasis on Pauline Anthropology* (Cambridge University Press, 1976; S.N.T.S. Monograph 29).
121. R. Bultmann, "Paulus" in *Die Religion in Geschichte und Gegenwart* IV (Mohr, Tübingen, ²1930), cols. 1019-45; English in *E.F.*, pp. 130-72.
122. R. Bultmann, *E.F.*, p. 152.
123. *Ibid.*, p. 153 (Bultmann's italics).
124. R. Bultmann, *T.N.T.* I, 192-203 and 232-46.
125. *Ibid.*, p. 235.

who are in the flesh cannot please God" (Rom. 8:8).[126] Existence "in the flesh" amounts to inauthentic existence, and "setting the mind on the things of the flesh" (Rom. 8:5) refers to "the pursuit of the merely human."[127]

Bultmann gives this a theological interpretation which accords both with Heidegger and with his concern about justification by faith. "Fixing the mind on the things of the flesh" (Rom. 8:7) means "to trust in one's self as being able to procure life by the use of the earthly and through one's strength."[128] Bultmann comments on the use of "flesh" in Galatians 3:3 and Philippians 3:3-7: "The attitude which orients itself by 'flesh' . . . is the self-reliant attitude of the man who puts his trust in his own strength and in that which is controllable by him."[129] It is "a life of self-reliant pursuit of one's own ends."[130] This leads not only to man's "boasting," but to his becoming a "debtor" to the flesh (Rom. 8:12) in the sense that he falls under the power of this mode of existence. He becomes "fleshly, sold under sin" (Rom. 7:14). Far from gaining the wholeness of authentic existence, " 'I' and 'I', self and self, are at war with each other . . . innerly divided" (Rom. 7:14-24).[131] Once again, from our chapters on Heidegger we can recognize the points of affinity with Heidegger's thought.

Before we try to assess how this interpretation relates to that of other New Testament scholars, we must glance briefly at Bultmann's interpretation of the Pauline uses of σῶμα. Bultmann insists that only in 1 Corinthians 15:35-44 does Paul use this term in the sense of outward physical form. The reason is only that here "Paul lets himself be misled into adopting his opponents' method of argumentation, and in so doing he uses the sōma-concept in a way not characteristic of him elsewhere."[132] Normally σῶμα stands for the whole person, as in such passages as "let not sin reign in your mortal sōma" (Rom. 6:12), or "Present your sōmata as living sacrifice" (Rom. 12:1). Bultmann asserts, "Man does not have a sōma; he is sōma."[133] "Man is called sōma in respect to his being able to make himself the object of his own action or to experience himself as the subject to whom something happens. He can be called sōma, that is, as having a relationship to himself."[134] As Macquarrie interprets Bultmann, a material thing such as a cricketball is purely an object. But man is "at

126. *Ibid.*, p. 236.
127. *Ibid.*, p. 238.
128. *Ibid.*, p. 239.
129. *Ibid.*, p. 240.
130. *Ibid.*, p. 241.
131. *Ibid.*, p. 245.
132. *Ibid.*, p. 192.
133. *Ibid.*, p. 194.
134. *Ibid.*, pp. 195-96.

once subject and object to himself. . . . He transcends the subject-object relationship. He understands himself, is open to himself in his being. He can be at one with himself or at war with himself; he can be himself or lose himself."[135] His existence is not to be described in terms of "properties," but of possibilities for the future. Σῶμα, like Dasein, stands for a way of being, in contrast to substance, nature, or object.

How are we to assess Bultmann's interpretation of σάρξ and σῶμα in Paul? His achievement can be fully appreciated only against the background of idealist interpretations of flesh in Paul at the hands of earlier New Testament scholars. Robert Jewett has demonstrated how firmly an idealist interpretation of Paul's view of man was embedded in the work of F. C. Baur, Carl Holsten, Hermann Lüdemann, Otto Pfleiderer, and H. J. Holtzmann.[136] Admittedly some writers prior to Bultmann, such as E. D. Burton, tried to do justice to the range and variety of Paul's uses of "flesh." But the quasi-Platonic interpretation of flesh in the New Testament had occupied some sort of place in Christian tradition since at least the time of Cyril of Alexandria. After Bultmann, however, as Jewett puts it, "the common view of *sarx* . . . is that it is the earthly sphere which becomes the source of sin only when man places his trust in it."[137] This perspective can be found in the work of many New Testament scholars, including E. Schweizer, W. G. Kümmel and E. Käsemann. Käsemann writes, for example, "The basic insight of Bultmann's interpretation was that the apostle's anthropological termini do not, as in the Greek world, characterize the component parts of the human organism; they apply to existence as a whole, while taking account of its varying orientation and capacity."[138]

It would admittedly be an exaggeration to claim that Bultmann's work alone was the decisive factor in leading to a unitary rather than dualist or partitive interpretation of Paul's view of man. The stress on so-called "Hebraic thought" associated with the era of the biblical theology movement also brought with it criticism of the attempt to find the basis of Paul's approach in the Hellenistic mind-body dualism. The distinctive insight of Bultmann about the term "flesh," however, was to call attention to its use in order to designate a mode of existence in which man trusted in his own resources in human self-sufficiency. Bultmann rightly pointed out that in Galatians, for example in Galatians 3:3, "ending with the flesh" meant ending "not in sensual passions but in observance of the

135. J. Macquarrie, *An Existentialist Theology*, p. 32.
136. R. Jewett, *Paul's Anthropological Terms. A Study of Their Use in Conflict Settings* (Brill, Leiden, 1971; Arbeiten zur Geschichte des antiken Judentums und des Urchristentums, Bd. X), especially pp. 50-57. Cf. Hermann Lüdemann, *Die Anthropologie des Apostels Paulus und ihre Stellung innerhalb seiner Heilslehre* (University Press, Kiel, 1872).
137. R. Jewett, *Paul's Anthropological Terms*, p. 67.
138. E. Käsemann, *Perspectives on Paul* (Eng. S.C.M., London, 1971), p. 7; cf. pp. 1-31.

Torah."[139] Several studies demonstrate that this approach is valid on exegetical grounds, including most recently Robert Jewett's excellent and detailed study of Paul's anthropological terms.

Jewett writes, "Our thesis is that the flesh-spirit dialectic has its root in the contrast Paul wishes to portray between boasting in the cross and boasting in the circumcised flesh."[140] Shifting one's boasting from the cross of Christ (Gal. 6:14) to the circumcised flesh (Gal. 6:13) "provides the key to the interpretation as well as the source of the *sarx* concept in Paul's theology. . . . One boasts in that upon which he finally depends."[141] Depending on one's own accomplishments stands in basic opposition to the whole principle of grace, of promise, of sonship, and of freedom. In Galatians 5:13-26 Paul turns from the legalists with their reliance on "religion" to the libertines. But even in this different context, the flesh still has the same theological significance. Jewett writes, "The key to the 'flesh' concept is not that it weakens man's will to do the good, but that it lures him to substitute his own good for God's. . . . The libertinist objects of desire . . . seem to offer man exactly what the law and circumcision offered—life."[142]

Jewett criticizes the existential interpretation, as he calls it, of Bultmann, Fuchs, and Schweizer, not on the grounds of what it says but on the grounds of what it fails to say. It fails to take account, Jewett claims, of the influence of apocalyptic on Pauline thought, and offers no explanation about the origins of Paul's use of the term flesh. Jewett's criticisms are valid as far as they go, but they do not challenge the value of Bultmann's approach in broad terms. Indeed, if the discussion is to be carried out at a detailed level, Jewett himself might be said to be open to criticism in not allowing for a sufficient range and variety in Paul's use of σάρξ.

My own conclusions about exegetical and semantic questions concerning σάρξ appear in two articles on this subject.[143] In the more recent of these articles I have argued that "the meaning of σάρξ varies radically from context to context."[144] "Fleshly" may take the form of a value-judgment of disapproval, the specific content of which may vary from case to case. Σάρξ, in other words, is a polymorphous concept. However,

---

139. R. Bultmann, *T.N.T.* I, 240.
140. R. Jewett, *Paul's Anthropological Terms*, p. 99.
141. *Ibid.*, p. 95.
142. *Ibid.*, pp. 103-04.
143. A. C. Thiselton, "The Meaning of Σάρξ in 1 Corinthians 5.5: A Fresh Approach in the Light of Logical and Semantic Factors" in *S.J.T.* XXVI (1973), 204-28; and "Flesh" (Supplement) in C. Brown (ed.), *The New International Dictionary of New Testament Theology* I (Paternoster, Exeter, 1975), 678-82.
144. A. C. Thiselton, "Flesh" in *The New International Dictionary of New Testament Theology* I, 678.

in the earlier article I also argued that not only was Bultmann's interpretation of flesh of primary importance, but that it was applicable to passages in 1 and 2 Corinthians, over and above those in Romans and Galatians which Bultmann himself cites.[145] In my exegetical discussions I took account of the work of E. Schweizer, A. Sand, and other scholars.[146]

Bultmann's interpretation of Paul's use of σῶμα has been even more influential than his work on σάρξ. A host of scholars have endorsed his view that "Man, his person as a whole, can be denoted by *soma*."[147] Robert Gundry comments, "We can hardly overestimate the importance of this definition, for Bultmann gives pride of place to Pauline theology, interprets Pauline theology as anthropology and makes *sōma* the key to that anthropology."[148] Gundry then offers detailed documentation to show that an overwhelming majority of scholars who have written on this subject have followed Bultmann in his conclusions, including for example Hans Conzelmann, M. E. Dahl, L. Cerfaux, and A. M. Hunter.[149] At the same time Gundry also notes that Bultmann's understanding of σῶμα as "self" or "person," in a way that parallels the personal pronoun, is due not so much to existentialist insights, but to Bultmann's following the work of his former teacher, Johannes Weiss.[150] This is not of course to deny that Bultmann's understanding of Heidegger may have underlined the importance of this approach for Bultmann, and encouraged him to emphasize and develop it.

Gundry challenges a number of assumptions in the holistic or unitary interpretation, however. He argues, first, that no inference about the semantic scope of σῶμα can be drawn from the fact that it is interchangeable with personal pronouns. He compares the sentences "She slapped his face" and "she slapped him," and comments that while "face" and "him" may be interchanged, "their interchangeability does not imply that 'face' has here become a technical term for the whole man."[151] We may speak of people as "souls" by synecdoche without implying any conclusion about the scope of the term "soul." On the other hand, passages such as Romans 6:12-14 and 16 suggest a reference to the physical body as the medium of action in the material world. Secondly, Gundry pays special attention to Paul's references to the body in the argument of 1 Corinthians 6:12-20. We cannot trace the details of his exegetical discussion here, but

145. A. C. Thiselton, "The Meaning of Σάρξ in 1 Corinthians 5.5" in *S.J.T.* XXVI , 212-15.
146. Cf. A. Sand, *Der Begriff 'Fleisch' in den paulinischen Hauptbriefen* (Pustet, Regensburg, 1967; Biblische Untersuchungen Bd. 2).
147. R. Bultmann, *T.N.T.* I, 195.
148. R. H. Gundry, *Sōma in Biblical Theology*, p. 4.
149. Cf. H. Conzelmann, *An Outline of the Theology of the New Testament* (Eng. S.C.M., London, 1968), p. 176; and R. H. Gundry, *Sōma in Biblical Theology*, pp. 5-8.
150. R. H. Gundry, *Sōma in Biblical Theology*, p. 4.
151. *Ibid.*, p. 30.

he concludes. "The *sōma* may *represent* the whole person simply because the *sōma* lives in union with the soul/spirit. But *sōma* does not *mean* 'whole person', because its use is designed to call attention to the physical object which is the body of the person rather than to the whole personality. Where used of whole people, *sōma* directs attention to their bodies, not to the wholeness of their being."[152] Thirdly, Gundry argues that there are terms in Paul which carry the flavor of a kind of dualism, in the sense that "outer man," "flesh," "body," and similar terms do duty for the corporeal part of man, while "inner man," "spirit," "mind," "heart," and "soul" all do duty for the incorporeal part.[153] Fourthly, Gundry gives detailed attention to Bultmann's claims about σῶμα, arguing that in more than one respect he tries "to squeeze the usage into a Heideggerian schema which fails to do justice to all the exegetical data. . . . The consistently substantival meaning of *sōma*, then, strikes at the heart of the anthropology of Bultmann, which, in turn, is his theology."[154]

Gundry does not for this reason entirely dismiss the value of Bultmann's labors. His effort, he observes, "has rewarded us richly. We shall never again be able to overlook the functional, operational elements in Pauline anthropology. . . . We have learned that they are more than descriptive of man. They are constitutive of man—but not to the exclusion of the substantival. Function must now be related to substance."[155] Gundry goes on to argue that by separating the realm of "responsibility" and "decision" from that of physical substance, it is Bultmann himself who is guilty, in the end, of a kind of dualism. This is precisely the point which we have urged in the present study, especially at the end of the previous chapter. Gundry concludes, "Ironically, what begins as an existentialist stress on human responsibility to decide the future ends in withdrawal from the only arena where we can exercise that responsibility—viz., the material world where objective events take place. . . ."[156]

We do not need to follow and endorse Gundry's argument in every exegetical detail in order to acknowledge that in the case of *many* (though not perhaps all) passages his claims are convincing. His criticism of Bultmann's interpretation of Paul's use of σῶμα is probably the most radical, but he is not entirely alone in arguing that Bultmann has failed to do full justice to the scope of Paul's language. E. Käsemann, for example, criticizes the individualistic nature of Bultmann's interpretation, claiming that body denotes "that piece of world which we ourselves are and for

152. *Ibid.*, p. 80.
153. *Ibid.*, p. 156.
154. *Ibid.*, p. 188.
155. *Ibid.*, p. 189.
156. *Ibid.*, p. 190.

which we bear responsibility. . . . For the apostle it signifies man in his worldliness and therefore in his ability to communicate. . . . In the bodily obedience of the Christian . . . in the world of every day, the lordship of Christ finds visible expression."[157]

The conclusion which all this suggests is that Bultmann's use of philosophical description enables him to notice important features of the subject-matter of the New Testament, but that his insights are sometimes selective, partial, and in need of complementation by work at the level of painstaking exegesis.

40. *Some Concluding Comments*

We may take as our point of departure for our concluding comments on Bultmann's hermeneutics a statement put forward by N. A. Dahl. In his essay entitled "Rudolf Bultmann's Theology of the New Testament" he writes, "The connection with Heidegger has helped him (Bultmann) to break through and to correct the earlier dominant understanding of New Testament anthropology that was determined by the idealistic tradition. Yet . . . the question arises whether or not Bultmann absolutizes his philosophical 'pre-understanding' in such a way that he decides in advance what the New Testament writings may or may not really say."[158] We agree with Dahl's verdict about the value of Bultmann's use of Heidegger's perspectives as a corrective to other approaches. However, he is both right and wrong in his comment about pre-understanding. He is right in the sense that the conceptuality with which Bultmann approaches the New Testament makes it possible to notice some things at the expense of overlooking others. He is wrong if he intends to say that the role which Bultmann *formally* assigns to the concept of pre-understanding in hermeneutics is itself responsible for undue selectivity in the handling of the New Testament. We do not criticize Bultmann's perfectly valid acceptance of the part played by an interpreter's own questions. We criticize the theological orientation which leads him to ask the particular questions that he does. We criticize not his *view* of pre-understanding, but the way in which he has allowed his own pre-understanding to be shaped in *practice*. This brings us to our first point.

---

157. E. Käsemann, *New Testament Questions of Today* (Eng. S.C.M., London, 1969), p. 135; cf. E. Käsemann, *Leib und Leib Christi* (Mohr, Tübingen, 1933; Beitrage zur historischen Theologie 9).
158. N. A. Dahl, *The Crucified Christ and Other Essays* (Augsburg Press, Minneapolis, 1974), p. 97.

(1) Methodologically Bultmann recognizes that pre-understanding constitutes no more than a starting-point which must be corrected in the light of the text. Neither the view of the hermeneutical circle which he finds in Schleiermacher and Heidegger nor even the view of "life" which he derives from Dilthey is responsible for the difficulty under discussion. Ironically, some of the problems raised by Bultmann's theology might have been avoided if the category of "life" had been allowed to play a part at the level of revelation and faith, rather than ranking merely as a "this-worldly" phenomenon. *What makes Bultmann foreclose in advance certain possibilities of interpretation is not his hermeneutical theory as such, but the theological response which he makes to the legacy of Neo-Kantian thought.* Any restricting features even in Heidegger's philosophy are restricting only in an almost secondary and incidental way. Heidegger's view of the historicity of Dasein, for example, encourages Bultmann to draw a radical contrast between past fact and present significance, just as his analysis of Dasein encourages an unduly individualistic perspective in Bultmann. But far more radical is Bultmann's insistence that acts of God belong to one realm, and this-worldly phenomena belong to a different realm. *This is a deeper and more persistent source of difficulty than Bultmann's use of Heidegger's conceptuality as such.* Dahl is therefore only partly right in talking about Bultmann's tendency to absolutize a philosophical pre-understanding. The absolute in Bultmann's thought, if such there is, is one of theology rather than philosophy.

(2) Bultmann's hermeneutics can be fully understood only in the light of his utilization of numerous "sources." We have discussed his relation to no less than ten figures or movements of thought: liberalism, Neo-Kantianism, Lutheranism (as mediated through Kähler and especially Herrmann), the History of Religions School, current biblical scholarship, dialectical theology, Heidegger, Dilthey, Collingwood, and Jonas. We could have added Kierkegaard and other thinkers to this list, but there are practical limits to this kind of exercise. Bultmann's originality lies in selecting elements of thought from each of these movements of thinkers and weaving them into a pattern which forms a coherent whole. It is true that he is not always successful in his attempt at consistency. Ogden and Macquarrie have made this point with reference to the question of the "scope" or limits of his demythologizing program. In spite of criticisms of their claims by Johnson, their comments have been vindicated by the sheer historical fact of the radical divergence between "left-wing" critics of Bultmann, such as Herbert Braun, Fritz Buri, and Schubert Ogden himself, and more orthodox "right-wing" critics. Ogden comments, "From both the 'right' and the 'left' responsible critics have repeatedly charged that Bultmann's view is, strictly speaking, not *a* view at all, but an uneasy synthesis of two different and ultimately incompatible

standpoints."[159] Johnson attacks this criticism on the ground that it "totally obscures the stringent theological focus that is present from the very beginning and consistently sustained in the whole of Bultmann's theology. . . . Bultmann is consistent and clear in his understanding of faith as always and only faith in the revelation of God in Jesus Christ."[160]

These two views of Bultmann's thought, however, are less contradictory than Johnson seems to think. *For the most part* the elements which Bultmann draws from his ten diverse "sources" serve to corroborate and support one another. The most obvious example of this relates to Bultmann's view of the relation between faith and history. Faith, we saw, must be said to rest neither on dogma nor on objective history, because this would entail a false security. This side of Bultmann's thought has affinities with Kähler. On the other hand, in *The History of the Synoptic Tradition* and in *Jesus and the Word* Bultmann reaches very pessimistic conclusions about historical inquiry. To borrow the phraseology of David Cairns, his "historical scepticism" is separate from his theological "flight from history"; but the two go easily together.[161] However, it would be surprising if such a wide sweep of the net failed to give ground for criticisms about inconsistency in certain particular respects. Our own view is that no less serious than the criticism expressed by Macquarrie and Ogden is Bultmann's inconsistency over the role played by the concept of "life." With Dilthey, he sees that the interpreter can only understand a text in relation to his own experience of life; but he supposes that acts of God will remain intelligible when they are relegated wholly to the realm of the Beyond outside this world. We shall explore this issue further in the next point.

(3) Bultmann has tried to respond to the epistemology of Marburg Neo-Kantianism, but in so doing has arrived at a dualism which in one respect reverses the concern of the Neo-Kantian philosopher, and brings him nearer to Kant himself. Kant, we might say, was more dualistic than the Neo-Kantians. The phenomenological realm was not co-terminous with reality. Ethics and value, for example, lie outside the phenomenological realm. Cohen, we saw, described it as "the fundamental weakness of Kant" that thinking has its beginning in some "given" outside itself. *Everything* becomes an object for thought, and is thus shaped and conditioned by the mind, seen through the grid of its objectifying laws. The Neo-Kantian concern with science, which we discussed in connection with Helmholtz, Hertz, and Boltzmann, arose not merely from a concern that philosophy should be up to date, but more radically from the urge to

159. S. M. Ogden, *Christ Without Myth*, p. 115. Cf. also Fritz Buri, "Entmythologisierung oder Entkerygmatisierung der Theologie" in *K.u.M.* II (1952), 85-101.
160. R. A. Johnson, *The Origins of Demythologizing*, pp. 17-18.
161. D. Cairns, *A Gospel without Myth?*, p. 140; cf. pp. 136-63.

arrive at a unified view of reality. Bultmann, however, reverses this concern by locating a second realm not, like Kant, in morality, but in the transcendent Beyond of revelation and faith. Thus when Pannenberg, for example, speaks about "the neo-Kantian distinction between being and value" it serves more as a comment on Bultmann's response to Neo-Kantian epistemology than as a description of the intention of the main Neo-Kantian thinkers themselves.[162]

Bultmann, however, makes a sharp division between God and his acts, on the one hand, and this-worldly phenomena on the other, including "religion." We have already discussed the criticisms of Ott, Pannenberg, and Young about the consequences of this for his view of history. This is also one of the factors, however, behind Bultmann's attitude to the Old Testament. This is made clear in his essay "The Significance of the Old Testament for Christian Faith."[163] The whole essay turns on the contrast between viewing the Old Testament as a source for reconstructing the religion of Israel and its possible status as revelation. From a theological viewpoint, Bultmann argues, "the relation of New Testament religion to Old Testament religion is not . . . relevant at all."[164] All that matters is "what basic possibility it presents for an understanding of human existence (*Daseinsverständnis*)."[165] Admittedly the Old Testament raises questions of law and grace, but "Jesus is God's demonstration of grace in a manner which is fundamentally different from the demonstrations of divine grace attested in the Old Testament."[166] In the Old Testament, Bultmann claims, to receive grace is seen as a matter of belonging to a particular people. In the New Testament it has nothing to do with a particular historical past, but "rather it is the Word which now addresses each person immediately as God's Word."[167]

Bultmann's approach to the Old Testament, then, rests on a dualism which draws a sharp line between two orders of reality. On the one hand, the Old Testament speaks about this-worldly history and religion. On the other hand, the New Testament speaks a word of personal address. But this raises questions in many areas of theology, and not least for hermeneutics. Who is this "God" who addresses us through the New Testament, unless he is the God of Abraham, of Isaac, and of Jacob? We shall see in a later chapter on Wittgenstein that this problem is really the problem of "private language." The Word of God must have a this-worldly cash-value; otherwise it is not a *word*. At times Bultmann seems

---

162. W. Pannenberg, *B.Q.T.* I, 86.
163. R. Bultmann, "The Significance of the Old Testament for Christian Faith" in B. W. Anderson (ed.), *The Old Testament and Christian Faith*, pp. 8-35.
164. *Ibid.*, p. 12.
165. *Ibid.*, p. 13.
166. *Ibid.*, p. 29.
167. *Ibid.*, p. 30.

to see this problem, especially when he talks about "life." I understand the Lordship of Christ through my everyday experience of obedience. Do I, then, understand what it means to be "redeemed" partly through Israel's historical experiences of redemption? If the answer is negative, we have reached a hermeneutical impasse. But if the answer is affirmative, why is Israel's redemption through this-worldly events (for example, the Exodus) not revelatory? Bultmann's dualism raises problems at every turn.

(4) The valuable feature behind Bultmann's dualism to which he is trying to give expression is partly his emphasis on the transcendence of God, and more specifically his concern about address, encounter, kerygma, decision, appropriation, and practical response. Hermeneutics, therefore, is never *only* a matter of understanding, but also of *hearing* and of *appropriation*. In the sense in which the term is so richly used by Martin Buber, hermeneutics brings about encounter and *dialogue*. Bultmann shares with Buber the valid and important recognition that the relationship of the I-Thou is different from that of the I-It. What Bultmann seems to overlook is Buber's realistic admission that it is "the exalted melancholy of our fate that every *Thou* . . . must become an *It*. . . . Without *It* man cannot live. But he who lives with *It* alone is not a man."[168] However, what Bultmann has in common with Buber is his stress on the role of personal address and dialogue, as between the I and the thou. Aubrey Hodes recalls Buber's oral remarks on the difference between propaganda and education in the sense of personal address. The one compels unthinking assent to dogmas and thereby closes the heart and stunts the mind. The other opens the heart and mind, so that a man comes to understand reality for himself and to appropriate it.[169] Bultmann's view of the Word of God is like the latter. It is a word of personal address that encounters the hearer, so that he responds by appropriating it for himself in decision. It is not propaganda-information about facts and concepts.

Even the study of history, for Bultmann, we saw, necessitates the historian's letting the text come alive with his own questions. For, following Dilthey and finding support in Collingwood, Bultmann insists that through history the interpreter comes to understand *himself*. His relationship to the text is not theoretical but *existentiell*. Only thus does the text "speak." We may recall in this connection Bultmann's very well-known words about the interpretation of the New Testament. Rather than interrogating the New Testament writings as "sources" for the reconstruction of "a picture of primitive Christianity as a phenomenon of the historical

---

168. Quoted and discussed in H. J. Paton, *The Modern Predicament*, p. 166; cf. pp. 162-73.
169. A. Hodes, *Encounter with Martin Buber* (Penguin Books, London, 1975), p. 135.

past," Bultmann prefers to say: "The reconstruction stands in the service of the interpretation of the New Testament writings under the presupposition that they have something to say to the present."[170] This perspective is nourished not only by dialectical theology, but also, as we have seen, by Heidegger's philosophy. We value this emphasis on the *existentiell* in hermeneutics, although we question whether it should necessarily carry with it a correspondingly radical devaluation of primarily cognitive, descriptive, or theoretical considerations.

(5) Our discussion of Bultmann's view of myth left several loose ends. We noted that the rejoinders of Thielicke, Schniewind, and Miegge about the nature of myth did not entirely meet Bultmann's point. However, we also noted that Bultmann's reply to their criticisms raised the question of how uncritically the New Testament writers used the medium of language which Bultmann calls myth. As John Knox rightly insists, on this issue hangs the question of how or when myth is distinguished from metaphor. Ancient man, Knox argues, actually believed that Aurora rose from the sea: "In a word, images which for us are metaphor were for him myth. . . . A myth is not an authentic myth if it is not believed."[171]

A number of scholars, however, have urged caution about assuming that biblical writers necessarily used mythical imagery uncritically. W. F. Albright, for example, challenges the assumptions which have been widespread in biblical scholarship since the Enlightenment about the logical capacities of the Hebrew mind. Albright insists that the biblical writers no more thought of heaven as literally "up" than modern man thinks of the sun as literally "rising."[172] Similarly in his examination of the ontology of the Book of Revelation Paul S. Minear concludes that the author did not in fact believe naively in a three-decker universe.[173] G. R. Beasley-Murray makes a similar point about the imagery of the Apocalypse, and G. B. Caird argues that while this book utilizes mythical imagery, the author does so with the critical awareness of the political cartoonist.[174] Brevard S. Childs has shown conclusively how in the Old Testament mythological imagery is repeatedly used not as myth, but as "broken myth."[175]

---

170. R. Bultmann, *T.N.T.* II, 251.
171. J. Knox, *Myth and Truth. An Essay on the Language of Faith* (Carey Kingsgate Press, London, 1966), pp. 25 and 27.
172. W. F. Albright, *New Horizons in Biblical Research* (Oxford University Press, 1966), pp. 17-35.
173. P. S. Minear, "The Cosmology of the Apocalypse" in W. Klassen and G. Snyder (eds.), *Current Issues in New Testament Interpretation* (S.C.M., London, 1962), p. 34; cf. pp. 23-37.
174. G. R. Beasley-Murray, "Demythologized Eschatology" in *Th.T.* XIV (1957), 66; cf. pp. 61-79; and G. B. Caird, "On Deciphering the Book of Revelation: Myth and Legend" in *Exp.T.* LXXIV (1962-63), 103; cf. pp. 103-05.
175. B. S. Childs, *Myth and Reality in the Old Testament* (S.C.M. London, ²1962), *passim*.

What is the bearing of this on Bultmann's arguments? First of all, these considerations make it hard to draw a clear line between myth and metaphor. If this is so, it opens the door again to a fresh consideration of the standard points put forward by Thielicke, Schniewind, and Miegge. It may be that in the light of this added factor their criticisms do not entirely miss the point, in the end. Secondly, if myth is to be understood not as a primitive world-view, but as imaginative imagery which functions with self-involving logic, it is no longer self-evident that such imagery is out-moded or obsolete. Karl Jaspers, Carl Jung, Mircea Eliade, and a number of biblical scholars including John Knox, A. N. Wilder and G. V. Jones—all insist that modern man *needs* myth, in this particular sense.[176] Eliade writes, for example, "We are at last beginning to know and under-stand the value of the myth. . . . The myth is not just an infantile or aberrant creation of 'primitive' humanity, but is the expression of a mode of being in the world. . . . It makes itself felt in the dreams, the fantasies, and the language of modern man. . . . Jung, for instance, believes that the crisis of the modern world is in great part due to the fact that the Christian symbols and 'myths' are no longer lived by the whole human being."[177] Karl Jaspers adds, "Mythical thinking is not a thing of the past, but characterizes man in any epoch. . . . How wretched how lacking in expressiveness our life would be if the langauge of myth were no longer valid. . . . The splendour and wonder of the mythical version is to be purified, but not be abolished."[178]

Bultmann would reply at once that he does not wish to eliminate myth, but only to interpret it. However, this brings us back to Ian Henderson's helpful contrast between interpreting a masterpiece when the original is preserved, and interpreting a code when the original is discarded. Is the original "myth" dispensable, or do we return to it again and again? Bultmann's answer to this question is not entirely clear, because of the ambiguity of his definition of myth. But his insistence that myth obscures and impedes its proper intention, together with the sugges-tion that it is somehow bound up with a primitive world-view, seems to imply that, as long as there is an interpretation in terms of self-understanding, the myth (though not the kerygma) is dispensable. How-ever, these very claims remain open to question. The belief about super-natural interventions in the affairs of men, for example, is not necessarily primitive or pre-scientific, as the Enlightenment view of myth would imply. This point is expressed admirably by Wolfhart Pannenberg. Pan-

---

176. J. Knox, *Myth and Truth*, pp. 34-50; A. N. Wilder, *Early Christian Rhetoric. The Language of the Gospel* (S.C.M., London, 1964), pp. 128-30; and G. V. Jones, *Christology and Myth* (Allen & Unwin, London, 1956), pp. 274-77.
177. M. Eliade, *Myths, Dreams, and Mysteries. The Encounter between Contemporary Faiths and Archaic Reality* (Eng. Fontana Library, London, 1968), pp. 23, 24, and 27.
178. K. Jaspers, "Myth and Religion" in *K.M.* II, 144.

nenberg asserts, "The acceptance of divine intervention in the course of events . . . is fundamental to every religious understanding of the world, including one which is not mythical in the sense in which comparative religion uses the term."[179] Even belief in demons, he claims, is not specifically mythical.[180] Thus in the New Testament "eschatology does not display mythical features," even though the cosmic significance of Jesus Christ is portrayed in terms which are "reminiscent of the archetypal elements of myth."[181]

(6) Central to Bultmann's claims about myth is his belief that the real intention behind myth is to express self-understanding, and that its objectifying pseudo-hypostatizing form is misleading as to its true function. The argument that is believed to clinch this point is an appeal to the supposed evidence of demythologizing within the New Testament itself. We need not add much to the criticism of this argument which we have already made. If every trace of objectifying language is regarded as uninterpreted myth, while all existential language on the same theme is regarded as demythologized myth, what kind of evidence *could* be adduced which would *count against* Bultmann's case? He has so loaded the terms of the discussion that any exegetical conclusions would seem to support his claim. Thus futurist eschatology is regarded as uninterpreted myth, while realized eschatology is demythologized myth. The conclusions are read off from the *form* of the argument, not from concrete particularities of exegesis. By the process of *Sachkritik*, any exegetical embarrassments, such as parts of 1 Corinthians 15, are dismissed as contrary to the true intention of the New Testament writer. Passages which do not fit in with Bultmann's overall interpretation of the New Testament are always interpreted in the light of others that do.

The growing emphasis among New Testament scholars on the pluriformity of the New Testament, however, has backfired on Bultmann's method of *Sachkritik*. It is seen that his approach raises questions about a canon within the canon. Is Luke-Acts, for example, simply a betrayal of the existential perspective of Paul and John? Is Romans 9-11 a historicizing lapse after the existential perspective of chapters 1-8? Even within the Synoptic Gospels what Bultmann has accepted as axiomatic has increasingly come under criticism. Graham Stanton, for example, has recently argued that Luke was not alone in recognizing that the story of Jesus was an essential part of the church's proclamation. He comments, "The gospels' rich portrait of Jesus cannot

179. W. Pannenberg, "Myth in Biblical and Christian Tradition" in *B.Q.T.* III, 14.
180. *Ibid.*, p. 67.
181. *Ibid.*, p. 68.
182. G. N. Stanton, *Jesus of Nazareth in New Testament Preaching* (Cambridge University Press, 1974; S.N.T.S. Monograph 27), p. 186.

be brushed aside . . . as a misunderstanding of their intention."[182] The work of Ebeling, Bornkamm, Käsemann, and Fuchs on the Gospels is not, as some have claimed, a step back from Bultmann's advance; but a recognition of the limitations of his holistic, even sweeping, approach to parts of the New Testament.

(7) Bultmann's use of Heidegger's conceptuality provides the basis for his more positive achievements as well as exaggerating certain difficulties. His dualism, his antipathy towards objectification, and his refusal to allow faith to rest on past history—all these themes were present in his theology whether or not he looked to Heidegger for further help in elucidating them. His understanding of Heidegger's work, however, enabled him to expound the theology of Paul with fresh clarity and power. We have already discussed his interpretation of "flesh" and "body" in Paul. The fact that it needs to be qualified and complemented in the light of work by Gundry and others does not call in question its fundamental value. No interpretation of the New Testament writings can ever claim to be definitive in the sense of achieving finality. Bultmann also sheds considerable light on man's relation to his past and his future. Out of his past, man has become what he is. Here is Heidegger's analysis of facticity. In order to be free, man must break the binding force of the past. Norman Young comments, "But this would be to get rid of himself, to become a 'new man'. . . . This, for Bultmann, is the meaning of the Christian claim that Jesus Christ is the eschatological event. He brings history to an end in the sense of ending a man's past history, his past understanding of himself, and grants him the possibility for free decision and thus new and authentic existence."[183] Bultmann writes, "For freedom is nothing else than being open for the genuine future, letting oneself be determined by the future. So Spirit may be called the power of futurity."[184]

The difficulty comes when insights which have been articulated through a conceptuality drawn from a particular philosophy are regarded as a comprehensive interpretation of the theology of the New Testament. Sometimes the criticism that Bultmann reduces theology to anthropology is made cheaply and simplistically, as when it is said, for example, that for Bultmann the gospel is merely good news about myself. This is a crude distortion of Bultmann's thought, which ignores what he says about talk of God and the event of grace. Nevertheless, when this criticism has been rejected in crude terms it remains true that Christ, in Bultmann's hermeneutics, can only be what he is *for me*. This brings us directly to the comments we made about Heidegger at the close of our two chapters on *Being and Time*. Disclosure *through* Dasein is too easily reduced to

183. N. Young, *History and Existential Theology*, p. 30.
184. R. Bultmann, *T.N.T.* I, 335.

disclosure *of* Dasein. We do not wish to reject the positive insight about the nature of knowledge and understanding to which Bultmann and Heidegger are eager to give due place. We cannot go back to the era before Kant. We must also be cautious about the kind of criticism voiced by Thielicke when he claims that "consciousness, not history, is what takes place in Bultmann."[185] This accords with Thielicke's persistent description of Bultmann's thought as "Cartesian theology," but overlooks the fact that self-understanding is not mere self-consciousness. Our criticism is that because Bultmann's perspective is fundamentally individualistic, he tends to assume that statements, for example, about the cosmic Lordship of Christ, or the acts of God in Israelite history, are mere objectifications which can be reduced to existential evaluations without loss. It would be nearer the truth, however, simply to say that language about God functions with self-involving logic. Bultmann, however, could not rest content with this, because he wishes to attack objectifying language in the realm of revelation even more radically than Heidegger attacks it in the realm of language about man. For whereas Heidegger allows that objectifying language may have some limited but legitimate place in relation to man, such as in the area of the sciences, Bultmann cannot allow room for any objectifying language about God or his acts, except insofar as this represents a clumsy attempt to express existential self-understanding through myth.

The conclusion to be drawn from these two sets of considerations is that, on the one hand, drawing on the conceptuality of a particular philosophy may lead, and has led, the New Testament interpreter to concrete insights into the text. On the other hand, it also leads to interpretations which are one-sided and partial, and which need to be complemented. The answer is not to abandon philosophical inquiry, for on this basis the positive side of Bultmann's work would have been lost. The answer is, rather, to draw a variety of conceptualities from other traditions, and critically to compare what each may achieve or fail to achieve. British philosophy, for example, provides finer tools with which to approach language. What is the relation between myth, metaphor, and the logic of self-involvement? Can self-involving language operate without a basis of "facts"? How does language (such as "Christ is Lord") relate to meta-language (such as "The early church confessed that 'Christ is Lord' ")? Is language merely a variable "medium" through which attitudes or ideas may be independently expressed? Most sharply of all, what is the particular status of the language of self-understanding which has no anchorage in this-worldly reality? We shall pursue this last question in our discussion of Wittgenstein.

185. H. Thielicke, *The Evangelical Faith*, I, 58.

CHAPTER XI

Gadamer's Philosophical Hermeneutics and Its Implications for New Testament Interpretation

In our second chapter we noted three points, among others, about the work of Hans-Georg Gadamer. We saw, first, that although he shared some of Heidegger's perspectives, Gadamer's approach is not identical with Heidegger's, and he is also more systematic and less elusive than the later thought of Heidegger. Secondly, in spite of Betti's criticisms, we noted that Gadamer regards his own work as descriptive rather than speculative. He writes, "I am not proposing a method, but I am describing *what is the case (Ich beschreibe,* was ist)."[1] What gave grounds for Betti's criticism was in reality due to Gadamer's recognition that one's view of "what is the case" is conditioned by one's place in tradition. Understanding occurs as an event within a tradition *(ein Überlieferungsgeschehen).* Thirdly, we saw that, in contrast to the role of theoretical thought, Gadamer is concerned to inquire about "modes of experience *(Erfahrungsweisen)* in which a truth is communicated."[2] This opens up the whole question of the relationship between truth and the experience of art, which constitutes the first of the three major sections of Gadamer's *magnum opus, Truth and Method.*

41. *The Relevance to Hermeneutics of Questions about Truth and Art*

We have observed that the use of the word "method" in Gadamer's title is ironical. In the experience of art, he writes, we are concerned with

1. H.-G. Gadamer, *T.M.*, p. 465 (German, p. 483).
2. *Ibid.*, p. xii (German, p. xxvi).

truths that go beyond the range of "methodical knowledge."[3] Understanding, or hermeneutics, is not a matter of mere technique in the narrower sense of the term. Gadamer wishes to go further here than Schleiermacher or Dilthey. Dilthey had separated the *Geisteswissenschaften* (the human sciences or the humanities) from *Naturwissenschaften* (the natural sciences), and had related hermeneutics only to the former. Nevertheless the human sciences were still "sciences," which invited the use of appropriate methods. By contrast, Gadamer writes in review of his own work, "I did not wish to elaborate a system of rules to describe, let alone direct, the methodical procedure of the human sciences. . . . My real concern was philosophic. . . . The investigation asks . . . how is understanding *(Verstehen)* possible?"[4] The investigation of the experience of art opens up a realm which transcends "method," as Gadamer understands it. Furthermore, it resists all attempts to reduce the problem of understanding to an examination of the subjective consciousness of either the author of the work of art or its interpreter.

Both in *Truth and Method* and in his more recent article "The Power of Reason," Gadamer strives to show that, far from being a permanent tradition in philosophy, a belief in the all-embracing power of theoretical reason is bound up with particular historical factors, such as the mood of the Enlightenment.[5] The Enlightenment, he argues, held as its ideal the achieving of knowledge of the world by pure reason. But this outlook, he claims, was exposed as invalid first by Hume's scepticism and then by Kant's *Critique of Pure Reason*. Since Hume and Kant, " 'science' has meant to us not so much Reason as empirical science."[6] But if this is the case regarding tradition after Kant, what can be said of the history of thought from the age of Greece to the Enlightenment? In the age of Aristotle, Gadamer argues, reason was not merely a theoretical capacity. "In order to be able to dedicate oneself wholly to the theoretical, one must presuppose 'practical knowledge'. . . . 'Reasonableness' is much rather a human attitude, something that one sticks to . . . in order to . . . build on common norms."[7]

In *Truth and Method* Gadamer shows how this broader, more practical approach finds expression not only in the Greek ideal of practical wisdom, but also in the ancient Roman concept of "Sensus Communis."[8] Aristotle allowed that the σοφία of the scholar depended on the φρόνησις of the wise man. Late Roman legal science, Gadamer urges, presupposed a view of the art and practice of law which was nearer to the practical

3. *Ibid.*, p. xiii.
4. *Ibid.*, pp. xvi-xviii (German, *W.M.*, pp. 19-29.
5. H.-G. Gadamer, "The Power of Reason" in *M.W.* III (1970), 5-15.
6. *Ibid.*, p. 6.
7. *Ibid.*, pp. 7-8.
8. H.-G. Gadamer, *T.M.*, pp. 19-29.

ideal of φϱόνησις than to the theoretical ideal of σοφία. The tradition articulated in the notion of *sensus communis* finds expression in the work of the Italian philosopher J. B. Vico. Gadamer writes, "For Vico the sensus communis is the sense of the right and the general good that is to be found in all men, moreover, a sense that is acquired through living in the community and is determined by its structures and aims." He then comments, "It was always known that the possibilities of rational proof and instruction did not fully exhaust the sphere of knowledge. Hence Vico's appeal to the sensus communis belongs . . . in a wider context that goes right back to antiquity and the continued effect of which into the present day is the subject of our book."[9]

Vico rejected the notion that any one method of inquiry should be regarded as the norm in every field of study. He illustrated his case from history, art, and law, and criticized Descartes for his complete lack of interest in history. The abstract methods which apply in mathematics, he urged, are not necessarily appropriate tools in philosophy. Standing in this same tradition, Gadamer follows Vico in singling out Descartes for attack. The emphasis on "method," he writes, which found its first great success in the mechanics of Galileo and Huygen, "found philosophical expression in Descartes' concept of method (and) totally changed the relationship between theory and practice."[10]

To illustrate this principle further, Gadamer refers to the work of Shaftesbury, Thomas Reid, and Henri Bergson.[11] Shaftesbury stressed the role of wit and humor in social intercourse to sift the true from the false, and explicitly appealed to the practical perspectives of ancient Rome to support his claim. Thomas Reid called attention to the role of common sense in arriving at judgments of truth. Henri Bergson criticized the tendencies in modern science towards undue abstraction, and associated man's most creative insights with intuition. However, the intellectual climate of nineteenth-century German thought, Gadamer admits, moved in the opposite direction. The one notable exception in Germany was that of pietism, as represented by Oetinger. Oetinger made the concept of *sensus communis* the subject of detailed investigation, viewing it as the gift of God.

Meanwhile, in the earlier German philosophical tradition, what was known in the English and French traditions as "common sense" appeared in altered form as "power of judgment" *(Urteilskraft)*. But Kant so transformed the meaning of the concept that in effect "the sensus communis plays no part in Kant."[12] Judgment that is related to the community

9. *Ibid.*, pp. 22 and 23.
10. H.-G. Gadamer, "The Power of Reason" in *M.W.* III, 8.
11. H.-G. Gadamer, *T.M.*, pp. 24-26.
12. *Ibid.*, p. 32.

becomes, for Kant, a matter of "taste." Common sense furnishes "judgments of taste" *(Geschmacksurteile)*. Taste operates in community, and in a specialized sense still constitutes a way of knowing or judging. However, in Kant's philosophy taste was relegated to a special area with the result that aesthetics underwent a radical subjectivization. This subjectivization, Gadamer insists, "was a completely new departure. In discrediting any kind of theoretical knowledge apart from that of natural science, it compelled the human sciences to rely on the methodology of the natural sciences in self-analysis."[13] Truth is a property of "concepts." How, then, Gadamer asks, are we to regard art?

Gadamer has now set the stage for his radical antithesis between *consciousness* and the *experience* of art. The notion of "aesthetic consciousness" is relatively modern. In Palmer's words, "It is a consequence of the general subjectivizing of thought since Descartes, a tendency to ground all knowledge in subjective self-certainty."[14] By contrast, Gadamer believes that experience of art is not merely a matter of subjective consciousness, but of ontological disclosure. It is unnecessary for us to follow closely his detailed arguments about the subjectivization of aesthetics in Kant.[15] Hegel's understanding of art, Gadamer argues, does better justice to history and to reality. He also notes the conclusion of Georg Simmel that in experience *(Erlebnis)* "the objective does not become, as in knowing *(Erkennen)*, an image and an idea *(Bild und Vorstellung)*, but an element in the life process itself *(Momenten des Lebensprozesses selbst)*."[16]

Experience, not abstraction, is the key to art. "Abstraction until only the 'purely aesthetic' is left is obviously a contradiction."[17] Gadamer concludes, "Our concern is to see the experience of art in such a way that it is understood as experience *(Erfahrung)*. The experience of art *(die Erfahrung der Kunst)* is not to be falsified by being turned into a possession of aesthetic culture. . . . This involves a far-reaching hermeneutic consequence."[18] This consequence is the recognition that encounter with the language of art is encounter with a still *unfinished* process *(Begegnung mit einem unabgeschlossenen Geschehen)*, which at the same time is a part of this same process. The work of art can never be reduced to the level of the consciousness of any one individual in history, but always transcends it. For it may yet disclose "something more" to subsequent generations. "The experience of art acknowledges that it cannot present the perfect truth of what it experiences in terms of final knowledge. . . .

13. *Ibid.*, p. 39.
14. R. E. Palmer, *Hermeneutics*, p. 167.
15. H.-G. Gadamer, *T.M.*, pp. 39-55.
16. *Ibid.*, p. 62; *W.M.*, p. 65.
17. *T.M.*, p. 80.
18. *Ibid.*, p. 88; *W.M.*, p. 94.

There is . . . no final exhaustion of what lies in a work of art."[19] This experience is essentially experience of reality *(Wirklichkeitserfahrung)*. Even the artist himself may come to see "something more" in his creation than had entered his consciousness at the moment of its production. Even if we could fuse together the conscious states of all who had beheld a work of art over a long period, this would not guarantee that we had an exhaustive disclosure of its own content.

All this has very close affinities with what Heidegger writes about language and art in his later work. "What is unsaid" is important both for Heidegger and for Gadamer, and for both of these thinkers it is crucial that neither language nor art be reduced to what can be contained in an individual's conscious awareness. Art is not aesthetics. It is neither a mere "thing" that cannot convey truth; nor mere "concepts" of the aesthetic realm. Gadamer, however, does not content himself with Heidegger's method of allowing his readers to find their own way in the light of quotations from Trakl and Hölderlin, or aphoristic statements of his own. Heidegger's method may do justice more adequately to his own premises about poetry and thinking, but his approach is also more obscure than that of Gadamer. Gadamer provides his readers with a more systematic discussion, and he readily illustrates what he wants to say about the ontology of art by means of an illuminating simile between art and games. Much can be learned from this simile about the outlook not only of Gadamer himself, but also of the later Heidegger, and the new hermeneutic, and in another study, I have discussed it in order to shed light on the hermeneutics of Ernst Fuchs.[20]

The key point, in Gadamer's words, is "the primacy of play over the consciousness of the player."[21] We can distinguish between play and the attitude of the player. "Play fulfils its purpose only if the player loses himself in his play."[22] Play "absorbs the player into itself. . . . The game tends to master the players."[23] What is important in a game is the "world" which it creates. When a player enters the world of the game, he accepts a nexus of presuppositions and aims which determine what he does. This acceptance of what the game demands amounts to "taking it seriously" and "not being a spoilsport." It is not simply a matter of the player's conscious thoughts. It is the game itself, not his thoughts, which determines the game's reality. At this point Gadamer suggests a parallel with art. "The work of art has its true being *(sein eigentliches Sein)* in the fact that it becomes an experience *(Erfahrung)* changing the person who

19. *T.M.*, p. 89.
20. A. C. Thiselton, "The Parables as Language-Event: Some Comments on Fuchs's Hermeneutics in the Light of Linguistic Philosophy" in *S.J.T.* XXIII (1970), 443; cf. pp. 437-68.
21. H.-G. Gadamer, *T.M.*, p. 94.
22. *Ibid.*, p. 92.
23. *Ibid.*, pp. 94-95.

experiences it. The 'subject' *(Subjekt)* of the experience of art, that which remains and endures, is not the subjectivity of the person who experiences it, but the work itself *(der Kunstwerk selbst).*"[24] Gadamer's conclusion applies equally to art and to play. "Play does not have its being in the consciousness *(Bewusstsein)* or the attitude *(Verhalten)* of the player, but on the contrary draws the latter into its area and fills him with its spirit. The player experiences the game as a reality that surpasses him *(als eine ihn übertreffende Wirklichkeit)."*[25]

Gadamer shows from the examples of music and drama that the work of art consists of the performance itself. What speaks to the audience is "the playing of the play" through its "presentation" *(Darstellung).*[26] A drama exists only when it is played. Music is experienced not simply in reading the composer's score privately, but in the actual event of the concert. Moreover, each performance is an event in its own right. It is not merely a "copy" of what went on in the consciousness of the composer. Indeed, we might say: it is not "merely" an interpretation; it is a creative event in its own right. Gadamer compares the phenomenon of celebrating a festival. A festival is neither an inferior copy of the original event, nor does it "have its being only in the subjectivity of those celebrating it." "A festival exists only in being celebrated."[27]

It is not difficult to see the relevance of all this to hermeneutics. First of all, truth is not to be reduced to a mere matter of concepts, but relates to experience in broader terms. We may compare with Shaftesbury's emphasis on humor and wit, for example, a work such as Edwin M. Good's admirable study *Irony in the Old Testament.*[28] In order to bring truth to light, Good points out, the Old Testament writers often use irony or humor to point out "the grotesque and absurd . . . in what we take for granted."[29] He discusses the use of this art-form in Judges 3, Amos 2, Hosea 6:3, 4, II Samuel 11 and 12, and in substantial sections of Isaiah and especially Jonah. In due course we shall note some similar claims made about the parables by D. O. Via. The work of Robert Funk and J. D. Crossan also presupposes a sharp contrast between experience and consciousness, or cognitive concepts. The parable, like the game or the work of art, opens up a "world" which dominates the hearer.

Secondly, this approach sets in a new light questions about the nature of *interpretation.* Gadamer insists that in the case of a work of art its actual being cannot be detached from its representation *(Darstellung).* Hence the *reality* of something written or presented in the past is not

24. *Ibid.,* p. 92; *W.M.,* p. 98.
25. *T.M.,* p. 98; *W.M.,* p. 104.
26. *T.M.,* p. 104; *W.M.,* p. 110.
27. *T.M.,* p. 110.
28. E. M. Good, *Irony in the Old Testament* (S.P.C.K., London, 1965).
29. *Ibid.,* p. 26.

recaptured by mere subjective recollection. Gadamer explicitly cites the Lutheran emphasis on preaching or the Catholic view of the mass as examples in which reality is disclosed *afresh*. Interpretation is not a mechanical reproduction of the past in the present, but a creative event in its own right. "The words of the sermon perform this total mediation (*Vermittlung*) which otherwise is the work of the religious rite, say, of the Mass. . . . 'Contemporaneity' (*Gleichzeitigkeit*) forms part of the being of the work of art. It constitutes the nature of 'being present' (*Dabeiseins*)."[30] The concert or the dramatic presentation which overwhelms and transforms a man today may be more faithful to the score or to the script by adopting a form not identical with that of two hundred years earlier. Drama and music "wait for the occasion in order to exist, and find their form only through that occasion."[31]

Gadamer concludes, "if my argument is correct . . . then the real problem of hermeneutics is quite different from its common acceptance. It . . . gives to the hermeneutical consciousness a breadth that surpasses even that of aesthetic consciousness. . . . Hermeneutics must be so determined as a whole that it does justice to the experience of art."[32] This also carries with it the reminder that "art is never simply past."[33] Gadamer illustrates this principle from music, painting, architecture, drama, and literature. A picture, he claims, is an ontological event in which truth is disclosed in the present. Even in the case of reading literature, "in its deciphering and interpretation a miracle takes place: the transformation of something strange and dead into a total simultaneity and familiarity. This is like nothing else that has come down to us from the past."[34] It achieves "the sheer presence of the past." Being, or truth, is disclosed to us, however, only when we allow ourselves to stand in the world created by the literature or other art-form. R. E. Palmer comments, "When we see a great work of art and enter the world, we do not leave home so much as 'come home'. We say at once: truly it is so! The artist has said what *is*."[35]

We have moved a long way from the Cartesian perspective according to which man, as active subject, scrutinizes the things around him as passive objects. In Gadamer's view, this is no model for hermeneutical understanding. The text, as Ernst Fuchs puts it, is not just the object of interrogation, but that which masters and shapes the interpreter by drawing him into its world. From the viewpoint of the new hermeneutic, by demonstrating the bankruptcy of subjectivized aesthetics, Gadamer has

30. H.-G. Gadamer, *T.M.*, p. 112; *W.M.*, p. 121.
31. *T.M.*, p. 130.
32. *Ibid.*, p. 146.
33. *Ibid.*, p. 147.
34. *Ibid.*, p. 145.
35. R. E. Palmer, *Hermeneutics*, p. 168.

also demonstrated the shallowness of subjectivized hermeneutics. Fuchs believes that only on the basis of this broader understanding of hermeneutics can the text of the New Testament "strike home" *(treffen)*, so that the interpreter is confronted with reality rather than with "concepts."

42. *Gadamer's Critique of Hermeneutics from Schleiermacher to Heidegger*

In the second main part of his study *Truth and Method* Gadamer attempts two further tasks. First of all, he examines the whole hermeneutical tradition as it stems from Schleiermacher and Dilthey, and submits it to careful criticism. Secondly, he reformulates his own approach to hermeneutics in the light of the problem of history and the interpreter's historical finitude.

Gadamer begins by considering what he calls the pre-history of the hermeneutics of Romanticism. The problem of the relationship between hermeneutics and tradition came to a head at the Reformation. Gadamer argues that the Reformers were not entirely consistent. On the one hand, they rejected the need for tradition in reaching a proper understanding of Scripture. On the other hand, however, they argued, first, that the understanding of individual passages depended on the witness of Scripture as a whole; and secondly, that Protestant credal formulae provided a guide concerning the understanding of this unity of the Bible. Thus, while they attempted to understand texts "in their own terms," in practice such interpretation was "always in need of support from a generally unacknowledged dogmatic guideline."[36] We shall return to Gadamer's claim again when we ask about the implications of his work for the relation between exegesis and systematic theology.

Gadamer next draws a contrast between two different approaches to hermeneutics, represented by Spinoza and Schleiermacher. Spinoza called "historical interpretation" into play only when and where the meaning of the text was obscure because of the interpreter's lack of familiarity with historical factors. We do not need to know about the life of the author, Spinoza argued, for the interpretation of moral maxims in the Bible, any more than we need to know about Euclid's life in order to understand his geometry. However, in contrast to the belief in the power of reason represented by the Enlightenment, Schleiermacher approaches the matter differently. Schleiermacher thought of hermeneutics, as we have seen, as a creative act in which truth hidden in the text is brought to light. "What is to be understood is now not only the exact words and their objective

36. H.-G. Gadamer, *T.M.*, p. 155.

meaning, but also the individuality of . . . the author. . . . It is ultimately a divinatory process, a placing of oneself within the mind of the author . . . a recreation of the creative act."[37]

The positive value of Schleiermacher's achievement, according to Gadamer, is the recognition that hermeneutics is an art, and not a mechanical process. He also approves of his maxim that "the object is to understand a writer better than he understood himself." Gadamer comments, "This statement contains the whole problem of hermeneutics."[38] For Schleiermacher himself this meant that the interpreter can become conscious of many things of which the writer may be unconscious. For example, even at the level of language, an interpreter who reads the text in a language of which he is not a native speaker may bring explicitly to consciousness grammatical and stylistic rules of which the original author may have been unaware, at least at a conscious level. At a theological level we have noted J. D. Smart's claims about a "Christian" understanding of Isaiah. Smart writes, "May there not be a meaning in the words of Scripture that was not fully known or understood by the person who spoke or wrote them? Since a prophet received his message from God, could it not be true that even the prophet himself did not grasp the full significance of what he was saying? The historical scholar is likely to deny any such possibility . . . and yet it must be recognized that the Biblical records, because they have to do with God . . . constantly point to realities that are far beyond the conscious grasp of any human being."[39] Gadamer's point, however, is that this principle need not rest on special theological considerations. He quotes the words of H. Steinthal, that "the literary critic understands the speaker and poet better than he understands himself, and better than his contemporaries understood him, for he brings clearly into consciousness what was actually but only unconsciously present in the other." Gadamer adds, "The artist who creates something is not the ideal interpreter of it."[40]

This has close connections with the claims of D. O. Via and others to view the parables of Jesus not simply in terms of their very earliest *Sitz im Leben,* but as works of art in their own right. While he allows that interpretations of the parables must not conflict with their original intention, Via insists that "the severely historical approach ignores the aesthetic nature of the parables and annuls their aesthetic function."[41] This issue also bears on our discussion of Bultmann's method of *Sachkritik* in the previous chapter. To return, however, to Schleiermacher, Gadamer offers several criticisms of his work, especially what he regards as his lack

37. *Ibid.,* p. 164.
38. *Ibid.,* p. 169.
39. J. D. Smart, *The Interpretation of Scripture,* pp. 34-35.
40. H.-G. Gadamer, *T.M.,* p. 170.
41. D. O. Via, *The Parables,* p. 24.

of understanding of the problem of history and historical distance. He observes, "Schleiermacher's problem is not historical obscurity, but the obscurity of the 'Thou'."[42] Hermeneutics remains a matter of "consciousness."

Gadamer proceeds to examine the contributions to hermeneutics made by Leopold von Ranke, J. G. Droysen, and Wilhelm Dilthey. We have already discussed the work of Ranke in our third chapter, on hermeneutics and history, and we looked at Dilthey's approach in connection with the work of Bultmann. Gadamer criticizes all three writers on two main grounds. First of all, they aimed at a kind of objectivity which really amounted in the end to an insufficiently critical objectivism, in spite of the influence of Kant. In his insistence that the *Geisteswissenschaften* still remained "sciences" Dilthey became trapped by the very objectivism which he sought to attack and overcome. Gadamer writes, "He (Dilthey) was always attempting to justify the knowledge of what was historically conditioned as the achievement of objective sciences, despite the fact of the knower's being conditioned himself. This was to be done by the theory of the structure. . . ." This presupposes, Gadamer continues, that the historical observer can overcome the fact that he is tied to a particular time and place. "But precisely this is the claim of historical consciousness, namely to have a truly historical standpoint to everything."[43] Dilthey was in fact aware of the problem, since he insisted, especially as against Hegel, that the interpreter must never forget his own finitude. But in the end he was no more successful than Ranke and Droysen in overcoming this problem.

Secondly, all three thinkers were able to conceal from themselves the radical nature of the problem by invoking what in Ranke's case amounted to a theology of history, and in Dilthey's case was a modified form of Hegelian idealism. Gadamer writes, "The hermeneutical self-understanding of the historical school, as we saw in Ranke and Droysen, has its ultimate foundation in the idea of universal history *(Universalgeschichte)*."[44] But, as we saw in our third chapter, Ranke depended in the end on theological considerations for such a view. Dilthey thought that he had escaped the problems left by Ranke and Droysen, and he also opposed Hegel's emphasis on the merely abstract. However, Gadamer argues that in the end he follows Hegel in resting the unity of history, which was necessary for his epistemology, on the notion of "absolute spirit."[45] Ultimately, in spite of his good intentions, Dilthey is entangled in the impasse left by the historical school, and tempted to assert the

42. H.-G. Gadamer, *T.M.*, p. 168.
43. *Ibid.*, p. 204.
44. *Ibid.*, p. 185; *W.M.*, p. 197.
45. *T.M.*, p. 202.

possibility of a standpoint "above" history, perhaps by the seductions of the claims made on behalf of scientific method. Gadamer concludes, "Thus Ernst Troeltsch quite rightly summed up Dilthey's life's work in the words: from relativity to totality."[46]

Gadamer believes that the true nature of the problem was unfolded successively by Husserl, Graf Yorck, and Heidegger. Although he acknowledges the work of other thinkers such as Nietzsche and Bergson, Gadamer declares, "The first man to bring to general awareness the radical challenge to historical being and knowledge presented by the inadequacy of the concept of substance was Heidegger. Only through him was the philosophical intention of Dilthey released."[47] But Heidegger built on the phenomenological method of Husserl, and especially on Husserl's notion of intentionality. Husserl insisted that all the beings given in one's world stand within the intentional horizon of consciousness. Thus his conception of intentionality "had spelled the end of old-style objectivism."[48] There is no need to elaborate this point, since we have already discussed in some detail the use to which Heidegger put this approach. Husserl's concept of the horizon becomes very important not only for Heidegger but also for Gadamer himself. Gadamer comments, "The phenomenon of horizon is of crucial importance for Husserl's phenomenological research. This concept, we too shall have occasion to use. . . . A horizon is not a rigid frontier, but something that moves with one and invites one to advance further."[49] Husserl's notion of "life-world" *(Lebenswelt)*, Gadamer adds, "is the antithesis of all objectivism *(Objektivismus)*. It is an essentially historical concept."[50] In this respect Husserl more truly achieves Dilthey's intention than Dilthey. Dilthey and Husserl are at one in their insistence that "No real blood runs in the veins of the knowing subject that Locke, Hume, and Kant constructed."[51]

The letters and posthumous papers of Graf Yorck, Gadamer argues, take us beyond both Dilthey and Husserl. All three thinkers, he claims go back behind the abstractions of Neo-Kantianism. Consciousness is to be understood as a life-attitude *(Lebensverhalten)*. Thought and philosophical "results" presuppose this life-attitude and depend on it, but as "results" they become detached from it. "Philosophy must reverse this process of detachment. It must repeat the experiment of life in the reverse direction "in order to know the conditions which govern the "results of life."[52] This is very close to Gadamer's own claim that what is important

46. *Ibid.*, p. 209.
47. *Ibid.*, pp. 214-15.
48. R. E. Palmer, *Hermeneutics*, p. 179.
49. H.-G. Gadamer, *T.M.*, p. 217.
50. *Ibid.*, p. 218; *W.M.*, p. 233.
51. Quoted from *Gesammelte Schriften* I, xviii and 217.
52. H.-G. Gadamer, *T.M.*, p. 223.

in the hermeneutical process is the interpreter's pre-judgments *(Vorur-teile)* rather than his conscious states of mind.

Gadamer regards Heidegger's philosophy both as the climax of the hermeneutical tradition of thought since Schleiermacher and as the point of departure for his own account of the relation between hermeneutics and historical finitude. Traditional hermeneutics, he argues, limits the horizon to which understanding belongs, and pays insufficient attention to human facticity.[53] As Palmer expresses the point, it is not simply a matter of how the world belongs to the human subject, but of how the human subject belongs to the world.[54] Hence, in Gadamer's words, the interpreter "must seek to be aware of (his) pre-judgments and to control (his) own pre-understanding," thereby avoiding "naive objectivism."[55]

We have already discussed Martin Heidegger's formulation of the principle of the hermeneutical circle, together with his comments concerning "fore-having," "fore-sight," and "fore-conception" *(Vorhabe, Vorsicht, und Vorgriff).*[56] Gadamer accepts this formulation of the issue, but he stresses more firmly than Heidegger the way in which the subject-matter itself invites the correction and revision of preliminary understanding. "Interpretation begins with fore-conceptions that are replaced by more suitable ones." "This pre-project *(Vorentwurf)* . . . is constantly revised *(revidiert)* in terms of what emerges."[57] Indeed we must "break the spell" of our own "fore-meanings," and avoid an understanding of the text which fits perfectly with our prior expectations. Here is one of Gadamer's most important insights. On the one hand there is no presuppositionless interpretation, on the other hand the text must be able to speak what is new. It must not merely reflect the interpreter's own lack of pre-judgments.

43. *The Task of Hermeneutics in the Light of Tradition and of Man's Historical Finitude*

Gadamer rightly insists that if this kind of understanding is to be achieved, two things are demanded of the interpreter. In the first place, he must remain *open* to the meaning of the text. Part of this openness shows itself in a willingness to revise and to correct pre-understandings. In an

53. *Ibid.*, p. 231.
54. R. E. Palmer, *Hermeneutics*, p. 180.
55. H.-G. Gadamer, "On the Scope and Function of Hermeneutical Reflection" in *Continuum* VIII (1970), 85; cf. pp. 77-95; translated from Gadamer's *Kleine Schriften* (4 vols.; Mohr, Tübingen, 1967, 1972, and 1977) I, 113-30, and *P.H.*, pp. 18-43.
56. Cf. M. Heidegger, *B.T.*, pp. 188-95 (sect. 32).
57. H.-G. Gadamer, *T.M.*, p. 236; *W.M.*, p. 251.

important statement Gadamer declares, *"A hermeneutically trained mind must be, from the start, sensitive to the text's quality of newness."*[58] Secondly, the interpreter must endeavor to become *aware* of the nature of the pre-judgments or pre-understanding which he brings to the text. He must inevitably come to the text with "anticipatory ideas"; but it is part of the hermeneutical task to make these conscious, in order to assess them against the text itself. Once again this assessment will never be a once-for-all definitive act, as if one could fully separate one's pre-understanding from his subsequent understanding of the text. But it is part of a process that must be begun.

"Prejudice" or "pre-judgment" *(der Begriff des Vorurteils)*, Gadamer insists, should not be made to bear the negative meaning which popular usage today derived from the Enlightenment. The word calls attention only to the *preliminary* or *provisional* nature of the judgment in question. "Actually prejudice means a judgment that is given before all the elements that determine a situation have been finally examined."[59] In German legal terminology the term signifies a provisional legal verdict before the final verdict is reached. It was only the rationalism of the Enlightenment, with its maxim, borrowed from Descartes, that nothing could be accepted which might in any way be doubted, that established the purely negative aspect of the term as the decisive one. Gadamer, by contrast, insists that pre-judgments are more far-reaching and fundamental for hermeneutics than conscious cognitive acts. He writes, "The self-awareness of the individual is only a flickering in the closed circuits of historical life. That is why the prejudices *(die Vorurteile)* of the individual, far more than his judgments *(seine Urteile)*, constitute the historical reality of his being *(die geschichtliche Wirklichkeit seines Seins)."*[60]

Prejudice, or pre-judgment, influences the individual through tradition, and often through his acceptance of certain values, attitudes, or institutions, as authoritative. Gadamer rejects the Enlightenment outlook which suspects all tradition and authority merely because it is tradition or authority. The acceptance of authority, he argues, is not necessarily blind or irrational obedience. It may be based on the thoroughly rational insight that as an individual of a particular historical generation I have my own built-in limitations, and may stand in need of learning from a source which has a better understanding of something than I do. Gadamer concludes that a clear-cut antithesis between tradition and historical knowledge must be rejected. He illustrates the point from the role played by "the classics" or "classical" literature and culture. The very word "classical"

58. *Ibid.*, p. 238 (my italics).
59. *Ibid.*, p. 240; *W.M.*, p. 255.
60. *T.M.*, p. 245; *W.M.*, p. 261.

conveys the idea that something from the past may still offer a model or norm which is relevant to the present.

Tradition, then, is no more a negative factor in hermeneutics than pre-judgment. Gadamer asserts, "Understanding is not to be thought of so much as an action of one's subjectivity, but as the placing of oneself within a process of tradition (*als Einrücken in ein Überlieferungsgeschehen*) in which past and present are constantly fused. This is what must be expressed in hermeneutical theory."[61] Tradition does not stand over against thinking as an object of thought, but is the horizon within which we do our thinking. To borrow Palmer's metaphor, we are immersed in the medium of our tradition which is as transparent to us, and therefore as invisible to us, as water to a fish.[62]

The consequence of this, in Gadamer's view, is that "every age has to understand a transmitted text in its own way, for the text is part of the whole of the tradition in which the age . . . seeks to understand itself."[63] We cannot, as it were, leave the present to go back into the past and to view the text *solely* on its own terms. The very meaning which the text has for us is partly shaped by our own place in a tradition which reaches the present. This does not mean that tradition is to be assimilated uncritically. We have seen that a "hermeneutically trained mind" will then be necessary to distinguish between those pre-judgments which are fruitful for the understanding of the text, and those which are unfruitful.

At this point Gadamer brings into play the concept of temporal distance (*Zeitenabstand*). Temporal distance is not simply, as many thinkers believe, an obstacle or difficulty in hermeneutics which must be overcome. In Gadamer's view it is of positive value in helping the interpreter to distinguish between fruitful and unfruitful pre-judgments. Temporal distance performs a "filtering process. . . . It not only lets those prejudices that are of a particular and limited nature die away, but causes those that bring about genuine understanding to emerge as such. It is only this temporal distance that can solve the really critical question of hermeneutics, namely of distinguishing the true prejudices, by which we understand, from the false ones by which we misunderstand. Hence the hermeneutically trained mind . . . will make conscious the prejudices governing our own understanding so that the text, as another's meaning, can be isolated and valued on its own."[64]

This raises some significant questions for the hermeneutics of the New Testament. Perhaps most urgently, it raises the whole fundamental issue of the relationship between exegesis and systematic theology, and the

61. *T.M.*, p. 258; *W.M.*, pp. 274-75.
62. R. E. Palmer, *Hermeneutics*, p. 177; cf. p. 183.
63. H.-G. Gadamer, *T.M.*, p. 263.
64. *Ibid.*, p. 266.

history of biblical interpretation. Systematic theology might be said to represent the end-process, to date, of that long growth of tradition in which the Christian community has struggled to arrive at an interpretation of the biblical texts which both does justice to its own present place in tradition and seeks to discard those false pre-judgments which have proved unfruitful. We shall explore this problem further in due course. Gadamer sharpens the problem still further by reiterating his earlier point, which we saw in connection with art, that "Not occasionally only, but always, the meaning of a text goes beyond its author."[65] We have already set out some of the implications of this issue.

Gadamer describes these effects of tradition and temporal distance as the principle of "effective-history" *(Wirkungsgeschichte),* or the actual operation of history on the process of understanding itself. The interpreter, he insists, cannot escape the impact of effective-history. This is what a naive historical objectivism overlooks. Gadamer drily remarks, "The power of effective-history does not depend on its being recognized."[66] In this connection Gadamer enters into discussion with questions about objectivism and objectivity in sociology. Is the use of statistics to describe sociological situations necessarily "objective," or is the sociologist's structuring and use of these statistics partly determined by his own place within tradition and history? Here he enters explicitly into dialogue with J. Habermas.[67]

In *Truth and Method* Gadamer illustrates this principle with reference to his striking simile of the merging or fusion of horizons. Moltmann and Pannenberg have both taken up this simile.[68] We have said that the tradition is not something that stands over against the interpreter, but constitutes his horizon of meaning. Gadamer now points out that this horizon is not closed and fixed, but moves as the interpreter himself moves. "The horizon is, rather, something into which we move and that moves with us. Horizons change for a person who is moving. Thus the horizon of the past . . . which exists in the form of tradition, is always in motion."[69] The hermeneutical situation, Gadamer urges, is determined by the pre-judgments that we bring with us, and which constitute "the horizon of a particular present." Genuine understanding takes place when there occurs a fusion of horizons *(Horizontverschmelzung)* between the past and the present, or between the text and the interpreter.

Gadamer is careful, however, to add a warning. Understanding does

65. *Ibid.,* p. 264.
66. *Ibid.,* p. 268.
67. H.-G. Gadamer, "On the Scope and Function of Hermeneutical Reflection" in *Continuum VIII,* 85. Cf. *T.M.,* pp. 495-96.
68. W. Pannenberg, "Hermeneutics and Universal History" in *B.Q.T.* I, 117-34; cf. 96-136; and J. Moltmann, *Theology of Hope* (Eng. S.C.M., London, 1967), p. 106.
69. H.-G. Gadamer, *T.M.,* p. 271.

not entail the kind of fusion in which critical distance and tension is entirely swallowed up. In an important statement he comments, "Every encounter with tradition that takes place within historical consciousness involves the experience of the tension between the text and the present. The hermeneutic task consists in not covering up this tension by attempting a naive assimilation, but consciously bringing it out."[70] Once again, this is relevant to the issue which we raised about exegesis and systematic theology. The subject matter of the text must not be simply assimilated into the horizon of a pre-existing theological tradition in the present.

Gadamer also holds that application *(Anwendung)* is integral to the whole experience of understanding a text. He illustrates this principle from the area of legal hermeneutics. Understanding in the area of law, far from constituting an exceptional problem in hermeneutics, actually provides a paradigm case of what understanding a text from the past involves. The jurist understands and interprets the meaning of a law, or a legal text, for the sake of a present legal case. But, as against Betti, Gadamer insists that the situation of the legal historian is not altogether different. "Understanding" it entails seeing how it applies "at every moment, in every particular situation, in a new and different way. Understanding here is always application."[71]

Heidegger's polemic against the objectivism of theoretical neutrality and detachment is invoked by Gadamer at this point. Understanding is not a theoretical activity, in which man scrutinizes the material before him as passive object. Indeed, in both legal and theological hermeneutics, Gadamer points out, the interpreter aims not at dominating the text, but at submitting to the will of the law or to the will of God. Perhaps the one major difference, he concedes, is that whereas a judge's verdict may actually supplement the law, "the gospel of salvation does not acquire any new content from its proclamation in preaching."[72] Nevertheless, understanding Scripture must involve more than "scientific or scholarly exploration of its meaning." Gadamer appeals here to the vexed question of the interpretation of the Old Testament. Clearly it is possible to understand the Old Testament in either a "Jewish" or a "Christian" way. Yet this does not imply that the interpreter is merely reading out of the text what he has put into it. "Neither the jurist nor the theologian regards the work of application as making free with the text."[73] In a way which reminds us of Wittgenstein, Gadamer compares the situation in which we "understand" an order: "To understand the order means to apply it to the specific situation to which it is relevant."[74] Similarly, he argues that the

70. *Ibid.*, p. 273.
71. *Ibid.*, p. 275; cf. pp. 290-305.
72. *Ibid.*, p. 295.
73. *Ibid.*, p. 297.
74. *Ibid.*, p. 298; cf. L. Wittgenstein, *P.I.*, sects. 139-155.

kind of understanding that is involved in intelligent reading also entails application. We may compare Wittgenstein's elucidation of understanding in terms of "Now I can go on," and of reading as relating to "situation."[75]

Gadamer brings this second major part of *Truth and Method* to a conclusion by setting beside the fact of historical finitude what he calls the hermeneutical priority of the question. A question places given subject-matter within a particular perspective or horizon. Moreover, it is in the process of the to-and-fro of question and answer that fresh insights may be said to "arise." They are not simply a product of one individual's conscious reflection, but "emerge" from the whole process of interrogation. Dialectic, in accordance with Plato's Socrates, "is the art of the formation of concepts as the working out of the common meaning. . . . The process of question and answer . . . performs that communication of meaning which . . . is the task of hermeneutics."[76] We shall return to this point in connection with Wittgenstein's work on the formation of concepts.

R. G. Collingwood earns Gadamer's approval for his observations on the logic of question and answer. Collingwood criticized an exclusive preoccupation with "statements" in British universities which failed, in Gadamer's words, to take account of the historicality that is part of understanding. Collingwood argued that we can understand a text only when we have understood the question to which it is an answer. Truth, Collingwood writes, belongs "not to any single proposition, nor even . . . to a complex of propositions taken together; but to a complex of questions and answers."[77] Had Gadamer written a little later, he might also have compared the work of F. Waismann in a chapter entitled "Towards a Logic of Questions." Waismann writes, "The question is the first groping step of the mind in its journeyings that lead towards new horizons. . . . Questions lead us on and over the barrier of traditional opinions. Questions seduce us, too, and lead us astray."[78] Collingwood, Waismann, and Gadamer all point to the method of Socrates.

Gadamer thus endorses the principle underlined by Bultmann that our understanding of a text is bound up with how we question it. "A person who thinks must ask himself questions."[79] However, he is also at pains to show that because our own questions will necessarily never be identical with those of the original author of the text, the process of understanding the text will be creative and not merely reproductive. Once

75. L. Wittgenstein, *P.I.*, sects. 151 and 166; cf. H.-G. Gadamer, *T.M.*, p. 304.
76. H.-G. Gadamer, *T.M.*, p. 331.
77. R. G. Collingwood, *An Autobiography*, p. 37; cf. *The Idea of History*, pp. 269-74 and 278-82.
78. F. Waismann, *The Principles of Linguistic Philosophy* (Macmillan, London, 1965), p. 405; cf. pp. 387-417.
79. H.-G. Gadamer, *T.M.*, p. 338.

again, this understanding is a matter of effective-history; and as such it is a genuinely creative event.

44. *Hermeneutics and Language in Gadamer*

Gadamer's view of language must be considered against the background of our earlier discussion of the relation between thought and language and its bearing on hermeneutics, which we set out in section 17 of the present study. There we examined the tradition of Humboldt and Cassirer, and compared the positive but very different insights represented on the one hand by the approach which finds its most extreme form in Whorf, and on the other hand by work in general linguistics from Saussure onwards.

Gadamer insists that understanding and language are inseparable. In the words of Gerhard Ebeling, hermeneutics is less the understanding *of* language than a matter of understanding *through* language.[80] In Gadamer's words, it is not that there already exists "a linguistic store-room" out of which we take ready-made concepts which must then be understood; rather, "language is the universal medium *(Medium)* in which understanding itself is realized. . . . All interpretation takes place in the medium of a language which would allow the object to come into words and yet is at the same time the interpreter's own language."[81] Hermeneutics, Gadamer adds, turns therefore on the relationship between thought and language, or between thinking and speaking.

What Gadamer has previously said about the present horizons of the interpreter is now expressed in terms of language. Whatever the interpreter *understands* necessarily comes to speech in the medium of *his* language. Here the issue, of course, must not be reduced to the question of understanding foreign languages as such. "Language" is used in the broader sense of the language-habits and language-world which condition the formation of concepts. However, even in the matter of linguistic translation Gadamer maintains that it is naive to imagine that the interpreter can leave his own concepts aside, and think only in the concepts of the epoch he is trying to understand. Understanding is impossible if it does not take place through the interpreter's own concepts. Hermeneutical translation "has meaning only in relation to one's own concepts. Historical consciousness fails to understand its own nature if, in order to understand, it seeks to exclude that which alone makes understanding possible.

80. G. Ebeling, *W.F.*, p. 318.
81. H.-G. Gadamer, *T.M.*, p. 350.

. . . No text and no book speaks if it does not speak the language that reaches the other person."[82]

Like Wittgenstein and even Gilbert Ryle, Gadamer stresses that thinking is not a kind of duplicate independent shadow-process that operates alongside the speaking of language. He comments, "The intimate unity of language and thought is the premise from which philosophy of language also starts."[83] We may compare Wittgenstein's words, "Thinking is not an incorporeal process which lends life and sense to speaking and which it would be possible to detach from speaking. . . ."[84] However, this does not mean that Gadamer, any more than Wittgenstein, entangles himself in the errors represented by T. Boman and attacked by James Barr, that thought is determined by accidents of grammar and lexicology. In a statement which is of major importance for this issue, Gadamer asserts, "If every language represents a view of the world, it is this primarily not as a particular type of language (in the way that philologists see it), but because of what is said or handed down in this language."[85]

Gadamer's discussion about the role of convention in language is very sophisticated and can all too easily be misunderstood. In his careful discussion of Plato's *Cratylus* it may seem as if he is equally firmly rejecting both the conventionalist and the naturalist views of language. If so, this would put him at odds with the general conclusions of linguistics. However, Gadamer is saying only that since language is handed down in tradition, it cannot now be altered arbitrarily by mere formal agreement. He rightly stresses the crucial role of linguistic habit. Thus when a group of children come to have a special language among themselves, "this is not so much because they have arbitrarily agreed on it, but because a linguistic habit has grown up between them. A common world— even if it is only an invented one—is always the presupposition of language."[86] This in no way conflicts with our own conclusions about this subject expressed above in section 17, and even points to what Wittgenstein is saying through his concept of language-games.

Only by means of a completely artificial language, or the language of mathematical signs, would it be possible to rise above the historical contingencies of linguistic tradition. As it is, language and the possibilities of thought are bound so closely together that we cannot think of some abstract "pre-given system of possibilities of being." "The word is not formed only after the act of knowledge has been completed . . . but is the

82. *Ibid.*, p. 358.
83. *Ibid.*, p. 364.
84. L. Wittgenstein, *P.I.*, sect. 339.
85. H.-G. Gadamer, *T.M.*, pp. 399-400.
86. *Ibid.*, p. 367.

act of knowledge itself."[87] The process of the development of language therefore goes hand in hand with that of concept formation (Begriffsbildung). Only in connection with the formation of concepts in science, Gadamer claims, can language be reduced to the level of mere instrumental signs, and its creative significance for thought overlooked.

Gadamer pays attention not only to the views of language held by Plato and Aristotle, but also to that of Wilhelm von Humboldt. Humboldt's importance for hermeneutics, he argues, lies in his recognition of the relation between language and world-view. "Language is not just one of man's possessions in the world, but on it depends the fact that man has a world at all."[88] But Gadamer recognizes that the inheritance of certain language-habits from tradition does not necessarily imprison men within a given linguistic world. Man's very use of language may give him freedom from the pressure of that world. As we shall see, this is a fundamental principle in the hermeneutics of Ernst Fuchs.

At the same time, Gadamer refuses to underestimate the significance of linguistic tradition and its bearing on human finitude. First of all, since a language-tradition highlights what is significant within a given language-community, this reinforces Heidegger's rejection of any merely objectivist understanding of "world" in terms of that which is present-at-hand. A language-world carries with it attitudes or pre-judgments which are prior to individual cognition and theoretical distancing. Secondly, language is "the record of finitude (der Endlichkeit)," because it is constantly being formed and developed.[89] Like Wittgenstein, Gadamer stresses that language lives, grows, and changes, just as human life lives, grows, and changes. Thirdly, "every word causes the whole language to which it belongs to resonate."[90] Man's use of words is inseparable from how he understands himself and the world as a whole, which in turn relates to the tradition in which he is placed.

The climax of Gadamer's work on the relation between hermeneutics and language comes in his conclusions about the ontological nature of language and its subject-matter. It is not simply that the interpreter is somehow "in control" of the words which reach him through a tradition. The emphasis is not on the interpreter or on the "method" by which he examines tradition, but on the coming into being of new subject-matter as language transmits a content which is understood, in turn, through the medium of the interpreter's own language. Something "emerges" (herauskommt) which transcends both the prior language of the commu-

---

87. Ibid., pp. 377 and 383.
88. Ibid., p. 401.
89. Ibid., p. 415 (German, p. 433).
90. Ibid., pp. 415-16.

nity and the prior consciousness of the interpreter, but is born out of interaction between them.

Gadamer traces the roots of this perspective first to Hegel, and then ultimately to the dialectic of Socrates and Plato. Plato loved to show how through the dialectic of question and answer what was false was exposed as false, while what was true "emerged." However, Gadamer criticizes Hegel for subordinating language as communication to the definitive use of statement (Aussage). Question and answer as a continuing process taps "the infinity of what is unsaid." But "in a statement the range of the meaning of what has to be said is concealed with methodical exactness; what remains is the 'pure' sense of the statements. That is what goes on record. But as meaning thus reduced to what is stated (das Ausgesagte) it is always a distorted meaning (ein entstellter Sinn)."[91] At this point we believe that Gadamer has been misled by undervaluing the range of logical functions that can be performed by statements of various kinds. We have argued this point elsewhere, and Gadamer's conclusion on this particular issue is also challenged by Wolfhart Pannenberg.[92] However, Gadamer's view finds parallel expression in Heidegger, Fuchs, and Ebeling.

On the basis of all that has been said, Gadamer now claims that he has reached a universal hermeneutics: "We are led to a universal hermeneutics that was concerned with the general relationship of man to the world. . . . With the ontological turn that our hermeneutical enquiry has taken, we are moving towards a metaphysical idea. . . ."[93] Truth emerges not by "the tool of method," but through the dialectical process of questioning in which language-tradition encounters and speaks to the historically-finite questioner in *his* language. The understanding that takes place in this encounter is an event in which, as the later Heidegger would say, "language speaks." Thus hermeneutics, to borrow Ebeling's phrase, is not a matter of finding a new *means* of speech, but of a new *coming* to speech.[94] For Gadamer, hermeneutics is concerned with "the coming-into-language of the thing itself (das Zur-sprache-kommen der Sache selbst)."[95]

By way of conclusion on the subject of Gadamer's view of language, it is worth noting how his work relates to that of Rudolf Bultmann. On the one hand, Gadamer corroborates the importance of how the interpreter questions the text, and of his own presuppositions or pre-judgments. There can be no such thing as presuppositionless exegesis. But Gadamer parts company from Bultmann on two major issues. In the first place,

91. *Ibid.*, p. 426 (German, p. 444).
92. A. C. Thiselton, "The Parables as Language-Event" in *S.J.T.* XXIII, 443; and W. Pannenberg, *B.Q.T.* I, 124-28.
93. H.-G. Gadamer, *T.M.*, pp. 433 and 434.
94. G. Ebeling, *The Nature of Faith*, p. 16.
95. H.-G. Gadamer, *T.M.*, p. 341 (German, p. 360).

language is not merely external clothing for thought, so that what is "meant" is somehow independent of its linguistic expression. Thought and language are intimately bound up with each other. In the second place, what is at issue in hermeneutics is not so much the interpreter's own self-understanding as the subject-matter of the language itself. The truth expressed in language is not simply or even primarily truth about the present situation of the interpreter and his own subjectivity. It communicates a content from the past, which tradition has handed down. Most certainly the understanding of the content is a creative process in which the interpreter and his own present are actively involved. But the truth communicated through language also concerns a subject matter which is handed down, no less than the interpreter himself.

45. *Some Implications of Gadamer's Work: The Relation between Exegesis and Theology as the Problem of Fusion and Distance*

The importance of Gadamer's philosophy for New Testament hermeneutics shows itself in at least two ways. First of all, we have already suggested that it bears on questions about the relation between exegesis and theology. We shall discuss this question in the present section. Secondly, it has close connections with the new hermeneutic and parable interpretation, and we shall consider these in the next chapter.

We may first note, however, that we are not concerned to try to defend Gadamer's work as an independent ontology. It may well be that, in contrast to the undue pessimism of the later Heidegger, Gadamer himself is too optimistic about the capacity of language, tradition, and temporal distance to filter out what is false and leave only what is true. Gadamer himself acknowledges that we must be careful not to ignore the part played by individual responsibility in relation to truth, so that, as in Heidegger, responsibility becomes merely responsiveness. He recognizes this danger in his own philosophy, although he considers that it is adequately met by his taking the human community (although not human subjectivity) as his point of departure. This emerges especially in his seminar at the close of his lecture on Schleiermacher.[96]

We suggested earlier in this chapter that systematic theology might be said to represent the end-process, to date, of the process of tradition in which the Christian community seeks to arrive at an understanding of the biblical text. This is especially the case if we accept Gadamer's maxim that interpretation necessarily involves application. The texts are under-

---

96. H.-G. Gadamer, "The Problem of Language in Schleiermacher's Hermeneutic" in *J.T.C.* VII (1970), 92; cf. pp. 68-95.

stood in terms of the horizons of history and the present, while tradition, as Gadamer puts it, is not merely a passive deposit but an active process of hermeneutical engagement with the text in which unfruitful pre-judgments are (at least, ideally) discarded, and fruitful ones retained as part of the ongoing tradition. But this raises two problems. In the first place, are unfruitful pre-judgments necessarily discarded? More pointedly: is tradition, as it were, always right? Secondly, Gadamer claims that the meaning of a text always goes beyond its author. But, on the one hand, does this open the door, as E. D. Hirsch claims, to a merely subjective understanding of the text?[97] On the other hand, how does it relate to Gadamer's own acknowledgment that in preaching, for example, "the gospel of salvation does not acquire any new content?"[98]

At first sight these questions seem to suggest that the exegete should attempt to interpret the text *without* reference to a prior theological tradition. He approaches it, so to speak, in its own right. But the whole thrust of Gadamer's hermeneutics is to show that such an approach is impossible and represents what he calls the outlook of naive objectivism. This point has been reinforced from a different direction recently by Geoffrey Turner's article on pre-understanding and New Testament interpretation.[99] Turner accepts the principle of the hermeneutical circle, and that exegesis cannot be carried out without pre-understanding, but he argues that this pre-understanding embraces "a whole conceptual world which the exegete brings to the text." These concepts, however, include not simply an existential question about man himself but " 'history,' 'revelation,' 'resurrection,' 'eschatology' and 'miracle.' "[100] Turner illustrates how different pre-understandings at this level influence the exegesis, for example, of Harnack and Barth. In his article he is especially concerned with pre-understandings about history. But the principle which his work seems to underline is that systematic theology, in the form of a nexus of theological assumptions, necessarily contributes to an exegete's pre-understanding. Pre-understanding is not simply a matter of one's non-theological attitudes or experiences of "life."

Yet when we look at the history of biblical interpretation, we can see that too often a theological pre-understanding has brought about a premature and uncritical understanding of the text, in which the text was forced to say only what was required by a given theological tradition. This was broadly true of the mediaeval period. Beryl Smalley shows us that there were exceptions to the rule, including especially Andrew of St. Victor,

97. E. D. Hirsch, "Gadamer's Theory of Interpretation" in *Validity in Interpretation* (Yale University Press, New Haven, 1967), pp. 245-264 (rpt. from *R.M.*).
98. H.-G. Gadamer, *T.M.*, p. 295.
99. G. Turner, "Pre-understanding and New Testament Interpretation" in *S.J.T.* XXVIII (1975), 227-42.
100. *Ibid.*, pp. 232 and 233.

who looked to Jewish sources for his interpretation of the Bible.[101] However, in general the mediaeval interpreter "subordinated scholarship . . . to mysticism and to propaganda."[102] The general tendency was to interpret the New Testament in such a way that it merely spoke back the current tradition of the church. In Gadamer's language, it could not bring new truth to speech. Some illustrations of this principle are provided by the older study by F. W. Farrar. The Pope, he argues, was "the doorkeeper of Scripture."[103] The words "nor do men light a lamp and put it under a bushel" (Matt. 5:15) were interpreted as a legitimation of the Pope's canonization of saints. "Thou hast put all things under his feet" (Ps. 8:6) was applied to the authority of the Pope. "Gather the weeds . . . to be burned" (Matt. 13:30) gave sanction to the methods of the Inquisition.[104]

It is against this theological and historical background that the Reformers sought a new objectivity in the interpretation of the Bible. But it was not an anti-theological stance. It is the kind of objectivity which T. F. Torrance described in his book *Theological Science*. Torrance writes, "It is once again to the Reformation that we must turn for the modern emphasis upon unbiased and disinterested truth. . . . Concentration upon the Word of God . . . inculcated a repentant readiness to rethink all preconceptions and presuppositions, to put all traditional ideas to the test face to face with the object. . . . It is this masterful objectivity that is one of the great contributions of the Reformation to the modern world."[105] Objectivity involves going where inquiry itself actually leads, and letting the object of inquiry determine the method of inquiry.

It is not difficult to find statements from the Reformers themselves which exemplify this point. In his commentary on Galatians, John Calvin insists that while Scripture is inexhaustible in wisdom, nevertheless "I deny that its fertility consists in the various meanings which anyone may fasten to it at his pleasure. Let us know, then, that the true meaning of Scripture is the natural and simple one (*verum sensum scripturae, qui germanus est et simplex*). . . . Let us boldly set aside as deadly corruptions those pretended expositions which lead us away from the literal sense (*a literali sensu*)."[106] In the Dedication which precedes his com-

101. B. Smalley, *The Study of the Bible in the Middle Ages* (Blackwell, Oxford, 1952), pp. 149-72.
102. *Ibid.*, p. 358.
103. F. W. Farrar, *History of Interpretation* (Dutton, New York, 1886; rpt. Baker, Grand Rapids, Mich., 1961), p. 296; cf. pp. 245-303.
104. *Ibid.*, pp. 297-99.
105. T. F. Torrance, *Theological Science*, p. 75.
106. J. Calvin, *The Epistles of Paul the Apostle to the Galatians, Ephesians, Philippians, and Colossians* (Eng. Oliver & Boyd, Edinburgh, 1965), pp. 84-85 (on Gal. 4:22).

mentary on Romans Calvin makes the same point.[107]

At the same time what more strikingly characterizes the commentaries of the Reformers is not, in practice, their ability to preserve a distance, or tension, between their own horizons and those of the text, but precisely the phenomenon of *a fusion of horizons in which often any tension is covered up.* It is this very fusion of horizons that Karl Barth commends in the work of the Reformers in the preface to the second edition to his own commentary on Romans. Barth sides with Calvin rather than with Jülicher and Lietzmann. Recent commentators, he complains, produce not commentaries "but merely the first step towards a commentary."[108] By contrast, "How energetically Calvin, having first established what stands in the text, sets himself to re-think the whole material and to wrestle with it, *till the walls which separate the sixteenth century from the first become transparent!* Paul speaks, and the man of the sixteenth century hears. The conversation between the original record and the reader moves round the subject-matter, *until a distinction between yesterday and today becomes impossible.*"[109] This is quite different, Barth declares, from Jülicher's over-hasty willingness to dismiss this or that passage as simply a difficult opinion of Paul's "without any real struggling with the raw material of the Epistle."[110]

The very fusion of horizons which is applauded by Barth is, however, criticized sharply by Krister Stendahl. To return to Gadamer, while understanding a text entails a fusion of horizons, this fusion must not be such that the tension between past and present is covered up. "The hermeneutic task consists in not covering up this tension . . . but consciously bringing it out."[111] Stendahl points out that the Reformers achieved a fusion of horizons with the text only by equating the problem of the Judaizers and the Torah in Paul with the problems of late mediaeval religious piety. He argues that this admittedly shed a flood of light on large stretches of the Pauline writings, "but left 20 per cent of Paul inexplicable—and consequently distorted in a certain sense the true picture of Pauline thought."[112] The problem, Stendahl continues, is even more serious than this. For we have formulated *"a problem which could not be detected, let alone criticized,* by Barth or any truly Barthian exegete."[113] This approach is "incapable of enough patience and enthusiasm for *keeping alive the tension between what the text meant and*

---

107. J. Calvin, *The Epistles of Paul the Apostle to the Romans and to the Thessalonians* (Eng. Oliver & Boyd, Edinburgh, 1960), pp. 1-4.
108. K. Barth, *The Epistle to the Romans*, p. 6.
109. *Ibid.*, p. 7 (my italics).
110. *Ibid.*
111. H.-G. Gadamer, *T.M.*, p. 273.
112. K. Stendahl, "Biblical Theology, Contemporary" in *The Interpreter's Dictionary of the Bible* 1 (Abingdon Press, New York, 1962), 420; cf. 418-32.
113. *Ibid.* (my italics).

what it means. There are no criteria by which they can be kept apart; what is intended as a commentary becomes a theological tractate expanding in contemporary terms what Paul should have said about the subject matter as understood by the commentator."[114]

It is possible that Stendahl may have overstated the case with respect to the particular writers concerned. But the general principle which he formulates is fundamentally important and valid. Objectivity is excluded when hermeneutical fusion becomes the *only* aim. In his article entitled "The Apostle Paul and the Introspective Conscience of the West," Stendahl endeavors to argue concretely that a fusion of horizons between Luther and Paul has led, in his view, to a one-sided and even distorted understanding of Paul by later generations who have seen Paul through Luther's eyes.[115] Stendahl argues, for example, that Paul's statement "I do not the good I want, but the evil I do not want to do is what I do" (Rom. 7:19) is made hermeneutically into a common denominator between Paul and the experience of modern man. It is interpreted, Stendahl suggests, in the light of Luther's struggle with his conscience. "But it is precisely at that point that we can discern the most drastic difference between Luther and Paul, between the sixteenth century and the first century."[116] For Paul, Stendahl insists, had a rather robust conscience. Paul "has nothing on his conscience" (1 Cor. 4:4); has a good conscience (Rom. 9:1; 2 Cor. 1:12); and as a Pharisee was blameless with respect to the righteousness of the law (Phil. 3:6). The failure of the Jews in Romans 2:17-3:20, Stendahl argues, was not a matter of individual conscience but of Israel's collective transgression. The key issue in Romans, he urges, is not the existential one of what happens to *me* now, but the status of *the law* now that Christ has come. The issue both in Romans 9-11 and in Galatians 3:24 is that of the course of salvation-history, not the individual's inner life.[117]

Stendahl's attack is not altogether fair to Luther and to the Reformation. T. F. Torrance warns us, for example, that it is a caricature of their position to interpret the necessary "for me" of appropriation as an egocentric and subjectivized "for *me*."[118] However, his general warning about the need to maintain a proper tension between the horizons of the text and the pre-understanding of the interpreter is valid, and we see the effects of an undue hostility towards objectification, if not in Luther, then certainly in Bultmann. Stendahl's attempt to distance himself from the

114. *Ibid.*, (my italics).
115. K. Stendahl, "The Apostle Paul and the Introspective Conscience of the West" in *H.T.R.* LVI (1963), 199-215; reprinted in *Paul Among Jews and Gentiles* (S.C.M., London, 1977), pp. 78-96.
116. *Ibid.*, p. 200.
117. *Ibid.*, pp. 204-07.
118. T. F. Torrance, *Theological Science*, p. 81.

traditional interpretation of Romans and Galatians provides a corrective which does justice to Gadamer's warnings against a premature fusion of horizons which fails to preserve any tension between the past and the present. In practice, Gerhard Ebeling reminds us that Luther himself was eager to ensure that this tension should not be ignored. Ebeling writes, *"According to Luther, the word of God always comes as* adversarius noster, *our adversary. It does not simply confirm and strengthen us in what we think we are, and in what we wish to be taken for. . . . This is the way, the only way, in which the word draws us into concord and peace with God."*[119] In other words, Luther saw that sufficient distance or tension between the text and the interpreter must be preserved in order to ensure that it did not merely mirror back his own human thoughts and attitudes. In this sense, man places himself "under" the word of God. But Luther also saw that there must be a fusion of horizons in which the interpreter is grasped and addressed, and can appropriate its truth as his own. Gadamer's work demonstrates at a theoretical level that these two sides must be held together. Can we go further and see more clearly how this can be done?

46. *Further Considerations of the Issue: Exegesis and Theology with Special Reference to Diem, Ott, and Stuhlmacher*

Robert Morgan has recently re-examined the relation between exegesis and Christian theology with particular reference to the claims of W. Wrede and A. Schlatter.[120] Wrede insisted that the biblical scholar must approach his subject-matter not as a systematic theologian but as a historian of religion. The exegete, according to Wrede, must approach his material "as objectively, correctly, and sharply as possible. That is all. How the systematic theologian gets on with its results and deals with them—that is his own affair. Could dogmatics teach New Testament theology to see the facts correctly? . . . To correct facts is absurd."[121] To appeal to the unity of Scripture as represented by the canon, or to appeal to theological tradition, is arbitrarily to put oneself under the ecclesiastical authority of the bishops or the early centuries of church history. Wrede wishes to aim at an "objective" understanding of the text and "that is all."

Clearly the kind of considerations raised by Gadamer about tradition and pre-understanding have no place at all in Wrede's thinking. His very

119. G. Ebeling, *I.T.T.L.,* p. 17 (my italics).
120. R. Morgan, *The Nature of New Testament Theology* (S.C.M., London, 1973).
121. W. Wrede, "The Tasks and Methods of 'New Testament Theology' " in *ibid.,* pp. 69-70.

attempt to be "historical" constitutes, from Gadamer's viewpoint, an attempt to ignore man's historicality. Morgan contrasts his outlook with that of Schlatter who approached the New Testament explicitly as a Christian theologian. Schlatter claimed that a theological approach was no less objective than an exclusively historical one, on the ground that "Dogmatic work demands . . . the strictest objectivity . . . no less than historical work."[122] His appreciation of the problem of objectivity was more advanced than Wrede's. For he saw that when the message of the New Testament makes a claim on man's will, it is inadequate to portray the interpreter of the New Testament as "a machine for observing."[123] However, he is not really motivated by the kind of issues that Gadamer raises. His argument is not, in the end, that the problem of tradition cannot be short-circuited, but that dogmatics is as objective a discipline as history.

Morgan argues that a way must be found of doing justice to the positive insights represented by both authors. Historical exegesis, he argues, does justice to the interpreter's integrity as a scholar; but theological exegesis takes account of the kerygmatic intention of the texts. For this reason, Wrede and Schlatter are "both so right in their own ways."[124] However, in Morgan's view, neither Wrede nor Schlatter, nor even Bultmann, Cullmann, or Käsemann, provides an adequate answer to the issue under discussion. His own contribution is to ask whether phenomenology might not provide a more hopeful way of approach. He is right to insist that history and theology are not exclusive alternatives in an approach to the New Testament. But we may still ask whether the phenomenological method is capable of achieving a genuine fusion of horizons, even though admittedly a fusion that does not cover up all tension and historical distance. Can phenomenology, with its emphasis on description alone, do justice to Gadamer's insight that understanding is inseparable from application? Does it really answer the point held in common by Barth and Bultmann that the Bible is not only information but also address; not only indicative, but also imperative? We are reminded of Wittgenstein's aphorism: " 'You can't hear God speak to someone else; you can hear him only if you are being addressed'—That is a grammatical remark."[125]

Before we turn to the writings of Hermann Diem and Heinrich Ott it is worth noting that the need to do justice to both sides in the discussion is widely recognized in current Roman Catholic theology. Karl Rahner insists that the gap between exegesis and systematic theology must be

122. A. Schlatter, "The Theology of the New Testament and Dogmatics" in *ibid.*, p. 119.
123. *Ibid.*, p. 125.
124. R. Morgan, *The Nature of New Testament Theology*, p. 28; cf. p. 35.
125. L. Wittgenstein, *Z.*, sect. 717.

bridged, but not simply by the dogmatic theologian. He addresses New Testament exegetes with the words "You must be critical—inexorably critical. You must not 'arrange' dishonest reconciliations between the results of your research and the Church's teaching."[126] But, he adds, New Testament scholars must not evade the responsibility of relating their work to the church's tradition. Questioning, discussing, and searching must not be replaced by the church's *magisterium,* but the *magisterium,* on the other hand, is no mere dead letter.

Heinrich Schlier, who writes both as a Roman Catholic theologian and as a former pupil of Bultmann, has an interesting comment on the problem. On the one hand, the New Testament writings "are entirely writings of their own age."[127] He even goes part of the way with Käsemann in accepting the theological pluriformity of the New Testament. To this extent he approaches the New Testament as a historian of religion. But on the other hand, he makes two points. First of all, there is, he claims, also a unity on the part of the New Testament which suggests that Scripture be interpreted in the light of Scripture. "One revelation-event has projected itself into manifold forms of believing thought."[128] Secondly, if we try to aim at historical objectivity in the sense which we have outlined in this study with reference to Wrede (and perhaps Nineham and Troeltsch), Schlier warns us that in the end the basis of our approach may turn out to be no more than "a very temporary attitude to past history," in which we "miss the past reality itself."[129] In a way which comes closer to Gadamer than Schlatter, Wrede, or Morgan, Schlier observes that hermeneutics involves entering into discussion "with what has already been thought in the Church on the basis of scripture. . . . So that this may yield up what has not been thought, and disclose further . . . the subject-matter itself."[130] He even alludes in the course of his discussion of this issue to the emphasis on the "wholeness" of what comes to speech according to Heidegger's later thought.

As a third and final example of Roman Catholic thinking on this subject we may note the interplay of exegesis and tradition found in the work of Nicolas Lash. He accepts the dictum of Schillebeeckx that the problem of doctrinal continuity is parallel to the hermeneutical problem in Protestant thought.[131] He fully accepts the implications of historical un-

126. K. Rahner, "Exegesis and Dogmatic Theology" in *Theological Investigations* V (Eng. Darton, Longman, & Todd, London, 1966), p. 71; cf. pp. 67-93.
127. H. Schlier, *The Relevance of the New Testament* (Eng. Burns & Oates, London, 1967), p. 27; cf. pp. 26-75.
128. *Ibid.,* p. 33; cf. p. 30.
129. *Ibid.,* p. 31 n. 3.
130. *Ibid.,* p. 73.
131. N. Lash, *Change in Focus. A Study of Doctrinal Change and Continuity* (Sheed & Ward, London, 1973), p. 180.

derstanding and historical particularity, but tries to work out the problem of theological interpretation against a view of tradition which is informed by the work of Gadamer and Pannenberg as well as of Y. Congar.[132] The past, he concludes, must be read and reread in the light of the present. In turn, this rereading becomes part of the historical tradition which is handed on. Like Gadamer himself, Lash may be too optimistic about the capacity of tradition to reject what is false in process of time. But he tries to hold together the various principles which we are discussing.

We come now to the work of Diem and Ott. Both theologians stand in the Barthian tradition, so it is worth recalling Karl Barth's own outlook on the relation between exegesis and systematic theology. Barth refers scathingly to the kind of quest for neutral detached objectivity associated with the Liberalism of Harnack. He writes, "For a short time, around 1910, this idea threatened to achieve almost canonical status in Protestant theology. But now we can quite calmly dismiss it as merely comical."[133] Scripture, Barth claims, is the interpreter of Scripture, and in any case the task of interpretation "is laid upon all members of the Church and not upon a specialized class of biblical scholars."[134] Barth himself aimed above all at a fusion of horizons in the understanding of the text: "If we rightly understand ourselves, *our problems are the problems of Paul* and if we be enlightened by the brightness of his answers, *those answers must be ours.*"[135] Barth recognized that his early commentary on Romans took interpretation much further than was customary, and suggested that it raised afresh the question: "What is exegesis?"[136] We have already pointed out that Bultmann supported Barth's approach. Barth rightly saw, Bultmann remarks, that Christianity is not merely "a phenomenon of the history of religion."[137]

Hermann Diem also attacks Harnack's contention that dogma represents an extraneous addition to the pure gospel.[138] He also deplores what he calls the loss of "the right relationship between dogmatics and exegesis."[139] He endorses Käsemann's complaint that it might often seem as if New Testament scholars and dogmatic theolgians have different Bibles in front of them. Diem stresses that dogmatics can never be final or definitive. "Dogmas must never be used to forestall the results of

132. *Ibid.*, pp. 38-43, 177-80 *et passim.*
133. K. Barth, *Church Dogmatics* I/2 (Eng. Clark, Edinburgh, 1956), 469.
134. *Ibid.*, p. 714.
135. K. Barth, *The Epistle to the Romans* (Eng. Oxford University Press, 1933 and 1968), p. 1.
136. *Ibid.*, p. ix; cf. p. 6.
137. R. Bultmann, *E.F.*, p. 340. Cf. "Karl Barths Römerbrief in zweiter Auflage" in *Christliche Welt* XXXVI (1922), 320-23, 330-34, 358-61, and 369-73.
138. H. Diem, *Dogmatics* (Eng. Oliver & Boyd, Edinburgh, 1959), p. 169.
139. *Ibid.*, p. 81.

exegesis."[140] On the other hand, dogmas may have to be revised in the light of exegesis. However: "this challenge cannot spring from the exegesis of any one particular Biblical passage, but only from a comprehensive survey of the Biblical testimony as a whole."[141] "In proclaiming one text we must at the same time listen to the voice of the other."[142]

There are two poles, then, in Diem's thought, around which moves a process which turns out to be little different from Gadamer's version of the hermeneutical circle. We begin with a provisional understanding of a particular text. This is interpreted in the light of what we already understand about Scripture as a whole, although "this must not happen in such a way that by one text we blunt the point of the other, and so level down the two of them."[143] We must not, for example, use Paul to weaken the message of James; or James, to weaken the message of Paul. Each must be allowed to speak to the appropriate historical moment. However, the interpreter must now return to the text itself. Diem criticizes Barth for making critical-historical exegesis a mere preliminary. It can never be left behind; but interpretation is never definitive or final. Hermeneutics is a process, not a once-for-all act.

This principle becomes even clearer and more explicit in the writings of Heinrich Ott. Ott declares, "Systematic theology finds its position . . . in the middle of the arch extending from the text to contemporary preaching."[144] But this does not mean that the particularity of the text must be renounced in favor of a definitive theological formulation. On the one hand, "there is no such thing as fixed dogmas by which exegetical reflection would be absolutely directed." But on the other hand, because, as Gadamer would put it, tradition and history move on, "there is no such thing as historical-critical results which stand unshakably, apart from theology's reflection upon its specific theme." Hence, Ott concludes, "Dogmatics and exegesis stand in a relation of interaction with one another."[145]

Once again, for Ott this principle is bound up with the hermeneutical circle. Understanding of the parts will always remain provisional on an understanding of the whole. But this is an ever ongoing process. "There is no final black-and-white distinction between 'having understood' and 'not having understood.' Rather . . . understanding by its very nature takes place at different levels."[146] As each event of provisional understanding

140. *Ibid.*, p. 304.
141. *Ibid.*
142. *Ibid.*, p. 237.
143. *Ibid.*
144. H. Ott, "What is Systematic Theology?" in J. M. Robinson and J. Cobb, Jr. (eds.), *New Frontiers in Theology: I, The Later Heidegger and Theology*, p. 81.
145. *Ibid.*, p. 83.
146. *Ibid.*, p. 80.

occurs and is subsequently revised, the whole process of interpretation deepens. We have seen that Ott criticizes what he regards as an ontological dualism in Bultmann's theology. By contrast, in the light of Heidegger's later thought he expresses approval of the way in which Barth and Ebeling explicate "the one and indivisible faith."[147] The gospel is like Heidegger's "one unspoken poem": each interpretation speaks from the whole.

This underlines for Ott the role of the community in hermeneutics. "Faith is not essentially a stance of the isolated individual but is by its nature the faith of the *communio sanctorum*." In this community "a common understanding is reached. . . . Communion *consists* in the common understanding of the one 'subject-matter' of faith. . . . The thinker . . . is not alone but finds himself in discussion with humanity."[148] This brings us straight back to Gadamer. Part of man's historicity is his place in the community and its tradition. Understanding is not only shaped by how an individual approaches a particular text, but also by how the community approaches a variety of texts. Pre-understanding depends partly on the theological tradition of the community; but corrected understanding also depends on the theology of the community. Nevertheless the rights of the text are not suppressed or ignored. For the process of understanding is provisional and remains open to listen anew to the voice of the text. In the face of criticism of his hermeneutics Ott asserts, "It is not at all the case that the outcome is the production of a uniformly harmonized standard theology of the New Testament. . . . The differences and antitheses between the Biblical authors continue to exist and must be taken very seriously."[149] Ott argues, for example, that the full understanding of the passage about the last judgment in Matthew 25:31-46 demands that its relation to justification by grace be considered; but not that it be harmonized into some final or definitive doctrine.

We are not concerned necessarily to commend Ott's theology as a whole. Some of the problems of his claims about "non-objectifying" language have been exposed, for example, by Paul van Buren.[150] However, Ott recognizes the provisional, progressive, and open-ended nature of hermeneutics when it is carried out on the one hand in relation to the horizons of tradition and the community, and on the other hand without overriding the rights of the text itself. Admittedly in his concern for the church community and the oneness of the gospel Ott may well have erred on the side of paying insufficient attention to the distance and tension which separates the text from the present. This defect characterizes other

147. *Ibid.*, p. 91.
148. *Ibid.*, pp. 94 and 102.
149. H. Ott, "Response to the American Discussion" in *ibid.*, p. 204.
150. Paul van Buren, *Theological Explorations* (S.C.M., London, 1968), pp. 81-105.

hermeneutical studies which stress the role of the churchly community, including, for example, John Wilkinson's otherwise helpful study *Interpretation and Community*.[151] Wilkinson recognizes the need for historical-critical inquiry but tends to separate exegesis and application into two self-contained areas.

Recently the debate has been taken a stage further by Peter Stuhlmacher in his notion of "a hermeneutics of consent."[152] Stuhlmacher writes as a former pupil of Käsemann, but he is also sympathetic with the outlook of kerygmatic theology, pietism, and "biblically-oriented Lutheranism."[153] In his own hermeneutical theory he is also heavily indebted to Gadamer, as R. A. Harrisville argues in his introduction to the American edition of Stuhlmacher's work.[154] He takes up Gadamer's principle of openness to the text, and accepts his formulation of effective historical consciousness. Moreover, Harrisville writes, "Even Stuhlmacher's commitment to *sola scriptura* has its counterpart in Gadamer's insistence upon the interpreter's submission to the text's claim to dominate the mind."[155] We may note that he also approves of Pannenberg's attempt to broaden hermeneutics beyond mere historical exegesis in the narrower sense.

Stuhlmacher emphasizes the primacy of the text, but he begins, negatively, with the recognition of the failure of the nineteenth-century attempt "at an objective, naturalistic view of history."[156] More positively, he insists that we need to lay hold of the insights of the new hermeneutic, including the work of Gadamer, Fuchs, and Ebeling. In this light, we must be willing to open ourselves anew to the claim of the text, *and* of tradition, *and* of the present, *and* of "transcendence." "We must again learn to ask what claim or truth about man, his world, and transcendence we hear from these texts."[157] This entails sensitivity and awareness concerning problems of historical and hermeneutical method. Such an approach, Stuhlmacher argues, witnesses to the sufficiency of Scripture, for "we remain open to the church's experience that the biblical texts disclose a truth which wakens faith and does not lie within the scope of human possibility."[158] It involves "openness to an encounter with the truth of God coming to us from out of transcendence."[159]

This approach contains the *theological* dimension which is entirely

151. J. Wilkinson, *Interpretation and Community* (Macmillan, London, 1963).
152. P. Stuhlmacher, *Historical Criticism and Theological Interpretation of Scripture. Towards a Hermeneutics of Consent* (Fortress Press, Philadelphia, 1977), especially pp. 83-91.
153. *Ibid.*, p. 13.
154. *Ibid.*, pp. 13-15.
155. *Ibid.*, p. 14.
156. *Ibid.*, p. 84.
157. *Ibid.*, p. 85.
158. *Ibid.*, p. 88.
159. *Ibid.*, p. 89.

lacking in the kind of perspective which we earlier discussed in connection with D. E. Nineham. Historical exegesis is essential, but it is not enough. We need *both* distancing *and* an *openness* to the text which will yield progress towards the fusion of horizons. The two principles are brought together in some comments of Walter Wink, to whose work we have already referred. Wink stresses the role of critical study in distancing the New Testament from theological tradition. He writes, "The Bible, wrenched from its matrix in ecclesiastical tradition, is thus objectified by critical scholarship."[160] Walter Wink observes, further, "The tradition is our world, prior to any separation of subject and object. . . . We can see nothing without it, since it provides the grid of meanings by which we filter the manifold of experience. It is our horizon." We can understand only in terms of our tradition. Tradition is necessary for the occurrence of a fusion of horizons with the text. But Wink, following Gadamer, goes on to stress the role of critical distancing; "distancing from prevailing cultural . . . pre-understandings."[161] Wink sees how Gadamer's two principles of fusion and distance apply to New Testament hermeneutics, but it is Diem and especially Ott who provide us with a vantage-point to see how this applies to the relationship between exegesis and systematic theology. There must be a sufficient tendency towards fusion to allow the interpreter, as Barth puts it, to see the problems of Paul as his problems. But there must be sufficient distance to do justice to the kind of warnings expressed by Stendahl, and to Luther's recognition that, far from mirroring back the interpreter's own thoughts, the Word of God may encounter men as his adversary. In Gadamer's words, "We speak of the fusion of horizons. . . . Understanding here is always application." Nevertheless: "Every encounter with tradition that takes place within historical consciousness involves the experience of the tension between the text and the present. The hermeneutic task consists in not covering up this tension . . . but consciously bringing it out."[162]

160. W. Wink, *The Bible in Human Transformation*, p. 23.
161. *Ibid.*, pp. 21 and 22.
162. H.-G. Gadamer, *T.M.*, pp. 273 and 275.

CHAPTER XII

The Later Heidegger, Gadamer, and the New Hermeneutic

In the second of our two introductory chapters we briefly considered the question of whether the new hermeneutic in theology is dependent on Heidegger's later thought, or only on his earlier work in *Being and Time*. We also noted that it is still a matter of controversy among Heidegger's interpreters whether his later thought is to be regarded as representing a "reversal" of his earlier work, or as a development which remains fundamentally in continuity with it. We must take this question further before examining the actual themes of Heidegger's later writings. Exponents of both views can easily be mentioned. Marjorie Grene draws a sharp contrast between Heidegger's earlier and later thought, and argues that while *Being and Time* has true philosophical power, the later work is thin, ill-organized, and even humdrum and dull.[1] Heinrich Ott also distinguishes sharply between the two periods; but only to praise the fuller insights of the later work in contrast to the more limited viewpoints of *Being and Time*.[2] Werner Brock, by contrast, adopts a different approach from both of these interpreters. Some writers, he remarks, "seem to think that there has been considerable change in Heidegger's outlook. . . . I for one do not share this opinion."[3]

One of the most emphatic writers to assert a radical discontinuity between Heidegger's earlier and later thought is Karl Löwith. Löwith goes so far as to maintain that a consistent follower of Heidegger could hardly participate in his later perspectives, and interprets the "turn"

1. M. Grene, *Martin Heidegger,* p. 117.
2. H. Ott, *Denken und Sein. Der Weg Martin Heideggers und der Weg der Theologie* (E.V.Z. Verlag, Zürich, 1959); cf. also his *Geschichte und Heilsgeschichte in der Theologie Rudolf Bultmanns,* pp. 173-93.
3. W. Brock, "An Account of 'The Four Essays' " in M. Heidegger, *E.B.,* p. 134.

(*Kehre*) as a "reversal" or an "about-face."[4] He stresses the existentialist character of *Being and Time* and claims that the ontological orientation of Heidegger's later thought is a "return to his theological beginning."[5] This conflicts, however, with Heidegger's own statements on the matter, and overlooks the fact that *Being and Time* is concerned with Being, even if from the standpoint of Dasein. Heidegger underlines the continuity of his thought not only in his "Letter on Humanism" in 1947, but also in a letter to William J. Richardson written in April 1962, and quoted in Richardson's book. He writes, "Only by way of what Heidegger I has thought does one gain access to what is to-be-thought by Heidegger II."[6] Admittedly the very fact that he can speak of "Heidegger I and II" shows that some change has occurred. In Richardson's own words, "There *is* a change, but it is in line with the subject-matter of *Being and Time*."[7]

The main point about the advances of Heidegger's later thought is not, as L. Landgrebe seems to suggest, that they are more obscure and esoteric.[8] This esoteric character springs from Heidegger's conviction that poetry may perhaps "show" what cannot be said in merely proposi-tional language, and is therefore only symptomatic of something more important. We may sum up the change in Heidegger's thinking under four headings. First of all, as Pöggeler and others suggest, the emphasis moves from that of an existential analytic to the nature of Being, although not in such a way as to imply that *Being and Time* did not concern ontology.[9] Michael Gelven rightly argues, as against W. J. Richardson and L. Versén-yi, that Heidegger's thought in *Being and Time* itself represents a steady progression towards an increasing emphasis on ontology, with the result that there are differences of *degrees* of ontological orientation between *Being and Time* in its first and second divisions and Heidegger's later writings, rather than a single difference of *kind* between the whole of *Being and Time*, on the one hand, and Heidegger's later thought, on the other hand.[10] Secondly, there is also some truth in J. G. Gray's argument that Heidegger moves "from human existence to nature."[11] However, even this comment could be misleading. It is true only if we interpret

4. K. Löwith, *Heidegger, Denker in dürftiger Zeit* (Vandenhoeck & Ruprecht, Göttingen, ²1960), p. 7.
5. *Ibid.*, p. 21. Cf. also J. M. Robinson, "The German Discussion of the Later Heidegger" in J. M. Robinson and J. B. Cobb, Jr. (eds.), *New Frontiers in Theology: I, The Later Heidegger and Theology*, pp. 3-76.
6. W. J. Richardson, *Heidegger: Through Phenomenology to Thought* (Nijhoff, The Hague, 1963), p. xxii.
7. *Ibid.*, p. xvi.
8. L. Landgrebe, "The Study of Philosophy in Germany: A Reply to Walter Cerf" in *J.Ph.* LIV (1957), 127-31 (especially p. 128).
9. O. Pöggeler, *Der Denkweg Martin Heideggers* (Neske, Pfullingen, 1963), p. 176.
10. M. Gelven, *A Commentary on Heidegger's 'Being and Time,'* pp. 137-42.
11. J. G. Gray, "Heidegger's Course: From Human Existence to Nature" in *J.Ph.* LIV (1957), 197-207.

"nature" broadly enough to describe the vision which Heidegger draws from Hölderlin and the poets. Thirdly, in his later writings Heidegger relates the problem of language to the question of Being, even though his diagnosis of the emptiness of the Western language-tradition is found in embryonic form in his view of "idle talk" in *Being and Time*. Fourthly, Heidegger's emphasis on pre-conceptual or non-objectifying thinking is now worked out in relation to art and poetry, rather than in terms of the problem of going beyond Kant's philosophy.

In spite of these four lines of advance, however, in his article "Heidegger's Earlier and Later Work Compared" J. Macquarrie stresses two important facts. First of all, the "turn" in Heidegger's thought is not a "reversal." It represents the working out of a dialectic that belongs to the very nature of Heidegger's problematic and of which he has been more of less aware from the beginning."[12] Secondly, since both the earlier and the later thought are part of a single whole, "we cannot separate them or exalt the one at the expense of the other."[13] Heidegger's own comments, not only in his two letters but also in his later work *On the Way to Language* would support these statements. Heidegger does speak of a "fundamental flaw" in *Being and Time,* but this concerns not its argument but the suggestion that "perhaps I ventured forth too far too early."[14] Elsewhere in the same work he comments, "I have left an earlier standpoint, not in order to exchange it for another one, but because even the former standpoint was merely a way-station along the way. The lasting element in thinking is the way."[15] Finally, Heidegger states thirty-two years after the publication of *Being and Time:* "What mattered then, and still does, is to bring out the Being of beings. . . ."[16]

The first systematic outline of Heidegger's later thought emerges in his book *An Introduction to Metaphysics.* Although first published in 1953, it represents lecture-material originally produced in 1935. Between 1935 and 1962 Heidegger published more than a score of writings. The two most important of these, for our purposes, are his *Unterwegs zur Sprache,* published in 1959 and his small address *Gelassenheit.* Heidegger's essay "Hölderlin and the Essence of Poetry," written in 1936, also has a significant bearing on his view of language.[17] We should perhaps also mention his short essay "The Way Back into the Ground of Metaphysics," which was written in 1949 as a self-contained introduction to the fifth edition of *What is Metaphysics?* In 1956 Heidegger singled this

12. J. Macquarrie, "Heidegger's Earlier and Later Work Compared" in *A.T.R.* XLIX (1967), 6; cf. pp. 3-16.
13. *Ibid.,* p. 7.
14. M. Heidegger, *O.W.L.,* p. 7.
15. *Ibid.,* p. 12.
16. *Ibid.,* p. 30.
17. In M. Heidegger, *E.B.,* pp. 291-315.

out as an important summary of his key ideas.[18] The three collections of
essays entitled respectively *Holzwege* (1950), *Vorträge und Aufsätze*
(1954), and *Wegmarken* (1967) all include significant material.[19] Some of
these essays have been translated into English in *Poetry, Language, and
Thought*.[20]

47. The Malaise of Language and Thinking
in the Western Language-Tradition

Heidegger begins his work *An Introduction to Metaphysics* with the
question "Why are there essents (entities, *Seienden*) rather than nothing?", and he constantly returns to this question.[21] He urges that this is
"the most fundamental of questions because it is the broadest and
deepest."[22] However, this problem, he believes, is approached more
constructively if we ask "the preliminary question 'How does it stand
with being?' (*Wie steht es um das Sein?*)"[23] But when we try, as it were,
to look directly at Being, we seem to find nothing to say. In this sense,
Heidegger asserts, Nietzsche went to the heart of the problem when he
described Being as a vapor or a haze *(Dunst)*. Certainly, viewed as a
"highest concept" Being is, in the words of Nietzsche, "the last cloudy
streak of evaporating reality."[24] The problem of Being thus brings us face
to face with the problem of language. The *word* "Being" seems
thoroughly empty and idle.

Nevertheless Heidegger asks: Is this the fault of Being? Or even: "Is
it the fault of the word that it remains so empty?" Does the fault not,
rather, lie with us in that "with all our efforts, with all our chasing after
the essent *(Seiendes),* we have fallen out of being *(Sein)?*"[25] It lies, he
claims, in something that runs through Western history from the very
beginning that we are "linked to being and yet had long fallen out of being,
without knowing it."[26] Had we not "fallen out of being," Heidegger

18. M. Heidegger, "The Way Back into the Ground of Metaphysics," translated in
W. Kaufmann (ed.), *Existentialism from Dostoevsky to Sartre (sic;* Meridian Books, The
World Publishing Co., New York, 1956, 1966), pp. 206-21.
19. M. Heidegger, *Holz.; Vorträge und Aufsätze* (Neske, Pfullingen, 1954); and *Wegmarken*
(Klostermann, Frankfurt, 1967).
20. M. Heidegger, *P.L.T.*
21. M. Heidegger, *I.M.,* pp. 1, 2, 12, 22, 29, 32, and elsewhere. The translator of this work,
R. Manheim, uses "essent" for *Seiendes* on the ground that "the word is deliberately alien
to everyday speech"; cf. pp. viii-ix.
22. *Ibid.,* p. 6.
23. *Ibid.,* p. 32; cf. pp. 39 and 41.
24. *Ibid.,* p. 36; Heidegger quotes from Nietzsche's work *The Twilight of Idols.*
25. *Ibid.,* pp. 36-37.
26. *Ibid.,* p. 37.

claims, it would have remained clear to us that Being was not a mere haze or emptiness, but a reality or a presence which is "the spiritual destiny of the Western world."[27]

How and on what basis can Heidegger suggest that the question of Being has anything to do with "the spiritual destiny of the Western World?" Fallenness from Being, he believes, is bound up with the disintegration and fragmentation of life, which in turn reflects a cultural tradition of technology and "levelling down." This is the time of "the spiritual decline of the earth" and "the darkening of the world, the flight of the gods, the destruction of the earth." This whole phenomenon is seen in "the transformation of men into a mass, the hatred and suspicion of everything free and creative."[28]

Heidegger has been criticized, with justice, for using this argument in order to justify the notion of German historical destiny as against Russia and America. Subsequent controversy over his address as the first National Socialist Rector of the University of Freiburg in 1933 is well known. However, given Heidegger's beliefs about "average everyday existence" already expressed in Being and Time, together with his growing conviction about the positive value of creative movements, his outlook is understandable. He equally criticizes American "gadgetry" (das Herstellbare), and the often dreary uniformity of Russian Marxist regimentation. He writes: "From a metaphysical point of view, Russia and America are the same; the same dreary technological frenzy, the same unrestricted organisation of the average man. . . . When a boxer is regarded as a nation's great man, when mass meetings attended by millions are looked on as a triumph . . . a question still haunts us like a spectre: What for?— Whither?—And what then?"[29] On the one hand, he believes, we are threatened with "the standardization of man, the pre-eminence of the mediocre."[30] "In Russia and America this development grew into a boundless etcetera of indifference and always-the-sameness."[31] On the other hand, "We ask the question 'How does it stand with being?' 'What is the meaning of being?' not in order to set up an ontology on the traditional style . . . (but) to restore man's historical being-there (Dasein) . . . in the totality of the history allotted to us, to the domain of being (Sein)."[32] This involves "re-calling" (wieder-holen) the beginning of our historical-spiritual existence "in order to transform it into a new beginning."[33]

27. Ibid.
28. Ibid., p. 38.
29. Ibid., pp. 37-38.
30. Ibid., p. 45.
31. Ibid., p. 46.
32. Ibid., pp. 41-42.
33. Ibid., p. 39.

All this has profound repercussions on questions about thought and language. Thinking, in the everyday orientation of technology, is reduced to mere calculation, while language is pressed into the service of day-to-day trivia. Day-to-day cash-value meanings are born out of man's purely functional and conventional concerns, and language is fragmented and debased. Worst of all, in Heidegger's view, language cannot articulate Being: "The word 'being' no longer applies to anything. . . . Everything . . . dissolves like a tatter of cloud in the sunlight."[34] "The destiny of language is grounded in . . . *relation to being.*"[35]

Thinking and language for Heidegger, as we saw in Gadamer, are intimately bound up with each other. In *Gelassenheit* Heidegger draws a clear-cut contrast between what he calls calculative thinking and meditative thinking.[36] Both are justified in their own way. But, Heidegger writes, "The approaching tide of technological revolution in the atomic age could so captivate, bewitch, dazzle, and beguile men that calculative thinking may someday come to be accepted and practised as the *only* way of thinking."[37] This contrast is presupposed in Heidegger's book *On the Way to Language,* where the powerlessness of language in the modern Western world is seen as symptomatic of the calculative frame of mind. He writes, "Modern thinking is ever more resolutely and exclusively turning into calculation. . . . We must . . . rid ourselves of the calculative frame of mind."[38]

The reduction of creative thinking to mere calculation is part and parcel of the splitting up of reality into self-contained compartments or specialist "fields." The degenerative process began with Plato. Heidegger writes, "It was in the Sophists and in Plato that appearance was declared to be mere appearance and thus degraded. At the same time being, as idea, was exalted to a suprasensory realm. A chasm, *chorismos,* was created between the merely apparent essent *(Seiendes)* here below and real being *(Sein)* somewhere on high. In that chasm Christianity settled down. . . . Nietzsche was right in saying that Christianity is Platonism for the people."[39] The first major division of reality, thus, was a dualism between the realm of things and the realm of ideas. This led, in Heidegger's view, to the split vision of subject-object thinking, where man views the world through the grid of his own concepts. Reality becomes a conceptualized object of thought.

An example of how this compartmentalizing affects man's relation to

34. *Ibid.,* p. 40.
35. *Ibid.,* p. 51.
36. M. Heidegger, *Discourse on Thinking. A Translation of Gelassenheit* (Harper & Row, New York, 1966), pp. 46 and 53.
37. *Ibid.,* p. 56 (Heidegger's italics).
38. M. Heidegger, *O.W.L.,* pp. 84 and 104.
39. M. Heidegger, *I.M.,* p. 106.

Being is seen in the reduction of art to "aesthetics." Heidegger's view of aesthetics and art is similar to that which we have examined in Gadamer, his pupil. On the basis of a Platonic dualism art is either brought into the "lower" realm of material objects, and reduced to the status of a mere "thing"; or else it is elevated into the realm of aesthetic concepts. But to do either of these two things is to rob it of its primeval power to disclose reality. Heidegger writes, "For us moderns, the beautiful . . . is intended for enjoyment and art is a matter for pastry cooks. . . . But . . . on the strength of a recaptured, pristine, relation to Being we must provide the word 'art' with a new content."[40] This point comes out in Heidegger's dialogue with Tezuka, "the Japanese," in *On the Way to Language*. The distinction between the sensuous and the supersensuous world is the basis of the Western presentation of art as aesthetics.[41] What Heidegger or "The Inquirer" calls "the complete Europeanization of the earth and man" leads to technological advances at every turn. But the Japanese admits that the impact of such a perspective on oriental art has the consequence that "the Japanese world is captured and imprisoned . . . in the objectness of photography. . . . Photographic objectification is already a consequence of the even wider outreach of Europeanization."[42] "Aesthetics . . . turns the art work into an object for our feelings and ideas. . . . Only then is it fit for exhibitions and museums . . . or . . . the art business."[43]

Just as the fragmentation of reality affects our understanding of art, so it also has dire consequences for our relation to language. Language, Heidegger complains, is reduced to the status of a technological, calculative tool. Day-to-day cash-value meanings are born out of the interests of specialized fields or narrow, purely pragmatic concerns. For example, "Time has ceased to be anything other than velocity, instantaneousness, and simultaneity, and time as history has vanished from the lives of all peoples."[44] According to Heidegger, the whole notion of the formation of concepts from Plato to Kant conceals an "attack on the nature of language" because it hides the fact that language is so much more than a means of labelling concepts.[45] Language is not simply a medium which serves to express ready-made ideas.[46] Moreover, language itself becomes objectified as a "thing." "Information about language is one thing; an experience we undergo with language is another."[47] Heidegger contrasts

40. *Ibid.*, pp. 131-32.
41. M. Heidegger, *O.W.L.*, p. 14.
42. *Ibid.*, p. 17; cf. pp. 15-16 and, more broadly, 18-54.
43. *Ibid.*, p. 43.
44. M. Heidegger, *I.M.*, p. 38.
45. M. Heidegger, *O.W.L.*, p. 25.
46. *Ibid.*, p. 35.
47. *Ibid.*, p. 59.

the traditional Western view of language with that which comes to expression in Stefan George's poem "The Word." Language, according to George, communicates not just "concepts" but reality: "Where word breaks off, no thing may be."[48] Heidegger also appeals to the poetry of Hölderlin and of Gottfried Benn. William Barrett, in attempting to convey Heidegger's vision to the English-speaking world, cites parallel expressions in the poetry of Yeats, T. S. Eliot, and Robert Graves. The language of nature, Graves complains, has been turned upside down, so that "trees" are merely timber for sawmills; "animals" belong to the circus or to the cannery. "Woman" no longer conveys the vision that delighted poets and knights, but fills the ranks of "auxiliary state personnel."[49] Language is caught up in the plight of modern Western man, who has fallen out of Being.

Heidegger discusses this situation in his essay "Hölderlin and the Essence of Poetry." He calls attention to the prophetic warning articulated by Hölderlin when he called language the "most dangerous of possessions . . . given to man."[50] Heidegger comments, "It is language which first creates the manifest conditions for menace and confusion to existence, and thus the possibility of the loss of existence."[51] In terms of man's actual present situation "language . . . is at his disposal for the purpose of communicating his experiences. . . . Language serves to give information." However, Heidegger continues: "But the essence of language does not consist entirely in being a means of giving information. . . . Language is not a mere tool. . . . Rather it is that event which disposes of the supreme possibility of human existence."[52]

In his *Introduction to a Theological Theory of Language* Gerhard Ebeling endorses Heidegger's view of the malaise of the Western language-tradition, although with scarcely one explicit reference to Heidegger himself. Language, he argues, has come to suffer from a lack of substance. Ebeling cites with approval the diagnosis of the sickness of language carried out by Hugo von Hofmannsthal. Language has, as it were, decomposed and fallen apart. It has become fragmented into compartments and atomized. "The atoms of speech, all that remain of language, the empty words, now produce not understanding but a strange alienation, and instead of offering you something, take hold of you like a whirlpool and carry you off into the void."[53] Ebeling quotes Hugo von Hofmannsthal's words, "Everything seemed to me to fall into fragments, the fragments into smaller fragments still, and nothing could any longer be

48. *Ibid.*, p. 60; cf. pp. 61-96.
49. W. Barrett, *What is Existentialism?* (Grove Press, New York, ²1964), p. 129.
50. M. Heidegger, *E.B.*, pp. 296-300; cf. pp. 293-315.
51. *Ibid.*, p. 298.
52. *Ibid.*, pp. 299-300.
53. G. Ebeling, *I.T.T.L.*, p. 71.

grasped by a concept. The individual words swam round me." Ebeling then comments: "The atomization of reality brings about the atomization of language."[54]

On this basis Ebeling speaks of "a profound crisis of language, and indeed a complete collapse of language."[55] Language "plays a decisive part in making man what he is." Hence it is a "sinister thing" that language has become reduced to the level of a "technical instrument. . . . It results in the neglect of whole dimensions of life. . . . What is disturbing above all is that language can become an instrument through which the human heart itself can be manipulated."[56] By contrast, we must seek a new coming-to-speech in which language regains its true creativity, spontaneity, and effectiveness. Hermeneutics is thus called into play to provide both "a theory of language with the widest possible horizon" and "a theory of how breakdowns in language can be overcome."[57] This is one of the central concerns of the new hermeneutic, shared especially by Fuchs and Ebeling. As it is, Ebeling asserts in his *God and Word*, "we threaten to die of language poisoning."[58] "With the dawn of the modern age . . . the path was clear for an unrestricted development of the mere sign-function of language. The logical result is that words are reduced to ciphers . . . and syntax to a question of calculus."[59]

Fuchs and Ebeling share Heidegger's view that a language which is dominated by the Cartesian perspective of subject and object can do nothing other than perpetuate established ways of seeing the world, which merely mirror back man's existing concerns and make him the helpless victim of his place in history. "He is always thrown back on the paths that he himself has laid out: he becomes mired in his paths, caught in the beaten track, and thus caught . . . excludes himself from being. He turns round and round in his own circle."[60]

48. *Language-Event and a New Coming to Speech*

In the later writings of Heidegger, it is possible to distinguish between three aspects of the quest for a new coming to speech. First of all, Heidegger believes that eventful language is grounded in Being rather than merely in human thought. Secondly, he calls attention to the gather-

54. *Ibid.*, pp. 71 and 72.
55. *Ibid.*, p. 76.
56. *Ibid.*, pp. 98 and 127.
57. *Ibid.*, pp. 156 and 157; cf. p. 36 and pp. 153-66.
58. G. Ebeling, *God and Word* (Eng. Fortress Press, Philadelphia, 1967), p. 2.
59. *Ibid.*, p. 17.
60. M. Heidegger, *I.M.*, pp. 157-58.

ing power of language, in connection with the notion of *logos* as collectedness. Thirdly, he examines the relation between Being, language, and man, according to which the role of man is that of listener rather than observer.

The first point, which turns on the contrast between Being and thought, is simply the converse side of what we have outlined in the previous section. Philosophy from Plato until Nietzsche, Heidegger believes, has viewed Being as a mere concept. Being as the object of thought is merely being-ness *(Seiendheit)*. In the pre-Socratic writings, he claims, Being is not a mere entity which is the object of thought, but an active eventful reality *(Sein)*. Heidegger constantly searches for ways of expressing this more dynamic perspective. Hence in his most recent writings, as James Robinson points out, "the verbal noun *Anwesen,* where the prefix accentuates the temporal meaning of arriving, tends to replace (even) the verbal noun *Sein.*"[61] Heidegger writes, "Essent *(Seiendes)* is only what, when correctly thought, stands up to correct thinking. . . . Being *(sein)* is the basic happening which first makes possible historical being-there. . . ."[62] "In this seemingly unimportant distinction between being and thinking we must discern the fundamental position of the Western spirit, against which our central attack is directed. It can be overcome only by a return to its *origins.*"[63] "The whole Western view of being (is) . . . summed up in the heading 'being and thought'. . . . In the beginning of Western philosophy the perspective governing the disclosure of being was time."[64] Heidegger claims that this is the case in Parmenides as well as Heraclitus.

This is the ground of eventful language. "Language is the primordial poetry in which a people speaks being."[65] Similarly in the writings of Ernst Fuchs, "Language . . . makes being into an event."[66] The word of God, Fuchs claims, is not a matter of human thought or concepts, but of "the meaning of being" *(der "Sinn" des Seins)*. The truth of God is the call of Being *(der Ruf zum Sein)*.[67] The language-event *(Sprachereignis)* which takes place through the New Testament constitutes not the communication of concepts, but a call *(Berufung)* or a pledge *(Einsatz)*.[68] Jesus does not simply pass on ideas, but *makes* a promise *(verheissen)*,

61. J. M. Robinson, *New Frontiers in Theology: I, The Later Heidegger and Theology,* p. 22.
62. M. Heidegger, *I.M.,* pp. 194 and 201.
63. *Ibid.,* p. 117 (Heidegger's italics).
64. *Ibid.,* p. 205.
65. *Ibid.,* p. 171.
66. E. Fuchs, *S.H.J.,* p. 207.
67. E. Fuchs, *Herm.,* p. 71.
68. E. Fuchs, *S.H.J.,* pp. 94 and 95 (German, pp. 291 and 293).

lays down a demand *(fordern)*, or *effects* a gift *(geben)*.[69] Clearly to pass on thoughts *about* promises, demands, or gifts is very different from actually *making* them. We might describe the latter as performative language, except for the fact that in J. L. Austin's sense of the term, performatives depend on the acceptance of conventions, whereas such an idea is absent from Heidegger and Fuchs. Indeed, one criticism which we shall be obliged to make of this approach is that it comes too near to word-magic. Thus Gerhard Ebeling actually speaks of the word-event as "an event in which God himself is communicated."[70]

Affinities between the new hermeneutic of Fuchs and Ebeling and the thought of Heidegger are usually closer and more explicit than possible connections with the hermeneutics of Gadamer. However, we have seen in the previous chapter that Gadamer strenuously resists any tendency to view language primarily as the communication of thought or the expression of ideas. Language for Gadamer is never a mere instrument for the manipulation of concepts. Ebeling and Gadamer are at one, we urged, in insisting that the real problem of language was not to find new *means* of speech, but to bring about a new *coming* to speech.[71] Constantly Gadamer has insisted that "reality" transcends the contents of human consciousness. Certainly Gadamer and Heidegger are completely at one in emphatically rejecting any equation of art with "aesthetics." Both thinkers are concerned to show that such a view is bound up with mistaken assumptions in the history of philosophy.

We come now to the second aspect of Heidegger's later thought about eventful language, namely that which concerns the gathering power of language. Heidegger writes, "language is logos, collection. . . . Pristine speech opens up the being of the essent in the structure of its collectedness."[72] Idle talk is dispersion, rather than gathering. "Because the esence of language is found in the act of gathering within the togetherness of being, language as everyday speech comes to its truth only when speaking and hearing are oriented toward logos as collectedness in the sense of being."[73] In accordance with his method of returning to primordial or, at least, pre-Socratic sources, Heidegger makes much of the actual meaning of logos as "collection" *(Sammlung)* in Heraclitus. "Just as the German word means (1) collecting and (2) collectedness, so *logos* means here (i.e. in Heraclitus) collecting collectedness, the primal gathering principle."[74]

69. *Ibid.*, pp. 91 and 93 (German, pp. 288 and 291); pp. 36 and 38 (German, pp. 224 and 226); and p. 141 (German, p. 347).
70. G. Ebeling, *The Nature of Faith*, p. 87.
71. *Ibid.*, p. 16.
72. M. Heidegger, *I.M.*, p. 172.
73. *Ibid.*, p. 173.
74. *Ibid.*, p. 128.

This emphasis on language as gathering persists in various writings, including Heidegger's book *On the Way to Language*. Saying, Heidegger writes, "gathers all things up." It constitutes a "gathering call."[75] The principle is perhaps most easily understood, however, with reference neither to Heraclitus nor to Heidegger's own difficult aphorisms about language, but to his statements about the gathering power of the work of art. In several different essays Heidegger discusses Van Gogh's paintings of the shoes of a peasant woman.[77] These paintings, he urges, do not present merely a pair of shoes in the abstract as things in themselves. Rather, they open up the whole world of the life of the peasant woman, bringing together its various elements. For example, "from the dark opening of the worn insides of the shoes the toilsome tread of the worker stares forth. In the stiffly rugged heaviness of the shoes there is the accumulated tenacity of her slow trudge through the far-spreading and ever-uniform furrows of the field swept by a raw wind. On the leather lie the dampness and richness of the soil. Under the soles slides the loneliness of the field-path as evening falls. In the shoes vibrates the silent call of the earth, its quiet gift of ripening grain. . . . This equipment is pervaded by uncomplaining anxiety as to the certainty of bread, the wordless joy of having once more withstood want. . . . This equipment belongs to . . . the *world* of the peasant woman."[78] In the painting, Heidegger claims, we see the "gathering within itself of all things" of the world of the peasant. This is achieved "not by a description . . . not by report . . . but only by bringing ourselves before Van Gogh's painting. This painting spoke. . . . The art work lets us know what shoes are in truth."[79]

Heidegger illustrates this gathering principle not only from painting but from architecture. In particular he discusses the gathering power mediated by the "presence" or "world" of a Greek temple. In silhouette it reveals not only its own shape, but also the expanse of the sky. A nearby pool reveals not only the lines of the temple, but thereby the capacity of the water to reflect these lines. The projections and cavities of the stonework reveal the contrast between the splendor of the sun and the darkness of shadow. The rocklike character of the temple as it stands there points to the stability of the earth on which it rests. "This resting of the work draws up out of the mystery of the rock's clumsy yet spontaneous support. . . . The temple-work, standing there, opens up a world. . . ."[80] Because a work of art brings together and "collects" reality into a

---

75. M. Heidegger, *O.W.L.*, p. 108.
76. *Ibid.*, p. 126.
77. M. Heidegger, *Holz.*, pp. 22-23; "The Origin of the Work of Art" in M. Heidegger, *P.L.T.*, pp. 32-37; cf. pp. 15-87; and *I.M.*, p. 35.
78. M. Heidegger, "The Origin of the Work of Art" in *P.L.T.*, pp. 33-34.
79. *Ibid.*, p. 35.
80. *Ibid.*, p. 42.

single eloquent presence, it makes things "more what they are." Works of art, therefore, as Gadamer also stresses, are not mere objects to be shipped around from museum to museum, or from gallery to gallery.[81]

A number of writers discuss Heidegger's claims in his essay "On the Origin of a Work of Art," including Vincent Vycinas, L. Versényi, and T. Langan.[82] The disclosure through art is not a matter of "concepts." As Langan comments, "The work of art is the field of combat between a Dasein, trying to open a world . . . and the 'matter' in which the Dasein must root its efforts. . . . The work of art is the meeting of a *World* which endows it with all of its desires and ideas and lights . . . and the *Earth,* the material from which the work is moulded. . . . The world absorbs these materials into its light, so that they yield up a meaning and become *Sein.* . . . Dasein is the earth's midwife."[83] What "speaks" in a work of art is the "world" and the "presence" of a single eloquent wholeness.

This applies not only to the visual and the plastic arts, but also to works of art in literature. It emerges, for example, in Heidegger's way of interpreting a chorus from the *Antigone* of Sophocles, or the poetry of Stefan George or Friedrich Hölderlin.[84] Heidegger makes the point explicitly in his discussion of the poetry of Georg Trakl. His task, he declares, is to see what "gathers" Trakl's "Saying" into his poetry: "Every great poet creates his poetry out of one single poetic statement only. . . . The poet's statement remains unspoken. . . . Nonetheless every poem speaks from the whole of the one single statement, and in each instance says that statement."[85] In other words, the creativeness and eventfulness of Trakl's poetry is bound up with its wholeness, its oneness, its capacity to "gather" into one.

Ernst Fuchs also lays stress on the gathering power of language. He writes, for example, *"The language of faith brings into language the gathering of faith, and thereby Christ"* (his italics).[86] "The proclamation gathers around Christ. . . . This community has its being, its 'togetherness,' in the possibility of its being able to speak the kind of language in

---

81. *Ibid.,* p. 19.
82. Cf. V. Vycinas, *Earth and Gods. An Introduction to the Philosophy of Martin Heidegger* (Nijhoff, The Hague, 1961), p. 243 (on the painting by Van Gogh); L. Versényi, *Heidegger, Being, and Truth,* pp. 95ff.; and T. Langan *The Meaning of Heidegger,* pp. 199-200.
83. T. Langan, *The Meaning of Heidegger,* pp. 199-200.
84. Heidegger expounds the *Antigone,* ll. 332-75, in *I.M.,* pp. 146-65; S. George's "The Word" in *O.W.L.,* pp. 60-108; and the writings of Hölderlin in *P.L.T.,* pp. 213-29. On Hölderlin see especially B. Allemann, *Hölderlin et Heidegger. Reserche de la relation entre poésie et pensée* (Presses Universitaires de France, Paris, 1959). Cf. also J. Macquarrie, *God-Talk. An Examination of the Language and Logic of Theology* (S.C.M., London, 1967), pp. 157-67.
85. M. Heidegger, "Language in the Poem. A Discussion of Georg Trakl's Poetic Work" in *O.W.L.,* p. 160; cf. pp. 159-98.
86. E. Fuchs, *S.H.J.,* p. 209.

which the event of its community is fulfilled."[87] Hence "everything" becomes new (II Cor. 5:17), and when the word is proclaimed "community is formed."[88] Fuchs and Ebeling also stress that, in Ebeling's words, "It is not a matter of understanding single words, but of understanding the word itself."[89] Heinrich Ott approvingly speaks of Ebeling's arrangement of his work in his book *The Nature of Faith* as making it "unmistakably clear that theology has to do with nothing other than the thinking explication of the one and indivisible faith."[90] In spite of their differences in other respects, Ott is in agreement with the two main exponents of the new hermeneutic in stressing the importance of this aspect of Heidegger's thought for biblical hermeneutics and theology. Each passage of the New Testament gives voice to the one gospel, although "the gospel itself— there is only one—remains unspoken."[91] Ott explicitly compares his own statement with Heidegger's remarks in his essay on Trakl.

The third major aspect of Heidegger's later thought on language concerns the role of man as *listener* rather than spectator. Negatively, Heidegger writes, "Words and language are not wrappings in which things are packed for the commerce of those who write and speak. It is in words and language that things first come into being and are. For this reason the misuse of language in idle talk, in slogans and phrases, destroys our authentic relation to things."[92] If language is to speak anew, there must be silent contemplative, receptive listening. It is this posture of receptive yieldedness *(Gelassenheit)* that distinguishes both the creative poet and the authentic thinker from the average man. The poet and the thinker must listen to language *questioningly*. Heidegger comments, "To know how to question means to know how to wait, even a whole lifetime. . . . For, as Hölderlin said, 'The mindful God abhors untimely growth.' "[93]

In his essays in *On the Way to Language* Heidegger develops the contrast between "speaking merely *about* language" and "letting language, *from within* language, speak to us."[94] "What the poet has learned to renounce is his formerly cherished view regarding the relation of thing and word. . . . The poet has learned renunciation. He . . . has experienced that only the word makes a thing appear as the thing it is, and thus lets it be present."[95] This is parallel to Heidegger's discussion of the contrast between calculative and meditative thinking in his book *Gelas-*

---

87. *Ibid.*, pp. 208-09.
88. *Ibid.*, pp. 202-03.
89. G. Ebeling, *The Nature of Faith*, p. 16.
90. H. Ott, "What is Systematic Theology?" in Robinson and Cobb, *New Frontiers in Theology: I, The Later Heidegger and Theology*, p. 91.
91. *Ibid.*, p. 87.
92. M. Heidegger, *I.M.*, pp. 13-14.
93. *Ibid.*, p. 206.
94. M. Heidegger, *O.W.L.*, p. 85.
95. *Ibid.*, p. 65.

senheit. He writes, "Meditative thinking demands of us not to cling one-sidedly to a single idea. . . . Releasement toward things and openness to the mystery never happen of themselves. . . . Both flourish through persistent courageous thinking."[96] However, Heidegger warns us, "Thinking is not a means to gain knowledge. Thinking cuts furrows into the soil of Being."[97]

Language, therefore, has ontological significance. It is "the house of Being" *(das Haus des Seins . . . die Hut des Anwesens).*[98] Elsewhere Heidegger speaks of language as the "custodian" of Being.[99] Man's task, is to let Being appear through language by putting himself in the "place" *(Ort)* where language will speak.[100] Hence, "Speaking is of itself a listening. . . . *Language* speaks . . . by saying, this is, by showing. . . . We hear Saying only because we belong within it. . . . Language needs human speaking, and yet it is not merely of the making or at the command of our speech activity. . . . The way to language . . . is language as Saying. . . . Saying is showing."[101]

We have already seen from the work of Gadamer how the linguistic tradition in which a man stands serves to shape his thought as well as express it. Language, as one writer has put it, cuts the grooves in which our thoughts move. Is it not, then, self-contradictory to claim that language speaks anew when man listens to it, rather than seeking actively to reshape it? There is indeed some truth, it seems, in the criticisms put forward by Hans Jonas to the effect that "thinking" is precisely an active attempt not to be at the mercy of fate and historical contingency.[102] The rejoinder of Charles Scott to Jonas's critical comments does not invalidate this particular point.[103] Jonas writes emphatically that theologians must not be beguiled and seduced into assuming that Heidegger's correlation between "thinking" and "thanking" has any connection with religious humility.[104]

It is possible to cite in support of Jonas's case some of the statements which have been made, even by Heidegger himself, about the relation of his later thought to Zen Buddhism. Heidegger is said to have remarked, on reading one of D. T. Suzuki's books on Zen, "This is what I have been

96. M. Heidegger, *Discourse on Thinking,* pp. 53 and 56.
97. M. Heidegger, *O.W.L.,* p. 70.
98. M. Heidegger, *Unterwegs zur Sprache,* p. 267; cf. *O.W.L.,* pp. 5, 21, 22, 26, 63, *et passim.*
99. M. Heidegger, *I.M.,* p. 185.
100. M. Heidegger, *U.S.,* p. 19.
101. M. Heidegger, *O.W.L.,* pp. 123, 124, 125, and 126.
102. H. Jonas, "Heidegger and Theology" in *R.M.,* XVIII (1964), 207-33.
103. C. E. Scott, "Heidegger Reconsidered: A Response to Professor Jonas" in *H.T.R.* LIX (1966), 175-85.
104. M. Heidegger, *Discourse on Thinking,* p. 85.

trying to say in all my writings."[105] More recently a careful and detailed comparison has been made by Peter Kreeft of parallels between Zen and Heidegger's *Gelassenheit*.[106] He concludes by suggesting no less than eight specific points of affinity between Heidegger and Zen: "A remarkably 'Zennish' character, Heidegger's 'released' man . . . will-lessly steadfast, voidedly joyful, objectlessly grateful, unattached to ideas or things. . . ."[107]

All the same, there are at least three aspects of this perspective, and probably more, which Fuchs and Ebeling try to take up in their approach to the New Testament, and they are assimilated still more eagerly by Heinrich Ott. First of all, Heidegger believes that language was born out of the wonder evoked in man by Being. Man must still himself in silence to wait for the vision that will once again fill him with wonder. This can be done only by sitting loose to well-worn conventions of thinking. Fuchs also believes that the language-event is bound up with the experience of wonder. Secondly, man's task is not merely to ask *about* language, or even to let language speak *about* a given subject-matter. The subject-matter of language *itself* comes to speech *through* language. Ebeling declares, *"The primary phenomenon in the realm of understanding is not understanding OF language, but understanding THROUGH language"* (his italics and capitals).[108] Thirdly, language, or the text, is accorded its rights over against man as the listener. Fuchs asserts, "The text is not just the servant that transmits kerygmatic formulations, but rather a master that directs us into the language-context of our existence in which we exist 'before God.' "[109] "In the tranquility of faith, where noise is reduced to silence, a *voice* is heard, the very voice which is of central significance for the texts."[110] "The text is itself meant to live."[111]

49. *Further Considerations about the Hermeneutics of Fuchs and Ebeling*

We have seen that Ebeling endorses Heidegger's diagnosis of the malaise of the Western language-tradition. Against this background Fuchs and Ebeling ask how the message of the New Testament may come-to-speech afresh, so that it will effectively "strike home" *(treffen)*.[112] In the

105. W. Barrett (ed.,) *Zen Buddhism* (Doubleday, New York, 1956), p. xi, and in N. W. Ross (ed.), *The World of Zen* (Collins, London, 1962), p. 344.
106. P. Kreeft, "Zen in Heidegger's *Gelassenheit*" in *I.P.Q.* XI (1971), 521-45.
107. *Ibid.*, p. 545.
108. G. Ebeling, *W.F.*, p. 318.
109. E. Fuchs, *S.H.J.*, p. 211.
110. *Ibid.*, p. 192.
111. *Ibid.*, p. 193.
112. *Ibid.*, pp. 196-98 and 202 (German, pp. 411-14 and 418); and *Herm.*, p. 91.

context of preaching, Ebeling seeks to avoid "pious words which have no bearing on reality."[113] He writes, "We have to bring a certain measure of good will to the average sermon if we are not to be bored or furious, sarcastic or melancholy in our reactions."[114] When the New Testament is expounded, it should not reach our ears as "nothing more than a tradition, a mere form of speech, a dead relic of the language of the past."[115] The language of Jesus, Fuchs writes, "singles out the individual and grasps him deep down."[116] "The text is meant to live."[117] The method of Jesus, Fuchs argues, was to enter the "world" of the hearer, and to speak from within that living world. Preaching the message of the New Testament today similarly demands a "translation" of language in which the message engages with the horizons of the hearers. Only then can there take place what Gadamer calls *das Zur-Sprache-Kommen der Sache selbst.*

We have already noted that for Fuchs and Ebeling hermeneutics is not a matter of understanding individual words, but of understanding the word. Furthermore, hermeneutics is not merely a mechanical matter of applying certain hermeneutical "rules."[118] The central question of hermeneutics is: how do I come to understand in practice? We cannot begin with a pre-formulated set of rules, because hermeneutics operates at the level of the living situation which is prior to theory or to subject-object cognition. Fuchs suggests a memorable analogy. We can define the properties of a cat, for example, in the abstract. But the "hermeneutical principle" that really causes a cat to show itself for what it is—is the mouse: ". . . *die Maus das hermeneutische Prinzip für das Verständnis der Katze zu sein.*"[119] We reach the heart of the matter in Ernst Fuchs' concept of *Einverständnis*, which is variously translated as "common understanding," "mutual understanding," and even as "empathy." The phrase "penetrative understanding" is suggested by Colin Brown as a paraphrase. In an important comment Fuchs remarks that his *Hermeneutik* constitutes "an attempt to bring the hermeneutical problem back into the dimension of language with the aid of the phenomenon of empathy *(des Phänomens des Einverständnisses)* as the foundation of all understanding."[120]

The phenomenon of *Einverständnis* is seen in the common under-

113. G. Ebeling, *God and Word*, p. 5; cf. pp. 33-36.
114. G. Ebeling, *The Nature of Faith*, p. 15.
115. G. Ebeling, *God and Word*, p. 3.
116. E. Fuchs, *S.H.J.*, p. 35.
117. *Ibid.*, p. 193.
118. G. Ebeling, *W.F.*, p. 313.
119. E. Fuchs, *Herm.*, p. 110.
120. E. Fuchs, "The Hermeneutical Problem" in J. M. Robinson (ed.), *The Future of Our Religious Past. Essays in Honour of Rudolf Bultmann* (S.C.M., London, 1971), pp. 267-68; cf. pp. 267-78; German in E. Dinkler (ed.), *Zeit und Geschichte. Dankesgabe an Rudolf Bultmann zum 80. Geburtstag* (Mohr, Tübingen, 1964), p. 357.

344 HEIDEGGER, BULTMANN, GADAMER, AND WITTGENSTEIN

standing shared by a close-knit family. A single word or phrase may convey a whole world of experience, because the language of the family is grounded in a network of shared attitudes, assumptions, and experiences. Thus "at home one does not speak so that people may understand, but because people understand."[121] The effective occurrence of language as language-event *(Sprachereignis)* or, to use Ebeling's term, as word-event *(Wortgeschehen) is grounded in something deeper than, and prior to, conscious thought.* The immediate harmony between what is said and what is grasped is not the result of a process of thought; it takes place at an earlier stage, as event. . . . The word 'gets home.' "[122]

The language-event which is grounded in, and also effects *Einverständnis* relates not to cognitive concepts so much as to "world." Here Fuchs comes very close to Gadamer. Where Fuchs uses the analogy of the language-world of the home, Gadamer refers to the world of children or of lovers. Gadamer writes, "Children and lovers likewise have 'their' language, by which they communicate with each other in a world that belongs to them alone. This is . . . because a linguistic habit has grown up between them. A common world *(die Gemeinsamkeit einer Welt)* . . . is always the presupposition of language."[123] We earlier discussed Gadamer's striking simile about the "world" of the game. In such a world, he argues, the reality of the game itself is more fundamental than the consciousness of the players. In this respect, the hermeneutics of both Gadamer and Fuchs are more orientated towards language than towards psychology. This is one reason why, in spite of the language-oriented aspect of Schleiermacher's earlier hermeneutics as re-discovered by Kimmerle, we cannot wholly accept C. E. Braaten's claim that the new hermeneutic is basically a return to Schleiermacher.[124]

In the parables, Fuchs argues, Jesus enters into the "world" of his hearers so that his language can reach home to them. It is important to note Fuchs' insistent comment that the picture-part *(Bildhälfte)* of the parable is no mere homiletical or illustrative device, simply used to make an ideational proposition more vivid. Jesus enters the world "of provincial and family life as it takes place in normal times." He enters the world of the farmer, the businessman, the housewife, the rich, and the poor. Fuchs asserts: "Jesus does not use the details of this world only as a kind of 'point of contact'; instead he has in mind *precisely this 'world.'* "[125] This is to be interpreted in the light of Fuchs' earlier comment, "We find

---

121. E. Fuchs, "The New Testament and the Hermeneutical Problem" in *N.H.*, p. 124.
122. E. Fuchs, *S.H.J.*, p. 196 (German, p. 411).
123. H.-G. Gadamer, *T.M.*, p. 367; *W.M.*, p. 384.
124. C. E. Braaten, "How New is the New Hermeneutic?" in *Th.T.* XXII (1965), 218-35.
125. E. Fuchs, "The New Testament and the Hermeneutical Problem" in *N.H.*, p. 126 (his italics).

existentialia wherever an understanding between men is disclosed through their having a common world."[126]

At the same time, Jesus enters the world of the hearer not only to stand alongside him, but also to bring him face to face with the substance *(Sachhälfte)* of the parable. A word that is creative, effective, and eventful is to take hold of him. Fuchs illustrates how the two principles operate together in the parable of the Laborers in the Vineyard (Matt. 20:1-16).[127] The hearers of the parable already live in the world where work is hard, and unemployment a hazard for casual laborers. When those who are hired last receive not only employment but a whole day's wage, the audience enjoys their good luck, and waits in suspense to see what will befall those who have worked through the heat of the day. Then comes the shock: "They receive the same. . . . It seems to them that the lord's action is unjust." But at this very point the *Sachhälfte* of the parable breaks through: "Is your eye evil because I am kind?" This is very different from an exposition on the theme of grace, or "the pallid requirement that sinful men should believe in God's kindness." A language-event takes place. Through his words Jesus meets the hearer, and pledges himself to those who "in the face of a cry 'guilty,' nevertheless found their hope on an act of God's kindness."[128]

What is at issue here is, in the words of Fuchs, that *"the truth has us ourselves as its object."*[129] The word is not simply "information," but a call, a pledge, a challenge, and a promise. In Ebeling's words, *"The text .. becomes a hermeneutical aid in the understanding of present experience."*[130] The hearer, Fuchs comments, "is drawn over on to God's side and learns to see everything with God's eyes."[131] "Jesus draws the hearer over to his side by means of the artistic medium, so that the hearer may think together with Jesus. Is not this the way of true love? Love does not just blurt out. Instead it provides in advance the sphere in which meeting takes place."[132]

Fuchs also comes near to Heidegger and Gadamer in his discussion of the way in which the authentic language-event may serve to challenge and shatter what previously were regarded as accepted and established ways of seeing the world. Thus we saw that the Parable of the Laborers in the Vineyard (Matt. 20:1-16) begins from within the horizons of conventional

---

126. E. Fuchs, *S.H.J.*, p. 97; cf. E. Fuchs, *Marburger Hermeneutik* (Mohr, Tübingen, 1968), pp. 171-81.
127. E. Fuchs, *S.H.J.*, pp. 32-38 and 154-56.
128. *Ibid.*, pp. 33-37.
129. E. Fuchs, "The New Testament and the Hermeneutical Problem" in *N.H.*, p. 143 (his italics).
130. G. Ebeling, *W.F.*, p. 33 (his italics).
131. E. Fuchs, *S.H.J.*, p. 155.
132. *Ibid.*, p. 129.

judgments about natural justice: "we, too, share the inevitable reaction of the first" (i.e. those who had worked all day). But in the language-event of the word of Jesus, this conventional mold is shattered by a pronounce-ment and pledge of grace to the undeserving. Fuchs is at pains to stress that in this respect the attitude and conduct of Jesus is intimately bound up with his language. Jesus' own conduct challenged accepted conven-tions. "Jesus acted in a very real way as God's representative, and said himself 'Blessed is he who takes no offence at me' (Matt. 11.6). . . . Jesus' proclamation . . . went along with his conduct."[133]

This emphasis on the oneness of word and deed in the person of Jesus serves to explain why Fuchs and Ebeling, as the leading exponents of the new hermeneutic, are also leading exponents of the so-called new quest of the historical Jesus, together with E. Käsemann and G. Bornkamm. The parables of Jesus are not just "teaching" but linguistic articulations of *how Jesus himself* reacted to the truth of God. The refusal of Fuchs and Ebeling to separate the language of Jesus from his deeds and his attitudes is part of their rejection of a purely cognitive view of language as that which merely conveys "thoughts." A speech-act is no less a commentary on the person who speaks than actions of other kinds. As Paul Achtemeier comments, "The parables reflect the way Jesus understood the present, and the way he himself reacted to it."[134] Or in the words of Norman Perrin, "It is not that Jesus created new concepts but rather that . . . in the parables Jesus verbalizes his understanding of his own existence in the world. . . . Fuchs sees the parables as verbalizing Jesus' own understand-ing of existence in such a way that the parable mediates the possibility of sharing Jesus' understanding of existence."[135]

On this basis the man who responds to the language-event of the parable may share the faith of Jesus. Entering the "world" of Jesus means to take up his own attitude of faith. Fuchs writes, "To have faith in Jesus now means essentially to repeat Jesus' decision."[136] "The so-called Christ of faith is none other than the historical Jesus."[137] Gerhard Ebeling adds, "The Kerygma . . . is not merely speech about man's existence. It is also a testimony to that which has happened."[138]

The christological implications of the new hermeneutic must not be allowed to obscure the extent to which it rests on a view of language which we find in Heidegger and Gadamer. "Reality" is determined, in effect, by language. For language determines how I see the world, and

133. *Ibid.*, pp. 36 and 37.
134. P. J. Achtemeier, *An Introduction to the New Hermeneutic*, p. 137. Cf. pp. 133-48.
135. N. Perrin, *Jesus and the Language of the Kingdom* (S.C.M., London, 1976), pp. 100-11.
136. E. Fuchs, *S.H.J.*, p. 28.
137. *Ibid.*, p. 30.
138. G. Ebeling, *Theology and Proclamation*, p. 38; cf. pp. 32-81.

how I understand myself. Therefore, if I am to see the world anew, a new language-event must take place which will break the bonds of my previous inherited self-understanding. This comes very close to some words of Gadamer. Gadamer writes, "The linguistic constitution of the world is far from meaning that man's relationship to the world is imprisoned within a linguistically schematized habitat. On the contrary, wherever language and men exist, there is not only a freedom from the pressure of the world, but this freedom from the habitat is also freedom in relation to the names that we give things, as stated in the profound account in Genesis according to which Adam received from God the authority to name creatures."[139] In a parallel way Fuchs comments on the *naming* of Christ in Philippians 2:9-11 with "the name which is above every name." "The language of faith . . . admits Christ into that existence which we ourselves enter upon in the *name* of Jesus. We are then repeatedly able to name Jesus as our Lord. . . . This is a language-event."[140] Fuchs then compares the event of naming another as "brother." He writes, "The other person is not simply called a brother because he is; he would not be a brother if I did not so call him. Through my calling him brother . . . I admit him as a brother among us by myself entering this community with him."[141]

Fuchs and Ebeling, we have seen, show many distinct points of affinity with the later Heidegger. There is the problem of the crisis of language in the Western language-tradition. There is the contrast between the relation of language to thought and language as event in relation to Being. Language gathers into one, and casts man in the role of listener rather than spectator. But all this comes to a head in the key concepts of *Einsverständnis* and especially "world," which can be found in the earlier Heidegger and also in Gadamer. This, in turn, is understood linguistically, so that Fuchs could say, with Gadamer: "Whoever has language 'has' the world." Language establishes "what man recognizes as existent and significant." Language is the horizon of a hermeneutic ontology.[142]

50. *Related Approaches to the Hermeneutics of the Parables: Funk, Via, and Crossan*

It is profitless to enter into the debate about the precise scope of the term "the new hermeneutic." By convention the term primarily describes the work of Fuchs and Ebeling. We have already seen that at certain specific points this has connections, through Heidegger's later thought,

139. H.-G. Gadamer, *T.M.*, p. 402.
140. E. Fuchs, *S.H.J.*, p. 209.
141. *Ibid*.
142. H.-G. Gadamer, *T.M.*, pp. 411, 413-14, and 397-431.

with the hermeneutics of Heinrich Ott. Pannenberg's theology is too different from that of Fuchs and Ebeling to invite inclusion under the same label; but in any case we have discussed his hermeneutics in a previous chapter.

The work of Eta Linnemann and Eberhard Jüngel admittedly stands broadly in the same tradition as Fuchs, and both writers are former pupils of his. Both writers make valuable points of their own; Linnemann especially on particular parables, and Jüngel especially on justification by faith in Jesus and Paul.[143] But from the point of view of the terms of reference of the present study, their hermeneutical method does not take us substantially beyond that of Fuchs himself. Two of Jüngel's most important theses about hermeneutics simply explicate more sharply points already made by Fuchs. First of all, as against Bultmann he argues that to try to distinguish between some outer mythical form *(Form)* and inner existential gist *(Inhalt)* is to do violence to the unity of language and thought.[144] Secondly, he develops the idea of language as "collection" *(Sammlung)*.[145]

We propose to consider briefly, however, work on the parables undertaken in America by Robert Funk, Dan Otto Via, and John Dominic Crossan, since there are important points of contact between their approach and the work of Heidegger, Gadamer, and Fuchs. Norman Perrin has, in our view, tended to exaggerate the differences between the German and American approaches.[146] What they have in common is perhaps more significant than the points at which they diverge.

Prior to his actual work on particular parables, Robert Funk makes four distinct points which reveal the extent of his indebtedness to Heidegger, Gadamer, and most directly to Fuchs. Indeed, later in his book he writes, "Ernst Fuchs' effort to grasp the parables as language-events is the underground spring that nourishes my own approach to the parables."[147] His first point concerns the relation between language and understanding. Language and understanding, he writes, give birth to each other, or may sometimes hold each other captive. There is a relationship of mutual dependence between "joint understanding" and understandable language.[148] Here, of course, we meet Gadamer, and Fuchs' concept of *Einverständnis*. Secondly, Funk endorses the view of the relation between language and reality which is shared by Heidegger, Gadamer, and

---

143. E. Jüngel, *Paulus und Jesus. Eine Untersuchung zur Präzierung der Frage nach dem Ursprung der Christologie* (Mohr, Tübingen, 1967); and E. Linnemann, *Parables of Jesus, Introduction and Exposition* (Eng. S.P.C.K., London, 1966).
144. E. Jüngel, *Paulus and Jesus*, p. 135.
145. *Ibid.*, p. 173.
146. N. Perrin, *Jesus and the Language of the Kingdom*, pp. 123-31 and 201.
147. R. W. Funk, *Language, Hermeneutic and Word of God*, p. 128.
148. *Ibid.*, pp. 3-4.

Fuchs. He writes, "if common language and joint understanding presuppose a shared reality, the failure of language and understanding betoken the failure of that reality. Tradition fails because the reality which has supported it fails."[149] A tradition fails when language and understanding become divorced. Thirdly, Funk follows Fuchs and Ebeling as well as Gadamer in his insistence that the word of the text "is not accessible to the exegete as an object for scrutiny. . . . The word of God is not interpreted—it interprets! . . . The direction of the flow between interpreter and text that has dominated modern biblical criticism from its inception is reversed, and hermeneutics . . . becomes hermeneutic. . . . It is not the text that requires interpretation but the interpreter."[150] Fourthly, the parables of Jesus, in Funk's judgment, operate at a pre-conceptual and pre-cognitive level. They are not just to convey "thoughts." Funk distinguishes, like Heidegger, between the primary function of speech in creating a world, and reflective language which is secondary and derivative. This theme recurs throughout his work.

Funk demonstrates how these four principles apply in the Parable of the Prodigal Son (Luke 15:11-32). The "righteous" find themselves in the world of the elder brother, endorsing his conventional ideas of rights and dues. "Sinners" find themselves alongside the prodigal son. Thus, "the word of grace and the deed of grace divide the audience into younger sons and elder sons—into sinners and Pharisees. This is what Ernst Fuchs means when he says that one does not interpret the parables; *the parables interpret him*. The auditors are not invited to consider their response; they either rejoice because as sinners they are glad to be dependent on grace, or they are offended because they want justice on top of grace. . . . It is man and not God who is on trial. . . . *The Pharisees are those who insist on interpreting the word of grace rather than letting themeselves be interpreted by it.*"[151]

In the central part of his book Funk takes the discussion further by a special consideration of the parable as metaphor. Norman Perrin is right when he describes this as "Funk's enormously important contribution to the discussion," which advances beyond the new hermeneutic in Germany.[152] Funk's point of departure here is C. H. Dodd's recognition of the fact that the parable should leave the mind in sufficient doubt about its application to tease it into active thought.[153] Funk writes, "The parable is not closed, so to speak, until the listener is drawn into it as participant." Metaphor, however, is not mere simile or illustration. Calling on the work

149. *Ibid.*, p. 5.
150. *Ibid.*, pp. 11-12.
151. *Ibid.*, pp. 16-17 (Funk's italics).
152. N. Perrin, *Jesus and the Language of the Kingdom*, p. 133.
153. C. H. Dodd, *The Parables of the Kingdom* (Nisbet, London, 1936), p. 16; and R. W. Funk, *Language, Hermeneutic and Word of God*, p. 133.

of Owen Barfield, Funk points out that "metaphor shatters the conventions of predication in the interests of a new vision." The subject-matter disclosed in the metaphor "is not 'there' except as it enters language. . . . The metaphor is a means of modifying the tradition."[154] In other words, metaphor not only invites the hearer to enter a new world; it also provides a means of extending language beyond its accustomed tracks. Unlike flat discursive speech "it embodies a 'world' in a 'soft' focus. . . . Language becomes event."[155]

Funk proceeds to work out this approach in terms of two concrete examples, expounding first the Parable of the Great Supper (Matt. 22:2-10; Luke 14:16-24) and then that of the Good Samaritan (Luke 10:29-37). In words which remind us of Gadamer, Funk writes concerning the Parable of the Great Supper, "Jesus does not preside over how the parable is heard. . . . He accords the parable a certain measure of independence over against himself."[156] Here we meet Gadamer on the autonomy of the text or the work of art. Funk is also at pains to stress that Jesus stands "with" his hearers in "their world." "He is initially one with them within the . . . world in which they both dwell."[157] Here we meet Fuchs once again. Finally, the parable operates as a pre-cognitive level. Understanding and application, as Gadamer would say, are part of the same process: "The first group now *knows* it has been accepted; the second group *knows* it has been embraced. But not a word of (separate) application has been spoken. . . . Each hearer is drawn into the tale as he wills."[158] Similarly the Parable of the Good Samaritan allows the hearer "to stake out his existence in the 'world' of the parable. . . . Insofar as the Samaritan's deeds 'communicate' his world to those attending the parable . . . the parable is a language-event that shapes their future decisively."[159]

If the work of Robert Funk calls to mind the work of Heidegger, Gadamer, and Fuchs on language, understanding, and reality, the approach of Dan Otto Via reminds us of the first main part of Gadamer's *Truth and Method,* in which he discusses the relation between truth and art. Via compares the parable with a novel in its capacity to operate at a pre-conceptual level. He writes, "A novel is the *pre-philosophical living-through of an experience* within an horizon, or the giving of a new configuration to *pre-conceptual existential forces*."[160] Because a parable

154. R. W. Funk, *Language, Hermeneutic and Word of God,* pp. 138 and 139.
155. *Ibid.,* p. 140.
156. *Ibid.,* p. 179.
157. *Ibid.*
158. *Ibid.,* pp. 191 and 192.
159. *Ibid.,* pp. 216 and 220.
160. D. O. Via, Jr., *The Parables. Their Literary and Existential Dimension* (Fortress Press, Philadelphia, 1967), p. 93 (my italics).

is a work of art, or, as Via unfortunately calls it, "an aesthetic object," it "should not be treated as an illustration of an idea or a dressing out of a 'point'. . . . They are genuine aesthetic objects."[161] Parables, therefore, should not be dominated by a hermeneutic which is based on what Via calls "the severely historical approach." He writes, "The severely historical approach ignores the aesthetic nature of the parables and annuls their aesthetic function."[162]

In his actual work on specific parables Via distinguishes between two main types. Some are structured as a comedy-plot moving in an upward direction towards well-being. This category includes the Laborers in the Vineyard (Matt. 20:1-16), the Unjust Steward (Luke 16:1-9), and the Prodigal Son (Luke 15:11-32). The comic movement of the Prodigal Son is from well-being, through fall, back to well-being. "The final help comes from beyond him and far exceeds his expectations."[163] Some parables, however, are tragedies, representing "a plot falling towards catastrophe and the isolation of the protagonist from society."[164] These include, for example, the Parable of the Talents (Matt. 25:14-30) and the Parable of the Ten Virgins (Matt. 25:1-13). In both cases the protagonist recognizes the painful truth only when it is too late.

In certain respects Via's hermeneutics are nearer to Bultmann, Dilthey, and Schleiermacher than to Fuchs, Gadamer, and Heidegger. The "existential dimension" in the subtitle of Via's book alludes to what he calls the common pool of human existence. The Parable of the Prodigal Son speaks to anyone who knows what it is to have lived in a family. The Parable of the Talents speaks to anyone who fears risk, or who experiences lost opportunity. The fate of the foolish virgins speaks to anyone who has ever felt that "the world would take care of them, that someone else would pay the bill . . . that well-being was guaranteed to them no matter what they did."[165] We have a hermeneutics of experience and human nature rather than a hermeneutics of language. Nevertheless, Via would be at one with Gadamer in stressing the capacity of art to disclose truth, and the relation between understanding and experience. He would be at one with Heidegger in stressing that what is expressed in flat discourse and theoretical propositions is less primal than language which is rooted in the whole of life and its worlds.

John Dominic Crossan also insists, like Fuchs and Funk, that a parable does not merely "convey concepts." "Parable casts fire upon the

161. *Ibid.*, p. 70.
162. *Ibid.*, p. 24.
163. *Ibid.*, p. 169.
164. *Ibid.*, p. 96.
165. *Ibid.*, p. 126.

earth."[166] Just as myths, he argues, are the agents of stability, so parable challenges the status quo. "Myth establishes world. Apologue defends world. . . . Satire attacks world. Parable subverts world."[167] Often the structure of expectation is diametrically opposed to what occurs in the parable. Crossan works this out brilliantly with reference to the Parable of the Good Samaritan (Luke 10:29-37). The operative point is that "Jews have no dealings with Samaritans" (John 4:9). Hence what Jesus is doing, Crossan urges, is "to put together two impossible and contradictory words for the same person: 'Samaritan' (10.33) and 'neighbour' (10.36). The whole thrust of the story demands that one say what cannot be said, what is a contradiction in terms: Good plus Samaritan. . . . When good (clerics) and bad (Samaritan) become, respectively, bad and good, a world is being challenged and we are faced with polar reversal."[168] The parable is not merely a moral lesson, Crossan urges, on "love your enemies." If so, why did Jesus choose the emotive figure of a Samaritan? He suggests that we imagine a story-teller narrating to a Catholic audience how a wounded man who lived on the Falls Road was passed by first by a member of the I.R.A. and then by a Catholic nun, until a Protestant terrorist stopped and helped him. Could such a story-teller convince the crowd which was about to lynch him that he was saying only "love your enemies?"[169]

Crossan considers a number of parables under the heading of "parables of reversal." In addition to the Good Samaritan, he includes the Rich Man and Lazarus (Luke 16:19-31); the Pharisee and the Publican (Luke 18:10-14); the Wedding Guest (Luke 14:7-11); the Great Supper (Matt. 22:1-10; Luke 14:16-24); and the Prodigal Son (Luke 15:11-32).[170] Because they subvert the world of accepted conventions and values, "Parables give God room. . . . They are stories which shatter the deep structure of our accepted world."[171] By placing a question-mark against established human values, they make way for the Kingdom of God.

51. *Further Assessments of the New Hermeneutic*

Although we value the work of Funk, Via, and Crossan as contributions to hermeneutics in their own right, we cannot accept Norman

166. J. D. Crossan, *The Dark Interval. Towards a Theology of Story* (Argus Communications, Niles, Illinois, 1975), p. 55.
167. *Ibid.*, p. 59.
168. J. D. Crossan, *In Parables. The Challenge of the Historical Jesus* (Harper & Row, New York, 1973), p. 64.
169. J. D. Crossan, *The Dark Interval*, pp. 106-07.
170. J. D. Crossan, *In Parables*, pp. 57-75.
171. J. D. Crossan, *The Dark Interval*, pp. 121-22.

Perrin's verdict that the strengths and weaknesses of this approach are quite separate from those of the new hermeneutic in Europe. Even work on the subject of metaphor is not the exclusive domain of literary criticism rather than philosophical description. In another study in which I have discussed metaphor in the biblical writings at greater length, I have alluded to work in this field carried out by a number of philosophers, including especially W. P. Alston, Max Black, J. Pelc, and B. Hester.[172] Some of the comments which are invited by the work of Fuchs and Ebeling, therefore, also apply to the work of these American writers. We may make the following points.

(1) While the new hermeneutic rightly faces the problem of how the interpreter may understand the text of the New Testament more deeply and more creatively, Fuchs and Ebeling are less concerned about how he may understand it correctly. Admittedly they insist on the need for historical-critical study, but we receive the impression that this is mainly a preliminary to the real task of hermeneutics. Fuchs and Ebeling are looking at *one* side, albeit a neglected and yet important side, of a two-sided problem. Rather than simply first using critical methods, is it not possible both to listen to the text as subject, and alongside this critically to test one's understanding of it? May not both attitudes be called into play successively and repeatedly as if in dialogue?

It will be suggested, by way of reply, that this is necessarily to surrender a vision of wholeness in exchange for a split conceptualizing perspective in which the text becomes, once again, a mere object of scrutiny. But while we may accept the warning of Heidegger and Gadamer that the subject-object "method" of Descartes is not always adequate, nevertheless conceptualizing thinking must be given some place in hermeneutics. As J. C. Weber asks, "If the criterion of truth is only in the language-event itself, how can the language-event be safeguarded against delusion . . .? Why cannot the language-event be a disguised event of nothingness?"[173] While Weber may perhaps overstate the difficulty, we have already met this problem in Heidegger's work, and discussed it in our assessment of *Being and Time*.

(2) The new hermeneutic tends to be one-sided or unduly selective in its approach to the New Testament. It tends to be more applicable to poetic and metaphorical language than to straight argument or discourse. The main application is to the parables of Jesus and to passages such as

172. A. C. Thiselton, "Semantics and New Testament Interpretation" in I. H. Marshall (ed.), *New Testament Interpretation*, pp. 75-104. Cf., for example, W. P. Alston, *Philosophy of Language* (Prentice-Hall, Englewood Cliffs, N.J., 1964), pp. 96-106; M. A. McCloskey, "Metaphor" in *Mind* LXXIII (1964), 215-33; and M. Black, *Models and Metaphors* (Cornell University Press, New York, 1962), pp. 25-47.
173. J. C. Weber, "Language-Event and Christian Faith" in *Th.T.* XXI (1965), 455; cf. pp. 448-57.

1 Corinthians 13 or Philippians 2:5-11. Fuchs has more to say about these passages and the parables than many others. This does not call in question the value of the new hermeneutic as such. It simply underlines the point that it is more relevant to some kinds of literature than others. Insofar as the epistles already presuppose a common world in which dialogue takes place between the writer and the community, this observation itself must be qualified. In my own work on 1 Corinthians elsewhere I have tried to show how Paul enters, and actively engages with, the horizons of his readers.[174] Robert Funk has fruitfully applied his own hermeneutical perspectives to 1 Corinthians 2:6-16 and to the whole of II Corinthians.[175] But at least it may be claimed that the results of applying the new hermeneutic to the New Testament are uneven. This is in no way surprising. One of the central arguments of the present study is that *particular* hermeneutical insights come through *particular* philosophical perspectives. No single philosophy provides a comprehensive theory of hermeneutics, even that of Gadamer.

(3) Just as it seems to be unduly one-sided in its conception of the hermeneutical task, and uneven in its actual handling of the New Testament material, so the new hermeneutic is one-sided in the view of language which it presupposes. On the positive side it pays more than adequate attention to the relationship between language, understanding, and reality. It also calls attention to the power of language to strike home at a pre-conscious, pre-conceptual level, rather than simply to convey "concepts." But the role of convention in language is largely ignored. Admittedly, Gadamer sees that language-use is bound with language-habit, and that this habit can be broken. Fuchs and Ebeling also believe that the language-event can lift a man, in a sense, out of a passive acceptance of tradition. But we had cause to criticize Ebeling's quasi-magical notion that in the language-event "God himself is communicated."

It is part of this one-sided view of language that, along with Gadamer himself, Fuchs and Ebeling undervalue the role of propositions as over against non-assertive language-uses. This distinction is often a merely arbitrary one. Robert Funk argues that this understanding of language "falls under the heading of what J. L. Austin called performative discourse. In this order of discourse, a person is not merely *saying* something, he is doing something."[176] Norman Perrin also declares, "Fuchs . . . is concerned with what in English came to be called the 'performa-

174. A. C. Thiselton, "Realized Eschatology at Corinth" in *N.T.S.* XXIV (1978), 510-26, and "The Meaning of Σάρξ in 1 Cor. 5.5" in *S.J.T.* XXVI, 204-28.
175. R. W. Funk, *Language Hermeneutic and Word of God*, pp. 275-306; and "The Hermeneutical Problem and Historical Criticism" in *N.H.*, pp. 164-97.
176. R. W. Funk, *Language, Hermeneutic and Word of God*, pp. 26-27.

tive' aspect of language.''[177] But this is misleading in that Austin made two points very clear. In the first place, performative language functions effectively only if certain conventions are accepted. For example, I cannot nowadays performatively make a challenge by saying "My seconds will call on you," because the conventions of duelling are not nowadays generally accepted. But the shipping-magnate's wife may say "I name this ship the *St. Clair*" performatively, given the conventions of smashing a bottle against the side of the ship, and so forth. Secondly, Austin insists, "for a certain performative utterance to be happy, certain statements have to be *true*.''[178]

In my article entitled "The Parables as Language-Event: Some Comments on Fuchs's Hermeneutics in the Light of Linguistic Philosophy" I have tried to argue with reference both to Austin and to Wittgenstein that assertions at the close of parables, for example, do not necessarily undermine their hermeneutical function as language-event.[179] Amos Wilder presses this kind of point in a different way. He writes, "Fuchs refuses to define the content of faith. . . . He is afraid of the word as convention or as a means of conveying information. . . . Fuchs carries this so far that revelation, as it were, reveals nothing. . . . Jesus calls, indeed, for decision. . . . But surely his words, deeds, presence, person, and message rested . . . upon dogma, eschatological and theocratic.''[180]

(4) There is some force in the criticism that the new hermeneutic lets "what is true *for me*" become the criterion of "what is true," and that its orientation towards the interpreter's subjectivity transposes theology too often into a doctrine of man. Fuchs' statement, which we quoted earlier, that "the texts must translate us before we can them" is double-edged. On the one hand it asserts the primacy of the text which has man as its "object." In this respect it stands in the Reformation tradition of placing the interpreter himself "under" the word. On the other hand, however, Fuchs insists that not only does the content of the text amount to "the interpretation of our own existence," but he adds: *"We should accept as true only that which we acknowledge as valid for our own person."*[181] We should beware of interpreting Fuchs himself one-sidedly. For example, he also writes, "Christian faith means to speak of God's act, not of . . . acts

177. N. Perrin, *Jesus and the Language of the Kingdom*, p. 110 cf. p. 185 n. 52.
178. J. L. Austin, *How to Do Things with Words* (Clarendon Press, Oxford, 1962), p. 45 (his italics).
179. A. C. Thiselton, "The Parables as Language-Event: Some Comments on Fuchs's Hermeneutics in the Light of Linguistic Philosophy" in *S.J.T.* XXIII (1970), 437-68 (especially pp. 438 and 451-68).
180. A. N. Wilder, "The Word as Address and Meaning" in *N.H.*, p. 213.
181. E. Fuchs, "The New Testament and the Hermeneutical Problem" in *N.H.*, p. 117 (my italics).

of men."[182] Perhaps we can only say that we find the very same difficulty and ambiguity in Bultmann's pupil as we have already discussed with reference to Bultmann himself. Although Ebeling also shares Fuchs' existential perspective, he writes at the same time, "When God speaks, the whole of reality as it concerns us enters language anew."[183]

(5) The exponents of the new hermeneutic would claim that they are concerned with what is sometimes called "the rights of the text." The text does not merely convey "concepts" which are then examined and re-shaped through the grid of the interpreter's own language-tradition. From a theological viewpoint this means that the New Testament message must not be domesticated and tamed by letting it filter through language and tradition as a mere "object" to be scrutinized and appraised. We see, from a theological viewpoint, the operation of both grace and judgment. In grace the word of Jesus, for example in the parables, enters the horizons of the "world" of the hearer. There is what Fuchs calls "a place of meeting." But there is not simply fusion without tension or distance. To go back once again to Ebeling's statement, "According to Luther, the word of God always comes as *adversarius noster,* our adversary. It does not merely confirm and strengthen us in what we think we are."[184] In the terminology of the new hermeneutic, it brings the word to speech anew, and takes place as language-event.

182. *Ibid.,* p. 114.
183. G. Ebeling, *The Nature of Faith,* p. 190.
184. G. Ebeling, *I.T.T.L.,* p. 17.

CHAPTER XIII

Philosophy and Language in Ludwig Wittgenstein

52. *The Contrast between Wittgenstein's Earlier and Later Writings and Its Significance for Hermeneutics*

Questions about the continuity and contrast between Wittgenstein's earlier and later writings are no less controversial among interpreters of Wittgenstein than questions about the earlier and later Heidegger are among interpreters of that thinker. As a provisional point of departure which may need qualification in the light of more detailed discussion we suggest the following way of formulating the contrast. In his earlier writings, for which the *Tractatus* constitutes the major source, Wittgenstein turned to logic for the answer to questions about the relationship between language and the world. From 1913 to 1929 the issues which he attacked with burning energy concerned the problem of logical necessity and the nature of the philosophy of logic. From 1929 or 1930 until his death in 1951 Wittgenstein continued to wrestle with logical problems, but now he placed them in the setting of human life. Language was now grounded not in a single comprehensive abstract calculus of formal logic, but in the varied and particular activities of human life.

It is tempting to jump to an immediate conclusion about the significance of this contrast for hermeneutics, in the particular way which is followed by Karl-Otto Apel.[1] Apel argues that the outlook of the *Tractatus* is incompatible with hermeneutics, while the later period shares with hermeneutical philosophy a belief in the priority of "life" over abstract logic. In the *Tractatus,* Apel tries to insist, everything revolves around

---

1. K.-O. Apel, *Analytic Philosophy of Language and the Geisteswissenschaften* (Eng. Reidel, Dordrecht, 1967; Foundations of Language Suppl. Series 4), pp. 4-13 and 35-37.

"objective" facts and "objective" knowledge, while in Wittgenstein's later writings, "It is . . . language which takes the place of 'a priori forms.' "[2] Apel compares Wittgenstein's grounding of language-games in "forms of life" with Dilthey's dictum that "in the veins of the knowing subject as constructed by Locke, Hume, and Kant, no real blood is flowing, but the diluted juice of 'reason' as the mere activity of thinking."[3] Following Peter Winch's interpretation of Wittgenstein, Apel writes, "Logic was understood to be dependent on the rules of the language-game actually in use."[4] He then quotes Winch's words, "Criteria of logic are not a direct gift of God, but arise out of . . . ways of living, or modes of social life."[5] Similarly, Apel concludes, "Hermeneutics deals with something that does not belong in the realm of formal logic."[6]

Apel's approach may perhaps have some usefulness as an impressionist picture of how the contrast between Wittgenstein's earlier and later thought relates to hermeneutics. But it needs to be corrected in the light of three sets of considerations which have occupied interpreters of Wittgenstein. First of all, it is possible to exaggerate the element of contrast between the two periods. Recently more attention has been given to the so-called middle period of 1929-1932, represented by the notes published in 1968 under the title *Ludwig Wittgenstein und der Wiener Kreis;* the *Philosophische Bemerkungen;* and the *Philosophical Grammar.*[7] These show that Wittgenstein's re-orientation towards the problem of language was not simply a sharp break that repudiated everything from the past. Indeed, Wittgenstein himself writes in his preface to the *Investigations,* "It . . . seemed to me that I should publish those old thoughts and the new ones together: that the latter could be seen in the right light only by contrast with, and against the background of, my old way of thinking."[8] Norman Malcolm recalls that Wittgenstein always thought of the *Tractatus* as an important book which provided "the *only* alternative to the viewpoint of the later work."[9] Secondly, while Apel sees Wittgenstein partly through the eyes of Peter Winch, as W. D. Hudson and others have pointed out, this is not the only possible way of interpreting Wittgenstein. Hudson warns us against interpreting language-games as

2. *Ibid.,* p. 41.
3. *Ibid.*
4. *Ibid.,* p. 42.
5. *Ibid.;* cf. P. Winch, *The Idea of a Social Science and its Relation to Philosophy* (Routledge & Kegan Paul, London, 1958), p. 100.
6. K.-O. Apel, *Analytic Philosophy of Language,* p. 43.
7. F. Waismann, *Ludwig Wittgenstein und der Wiener Kreis* (Blackwell, Oxford, 1967); L. Wittgenstein, *P.B.;* and L. Wittgenstein, *P.G.*
8. L. Wittgenstein, *P.I.,* p. x.
9. N. Malcolm, *Ludwig Wittgenstein. A Memoir* (Oxford University Press, 1939 and 1966), p. 69.

self-contained universes of discourse which each have their own autonomous rules of logic.[10] Paul van Buren, for example, expresses a half-truth when he claims that "Wittgenstein's game theory works, if it works at all, in a pluralistic and relativistic world."[11] Thirdly, the publication of Wittgenstein's letters to Paul Engelmann, as well as his letters to Russell, Keynes, and Moore, and especially the publication of *Wittgenstein's Vienna* by Allan Janik and Stephen Toulmin, suggest that the *Tractatus* should be seen in a new light. Janik and Toulmin convincingly argue that far from interpreting the *Tractatus* in the tradition of Russell and British empirical philosophy, the earlier Wittgenstein should be seen as "a Viennese thinker whose intellectual problems and personal attitudes alike had been formed in the neo-Kantian environment of pre-1914, in which logic and ethics were essentially bound up with each other and with the critique of language *(Sprachkritik)*."[12] Wittgenstein's letters to Engelmann and Russell provide support for this conclusion.[13]

If Janik and Toulmin are right, the outlook of the *Tractatus* is much closer to the Neo-Kantian dualism of Bultmann than any interpreter of either thinker has yet noticed. We have seen again and again that Bultmann's entire system of thought, including his hermeneutics, is built on the assumption of a radical disjunction between the transcendent activity of God and "this-worldly" phenomena. In a parallel way, Wittgenstein writes in the *Tractatus:* "The sense of the world *(der Sinn der Welt)* must lie outside the world. . . . *In* it no value *(keinen Wert)* exists. . . . If there is any value that does have value, it must lie outside the whole sphere of what happens and is the case. For all that happens and is the case is accidental. . . . And so it is impossible for there to be propositions of ethics. Propositions can express nothing that is higher."[14] Wittgenstein adds, *"How* things are in the world is a matter of complete indifference for what is higher. God does not reveal himself *in* the world."[15]

Those who interpret the *Tractatus* in line with Ayer's Logical Positivism or the philosophy of the Vienna Circle assume that Wittgenstein is here stripping away questions about the beyond in order to leave room for the really important question of propositions about the natural world and their logical relationship to one another. But this is to turn the

10. W. D. Hudson, "Some Remarks on Wittgenstein's Account of Religious Belief" in *Royal Institute of Philosophy Lectures II, Talk of God* (Macmillan, London, 1969), pp. 45-49; cf. pp. 36-51.
11. P. M. van Buren, *Theological Explorations* (S.C.M., London, 1968), p. 19.
12. A. Janik and S. Toulmin, *Wittgenstein's Vienna*, p. 22.
13. P. Engelmann, *Letters from Ludwig Wittgenstein. With a Memoir* (Blackwell, Oxford, 1967), pp. xiv, 6, 31, 96-97, 110, 117, 123-27, 135, and 143. Cf. L. Wittgenstein, *Letters to Russell, Keynes, and Moore.* (Blackwell, Oxford, 1974), e.g. pp. 71 and 82.
14. *T.* 6.41 and 6.42.
15. *Ibid.* 6.432 (Wittgenstein's italics).

concerns of Wittgenstein's own life and thought upside down. The man who read Kierkegaard, Schopenhauer, Tolstoy, and Dostoevski does not wish to *eliminate* value, but, like Bultmann, to insure that it is *not reduced* to the level of empirical propositions. Janik and Toulmin rightly argue, "The fundamental point of this whole critique was to underline the ethical point that all questions about value lie *outside* the scope of such ordinary factual or descriptive language. . . . The half that he did not write ('this second part, that is the important one') comprises the corpus of Karl Kraus's writings. . . . Wittgenstein's radical separation of facts from values can be regarded as the terminus of a series of efforts to distinguish the sphere of natural science from the sphere of morality, which had begun with Kant, had been sharpened by Schopenhauer, and had been made absolute by Kierkegaard. Like Kant, Wittgenstein was concerned at the same time to defend the adequacy of language as a scientific instrument from Mauthner's scepticism . . . while drawing an absolute distinction between what language *says* and what it *shows*—that is, what is 'higher.' "16

The importance of all this for the argument of the present study is not that the *Tractatus* lends any support to Bultmann's approach. The point is, in the first place, that increasingly after 1929 Wittgenstein came to see that far from being what he had called "the final solution of the problems," the dualism of the *Tractatus* simply failed to do full justice to the diversity of particular ways in which language is actually used by human beings. Language itself is a this-worldy phenomenon; but it does more than communicate descriptive propositions about the world which are interrelated together in a single system of logical calculus. The "bedrock" of language is human life. The abandonment of the dualism of the *Tractatus* therefore prompts us to ask the question: can Bultmann escape those problems which *forced* Wittgenstein to adopt a different perspective, almost, as it were, against his will?

Secondly, as soon as the emphasis moves from a single calculus of logic to a diversity of language-games embedded in human life, the problem of hermeneutics emerges. For hermeneutics is the recognition of Wittgenstein's point that we cannot use language "outside" a given language-game. *All* language is part of a *given* language-game. In *this* sense, there is no such thing as presuppositionless exegesis, or understanding without pre-understanding. Meaning, in a large class of cases, depends on use (*Gebrauch*), but use, in turn, depends on training (*Abrichtung*).17 "To imagine a language means to imagine a form of life (*Lebensform*). . . . Problems arise when language goes on holiday."18

16. A. Janik and S. Toulmin, *Wittgenstein's Vienna*, pp. 196 and 197.
17. *P.I.*, sects. 43 and 86.
18. *Ibid.*, sects. 19 and 38.

Asking an inappropriate question is asking it "outside a particular language-game," like asking what the time is on the sun, or where the past goes to, or where the flame goes when the gas goes out.[19] Wittgenstein insists that this approach does not abandon logic. Nevertheless, he adds, the idea of logic's "crystalline purity" was only a preconceived idea in the *Tractatus*. It was not the *result* of the investigation but its assumption. "The preconceived idea of crystalline purity can only be removed by turning our whole examination round. (One might say: the axis of reference of our examination must be rotated, but about the fixed point of our real need.")[20] Hence the standpoint of the later writings is that "Only in the stream of thought and life *(Leben)* do words have meaning."[21] "When language-games change, then there is a change in concepts, and with the concepts the meanings of words change."[22]

Thirdly, there is a connection between "showing" in the earlier writings and Wittgenstein's later work on the relation between the formation of concepts and grammatical utterances. His earlier work on tautologies stands in continuity with his later observations about analytical statements and formal concepts. This reaches a climax in Wittgenstein's last notes published under the title *On Certainty*. A statement like "Every body is extended" or "Water boils at 100° C" does not "say" anything, in the sense that it does not constitute a descriptive assertion about a state of affairs *(der Sachverhalt)*. But it may nevertheless enable us to notice *(bemerken)* something. Moreover, propositions of this type sometimes express what "has belonged to the scaffolding of our thoughts (Every human being has parents)."[23] We shall try to see the bearing of this approach in due course on certain stretches of language in the New Testament itself.

Other aspects of Wittgenstein's thought are bound up with these three sets of questions. For example, we have already begun to inquire about the relation between Bultmann's dualism and Wittgenstein's later emphasis on public criteria of meaning. However, now that we have suggested certain corrections, or at least complementations, to Apel's statements, we may return to the basic contrast which he formulates. In the earlier writings of Wittgenstein, the justification for everything that can be "said" rather than "shown" falls within the domain of propositional logic. "Logic is prior to every experience."[24] But in *On Certainty* Wittgenstein writes, "Giving grounds, justifying the evidence, comes to an end—but the end is not certain propositions' striking us immediately as

19. *Ibid.*, sect. 47.
20. *Ibid.*, sect. 108.
21. *Z.*, sect. 173.
22. L. Wittgenstein, *Cert.*, sect. 65.
23. *Ibid.*, sect. 211.
24. *T.*, 5.552.

true. . . . It is our *acting* which lies at the bottom of the language-game."[25] Or, in the more familiar words of the *Investigations*, "If I have exhausted the justifications I have reached bedrock, and my spade is turned. Then I am inclined to say: 'This is simply what I do.' "[26] It will become clear that although Wittgenstein by no means stands in the tradition of Heidegger, this is not very far from Heidegger's belief that on the question of understanding life is prior to conscious thought.

53. The Earlier Writings: Propositions, the Picture Theory, and the Limits of Language

In his preface to the *Tractatus* Wittgenstein declares that "the aim of the book is to set a limit to thought, or rather—not to thought, but to the expression of thoughts."[27] Later he writes, "All philosophy is a 'critique of language' *(Sprachkritik)*."[28] On this basis some philosophers have viewed the *Tractatus* as "Kantian from beginning to end."[29] Just as Kant constructed a critique of theoretical reason and established its limits, so Wittgenstein, it is sometimes argued, marked out the limits of language. In Wittgenstein's own words, "*The limits of my language* mean the limits of my world."[30] "What we cannot speak about we must pass over in silence."[31]

But what gives rise to this kind of conclusion? First and foremost, the problems which pervade both the *Notebooks* and the *Tractatus* concern logical necessity. Wittgenstein notes, as we have seen, that "logic is prior to every experience."[32] Logic must be "irrefutable by any possible experience, but it must also be unconfirmable by any possible experience."[33] Experience may, for example, serve to establish "*p*," the contingent proposition "it is raining." But the logically necessary proposition "*p* v ~ *p*" ("either it is raining or it is not raining") remains independent

25. *Cert.*, sect. 204.
26. *P.I.*, sect. 217.
27. *T.*, 3.
28. *Ibid.* 4.0031.
29. D. Pears, "Wittgenstein and Austin" in B. Williams and A. Montefiore (eds.), *British Analytical Philosophy* (Routledge & Kegan Paul, London, 1966), p. 25; cf. pp. 17-39. See also D. Pears, *Wittgenstein* (Fontana, Collins, London, 1971), pp. 25-47; and D. S. Shwayder, "Wittgenstein on Mathematics" in P. Winch (ed.), *Studies in the Philosophy of Wittgenstein* (Routledge & Kegan Paul, London, 1969), p. 66.
30. *T.*, 5.6 (Wittgenstein's italics).
31. *Ibid.* 7.
32. *Ibid.* 5.552.
33. *Ibid.* 6.1222. Cf. L. Wittgenstein, *N.*, pp. 34-35.

of experience for corroboration or refutation. But how, then, do we ever arrive at a logically necessary proposition in the first place?

Wittgenstein believed that, in the words of David Pears, "logical necessity could be explained only if it were traced back to its source in the essential nature of propositions."[34] In the *Notebooks* he exclaims, "My *whole* task consists in explaining the nature of the proposition. That is to say, in giving the nature of all facts, whose picture the proposition *is*."[35] "The question about the possibility of existence propositions does not come in the middle but at the very first beginning of logic."[36] How do propositions relate to reality? How do they "reach out through . . . logical space?"[37]

In practice in the final arrangement of the *Tractatus* Wittgenstein begins with considerations about facts, or states of affairs, moves on to the relations between states of affairs and propositions, and turns finally to logical questions about the rôle of propositions as truth-functions. Thus he sets out the first of his seven main statements as follows:

"1. The world is all that is the case.

"2. What is the case—a fact *(die Tatsache)*—is the existence of states of affairs *(Sachverhalten)*.

"3. A logical picture of facts is a thought.

"4. A thought is a proposition with a sense *(der sinvolle Satz)*."

The fifth and sixth propositions concern truth-functions and the general form of a proposition, while the seventh relates to the limits of language.

A large part of the argument, especially in this first half of the *Tractatus*, hinges on the notion of a structural correspondence, or as Rush Rhees insists, a relation of "projection" *(Abbildung)* between propositions and the states of affairs which they portray.[38] In the *Notebooks* Wittgenstein had written, "The difficulty of my theory of logical portrayal was that of finding a connexion between the signs on paper and a situation outside in the world."[39] But then he asserts, "The proposition is a model of reality as we imagine it."[40] Similarly, in the *Tractatus* he writes, "A proposition is a picture of reality."[41] "A picture presents the existence and non-existence of states of affairs."[42] He concludes, "Pictorial form is

34. D. Pears, *Wittgenstein*, p. 60.
35. L. Wittgenstein, *N.*, p. 39 (22.1.15).
36. *Ibid.*, p. 10 (9.10.14).
37. *Ibid.*, p. 36 (16.12.14); cf. pp. 31-34 and 37-42.
38. R. Rhees, " 'Ontology' and Identity in the *Tractatus*" in P. Winch (ed.), *Studies in the Philosophy of Wittgenstein*, p. 55. Cf. E. Stenius, *Wittgenstein's Tractatus. A Critical Exposition of its Main Lines of Thought* (Blackwell, Oxford, 1960), pp. 91-96.
39. L. Wittgenstein, *N.*, p. 19 (27.10.14).
40. *Ibid.*, p. 20 (27.10.14).
41. *T.*, 4.01.
42. *Ibid.* 2.11; cf. 2.15.

the possibility that things are related to one another in the same way as the elements of the picture. *That* is how a picture is attached to reality."[43]

According to his biographers, Wittgenstein's formulation of the picture theory of meaning owed something of its origin to a report in 1914 of some court proceedings in which claims about the events of a car accident were portrayed by means of a model.[44] In the *Notebooks* Wittgenstein comments, "In the proposition a world is as it were put together experimentally. (As when in the law-court in Paris a motor-car accident is represented by means of dolls, etc.)."[45] He repeats the substance of the point in the *Tractatus*.[46] In essence, three principles seem to be involved:

(i) each of the constituent elements of the model corresponds with an element in the situation which it depicts;

(ii) these elements can be arranged in various ways to portray possible states of affairs; and

(iii) a given arrangement of elements in the model represents a determinate state of affairs.

These principles apply, with one possible qualification, to the function of a proposition in portraying a state of affairs.[47] "In a proposition there must be exactly as many distinguishable parts as in the situation that it represents."[48] This can be seen most clearly in propositions of the simplest kind, namely elementary propositions. Irving Copi argues convincingly that in fact "Wittgenstein's picture theory of meaning . . . applies not to *all* propositions, but to elementary propositions alone."[49] It should be noted that this conclusion meets with controversy in some quarters, in spite of G. E. M. Anscombe's support for it. But we may take it for granted that the picture theory applies *at least* to elementary propositions, before we consider questions about its further application.

An elementary proposition portrays a configuration of "simples." It should be stressed, however, that in contrast to the logical atomism of Russell, Wittgenstein is concerned exclusively with logic rather than with any implication for ontology or epistemology. His three very close interpreters, Rush Rhees, G. E. M. Anscombe, and Norman Malcolm, all call

---

43. *Ibid.* 2.151.
44. N. Malcolm and G. H. von Wright, *Ludwig Wittgenstein,* pp. 7-8. But cf. the editors' comments in *N.,* p. 7.
45. *N.,* p. 7 (29.9.14).
46. *T.* 4.031.
47. The qualification concerns Rush Rhees's warning about the difference between correspondence and "projection" *(Abbildung)* noted above.
48. *T.* 4.04.
49. I. M. Copi, "Objects, Properties, and Relations in the *Tractatus*" in I. M. Copi and R. W. Beard (eds.), *Essays on Wittgenstein's Tractatus* (Routledge & Kegan Paul, London, 1966), p. 170; cf. pp. 167-86.

attention firmly to this point.[50] For this reason, Wittgenstein never felt the need to specify what might constitute a simple object by way of example. If there is to be *logical* determinacy, "there must be objects. . . . Objects are what is unalterable and subsistent."[51] In the *Notebooks* Wittgenstein writes, "We do not infer the existence of simple objects from the existence of particular simple objects, but rather . . . as the end-product of analysis, by means of a process that leads to them."[52] In G. E. M. Anscombe's words, "The simple objects are presented as something demanded by the nature of language."[53]

When elementary propositions are linked together to form complex propositions, the structure of "picturing" is certainly not always an obvious one. But Wittgenstein argues that here "Language disguises thought. . . . It is impossible to infer the form of the thought beneath it."[54] As early as 1913 he had remarked, "Distrust of grammar is the first requisite for philosophizing."[55] However, Wittgenstein stresses that the pictorial form "is *not* impaired by apparent irregularities. . . . A gramophone record, the musical idea, the written notes, and the sound-waves, all stand to one another in the same internal relation of depicting that holds between language and the world."[56] Similarly, although hieroglyphic script depicts what it represents in an obvious way, nevertheless "alphabetic script developed out of it without losing what was essential to depiction *(Abbildung)*."[57] It is not necessary to our purpose to enter into discussion about the relation between pictorial form or form of projection *(die Form der Abbildung)* and representational form *(die Form der Darstellung)*. This is done by Max Black, E. Stenius, and especially James Griffin.[58] In view of our earlier consideration of Neo-Kantianism, it is of greater interest to note Wittgenstein's indebtedness to Hertz at this point.

Wittgenstein's next step is to show that each elementary proposition contributes not simply to a complex proposition, but ultimately to a single

50. R. Rhees, " 'Ontology' and Identity in the *Tractatus*" in *Essays on Wittgenstein's Tractatus;* N. Malcolm and G. H. von Wright, *Ludwig Wittgenstein*, p. 86; and G. E. M. Anscombe, *An Introduction to Wittgenstein's Tractatus* (Hutchinson, London, 1959), pp. 27-31.
51. *T.* 2.026. Cf. 2.011, 2.012, 2.0123, and 2.02ff.
52. *N.*, p. 50.
53. G. E. M. Anscombe, *An Introduction to Wittgenstein's Tractatus*, p. 29. But cf. J. Griffin, *Wittgenstein's Logical Atomism* (Oxford, 1964), pp. 39-71.
54. *T.* 4.002.
55. "Notes on Logic" in *N.*, p. 93.
56. *T.* 4.013 and 4.014.
57. *Ibid.* 4.016. Cf. E. Stenius, *Wittgenstein's Tractatus.*
58. M. Black, *A Companion to Wittgenstein's 'Tractatus'* (Cambridge University Press, 1964), pp. 98-101; and J. Griffin, *Wittgenstein's Logical Atomism*, pp. 99-102. Cf. G. E. M. Anscombe, *An Introduction to Wittgenstein's Tractatus*, pp. 67-70; and E. Stenius, *Wittgenstein's Tractatus*, pp. 88-116.

comprehensive system of logical calculus. He writes: "If all true elementary propositions are given, the result is a complete description of the world."[59] Arriving at the first expression in the *Tractatus* of what has often been called "the thesis of extensionality," he writes, "A proposition is an expression of agreement and disagreement with truth-possibilities of elementary propositions."[60] Thus, more explicitly, "Propositions comprise all that follows from the totality of all elementary propositions."[61] Echoing an earlier reflection from his "Notes on Logic," Wittgenstein concludes: "If a god creates a world in which certain propositions are true, then by that very act he also creates a world in which all the propositions that follow from them come true."[62]

This paves the way for Wittgenstein's work in the main body of the *Tractatus* on truth-possibilities, truth-functions, and finally truth-tables. To set out the details of Wittgenstein's thought at this point would take us far beyond the concerns of the present study, including the need to make some reference to Frege's notion of truth-functions in logic. The main point, however, is clearly summed up by Anthony Kenny. He writes, "Propositions of great length and complexity may be built up by repeated use of connectives such as 'and' and 'or'; but, however complex they are, their truth-value can always be determined from the truth-values of the simple propositions which make them up. This is done by repeated applications of the tables belonging to the particular connectives."[63] To show the effects of the truth or falsity of their constituent-statements on non-elementary propositions is, more technically, to show what is the effect of the truth-conditions of elementary propositions on their truth-functions. If we take just one elementary proposition "p" ("it is raining"), in schematic form we may set out the effect of its truth-conditions on the complex proposition "not-p" ("it is not raining") as well as on the tautology "either p, or not-p" and the contradiction "p and not-p." We should then have:

P	$\sim P$	$P \lor \sim P$	$P \sim P$
T	F	T	F
F	T	T	F

On this basis a vast logical calculus can be built up.[64] The truth-possibilities of n elementary propositions become 2 to the power of n, while their truth-functions would amount to 2 to the power of 2^n.

59. *T.* 4.26.
60. *Ibid.* 4.4. Cf. M. Black, *A Companion to Wittgenstein's 'Tractatus,'* p. 219.
61. *T.* 4.52.
62. *Ibid.* 5.123; cf. "Notes on Logic" in *N.*, p. 98.
63. A. Kenny, *Wittgenstein* (Penguin Books, London, 1975), pp. 30-31.
64. *T.* 4.31 and 5.101 include two schematic tables, but cf. the whole section from 4.26 to 5.521.

One consequence of this is that every complex proposition can be reduced, by means of *analysis*, into a series of elementary propositions, which have a *determinate* or exact meaning and truth-value. Thus Wittgenstein asserts: "A proposition has one and only one complete analysis. What a proposition expresses, it expresses in a determinate manner which can be set out clearly."[65] Whenever we encounter the appearance of indeterminacy in a proposition, this is simply symptomatic of the fact that it is unanalyzed and complex. Wittgenstein writes, "When a propositional element signifies a complex, this can be seen from an indeterminateness *(Unbestimmtheit)* in the propositions in which it occurs."[66] Even in the *Philosophische Bemerkungen,* although his interest has now shifted explicitly to "grammar," he begins his opening sentence with the notion of a *final* analysis, or of complete clarity. He declares, "Der Satz is vollkommen logisch analysiert, dessen Grammatik vollkommen klargelegt ist."[67]

This brings us to Wittgenstein's final section in the *Tractatus* which reaches its climax in his seventh and final proposition "What we cannot speak about we must pass over in silence." *Either* a stretch of language turns on elementary propositions which depict states of affairs *(Sachverhalten) or else* it neither affirms nor denies any state of affairs, in which case it fails to "say" *(sagen)* anything. This is not to say, however, that "what cannot be said" has no reality or existence. Wittgenstein insists, "What *can* be shown (gezeigt) *cannot be said (gesagt).*"[68] He declares, "There are indeed things that cannot be put into words. They *make themselves manifest.* They are what is mystical. *(Dies* zeigt *sich, es ist das Mystische).*"[69]

The statement that "What *can* be shown *cannot* be said" comes in a particular context in the pages of the *Tractatus.* Wittgenstein has been discussing the role of propositions as pictures of reality. He then states, "Propositions can represent the whole of reality, but they cannot represent what they must have in common with reality in order to be able to represent it—logical form."[70] "Propositions cannot represent logical form: it is mirrored in them. What finds its reflection in language, language cannot represent. What expresses *itself* in language, *we* cannot express by means of language."[71] Hence, "Propositions *show* the logical form of reality."[72] The point is that we cannot step outside our own logic and

65. *Ibid.* 3.25 and 3.251.
66. *Ibid.* 3.24.
67. L. Wittgenstein, *P.B.* I, sect. 1, p. 51; cf. also IV, sect. 46, p. 79.
68. *T.* 4.1212.
69. *Ibid.* 6.522 (Wittgenstein's italics).
70. *Ibid.* 4.12.
71. *Ibid.* 4.121.
72. *Ibid.* (Wittgenstein's italics).

language, and talk about it from some Archimedean point. If a map or a chart depicts a state of affairs it cannot also *thereby* depict its own method of depiction. To do so requires some kind of supplementary inset. But language is all that we have both to depict states of affairs and to *show* us what is happening.

We must now note a crucial distinction drawn by Wittgenstein between propositions that lack sense *(sind sinnlos)*, and things that cannot even be formulated in thought because they cannot be other than nonsensical *(unsinnig)*. To the former category belong tautologies and contradictions, or analytical and logical truths. These propositions lack sense in that they have no poles of truth-or-falsity. A tautology, for example, remains true whatever its functions; it has only one truth-possibility. But the importance of this category in Wittgenstein's work is acknowledged even by his fiercest critics. C. W. K. Mundle, for example, admits: "That all necessary truths are analytic propositions which unfold the (often unnoticed) implications of what men have packed into definitions, is a very important thesis. Its formulation by Wittgenstein was a major contribution to a critique of language."[73]

Wittgenstein argues that mathematical equations come under this category. Calculation, he insists, is different from experiment.[74] "Equations express the substitutionability of two expressions."[75] But they are not therefore unimportant or insignificant. Great discoveries may be made possible because of them. Similarly the propositions of logic have no subject-matter *(sie handeln von nichts)*. They are tautologies. "One can recognize that they are true from the symbol alone."[76] But they are not unimportant. What is involved is *not information but understanding*. They enable us to "see" what is there. Wittgenstein insists that on this basis the *concepts* involved in such proposition are *formal* concepts. G. E. M. Anscombe remarks, "Not only 'concept,' 'function,' 'object,' but also 'number,' 'fact,' 'complex' are formal concepts; and, in opposition to Carnap, Wittgenstein would maintain that such linguistic concepts as 'name,' 'predicate,' 'proposition,' 'relational expression' are also formal concepts. In none of these cases can it be *informatively* said of something that it falls under the concept."[77] The propositions of the *Tractatus* itself are described by Wittgenstein as "elucidations" *(erläutern)*. Even though strictly they may be "nonsensical" *(unsinnig)*, they

73. C. W. K. Mundle, *A Critique of Linguistic Philosophy* (Clarendon Press, Oxford, 1970), pp. 183-84.
74. *T.*, 6.2331.
75. *Ibid.* 6.24.
76. *Ibid.* 6.113.
77. G. E. M. Anscombe, *An Introduction to Wittgenstein's Tractatus*, p. 123 (my italics).

can be used to offer an insight which allows the reader to climb beyond them.[78]

Wittgenstein's remarks about the limits of language, then, pave the way for his work on grammatical utterances in the later writings. But they also do more than this. They show the *limits* of language in the sense that Wittgenstein stresses what A. Maslow calls "the fallacy of the angelic point of view."[79] This is what lies behind Wittgenstein's rather obscure remark: "What the solipsist *means* is quite correct; only it cannot be *said*."[80] The world can only be "*my* world." Hence: "The limits of my language mean the limits of my world."[81]

Thus we arrive at the insight which is central for hermeneutics that the problem of language is bound up with human finitude. As Janik and Toulmin point out, to anyone who was a follower of Russell and British empiricism, this aspect of the *Tractatus* seemed paradoxical; an almost inexplicable appendage to an otherwise fine work on logic. But Wittgenstein's own letters, as we have noted, showed that Russell's understanding of the *Tractatus* missed Wittgenstein's main intention. Janik and Toulmin write, "Wittgenstein was convinced that he had solved 'the problem of philosophy.' The model theory explained how knowledge of the world was possible. The mathematical (logical) basis of that theory explained how the very structure of propositions *showed* their *limitations* . . . (and) determined the limits of scientific (rational) inquiry. . . . Subjective truth is communicable only indirectly, through fable, polemics, irony, and satire. . . . Ethics is taught not by arguments, but by providing examples of moral behaviour."[82] The tradition of the *Tractatus* is not that of Russell, Moore, Ayer, and Carnap, but of Kraus, Schopenhauer, Kierkegaard, and Tolstoy. This not only explains how the last pages of the *Tractatus* fit the rest, but how the whole *Tractatus* fits the man who wrote it.

Even the *Tractatus,* then, raises questions which are relevant to hermeneutics. In chapter two of this study we alluded to the "Symposium on Saying and Showing in Heidegger and Wittgenstein" which appeared in 1972.[83] In this discussion Eva Schaper points out a crucial contrast between Heidegger and the earlier Wittgenstein. Both Heidegger and Wittgenstein express their astonishment and wonder that anything exists. But whereas Heidegger writes more than one volume on this question, the

---

78. *T.* 6.54.
79. A. Maslow, *A Study in Wittgenstein's Tractatus* (University of California Press, Berkeley, 1961; originally written in 1933), p. 148.
80. *T.* 5.62 (Wittgenstein's italics).
81. *Ibid.* 5.6.
82. A. Janik and S. Toulmin, *Wittgenstein's Vienna*, p. 198.
83. P. McCormick, E. Schaper, and J. M. Heaton, "Symposium on Saying and Sharing in Heidegger and Wittgenstein" in *J.B.S.P.* III (1972), 27-45.

earlier Wittgenstein insists: "This astonishment cannot be expressed in the form of a question. . . . Anything we say on this must *a priori* be only nonsense."[84] However, in his introductory paper Peter McCormick argues suggestively that Wittgenstein's notion of what can be *shown* (but not said) is closely parallel in practice to what Heidegger puts under the heading of authentic and primal *Saying,* in the sense that it is a non-objectifying letting-be-seen.[85] Unfortunately he does not develop this point. But in spite of the huge differences between their philosophical orientations, it does indeed seem to be legitimate to compare these two thinkers at this point. Heidegger draws a contrast between merely "using" language to describe or to objectify the things in the world and undergoing "an experience" with language.[86] Objectifying language operates with a logical calculus and rests on a correspondence view of truth. When "language speaks," there is a letting-be-seen of something otherwise hidden. Wittgenstein draws a contrast between the language which describes the world because it depends on elementary propositions about states of affairs, and a "showing" of the mystical or, as Black expounds it, "the Beyond," which occurs not *in* language but *through* language. The "mystical," or the "Beyond," does not appear in the *Investigations* in this way. But the notion of how language "shows" what is already there to be seen is developed in terms of "grammatical" utterances.

54. *Hermeneutics and the Later Writings: Language-Games and Life*

The radical difference of style between the *Tractatus* and the *Investigations* underlines their difference of orientation and approach. Anthony Kenny observes that the *Investigations* contains 784 questions, of which only 110 are answered. Of these 110 answers, he adds, no less than seventy are *meant* to be wrong.[87] In a striking article on the nature of the later writings Stanley Cavell argues that this distinctive style serves "to prevent understanding which is unaccompanied by inner change."[88] We have already noted D. M. High's comments about the propriety of "using" the later writings as a means of fulfilling Wittgenstein's stated aim that he wished them "to stimulate someone to thoughts of his own."[89]

84. *Ibid.*, p. 38; cf. L. Wittgenstein, "A Lecture on Ethics" (1929) in *Ph.R.* LXXIV (1965), 3-26.
85. P. McCormick, in *J.B.S.P.* III, 34-35.
86. M. Heidegger, *O.W.L.,* pp. 65 and 77; cf. pp. 57-108.
87. A. Kenny, "Aquinas and Wittgenstein" in *The Downside Review* LXXVII (1959), 235.
88. S. Cavell, "The Availability of Wittgenstein's Later Philosophy" in G. Pitcher (ed.) *Wittgenstein. The Philosophical Investigations* (Macmillan, London, 1968), p. 184; cf. pp. 151-85 (rpt. from *Ph.R.* LXXI [1962], 67-93).
89. *P.I.,* p. x.

Alluding to this statement, Renford Bambrough adds: "No book was more deliberately designed than the *Investigations* to be 'a machine to think with.' "[90] The *Philosophical Investigations,* then, are not concerned simply with "results." Like Kierkegaard, Wittgenstein believed that it was not enough simply to state the truth: "One must also find the way from error to truth."[91]

Expressed in Heidegger's terms, Wittgenstein's aim was to allow what was already there to be "seen" by viewing it from the appropriate angle of vision. But unlike the later Heidegger, he did not believe that this angle of vision could be achieved by passive yieldedness. To be sure, for both thinkers the task was to emancipate oneself from the well-worn grooves of tradition. But, as Malcolm recalls, Wittgenstein declared, "You can't think decently if you don't want to hurt yourself."[92] As a final witness to Wittgenstein's aims in his later writings we may appeal to his close disciple Rush Rhees. Rhees recalls Wittgenstein's comment to his students, "What I should like to get at is for you not to agree with me in particular opinions, but to investigate the matter in the right way. To notice the interesting kind of thing (that is, the things which will serve as keys if you use them properly). . . . What I want to teach you isn't opinions but a method . . . a way of investigating central problems."[93]

This at once suggests a connection between Wittgenstein's conception of philosophy and the task of hermeneutics. Hermeneutics is concerned with the opening up of a perspective which allows the interpreter to see what is there. Biblical exposition, for example, is not concerned primarily with discovering new facts, but with opening the eyes of the hearer to see what was there all the time. But this is exactly Wittgenstein's point about the purpose of philosophy. He writes: "The aspects of things that are most important for us are hidden because of their simplicity and familiarity. (One is unable to notice *(bemerken)* something—because it is always before one's eyes.)"[94] Problems are solved, not by acquiring new information, "but by arranging what we have always known."[95] But there is nothing trivial about this activity. Wittgenstein's *Remarks on the Foundations of Mathematics,* for example, contain observations "on facts which no one has doubted, and which have only gone unremarked because they are always before our eyes."[96] The form of account which

90. R. Bambrough, "How to Read Wittgenstein" in *Royal Institute of Philosophy Lectures VII: Understanding Wittgenstein* (Macmillan, London, 1974), p. 118; cf. pp. 117-32.
91. L. Wittgenstein, "Bemerkungen über Frazers *The Golden Bough*" in *Synthese* XVII (1967), 233.
92. N. Malcolm and G. H. von Wright, *Ludwig Wittgenstein,* p. 40; cf. pp. 26-27.
93. R. Rhees, *Discussions of Wittgenstein* (Routledge & Kegan Paul, London, 1970), pp. 42-43.
94. *P.I.,* sect. 129.
95. *Ibid.,* sect. 109.
96. L. Wittgenstein, *R.F.M.* I, sect. 141.

Wittgenstein gives relates directly to "the way we look at things."[97] He continues, "Philosophy simply puts everything before us, and neither explains nor deduces anything. . . . The work of the philosopher consists in assembling reminders for a particular purpose."[98] "We want to replace . . . explanations by quiet weighing of linguistic facts."[99] "The philosopher is not a citizen of any community of ideas. That is what makes him into a philosopher."[100] Richard H. Bell observes in connection with this passage, "Wittgenstein's philosophical method . . . was as close to a purely 'descriptive' method as can be found."[101]

It would be a mistake to interpret these remarks in a quasi-empirical way, as if Wittgenstein was only concerned to construct a kind of empirical linguistics. This is precisely *not* what Wittgenstein is saying. We must go back to Cavell's point about "inner change." Wittgenstein believes that a grasp of what "grammar" *shows* can, as he puts it, change our way of looking at things *(Anschauungsweise)*.[102] Thus while he does not give new "facts" about the nature of logical contradiction, Wittgenstein states in his *Remarks,* "My aim is to alter the *attitude* to contradiction."[103] Nothing could be closer to the hermeneutical concern with subjectivity.

We must now move on to a second main consideration. Whereas formal logic is concerned with system, with calculus, and with generality, hermeneutics concerns problems of historical and cultural particularity. But the movement from the general to the particular is precisely what characterizes Wittgenstein's middle and later thought. In the *Blue Book* he declares that what often leads the philosopher into darkness is "our craving for generality . . . our preoccupation with the method of science."[104] He refers in particular to "the method of reducing the explanation of natural phenomena to the smallest possible number of primitive natural laws . . . of unifying the treatment of different topics by using a general label." He adds, "Instead of 'craving for generality' I could also have said 'the contemptuous attitude towards the particular case.' "[105]

These remarks apply, above all, to language. Alluding to the more "scientific" orientation of his earlier work, Wittgenstein declares, "It is interesting to compare the multiplicity of the tools in language and of the ways they are used, the multiplicity of the kinds of word and sentence *(die Mannigfaltigkeit der Wort und Satzarten),* with what logicians have said about the structure of language. (Including the author of the *Tractatus*

97. *P.I.,* sect. 122.
98. *Ibid.,* sects. 126-27. Cf. also *Z.,* sects. 447 and 456-60; and *Cert.,* sects. 12, 21, and 481.
99. *Z.,* sect. 447.
100. *Ibid.,* sect. 455.
101. R. H. Bell, "Wittgenstein and Descriptive Theology" in *R.St.* V (1969), 4.
102. *P.I.,* sect. 144, and *Z.,* sect. 461.
103. *R.F.M.* II, sect. 82, p. 106 (Wittgenstein's italics).
104. *B.B.,* p. 18.
105. *Ibid.*

Logico-Philosophicus.)"[106] Negatively, he makes "a radical break with the idea that language always functions in one way, always serves the same purpose; to convey thoughts—which may be about houses, pains, good and evil, or anything else you please."[107] In one of his most famous and important similes he writes, "Think of the tools in a tool-box: there is a hammer, pliers, a saw, a screw-driver, a ruler, a glue-pot, nails and screws.—The functions of words are as diverse as the functions of these objects."[108] The error, he urges, is "to look for something in common to all the entities which we commonly subsume under a general term."[109]

Wittgenstein sets in contrast the generality of the abstract *a priori* (or supposed *a priori*) with the particularity of human life and experience. When he looks back, for example, to the general questions which he had asked in the *Tractatus,* "questions as to the *essence* of language, of propositions, of thought," he remarks: "We ask: '*What is* language?', '*What is* a proposition?' And the answer to these questions had to be given once for all; and *independently of any future experience*."[110] But in his later thought, as Rush Rhees comments, "These words— 'proposition', 'grammar', 'rule', 'proof', and so on—have their meanings *in particular surroundings* or environments."[111] As we suggested in chapter two, Wittgenstein's adoption of this perspective may well have owed something to the influence of the paper given by Brouwer in 1928, in which he insisted that mathematics, science, and language should be viewed as human activities with a social and historical context. S. Toulmin, J. T. E. Richardson, and P. M. S. Hacker, we saw, underlined this point.

It is partly to meet these two points that Wittgenstein introduces his key term "language-game" *(Sprachspiel).* The term is partly meant to call attention to the fact that language-uses are grounded in the *particular surroundings* of situations in human life. It also points to the fact that language is not used in a single uniform way, as, for example, "to describe the world." Thus, comparing "language" with "game" he writes, "Instead of producing something common to all that we call language, I am saying that these phenomena have no one thing in common which makes us use the same word for all,—but that they are *related* to one another in many different ways. . . . Consider, for example, the proceedings that we call 'games'. . . . If you look at them you will not see something that is common to *all,* but similarities, relationships, and a whole series of them at that. . . .—Are they all 'amusing'? Compare chess with noughts and

106. *P.I.,* sect. 23.
107. *Ibid.,* sect. 304.
108. *Ibid.,* sect. 11.
109. *B.B.,* p. 17.
110. *P.I.,* sect. 92 (my italics).
111. R. Rhees, *Discussions of Wittgenstein,* p. 48 (my italics).

crosses. Or is there always winning and losing . . .? Think of Patience.
. . ."[112] Admittedly there are "similarities" between particular games.
Otherwise they would not all be games. But Wittgenstein believes that
these are best described as "family resemblances," not as members of a
class which represents the essence of all games.

It is in keeping with this approach that Wittgenstein refuses to define
the essence of a language-game. What it means depends on how it is used
in particular contexts. Sometimes, for example, Wittgenstein uses the
notion of language-games to describe a simplified working model of language in action. This notion emerges in the middle period and especially in
the *Blue Book,* but is never left behind in the later writings. In the
transitional *Philosophische Bemerkungen* Wittgenstein begins to conceive
of language as a network of interrelated sub-systems, rather than as one
uniform system.[113] In the *Blue Book* Helen Hervey's verdict seems to
hold good that "the chief purpose of the model language-games . . . is to
weaken the hold of the denotative theory of meaning, by paying attention
to particular cases."[114] But they seem to retain the status of simplified
examples which have been abstracted from a more complex language.[115]
In the *Brown Book* and the *Investigations,* as Rhees puts it, the language-
games "are not stages in the development of a more complicated language. . . . But they are stages in a discussion leading up to the 'big
question' of what language is."[116]

Thus there is a second main point behind Wittgenstein's discussion of
language-games. It calls attention to the close connection between *language and life; to* speaking as an *activity.* He states, "The term
'language-*game*' is meant to bring into prominence the fact that the
speaking of language is part of an activity, or of a form of life."[117] He
applies the term not simply to language, but to a totality "consisting of
language and the actions into which it is woven."[118] "To imagine a
language is to imagine a form of life *(Lebensform).*"[119] For, as he expresses it in the *Zettel,* "Only in the stream of thought and life do words have
meaning."[120]

Superficially it might appear that all Wittgenstein is doing is endorsing what was long before recognized by linguists such as Ferdinand de
Saussure that language is "a set of linguistic habits," and "its social

112. *P.I.,* sect. 65.
113. *P.B.,* II, sects. 13-15.
114. H. Hervey, "The Problem of the Model Language-Game in Wittgenstein's Later
Philosophy" in *Philosophy* XXXVI (1961), 345.
115. Cf. *B.B.,* p. 17.
116. *Ibid.,* p. ix.
117. *P.I.,* sect. 23.
118. *Ibid.,* sect. 7.
119. *Ibid.,* sect. 19.
120. *Z.,* sect. 173.

nature is one of its main characteristics."[121] But this would be entirely to miss Wittgenstein's point. Wittgenstein is talking about language from the point of view of its content, its logic, or its "grammar" in the philosophical sense. He observes, "We talk about it as we do about the pieces in chess when we are stating the rules of the game, not describing their physical properties."[122] The key point is, therefore, that "When language-games change, then there is a change in concepts, and with the concepts the meanings of words change."[123] Indeed what speaking *is*, and what meaning *is*, depends on the surroundings in which language is being spoken.

Much of Wittgenstein's work in the *Philosophical Investigations* consists of showing how changes of linguistic surroundings affect particular concepts which are of importance for philosophy. Thus he asks: "What would it mean to cry 'I am not *conscious*'? . . . A man can pretend to be unconscious; but *conscious?*"[124] Uses of "believe" are also embedded in life-situations: "If there were a verb meaning 'to believe falsely', it would not have any significant first person present indicative. . . . My relation to my own words is wholly different from other people's."[125] Or: "Love is not a feeling. Love is put to the test, pain not. One does not say: 'That was not true pain, or it would not have gone off so quickly.' "[126] On the other hand, "Could someone have a feeling of ardent love or hope for the space of one second—*no matter what* preceded or followed this second? . . . The surroundings give it its importance. And the word 'hope' refers to a phenomenon of human life. (A smiling mouth *smiles* only in a human face.)"[127] If we can speak of one man's having another man's gold tooth, why can we not also speak of his having the other man's toothache?[128] Part of the answer turns on the grammar of the word "pain": "The concept of pain is characterized by its particular function in our life. Pain has *this* position in our life; has *these* connexions. . . . Only surrounded by certain normal manifestations of life, is there such a thing as an expression of pain."[129]

It is on this kind of basis that Rhees comments of Wittgenstein's work, "Speaking is not *one thing*, and 'having meaning' is not one thing either."[130] This is emphatically not to say that language-games are self-contained systems, as we noted would tend to be the case in van Buren's

121. F. de Saussure, *Course in General Linguistics*, p. 77.
122. *P.I.*, sect. 108.
123. *Cert.*, sect. 65.
124. *Z.*, sects. 394-95.
125. *P.I.* II.x, pp. 190 and 192.
126. *Z.*, sect. 504.
127. *P.I.*, sect. 583; cf. *Z.*, sects. 53-68.
128. *B.B.*, pp. 48-55.
129. *Z.*, sects. 532-34.
130. R. Rhees, *Discussions of Wittgenstein*, p. 75; cf. pp. 71-84.

interpretation of Wittgenstein, and might almost be implied by Peter Winch and William Hordern in their otherwise illuminating studies.[131] It is rather that, as Wittgenstein notes in the *Zettel,* "What determines . . . our concepts and reactions is . . . the whole hurly-burly of human actions, the background against which we see any action."[132] Or in the *Remarks:* "The kinds of use we feel to be 'the point' are connected with the rôle that such-and-such a use has in our whole life."[133]

We have noted that this emphasis on particularity and on "life" is characteristic of a hermeneutical approach to language. We may now note two further points of connection between Wittgenstein and hermeneutics. First of all, Wittgenstein sees language-games as operating within a context that lives, grows, and moves on. In other words, while he does not give the kind of place to history and time that Heidegger does, nevertheless he indirectly takes account of *historical and temporal change.* Thus, commenting on the multiplicity of its language-games, Wittgenstein remarks, "This multiplicity is not something fixed, given once for all; but new types of language, new language-games . . . come into existence, and others become obsolete and get forgotten."[134] This is why (in spite of Strawson's subsequent criticism) he speaks here of "*countless* kinds."[135] These include, for example, "giving orders and obeying them, describing the appearance of an object, or giving its measurements, constructing an object from a description . . . , reporting an event . . . making up a story and reading it . . . guessing a riddle, making a joke . . . asking, thanking, cursing, greeting, praying."[136] He compares language with an ancient city: "a maze of little streets and squares, of old and new houses, or houses with additions from various periods; and this surrounded by a multitude of new boroughs with straight rectangular streets and uniform houses."[137]

Secondly, Wittgenstein grounds his notion of language-games in human practice, use, application, or training. Norman Malcolm rightly warns us that in holding that (in many cases) the meaning of an expression is its use, "Wittgenstein was not declaring that the words 'meaning' and 'use' are general synonyms. By the 'use' of an expression he meant the special circumstances, the 'surroundings', in which it is spoken or writ-

131. Cf. W. Hordern, *Speaking of God. The Nature and Purpose of Theological Language* (Epworth Press, London, 1964), pp. 81-92 *et passim.*
132. *Z.,* sect. 567.
133. *R.F.M.* I, sect. 16, p. 8.
134. *P.I.,* sect. 23.
135. *Ibid.* Cf. P. F. Strawson, "Critical Notice of Wittgenstein's *Philosophical Investigations*" in H. Morick (ed.), *Wittgenstein and the Problem of Other Minds* (McGraw-Hill, New York, 1967), pp. 6-7; cf. pp. 3-42.
136. *P.I.,* sect. 23.
137. *Ibid.,* sect. 18.

ten. The use of an expression is the *language game* in which it plays a part."[138]

Wittgenstein does say, "For a *large* class of cases—though not for all—in which we employ the word 'meaning' *(Bedeutung),* it can be defined thus: the meaning of a word is its use in the language *(sein Gebrauch in der Sprache)."*[139] But this is not to be interpreted as a generalizing slogan about meaning. It is a way of making a particular point. It is also true that, as Garth Hallett carefully argues, the notion of "use" does enter into the *Tractatus.*[140] Wittgenstein explicitly states there: "If a sign is useless *(nicht gebraucht),* it is meaningless."[141] In the later period, however, the emphasis is especially on the contrast between what may come "before our minds" and the application of language, with special reference to the contrast between picture and application. "The same thing can come before our minds . . . and the application *(Anwendung)* still be different."[142] Wittgenstein illustrates the point by means of an example. He writes, "Imagine a picture representing a boxer in a particular stance. Now, this picture can be used to tell someone how he should stand, should hold himself; or how he should not hold himself; or how a particular man did stand in such-and-such a place, and so on. . . ."[143]

The hermeneutical significance of this point emerges most clearly in Wittgenstein's rejection of the view that ostensive definition is the basis of language and understanding, in favor of his later realization that the decisive factor is "training" *(Abrichtung).* We noted his criticism of ostensive definition in our consideration of meaning as reference in our earlier chapter on hermeneutics and language. In the *Blue Book* he comments, "The ostensive definition 'this is tove' can be interpreted in all sorts of ways. . . . 'This is a pencil'; 'This is round'; 'This is wood'; 'This is one'; 'This is hard', etc."[144] In the *Investigations* he suggests, "Point to a piece of paper.—And now point to its shape—now to its colour—now to its number. . . . How did you do it?" He insists, "An ostensive definition can be variously interpreted in *every* case."[145] In Strawson's words, "The efficacy of these procedures depends on the existence of a prepared framework of linguistic training."[146]

138. N. Malcolm, "Wittgenstein" in P. Edwards (ed.), *The Encyclopedia of Philosophy* VIII, 337.
139. *P.I.,* sect. 43.
140. G. Hallett, *Wittgenstein's Definition of Meaning as Use* (Fordham University Press, New York, 1967), pp. 8-32.
141. *T.,* 3.328; cf. 3.326.
142. *P.I.,* sect. 140.
143. *Ibid.,* p. 11 (additional note).
144. *B.B.,* p. 2.
145. *P.I.,* sects. 33 and 28.
146. P. F. Strawson, "Critical Notice" in *Wittgenstein and the Problem of Other Minds,* p. 5.

Wittgenstein insists that when a child is learning to talk, "the teach-ing of language is not explanation but training *(Abrichtung)*." Everything turns on "the role which the demonstration (pointing and pronouncing) plays in the whole training and in the use which is made of it in the practice of communication."[147]

Wittgenstein's most devastating application of this insight is to his own earlier work in the *Tractatus*. The point of departure was his notion of "simples" or simple objects, which combined to form a state of affairs that could be portrayed by an elementary proposition. From this followed the conclusion that all meaning must be determinate and exact. But now Wittgenstein asks: What do we mean by "simple" or "exact"? He had imagined that he was beginning from some *a priori* understanding of simples and exactitude. But now he sees that these words have no use "outside a particular language-game."[148] Thus he returns to the question: What *are* "simple constituent parts"? Similarly the concept of "exact-ness" depends on the surroundings in life in which it is used. "Am I inexact when I do not give our distance from the sun to the nearest foot, or tell a joiner the width of a table to the nearest thousandth of an inch?" Wittgenstein concludes, " 'Inexact' is really a reproach, and 'exact' is praise."[149] Questions about logical determinacy, then, are not *a priori* issues, but rest on concepts which have themselves been shaped within particular language-games.

We have now observed at least four points of connection between Wittgenstein's later writings and the hermeneutical problem. First of all, he is concerned to open up a perspective which allows us to notice what was always there to be seen. Secondly, he is concerned not with the generalities of formal logic, but with the particularities of specific language-situations, which may bring about changes in concepts. Thirdly, language-games are grounded in human life and human activities, which are open-ended towards the future and may therefore undergo temporal or historical change. Fourthly, there is no logical *a priori* "behind" training and upbringing in human life which places us in the situations in which we employ language. This comes near to Heidegger's belief that the "world" of Dasein is something prior to subject-object thinking and to cognitive propositions. Indeed, although Wittgenstein's notion of language-games is not identical with Heidegger's notion of worldhood, it has become clear that there are close parallels between the two concepts.

In practice, although I do not think that he uses the actual term "hermeneutics," Peter Winch's work, especially in his essay "Understand-ing a Primitive Society," amounts to what we might describe as a her-

147. *P.I.*, sect. 5 and *B.B.*, p. 80.
148. *P.I.*, sect. 47.
149. *Ibid.*, sect. 88.

meneutical approach to anthropology and the social sciences on the basis of Wittgenstein's philosophy.[150] We alluded at the beginning of this chapter to Apel's discussion of Winch's approach. The strengths as well as some of the difficulties of this approach have been recently discussed by Alan Keightley, with special reference to the whole question of the relation between the particularity of life and culture and the "general" idea of rationality.[151] In one or two statements Keightley recognizes that Wittgenstein's approach moves back beyond the distinction between the wholly "objective" and the purely "subjective." In comparing the more "objective" interpretations of religious language in J. Hick and K. Nielsen with the more "subjective" accounts of Ian Ramsey and others, Keightley states that this is "an *either/or* which would never satisfy the Wittgensteinians" (i.e. especially Peter Winch and D. Z. Phillips). What these writers cannot accept is the alternative "that if religious beliefs do not make claims about an 'objective reference', they are merely subjective attitudes to the world."[152] We are not necessarily endorsing the approaches of Winch and Phillips, and we do not claim that they are without difficulty. However, the point to which Keightley rightly draws attention is that this approach calls for a re-assessment of what we actually mean by such concepts as "objectivity" and "rationality" especially in the context of understanding other cultures and "forms of life." We have seen already that this is one of the major questions posed by the hermeneutics of Heidegger.

55. *The Hermeneutical Significance of the Argument about Private Language and Public Criteria of Meaning*

A vast secondary literature has arisen on the private language argument. In addition to the standard discussions by Malcolm, Strawson, Rhees, Ayer, and many others, O. R. Jones helpfully introduces the subject in a volume of essays entirely on this issue.[153] It is an axiom of modern language-study that language operates on the basis of rules, regularities, or what Fodor and Katz call "mechanisms which are recur-

150. P. Winch, "Understanding a Primitive Society" in D. Z. Phillips (ed.), *Religion and Understanding* (Blackwell, Oxford, 1967), pp. 9-42.
151. A. Keightley, *Wittgenstein, Grammar and God* (Epworth Press, London, 1976).
152. *Ibid.*, p. 108.
153. O. R. Jones (ed.), *The Private Language Argument* (Macmillan, London, 1971). Cf. especially R. Rhees, *Discussions of Wittgenstein*, pp. 55-70, which includes an attack on some of A. J. Ayer's assumptions, and L. Wittgenstein, "Notes for Lectures on 'Private Experience' and 'Sense Data' " in *Ph.R.* LXXVII (1968), 271-320, also rpt. in O. R. Jones (ed.), *The Private Language Argument*, pp. 232-75.

sive."[154] John Searle speaks of language as a "rule-governed form of behaviour."[155] Wittgenstein, however, is cautious about the extent to which speaking a language is rule-*governed*. There are indeed rules, but these are neither entirely prescriptive nor part of a closed system. He writes, "The application of a word is not everywhere bounded by rules. . . . A rule stands there like a signpost."[156] "Our rules leave loop-holes open, and the practice has to speak for itself."[157] Rush Rhees comments, "In some ways it is misleading to talk of rules at all here. But it does make some things clearer—that it is possible to use an expression wrongly, for instance. A rule is something that is *kept*. That is why we can know what we are talking about."[158] In Wittgenstein's words, "A person goes by a sign-post only in so far as there exists a regular use of sign-posts, a custom. . . . It is not possible that there should have been only one occasion on which someone obeyed a rule. . . . To obey a rule, to make a report, to give an order . . . are *customs* (uses, institutions)."[159]

If communication is to take place, if words are to function as *language,* it must be possible to see what kind of thing would count as a check on its application. It would not be sufficient, Wittgenstein urges, for a single speaker to be under the impression that he was following a rule; he must actually follow it. He writes, " 'obeying a rule' is a practice. And to *think* one is obeying a rule is not to obey a rule. Hence it is not possible to obey a rule 'privately': otherwise thinking one was obeying a rule would be the same thing as obeying it."[160] In this connection Malcolm comments, "If the distinction between 'correct' and 'seems correct' has disappeared, then so has the concept *correct*."[161] Effective language presupposes a distinction between correct and mistaken applications of words. For "correct" has no substance unless it carries with it the conception of what being "incorrect" in the same case might amount to.

On this very issue hangs even the capacity to identify, to recognize, to exercise, or to apply concepts. If people could not be brought to use the word "red," for instance, in a regular way, how could I ever say, or even think, "No, that is not red; this word is wrongly applied here"? How can I identify "red" as a concept? Rhees declares, "No one can get the concept

154. J. A. Fodor and J. J. Katz (eds.), *The Structure of Language. Readings in the Philosophy of Language* (Prentice-Hall, Englewood Cliffs, N.J., 1964), p. 11; cf. pp. 1-18 and 479-518.
155. J. R. Searle, *Speech Acts. An Essay in the Philosophy of Language* (Cambridge University Press, 1969), p. 12; cf. pp. 33-42.
156. *P.I.*, sects. 84 and 85.
157. *Cert.*, sect. 139.
158. R. Rhees, *Discussions of Wittgenstein*, p. 56 (his italics).
159. *P.I.*, sects. 198-99 (Wittgenstein's italics).
160. *Ibid.*, sect. 202.
161. N. Malcolm, "Wittgenstein's *Philosophical Investigations*" in *Wittgenstein and the Problem of Other Minds*, p. 48.

of colour just by looking at colours, or of red just by looking at red things. If I have the concept, I know how the word 'red' is used. There must *be* a use, though. . . . The phrase 'the same colour' must mean something and be generally understood, and also 'a different colour.' "[162] Earlier he writes, "The agreement of which I am speaking is something without which it would not be possible for people to 'see' that their reactions . . . or anything else tallied."[163] Wittgenstein observes in *On Certainty*, "A child must learn the use of colour words before it can ask for the name of a colour."[164] "In order to make a mistake, a man must already judge in conformity with mankind."[165] This is also part of the point behind Wittgenstein's memorable aphorism in the *Investigations*, "If a lion could talk, we could not understand him."[166]

The stage has now been set for the problem of private language. It is easy to see what kind of thing would count as a check on the application of language about public or empirical objects. As O. R. Jones comments, "If you think you are using the word 'chair' regularly to refer to the same kind of thing on various occasions, someone else could soon tell you if you are not."[167] But what kind of thing counts as a check on the application of words to feelings, sensations, or "private" experiences? If I know what it is to feel pain, or to feel joy, or to experience "inner" peace *only from my own case*, how can I be aware of any regularity or agreement about the use of "pain," "joy," or "inner peace"? How can I retain any distinction between "correct" and "*seems* correct to me"? What kind of thing would it *be* to make a genuine mistake in the application of such language? What would *count* as a mistake?

According to Wittgenstein, if sensations, feelings, states of mind, and the like were *wholly* or *necessarily* "private," language about them could never have arisen. Since, however, as a matter of fact we do talk intelligibly about them, such an account of private experience can only be rejected.

Because the term "private" has a technical and sometimes ambiguous meaning in the wider debate, several writers suggest other ways of expressing the point behind the term. David Pears, for example, regularly uses the word "unteachable."[169] For what makes language teachable is *its connection with observable regularities in human behavior*. Wittgenstein writes, "What would it be like if human beings showed no outward

162. R. Rhees, *Discussions of Wittgenstein*, pp. 57-58.
163. *Ibid.*, p. 56.
164. *Cert.*, sect. 548. Cf. sects. 527-49.
165. *Ibid.*, sect. 156.
166. *P.I.* II,xi, p. 223. Cf. S. P. Carse, "Wittgenstein's Lion and Christology" in *Th.T.* XXIV (1967), 148-59.
167. O. R. Jones (ed.), *The Private Language Argument*, p. 17.
168. D. Pears, *Wittgenstein*, pp. 142-52.
169. *Ibid.*, p. 147.

signs of pain (did not groan, grimace, etc.)? Then it would be impossible to teach a child the use of the word 'toothache'."[170] Hence, in Malcolm's words, "By a 'private' language is meant one that not merely is not but *cannot* be understood by anyone other than the speaker."[171]

It would be possible at this point to follow most interpreters of Wittgenstein by developing the consequences of this view for the philosophy of mind. Wittgenstein is, in effect, attacking a Cartesian view of mind, according to which sensations and feelings are only contingently related to behavior. Jones, Kenny, and others take up this point.[172] Our present interest, however, is not in the philosophy of mind as such, but in the consequences of this approach for hermeneutics. What is being said is that concepts like "being redeemed," "being spoken to by God," and so on, are made intelligible and "teachable" *not on the basis of private existential experience but on the basis of a public tradition of certain patterns of behavior*. Just as what "pain" means depends on observable regularities in pain-behavior, so what "redemption" means depends on observable regularities in redemption-behavior. To express the point more sharply: *if with Bultmann we substitute an emphasis on the other-worldly and "my" existential experience in place of the public tradition of Old Testament history, the problem of hermeneutics becomes insoluble.* What redemption, for example, is, can best be seen not from "my own experience" but from recurring salvation-patterns in the Exodus, the wilderness wanderings, the Judges, and so on. These model language-games are of course revised and corrected in the light of subsequent history, in accordance with the principle of the hermeneutical circle. But from the point of view of New Testament hermeneutics, Old Testament history provides a necessary starting-point for the elucidation of concepts.

Wittgenstein imagines a critic offering the rejoinder: but I can know what a concept means from my own case. He writes, "Someone tells me that *he* knows what pain is only from his own case!—Suppose everyone had a box with something in it: we call it a 'beetle'. No one can look into anyone else's box, and everyone says he knows what a beetle is only by looking at *his* beetle.—Hence it would be quite possible for everyone to have something different in his box." The thing in the box is not *relevant* to other considerations. It "has no place in the language-game at all; not even as a something: for the box might even be empty.—No, one can 'divide through' by the thing in the box; it cancels out, whatever it is."[173] To try to check the difference between "is correct" and "seems correct"

---

170. *P.I.*, sect. 257.
171. N. Malcolm in *Wittgenstein and the Problem of Other Minds*, p. 46.
172. Cf. O. R. Jones, *The Private Language Argument*, p. 14; and A. Kenny, "Cartesian Privacy" in G. Pitcher (ed.), *Wittgenstein: The Philosophical Investigations*, sect. 293.
173. *P.I.*, sect. 293.

only from my case is, Wittgenstein urges, "as if someone were to buy several copies of the morning paper to assure himself that what it said was true."[174] It is like someone's saying "But I know how tall I am," and laying his hand on top of his head to prove it.[175]

We may now take this point a stage further. Once again the hermeneutical issue is parallel to, but not identical with, that which arises in the philosophy of mind. We have claimed that certain concepts depend for their *intelligibility* on their anchorage in a public historical tradition, such as the life of the Israelite nation. We may now go further, and say that on Wittgenstein's view *these public features are themselves part of the grammar of the concept.* When the Christian says "God has redeemed me," part of the grammar of "redemption," i.e. part of the meaning of the concept, is necessarily bound up with Israel's experiences at the Exodus and in the wilderness. The operation and validity of this principle can best be seen in terms of Wittgenstein's own examples concerning such concepts as "thinking," "meaning," "understanding," "believing," and "expecting." We shall restrict our attention to the last two examples.

Wittgenstein writes, "An expectation is embedded in a situation from which it takes its rise."[176] He admits that we *can* think of expectation as a kind of state or sensation, such as a feeling of tension, for instance.[177] "But in order to understand the grammar of these states it is necessary to ask: 'What counts as a criterion for anyone's being in such a state?' "[178] In this sense, however, a considerable variety of activities may be involved. In the *Blue Book* Wittgenstein examines the phenomenon of "expecting B to come to tea from 4 to 4.30." The variety of significant factors may include: (i) seeing his name in my diary; (ii) preparing tea for two; (iii) wondering whether he smokes, and putting out cigarettes; (iv) beginning to feel impatient towards 4:30; and so on. "All this is called 'expecting B from 4 to 4.30'. And there are endless variations to this process which we all describe by the same expression. . . . There is no single feature in common to all of them."[179]

Wittgenstein insists, on this basis, that "psychological—trivial—discussions about expectation, association, etc., always pass over what is really noteworthy . . . without touching the *punctum saliens.*"[180] For even "the process of thinking will be *very various.* I whistle and someone asks me why I am so cheerful. I reply, 'I'm hoping N. will come

174. *Ibid.*, sect. 265.
175. *Ibid.*, sect. 279.
176. *Z.*, sect. 67. On "expect" see *P.I.*, sects. 572-86; *Z.*, sects. 58-68 and 71-77; *B.B.*, pp. 20-21 and 35-36; and *P.B.*, sects. 21-31.
177. *B.B.*, pp. 20-21.
178. *P.I.*, sect. 572.
179. *B.B.*, p. 20.
180. *Z.*, sect. 66. Cf. *P.B.*, sect. 31.

today'.—But while I whistled I wasn't thinking of him. All the same, it would be wrong to say: I stopped hoping when I began to whistle."[181] "I watch a slow match burning, in high excitement follow the progress of the burning and its approach to the explosive. Perhaps I don't think anything at all, or have a multitude of disconnected thoughts. This is certainly a case of expecting."[182] If I say "I am expecting him," I might mean only: "I should be surprised if he didn't come"; and this "will not be called the description of a state of mind."[183] I may replace the words "I expect an explosion," by "it will go off now"; and this does "not describe a feeling," even if it may admittedly manifest it.[184]

Wittgenstein's observations suggest that we cannot say what "expecting" *amounts to* without reference to its surroundings in the public domain of human behavior. This is therefore part of the grammar of the concept. The same principle applies to "believing." Wittgenstein readily admits that, as in the case of "expecting," in an obvious sense "believing is a state of mind."[185] But what "believing" really amounts to "is shown me in the case of someone else by his behaviour and by his words."[186] In religion, "the strength of a belief is not comparable with the intensity of a pain. . . . A belief isn't like a momentary state of mind. 'At 5 o'clock he had a very bad toothache.' "[187] What it is to have an unshakable religious belief may be seen perhaps in how it regulates "for all in his life."[188]

Even our everyday ways of talking about belief, Wittgenstein seems to imply, suggest that "believing" is not primarily a matter of having certain mental states. He comments, "Really one hardly ever says that one has believed . . . 'uninterruptedly' since yesterday. An interruption of belief would be a period of unbelief, not e.g. the withdrawal of attention from what one believes—e.g. sleep."[189] Similarly: "Does it make sense to ask 'How do you know that you believe?'—and is the answer: 'I know it by introspection?' In *some* cases it will be possible to say some such thing, in most not."[190] The repercussions of adopting this kind of approach to the grammar of "belief" has been discussed both sympathetically and critically by H. H. Price.[191]

Wittgenstein further illustrates the integral connection between con-

181. *Z.*, sects. 63-64.
182. *P.I.*, sect. 576.
183. *Ibid.*, sect. 577.
184. *Ibid.*, sect. 582.
185. *Ibid.* II.x, p. 191. On believing see *ibid.*, sects. 574-75, 577-78, 587, and 589; II.x, pp. 190-93; *B.B.*, pp. 143-47 and 132; *Z.*, sects. 75, 85, and 471; and *L.C.A.P.R.*, pp. 53-64.
186. *P.I.*, pp. 191-92.
187. *L.C.A.P.R.*, p. 54.
188. *Ibid.*
189. *Z.*, sect. 85.
190. *P.I.*, sect. 587.
191. H. H. Price, *Belief* (Allen & Unwin, London, 1969).

cepts and their settings in life with reference to the distinctive logic of certain first-person utterances. The logical grammar, for example, of "I believe," "I understand," or "I am in pain," is not the same as that of the corresponding third-person verbs, and Wittgenstein demonstrates this with reference to considerations about pain-behavior, or how belief or understanding is related to action. Thus the utterance "I am in pain," Wittgenstein claims, "replaces crying," rather than describing either some mental state or the act of crying itself.[192] Similarly the words "Now I understand" correspond to the act of picking up a pen with a flourish and writing down a series of numbers or words. It is like "a glad start."[193] To pursue these points further here, however, would take us beyond the purpose of this chapter.

We have seen that Wittgenstein's concern about the particular case in language, together with his anchoring of language-games in life, both brings us close to the perspectives of hermeneutics, and effectively challenges the more abstract and generalizing approach of the *Tractatus* which led to a sharp dualism between fact and value. In elucidating how Wittgenstein's philosophy of language relates to hermeneutics, therefore, it has also become clear that there are two fundamental weaknesses in Bultmann's hermeneutics, which at bottom turn on the same difficulty. First of all, a sharp dualism between fact and value cannot be sustained against the given ways in which language actually operates in life. Secondly, any attempt to reject the "this-worldly" dimension of the language of revelation and to substitute individual self-understanding for public tradition and history raises insuperable problems for hermeneutics. For the very grammar of the concepts involved is embedded in a history of events and behavior. It is part of the grammar of the concept of "God" that he is the God of Abraham, of Isaac, and of Jacob (Exod. 3:6).

192. *P.I.*, sect. 244.
193. *Ibid.*, sect. 323; cf. sects. 151 and 179-80.

CHAPTER XIV

Wittgenstein, "Grammar," and the New Testament

56. *Grammar, Insight, and Understanding: Examples of a First Class of Grammatical Utterances*

In the *Philosophical Investigations* Wittgenstein remarks that in a certain way of looking at things we find "a whole cloud of philosophy condensed into a drop of grammar."[1] Grammatical clarifications and observations constitute the subject-matter of Wittgenstein's whole work. As we have already suggested, the roots of what he later says about grammar go back to his statements about logic in the *Tractatus,* and especially to his observations about mathematical equations and tautologies. At the end of the *Zettel* he writes, " 'You can't hear God speak to someone else, you can hear him only if you are being addressed'.—That is a grammatical remark."[2] In other words, *its function is not to give information about a state of affairs, but to elucidate the logical grammar of a concept.*

Wittgenstein offers numerous examples of aphorisms or short statements which are very clearly grammatical utterances. He writes, "The proposition 'sensations are private' is comparable to: 'One plays patience by oneself'."[3] These statements give no information above and beyond what is implied by the concepts in question; but they do elucidate what kind of concepts are at issue. Similarly, Wittgenstein writes, "Every rod has a length" says only: "we call something . . . 'the length of a rod' but nothing 'the length of a sphere'."[4] To say that "three" is a numeral, or

1. *P.I.* II.xi, p. 222.
2. *Z.,* sect. 717.
3. *P.I.,* sect. 248.
4. *Ibid.,* sect. 251.

that "green" is a color-word, or that water boils at 100° C is to make a grammatical remark. Often, Wittgenstein comments, when we want to say "I can't imagine the opposite," "these words are a defence against something whose form makes it look like an empirical proposition, but which is really a grammatical one."[5]

Nevertheless it should not be thought that grammatical remarks are necessarily trivial or obvious. The grammar of a concept is not always apparent at first sight. Indeed it is Wittgenstein's claim that traditionally in philosophy the grammar of such concepts as "meaning," "thinking," and even "language" has frequently been misunderstood. Hence he urges that we must distinguish between "surface grammar" and "depth grammar." "Compare the depth grammar, say, of the word, 'to mean', with what its surface grammar would lead us to suspect."[6] In this sense Wittgenstein writes: "Grammar tells what kind of object anything is. (Theology as grammar.)"[7]

Wittgenstein's description of *theology* as grammar reminds us that we have now moved away some distance from the notion of tautologies and logical equations in the *Tractatus*. E. K. Specht discusses the different ways in which it is possible to understand the statement "all grammatical propositions are *a priori;* a grammatical proposition does not depend for its truth value on any empirical fact."[8] From the viewpoint of the *Tractatus* grammatical utterances are simply *analytical* utterances which are *a priori* rather than culture-relative. "All bachelors are unmarried" accords even with Quine's rigid criteria of analyticity, having a form comparable with the statement $\sim (p.\sim p)$. But in his later thought, Specht comments, "Wittgenstein's theory of the *a priori* starts from the language-game model. . . . The world confronts us only within language-games and is thus already articulated in detail. . . . The *a priori* proposition expresses those properties of an object which necessarily belong to it on the basis of the linguistic rules for its name; its truth-value thus depends on the way in which we have gathered objects together and on the linguistic rules that are consequently fixed. An *a priori* proposition thus makes an assertion both about the objects and also about the linguistic rules for the name of the object; for this reason it is a 'grammatical proposition'."[9]

Two consequences follow from this which are significant for the argument of the present chapter. First of all, not all grammatical utterances are "universal" or topic-neutral, in the sense of not being culture-

5. *Ibid.*
6. *Ibid.*, sect. 664.
7. *Ibid.*, sect. 373.
8. E. Specht, *The Foundations of Wittgenstein's Late Philosophy* (Eng. Manchester University Press, 1969), p. 153.
9. *Ibid.*, pp. 154-55.

relative; or, we might say, relative to *certain* language-games rather than to *all* language-games. Secondly, grammatical utterances relate not to information but to *understanding*. To understand a language-game entails knowledge of its grammar. In this sense, grammar is bound up with hermeneutics. We may comment on this second point further before we return to the first.

In the course of his many criticisms of linguistic philosophy, Ernest Gellner refers disparagingly to a noticeable tendency among admirers of Wittgenstein to describe his various observations or views as "in-sights."[10] Characteristically, Gellner assumes that this must be "in view of their elusiveness."[2] A more adequate explanation for the use of the term "insight," however, is that Wittgenstein's remarks amount to grammatical statements; and these convey insights, rather than informa-tion about the world. Stuart Brown admirably shows what is achieved, in this sense, by "insight." He explains, "There are . . . two different kinds of advance in knowledge. One of them, which *consists* in the acquisition of new pieces of information, takes place only *within* an accepted concep-tion of reality. It involves, that is to say, no alteration of the conceptual apparatus in terms of which experience is understood." However, "There is another kind which *makes possible* the finding of new information by providing a change in, or extension of, concepts already available. It is, first and foremost, an *advance in understanding*."[11] In a section entitled "Theology as Grammar" Brown illustrates his point with reference to C. H. Dodd's interpretation of the relation between sin and divine retribu-tion in Romans 1:18-32.[12] If Dodd is correct, retribution stands not in an external relation to sin, but serves to elucidate the very grammar of what sin *is*. Thereby it extends the horizons of the reader to *understand* the concept more adequately.

To return now to the first of our two points: if grammatical utterances are not all universal or analytical, is it perhaps possible to distinguish between different types or classes of grammatical utterances? We shall try to show that it is, and moreover that it is also possible to distinguish between characteristic settings in which these occur. From the point of view of New Testament studies this will take us into what amounts to a form-critical discussion of certain passages in the New Testament itself. Part of the purpose of this investigation will be to throw light on the function of a type of utterance that is usually neglected in biblical studies. But it will also bring us back to the question which we raised in connec-tion with the hermeneutics of Troeltsch, Nineham, and Pannenberg, about

10. E. Gellner, *Words and Things* (Pelican edn., London, 1968), p. 180.
11. S. C. Brown, *Do Religious Claims Make Sense?* (S.C.M., London, 1969), p. 118.
12. *Ibid.,* pp. 147-52.

whether certain axioms in the New Testament could be better described as culture-relative or as expressing particular *religious* convictions.

We begin by marking off eight clear examples of "universal," topic-neutral, or "class-one" grammatical utterances. For the sake of convenience we shall restrict our selection to the Pauline epistles. We shall see that all of these amount to being analytical utterances, which are not culture-relative.

(1) In Romans 11:6 Paul writes: εἰ δὲ χάριτι, οὐκέτι ἐξ ἔργων, ἐπεὶ ἡ χάρις οὐκέτι γίνεται χάρις. C. K. Barrett observes, "Paul is here defining his terms. . . . If you confuse such opposites as faith and works, then words will simply lose their meaning."[13] The opposition, or mutual exclusion, between the two concepts under discussion in this verse provides a paradigm case of what grace amounts to. If grace does not exclude the notion of works, it can mean either nothing or everything. Other commentators make this point equally clearly. What is at issue is, as Otto Michel puts it, the "concept" of grace.[14] Paul is not giving any information of which his readers are unaware, but he is clarifying their *concept* of grace. In other words, he is making a grammatical remark. But it is impossible to conceive of a language-situation in which the function of the utterance would become different.

(2) In Romans 4:4 Paul states: τῷ δὲ ἐργαζομένῳ ὁ μισθὸς οὐ λογίζεται κατὰ χάριν ἀλλὰ κατὰ ὀφείλημα. Here the very same principle operates. Indeed Otto Kuss explicitly describes the statement as "analytical" rather than synthetic.[15] Although he reformulates the notion of "counted" as it occurs in Genesis 15:6 (LXX), Paul is not so much putting a case as laying down a paradigm. Just as "due" is implied in the grammar of the concept "wages," so it is excluded from the grammar of "grace."

(3) In Romans 8:24 Paul declares: ἐλπὶς δὲ βλεπομένη οὐκ ἔστιν ἐλπίς. ὃ γὰρ βλέπει τίς ἐλπίζει; Barrett paraphrases this with "Hope really means hope," and Bultmann describes it as an appeal to formal logic.[16]

(4) In 1 Corinthians 13:10 Paul writes: ὅταν δὲ ἔλθῃ τὸ τέλειον, τὸ ἐκ μέρους καταργηθήσεται. The logical status of this verse may be less clear than in the previous cases. If, with C. K. Barrett, we interpret τὸ τέλειον in terms of "totality," its analytical character can perhaps hardly be in

---

13. C. K. Barrett, *A Commentary on the Epistle to the Romans* (Black, London, [2]1962), p. 209.
14. O. Michel, *Der Römerbrief* (Vandenhoeck & Ruprecht, Göttingen, [4]1966), pp. 267-68; cf. W. Sanday and A. C. Headlam, *A Critical and Exegetical Commentary on the Epistle to the Romans* (Clark, Edinburgh, [5]1902), p. 313; and F. J. Leenhardt, *The Epistle to the Romans* (Eng. Lutterworth, London, 1961), p. 279.
15. O. Kuss, *Der Römerbrief* (2 vols., continuing; Pustet, Regensburg, [2]1963), pp. 181-82.
16. C. K. Barrett, *Romans*, p. 167; R. Bultmann in *Theological Dictionary of the New Testament* II, 531.

question.[17] Similarly, Hans Lietzmann and H. D. Wendland view the contrast in question in terms of the mutual exclusion implicit in *Stückwerk* and *Vollkommenheit;* and Johannes Weiss, in terms of the opposition between *"Ganze"* and *"Teile."*[18] Even if τὸ τέλειον is understood differently, however, the context of thought seems to suggest that the statement is still analytical. Prophecy is associated with the imperfect or fragmentary; love can never lose its relevance, even in the consummation of the new age. The contrast and its implications are brought into focus and elucidated by means of a statement about the grammar of two opposing concepts, namely τὸ τέλειον and τὸ ἐκ μέρους.

(5) In spite of the admitted difficulty of the verse, we clearly have a further instance of a straightforward analytical statement in Paul's words in Galatians 3:20, ὁ δὲ μεσίτης ἑνὸς οὐκ ἔστιν. In his commentary on this epistle, E. D. Burton, for one, concludes that this sentence amounts to "a general statement deduced from the very definition of a mediator." He explains, "From the duality of the persons between whom the mediator acts and the fact that God is but one person, the inference intended to be drawn is that the law, being given through a mediator, came from God indirectly. . . . The promise came directly. . . ."[19] A. Oepke also considers that Paul's aim is to elucidate "the concept" of mediator, while D. Guthrie says that he expresses "a truism."[20] However, whereas G. S. Duncan, seeing that the words convey no information, claims that the sentence "seems to add nothing of real value to Paul's argument," Guthrie rightly sees that the truism enables the readers to put the law in a different category from the promise.[21] It affects not *what* they see but *how* they see.

(6) In some instances it may be tempting to overlook the grammatical character of an utterance on the grounds that its formulation owes more to stylistic considerations than to other factors. This may apply, for example, to Paul's use of cognate forms in Galatians 5:1: τῇ ἐλευθερίᾳ ἡμᾶς Χριστὸς ἠλευθέρωσεν. P. Bonnard, for instance, explains the form in terms of the emotion felt by its author.[22] Alternatively, might this not be simply a linguistic pleonasm which carries no particular significance? A. Oepke

17. C. K. Barrett, *A Commentary on the First Epistle to the Corinthians* (Black, London, 1968), p. 306.
18. H. Lietzmann, *An die Korinther* I-II (Mohr, Tübingen, 1949), p. 66. H. D. Wendland, *Die Briefe an die Korinther* (Vandenhoeck & Ruprecht, Göttingen, 1910), p. 318.
19. E. de Witt Burton, *A Critical and Exegetical Commentary on the Epistle to the Galatians* (Clark, Edinburgh, 1921), pp. 190-92.
20. A. Oepke, *Der Brief des Paulus an die Galater* (Evangelische Verlag, Berlin, ³1964), pp. 82-84; and D. Guthrie, *Galatians* (Nelson, London, 1969), p. 110.
21. G. S. Duncan, *The Epistle of Paul to the Galatians* (Hodder & Stoughton, London, 1934), p. 115; cf. D. Guthrie, *Galatians.*
22. P. Bonnard, *L'épitre de Saint Paul aux Galates* (Delachaux et Niestlé, Neuchâtel, 1953), pp. 101-02.

and D. Guthrie, however, convincingly argue that it is otherwise.[23] The apostle demands of his readers how it can *make sense* to speak of having been "freed" by Christ, if this freedom does not entail their release from bondage and subsequent status as free men. If they relapse into bondage they cannot *also* claim to be free, except in some purely private and esoteric sense of the term. Paul is concerned to open their understanding by elucidating the grammar of a concept.

(7) Another example comes in Romans 13:10: ἡ ἀγάπη τῷ πλησίον κακὸν οὐκ ἐργάζεται. Admittedly C. K. Barrett argues that the statement "is regarded by Paul as the ground for the claim of v. 8," namely ὁ γὰρ ἀγαπῶν τὸν ἕτερον νόμον πεπλήρωκεν. Further, it may be that he wishes to show that "love" also does not entail less than obedience to the civil law, which was the main subject of discussion in vv. 1-7. F. J. Leenhardt also argues for this conclusion.[24] On this or on any other basis, however, the statement in v. 10b, πλήρωμα οὖν νόμου ἡ ἀγάπη, no more rests on empirical observations about conduct, than ἡ ἀγάπη τῷ πλησίον κακὸν οὐκ ἐργάζεται. The point can *only* be a conceptual one. For if anyone attempted to appeal to empirical phenomena in order to show that love could in practice bring harm to someone, the reply could always be made, "*That* wasn't a genuine example of the concept under discussion."

(8) In 1 Corinthians 14:11 Paul writes, ἐὰν οὖν μὴ εἰδῶ τὴν δύναμιν τῆς φωνῆς, ἔσομαι τῷ λαλοῦντι βάρβαρος καὶ ὁ λαλῶν ἐν ἐμοὶ βάρβαρος. Among other things, Paul is concerned to point out that the concept of "foreigner" is double-edged. Ovid notes that not only do foreigners appear as βάρβαροι to the Roman citizen; but also "barbarus hic ego sum, quia non intellegor ulli."[25] Hence Paul believes that the very *concept* has no application, without self-contradiction, as a description of relations between different fellow-believers. His argument to the Corinthians, then, turns on a grammatical remark about the concept of "foreigner."

These eight examples could easily be extended. Other instances might include Galatians 6:3: "if anyone thinks he is something when he is nothing, he deceives himself" (which finds a parallel in Plato); 1 Corinthians 12:14: "a body is not one member but many" (which also finds a parallel in Epictetus); Romans 6:16; 10:14; 2 Corinthians 13:8; and Galatians 3:18.[26] Other examples could be added from outside the Pauline epistles. The function of these utterances is not to give fresh information, but simply to expand the horizons of the reader's *understanding*. In this sense they are *hermeneutical*. However, the purpose of noting these examples is not only to list occurrences of a certain type of statement; it is

23. A. Oepke, *Der Brief des Paulus an die Galater*, p. 118; and D. Guthrie, *Galatians*, p. 135.
24. C. K. Barrett, *Romans*, p. 251; F. J. Leenhardt, *Romans*, p. 338.
25. Ovid, *Tristia* V.10.37.
26. Plato, *Apology* 33.41 E; and Epictetus, *Discourses* II.5.24, 25.

also to mark off this particular type of grammatical utterance from other types, with a view to suggesting certain conclusions about their settings.

57. A Second Class of Grammatical Utterances and the Respective Life-Settings of the Two Classes

In his last notes published under the title *On Certainty* Wittgenstein considers a special class of statement about which the speaker would, as it were, "like to say: 'If I am wrong about *this*, I have no guarantee that anything I say is true'."[27] As in the case of our first class of grammatical utterances, a speaker would be tempted to say: "I cannot imagine the opposite." But in this case, he would be *expressing the attitude of a particular tradition*. The opposite would be inconceivable *within* a given cultural or perhaps religious tradition. Nevertheless, the grammatical character of formulations within this class should not be overlooked, simply because they might cease to be "grammatical" outside the tradition in question. In Wittgenstein's words, they amount to "hinges" on which other statement or inquiries turn.[28] They articulate "the scaffolding of our thoughts."[29]

Wittgenstein compares this type of utterance with propositions which have the status or function of the words "It is written. . . ."[30] Within particular communities they have become virtually unquestioned or even unquestionable axioms; they function "as a *foundation* for research and action," but are often simply "isolated from doubt, though not according to any explicit rule."[31] Wittgenstein seems to suggest that in any culture, including our own, "all enquiry . . . is set so as to exempt certain propositions from doubt. . . . They lie apart from the route travelled by enquiry."[32] In due course, an axiom may become "fossilized."[33] "It is removed from the traffic. It is so to speak shunted onto an unused siding."[34] But it does not thereby lose its significance; rather, its significance has changed into that of a grammatical proposition. "Now it gives our way of looking at things, and our researches, their form *(unsern Betrachtungen, unsern Forschungen, ihre Form)*. Perhaps it was once

27. *Cert.*, sect. 69 (Wittgenstein's italics).
28. *Ibid.*, sects 343 and 655.
29. *Ibid.*, sect. 211.
30. *Ibid.*, sect. 216.
31. *Ibid.*, sect. 87.
32. *Ibid.*, sect. 88.
33. *Ibid.*, sect. 657.
34. *Ibid.*, sect. 210.

disputed. But perhaps, for unthinkable ages, it has belonged to the *scaffolding* of our thoughts. (Every human being has parents.)"[35]

Such utterances, Wittgenstein notes, "have a peculiar logical role in the system of our empirical propositions."[36] We "discover" them, "like the axis around which a body rotates. . . . The movement around it determines its immobility."[37] For, in practice, "what I hold fast to is not *one* proposition but a nest of propositions."[38] Each twig, as it were, is "held fast by what lies around it."[39] Thus, as in the case of ordinary *grammatical* statements, if someone challenges an unshakable "hinge" proposition from within the community or culture in question, "I would not know what such a person would still allow to be counted as evidence and what not."[40] "What *counts* as a test?"[41] The decisive point is that "our talk gets its meaning from the rest of our proceedings."[42]

(1) In Romans 3:4, 5b, 6, Paul declares: γινέσθω δὲ ὁ θεὸς ἀληθής, πᾶς δὲ ἄνθρωπος ψεύστης . . . μὴ ἄδικος ὁ θεὸς ὁ ἐπιφέρων τὴν ὀργήν; κατὰ ἄνθρωπον λέγω. μὴ γένοιτο; ἐπεὶ πῶς κρινεῖ ὁ θεὸς τὸν κόσμον; Both for Paul and for most, if not all, of his readers, the justice and truthfulness of God constitutes an unshakable axiom which cannot be questioned without, among other things, calling in question the very tradition of life and thought to which they belong. It has itself become a fixed hinge on which further statements or inquiries turn. Thus in v. 6 Paul exclaims, "If God were unjust, how could he judge the world?" Although strictly the "must" and "could" of the N.E.B. have no isomorphic counterpart in the Greek, the words admirably reflect the logical force of the passage. The twice-repeated μὴ γένοιτο of vv. 4 and 6 amount, in net effect, to the *grammatical* use of "cannot" in "God cannot lie."

Paul gives expression to a fixed point which lies, as it were, apart from the route travelled by inquiry because so much revolves around it. Thus C. H. Dodd comments, "It is not, of course, an argument. . . . At best all that Paul says is, 'You and I both agree that it is inconceivable that God should be unjust, and you must understand all that I say in that sense.' "[43] Certainly it would be very difficult to see what might "count as a test" of the truth-or-falsity of the axiom within the primitive Christian tradition. This is partly why Paul seems to feel obliged to offer an apology

35. *Ibid.*, sect. 211.
36. *Ibid.*, sect. 136.
37. *Ibid.*, sect. 152.
38. *Ibid.*, sect. 225.
39. *Ibid.*, sect. 144; cf. sect. 142.
40. *Ibid.*, sect. 231; cf. sect. 343.
41. *Ibid.*, sect. 110.
42. *Ibid.*, sect. 229.
43. C. H. Dodd, *The Epistle of Paul to the Romans* (Hodder & Stoughton, London, 1932), p. 45.

for even raising the issue: κατὰ ἄνθρωπον λέγω (v. 5). Commenting on the use of μή rather than οὐ in framing the hypothetical objection μὴ ἄδικος ὁ θεός, C. K. Barrett notes, "Paul . . . cannot bring himself to put on paper even the grammatical implication that God is unjust." "The truth, or faithfulness, of God is to be believed, even though maintaining it . . . leads to the conclusion that all men are liars."[44] Paul might have said, in Wittgenstein's words, "If I am wrong about *this*, I have no guarantee that anything I say is true."[45] "I can't imagine the opposite."[46] "I have reached bedrock, and my spade is turned."[47]

(2) A close parallel is provided by Romans 9:14-24. Paul exclaims, again, μὴ ἀδικία παρὰ τῷ θεῷ; μὴ γένοιτο (v. 14). God has mercy, Paul states, on whom he wills, and whom he will he "hardens" (v. 18). He considers the objection, "You will say to me, 'If this is so, why does he (God) still make complaints? For who can resist his will?' " (v. 19). But Paul questions the very propriety of the critic's question: If God is *God*, "who are you to answer back to God?" (v. 20). Borrowing the analogy from the Old Testament (cf. Jer. 18:1 and Isa. 45:9), Paul insists that the reader can no more challenge God's justice than the clay may challenge the decision of the potter.

C. H. Dodd argues that "The objection is right. . . . It is the weakest point in the whole epistle." He adds, "When Paul, normally a clear thinker, becomes obscure, it usually means that he is embarrassed by the position he has taken up. It is surely so here."[48] But Paul's purpose here is, in Leenhardt's words, "to help his readers *to adjust their field of vision.*"[49] Paul is drawing on a tradition of thought, familiar in first-century Judaism, within which part of what is entailed in God's being God is that his verdicts cannot be challenged by guilty men. Thus in the Wisdom of Solomon the writer asserts: "For to thee no one can say, 'What hast thou done?' or dispute thy verdict. Who shall bring a charge against thee for destroying nations which were of thy own making? . . . For there is no other god but thee . . ." (Wis. 12:12, 13; cf. vv. 14-18).

(3) In several cases, further examples from this class of grammatical utterances are indicated by Paul's use of δύναμαι. In Romans 8:7, 8, for instance, it is already largely implicit in Paul's use of σάρξ (in certain contexts) that οἱ δὲ ἐν σαρκὶ ὄντες θεῷ ἀρέσαι οὐ δύνανται. The use of "cannot" does not mark an *empirical* limitation so much as a grammatical one. In C. K. Barrett's words, "For the flesh to be obedient to God is a contradiction in terms, for 'flesh' in this context means a mind from which

44. C. K. Barrett, *Romans*, p. 64.
45. *Cert.*, sect. 69.
46. *P.I.*, sect. 251.
47. *Ibid.*, sect. 217; cf. *Cert.*, sects. 204-16.
48. C. H. Dodd, *Romans*, pp. 158-59.
49. F. J. Leenhardt, *Romans*, p. 255 (my italics).

God is excluded."[50] But since this understanding of σάρξ remains relative to a particular theological tradition or frame, this would hardly amount to a topic-neutral grammatical utterance. This last point is perhaps still clearer in 1 Corinthians 2:14, where the theme is partly parallel to that of Romans 8:7, 8: οὐ δύναται γνῶναι ὅτι πνευματικῶς ἀνακρίνεται.

(4) The corollary of this theme appears in 1 Corinthians 12:3: οὐδεὶς δύναται εἰπεῖν Κύριος Ἰησοῦς, εἰ μὴ ἐν πνεύματι ἁγίῳ. The use of δύναμαι with an infinitive is matched by an ordinary indicative in the parallel clause (v.3a, λέγει). "Cannot" in the second part of the verse is hardly empirical, especially since questions about the Spirit constitute the focus of attention, rather than the human activity of making a confession of faith. Paul is not inviting his readers to imagine that someone tries hard to make such a confession, but fails to bring it off, in the event, without the aid of the Spirit. Paul's concern, rather, is with the grammar of Christian "spirituality"; with what being inspired by the Spirit amounts to. The heart of the matter, F. F. Bruce suggests, is that "every true Christian, in short, is a 'spiritual person'."[51] The hinge on which all subsequent inquiries turn is the unshakable conviction that the Spirit is the Spirit of Christ in the sense which Paul outlines, for example, in Romans 8:14, 15. Thus "cannot" in 1 Corinthians 12:3 expresses a conviction which has now become a settled part of the grammar of Paul's statements about the Spirit.

We have been considering examples of a second class of grammatical utterances of which Wittgenstein says that "they lie apart from the route travelled by inquiry"; they articulate "the scaffolding of our thoughts"; they give us "our way of looking at things." They are "hinges" on which other propositions turn. In chapter three (especially sect. 9) we discussed D. E. Nineham's claims, made in the light of work by T. E. Hulme, that certain presuppositions lie so far back in the outlook of a given culture that the people of that culture "are never really conscious of them. They do not see them, but rather other things *through* them."[52] They are "doctrines seen as facts." This is exactly the kind of thing that Wittgenstein has in mind in *On Certainty*. The propositions that express them so take their truth for granted that *within a given tradition* their denial is inconceivable. More than this, they are so axiomatic that they "lie apart from the route travelled by inquiry."

Does this mean that our attempt to isolate a second class of grammatical utterances serves to confirm Nineham's claims? The answer is

50. C. K. Barrett, *Romans*, p. 158. Cf. O. Kuss, *Der Römerbrief* II, 500; O. Michel, *Der Römerbrief*, pp. 191-92; and A. Sand, *Der Begriff "Fleisch" in den Paulinischen Hauptbriefen*, pp. 196-97.
51. F. F. Bruce, *I and II Corinthians* (Oliphants, London, 1971), p. 118. Cf. H. Lietzmann, *An die Korinther*, p. 61; and C. K. Barrett, *I Corinthians*, pp. 279-81.
52. See above, chapter three, sect. 9.

both yes and no. It does seem to confirm Nineham's claim that such outlooks are presupposed in the New Testament itself. However, it does not corroborate Nineham's claim that these are *cultural* axioms. The examples which we have considered are in fact in each case those which express a distinctively *theological* subject-matter. What is significant about the tradition within which these propositions function grammatically is that they are *theological* traditions. But this was precisely the point at issue in Pannenberg's critique of Troeltsch, and thereby, indirectly, of Nineham.

The weakest point about our own case is that admittedly it rests only on selective examples. It would take us far beyond the confines of the present study to attempt an exhaustive classification of all grammatical utterances in the New Testament. Even then, such a classification would not establish a definitive case, for not all beliefs of this kind find explicit expression in grammatical utterances. However, it is possible to argue, along the lines of a form-critical analysis, that the *distinctive* setting of this second class of grammatical utterances seems to be that of theological argument or belief, as against the first class of topic-neutral grammatical utterances, which occur in settings which may or may not be theological. If so, the balance of evidence would be against Nineham's use of the term "cultural" where Pannenberg and probably others would prefer to speak of religious beliefs or theological convictions. We are not suggesting that the New Testament writers are somehow exempt from taking for granted certain culture-relative assumptions of which they are scarcely aware. But we do suggest that some assumptions which are articulated in class-two grammatical utterances are distinctively theological, and that it is therefore misleading to describe *all* such assumptions as *culture*-relative.

The present inquiry differs from normal form-critical procedure in at least one important respect. Instead of determining "form" in terms of what Wittgenstein would call "the physical properties" of language, we are attempting to classify forms on the basis of their logical function. This is not to abandon form-critical method, but to try to make it less arbitrary and more soundly based, since the actual "physical properties" of a stretch of language are more likely to have been determined by accidental factors than would be the case with logical function. Just as John Sawyer has argued that there is a parallel between *Sitz im Leben* in form-criticism and context of situation in semantics, we are suggesting that there is a parallel between *Sitz im Leben* and the settings in which given logical functions are grounded.[53] In other words, *Sitz im Leben* is a parallel to the concept of language-games.

A comparison between the New Testament material and other con-

---

53. J. F. A. Sawyer, "Context of Situation and *Sitz im Leben*" in *Proceedings of the Newcastle-upon-Tyne Philosophical Society* I (1967), 137-47.

temporary literature suggests that class-one topic-neutral grammatical utterances regularly feature in the setting of a dialogue or argument which is based on an open-ended rational appeal, while class-two grammatical utterances regularly occur in the context of an appeal which presupposes a given religious or ethical "common understanding." Class-one grammatical utterances simply pave the way for an extension or clarification of concepts that leads to fresh understanding. Thus with our eight or more examples of class-one grammatical utterances in the Pauline epistles we may compare the following, from Greek or Latin writers outside the New Testament.

In Plato's *Gorgias* Socrates clarifies the difference in logical grammar between the concept of belief (πίστις) and knowledge (ἐπιστήμη) by stating that while belief may be true or false, we cannot speak of a "knowledge" which may be true or false.[54] Similarly the stranger in *The Sophist* is not making a merely trivial comment, but calling attention to the grammar of a concept when he says: τὸ ἀληθινὸν ὄντως ὂν λέγων; . . . τὸ μὴ ἀληθινὸν ἆρ' ἐναντίον ἀληθοῦς;[55] Horace, Seneca, and Quintilian all make grammatical statements about the concepts of virtue and vice. Horace writes, "Virtus est vitium Fugere et sapientia prima stultitia caruisse."[56] Quintilian similarly asserts, "Prima virtus est vitio carere."[57] Seneca adds, "Nihil invenies rectius recto, non magis quam verius vero, quam temperator temperatius. . . ."[58] None of these statements presupposes a particular ethical tradition, unlike other grammatical utterances about ethics which we shall consider. From any point of view, nothing is more right than "right"; otherwise it would not be "right." Similarly the writer of *Corpus Hermeticum* Tractate 13 is making a conceptual point, not a religious or theological one, when he states that knowledge excludes ignorance, joy takes away grief, and truth drives out deceit.[59] Similarly the writer in the Gospel of Truth declares, "When one comes to know, then one's ignorance is wont to melt away. . . . The lack is wont to melt away in completion."[60]

The New Testament itself provides further parallels outside the Pauline epistles. For example, ὁ ποιῶν τὴν δικαιοσύνην δίκαιός ἐστιν (1 John 3:7) is a grammatical not an empirical statement, like a number of others in this epistle. But examples of this first class of grammatical utterances also occur in the Wisdom literature of the Old Testament and Judaism. In Proverbs 18:2 a fool (*kᵉsîl*) has no delight in understanding

54. Plato, *Gorgias* 454D.
55. Plato, *The Sophist* 240B.
56. Horace, *Epistles* I.1.41, 42.
57. Quintilian, *Institutio oratoria* VIII.3.41.
58. Seneca, *Ad Lucilium epistulae morales* 66.8, 9; cf. 11, 12.
59. *Corpus Hermeticum* 13.8, 9.
60. Evang. Ver. 24.35 and 25.3.

(tᵉḇûnâ). In Proverbs 14:24, the foolishness of fools is folly. In Ben Sirach a patient man is the man who can wait for the right time: ἕως καιροῦ ἀνθέξεται μακρόθυμος (Ecclus. 1:22, LXX; 23 English). Many other examples of this kind can easily be found.[61] It is no accident, however, that class-one grammatical utterances are found in the setting of the Wisdom literature rather than elsewhere in the Old Testament. William McKane sums up the conclusions of R. B. Y. Scott, R. N. Whybray, and others when he points out that this type of literature embodies "an open uncommitted approach which employed strict intellectual probity."[62]

Many scholars insist that the particularity of Israel's faith and history does not destroy the role of rational appeal in these writings. Otto Eissfeldt observes, for example, "The basis for the commendation of wisdom and piety is on the one hand purely secular and rational." Even in Proverbs, it turns on "the unfortunate consequences of foolish and impious action . . . and the reward of right action."[63] Still more pointedly, Gerhard von Rad argues that the "advice" or "counsel" *('ēṣâ)* offered in Proverbs "does not demand obedience, but it appeals to the judgment of the hearer; it is intended to be *understood,* to make decisions easier."[64] He adds, "For wisdom, questions of faith entered in only on the periphery of its field. It works with reason, in its simplest form as sound common sense." Because its concern is with right questioning and effective understanding, rather than simply with cut-and-dried doctrines, "wisdom is always *open* and never brought to conclusion."[65] Its basis of appeal is "what is common to *all* men."[66]

Although Bultmann's very early work is now dated, and although he also draws heavily on P. Wendland, C. F. G. Heinrici, and J. Weiss, the book *Der Stil der paulinischen Predigt und die kynisch-stoische Diatribe* still constitutes the standard work for demonstrating not only Paul's use of the diatribe style, but also the place of rational appeal and dialogue in his approach to the churches.[67] In the first half of his study Bultmann shows that the diatribe is dialogical and is characterized by particular

61. Cf. Proverbs 1:7; 12:15; 15:2, 14; 24:7; Ecclesiasticus 3:18, 29; 6:20; 21:12, 18.
62. W. McKane, *Prophets and Wise Men* (S.C.M., London, 1965), p. 46. Similarly cf. R. B. Y. Scott, *Proverbs, Ecclesiastes* (Doubleday, New York, 1965), pp. xv-lii, especially xvi-xvii; J. Lindblom, "Wisdom in the Old Testament Prophets" in *Supplement to Vetus Testamentum* III (1955): *Wisdom in Israel and in the Ancient Near East. Essays Presented to H. H. Rowley* (ed. by M. Noth and D. W. Thomas), which includes comments on the use of question-and-answer forms; R. N. Whybray, *Wisdom in Proverbs* (S.C.M., London, 1965), pp. 14-29.
63. O. Eissfeldt, *The Old Testament, An Introduction* (Eng. Blackwell, Oxford, 1965), p. 477.
64. G. von Rad, *Wisdom in Israel,* p. 434 (my italics).
65. *Ibid.,* pp. 435 and 422.
66. *Ibid.,* p. 433 (my italics).
67. R. Bultmann, *Der Stil der paulinschen Predigt und die kynisch-stoische Diatribe* (Vandenhoeck & Ruprecht, Göttingen, 1910; F.R.L.A.N.T. 13).

modes of argumentation, and he illustrates his case with numerous examples from Musonius, Teles, Horace, Seneca, Plutarch, Dio Chrysostom, and especially Epictetus. In the second half of his study he lists Pauline passages which afford parallels to each of the characteristics he has listed for the diatribe. In particular we may mention the striking frequency of direct questions both in Paul and the diatribe (I calculate that there are at least 220 in the four major epistles, excluding purely rhetorical questions for stylistic effect); and the use of slogans or catch-phrases borrowed from the readers or from opponents. Examples of such slogans include, for instance, such phrases as πάντα μοι ἔξεστιν (1 Cor. 6:12; 10:23); πάντες γνῶσιν ἔχομεν (1 Cor. 8:1); or single words such as πίστις (Rom. 3:21-26) or λογίζεσθαι (Rom. 4:1-8). Heinrici lists numerous examples, to which Bultmann adds yet more.[68]

More recently A. N. Wilder has endorsed Bultmann's verdict about Paul and the diatribe, and G. Bornkamm takes up the point that Paul often, indeed regularly, appeals to man's rational capacity to consider and respond to argument.[69] Bornkamm points out that Paul specifically avoids a "revelation" mode of address, such as we find characteristically in many of the Gnostic writings. This element of Pauline thought, we have seen, stands in continuity with the Wisdom tradition in the Old Testament, and it provides the characteristic setting for class-one grammatical arguments. But it would be a mistake to follow Robert Funk in contrasting the "primal" language of the parables as metaphor with the "secondary" language of discursive argument in the epistles. For we have seen that grammatical utterances, like the logical propositions of Wittgenstein's *Tractatus*, do not merely *inform* or even *argue*, but *show*. In this respect, they are more than distantly related to Funk's metaphors. It is not just what Weiss calls sharing "in reflection"; it is also sharing in understanding.[70]

We have already seen that within the Pauline writings class-two grammatical utterances occur not simply in the setting of open dialogue, but in the context of a theological tradition. The same principle emerges, with reference either to theology or to ethics, in the writings of Epictetus and Philo. For example, Epictetus writes, τίσ οὖν οὐσία θεοῦ; σάρξ; μὴ γένοιτο. ἀργός; μὴ γένοιτο (Discourse II.8.2). This is not a class-one grammatical utterance, since within certain traditions it would be an

68. C. F. G. Heinrici, *Der litterarische Charakter der neutestamentlich Schriften* (Durrsche Buchhandlung, Leipzig, 1908), p. 68; and R. Bultmann, *Der Stil der paulinischen Predigt*, p. 98.
69. A. N. Wilder, *Early Christian Rhetoric*, p. 54; and G. Bornkamm, "Faith and Reason in Paul" in *Early Christian Experience* (Eng. S.C.M., London, 1969), pp. 29-46.
70. J. Weiss, *Earliest Christianity* (Eng. Harper, New York, 1959) II, 417-18; and "Beiträge zur paulinischen Rhetorik" in *Theologische Studien—Bernhard Weiss* (Vandenhoeck & Ruprecht, Göttingen, 1897), pp. 165-247, especially 168 and 183ff.

informative, not a grammatical, statement to say that God is not a material object. But for Epictetus the denial of the proposition is inconceivable, and not merely false. The immateriality of God is part of the scaffolding of his thought about which he need not inquire. However, the grammar is *theological* grammar, not merely culture-relative grammar. Similarly in the sphere of ethics Epictetus writes: ἀνὴρ καλὸς καὶ ἀγαθὸς οὐδὲν ποιεῖ τοῦ δόξαι ἕνεκα, ἀλλὰ τοῦ πεπρᾶχθαι καλῶς (Discourse III.24.50). There are a number of parallels to this statement.[71] On the one hand it is a grammatical utterance, for its purpose is to elucidate the grammar of "goodness," and the opposite is inconceivable. However, it is not a class-one grammatical utterance, for the opposite would not be inconceivable in another ethical system such as a version of hedonism. The same point might be argued about the conceptual elucidation of certain vices by Epictetus, in which he shows that certain penalties are entailed in the grammar of the concept. Anger carries with it the penalty of loss of reason; adultery, loss of self-respect; and so on.[72] These observations would cease to be "grammatical," however, outside his own high ethical tradition.

Philo has a closely parallel set of statements about the way in which acts of obedience or disobedience to the law carry their own penalties with them. The refusal to worship other gods, he states, carries its own reward (γέρας) with it.[73] Similarly "wisdom is the reward of wisdom." Elsewhere he urges that it is part of the very concept of "resting at the sabbath" that body and soul is thereby refreshed.[74] In the same kind of way he makes a point about the grammar of a theological concept when he says that the first reward (τὰ πρῶτα τῶν ἄθλων) in seeking God is God himself.[75] Thus Abraham, for Philo, as the friend of God, illustrates a point about the grammar of the concept "God." But the point is "grammatical" only from the viewpoint of Philo's own theological tradition.

There seems to be a reasonable case, then, for accepting the suggestion that our two different classes of grammatical utterances regularly or at least often occur in the distinctive settings that we have outlined. If this form-critical analysis is correct, two consequences follow. First of all, claims about the place of reason in Paul should be modified to give due regard to the role of Pauline language in extending/or clarifying concepts for *understanding*. Concepts which facilitate understanding are "shown" by grammatical utterances and are not merely the end-product of fresh information or a discursive chain of argument about facts and inferences.

71. Epictetus, *Discourses* II.10.18, 19; III.17.3; 20.2, 3, 16; 22.35.
72. Epictetus, *Discourses* II.10.19; cf. 10.10-23; III.17.3; and IV.9.6-10.
73. Philo, *De specialibus legibus* II.258.
74. *Ibid.* II.259-60.
75. Philo, *De Abrahamo* 127-30.

They turn on how things are "seen." Secondly, if even some of our examples hold, we need to be hesitant about describing *all* assumptions which "lie apart from the route travelled by inquiry" as necessarily being *culture* relative rather than as belonging to a given *theological* tradition.

58. *Class-Three Grammatical Utterances: Linguistic Recommendations, Pictures, and Paradigms*

It is possible to distinguish a third class of grammatical utterances, which is neither simply topic-neutral nor an expression of what constitutes "the scaffolding of our thoughts." In Galatians 3:29 Paul states, εἰ δὲ ὑμεῖς Χριστοῦ, ἄρα τοῦ ᾿Αβραὰμ σπέρμα ἐστέ, κατ᾿ ἐπαγγελίαν κληρονόμοι. His subject, in G. S. Duncan's phrase, is "the *true* offspring of Abraham."[76] Philo makes a parallel statement in the course of his extended commentary on Genesis 15:2-18. The *true* heir of Abraham, he urges, is the sage (ὁ σοφός).[77] In Romans 2:28, 29 Paul defines, in Barrett's words, the "real" Jew; or, as Otto Michel expresses it, the "true" Jew.[78] Paul writes: οὐ γὰρ ὁ ἐν τῷ φανερῷ ᾿Ιουδαῖός ἐστιν, οὐδὲ ἡ ἐν τῷ φανερῷ ἐν σαρκὶ περιτομή · ἀλλ᾿ ὁ ἐν τῷ κρυπτῷ ᾿Ιουδαῖος, καὶ περιτομὴ καρδίας.

A. J. Ayer argues that analytic propositions "simply record our determination to use words in a certain fashion. We cannot deny them without infringing the conventions which are presupposed by our very denial. . . . This is the sole ground of their necessity."[79] He implies that what is at issue in such statements is "merely verbal." But Ayer's approach involves three difficulties. First of all, it covers up the distinctions of logical function between the three classes of grammatical utterances under discussion. Linguistic recommendations about the terms "Jew" and "seed of Abraham" are not simply straightforward analytical utterances of the same class as "to see is no longer to hope" (Rom. 8:24) or "an intermediary is not needed for one party acting alone" (Gal. 3:20). These class-one examples are hardly *recommendations* about the use of "hope" or "intermediary"; they articulate what is universally agreed already about the concepts in question. However, class-three grammatical utterances remain *grammatical* utterances, since they concern the elucidation and the application of certain *concepts,* and are not statements about the world. Secondly, class-three grammatical utterances often turn

76. G. S. Duncan, *Galatians*, p. 124.
77. Philo, *Quis rerum divinarum heres* 313.
78. C. K. Barrett, *Romans,* p. 59; and O. Michel, *Der Römerbrief,* p. 92.
79. A. J. Ayer, *Language, Truth and Logic* (Gollancz, London, ²1946; Penguin edn. 1971), p. 112.

not simply on linguistic convention or habit, but on what John Searle calls "institutional facts."[80] Searle argues, for example, that sentences such as "Mr. Smith married Miss Brown" or "Jones scored two goals" count as events only against the background of certain institutions, such as marriage or football. In the same way, Paul's language about the true Jew functions against the background of the privileges instituted for Israel in the Old Testament. Thirdly, as Wittgenstein often stressed, how language is used affects how a thing is "seen." How something is pictured often determines its place in our wider system of concepts, and hence also our attitudes towards it.

We have already referred to Bultmann's work on Pauline preaching and the diatribe. In this work a special section is included on Paul's revaluation *(Umwertung)* of words.[81] Here Bultmann refers in particular to Paul's reappraisal of the terms "Jew," "son of Abraham," and "Jerusalem." In Galatians 3:7, for example, Paul writes οἱ ἐκ πίστεως, οὗτοι υἱοί εἰσιν Ἀβραάμ. In Romans 4:11, 12 he states that Abraham is the father of all who have faith, even when uncircumcised. But behind these sentences lies the institutional fact that "the promises were pronounced to Abraham and to his 'issue' " (Gal. 3:16). Hence the point at stake in Paul's discussion is not simply a verbal one. An illustration of the principle can be found in everyday modern life with reference to the seemingly trivial question of whether tomatoes are to be called fruit or vegetables. One description is "correct" from a culinary viewpoint; the other is "correct" from a biological viewpoint. So far the issue turns on linguistic convention or habit. But if a tax or import surcharge is placed on, say, fruit but not vegetables, the introduction of an institutional fact relevant to the linguistic situation turns the issue into a very practical question.

We cannot enter here into the technical discussion about Paul and "the true Jew" provided by Peter Richardson.[82] We do not find Richardson's case entirely convincing. Paul's approach seems to be better expressed in the words of E. Käsemann: "The only true Jew is the Christian."[83] The logic of Paul's statements is that of a grammatical utterance. But it belongs to the third class, namely linguistic recommendations which may or may not be based on institutional facts. There are many examples of class-three grammatical utterances which are not based on institutional facts, in Greek authors of Paul's time. For example,

80. J. R. Searle, *Speech-Acts*, pp. 50-53.
81. R. Bultmann, *Der Stil der paulinischen Predigt und die kynisch-stoische Diatribe*, pp. 27-30 and 80-85.
82. P. Richardson, *Israel in the Apostolic Church* (Cambridge University Press, 1969), especially pp. 70-158.
83. E. Käsemann, *Perspectives on Paul* (Eng. S.C.M., London, 1971), p. 144.

Epictetus states that *real* "having" is not having riches or property, but precisely the opposite: "having" is τὸ μὴ χρείαν ἔχειν πλούτου.[84] Similarly the true "diviner" is not the professional consultant, but ὁ μάντις ἔσω.[85] Similarly, just as a number of class-three grammatical utterances in Paul turn on the application of "the true Jew," in Epictetus many turn on linguistic recommendations about "true freedom."[86]

In an article on the meaning of "flesh" and "spirit" in 1 Corinthians, I have argued that some of Paul's statements turn on the issue of what some philosophers term "persuasive definition."[87] John Hospers explains the meaning of this term when he comments: "When a word or phrase has already acquired a favourable emotive meaning, people often want to see the word or phrase to carry a cognitive meaning different from its ordinary one, so as to take advantage of the favourable emotive meaning that the word already has. . . . The same thing can happen with unfavourable emotive meaning."[88] For example, in certain political circles "moderates" is used with a favorable emotive meaning. A politician will then provide the term with a particular cognitive content by suggesting that "moderates will wish to support these proposals."

The Corinthians were quick to see that "spiritual" carried with it strong approval, while "fleshly" functioned in the opposite way. Language about the "spiritual" man became highly emotive. All things were lawful to him; he reigned like a king; he judged others but no one could judge him (1 Cor. 2:10-15; 4:8; 6:12). I have argued this point in detail in another article entitled "Realized Eschatology at Corinth."[89] Paul enters the readers' horizons, and at first even seems to endorse their language about the spiritual man (2:10-15). But then comes the crucial reversal of their perspective: "I could not address you as spiritual men. . . . You are still of the flesh" (3:1, 3). An example of a class-three grammatical utterance comes in 3:3: ὅπου γὰρ ἐν ὑμῖν ζῆλος καὶ ἔρις, οὐχὶ σαρκικοί ἐστε. The utterance is grammatical because it concerns the grammar of a concept, and does not give information about a state of affairs. But it is different from class-one and class-two grammatical utterances. For its purpose is to define the grammar of "fleshly" and "spiritual" in cognitive terms, in a way which will lead to a reappraisal of the theological situation of the readers. We might say, in Wittgenstein's words, that a "picture"

---

84. Epictetus, *Discourses* IV.9.2; cf. I.60-61.
85. *Ibid.* II.7.3.
86. *Ibid.* IV.1.8, 11-14, 24.
87. A. C. Thiselton, "The Meaning of Σάρξ in 1 Corinthians 5.5. A Fresh Approach in the Light of Logical and Semantic Factors" in *S.J.T.* XXVI (1973), 204-28, especially pp. 217-18.
88. J. Hospers, *An Introduction to Philosophical Analysis* (Routledge and Kegan Paul, London, ²1967), pp. 53-54.
89. A. C. Thiselton, "Realized Eschatology at Corinth" in *N.T.S.* XXIV (1978), 510-26.

had held the Corinthians captive; a picture of themselves as spiritual men. In place of this picture Paul substitutes another. In my second article I have argued that this new picture is of the Corinthians *on the way* to salvation.[90]

This brings us to Wittgenstein's own remarks on the extent to which a "picture" can determine our way of seeing things. Looking back on his own use of the picture theory in the *Tractatus,* Wittgenstein himself sees that he was held captive by what was, in effect, only a model: "A *picture* held us captive, and we could not get outside it, for it lay in our language and language seemed to repeat it to us inexorably."[91] Wittgenstein remarks that one thinks one is looking at the nature of something, but "one is merely tracing round the frame through which we look at it."[92] It is in this context, and in this sense, that he observes, "The problems are solved not by giving new information, but by arranging what we have always known. Philosophy is a battle against the bewitchment of our intelligence by means of language."[93] Wittgenstein illustrates the principle with reference to language about abstract nouns, such as time, and language about "inner" states, such as pain. It is the *picture* of time as a stream flowing from the future into the past that allows such confusing questions as "Where does the past go to?" or even "What *is* time?" The whole philosophical problem about pain and inner states, he insists, is caused by the *picture* of an "inner process" which "tries to force itself on us," together with a whole "grammar" of pain.[94] The picture and the grammar which it suggests "commits us to a particular way of looking at the matter."[95] It is only by breaking the spell of a misleading picture that Wittgenstein can "show the fly the way out of the fly-bottle."[96] As he puts it in *The Blue Book,* although a "new notation" changes no facts, we may be "irresistibly attracted or repelled by a notation. . . . A change of names . . . may mean a great deal."[97]

Neither linguistic recommendations nor pictures, then, are a "merely verbal" matter, in the sense of being in any way trivial or unimportant. This is especially the case when, as happens in some class-three grammatical utterances, linguistic recommendations relate to institutional facts. But even apart from questions about institutional facts, Wittgenstein shows that linguistic recommendations may profoundly affect the way in which we see things. This applies particularly to language-uses

90. *Ibid.*
91. L. Wittgenstein, *P.I.*, sect. 115.
92. *Ibid.*, sect. 114.
93. *Ibid.*, sect. 109.
94. *Ibid.*, sects. 300-307.
95. *Ibid.*, sect. 308.
96. *Ibid.*, sect. 309.
97. L. Wittgenstein, *B.B.*, p. 57.

which constitute paradigms or examples of paradigm cases.

The notion of a paradigm case in language can perhaps best be explained against the background of G. E. Moore's philosophy. Moore would argue: when I say that I *know* that I have a hand, if *that* kind of thing is not "knowing," what is?[98] This is precisely the kind of everyday utterance from which "know" derives its rock-bottom linguistic currency. To try to argue that the paradigm-case is self-contradictory is to ignore Wittgenstein's later warning, "I must not saw off the branch on which I am sitting."[99] For Moore insists that he has selected for consideration "the very type of an unambiguous expression, the meaning of which we all understand." This type of argument has often been illustrated with reference to uses of the word "solid" in the light of modern physics. It may be suggested that a slab of marble or an oak table is not "really" solid. But slabs of marble and oak tables provide paradigm cases of what it is to *be* solid. To say that something is not solid is to say that it is unlike slabs of marble or oak tables.

If Moore's contribution was to show that, in effect, such an argument constitutes an appeal to a paradigm case, Wittgenstein's contribution in *On Certainty* was to show that Moore's argument entailed *no more* than this. It was still *a way of looking at things,* even if it was so deeply embedded in human tradition that its grammatical status went unnoticed. At the same time Wittgenstein saw the profound consequences that the acceptance of such paradigms had for one's view of life as a whole. More recently, special attention has been given to the far-reaching role of paradigms in the sciences, especially by Thomas S. Kuhn. Kuhn argues, for example, that the men who called Copernicus mad because he claimed that the earth moved were not "just wrong." The point was that "part of what they meant by 'earth' was fixed position." If "earth" was a paradigm-case of fixity, Copernicus seemed to be making a self-contradictory claim.[100] Only by changing their way of looking at things, and substituting a new paradigm, could the way be opened for an acceptance of his claims.

As Alan Keightley shows, this brings us back to our earlier discussions about the approach of Peter Winch and D. Z. Phillips, and their interpretation of Wittgenstein.[101] However, we are not obliged to invoke Winch or even Wittgenstein himself for proof of the importance of this point. A number of writers from more than one philosophical tradition have underlined the importance of paradigms in both science and religion,

98. G. E. Moore, *Philosophical Papers* (Allen & Unwin, London, 1959), p. 37.
99. L. Wittgenstein, *P.I.*, sect. 55.
100. T. S. Kuhn, *The Structure of Scientific Revolutions* (University of Chicago Press, ³1973), pp. 149-50.
101. A. Keightley, *Wittgenstein, Grammar and God*, pp. 102-09.

including especially Ian Barbour.[102] Models and paradigms, Barbour argues, offer "ways of ordering experience."[103] Paradigm-shifts accompany or even herald revolutions in science and transformations in religion. Such a paradigm-shift occurs in Paul's handling of the great paradigms of the Old Testament. The righteousness of Abraham, he agrees with his Jewish readers, provides a paradigm-case of what it means to *be* righteous. But "true" righteousness is therefore independent of the law, since Abraham was accounted righteous before the advent of the law (Rom. 4:9-25).

This means that in one particular respect class-three grammatical utterances are not, in the end, greatly different in their function from class-one grammatical utterances. Both extend understanding by "showing." In this sense all grammatical utterances are hermeneutical. But in examining class-three grammatical utterances we have seen that Wittgenstein, like Heidegger and especially Gadamer, takes account of the power of linguistic habit as a means of perpetuating a given view of the world. In Gadamer's words, "The intimate unity of language and thought is the premise from which philosophy of language starts. . . . If every language represents a view of the world it is this primarily not as a particular type of language in the way that philologists see it, but because of what is said or handed down in this language."[104] In Wittgenstein's words, *grammar* may either lead us to new insights or else seduce us into confusion and ignorance. In the New Testament the element of both continuity and discontinuity with Israelite and Jewish faith is displayed when Paul takes up language-paradigms relating to "righteousness," "worship," "freedom," and even "Jew," and reformulates them christocentrically, often in class-three grammatical utterances. In the same way, the great paradigm-concepts of light, bread, life, and so on, are taken up and reapplied in the Fourth Gospel. In the Christian tradition to detach these paradigms from their christological setting would be, in Wittgenstein's words, "to saw off the branch on which I am sitting."

The settings of class-three grammatical utterances, we have seen, may vary. Sometimes they operate against the background of what we have called institutional facts. At other times they occur when what is at issue is a paradigm-shift against the background of a particular linguistic habit or tradition which affects the way in which the readers order their beliefs and experience. The fact that class-three grammatical utterances, however, serve to "show" by means of pictures or paradigms should invite caution about uncritically accepting Robert Funk's rather too clear-cut distinction between the primal power of metaphor in the para-

102. I. G. Barbour, *Myths, Models, and Paradigms* (S.C.M., London, 1974).
103. *Ibid.,* pp. 22 and 45.
104. H.-G. Gadamer, *T.M.,* pp. 364 and 399-400.

bles and the more argumentative and discursive approach of the epistles. When Paul gives a reappraisal of the term "spiritual" in 1 Corinthians, he is not so much "arguing" as breaking the spell of a picture that was misleading his readers.

59. *Language-Games, "the Particular Case," and Polymorphous Concepts*

It should not be thought that the application of Wittgenstein's insights to the interpretation of the New Testament does no more than call attention to the logic of grammatical utterances, in the narrower sense of the term. Nor are we suggesting that the whole of the New Testament should be interpreted in non-cognitive terms. Christian faith, for the New Testament writers, was far more than a way of viewing the world. Indeed the net effect of marking off three classes of grammatical utterances is to show that it is *these* types of utterance (as against others) which function in the ways that we have indicated. By way of illustrating a different point which emerges from Wittgenstein's writings, we shall first return, briefly, to his warnings about the importance of the particular case.

In the previous chapter we noted how Wittgenstein rejected what he called "the craving for generality" and "the contemptuous attitude towards the particular case."[105] We saw that, in his own view, language itself, for example, is not just "one thing." What language *is* depends on the setting or language-game in which the term "language" is used. He writes, "We ask: *'What is* language?', *'What is* a proposition?' And the answer to these questions is to be given once for all, and independently of any future experience." But this rests on the illusion that words like "language," "experience," and so on are *"super-*concepts" *(Über-*Begriffen). "The language-game in which they are to be applied is missing."[106]

Most of Wittgenstein's considerations of particular concepts illustrate this principle, for it is a theme which dominates all his later work. We have already seen how it operates in the case of the words "exact" and "expect." What "exactness" *is* varies from situation to situation. If I am measuring the distance from the earth to the sun, it is quantitatively different from what it is when I am giving a joiner instructions about mending a piece of furniture. "Expecting" when someone is due to come to tea is not exactly the same as it is when I am expecting an explosion.[107]

105. L. Wittgenstein, *B.B.*, p. 18.
106. L. Wittgenstein, *P.I.*, sects. 92, 96, and 97.
107. L. Wittgenstein, *Z.*, sects. 58-68 and 71-72, and *P.I.*, sects. 572-86. See above, sect. 55.

In the same way Wittgenstein shows how misleading it is simply to ask, "What is *thinking?*" In the sections which follow this question he distinguishes between a diversity of concrete situations in which to ask "What was 'thinking?' " would invite different answers.[108] For example: "Thinking is not an incorporeal process . . . which it would be possible to detach from speaking. . . . One might say 'Thinking is an incorporeal process', however, if one were using this to distinguish the grammar of the word 'think' from that of, say, the word 'eat'."[109] This, of course, was Wittgenstein's point about the word "game": "Don't say 'there *must* be something common, or they would not be called 'games'—but *look and see* whether there is anything common to all." Wittgenstein's own term for the similarities between particular examples of games was "family resemblances."[110]

Wittgenstein's observations came to have the status of a standard methodological device in linguistic philosophy. F. Waismann, for example, argues that "to try" is something different in "trying to lift a weight," "trying to do a calculation," and "trying to go to sleep."[111] Gilbert Ryle applies the principle to a whole range of mental activities such as thinking or attending, while G. E. M. Anscombe pays special attention to "intention," and A. R. White specially considers "attention."[112] In some circles the term "polymorphous concepts" is used to indicate the kind of concepts which have this kind of logical grammar.

I now suggest that the theological vocabulary of the New Testament contains some polymorphous concepts. The clearest examples are perhaps "faith" (πίστις), "flesh" (σάρξ), or "fleshly" (σαρκικός), and "truth" (ἀλήθεια). What does it mean to "have faith"? It is well known that Rudolf Bultmann declares, *"Paul understands faith primarily as obedience;* he understands the act of faith as an act of obedience." He adds, "This is shown by the parallelism of two passages in Romans: 'because your faith is proclaimed in all the world' (16:19). Thus he can combine the two in the expression ὑπακοὴ πίστεως ('the obedience which faith is', Rom. 1.5) to designate that which it is the purpose of his apostleship to bring about."[113] We have seen in our three chapters on Bultmann that there are important reasons why he wishes to view faith as obedience rather than, for example, as intellectual assent. What Bultmann is doing, however, in arguing that this meaning is "primary," is viewing

108. L. Wittgenstein, *P.I.*, sects. 327-49.
109. *Ibid.*, sect. 339.
110. *Ibid.*, sect. 66-67.
111. F. Waismann, *Ludwig Wittgenstein und der Wiener Kreis*, pp. 183-84.
112. G. Ryle, *The Concept of Mind* (Hutchinson, London, 1949; Penguin Books, 1963); G. E. M. Anscombe, *Intention* (Blackwell, Oxford, ²1963); and A. R. White, *Attention* (Blackwell, Oxford, 1964).
113. R. Bultmann, *T.N.T.* I, 314 (his italics).

the concept of faith "outside *a particular language-game.*" "The language-game in which (it) is to be applied is missing."

It does violence to the situational character of the New Testament writings to insist on isolating the "essence" of faith. For what faith *is* is only answered by the New Testament writers, including Paul, in relation to what is *the issue at stake*. In Romans 4:5, "faith," especially in relation to the faith of Abraham, is the activity or disposition of "one who does not work but trusts him who justifies the ungodly." As J. Weiss comments, "Faith is not 'a work' to be substituted for other works. . . . It is nothing but a giving up of one's own activity."[114] J. Jeremias makes the same point with reference to Romans 3:28: "a man is justified by faith apart from works of the law." Here faith means, Jeremias urges, a renunciation of one's own achievement, and an attitude which attends solely to God.[115] On the other hand, in 2 Corinthians 5:7 the issue is a different one: "we walk by faith, not by sight." Here faith has a future orientation, as it does in Hebrews 11:1. Yet again, in Romans 10:9 faith entails an intellectual conviction, even if it is also belief in the truth of a self-involving confession: "if you confess with your lips that Jesus is Lord and believe in your heart that God raised him from the dead, you will be saved." In Galatians 1:23 "the faith" means simply "Christianity"; while in 1 Corinthians 13:2 faith that can move mountains seems to be a gift that is given only to certain Christians and not to all. We must agree with A. Schweitzer that when Paul speaks of faith, he does not speak of it "in the abstract."[116] G. Bornkamm provides a point of departure when he says, "The nature of faith is given in the object to which faith is directed."[117] But this must be taken much further. Faith in the New Testament is a polymorphous concept, and therefore questions about faith must not be answered "outside a particular language-game."

The same principle applies to Paul's language about "flesh" and "fleshly." Sometimes Paul uses the term to denote physical substance, as in 1 Corinthians 15:39 and 2 Corinthians 3:2, 3. The phrase "a thorn in the flesh" (2 Cor. 12:7) is rendered by the N.E.B. as "a sharp physical pain." In Romans 1:3 "seed of David according to the flesh" may either refer to physical descent, or else to the parentage of Jesus "from an ordinary point of view". At all events, this second alternative is the meaning of σοφοὶ κατὰ σάρκα in 1 Corinthians 1:26. In 2 Corinthians 11:18 "glorying after the flesh" means glorying in such ordinary human phenomena as pedigree, rhetoric, recommendation, and "success." In numerous pas-

114. J. Weiss, *Earliest Christianity* II, 508.
115. J. Jeremias, *The Central Message of the New Testament* (S.C.M., London, 1965), pp. 55 and 68.
116. A. Schweitzer, *The Mysticism of Paul the Apostle* (Eng. Black, London, 1931), p. 206.
117. G. Bornkamm, *Paul* (Eng. Hodder & Stoughton, London, 1972), p. 141.

sages Paul borrows the Old Testament emphasis on "flesh" as that which is creaturely, weak, and fallible. As J. A. T. Robinson puts it, "Flesh represents mere man, man in contrast with God—hence man in his weakness and mortality."[118] Fleshly wisdom (2 Cor. 1:12) is merely human wisdom. "Walking according to the flesh" (2 Cor. 10:2) is not sensuality but ineffectiveness. In Galatians 5:19, 20, "the works of the flesh" include attitudes which are not restricted to the physical or sensual, but simply receive an adverse ethical evaluation. Finally in Romans 8:7, 13, and elsewhere, Bultmann rightly defines "flesh" as "trust in oneself as being able to procure life by the use of the earthly, and through one's own strength." It is "the self-reliant attitude of the man who puts his trust in his own strength."[119]

In chapter ten we argued that the recent study by Robert Jewett serves to confirm the value of Bultmann's work on the concept of "flesh," which was illuminated in turn by Heidegger. However, this point must now be qualified. Both Bultmann and even Jewett aim to suggest a unifying category which somehow binds together these varied uses of "flesh" into a single whole. Bultmann does this by applying *Sachkritik* in order to distinguish characteristic from uncharacteristic meanings; Jewett does it by postulating a particular theory about the origins of Paul's own concept of "flesh" in relation to the Galatian debate about circumcision. Thus Jewett attacks and criticizes the careful account of seven different categories of meaning arrived at by E. D. Burton, and looks for *one* situation which would account for Paul's varied uses.[120] Admittedly Jewett is usually aware of the need to pay attention to a wide range of settings behind Paul's uses of anthropological terms. But in the case of "flesh" he seems reluctant to give adequate emphasis to the variety of language games in which "flesh" actually occurs, and which determine its meaning in particular passages. Thus he argues that the legalist error of "shifting one's boasting from the cross of Christ (Gal. 6.14) to the circumcised flesh (Gal. 6.13)" is really the same error as the libertinist one of seeking satisfaction in sensuality, since both aim at securing "life" in one's own strength. This provides *"the* key to the interpretation as well as *the* source of the *sarx* concept in Paul's theology."[121] But it is no more necessary to seek for a common "essence" of the fleshly attitude than it is to find the essence of "exact," "expecting," "thinking," "trying," or "game." Paul does not wish to say that being "fleshly" is one *thing*. The "fleshliness" of the Corinthians was evident in a *variety* of ways; the

118. J. A. T. Robinson, *The Body. A Study in Pauline Theology* (S.C.M., London, 1952), p. 19.
119. R. Bultmann, *T.N.T.* I, 239 and 240.
120. R. Jewett, *Paul's Anthropological Terms*, pp. 59-60.
121. *Ibid.,* p. 95 (my italics); cf. pp. 103-04.

"fleshliness" of the two groups in Galatians was perhaps exactly identical with none of them. Indeed what Paul attacks in 1 Corinthians is a generalizing and hence undiscriminating application of the correlative term "spiritual." What it *is* to be "fleshly" depends on the nature of the issue, which is in turn determined by the situation or language-game. Questions of interpretation cannot be asked "outside" given language-games.

As a third example of a polymorphous concept in the New Testament we may consider the varied uses of the word "truth." Is it possible to say what the "essence" of truth is in the biblical writings, apart from its meanings in given language-games? Or does the meaning of the word, in the sense of what *constitutes* truth, vary from context to context?

Certainly in the case of the history of philosophical thought and even in ordinary language no *single* uniform concept of truth exists. In the context of considering a descriptive report, truth is a matter of correspondence with the facts. But when Kierkegaard declares that subjectivity is truth, what is at issue is something different from correspondence with facts. What may be said to constitute truth varies again in the context of Heidegger's thought, as we have already seen. Similarly the truth of a poem is not the same kind of thing as the truth of a proposition in the *Tractatus*. Do we not meet the same multiform phenomena in the New Testament? I have discussed the use of the various words for truth in the biblical writings in considerable detail elsewhere.[122] In this study I have distinguished between the following uses of the word.

(1) In Greek literature and in the Old and New Testaments there are abundant examples of uses of the word "truth" in which the point at issue is correspondence with the facts of the matter. In Homer Achilles sets an umpire to tell the truth of a race, i.e. to report the state of affairs as it really was (*Iliad* 23.361). Plato uses "truth" to mean simply "the facts of the matter" (*Epistles* 7.330). More explicitly Aristotle declares, "We call propositions only those sentences which have truth or falsity in them" (*On Interpretation* IV.17a, 4). "The truth of a proposition consists in corresponding with facts" (*ibid.* IX.19a, 33). Many scholars expect to find this usage in Aristotle, but tend to play down examples of the same use in the Old Testament. However, the Old Testament offers many examples of this "factual" use. In Genesis 42:16 Joseph wishes to establish whether his brothers have told the truth. In Exodus 18:21 the men of truth who hate a bribe are not only "reliable"; they also take account of all the facts and hide nothing. In Proverbs 12:19, truthful lips stand in contrast to a false testimony about the facts of the matter; while the injunction to

---

122. A. C. Thiselton, "Truth *(Alētheia)*" in C. Brown (ed.), *The New International Dictionary of New Testament Theology* III (Paternoster, Exeter, 1978), 874-902.

"buy" truth (Prov. 23:23) refers to the acquisition of knowledge, not primarily here to stability of character. As a champion of truth, the king in the Psalms is to expose whatever is shady, underhanded, or false (45:4). In Tobit 7:10, "truth" is used of giving a true report. The New Testament, equally, uses "truth" in opposition to a false report. "Putting away falsehood, let every one speak the truth with his neighbour" (Eph. 4:25). Paul declares that everything he said was true (2 Cor. 7:14). The woman of Samaria speaks factual truth about her marital status (John 4:18). Everything that John the Baptist says about Jesus is true (John 10:41). It is clear that very often in the biblical writings "truth" draws its meaning from its function within the language-game of factual report.

(2) In other passages, however, a different language-game determines a different meaning for the same word. It is well known that the Hebrew word $'^{e}met$ can mean either truth or faithfulness. This does not of course mean that it bears *both* of these meanings in the *same* set of contexts. There is no doubt, however, that in *certain* contexts "truth" is used in the sense of faithfulness, honesty, or reliability. The collectors in Josiah's reformation deal "honestly" (2 Kings 22:7). Most notably, when it is said that God is true, the writer means that God proves his faithfulness to men afresh. This connection between faithfulness and truth depends, however, not on any semantic factors which are peculiar to the Hebrew language, but on the fact that when God or man is said to act faithfully the issue at stake is a correspondence between his word and deed. We are now in a different language-game from that of factual report. When the Psalmist exclaims that "all the paths of the Lord are mercy and truth" (Ps. 25:10), he is testifying that God's dealings with his people are utterly trustworthy, because they are characterized by loyalty to the covenant. In the context of this kind of language-game, Pannenberg is correct when he says that in the Old Testament "the truth of God must prove itself anew."[123] This is because of the nature of the language-game, not because of some supposedly "Hebraic" peculiarity of thought. What is "Hebraic" is simply the frequency with which this particular language-game is used, as against others. This meaning of "truth" finds its way also into the New Testament. Truth, especially in certain parts of 2 Corinthians, means that kind of integrity in which there is a total correspondence between word and deed (2 Cor. 6:4-7).

(3) There are other contexts in which "truth" means neither correspondence with the facts, nor faithfulness and integrity, but the gospel of Christ in contrast to some other gospel or view of the world. As J. Murphy-O'Connor convincingly argues, "truth" occurs in the writings of Qumran with the meaning of "revealed doctrine" (1 QS 6:15; cf. 1:15;

---

123. W. Pannenberg, "What is Truth?" in *B.Q.T.* II, 8; cf. pp. 1-27.

3:24), and this meaning is retained in parts of the New Testament.[124] Thus "truth" cleanses a man from sin (1 QS 4:20, 21). What is at issue between Paul and the Judaizers is "the truth" (Gal. 2:5). Truth, for Paul, stands in contrast to "another gospel" (2 Cor. 11:4). This is almost certainly the meaning of "knowledge of the truth" in the Pastorals (1 Tim. 2:4; 2 Tim. 3:7), where the word cannot simply mean knowledge of true facts. Men will turn away from hearing "the truth" in order to listen to more myths (2 Tim. 4:3, 4).

(4) Philo describes God as the God who is true, in the sense that he is "real," like a coin that is genuine rather than counterfeit, or an article which is what it seems and not merely veneer (*The Preliminary Studies*, 159). In the Fourth Gospel, Jesus says that his flesh is "real" food and his blood is "real" drink (John 6:55). Those who worship God must worship him in Spirit and reality (John 4:23, 24). The context of this passage makes it plain that what is at issue is not "sincerity" but worshipping God on the basis of the reality disclosed through divine revelation, rather than on the speculations of human religious aspiration. If we extend our investigation of ἀληθής and ἀλήθεια in order to include ἀληθινός, there are a number of further examples in John. Jesus is the real light, in contrast to John the Baptist (John 1:9). He is the real bread, in contrast to the manna (6:32). He is the real vine, in contrast to Israel (15:1). This remains a conceptual rather than a lexicographical point, however, for in a different context ἀληθινός may also denote a saying which corresponds with the facts (John 4:37).

(5) Sometimes truth is used in contrast to that which is hidden. Whereas the devil has no truth in him because he is a deceiver (John 8:44, 45), the Spirit of truth "exposes" what is the case; he "brings things to the light of day" and "shows a thing in its true colors" (John 14:17; 15:26; 16:13; cf. 1 John 4:6; 5:6).[125]

(6) It is possible to distinguish other nuances of meaning, such as that of "valid" witness (John 5:31, 32). Yet we must also allow for the use of the word "truth" in an over-arching way that holds together several of these other uses. We find this over-arching meaning, for example, when Jesus in the Fourth Gospel says that he *is* the truth (John 14:6). John has already introduced his readers to the idea that the testimony of Jesus is valid; that he reveals the truth of the gospel; that his words correspond with his deeds; and that his statements correspond with the facts. Hence none of these concepts of truth can be excluded. Nevertheless, this in no way invalidates our argument that truth in the New Testament is a

---

124. J. Murphy-O'Connor, "Truth: Paul and Qumran" in *Paul and Qumran* (Chapman, London, 1968), pp. 179-230.
125. C. K. Barrett, *The Gospel according to St. John* (S.P.C.K., London, 1955), p. 76.

polymorphous concept. For in the first place, even this over-arching use occurs only in a given type of context, for example in the context of Christology. In the second place, even then it is hardly possible to define the "essence" of truth in a single uniform way. We cannot ask questions about "the New Testament concept of truth," or even "John's concept of truth," *outside* a given context of language-game.

We have only to look at the history of research into the subject to see how some scholars have been led astray by failing to understand this point. The basic procedure in the nineteenth century was first of all to draw a clear-cut contrast between the "theoretical" concept of truth in Greek thought and the "practical" concept in Hebraic thinking. The theoretical view was based on the correspondence theory of truth, while the practical view was connected first of all with the semantic accident that 'ᵉmeṭ could mean either truth or faithfulness, and partly with the interest of the Old Testament writers in the reliability of God. Research on Paul is still today dominated by the question raised by H. H. Wendt in 1883 about which of the New Testament writers was most influenced by this supposedly "Hebraic" concept of truth.[126] In a study of 1928, Bultmann argued that Wendt's thesis of Hebraic influences applied to Paul, but not to John.[127] The same clear-cut contrast is the basis for D. J. Theron's study of truth in Paul, published in 1954, and L. J. Kuyper's article of 1964 on truth in John.[128] A whole body of literature is influenced by this methodology, and writers insist on trying to get at the essence of "the" Johannine concept, in order to assess whether its main affinity is with Greek or Hebrew thought. The truth of the matter is not that the Hebrews had a special concept of truth but that they employed the concept in certain contexts or language-games more frequently than these language-games were used in Greek literature. But the same language-games *could* be employed in both traditions.

The failure to notice the polymorphous character of this concept led many scholars into a blind alley. They looked for what Paul saw as the *essence* of the concept, or what the Hebrews or John saw as its *essence*. But what truth *is* or *consists in* varies from language-game to language-game, whichever writer is in view. Sometimes what is at issue is correspondence between statements and facts. Truth *is* this, in this context. At

126. H. H. Wendt, "Der Gebrauch der Worter alētheia, alēthēs, und alēthinos im N.T. auf Grund der altestamentlichen Sprachgebrauches" in *Theologische Studien und Kirtiken, eine Zeitschrift für das gesamt der Theologie* LXV (1883), 511-47.
127. R. Bultmann, "Untersuchungen zum Johannesevangelium" in *Z.N.W.* XXVII (1928), 113-63; cf. Bultmann's article in *Theological Dictionary of the New Testament* I, 242-50.
128. D. J. Theron, "Alētheia in the Pauline Corpus" in *E.Q.* XXVI (1954), 3-18; and L. J. Kuyper, "Grace and Truth" in *Reformed Review* XVI (1962), 1-16, and "Grace and Truth. An Old Testament Description of God and its Use in the Johannine Gospel" in *Int.* XVIII (1964), 3-19.

other times what is at issue is correspondence between word and deed. In other contexts what truth *is* depends on the nature of revealed doctrine; while in others, what truth *is* depends on holding together several different strands of a multiform concept. The question "What is truth?" cannot be asked outside a given language-game. For, as Wittgenstein conclusively showed about such concepts as "expect," "think," "mean," and "understand," every use of the term is embedded in a particular situation, and attempts to ask questions about these concepts in the abstract can lead only to confusion and misunderstanding. The point we are making is not simply a point about lexicography, although clearly it involves lexicography. The primary point is a logical one, about the grammar of the concept in the New Testament writings. This does not mean, of course, that the systematic theologian cannot inquire about truth in the New Testament; only that his work must be guided by exegesis which takes full account of the logical particulars of each passage.

60. *Language-Games and "Seeing-as": A Fresh Approach to Some Persistent Problems about Justification by Faith in Paul*

The history of Pauline research over the last hundred years has raised at least five related problems about the nature of justification by faith. (1) Are the terms for "to justify" (δικαιόω) and "justified" or "righteous" (δίκαιος) primarily declaratory (to count righteous) or behavioral (to make righteous)? Whichever view is taken, does this mean that the believer is no longer in status or in actuality a sinner? *How do we hold together the so-called paradox of his being both righteous and a sinner?* (2) How central is justification in Pauline thought? This question tends to mean, in effect: to what conceptual scheme does it belong? (3) Is justification a present experience, or does it belong, more strictly, to the future, as an anticipated verdict of the last judgment? (4) What kind of faith is justifying faith? How do we avoid making "faith" a special kind of substitute for "works," which is somehow a more acceptable sort of human activity? (5) If we can arrive at a concept of faith which escapes this problem, how does it relate to the concept of faith in the Epistle of James?

Various attempts at solutions to these problems have been offered. However, the fact that scholars repeatedly return to them suggests that none of the proposed solutions is entirely satisfactory. We shall try to use some of Wittgenstein's own concepts and categories in order to approach these questions from a fresh angle. Our approach is by no means an alternative to traditional or more recent approaches, and it is not intended to undermine them. However, we do suggest that a new perspective is

416   HEIDEGGER, BULTMANN, GADAMER, AND WITTGENSTEIN

needed in the light of which certain conceptual clarifications may become possible.

The first problem concerns the declaratory or behavioral meaning of the δικαιόω terms. Some of the arguments on this question are primarily or at least partly linguistic. Thus in his recent study J. A. Ziesler argues that the traditional Protestant interpretation, in terms of status, rests primarily on the evidence of the verbal form δικαιόω, while the traditional Roman Catholic interpretation, in terms of behavioral or ethical righteousness, rests mainly on the use of the noun δικαιοσύνη and the adjective δίκαιος.[129] Both aspects, he argues, can be found in the Hebrew form ṣāḍaq, although in the Hebrew the forensic is probably primary. Yet even Ziesler, whose study is largely linguistic, finds the logical and theological factors the decisive ones. He writes, "If God looks on believers only as they are found in Christ, he may properly declare them righteous, for in him . . . they are righteous. . . . There is nothing fictional here."[130]

We need not delay on the question of whether Ziesler overpresses the contrast between the noun and the verb. We are more concerned with his theological arguments. Can we actually *ask* whether the believer is "really" righteous in Paul's view? We shall argue shortly that the believer becomes righteous *within the context of one language-game,* but that in *another context,* or language-game, even the Christian believer still remains a sinner. Ziesler, like most Pauline interpreters, tends to ask the question about righteousness *outside* a given language-game. There is no escaping the Lutheran formulation that, according to Paul, the believer is *simul iustus et peccator,* or *"semper peccator, semper penitens, semper iustus."*[131] However firmly a behavioral interpretation is pressed, Paul would *not* have been willing to accept the assertion *that Christians are no longer sinners.* This possibility must be rejected in the light of such passages as 1 Corinthians 3:3; 4:4; 11:17, 28-32; 2 Corinthians 12:20b; and Philippians 3:12, 13.[132] This theological point lies behind many of the approaches which defend the forensic view. Thus J. Weiss writes that justification "does not say what a man is in himself, but it states what he is considered to be in the eyes of God."[133] Similarly H. Ridderbos asserts, "It is a matter of man as a sinner, and not yet of his future inner renewal."[134]

129. J. A. Ziesler, *The Meaning of Righteousness in Paul. A Linguistic and Theological Enquiry* (Cambridge University Press, 1972), pp. 128-210 *et passim*.
130. *Ibid.,* p. 169.
131. On Luther's language, cf. G. Rupp, *The Righteousness of God: Luther Studies* (Hodder & Stoughton, London, 1953), e.g. pp. 225 and 255; and P. Stuhlmacher, *Gerechtigkeit Gottes bei Paulus* (Vandenhoeck & Ruprecht, Göttingen, 1965), pp. 19-23.
132. Cf. further R. Bultmann, "Das Problem der Ethik bei Paulus" in *Z.N.W.* XXIII (1924), 123-40.
133. J. Weiss, *Earliest Christianity* (Eng. 2 vols.; Harper, New York, 1959) II, 499.
134. H. Ridderbos, *Paul. An Outline of his Theology* (Eerdmans, Grand Rapids, 1977, and S.P.C.K., London, 1977), p. 175.

This, however, does not solve our problem as advocates of the behavioral view are quick to note. Fernand Prat, for one, regards what he calls the "official" Protestant doctrine as flatly self-contradictory. He writes, *"How can the false be true,* or how can God declare true what he knows to be false?"[135] Similarly F. Amiot and L. Cerfaux consider that this difficulty is a fatal objection to the traditional Protestant view.[136] E. Käsemann speaks of the "tensions" of Paul's language, and the "logical embarrassment" in which he places the modern reader.[137] Even Bultmann's "relational" concept of righteousness does not fully answer this particular problem.[138] For if man's relationship to God is right, is he still a sinner or not? Ziesler comments, "The resulting position is . . . very similar to the usual Protestant one."[139] We seem, then, to have come up against a brick wall. The behavioral interpretation makes it difficult to see how man can still be regarded as a sinner from a *logical* viewpoint. For behavioral righteousness seems logically to exclude his still being a sinner, although this is patently at variance with other Pauline statements. On the other hand, the forensic interpretation makes it difficult to see how man can still be regarded as a sinner from a theological viewpoint. For forensic righteousness seems logically to exclude his being even considered a sinner.

At this point we may turn to examine Wittgenstein's remarks about the phenomenon of "seeing . . . as . . . ," of seeing *x* as *y*.[140] In his *Zettel* Wittgenstein writes, "Let us imagine a kind of puzzle picture. . . . At first glance it appears to us as a jumble of meaningless lines, and only after some effort do we see it as, say, a picture of a landscape.—What makes the difference . . . ?"[141] What makes the difference, Wittgenstein asks, between seeing a diagram as a chaotic jumble of lines, and seeing it as representing the inside of a radio receiver?[142] How does someone who is unfamiliar with the conventions of how a clock signifies the time, suddenly come to see the hands as pointers which tell the time? Wittgenstein declares: "It all depends on the *system* to which the sign belongs."[143] We

135. F. Prat, *The Theology of St. Paul* (Eng. 2 vols.; Burns, Oates, & Washbourne, London, 1945) II, 247 (my italics).
136. F. Amiot, *The Key Concepts of St. Paul* (Eng. Herder, Freiburg, 1962), pp. 120-25; and L. Cerfaux, *The Christian in the Theology of St. Paul* (Eng. Chapman, London, 1967), pp. 391-400.
137. E. Käsemann, *New Testament Questions of Today* (Eng. S.C.M., London, 1969), p. 171.
138. R. Bultmann, *T.N.T.* I, 270-85.
139. J. A. Ziesler, *The Meaning of Righteousness in Paul*, p. 3.
140. L. Wittgenstein, *P.I.*, sect. 74 and II.xi, pp. 193-214; *B.B.*, pp. 163-74; and *Z.*, sects. 195-235.
141. L. Wittgenstein, *Z.*, sect. 195.
142. *Z.*, sect. 201.
143. *Z.*, sect. 228 (Wittgenstein's italics).

see a puzzle picture at first as a jumble of lines. Then suddenly *we provide a certain context,* and the lines portray a landscape. Only the person who knows the *system* of representation in radio circuitry can see the diagram as that of a radio receiver.

But Wittgenstein also asks, What is it about a special situation that allows me to see something *either as this, or as that?* He writes, "When I interpret, I step from one level of thought to another. If I see the thought symbol 'from outside', I become conscious that it *could* be interpreted thus or thus."[144] Wittgenstein's most famous example of this phenomenon comes not in the *Zettel* but in the *Investigations,* where he speaks about "the 'dawning' of an aspect."[145] He cites the example of the "duck-rabbit" suggested in Jastrow's *Fact and Fable in Psychology.* The

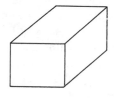 

same figure can be seen either as a duck facing to the left, or as a rabbit facing upwards and a little to the right. The same lines that represent the beak in the duck-system also represent the ears in the rabbit-system. *What* is seen remains the same; *how* it is seen depends on the significance or function of the phenomenon within a given system, frame of reference, or setting in life. Wittgenstein also suggests the example of a two-dimensional drawing of a cube. It may be seen now as a glass cube, now as three boards forming a solid angle, now as a wire frame, now as an open box. Our interpretation depends on the context from life what we choose as the system of reference.[145] Another common experience is that of seeing a face in a crowd that we think we recognize. We slot it into a given context, and we think it is our friend, and then suddenly we realize that we are mistaken and the context is irrelevant.

This principle is of course highly suggestive for hermeneutics. Interpretation depends, as Schleiermacher saw, on relating what we see to aspects of our own experience. But this is not the primary point which concerns us here. Nor am I unaware that other interpreters of Wittgenstein have sometimes stressed other aspects of Wittgenstein's work on "seeing . . . as. . . ."[147] Our concern here is with the relationship be-

144. *Z.,* sects. 234-35.
145. *P.I.,* p. 194.
146. *P.I.,* p. 193.
147. Cf. V. C. Aldrich, "Pictorial Meaning, Picture Thinking, and Wittgenstein's Theory of Aspects" in *Mind* LXVII (1958), 70-79.

tween "seeing . . . as . . ." and a system or context. In a valuable discussion Donald Evans make the same point under the heading of what he calls "onlooks."[148] He writes, " 'Looking on *x* as *y*' involves placing *x* within a structure, organization, or scheme. This often involves the description of a status . . . to *x*." He adds, "Sometimes *x* is placed in a futural structural context rather than a present one."[149]

We return now to Pauline thought. The believer is "seen as" righteous, we shall argue, specifically within the context of eschatology or at least in the context of the new age. Yet in the context, or frame of reference, of history and law, he remains a sinner. In order to elucidate this point, however, we must first move on to two other aspects of these persistent problems about the subject.

One of the key questions raised by this subject is whether justification in Paul is present or future. Some passages suggest that it is a present experience for the believer: δικαιωθέντες οὖν ἐκ πίστεως εἰρήνην ἔχομεν πρὸς τὸν θεόν (Rom. 5:1; cf. 5:9; 9:30; 1 Cor. 6:11). But Paul also declares unambiguously: ἐκ πίστεως ἐλπίδα δικαιοσύνης ἀπεκδεχόμεθα (Gal. 5:5). Many interpreters of Paul, following J. Weiss and A. Schweitzer, urge that righteousness "belongs strictly speaking" to the future, even though it is effective in the present.[150] Both Bultmann and Barrett speak of the "paradoxical" nature of the situation when an eschatological verdict is pronounced in the present.[151] The importance of this eschatological frame is further underlined by recent attempts to ground justification in the context of apocalyptic. E. Käsemann has stressed the significance of such passages as Testament of Dan 6:10 and 1QS 11.12, while C. Müller argues that Paul's thought on this subject is decisively influenced by apocalyptic-Jewish conceptions of the cosmic juridical trial in which God judges Israel and the nations.[152] The apocalyptic context of the concept is also emphasized by P. Stuhlmacher and K. Kertelge.[153] Kertelge shows how the forensic and eschatological aspects are brought together in the expectation of God's rightwising verdict at the end of time.

The fact that we have to do with the logic of evaluation or *verdict*, especially in an eschatological context, explains an important point. If we are confronted with two *statements*, one of which asserts *p* and the other

148. D. D. Evans, *The Logic of Self-Involvement. A Philosophical Study of Everyday Language with Special Reference to the Christian Use of Language about God as Creator* (S.C.M., London, 1963), pp. 124-41.
149. *Ibid.*, p. 127.
150. A. Schweitzer, *The Mysticism of Paul the Apostle*, p. 205; cf. J. Weiss, *Earliest Christianity* II, 502.
151. R. Bultmann, *T.N.T.* I, 276; C. K. Barrett, *Romans*, p. 75.
152. C. Müller, *Gottes Gerechtigkeit und Gottes Volk* (F.R.L.A.N.T. 86; Vandenhoeck & Ruprecht, Göttingen, 1964).
153. P. Stuhlmacher, *Gerechtigkeit Gottes bei Paulus;* and K. Kertelge, *'Rechtfertigung' bei Paulus*, pp. 112-60.

of which denies p, we are faced with a *contradiction*. If one man claims *"x is black"* and another claims *"x is white,"* one of them must be wrong. But the situation is different when we are faced with the logic of *evaluation* or *verdict*. If one man claims, *"x is satisfactory,"* or *"x is fast,"* and the other claims, *"x is unsatisfactory,"* or *"x is slow,"* each may be a valid assessment *in relation to a different frame of reference*. In the same way, if justification is a verdict, for God to declare the believer righteous in the context of eschatology does not contradict his declaring him a sinner in the context of history, or in terms of what he is in the natural world. In the context of the new age, the eschatological verdict of "righteous" which belongs to the last judgment is brought forward and appropriated by faith. In this sense, justification, although strictly future, is operative in the present "apart from the law" (Rom. 3:21; cf. Gal. 2:16; Phil. 3:9). In as far as the believer is accorded his eschatological status, viewed in that context he is justified. In as far as he still lives in the everyday world, he remains a sinner who awaits future justification. History and eschatology each provide a frame of reference in which a different verdict on the believer is valid and appropriate. This is neither contradiction nor even "paradox." In Wittgenstein's sense of the "home" setting of a language-game, eschatology is the home setting in which the logic of justification by faith properly functions.

We are now in a position to respond to the first three of our five questions. First of all, there is no contradiction involved in the verdict *simul iustus et peccator,* because there is room for a difference of verdict, "seeing . . . as . . .", or "onlook," when each operates within a different system or frame of reference. Thus the declarative view of justification is not involved in legal fiction or paradox. But it is a mistake to try to arbitrate between the declarative and behavioral views of righteousness by asking whether the believer is "really" righteous, as if this question could be asked *outside* a given language-game. The behavioral interpretation too often obscures this point, although it derives a measure of plausibility when, as in the work of Kertelge, a writer concentrates almost exclusively on the eschatological or apocalyptic context, since in *that* context "righteous" is indeed the only possible verdict.

Secondly, claims about the centrality of justification by faith in Paul have been bound up with the question, since the work of L. Usteri (1824) and H. E. G. Paulus (1831), of the relationship between a juridical conceptual scheme and that which centers on new creation and participation. As Schweitzer showed in his survey *Paul and his Interpreters*, this was a major issue for R. A. Lipsius (1853), H. Lüdemann (1872), and Richard Kabisch (1893)[154]; and when Schweitzer himself discusses the place of

---

154. A. Schweitzer, *Paul and his Interpreters. A Critical History* (Eng. Black, London, 1912), pp. 9-11, 19, 28-31, and 58-65.

justification in Pauline thought, it is not only the concept itself that is in question, but also the conceptual scheme to which it belongs.[155] What emerges from our discussion is that from a conceptual or logical point of view, justification has a role within *both* schemes of thought. The juridical scheme underlines, in the best or perhaps the only way available to Paul, that we have to do with *verdictive* logic, not with the logic of assertion or statement. The "new creation" or "participation" scheme of thought underlines the point that this verdict is *eschatological*. The point of the "participational" conceptual scheme, as writers from Schweitzer to E. P. Sanders have emphasized, is that in union with Christ the believer is lifted out of the frame of law and history, even though in another sense he still lives in the world.[156] If this is correct, many of the standard attempts to devalue the importance of justification for Paul must fail. At least this is the case with those arguments which view justification only as a concept within the juridical scheme.[157] Even Schweitzer's criticisms were directed more against the importance of the juridical scheme as such, than against the concept of justification in itself.[158]

Thirdly, we have seen *why* the problem arises about whether justification in Paul is present or future, and why there is truth in both claims. Since the frame of reference of eschatology, rather than of history, is the decisive one, the eschatological verdict can be anticipated even in the present by faith. But it is still a verdict which is appropriated in *faith*. As one who lives in the everyday world and as the product of his own historical decisions, the believer cannot deny that he is also a sinner. He has not yet been delivered out of the world. The notion that justification by faith is a legal fiction rests on viewing the problem *only* from the historical frame of reference, from which it appears that the believer is "counted" righteous, but is "really" a sinner. However, from the eschatological perspective the situation is seen differently. Thus from the historical viewpoint justification is still future, but by appropriation of the eschatological verdict it is possible to live by faith in the present experience of being justified. Thus J. Weiss speaks of a "pre-dating of what is really an eschatological act."[159]

This at once, however, leads us on to our fourth question. How is "faith" capable of doing this? How is it possible to speak of faith in such a

[margin note: the angle of vision]

155. A. Schweitzer, *The Mysticism of Paul the Apostle*, pp. 220-21 and 225.
156. E. P. Sanders, *Paul and Palestinian Judaism* (S.C.M., London, 1977), pp. 453-72.
157. This is not to deny the importance of critiques of the traditional approach made from a different angle; cf. K. Stendahl, *Paul among Jews and Gentiles* (S.C.M., London, 1977). I am convinced that room must be found to hold together what is correct in Stendahl's analysis with the valid insights of Käsemann and the Reformers.
158. I have argued this point in A. C. Thiselton, "Schweitzer's Interpretation of Paul," forthcoming in *Exp. T.* XC (1979), 132-37.
159. J. Weiss, *Earliest Christianity*, II, 502.

way that it does not become a special kind of work? We shall now examine this question, together with the fifth issue, of the relationship between faith in Paul and faith in James.

61. *Grammatical Relations and Dispositions: Faith in Paul and in James*

In the light of our discussions in the previous section we can now see that in Paul faith is related to justification *internally* or *grammatically*. This is why Paul can set the concept in contrast to works (Rom. 3:27-28; 4:2-6; 9:30-32). D. E. H. Whiteley correctly observes, "Faith is not 'another kind of work' which is a species of the same genus and operates in the same way: faith and works do not belong to the same genus at all."[160] G. Bornkamm makes a similar point.[161] This is not to deny our earlier conclusion about faith as a polymorphous concept, for we are speaking about faith only as it is used in this present context or language-game. In this context it means the acceptance of this future-oriented outlook as being effectively relevant in the present. The verdict that will be openly valid at the judgment day *is valid for faith now*. From a purely external or historical viewpoint, justification remains future; but faith involves stepping out of a purely historical frame of reference into that of eschatology. Thus Paul may not be as far as is sometimes assumed from the definition of faith in Hebrews 11:1 as ἐλπιζομένων ὑπόστασις. As Cullmann insists, the temporal contrast is no less important than the spatial one in primitive Christianity.[162] If this is correct, however, it shows that faith is not merely an external *instrument* which somehow "procures" justification; it is an indispensable feature of justification itself. *To have this faith is part of what justification is and entails.* It is part of the experience of it.

In Wittgenstein's language, to say that justification requires faith is to make a grammatical or analytical statement comparable to "every rod has a length," "green is a color," or "water boils at 100° C." Faith is part of the *concept* of justification, just as "works" are part of the *concept* of law. Certainly faith is not a special kind of work. The two categories stand in contrast to each other only because each is internally or analytically related to the system of concepts to which it belongs. Perhaps, strictly, the kind of grammar in question is more like that of class-two grammatical utterances than straightforward topic-neutral grammatical utterances.

160. D. E. H. Whiteley, *The Theology of St. Paul* (Blackwell, Oxford, 1964 and revised edn.), p. 164.
161. G. Bornkamm, *Paul,* pp. 141-46.
162. O. Cullmann, *Christ and Time* (Eng. S.C.M., London, 1951), p. 37.

Those outside the New Testament or Pauline tradition might view the grammar of the concepts differently. But for Paul himself the grammar of the concepts in question is part of "the scaffolding of his thought"; "the hinges on which other propositions turn."

The conclusion that faith means, for Paul, the appropriation of an eschatological verdict as being effective in the present depends on the arguments put forward in the previous section. Given the validity of those arguments, faith assumes this role within the language-game. But this does not exclude us from viewing faith in a closely parallel but slightly different way as well. For Paul, the believer can anticipate by faith the verdict "not guilty" only because he has become part of the new creation and has entered the new age in union with Christ. Our argument, then, in no way denies the fact that faith is also closely related to the concept of Christ-union. Once again, it is internally or grammatically related to "Being-in-Christ," for faith is the appropriation of Christ-union rather than some external instrument which makes it possible. Once again, faith is not a special kind of work, but part of what is *entailed* in being united with Christ as part of the new creation. Faith does not *make* a man a Christian; but he cannot be a Christian without faith, for faith in Christ is part of the definition of what it means to be a Christian.

When we turn to the Epistle of James we enter a different world. We are especially concerned with the argument of James in 2:14-26: "What does it profit, my brethren, if a man says he has faith but has not works? Can his faith save him? . . . Faith by itself, if it has no works, is dead. But, some one will say, 'You have faith and I have works'. Show me your faith apart from your works, and I by my works will show you my faith. . . . Faith apart from works is barren (ἀργή)" (14, 17, 18, 20). Both Paul and James appeal to the verse, "Abraham believed God and it was reckoned to him as righteousness" (Gen. 15:6; Rom. 4:3, 9; Jas. 2:21). But whereas Paul understands this verse to refer to faith *in contrast to* works (Rom. 4:2-25), James declares that faith needs to be evidenced *by* works (Jas. 2:22-26). As J. Jeremias points out, the problem comes to a head most sharply when we compare Romans 3:28 with James 2:24.[163] Paul asserts, λογιζόμεθα γὰρ δικαιοῦσθαι πίστει ἄνθρωπον χωρὶς ἔργων νόμου (Rom. 3:28). James declares, ὁρᾶτε ὅτι ἐξ ἔργων δικαιοῦται ἄνθρωπος καὶ οὐκ ἐκ πίστεως μόνον (Jas. 2:24).

Jeremias is correct in his claim that this apparent contradiction is to be explained not in terms of a head-on clash between Paul and James, but partly in terms of their difference of concerns, and partly in terms of the radically different ways in which they use the same terminology. Jeremias argues that the concept of faith which James attacks is merely "the

---

163. J. Jeremias, "Paul and James" in *Exp.T.* LXVI (1955), 368-71.

intellectual acceptance of monotheism," whereas the concept of faith which Paul defends is "the confidence that Christ died for my sins."[164] In broad terms, this is true. But it tends to suggest that James is merely the negative corollary of Paul, as if James merely accepted his opponent's inadequate concept of faith, and then argued that such faith (intellectual assent) must be supplemented by works. Thus in his commentary on James, Martin Dibelius asserts, "James . . . cannot possibly be concerned about a theologically refined concept of faith. There is no special doctrine presupposed here, but rather the common meaning of the word 'faith'."[165] What some commentators have missed, however, is that especially in 2:18-26 James is not merely attacking an inadequate view of faith, but is also giving what amounts to a fairly sophisticated and positive account of the logical grammar of his own concept of faith. James is neither merely attacking someone else's view of faith, nor is he merely saying that faith must be supplemented by works. He is saying that his *concept* of faith would *exclude* instances of supposed belief which have no observable backing or consequences in life. In other words, whereas in Paul we see an internal or grammatical relation between faith and justification (because faith is entailed in the very concept of justification for Paul), in James we see an internal or grammatical relation between faith and works, because the very concept of faith entails *acting* in a certain way.

This principle receives clarification and illumination when we turn to Wittgenstein's remarks about belief-utterances. Wittgenstein argues that belief "is a kind of *disposition* of the believing person. This is shown me in the case of someone else by his *behavior;* and by his works."[166] It is of course possible, Wittgenstein allows, to think of belief as a state of mind. But this does not get at the heart of the matter, and even gives rise to conceptual confusions. For example, does a believer stop believing when he falls asleep? Wittgenstein writes in the *Zettel:* "Really one hardly ever says that one has believed . . . 'uninterruptedly' since yesterday. An interruption of belief would be a period of unbelief, not e.g. the withdrawal of attention from what one believes—e.g. sleep."[167] "I can attend to the course of my pains, but not in the same way to that of my belief."[168] What *counts* as belief, then, is not simply what is going on in my head. Otherwise I become an unbeliever at some point every night.

The other way of approaching the grammar of the concept is to understand belief in terms of a disposition to respond to certain cir-

164. *Ibid.,* p. 370.
165. M. Dibelius and H. Greeven, *James. A Commentary on the Epistle of James* (Hermeneia series; Eng. Fortress Press, Philadelphia, 1976), pp. 151-52.
166. L. Wittgenstein, *P.I.* II.x, pp. 191-92 (my italics).
167. L. Wittgenstein, *Z.,* sect. 85.
168. *Ibid.,* sect. 75.

cumstances in certain situations. If I hold the belief "p," I shall act in certain ways, given the appropriate situation. Wittgenstein points out that belief, if it is genuine belief, carries certain *consequences* with it, or else it is not, after all, genuine. For example, I may say: "He believes it, but it is false"; but it would be nonsense to say: "I believe it, but it is false." Wittgenstein writes, "If there were a verb meaning 'to believe falsely', it would not have any significant first person present indicative."[169] What would it *mean* if a man said that he *believed* the New Testament, but was an atheist or an agnostic? If I say that I believe, "my own relation to my words is wholly different from other people's."[170]

The importance and validity of Wittgenstein's analysis of belief has been defended by D. M. High. In a valuable chapter High refers to certain points of similarity between Wittgenstein's view of belief and that of M. Polanyi. Both writers, he urges, view belief not primarily in terms of mental states, but as a matter of personal accreditation . . . personal backing, or signature."[171] This aspect of belief emerges not only in the *Investigations* and the *Zettel*, but also in Wittgenstein's *Lectures and Conversations*. Here, religious belief is seen as something which by definition cannot be isolated from given *attitudes*. As Wittgenstein says elsewhere, "The surroundings give it its importance . . . (A smiling mouth *smiles* only in a human face)."[172] D. M. High points out that Wittgenstein's work on the grammar of belief is part and parcel of his all-out attack on various kinds of dualism; between fact and value, between mind and body, between faith and reason, and between knowledge and belief.[173] Belief is not simply a mental state. It is no more possible to abstract believing from attitudes and actions than it is to extract the utterance "I promise" from questions about one's future conduct.

This is not of course to deny that in certain circumstances a man may act inconsistently with his beliefs, or be hypocritical or insincere when he affirms what he believes. But if his conduct were *consistently* unrelated to his belief, in what would his belief consist? What would it amount to? This question is discussed in detail by H. H. Price.[174] In very broad terms we may say that, with some of the qualifications which Price formulates, "When we say of someone 'he believes . . .' it is held that we are making a dispositional statement about him, and that this is equivalent to a series of conditional statements describing what he *would* be likely to say or do or feel if such and such circumstances were to arise."[175] For example, he

169. *P.I.*, p. 190.
170. *P.I.*, p. 192.
171. D. M. High, *Language, Persons and Belief*, p. 142.
172. *P.I.*, sect. 583. The metaphor refers primarily here to "hope."
173. D. M. High, *Language, Persons and Belief*, pp. 137-39.
174. H. H. Price, *Belief* (Allen & Unwin, London, 1969), pp. 27-28 and 290-314.
175. *Ibid.*, p. 20.

might be likely to assert his belief if he heard someone else denying it or expressing doubt about it; or if circumstances arose in which it made a practical difference whether he held the belief in question, he would act as if it were true.

As we have said, this action need not always be consistent. Price discusses the phenomenon of "half-belief" when a man acts in accordance with his belief on some occasions, but on other occasions he acts in the same way as someone who did not hold this belief.[176] The Book of Jonah, for example, could be described as a satire on half-belief. Jonah believes that God "made the sea and the dry land," yet he flees to Tarshish "from the presence of the Lord" (Jon. 1:3, 9). He cries to the Lord in his distress, yet seems ready to throw away his life (1:12; 2:1-9; 4:3). He feels deep concern for the plant which shields him from the sun, but cannot understand why God should feel concern for the people of Nineveh (4:10, 11). The book is addressed to those who "believe in" missionary activity, but whose belief is belied by the fact that they fail to take it seriously in practice. "This is a satire. . . . We are supposed to laugh at the ludicrous picture."[177]

What, then, does faith without action *amount to?* This is precisely James's question. The opponents whom James criticizes may well have been thinking of faith as, in effect, "a mental state" to be set in contrast to outward "acts." If so, James is not simply saying that the outward act must *match* the inward faith, but that faith which has no backing in attitude and action is not true *faith* at all. This explains the point behind James's statement about Abraham, and why he introduces into the discussion the question of how a believer responds to the brother or sister who is in need. Thus C. L. Mitton declares, "If a Christian claims to have faith, but is, for instance, dishonest, or harsh and callous to others in their need, it shows that his so-called faith is not true faith."[178] We cannot enter here into a detailed discussion of the Johannine epistles, but there is some kind of parallel between this dispositional perspective and the series of contrasts between word and deed in 1 John: "if we say we have fellowship with him while we walk in darkness, we lie . . ." (1:6); "He who says he is in the light and hates his brother is in the darkness still" (2:9; cf. 2:4; 2:6; 3:9, 10, 17, 18, 24; 4:20; 5:18). That John is not teaching "sinless perfection," or that faith is *the same as* works, is clear from his recognition in 1:8-10 that even the believer sins.

An elucidation of the grammar of the concept of faith has helped us to see at least part of what is at issue in the apparent contradiction between

---

176. *Ibid.*, pp. 305-07.
177. E. M. Good, *Irony in the Old Testament* (S.P.C.K., London, 1965), pp. 49-50; cf. pp. 39-55.
178. C. L. Mitton, *The Epistle of James* (Marshall, Morgan & Scott, London, 1966), p. 109.

Paul and James. We have seen that, as most writers urge, they do not contradict each other. But more than this, each has a rich and positive view of the grammar of faith, which emerges in the context of a given language-game or language-situation. It would be a mistake, as we saw in our section on polymorphous concepts, to ask what faith is in the New Testament, or even in Paul or in James, *in the abstract*. This is one of many reasons why systematic theology must always return to the text of the New Testament. But this does not mean that, on the other side, what Paul or James says about faith is only relevant to the situation for which they were writing. For the situations which they address have parallels today, and their words still speak to those who find themselves in these parallel circumstances. The use of categories and perspectives drawn from Wittgenstein has not imposed something alien onto the text of the New Testament. It has simply helped us to see more clearly the logical grammar of what the New Testament writers are actually saying, and provided tools which contribute towards a progressive interrelation and fusion between the horizon of the text and the horizon of the modern interpreter.

Wittgenstein and Structuralism

It may seem hazardous to try to embark on the subject of structuralism in only three or four pages. There are considerable variations of approach between different structuralist writers, and even some who are called structuralists by other scholars reject the use of this label as a description of their approach. However, in recent years structuralism has entered biblical studies, and in this short note my very limited objective is simply to note one or two points at which the work of Wittgenstein suggests certain assessments of the structuralist perspective. I shall not try to define the effect structuralism has on biblical studies, nor try to introduce it to readers who may still be unfamiliar with the movement. I have attempted this task in an article published elsewhere.[1]

We may first note the following points of affinity between Wittgenstein's later work and many structuralist writers. (1) Both approaches view language in a functional way, and see language-functions as deriving their force from interrelationships within a larger network of linguistic functions. Most structuralist writers would endorse Saussure's principle that "language is a system of interdependent terms in which the value of each term results solely from the simultaneous presence of the others."[2] What determines meaning is the interrelationship of similarities and differences within what structuralists call the system and what Wittgenstein calls the language-game. (2) Because language is based on convention or "rules," both Wittgenstein and the structuralists acknowledge the serious limitations of theories of reference, or ostensive definition, as an explanation of meaning, except in the context of certain special questions. Language,

---

1. A. C. Thiselton, "Structuralism and Biblical Studies: Method or Ideology?" *Exp.T.* LXXXIX (1978), 329-335.
2. F. de Saussure, *Cours de linguistique générale*, p. 114 (édition critique, Fasc. 2, p. 259).

many structuralists would say, is a self-referring and self-regulating system. (3) Wittgenstein and many structuralists also reject any sharp dualism between language and thought. Wittgenstein observes, "Thinking is not an incorporeal process . . . which it would be possible to detach from speaking, rather as the Devil took the shadow of Schlemiehl from the ground."[3] Structuralists tend to resist the notion that a text "contains" a series of "thoughts," as if "the text had to *express* a pre-established meaning," or as if "the meaning existed beyond or beneath the text."[4] Similarly Wittgenstein writes, "Meaning is not a process which accompanies a word."[5] (4) Wittgenstein is concerned that we should look at language from as many different angles as possible. Structuralism provides an angle of vision which is very different from that of traditional interpretation theory. Perhaps, in Wittgenstein's terms, such an angle of vision will allow us to *notice* features of language which we have failed to see before, even because of their very familiarity. (5) Both Wittgenstein and many structuralists draw on a contrast between "deep" grammar and "surface" grammar.[6] In both there is a sense that we must somehow reach "behind" the surface of language to something deeper, although this is not some "inner" or "mental" process.

On closer inspection, however, we find that with the important exception of the first and the fourth of these points, the difference between Wittgenstein and structuralism is more fundamental than their points of affinity.

(1) To begin with the last point, it is clear what Wittgenstein means by "deep" grammar. He is talking about the fundamental contrast between the grammar of language-*uses,* and accidents of surface-grammar which are determined solely by convention. Wittgenstein's contrast is vindicated by the conceptual clarifications which emerge on the basis of his work. In structuralism, however, we have a different type of contrast, between "message" and "code." But here the difficulty is that different structuralists discover different types of codes behind or beneath each message. Sometimes these coincide with Freudian or Jungian symbolism; sometimes the code is expounded in terms of the narrative grammar of V. I. Propp or of A. J. Greimas; sometimes it takes a form which is determined by Lévi-Strauss's theory of myth. All three versions of the code have found their way into biblical studies.[7] But it is seldom clear what status this code possesses, or what is its actual relation to the

3. *P.I.*, sect. 339.
4. J.-M. Benoist, *The Structural Revolution* (Weidenfeld & Nicolson, London, 1978), pp. 11-12.
5. *P.I.* II.xi, p. 21.
6. *P.I.*, sect. 664.
7. E.g. J. Calloud, *Structural Analysis of Narrative* (Fortress Press, Philadelphia, and Scholars Press, Missoula, 1976), pp. 47-108 (using models from Greimas); D. O. Via, "The

meaning of the "surface" message. Rejoinders about the importance of polysemy do not entirely answer this question.

(2) More serious still is the attempt of many structuralists to abstract their analyses of particular texts from *history,* or from human life. This is not simply a matter of our accepting Saussure's warnings about the relationship between synchrony and diachronic meaning. *This* point is valid. It is bound up, rather, with the a-historical nature of *the code* (cf. Saussure's *langue*). But if the code is divorced from historic human life, how is it still related to language as a *human* activity? Wittgenstein rightly insists as his most central axiom that language is grounded in life. "The speaking of language is part of an activity, or of a form of life."[8] Language-games comprise "the whole, consisting of language and the actions into which it is woven."[9] This is not to deny Saussure's insight that the connection between the signifier and the signified is "arbitrary," or based on convention. Many structuralists seem to forget that "Only in the stress of life and thought do words have meaning."[10] If by way of reply it is urged that here we are concerned only with the code, we return to our previous point. How does the structuralist code relate to the "meaning" of the text in any acceptable sense of the word "meaning"?

(3) Our third main point arises from the second. If language is grounded in human life, Wittgenstein shares with the hermeneutical tradition a recognition of the importance of the particular case. Human beings use language creatively, and therefore constantly transcend the boundaries of generalizing models. This is precisely what marks the most crucial point of difference between the *Tractatus* and the *Investigations,* and between linguistics and hermeneutics. In the *Tractatus* Wittgenstein bases language on general principles which function in the abstract. In the *Blue Book* he violently attacks what he calls "our pre-occupation with the method of science" with its "craving for generality" and "contemptuous attitude towards the particular case."[11] In the *Investigations* he grounds language-uses in the particularities or "surroundings" of language-games, rather than "systems," because these in turn rest on forms of *life*. We do not dispute, as Wittgenstein did not dispute, that *regularities* occur in language. Otherwise communication could not take place at all. But many structuralists constantly try to squeeze stretches of human language or of

---

Parable of the Unjust Judge: A Metaphor of the Unrealized Self" in D. Patte (ed.), *Semiology and Parables. An Exploration of the Possibilities Offered by Structuralism for Exegesis* (Pickwick Press, Pittsburgh, 1976), pp. 1-33 (using Jung); and E. Leach, "Structuralism in Social Anthropology" in D. Robey (ed.), *Structuralism* (Clarendon Press, Oxford, 1973), pp. 53-56 (using Lévi-Strauss).
8. *P.I.,* sect. 23.
9. *P.I.,* sect. 7.
10. *Z.,* sect. 173.
11. *B.B.,* p. 18.

the written text into the pre-cast molds of their structuralist models and categories. Characters in the New Testament have their structural roles reduced to *general* terms. For example, in accordance with Greimas' model of narrative grammar, each character assumes the role of "helper," "sender," "receiver," "opponent," and so on. But too often the use of these general categories is forced onto the text without regard for its particularities.[12]

We are not suggesting that Wittgenstein has provided any single decisive argument against the validity of structuralism as such. For, as I have argued in my article on the subject, it is possible to select certain structuralist methods judiciously, without subscribing to a structuralist ideology. Furthermore, Wittgenstein is concerned with a largely different set of problems from those which occupy the attention of structuralists. However, some of Wittgenstein's remarks do suggest that we should exercise caution before welcoming structuralism into biblical studies as a proven and entirely valid method of *exegesis*. We must add that structuralism is still relatively young, especially in terms of its introduction to biblical studies. We still wait to see what its more mature contribution to biblical hermeneutics may turn out to be. As a preliminary assessment, however, Wittgenstein's work suggests that while there is some value in its emphasis on the role of interrelated functions in language, and while it may provide a fresh angle of vision from which to view the text, some of the other claims made by structuralists must be considered with caution.

12. See the valid criticism of J. L. Crenshaw in *Semiology and Parables*, pp. 54-55.

Wittgenstein and the Debate about Biblical Authority

Wittgenstein does not discuss questions about the authority of a written text, nor does he anywhere express concern about the status of the Bible. However, several major points which he makes do suggest certain warnings or lessons about the shape of the modern debate about biblical authority. The purpose of this short note is not so much to enter into the debate itself, as to suggest ways in which, through conceptual investigations stimulated by Wittgenstein, certain pitfalls may perhaps be avoided, and the argument carried forward more constructively.

(1) We have seen that Wittgenstein lays down a very solemn warning about the power which a *picture* possesses to seduce us, to lead us astray, or at the very least to dictate our way of marking out the terms of a problem. He writes concerning the spell of a picture over his own earlier work: "A *picture* held us captive. And we could not get outside it."[1] "The picture was the key. Or it *seemed* like a key."[2] What misleads us is not simply the power of a model or metaphor as such, but the fact that all too often our way of seeing a particular problem is wholly dictated by a *single controlling* picture which excludes all others. In these circumstances it exercises a spell over us, which bewitches our intelligence and blinds us to other ways of seeing the problem.

In the history of the debate about the nature of biblical authority, often each side has operated with a controlling picture on the basis of which it makes out the entire ground of the debate. The most obvious example concerns a one-sided picture of the Bible either as exclusively a divine Word of God, or else as exclusively a merely human word of religious men. James Smart observes that during the first sixteen or more

1. L. Wittgenstein, *P.I.*, sect. 115.
2. *Z.*, sect. 240.

centuries of tradition, "the church in its zeal to exalt the Scriptures so emphasized their divinity as to deny the actuality of the human element in them. . . . The great and abiding achievement of historical scholarship has been to discover and establish the human character of the Scriptures. So obsessed, however, did scholars become with the importance of this discovery that in very large degree they lost sight of the divine character of Scripture. It became for them the human story of man's religious and ethical achievements."[3] Even today, one writer is exclusively preoccupied with following through the consequences of the picture of divinely authored Scripture, while another explores and sees only what the human picture allows for. Each accords to his picture the status of a comprehensive account of all the facts of the matter.

Recently James Barr has criticized the use of the model of Chalcedonian Christology as an attempt to do justice to both the human and divine aspects of Scripture.[4] On one side, Wittgenstein's warnings about the spell of a controlling picture justify Barr's warning, if what is at issue is the adoption of this model as a *controlling* one. But on the other side, the very purpose of this model as traditionally conceived, was to prevent either a Docetic or Arian picture of the Bible from dominating the debate one-sidedly. In this respect, the traditional model still serves a useful purpose, provided that it, in turn, does not become our only model. Thus, while he accepts the validity of the christological model up to a point, J. T. Burtchaell argues that "the real issue here is what confounds scholars in so many areas: the manner in which individual human events are jointly caused by both God and man."[5] His argument is that static models, including a static model of inerrancy, must be replaced by dynamic ones.[6] Burtchaell's allusion to the question of inerrancy also reminds us that many writers work with one over-narrow model of truth when discussing the truth-claims of the Bible. Once again, this has led to an unhelpful polarization in the debate. Many writers work exclusively with the model of correspondence between propositions and facts. Others over-react against this approach, so that Oswald Loretz, for example, argues that the truth of the Bible is *solely* a matter of existential truth, in accordance with the supposedly Hebraic tradition.[7] But we have seen in the course of our discussion of polymorphous concepts that "truth" is employed in the New Testament in a variety of language-games.

The question of the nature of biblical authority is a highly complex

3. J. Smart, *The Interpretation of Scripture*, p. 15.
4. J. Barr, *The Bible in the Modern World*, pp. 20-22.
5. J. T. Burtchaell, *Catholic Theories of Biblical Inspiration Since 1810* (Cambridge University Press, 1969), p. 279.
6. *Ibid.*, p. 303.
7. O. Loretz, *The Truth of the Bible* (Burns & Oates, London, 1968), pp. 9-21 *et passim*.

one. Any attempt, therefore, to pre-empt the debate and to dictate the terms of the discussion on the basis of some *single* picture of the shape of the problem must be firmly resisted. For such a picture, Wittgenstein warns us, will blinker our eyes against *noticing* some of the varied phenomena that are before us. This leads to a stalemate in the debate, for each side is working with a different picture.

(2) We have seen that in his book *On Certainty* Wittgenstein discussed the special status of propositions which function "as *a foundation* for research and action."[8] Such propositions belong "to the scaffolding of our thoughts."[9] They are "like the axis around which a body rotates."[10] Wittgenstein himself described such propositions as having the function of the words "It is written."[11]

At first sight this seems to raise a peculiar problem about the attitude of the New Testament writers towards the authority of the Old Testament. This attitude, we may note, has always formed a major plank in the conservative argument about the authority of Scripture, as represented for example in the writings of B. B. Warfield. If Jesus and the apostolic church regarded the Old Testament as authoritative Scripture, it is argued, this attitude is normative for all Christians who claim to stand in the apostolic tradition and to yield obedience to Jesus Christ. It is then argued, in turn, that the New Testament can hardly be less authoritative than the Old. But these arguments invite a standard rejoinder. It is argued, by way of reply, that Jesus and the apostolic church regarded the Old Testament as authoritative only because they *could do no other.* They inherited this attitude as a *cultural presupposition* which they accepted uncritically. The Hellenistic world, it is argued, was familiar with the notion of divinely inspired writings, and the Old Testament possessed absolute authority in Judaism. Wittgenstein's remarks in *On Certainty* seem at first sight to confirm the standard arguments directed against the conservative case. For if the authority of the Old Testament is a "hinge" on which other arguments turn, then is it not also the kind of axiom of which it may be said: "I cannot imagine the opposite"?[12] "It is removed from the traffic."[13] It is an inherited assumption, built into the fabric of thought because "every human being has parents."[14] It "lies apart from the route travelled by inquiry."[15]

We need not question the fact that the authority of the Old Testament

8. L. Wittgenstein, *Cert.,* sect. 87.
9. *Ibid.,* sect. 211.
10. *Ibid.,* sect. 152.
11. *Ibid.,* sect. 216.
12. *Ibid.,* sects. 231, 343, and 655.
13. *Ibid.,* sect. 210.
14. *Ibid.,* sect. 211.
15. *Ibid.,* sect. 88.

had the status of a "certainty," in Wittgenstein's sense of the term, for the primitive church. The Old Testament provided a "foundation" on which further thought and inquiry rested. C. K. Barrett rightly comments, "The New Testament . . . authors regarded the Old Testament as an authoritative body of literature which claimed . . . the obedience of Christians. It was used as a basis of theological argument and of ethical instruction."[16] However, there are two sets of factors which suggest to us that this was not merely due to the *uncritical* acceptance of a *cultural* assumption. First of all, there are factors which suggest that while the authority of the Old Testament was never in *doubt*, it was nevertheless the subject of *thought*. Secondly, we have already argued in some detail in the previous chapter that class-two grammatical utterances characteristically express *religious* connections, and not simply cultural ones.

The first point sub-divides into at least four considerations. In the first place, some scholars make much of the supposed claim of Jesus to interpret the will of God in a radically different way from Moses: "You have heard that it was said to the men of old. . . . But I say to you . . ." (Matt. 5:33, 38, and 43). Secondly, C. F. Evans and others argue that the trend towards "secularization" initiated by Jesus and Paul ought quite naturally to have challenged the idea of a "holy" book.[17] Jesus "proclaimed the rule of God in terms largely free from the cultic or ecclesiastical. . . . One thinks of Paul's passionate refusal of the sacral badge of circumcision as a sine qua non of salvation."[18] Thirdly, there is the whole question of the status of the Jewish law for the Gentile churches. Fourthly, there is the emergence at Corinth and presumably elsewhere of a "charismatic" emphasis on a direct appeal to the experience of the Holy Spirit which might be thought to assume a position of precedence over documents belonging to the past. Even if the first two claims are often exaggerated, there need only be a small grain of truth in each of these four points to suggest that the acceptance of a Jewish book as authoritative Scripture for the primitive communities *could not* have occurred without thought and critical reflection. The status of the Old Testament as an authoritative book is more than an *inherited* assumption for the Gentile churches who already knew that the Jewish law was not in every respect binding on them.

This conclusion accords with our earlier arguments about the significance of class-two grammatical utterances.[19] We argued that the kind of convictions expressed in class-two grammatical utterances usually repre-

16. C. K. Barrett, "The Interpretation of the Old Testament in the New" in P. R. Ackroyd and C. F. Evans (ed.), *The Cambridge History of the Bible* I (Cambridge University Press, 1970), p. 377.
17. C. F. Evans, *Is 'Holy Scripture' Christian?*, pp. 34-36.
18. *Ibid.*, p. 34.
19. Above, sect. 57.

sents *religious* or *theological* beliefs, rather than simply axioms of the prevailing culture, at least in the cases of first-century literature that we examined. Thus the reason why there is no active or prolonged controversy about the status of the Old Testament within the pages of the New is not because it was never the object of serious *thought*, but because it was never the object of serious *doubt*. It remains a foundational "certainty" on the basis of which other thought and action is carried out, but not because it is merely a cultural axiom accepted uncritically. It was a *religious* conviction that through the Old Testament God had spoken and still continued to speak. These considerations, coupled with the fact that the authority of the Old Testament retains the characteristics of a genuine "certainty," suggest that the traditional Warfield-type arguments about the status of the Old Testament in the New Testament writings must still be accorded respect.

(3) We have seen that for Wittgenstein "the speaking of language is part of an activity."[20] "Only in the stream of thought and life do words have meaning."[21] This means that the actual experience of the authority of the biblical text is something which occurs in concrete and dynamic terms. This is seen in many different ways and experienced at different levels. Biblical authority is not simply an abstract and monolithic concept. We have seen, for example, that the biblical writers address themselves to different particular situations, and that, in turn, they write out of their own particular situations. This means that the biblical text comes alive as a "speech-act" (cf. Heidegger's "language-event") when some kind of correspondence or inter-relation occurs between the situation addressed by the biblical writer and the situation of the modern reader or hearer. This looks at first sight as if it opens the door to subjectivism or at the very least to what Barr calls a "soft" idea of authority.[22] But to describe such a view of authority as "soft" is a grave mistake. To recognize the interrelationship between authority and hermeneutics is precisely to give authority cash-value and a cutting edge. It means that far from seeing the biblical message as something packaged up in neat containers and abstracted from life, it is in the stream of life and thought that it makes its impact, from situation to situation. The experience of biblical authority is concrete and dynamic, because it is not experienced *outside* a given language-game.

There is a danger that both sides in the debate will read too much, or perhaps not enough, out of this point. We are not saying that the Bible is authoritative only when it "rings a bell" for the hearer. For we are speaking here not of authority as such, but of the *experience* of authority. At one level, what the Bible says *about* forgiveness, for example, is

20. *P.I.*, sect. 23.
21. *Z.*, sect. 173.
22. J. Barr, *The Bible in the Modern World*, p. 27.

authoritative for the Christian regardless of his situation (in a way which we shall explain shortly). But at the level of experience, it is when a man so reads the texts that he hears God, for example, *forgiving* him that the authority of the text is fully experienced. In this sense, the language-games of the Bible embrace a whole range of dynamic speech-acts: commanding, promising, asking, judging, blessing, warning, pardoning, acclaiming, and so on. But at another level all these broadly "performative" acts can be effective only because certain states of affairs are true. Thus Jesus can say "Your sins be forgiven you" only because he is the one who can forgive sins. In *this* sense, the authority of the words of Jesus rests on something that lies *behind* the particular speech-act and its interpretation.

The point which is correct behind the so-called "non-propositional" view of revelation is that the Bible is not merely a handbook of information and description, along the lines of propositions in the *Tractatus*. But the point behind the so-called "propositional" view is even more important, even if it is badly expressed in the traditional terms which are often used. It is that the dynamic and concrete authority of the Bible rests, in turn, on the truth of certain states of affairs in God's relation to the world. As J. L. Austin succinctly put it, for performative language to function effectively, "certain statements have *to be true*."[23]

Biblical authority is experienced, then, not in the abstract but in the dynamic and concrete speech-acts of particular language-games. But the basis of this authority is something broader and more comprehensive which concerns God's relationship to his world. It is a mistake to polarize these two aspects of authority into alternatives, as when Barr speaks of "hard" and "soft" views of authority.

(4) Wittgenstein uses the concept of the paradigm case, following the work of G. E. Moore. As we earlier recalled, Moore would argue: when I say that I *know* that I have a hand, if *that* kind of thing is not "knowing," what is?[24] We also considered in this connection the claim that in the light of modern physics, marble slabs and oak beams were not "really" solid. But marble and oak provide paradigm cases of what it is to *be* "solid." Wittgenstein remarks about such paradigm cases: "I must not saw off the branch on which I am sitting."[25]

From the point of view of logical grammar, there is a close connection between the notion of a paradigm case and some of the admirable comments which John Bright puts forward about the authority of the Bible. He writes, "The Bible provides us with the primary, and thus the normative, documents of the Christian faith. . . . To ask, as we continu-

23. J. L. Austin, *How to Do Things with Words*, p. 45.
24. G. E. Moore, *Philosophical Papers*, p. 37; cf. above, sect. 58.
25. *P.I.*, sect. 55.

ally do, Is this teaching truly Christian? . . . is to be driven back to the Bible. . . . On what basis can we say what is truly in accord with the Christian faith if we fail to consult the only documents that tell us *what the Christian faith originally was?*"[26] I have already argued in this study and elsewhere that the publicly accessible tradition of the Old Testament, through events such as the Exodus and the work of the Judges, provides primary models of what is meant by God's saving activity. To try to redefine our basic Christian concepts in such a way that they undermine or contradict the witness of the Bible would be to "saw off the branch on which I am sitting." The Bible provides paradigms in the light of which given concepts or experiences may be *identified* as genuinely "Christian," or otherwise.

26. J. Bright, *The Authority of the Old Testament* (S.C.M., London, 1967), p. 30 (my italics).

CHAPTER XV

Conclusions

We have seen that the problem of hermeneutics is two-sided, relating to the interpreter as well as to the text. This principle raises questions about the nature of pre-understanding, about the role of tradition in interpretation, and about whether and in what sense we may properly speak of the present meaning of a text. We saw that the problem of pre-understanding is a genuine one, and that it is by no means exclusively connected with Bultmann's hermeneutics. Thinkers from Schleiermacher to Ricoeur, and from Freud to the Latin-American theologians of liberation, have tried to grapple with the issues which are raised by this aspect of the subject. The problem of pre-understanding, however, does not give grounds for the cynical response that the modern interpreter understands the Bible only on the basis of his own presuppositions. For there is an ongoing process of dialogue with the text in which the text itself progressively corrects and reshapes the interpreter's own questions and assumptions.

Nor should we be unduly pessimistic about the problem of tradition. We have seen that tradition affects understanding both negatively and positively. The former aspect emerged most clearly in the later writings of Heidegger; the latter aspect, in the work of Gadamer. In this latter context we saw that it raised positive and fruitful questions about the relations between exegesis and systematic theology as expressing the ongoing tradition of the Christian community. In Gadamer's view tradition is not only a bridge between the past and the present, but also a filter which passes on interpretations and insights which have stood the test of time.

That the problem of present meaning cannot be excluded from interpretation in Christian theology is suggested partly by the attitude of the New Testament writers towards the Old Testament. This attitude, we have argued, is not due to pre-critical naïveté. The interpreter, in any case, cannot simply step out of his own horizons, and look at the text as if he

439

were detached from his own time and his own tradition. While his subjectivity should be critically controlled, the hermeneutical task involves both *distance,* in which account is taken of the particularity of the text, and also a progress towards as close a *fusion* of horizons with the text as the relation between text and interpreter will allow.

Certain conclusions were suggested about the problem of hermeneutics and history. We must recognize the seriousness of the problem of historical relativity and distance. But this does not mean that we are obliged to accept the claims of D. E. Nineham about its nature and difficulty. Nineham, we argued, has exaggerated the problem of historical distance, and introduced an unnecessarily positivistic flavor into the debate. We offered six specific criticisms of his position. Moreover, when we looked at the rise of historical consciousness in thinkers from Lessing and Herder to Ranke, the contribution of these thinkers did not seem to undermine these criticisms. More positively, we saw in the work of Wolfhart Pannenberg a much more adequate attempt to grapple with the relation between hermeneutics and history. Pannenberg sees the seriousness of the problem in question, but he capitulates neither to positivism nor to the dualism of fact and value which has vitiated so much modern theological thinking.

Arguments from theology do not invalidate the necessity for hermeneutics, nor do they call in question the urgency of the hermeneutical task. For example, appeals to the Holy Spirit do not bypass hermeneutics. For the Spirit works *through* human understanding, and not independently of it. Appeals to the need for faith and claims about so-called timeless truth demand careful clarification and assessment. But when this is done, rather than challenging the need for hermeneutical theory, these considerations underline its importance.

Hermeneutics cannot bypass semantics and traditional language-study. Nevertheless we must also move beyond this area. The work of Ricoeur admirably illustrates this point. The relation between hermeneutics and language introduces the questions about language and thought. Two sides have to be held together. On the one hand, accidents of surface-grammar and vocabulary stock do not usually determine thought in a decisive way. In this respect the claims of Saussure and his successors in linguistics are correct. Similarly Barr's attack on Boman, which is based on them, is also valid. But this is only half of the problem. On the other side, language-uses, as language habits, can and do influence thought in the way suggested by Gadamer and Wittgenstein. There is a half-truth in the Whorf hypothesis, which is significant for hermeneutics, especially for the problem of pre-understanding.

We may turn now to Heidegger. There is truth in Heidegger's claim that man is already placed in a given "world," prior to his reflection on his situation. Hermeneutics must take account of this. We cannot put the clock back to the era before Kant. Objectivity is not the same as objectivism, and the relevance to hermeneutics of the Cartesian model of knowledge must not be assumed without question and accorded a privileged position.

At the same time, Heidegger's own position is not without problems. There is still a place for subject-object thinking in hermeneutics. Ryle's criticism of Heidegger may fail to do justice to the importance of feeling-states, but there is a measure of truth in his complaint about Heidegger's devaluing of the role of cognition. Heidegger's work on the nature of truth suggests that he wishes to *broaden* the basis of epistemology. But in practice to reject the role of subject-object thinking in critical testing is unwarrantably to *narrow* this basis. Feeling states and the priority of worldhood are important in hermeneutics, and the Cartesian model is too limited as a model for the interpretation of texts. Nevertheless there is room *both* for critical reflection on the text as object and *also* for submission to the text in order that it may speak to man in his "world."

Heidegger's approach leads both to difficulties and to insights in Bultmann's work on the New Testament. One insight connected with Heidegger's thought is Bultmann's view of man as a unity, in terms of his possibilities rather than in terms of substances or "parts." But his notion of authentic existence raises difficulties, not least because of its individualism. Moreover, truth disclosed *through Dasein* too easily becomes truth *about Dasein*. In addition to this, there are claims about the "present" status of history which need to be clarified carefully.

When we turn to Bultmann's own work in greater detail, we find that the terms of the hermeneutical problem were virtually set and established for Bultmann *prior* to Heidegger's philosophy. Bultmann was influenced by a whole range of factors, which we have enumerated in chapters eight and nine. Of special importance is the influence of Herrmann and of Neo-Kantian philosophy. This latter suggests for Bultmann a radical dualism between the this-worldly and the Beyond, which becomes a major source of difficulty when combined with his theological assumptions. This-worldly knowledge remains knowledge of an objectified realm. Man knows this realm, as it were, on his own terms. For Bultmann this cannot be the realm of faith and of revelation. His view of faith and history and his relation to nineteenth-century Lutheranism compound the problem.

Liberalism, with its concern about modern man, and the History of Religions School, with its stress on the strangeness of the New Testament world, made the problem of hermeneutics more urgent for Bultmann. Above all, dialectical theology nourished Bultmann's belief that anything in the New Testament which is merely "descriptive" must be re-interpreted in order to give it a kerygmatic thrust. His conception of myth derives from several sources, but this contrast between the objective and the existential was already applied to the problem of myth in the work of Hans Jonas. Heidegger's work offered to Bultmann a conceptuality which seemed to solve the hermeneutical problem set for Bultmann by this large variety of other factors and influences.

Bultmann draws on the work of Dilthey and Yorck, and finds parallels between his own work and that of Collingwood. He endorses Dilthey's view of pre-understanding and the constancy of human nature, but it is a mistake to identify self-understanding in Bultmann with "inner" life in Dilthey. From Yorck Bultmann draws the insight that the interpreter not only examines the text, but the text examines the interpreter. This is an insight which he passes on to his pupils, especially Ernst Fuchs. Too much should not be made of the relation between Bultmann and Collingwood, for which Bultmann perhaps claims more than he should.

Bultmann's view of myth raises very serious difficulties. These are partly bound up with his notion of the relation between language and thought. But the real difficulty is that *within his own system* it is impossible either to confirm or to deny his claims on the basis of an *exegesis* of the relevant New Testament passages. For every passage is regarded by Bultmann as representing *either* myth that has already been demythologized, *or* myth which obscures the true intention of the text. Very often Bultmann allows that the text represents the biblical writer's own true intention *only when it accords with Bultmann's view of the New Testament,* at least in Paul and John. Thus *Sachkritik* is employed in order to support a holistic view of the New Testament, which precludes the possibility of falsifying Bultmann's case on the basis of exegesis. Of course, exegetical assessments may be offered from *outside* Bultmann's system, but he would always claim that such assessments failed to meet his point.

There are numerous other difficulties, which are widely known. For example, we must ask whether his three definitions of myth are mutually consistent. But two criticisms relate to the problem of language and meaning. First of all, Bultmann tends to view language as outer clothing which can be detached from the thought or intentions behind it. But both Gadamer and Wittgenstein show the difficulties of such a view. Secondly, because of his dualism between fact and value, Bultmann cannot meet Wittgenstein's warnings about public criteria of meaning. The Old Testament is devalued as a source of publicly-accessible tradition, and revelation, which is restricted to a realm beyond objectification, loses the basis on which its meaningfulness is grounded.

Gadamer rightly stresses the role of experience, tradition, and pre-judgment in hermeneutics. His emphasis on experience is corroborated by his discussions of art, of games, and of the history of philosophy. He rightly calls for a fresh sensitivity in hermeneutics, in which there is an openness to new truth, and an attempt to reach a maximum awareness of one's own pre-judgments. Gadamer's concept of the fusion of horizons is constructive for hermeneutical theory and practice.

The emphasis on both distance and (as far as possible) fusion suggests certain conclusions about the relation between exegesis and systematic theology. When exegesis is subordinated to a theological tradition, the need for distancing becomes all the more urgent. But it is theologically sterile to aim only at achieving distance, as was the aim of some nineteenth-century biblical scholars. Neither exegesis nor systematic theology can ever be final, or totally independent of the other. The problem is constructively elucidated by Diem, Ott, and Stuhlmacher.

The new hermeneutic owes much to Heidegger's later thought, as well as to Gadamer. Fuchs fruitfully explores the categories of language-event and *Einverständnis*. There are points of similarity between the work of Fuchs and Ebeling and that of Funk and Crossan in America. Nevertheless, in spite of its promise and its value, the new hermeneutic is one-sided. Its view of language comes too near at times to word-magic, and tends to ignore the fact that language is founded on convention. Moreover, in devaluing the place of assertions, it overlooks the complexity and variety of functions performed by statements. Even performative language presupposes certain conventions and states of affairs. More seriously, it is difficult to reconcile Fuchs' valid insight that the word of God judges the hearer with his claim that somehow the hearer himself remains the criterion of truth. Truth has become a matter of what is true for me. Finally, the relevance of the new hermeneutic to the New Testament varies drastically from passage to passage, or perhaps from genre to genre.

There is a growing body of secondary literature on the subject of the relationship between Heidegger and Wittgenstein. We introduced some of the claims of this literature in our introductory remarks in chapter two. The *Tractatus* reflects a dualism of fact and value which has the same Neo-Kantian background as that which lies behind the work of Bultmann. The *Tractatus* is far from being a work of positivism. Value for the earlier Wittgenstein transcends the limitations of propositions about facts. But this does not mean that value is unimportant. Indeed the reverse is the case. "Showing" in the *Tractatus* is like "saying" in the later Heidegger. Both concern what really matters.

However, Wittgenstein, unlike Bultmann, abandons this dualism. All language, he sees, is grounded not simply in formal logic, but in the stream of human life. Language-games, like Heidegger's "world," are givens." We cannot make generalizations about language which are independent of future experience, for language lives and grows. Hence language-games constitute a key category in hermeneutics. Hermeneutics avoids asking questions *outside* a particular language-game. The concepts, or language-uses, of the interpreter, and equally those of the text, belong to particular games. Language-games, and the concepts which they shape, change with changing situations over the course of time. Wittgenstein does not, as some of his interpreters claim, open the door to pluralism and relativism. But he does recognize the importance of the particular case, and the particularity of each of the two horizons is the first principle of hermeneutics.

Wittgenstein's warnings about private language pinpoint a major difficulty in Bultmann's hermeneutics. Rules in language, Wittgenstein urges, presuppose a publicly accessible tradition of behavior and language-uses. Such a tradition is provided in the Bible by the Old Testament accounts of God's saving acts in the life and traditions of Israel. But Bultmann, as we have seen, devalues the "this-worldly." Indeed in this context the dualism of Neo-Kantian thought imposes an impossible dilemma. Either revelation involves the kind of objectification presupposed by a publicly accessible tradition, or it remains incommunicable as "private" language. Bultmann's use of Dilthey's category of "life" suggests that he has some awareness of the problem, but it is insufficient to rescue him from the difficulty.

Wittgenstein's remarks about conceptual and logical problems shed light on some quite specific issues in the New Testament. It is illuminating to distinguish between various classes of "grammatical" utterances in the Pauline writings, and to suggest certain conclusions about their life-settings. This suggests caution about describing all assumptions which form "the scaffolding of our thought" as necessarily culture-relative rather than the product of genuinely theological convictions. It also suggests caution in assuming that there is a clear-cut contrast between "showing" in the parables of Jesus and "argument" in the epistles of Paul. Perhaps these two modes of discourse are not as far apart as is usually imagined. Pictures and linguistic recommendations profoundly affect how we see the world and order our lives.

Some of the concepts used in the New Testament are multiform or polymorphous. Some serious mistakes might have been avoided if scholars had noticed how this principle operates in the case of "faith," "flesh," and "truth" in the New Testament. We concluded our study by applying several elements from Wittgenstein's thought to the clarification of five persistent problems about justification by faith in the Pauline writings. These include Wittgenstein's remarks about "seeing . . . as. . . ." *Simul iustus et peccator* represents not two contradictory assertions, but two evaluations made from within different language-games. In

Paul, faith is related to justification not instrumentally but internally as part of the grammar of the concept.

At the beginning of our study we claimed that the use of philosophical description would serve the interpreter of the New Testament in three ways. First of all, it would help him to define the nature of the hermeneutical task. Secondly, it would provide conceptual tools for the interpretation of parts of the text. Thirdly, it would help the interpreter to detect his own presuppositions and enlarge his own critical capacities. If these three aims have been fulfilled to any extent, this means that the introduction of philosophical consideration into the hermeneutical debate, far from leading to a one-sided or distorted interpretation of the New Testament, will provide the interpreter with a broader pre-understanding in relation to which the text may speak more clearly in its own right. The hermeneutical goal is that of a steady progress towards a fusion of horizons. But this is to be achieved in such a way that the particularity of each horizon is fully taken into account and respected. This means *both* respecting the rights of the text *and* allowing it to speak.

Bibliography of Works Cited

Paul J. ACHTEMEIER, "How Adequate is the New Hermeneutic?" in *Th.T* XXIII (1966), 105-11.

_____, *An Introduction to the New Hermeneutic*. Westminster Press, Philadelphia, 1969.

W. F. ALBRIGHT, *New Horizons in Biblical Research*. Oxford University Press, 1966.

V. C. ALDRICH, "Pictorial Meaning, Picture-Thinking, and Wittgenstein's Theory of Aspects" in *Mind* LXVII (1958), 70-79.

Bede ALLEMANN, *"Hölderlin et Heidegger. Recherche de la relation entre poésie et pensée*. Presses Universitaires de France, Paris, 1959.

E. L. ALLEN, *Existentialism from Within*. Routledge & Kegan Paul, London, 1953.

William P. ALSTON, *Philosophy of Language*. Prentice-Hall, Englewood Cliffs, N.J., 1964.

Stephen AMDUR and Samuel A. HORINE, "An Index to Philosophically Relevant Terms in Wittgenstein's *Zettel*" in *I.P.Q.* X (1970), 310-22.

F. AMIOT, *The Key Concepts of St. Paul*. Eng. Herder, Freiburg, 1962.

G. E. M. ANSCOMBE, *An Introduction to Wittgenstein's Tractatus*. Hutchinson, London, 1959.

_____, *Intention*. Blackwell, Oxford, ²1963.

Karl-Otto APEL, "Wittgenstein und das Problem des hermeneutischen Verstehen" in *Z.Th.K.* LXIII (1966), 49-87.

_____, *Analytic Philosophy of Language and the Geisteswissenschaften*. Reidel, Dordrecht, 1967 (Foundations of Language, Supplementary Series 4).

John L. AUSTIN. *Philosophical Papers*. Clarendon Press, Oxford, 1961 and ²1971.

_____, *How to Do Things with Words*. Clarendon Press, Oxford, 1962.

A. J. AYER, *Language, Truth, and Logic*. Gollancz, London, ²1946, Penguin edn. 1971.

Renford BAMBROUGH, "How to Read Wittgenstein" in *Royal Institute of Philosophy Lectures VII: Understanding Wittgenstein*. Macmillan, London, 1974, pp. 117-32.

Ian G. BARBOUR, *Myths, Models and Paradigms. The Nature of Scientific and Religious Language*. S.C.M., London, 1974.

James BARR, *The Semantics of Biblical Language*. Oxford University Press, 1961.

—————, *Old and New in Interpretation. A Study of the Two Testaments*. S.C.M., London, 1966.

—————, *The Bible in the Modern World*. S.C.M., London, 1973.

C. K. BARRETT, *The Gospel according to St. John*. S.P.C.K., London, 1958.

—————, *A Commentary on the Epistle to the Romans*. Black, London, ²1962.

—————, *A Commentary on the First Epistle to the Corinthians*. Black, London, 1968.

William BARRETT, *What is Existentialism?* Grove Press, New York, 1964.

Karl BARTH, *The Word of God and the Word of Man*. Eng. Hodder & Stoughton, London, 1928.

—————, *The Epistle to the Romans*. Eng. Oxford University Press, 1933 and 1968.

—————, *Church Dogmatics* I/2. Eng. Clark, Edinburgh, 1956.

—————, *From Rousseau to Ritschl*. Eng. S.C.M., London, 1959.

Hans-Werner BARTSCH (ed.), *Kerygma und Mythos. Ein theologisches Gespräch* (6 vols. with supplements). Reich & Heidrich, Evangelischer Verlag, Hamburg, 1948 onwards. Selections in English in *Kerygma and Myth* (2 vols.). S.P.C.K., London, ²1964 and 1962.

G. R. BEASLEY-MURRAY, "Demythologized Eschatology" in *Th.T.* XIV (1957), 61-79.

Lewis White BECK, "Neo-Kantianism" in P. Edwards (ed.), *The Encyclopedia of Philosophy*. 8 vols.; Macmillan & Free Press, New York, 1967, V, 468-73.

Michael BEINTKER, *Die Gottesfrage in der Theologie Wilhelm Herrmanns*. Evangelische Verlagsanstalt, Berlin, 1976.

Richard H. BELL, "Wittgenstein and Descriptive Theology" in *R.St.* V (1969), 1-18.

Jean-Marie BENOIST, *The Structural Revolution*. Weidenfeld and Nicolson, London, 1978.

Max BLACK, "Linguistic Relativity: The Views of Benjamin Lee Whorf" in *Ph.R.* LXVIII (1959), 228-38.

—————, *Models and Metaphors: Studies in Language and Philosophy*. Cornell University Press, Ithaca, New York, 1962.

—————, *The Labyrinth of Language*. Pall Mall Press, London, 1968.

H. J. BLACKHAM, *Six Existentialist Thinkers*. Routledge & Kegan Paul, London, ²1961.

E. C. BLACKMAN, *Biblical Interpretation*. Independent Press, London, 1957.

—————, "New Methods of Parable Interpretation" in *C.J.T.* XV (1969), 3-13.

José Míguez BONINO, *Revolutionary Theology Comes of Age*. Eng. S.P.C.K., London, 1975.

—————, "Theology and Theologians of the New World: II, Latin America" in *Exp.T.* LXXXVII (1976), 196-200.

Pierre BONNARD, *L'épitre de Saint Paul aux Galates*. Delachaux et Niestlé, Neuchâtel, 1953.

G. BORNKAMM, "Faith and Reason in Paul" in *Early Christian Experience*. Eng. S.C.M., London, 1969, pp. 29-46.

—————, *Paul*. Eng. Hodder and Stoughton, London, 1972.

Maurice BOUTIN, *Relationalität als Verstehensprinzip bei Rudolf Bultmann*, Beiträge zur evangelischen Theologie 67. Kaiser, Munich, 1974.

Carl E. BRAATEN, "How New is the New Hermeneutic?" in *Th.T.* XXII (1965), 218-35.

—————, *History and Hermeneutics* (New Directions in Theology Today 2). Lutterworth Press, London, 1968.

Herbert E. BREKLE, *Semantik. Eine Einführung in die sprachwissenschaftlich Bedeutungslehre*. Fink, Munich, 1972.

John BRIGHT, *The Authority of the Old Testament*. S.C.M., London, 1967.

Colin BROWN, *Philosophy and the Christian Faith*. Tyndale Press, London, 1969.

————— ed., *History, Criticism, and Faith*. Inter-Varsity Press, London, 1976.

James BROWN, *Subject and Object in Modern Theology*. S.C.M., London, 1955.

R. L. BROWN, *Wilhelm von Humboldt's Conception of Linguistic Relativity*. Mouton, The Hague, 1967.

Stuart C. BROWN, *Do Religious Claims Make Sense?* S.C.M., London, 1969.

F. F. BRUCE, *I and II Corinthians*. Oliphants, London, 1971.

F. F. BRUCE and E. G. RUPP (eds.), *Holy Book and Holy Tradition*. Manchester University Press, 1968, p. 130.

Karl BÜHLER, *Sprachtheorie. Die Darstellungsfunktion der Sprache*. Fischer, Jena, 1934.

Rudolf BULTMANN, *Der Stil der paulinischen Predigt und die kynische-stoische Diatribe*. Vandenhoeck & Ruprecht, Göttingen, 1910.

—————, "Das Problem der Ethik bei Paulus" in *Z.N.W.* XXIII (1924), 123-40.

—————, "Die Geschichtlichkeit des Daseins und der Glaube: Antwort an Gerhardt Kühlmann" in *Z.Th.K.* N.F. XI (1930), 339-64; Eng. "The Historicity of Man and Faith" in *Existence and Faith*, 107-29.

—————, "Paulus" in *Religion in Geschichte und Gegenwart* 4. Mohr, Tübingen, ²1930, cols. 1019-45; Eng. in *E.F.*, 130-72.

—————, "To Love your Neighbour" in *Scottish Periodical* I (1947), 42-56.

—————, *Jesus*. Mohr, Tübingen, ³1951. Eng. *Jesus and the Word*. Fontana edn., Collins, London, 1958.

—————, "History and Eschatology in the New Testament" in *N.T.S.* I (1954) 5-16.

—————, *Essays Philosophical and Theological* (Eng. of *Glauben und Verstehen* II). S.C.M., London, 1955.

—————, *Theology of the New Testament* (2 vols.). Eng. S.C.M., London, 1952 and 1955.

—————, *History and Eschatology*. Edinburgh University Press, 1957.

—————, "Milestones in Books" in *Exp.T.* LXX (1959), 125.

—————, *Jesus Christ and Mythology*. S.C.M., London, 1960.

—————, *This World and Beyond. Marburg Sermons*. Lutterworth Press, London, 1960.

—————, *The History of the Synoptic Tradition*. Eng. Blackwell, Oxford, 1963.

——————, *Existence and Faith. Shorter Writings of Rudolf Bultmann* (ed. by S. M. Ogden). Eng. Fontana edn., Collins, London, 1964.

——————, "The Significance of the Old Testament for the Christian Faith" in B. W. Anderson (ed.), *The Old Testament and Christian Faith.* S.C.M., London, 1964, pp. 8-35.

——————, *Glauben und Verstehen. Gesammelte Aufsätze* (4 vols.). Mohr, Tübingen, 1964-65.

——————, *Faith and Understanding* I (Eng. of *Glauben und Verstehen* I). S.C.M., London, 1969.

——————, *The Gospel of John. A Commentary.* Eng. Blackwell, Oxford, 1971.

Paul M. van BUREN, *Theological Explorations.* S.C.M., London, 1968.

——————, *The Edges of Language.* S.C.M., London, 1972.

James T. BURTCHAELL, *Catholic Theories of Biblical Inspiration since 1810.* Cambridge University Press, 1969.

Herbert BUTTERFIELD, *Man on his Past. The Study of the History of Historical Scholarship.* Cambridge University Press, 1955.

Henry J. CADBURY, *The Peril of Modernizing Jesus.* Macmillan, 1937; rpt. S.P.C.K., London, 1962.

G. B. CAIRD, "On Deciphering the Book of Revelation: Myth and Legend" in *Exp.T.* LXXIV (1962-63), 103-05.

David CAIRNS, *A Gospel without Myth? Bultmann's Challenge to the Preacher.* S.C.M., London, 1960.

Jean CALLOUD, *Structural Analysis of Narrative.* Fortress Press, Philadelphia, and Scholars Press, Missoula, 1976.

John CALVIN, *The Epistles of Paul the Apostle to the Romans and to the Thessalonians.* Eng. Oliver & Boyd, Edinburgh, 1960.

——————, *The Epistles of Paul the Apostle to the Galatians, Ephesians, Philippians, and Colossians.* Eng. Oliver & Boyd, Edinburgh, 1965.

S. P. CARSE, "Wittgenstein's Lion and Christology" in *Th.T.* XXIV (1967), 148-59.

Ernst CASSIRER, *Language and Myth.* Eng. Harper, New York, 1946.

Charles E. CATON (ed.), *Philosophy and Ordinary Language.* University of Illinois Press, Urbana, 1963.

Stanley CAVELL, "Existentialism and Analytical Philosophy" in *Daedalus* XCIII (1964), 946-74.

——————, "The Availability of Wittgenstein's Later Philosophy" in George Pitcher (ed.), *Wittgenstein. The Philosophical Investigations* (Macmillan, London, 1968), pp. 151-85.

——————, *Must We Mean What We Say?* Cambridge University Press, 1976.

Albert CHAPELLE, *L'ontologie phénoménologique de Heidegger. Un commentaire de "Sein und Zeit."* Editions universitaires, Paris, 1962.

Brevard S. CHILDS, *Myth and Reality in the Old Testament.* S.C.M., London, [2]1962.

——————, *Biblical Theology in Crisis.* The Westminster Press, Philadelphia, 1970.

Hermann COHEN, *Logik der reinen Erkenntniss.* Bruno Cassirer, Berlin, 1902.

R. G. COLLINGWOOD, *An Autobiography.* Oxford University Press, 1939.

——————, *The Idea of History.* Clarendon Press, Oxford, [2]1946; rpt. 1961.

H. CONZELMANN, *An Outline of the Theology of the New Testament*. Eng. S.C.M., London, 1968.

Christopher COOPE et al., *A Wittgenstein Workbook*. Blackwell, Oxford, 1971.

I. M. COPI, "Objects, Properties, and Relations in the *Tractatus*" in I. M. Copi and R. W. Beard (eds.), *Essays on Wittgenstein's Tractatus*. Routledge & Kegan Paul, London, 1966.

John D. CROSSAN, *In Parables. The Challenge of the Historical Jesus*. Harper & Row, New York, 1973.

—————, *The Dark Interval. Towards a Theology of Story*. Argus Communications, Niles, Illinois, 1975.

David CRYSTAL, *Linguistics, Language, and Religion*. Burns & Oates, London, 1965.

N. A. DAHL, *The Crucified Christ and Other Essays*. Augsburg Press, Minneapolis, 1974.

Martin DIBELIUS and Heinrich GREEVEN, *James. A Commentary on the Epistle of James*. Eng. Fortress Press, Philadelphia, 1976.

John DILLENBERGER, "On Broadening the New Hermeneutic" in J. M. Robinson and J. B. Cobb, Jr. (eds.), *New Frontiers in Theology: II, The New Hermeneutic* (cited below).

Wilhelm DILTHEY, *Gesammelte Schriften* (12 vols.). Teubner, Stuttgart, 1962 edn., especially Vol. VII.

Erich DINKLER, "Martin Heidegger" in Carl Michaelson (ed.), *Christianity and the Existentialists*. Scribner, New York, 1956, pp. 97-127.

————— (ed.), *Zeit und Geschichte. Dankesgabe an Rudolf Bultmann zum 80. Geburtstag*. Mohr, Tübingen, 1964.

C. H. DODD, *The Epistle of Paul to the Romans*. Hodder & Stoughton, London, 1932.

—————, *The Parables of the Kingdom*. Nisbet, London, 1936.

William H. DRAY, *Philosophy of History*. Prentice-Hall, Englewood Cliffs, N.J., 1964.

Gerhard EBELING. "Hermeneutik" in *Die Religion in Geschichte und Gegenwart*, 3rd edn. Mohr, Tübingen, III (1959), cols. 242-62.

—————, *The Nature of Faith*. Eng. Collins, London, 1961.

—————, *Word and Faith*. Eng. S.C.M., 1963, especially "Word of God and Hermeneutics," pp. 305-32.

—————, *Theology and Proclamation. A Discussion with Rudolf Bultmann*. Collins, London, 1966.

—————, *God and Word*. Eng. Fortress Press, Philadelphia, 1967.

—————, *The Problem of Historicity in the Church and its Proclamation*. Fortress Press, Philadelphia, 1967.

—————, *The Word of God and Tradition*. Eng. Collins, London, 1968.

—————, "Time and Word" in James M. Robinson (ed.), *The Future of Our Religious Past. Essays in Honour of Rudolf Bultmann*. S.C.M., London, 1971, pp. 247-66; from E. Dinkler (ed.), *Zeit und Geschichte* (cited above), pp. 341-56.

—————, *Luther. An Introduction to his Thought*. Eng. Collins, London, 1972.

—————————, *Introduction to a Theological Theory of Language*. Eng. Collins, London, 1973.

Paul EDWARDS (ed.), *The Encyclopedia of Philosophy*. Macmillan and Free Press, New York, 1967. 8 vols.

Mircea ELIADE, *Myths, Dreams, and Mysteries. The Encounter between Contemporary Faiths and Archaic Reality*. Eng. Fontana Library, Collins, London, 1968.

Paul ENGELMANN, *Letters from Ludwig Wittgenstein. With a Memoir*. Blackwell, Oxford, 1967.

Christopher F. EVANS, *Is 'Holy Scripture' Christian? And Other Questions*. S.C.M., London, 1971.

Donald D. EVANS, *The Logic of Self-Involvement. A Philosophical Study of Everyday Language with Special Reference to the Christian Use of Language about God as Creator*. S.C.M., London, 1963.

K. T. FANN (ed.), *Ludwig Wittgenstein, The Man and his Philosophy*. Delta Books, Dell, New York, 1967.

Frederick W. FARRAR, *History of Interpretation*. Dutton, New York, 1886; rpt. Baker, Grand Rapids, Mich., 1961.

Thomas FAWCETT, *Hebrew Myth and Christian Gospel*. S.C.M., London, 1973.

A. G. N. FLEW and A. MACINTYRE (eds.), *New Essays in Philosophical Theology*. S.C.M., London, 1955.

J. A. FODOR and J. J. KATZ (eds.), *The Structure of Language. Readings in the Philosophy of Language*. Prentice-Hall, Englewood Cliffs, N.J., 1964.

Hans FREI, *The Eclipse of Biblical Narrative. A Study in Eighteenth and Nineteenth Century Hermeneutics*. Yale University Press, New Haven, 1974.

Ernst FUCHS, *Zum hermeneutischen Problem in der Theologie*. Mohr, Tübingen, 1959.

—————————, *Zur Frage nach dem historischen Jesus*. Mohr, Tübingen, 1960. Partly translated as *Studies of the Historical Jesus*. S.C.M., London, 1964.

—————————, "The New Testament and the Hermeneutical Problem" in James M. Robinson and J. B. Cobb, Jr. (eds.), *New Frontiers in Theology: II, The New Hermeneutic*. Harper & Row, New York, 1964, 111-45.

—————————, *Marburger Hermeneutik*. Mohr, Tübingen, 1968.

—————————, *Hermeneutik*. Mohr, Tübingen, ⁴1970.

—————————, "The Hermeneutical Problem" in J. M. Robinson (ed.), *The Future of Our Religious Past. Essays in Honour of Rudolf Bultmann*. S.C.M., London, 1971, pp. 267-78; from E. Dinkler (ed.), *Zeit und Geschichte* (cited above), pp. 357-66.

Robert W. FUNK, "Colloquium on Hermeneutics" in *Th.T.* XXI (1964), 287-306.

—————————, *Language, Hermeneutic and Word of God. The Problem of Language in the New Testament and Contemporary Theology*. Harper & Row, New York, 1966.

—————————, *Jesus as Precursor* (Society of Biblical Literature, *Semeia* Supplement no. 2. Scholars Press, Missoula, and Fortress Press, Philadelphia, 1975.

Hans-Georg GADAMER, "Vom Zirkel des Verstehens" in *Festschrift Martin Heidegger zum siebzigsten Geburtstag*. Neske, Pfullingen, 1959, pp. 24-34.

——————, "Martin Heidegger und die Marburger Theologie" in E. Dinkler (ed.), *Zeit und Geschichte. Dankesgabe an Rudolf Bultmann zum 80. Geburtstag.* Mohr, Tübingen, 1964, pp. 479-90.

——————, *Wahrheit und Methode. Grundzüge einer philosophischen Hermeneutik.* Mohr, Tübingen, ²1965. Eng. *Truth and Method.* Sheed and Ward, London, 1975.

——————, *Kleine Schriften* (4 vols.). Mohr, Tübingen, 1967, 1972, and 1977; Vols. I-III partly translated as *Philosophical Hermeneutics.* University of California Press, Berkeley, 1976.

——————, "The Problem of Language in Schleiermacher's Hermeneutic" in *J.T.C.* VII (1970), 68-95.

——————, "The Power of Reason" in *M.W.* III (1970), 5-15.

——————, "On the Scope and Function of Hermeneutical Reflection" in *Continuum* VIII (1970), 77-95, and in *Philosophical Hermeneutics* (above).

Allan D. GALLOWAY, *Wolfhart Pannenberg.* Allen & Unwin, London, 1973.

Peter GEACH, "The Fallacy of 'Cogito Ergo Sum'," reprinted from *Mental Acts.* Routledge & Kegan Paul, London, 1957 in H. Morick (ed.), *Wittgenstein and the Problem of Other Minds.* McGraw-Hill, New York, 1967, pp. 211-14.

Peter GEACH and Max BLACK (eds.), *Translations from the Philosophical Writings of Gottlob Frege.* Blackwell, Oxford, 1952.

Claude GEFFRÉ, "Bultmann on Kerygma and History" in Thomas F. O'Meara and Donald M. Weisser (eds.), *Rudolf Bultmann in Catholic Thought.* Herder & Herder, New York, 1968.

Ernst GELLNER, *Words and Things.* Pelican edn., London, 1968.

Michael GELVEN, *A Commentary on Heidegger's 'Being and Time'.* Harper & Row, New York, 1970.

A. Boyce GIBSON, *Theism and Empiricism.* S.C.M., London, 1970.

Jerry H. GILL, "Wittgenstein and Religious Language" in *Th.T* XXI (1964), 59-72.

——————, "Saying and Showing: Radical Themes in Wittgenstein's *On Certainty*" in *R.S.* X (1974), 279-90.

Hans Theodor GOEBEL, *Wort Gottes als Auftrag. Zur Theologie von Rudolf Bultmann, Gerhard Ebeling, und Wolfhart Pannenberg.* Neukirchener Verlag, Neukirchen-Vluyn, 1972.

Friedrich GOGARTEN, *Demythologizing and History.* Eng. S.C.M., London, 1955.

Edwin M. GOOD, *Irony in the Old Testament.* S.P.C.K., London, 1965.

Anton GRABNER-HAIDER, *Semiotik und Theologie. Religiöse Rede zwischen analytischer und hermeneutischer Philsophie.* Kösel-Verlag, Münich, 1973.

J. G. GRAY, "Heidegger's Course: From Human Existence to Nature" in *J.Ph.* LIV (1957), 197-207.

Prosper GRECH, "The 'Testimonia' and Modern Hermeneutics" in *N.T.S.* XIX (1973), 318-24.

Marjorie GRENE, *Martin Heidegger.* Bowes & Bowes, London, 1957.

Robert H. GUNDRY, *Sōma in Biblical Theology with Emphasis on Pauline Anthropology.* Cambridge University Press, 1976; S.N.T.S. Monograph 29.

Donald F. GUSTAFSON (ed.), *Essays in Philosophical Psychology*. Anchor Books, Doubleday, New York, 1964.

D. GUTHRIE, *Galatians*. Nelson, London, 1969.

Gustavo GUTIÉRREZ, *A Theology of Liberation*. Eng. Orbis Books, Maryknoll, New York, 1973.

E. GÜTTGEMANNS, *Studia Linguistica Neotestamentica. Gesammelte Aufsätze zur linguistischen Grundlage einer Neutestamentlichen Theologie;* Beiträge zur evangelischen Theologie Bd. 60. Kaiser, Münich, 1971.

P. M. S. HACKER, *Insight and Illusion: Wittgenstein on Philosophy and the Metaphysics of Experience*. Oxford University Press, 1972.

Garth HALLETT, *Wittgenstein's Definition of Meaning as Use*. Fordham University Press, New York, 1967.

E. HALLER, "On the Interpretative Task" in *Int*. XXI (1967), 158-67.

P. P. HALLIE, "Wittgenstein's Grammatical-Empirical Distinction" in *J.Ph*. LX (1963), 565-78.

R. P. C. HANSON, *The Bible as a Norm of Faith*. Durham University Press, 1963.

R. HARRÉ, "Tautologies and the Paradigm-Case Argument" in *Analysis* XIX (1958), 94-96.

Christian HARTLICH and Walter SACHS, *Der Ursprung des Mythosbegriffes in der modernen Bibelwissenschaft*. Mohr, Tübingen, 1952.

Justus HARTNACK, *Wittgenstein and Modern Philosophy*. Eng. Methuen, London, 1965.

Van Austin HARVEY, *The Historian and the Believer. The Morality of Historical Knowledge and Christian Belief*. S.C.M., London, 1967.

John M. HEATON, "Symposium on Saying and Showing in Heidegger and Wittgenstein—III" (with P. McCormick and E. Schaper) in *J.B.S.P*. III (1972), 42-45.

G. W. F. HEGEL, *The Phenomenology of Mind*. Eng. Allen & Unwin, London, ²1964.

Martin HEIDEGGER, *Being and Time*. Eng. Blackwell, Oxford, 1962, rpt. 1973.

_____, *Kant and the Problem of Metaphysics*. Eng. Indiana University Press, Bloomington, 1959, and London, 1962.

_____, *An Introduction to Metaphysics*. Eng. Yale University Press, New Haven, 1959, and London, 1959.

_____, *Existence and Being*. With an introduction by W. Brock. Vision Press, London, ³1968. (including "Hölderlin and the Essence of Poetry").

_____, "The Way Back into the Ground of Metaphysics," English in Walter Kaufmann (ed.), *Existentialism from Dostoevsky to Sartre*. World Publishing Co., Meridian Books, Cleveland and New York, 1956, pp. 206-21.

_____, *Hegel's Concept of Experience*. Eng. Harper & Row, New York, 1970.

_____, *Holzwege*. Klostermann, Frankfurt, 1950.

_____, *Vorträge und Aufsätze*. Neske, Pfullingen, 1954.

_____, *Vom Wesen der Wahrheit*. Klostermann, Frankfurt, 1954, ⁴1961; also reprinted in *Wegmarken* (cited below).

——————, *Unterwegs zur Sprache*. Neske, Pfullingen, ²1960; all but one essay in English in *On the Way to Language*. Harper & Row, New York, 1971.

——————, *Gelassenheit*. Neske, Pfullingen, 1959. Translated into English in *Discourse on Thinking*. Harper & Row, New York, 1966.

——————, *Wegmarken*. Klostermann, Frankfurt am Main, 1967.

——————, *Poetry, Language, and Thought*. Harper & Row, New York, 1971.

——————, *On Time and Being*. Eng. Harper & Row, New York, 1972.

Karl HEIM, *The Transformation of the Scientific World View*. Eng. S.C.M., London, 1953.

C. F. G. HEINRICI, *Der litterarische Charakter der neutestamentliche Schriften*. Durrsche Buchhandlung, Leipzig, 1908.

Paul HELM, "Revealed Propositions and Timeless Truths" in *R.St.* VIII (1972), 127-36.

Ian HENDERSON, *Myth in the New Testament*. S.C.M., London, 1952.

——————, *Rudolf Bultmann*. Carey Kingsgate Press, London, 1965.

R. W. HEPBURN, "Demythologizing and the Problem of Validity" in A. Flew and A. MacIntyre (eds.), *New Essays in Philosophical Theology*. S.C.M., London, 1955, pp. 227-42.

——————, *Christianity and Paradox*. Watts, London, 1958.

Wilhelm HERRMANN, *Die Religion im Verhältnis zum Welterkennen und zur Sittlichkeit*. Niemeyer, Halle, 1879.

——————, *Systematic Theology*. Eng. Allen & Unwin, London, 1927.

——————, *The Communion of the Christian with God Described on the Basis of Luther's Statements*. Eng. S.C.M., London, 1972.

Helen HERVEY, "The Problem of the Model Language-Game in Wittgenstein's Later Philosophy" in *Philosophy* XXXVI (1961), 333-51.

Marcus B. HESTER, *The Meaning of Poetic Metaphor. An Analysis in the Light of Wittgenstein's Claim that Meaning is Use*. Mouton, The Hague, 1967.

Dallas M. HIGH, *Language, Persons and Belief. Studies in Wittgenstein's 'Philosophical Investigations' and Religious Uses of Language*. Oxford University Press, New York, 1967.

E. D. HIRSCH, *Validity in Interpretation*. Yale University Press, New Haven, 1967.

——————, "Current Issues in Theory of Interpretation" in *J.R.* LV (1975), 298-312.

——————, *The Aims of Interpretation*. University of Chicago Press, Chicago and London, 1976.

H. A. HODGES, *Wilhelm Dilthey. An Introduction*. Kegan Paul, Trench, & Trubner, London, 1944.

——————, *The Philosophy of Wilhelm Dilthey*. Routledge & Kegan Paul, London, 1952.

Peter HOMANS, "Psychology and Hermeneutics" in *J.R.* LV (1975), 327-47.

Jasper HOPKINS, "Bultmann on Collingwood's Philosophy of History" in *H.T.R.* LVIII (1965), 227-33.

William HORDERN, *Speaking of God. The Nature and Purpose of Theological Language*. Epworth Press, London, 1965.

Ingvar HORGBY, "The Double Awareness in Heidegger and Wittgenstein" in *Inquiry* II (1959), 235-64.

John HOSPERS, *An Introduction to Philosophical Analysis*. Routledge & Kegan Paul, London, ²1967.

W. Donald HUDSON, *Ludwig Wittgenstein. The Bearing of his Philosophy upon Religious Belief*. Lutterworth Press, London, 1968.

—————, "Some Remarks on Wittgenstein's Account of Religious Belief" in *Royal Institute of Philosophy Lectures II, Talk of God*. Macmillan, London, 1969, 36-51.

Hans JAEGER, *Heidegger und die Sprache*. Francke Verlag, Berne & Münich, 1971.

Allan JANIK and Stephen TOULMIN, *Wittgenstein's Vienna*. Wiedenfeld and Nicolson, London, 1973.

Joachim JEREMIAS, "Paul and James" in *Exp.T*. LXVI (1955), 368-71.

—————, *The Parables of Jesus*. Eng. S.C.M., London, rev. edn. 1963.

—————, *The Central Message of the New Testament*. Eng. S.C.M., London, 1965.

Robert JEWETT, *Paul's Anthropological Terms. A Study of Their Use in Conflict Settings*. Brill, Leiden, 1971.

Roger A. JOHNSON, *The Origins of Demythologizing. Philosophy and Historiography in the Theology of Rudolf Bultmann*. Brill, Leiden, 1974.

Hans JONAS, *Gnosis und spätantiker Geist: II, 1, Von der Mythologie zur mystischen Philosophie*. Vandenhoeck & Ruprecht, Göttingen, 1954 (F.R.L.A.N.T. 45)

—————, "Epilogue: Gnosticism, Existentialism, and Nihilism" in *The Gnostic Religion*. Beacon Press, Boston, ²1963, pp. 320-40.

—————, "Heidegger and Theology" in *R.M.* XVIII (1964), 207-33.

Geraint Vaughan JONES, *Christology and Myth in the New Testament*. Allen & Unwin, London, 1956.

—————, *The Art and Truth of the Parables*. S.P.C.K., London, 1964.

O. R. JONES (ed.), *The Private Language Argument*. Macmillan, London, 1971.

Peter R. JONES, "Biblical Hermeneutics" in *R.E.* LXXII (1975), 139-47.

M. JOOS, "Semantic Axiom Number One" in *Language* XLVIII (1972), 258-65.

Paul Henning JØRGENSEN, *Die Bedeutung des Subjekt-Objektverhältnisses für die Theologie. Der Theo-onto-logische Konflikt mit der Existenzphilosophie*. Theologische Forschung 46. Herbert Reich, Evangelischer Verlag, Hamburg, 1967.

Adolf JÜLICHER, *Die Gleichnisreden Jesu* (2 vols.). Mohr, Tübingen and Freiburg, ²1899.

Eberhard JÜNGEL, *Paulus und Jesus. Eine Untersuchung zur Präzierung der Frage nach dem Ursprung der Christologie*. Mohr, Tübingen, ³1967.

Martin KÄHLER, *The So-Called Historical Jesus and the Historic Biblical Christ*. Eng. ed. by Carl E. Braaten. Fortress Press, Philadelphia, 1964.

Ernst KÄSEMANN, *Leib und Leib Christi*. Mohr, Tübingen, 1933; Beiträge zur historischen Theologie 9.

—————, *New Testament Questions of Today*. Eng. S.C.M., London, 1969.

—————, *Perspectives on Paul*. Eng. S.C.M., London, 1971.

Charles W. KEGLEY (ed.), *The Theology of Rudolf Bultmann*. S.C.M., London, 1966.
Alan KEIGHTLEY, *Wittgenstein, Grammar and God*. Epworth Press, London, 1976.
David H. KELSEY, *The Uses of Scripture in Recent Theology*. S.C.M., London, 1975.
Anthony KENNY, *Wittgenstein*. Penguin Books edn., London, 1975.
F. KERR, "Language as Hermeneutic in the Later Wittgenstein" in *Tijdskrift voor Filosophie* XXVII (1965), 491-520.
R. KIEFFER, *Essais de méthodologie néotestamentaire*. Gleerup, Lund, 1972.
S. KIERKEGAARD, *Concluding Unscientific Postscript to the Philosophical Fragments*. Eng. Princeton University Press, 1941.
————, *Purity of Heart is to Will One Thing*. Eng. Fontana, Collins, London, 1961.
Heinz KIMMERLE, "Hermeneutical Theory or Ontological Hermeneutics" in *J.T.C.* IV (1967), 107-21.
Magda KING, *Heidegger's Philosophy. A Guide to his Basic Thought*. Blackwell, Oxford, 1964.
Andrew KIRK, *The Theology of Liberation in the Latin American Roman Catholic Church Since 1965: An Examination of its Biblical Basis*. Unpublished Ph.D. thesis, University of London, 1975.
————, *Liberation Theology: An Evangelical View From the Third World*. Marshall, Morgan, & Scott, London, 1979.
Theodore KISIEL, "The Happening of Tradition: The Hermeneutics of Gadamer and Heidegger" in *M.W.* II (1969), 358-85.
John KNOX, *Myth and Truth, An Essay on the Language of Faith*. Carey Kingsgate Press, London, 1966.
Peter KREEFT, "Zen in Heidegger's *Gelassenheit*" in *I.P.Q.* XI (1971), 521-45.
W. G. KÜMMEL, *The New Testament. The History of the Interpretation of its Problems*. Eng. S.C.M., London, 1973.
Gerhardt KULHMANN, "Zum theologischen Problem der Existenz: Fragen an Rudolf Bultmann" in *Z.Th.K.* N.F. X (1929), 28-57.
Otto KUSS, *Der Römerbrief* (2 vols. to date). Pustet, Regensburg, ²1963.
G. E. LADD, "Eschatology and the Unity of New Testament Theology" in *Exp.T* LXVIII (1957), 268-73.
Samuel LAEUCHLI, *The Language of Faith. An Introduction to the Semantic Dilemma of the Early Church*. Epworth Press, London, 1965.
L. LANDGREBE, "The Study of Philosophy in Germany. A Reply to Walter Cerf" in *J.Ph.* LIV (1957), 127-31.
Thomas LANGAN, *The Meaning of Heidegger. A Critical Study of an Existentialist Phenomenology*. Routledge & Kegan Paul, London, 1959.
Roger LAPOINTE, "Hermeneutics Today" in *B.T.B.* II (1972), 107-54.
Nicolas LASH, *Change in Focus. A Study of Doctrinal Change and Continuity*. Sheed & Ward, London, 1973.
F. J. LEENHARDT, *The Epistle to the Romans*. Eng. Lutterworth, London, 1961.

G. E. LESSING, "On the Proof of the Spirit and of Power" in H. Chadwick (ed.), *Lessing's Theological Writings*. Black, London, 1956, pp. 51-56.

Hans LIETZMANN, *An die Korinther I-II*. Mohr, Tübingen, 1949.

Eta LINNEMANN, *Parables of Jesus. Introduction and Exposition*. Eng. S.P.C.K., London, 1966.

Bernard J. F. LONERGAN, *Insight. A Study of Human Understanding*. Longmans, Green & Co., London, ²1958.

—————, *Method in Theology*. Darton, Longman & Todd, London, 1972.

Hermann LÜDEMANN, *Die Anthropologie des Apostels Paulus und ihre Stellung innerhalb seiner Heilslehre*. University, Kiel, 1872.

John LYONS, *Introduction to Theoretical Linguistics*. Cambridge University Press, 1968.

John MACQUARRIE, *An Existentialist Theology. A Comparison of Heidegger and Bultmann*. S.C.M., London, 1955; rpt. by Pelican Books, London, 1973.

—————, *The Scope of Demythologizing. Bultmann and his Critics*. S.C.M., London, 1960.

—————, "Modern Issues in Biblical Studies: Christian Existentialism in the New Testament" in *Exp.T*. LXXI (1960), 177-80.

—————, *Studies in Christian Existentialism*. S.C.M., London, 1966.

—————, "Philosophy and Theology in Bultmann's Thought" in C. W. Kegley (ed.), *The Theology of Rudolf Bultmann* (cited above), pp. 127-43.

—————, *God-Talk. An Examination of the Language and Logic of Theology*. S.C.M., London, 1967.

—————, "Heidegger's Earlier and Later Work Compared" in *A.T.R*. XLIX (1967), 3-16.

—————, *Martin Heidegger*. Lutterworth Press, London, 1968.

—————, *Existentialism*. World Publishing Co., New York, 1972; rpt. by Pelican Books, London, 1973.

Rudolf A. MAKKREEL, "Wilhelm Dilthey and the Neo-Kantians" in *J.H.P*. VII (1969), 423-40.

Norman MALCOLM, *Ludwig Wittgenstein. A Memoir*. With G. H. von Wright. Oxford University Press, 1958.

—————, "Wittgenstein, Ludwig Josef Johann" in Paul Edwards (ed.), *The Encyclopedia of Philosophy* (cited above), VIII, 327-40.

—————, "Wittgenstein's *Philosophische Bemerkungen*" in *Ph.R*. LXXVI (1967), 220-29.

André MALET, *The Thought of Rudolf Bultmann*. Eng. Doubleday, New York, 1971.

L. MALEVEZ, *The Christian Message and Myth. The Theology of Rudolf Bultmann*. Eng. S.C.M., London, 1958.

René MARLÉ, *Introduction to Hermeneutics*. Burns & Oates, London, 1967.

A. MASLOW, *A Study in Wittgenstein's Tractatus*. University of California Press, Berkeley, 1961.

P. McCORMICK, E. SCHAPER, and J. M. HEATON, "Symposium on Saying and Sharing in Heidegger and Wittgenstein" in *J.B.S.P*. III (1972), 27-45.

John McGINLEY, "Heidegger's Concern for the Lived-World in his Dasein-Analysis" in *Ph.T*. XVI (1972), 92-116.

Manfred MEZGER, "Preparation for Preaching: the Route from Exegesis to Proclamation" in *J.T.C.* II (1965), 159-79.

Otto MICHEL, *Der Römerbrief.* Vandenhoeck & Ruprecht, Göttingen, ⁴1966.

Giovanni MIEGGE, *Gospel and Myth in the Thought of Rudolf Bultmann.* Eng. Lutterworth Press, London, 1960.

Paul S. MINEAR, "The Cosmology of the Apocalypse" in W. Klassen and G. Snyder (eds.), *Current Issues in New Testament Interpretation.* S.C.M., London, 1962, pp. 23-37.

José Porfirio MIRANDA, *Marx and the Bible. A Critique of the Philosophy of Oppression.* Eng. Orbis Books, Maryknoll, New York, 1974.

C. L. MITTON, *The Epistle of James.* Marshall, Morgan & Scott, London, 1966.

J. MOLTMANN, *Theology of Hope.* Eng. S.C.M., London, 1967.

—————, "Towards a Political Hermeneutics of the Gospel" in *U.S.Q.R.* XXIII (1968), 303-23.

A. L. MOORE, *The Parousia in the New Testament.* Brill, Leiden, 1966.

G. E. MOORE, *Philosophical Papers.* Allen & Unwin, London, 1959.

Robert MORGAN, *The Nature of New Testament Theology.* S.C.M., London, 1973.

Harold MORICK (ed.), *Wittgenstein and the Problem of Other Minds.* McGraw-Hill, New York, 1967.

C. MÜLLER, *Gottes Gerechtigkeit und Gottes Volk.* Vandenhoeck & Ruprecht, Göttingen, 1964.

C. W. K. MUNDLE, *A Critique of Linguistic Philosophy.* Clarendon Press, Oxford, 1970.

Franz MUSSNER, *The Historical Jesus in the Gospel of St. John.* Eng. Herder, Freiburg, and Burns & Oates, London, 1967.

Vernon H. NEUFELD, *The Earliest Christian Confessions.* Brill, Leiden, 1963.

Eugene A. NIDA, "The Implications of Contemporary Linguistics for Biblical Scholarship" in *J.B.L.* XCI (1972), 73-89.

Eugene A. NIDA and Charles R. TABER, *The Theory and Practice of Translation.* Brill, Leiden, 1969.

Dennis E. NINEHAM, "The Use of the Bible in Modern Theology" in *B.J.R.L.* LII (1969), 178-99.

—————, *New Testament Interpretation in an Historical Age* (Ethel M. Wood Lecture). Athlone Press, London, 1976.

—————, *The Use and Abuse of the Bible. A Study of the Bible in an Age of Rapid Cultural Change.* Macmillan, London, 1976.

————— (ed.), *The Church's Use of the Bible Past and Present.* S.P.C.K., London, 1963.

Albrecht OEPKE, *Der Brief des Paulus an die Galater.* Evangelische Verlag, Berlin, ³1964.

Schubert OGDEN, "Bultmann's Project of Demythologization and the Problem of Theology and Philosophy" in *J.R.* XXXVII (1957), 156-73.

—————, *Christ Without Myth. A Study Based on the Theology of Rudolf Bultmann.* Collins, London, 1962.

Heinrich OTT, *Geschichte und Heilsgeschichte in der Theologie Rudolf Bultmanns.* Beiträge zur historischen Theologie 19. Mohr, Tübingen, 1955.

_____, *Denken und Sein. Der Weg Martin Heideggers und der Weg der Theologie*. E.V.Z. Verlag, Zürich, 1959.

_____, "What is Systematic Theology?" in James M. Robinson and John Cobb, Jr. (eds.), *New Frontiers in Theology: I, The Later Heidegger and Theology* (cited below), 77-111.

_____, *Theology and Preaching*. Eng. Lutterworth Press, London, 1965.

David PAILIN, "Lessing's Ditch Revisited: The Problem of Faith and History" in Ronald H. Preston (ed.), *Theology and Change. Essays in Memory of Alan Richardson*. S.C.M., London, 1975, pp. 78-103.

Richard E. PALMER, *Hermeneutics. Interpretation Theory in Schleiermacher, Dilthey, Heidegger, and Gadamer*. Northwestern University Press, Evanston, 1969 (Studies in Phenomenology and Existential Philosophy).

_____, "Towards a Post-Modern Interpretive Self-Awareness" in *J.R.* LV (1975), 313-26.

Wolfhart PANNENBERG, "The Revelation of God in Jesus of Nazareth" in James M. Robinson and John B. Cobb, Jr. (eds.), *New Frontiers in Theology: III, Theology as History* (cited below), 101-33.

_____, *Jesus—God and Man*. Eng. S.C.M., London, 1968.

_____, *Basic Questions in Theology* (3 vols.). Eng. S.C.M., London, 1970, 1971, and 1973.

_____ (ed.), *Revelation as History*. Eng. Sheed & Ward, London, 1969.

H. J. PATON, *The Modern Predicament*. Allen & Unwin, London, 1955.

Daniel PATTE, *Early Jewish Hermeneutic in Palestine*. Scholars Press, University of Montana, 1975.

_____ (ed.), *Semiology and Parables*, Pickwick Press, Pittsburgh, 1976.

_____, *What is Structural Exegesis?* Fortress Press, Philadelphia, 1976.

David PEARS, "Wittgenstein and Austin" in B. Williams and A. Montefiore (eds.), *British Analytical Philosophy*. Routledge & Kegan Paul, London, 1966, pp. 17-39.

_____, *Wittgenstein*. Fontana, Collins, London, 1971.

Norman PERRIN, "The Interpretation of a Biblical Symbol" in *J.R.* LV (1975), 348-70.

_____, *Jesus and the Language of the Kingdom. Symbol and Metaphor in New Testament Interpretation*. S.C.M., London, 1976.

Ted PETERS, "Truth in History: Gadamer's Hermeneutics and Pannenberg's Apologetic Method" in *J.R.* LV (1975), 36-56.

Norman R. PETERSEN, *Literary Criticism for New Testament Critics*. Fortress Press, Philadelphia, 1978.

C. A. van PEURSEN, *Ludwig Wittgenstein: An Introduction to his Philosophy*. Eng. Faber, London, 1969.

D. Z. PHILLIPS, *Faith and Philosophical Inquiry*. Routledge & Kegan Paul, London, 1970.

_____ (ed.), *Religion and Understanding*. Blackwell, Oxford, 1967.

George PITCHER, *The Philosophy of Wittgenstein*. Prentice-Hall, Englewood Cliffs, N.J., 1964.

_____ (ed.), *Wittgenstein: The Philosophical Investigations*. Macmillan, London, 1968.

Otto PÖGGELER, *Der Denkweg Martin Heideggers*. Neske, Pfullingen, 1963.

Blanche I. PREMO, "The Early Wittgenstein and Hermeneutics" in *Ph.T.* XVI (1972), 43-65.

H. H. PRICE, *Belief*. Allen & Unwin, London, 1969.

Karl RAHNER, "Exegesis and Dogmatic Theology" in *Theological Investigations* V. Eng. Darton, Longman, & Todd, London, 1966, 67-93.

Ian T. RAMSEY, *Religious Language. An Empirical Placing of Theological Phrases*. S.C.M., London, 1957.

_____, *Models and Mystery*. Oxford University Press, 1964.

_____, *Christian Discourse. Some Logical Explorations*. Oxford University Press, 1965.

Leopold von RANKE, "Preface to the History of the Latin and Teutonic Nations," translated in Fritz Stern (ed.), *The Varieties of History*. Macmillan, London, ²1970, pp. 55-62.

Rush RHEES, *Discussions of Wittgenstein*. Routledge & Kegan Paul, London, 1970.

Alan RICHARDSON, *The Bible in the Age of Science*. S.C.M., London, 1961.

_____, *History Sacred and Profane*. S.C.M., London, 1964.

John T. E. RICHARDSON, *The Grammar of Justification. An Interpretation of Wittgenstein's Philosophy of Language*. Sussex University Press, and Chatto and Windus, London, 1976.

Peter RICHARDSON, *Israel in the Apostolic Church*. Cambridge University Press, 1969.

William J. RICHARDSON, *Heidegger: Through Phenomenology to Thought*. Martinus Nijhoff, The Hague, 1963.

Paul RICOEUR, *Freud and Philosophy. An Essay on Interpretation*. Eng. Yale University Press, New Haven and London, 1970.

_____, *The Conflict of Interpretations. Essays in Hermeneutics* (ed. by D. Ihde). Northwestern University Press, Evanston, 1974 (Studies in Phenomenology and Existential Philosophy).

_____, "Biblical Hermeneutics" in *Semeia* IV (1975), 29-145.

Georges Van RIET, "Exégèse et Réflexion Philosophique" in G. Thils and R. E. Brown (eds.), *Exégèse et Théologie. Les saintes Écritures et leur interpretation théologique;* Iosepho Coppens III. Duculot, Gembloux, 1968, 1-16.

Robert C. ROBERTS, *Rudolf Bultmann's Theology. A Critical Interpretation*. Eerdmans, Grand Rapids, 1977, S.P.C.K., London, 1977.

James M. ROBINSON, "The Pre-history of Demythologization" in *Int.* XX (1966), 65-77.

_____ (ed.), *The Future of Our Religious Past. Essays in Honour of Rudolf Bultmann*. S.C.M., London, 1971. Part-translation of E. Dinkler (ed.), *Zeit und Geschichte* (cited above).

_____ and John B. Cobb, Jr. (eds.), *New Frontiers in Theology: I, The Later Heidegger and Theology*. Harper & Row, New York, 1963.

_____, *New Frontiers in Theology: II, The New Hermeneutic*. Harper & Row, New York, 1964.

_____, *New Frontiers in Theology: III, Theology as History*. Harper & Row, New York, 1967.

462 BIBLIOGRAPHY

John A. T. ROBINSON, *The Body. A Study in Pauline Theology*. S.C.M., London, 1952.

—————, *The Human Face of God*. S.C.M., London, 1973.

Richard RORTY (ed.), *The Linguistic Turn: Recent Essays in Philosophical Method*. University of Chicago Press, 1967.

Klaus ROSENTHAL, *Die Überwindung des Subjekt-Objekt-Denkens als philosophisches und theologisches Problem*. Forschungen zur systematischen und ökumenischen Theologie Bd. 24. Vandenhoeck & Ruprecht, Göttingen, 1970.

ROYAL INSTITUTE OF PHILOSOPHY LECTURES: *Vol. 2. Talk of God*. Macmillan, London, 1969.

—————: *Vol. 7. Understanding Wittgenstein*. Macmillan, London, 1974.

Lionel RUBINOFF, "Collingwood's Theory of the Relation between Philosophy and History: A New Interpretation" in *J.H.P.* VI (1968), 363-80.

Gilbert RYLE, *The Concept of Mind*. Hutchinson, London, 1949; Penguin Books, 1963.

—————, *Collected Papers* (2 vols.). Hutchinson, London, 1971.

A. SAND, *Der Begriff "Fleisch" in den Paulinischen Haupbriefen*. Pustet, Regensburg, 1967; Biblische Untersuchungen Bd. 2.

W. SANDAY and A. C. HEADLAM, *A Critical and Exegetical Commentary on the Epistle to the Romans*. Clark, Edinburgh, ⁵1902.

E. P. SANDERS, *Paul and Palestinian Judaism*. S.C.M., London, 1977.

Jean-Paul SARTRE, *Being and Nothingness*. Eng. Methuen, London, 1957.

Ferdinand de SAUSSURE, *Cours de linguistique générale*. Édition critique par R. Engler. Harrasowitz, Wiesbaden, 1967. The English translation, *Course in General Linguistics*, Owen, London, 1960, has been the subject of criticism.

John F. A. SAWYER, "Context of Situation and *Sitz im Leben*" in *Proceedings of the Newcastle-upon-Tyne Philosophical Society* I (1967), 137-47.

—————, *Semantics in Biblical Research. New Methods of Defining Hebrew Words for Salvation*. S.C.M., London, 1972.

Edward SCHILLEBEECKX, *The Understanding of Faith. Interpretation and Criticism*. Eng. Sheed & Ward, London, 1974.

F. D. E. SCHLEIERMACHER, *Hermeneutik, nach den Handschriften neu herausgegeben und eingeleitet von Heinz Kimmerle*. Carl Winter, Heidelberg, 1959.

Heinrich SCHLIER, *The Relevance of the New Testament*. Eng. Burns & Oates, London, 1967.

Walter SCHMITHALS, *An Introduction to the Theology of Rudolf Bultmann*. Eng. S.C.M., London, 1968.

Luis ALONSO SCHÖKEL, *The Inspired Word. Scripture in the Light of Language and Literature*. Eng. Burns and Oates, London, 1967.

Albert SCHWEITZER, *The Quest of the Historical Jesus*. Eng. Black, London, 1910.

—————, *The Mysticism of Paul the Apostle*. Eng. Black, London, 1931.

Charles E. SCOTT, "Heidegger Reconsidered: A Response to Professor Jonas" in *H.T.R.* LIX (1966), 175-85.

John R. SEARLE, *Speech Acts. An Essay in the Philosophy of Language.* Cambridge University Press, 1969.

George F. SEFLER, *Language and the World. A Methodological Synthesis Within the Writings of Martin Heidegger and Ludwig Wittgenstein.* Humanities Press, Atlantic Highlands, N.J., 1974.

George Joseph SEIDEL, *Martin Heidegger and the Pre-Socratics. An Introduction to his Thought.* University of Nebraska Press, Lincoln, Neb., 1964.

Beryl SMALLEY, *The Study of the Bible in the Middle Ages.* Blackwell, Oxford, 1952.

James D. SMART, *The Interpretation of Scripture.* S.C.M., London, 1961.

—————, *The Strange Silence of the Bible in the Church. A Study in Hermeneutics.* S.C.M., London, 1970.

Ernst Konrad SPECHT, *The Foundations of Wittgenstein's Late Philosophy.* Eng. Manchester University Press, 1969.

Günter STACHEL, *Die neue Hermeneutik. Ein Überblick.* Kösel-Verlag, Munich, 1960.

Graham N. STANTON, *Jesus of Nazareth in New Testament Preaching.* Cambridge University Press, 1974; S.N.T.S. Monograph 27.

Krister STENDAHL, "Biblical Theology, Contemporary" in *The Interpreter's Dictionary of the Bible,* Abingdon Press, New York, 1962, pp. 418-32.

—————, *Paul Among Jews and Gentiles.* S.C.M., London, 1977.

Erik STENIUS, *Wittgenstein's Tractatus. A Critical Exposition of its Main Lines of Thought.* Blackwell, Oxford, 1960.

Charles L. STEVENSON, "Persuasive Definition" in *Mind* XLVII (1938), 331-50.

H. L. STRACK and P. BILLERBECK, *Kommentar zum Neuen Testament aus Talmud und Midrasch* (6 vols.). Beck, Munich, 1922 onward.

Peter F. STRAWSON, *Individuals. An Essay in Descriptive Metaphysics.* Methuen, London, 1959.

—————, "Critical Notice of Wittgenstein's *Philosophical Investigations*" in Harold Morick (ed.), *Wittgenstein and the Problem of Other Minds.* McGraw-Hill, New York, 1967, pp. 3-42.

P. STUHLMACHER, *Gerechtigkeit Gottes bei Paulus.* Vandenhoeck & Ruprecht, Göttingen, 1965.

—————, *Historical Criticism and Theological Interpretation of Scripture.* Fortress Press, Philadelphia, 1977.

Helmut THIELICKE, "Reflections on Bultmann's Hermeneutic" in *Exp.T.* LXVII (1956), 154-57.

—————, *Offenbarung, Vernunft, und Existenz. Studien zur Religionsphilosophie Lessings.* Gutersloher Verlagshaus, ⁴1957.

—————, *The Evangelical Faith: Vol. I, The Relation of Theology to Modern Thought-Forms.* Eng. Eerdmans, Grand Rapids, Mich. 1974.

Anthony C. THISELTON, "The Parables as Language-Event. Some Comments on Fuchs's Hermeneutics in the Light of Linguistic Philosophy" in *S.J.T.* XXIII (1970), 437-68.

—————, "The Meaning of Σάρξ in I Corinthians 5.5: A Fresh Approach in the Light of Logical and Semantic Factors" in *S.J.T.* XXVI (1973), 204-28.

——————, "The Use of Philosophical Categories in New Testament Hermeneutics" in *The Churchman* LXXXVII (1973), 87-100.

——————, "The Supposed Power of Words in the Biblical Writings" in *J.T.S.* N.S. XXV (1974), 283-99.

——————, *Language, Liturgy, and Meaning* (Grove Liturgical Studies 2). Grove Books, Nottingham, 1975.

——————, "Explain, Interpret *(exēgeomai, hermēneuō)"* and "Flesh *(sarx):* Supplement" in C. Brown (ed.), *The New International Dictionary of New Testament Theology* (3 vols.). Paternoster Press, Exeter, and Zondervan, Grand Rapids, Mich. 1975-78, I, 573-84 and 678-82.

——————, "The Parousia in Modern Theology. Some Questions and Comments" in *T.B.* XXVII (1976), 27-54.

——————, "The Semantics of Biblical Language as an Aspect of Hermeneutics" in *Faith and Thought* CIII (1976), 108-20.

——————, "Semantics and New Testament Interpretation" in I. H. Marshall (ed.), *New Testament Interpretation.* Paternoster Press, Exeter, and Eerdmans, Grand Rapids, Mich., 1977, pp. 75-104.

——————, "The New Hermeneutic" in *ibid.,* pp. 308-333.

——————, "Realized Eschatology at Corinth" in *N.T.S.* XXIV (1978), 510-26.

——————, "Truth *(Alētheia)"* in C. Brown (ed.), *The New International Dictionary of New Testament Theology* III (1978), 874-902.

——————, "Word *(Logos):* Language and Meaning in Religion" in *ibid.,* pp. 1123-43.

——————, "Structuralism and Biblical Studies: Method or Ideology?" in *Exp.T.* LXXXIX (1978), 329-35.

Paul TILLICH, "Existential Philosophy" in *J.H.I.* V (1944), 44-68.

——————, *Theology and Culture.* Galaxy Books, New York, 1964.

James TORRANCE, "Interpretation and Understanding in Schleiermacher's Theology: Some Critical Questions" in *S.J.T.* XXI (1968), 268-82.

Thomas F. TORRANCE, "Hermeneutics according to F. D. E. Schleiermacher" in *S.J.T.* XXI (1968), 257-67.

——————, *Theological Science.* Oxford University Press, London, 1969.

——————, *God and Rationality.* Oxford University Press, London, 1971.

Ernst TROELTSCH, "Historiography," reprinted from James Hastings (ed.), *Encyclopedia of Religion and Ethics* VI (1913), 716-23 in John Macquarrie (ed.), *Contemporary Religious Thinkers.* S.C.M., London, 1968, pp. 76-97.

——————, *Die Bedeutung der Geschichtlichkeit Jesus für den Glauben.* Mohr, Tübingen, 1929.

E. Frank TUPPER, *The Theology of Wolfhart Pannenberg.* S.C.M., London, 1974.

Geoffrey TURNER, "Pre-understanding and New Testament Interpretation" in *S.J.T.* XXVIII (1975), 227-42.

Howard N. TUTTLE, *Wilhelm Dilthey's Philosophy of Historical Understanding. A Critical Analysis.* Brill, Leiden, 1969.

Stephen ULLMANN, *The Principles of Semantics.* Blackwell, Oxford, ²1957.

W. M. URBAN, *Language and Reality. The Philosophy of Language and the Principles of Symbolism.* Allen & Unwin, London, 1939.

Cornelius VAN TIL, *The Defense of the Faith*. Presbyterian & Reformed Publishing Co., Philadelphia, 1955.

L. VERSÉNYI, *Heidegger, Being, and Truth*. Yale University Press, New Haven, 1965.

Dan Otto VIA, Jr., *The Parables. Their Literary and Existential Dimension*. Fortress Press, Philadelphia, 1967.

Vincent VYCINAS, *Earth and Gods. An Introduction to the Philosophy of Martin Heidegger*. Nijhoff, The Hague, 1961.

A. de WAELHENS, *La Philosophie de Martin Heidegger*. Université Catholique de Louvain; éditions de l'institut superieur de philosophie. Louvain, 1942.

F. WAISMANN, *The Principles of Linguistic Philosophy*. Macmillan, London, 1965.

_____, *Ludwig Wittgenstein und der Wiener Kreis*. Blackwell, Oxford, 1967.

W. H. WALSH, *An Introduction to Philosophy of History*. Hutchinson, London, 1951.

J. C. WEBER, "Language-Event and Christian Faith" in *Th.T.* XXI (1965), 448-57.

J. WEISS, "Beiträge zur paulinischen Rhetorik" in *Theologische Studien*. Bernhard Weiss, Vandenhoeck & Ruprecht, Göttingen, 1897, pp. 165-247.

Merold WESTPHAL, "Hegel, Pannenberg, and Hermeneutics" in *M.W.* IV (1971), 276-93.

Philip WHEELWRIGHT, *The Burning Fountain*. Indiana University Press, Bloomington, 1954.

_____, *Metaphor and Reality*. Indiana University Press, Bloomington, 1962.

B. L. WHORF, *Language, Thought, and Reality: Selected Writings of Benjamin Lee Whorf* (ed. by J. B. Carroll). M.I.T. Press, Cambridge, Mass., 1956.

Amos N. WILDER, *Early Christian Rhetoric. The Language of the Gospel*. S.C.M., London, 1964.

M. F. WILES et al., *Christian Believing. A Report by the Doctrine Commission of the Church of England*. S.P.C.K., London, 1976.

John WILKINSON, *Interpretation and Community*. Macmillan, London, 1963.

Peter WINCH, "Understanding a Primitive Society" in D. Z. Phillips (ed.), *Religion and Understanding*. Blackwell, Oxford, 1967, pp. 9-42.

_____ (ed.), *Studies in the Philosophy of Wittgenstein*. Routledge & Kegan Paul, London, 1969.

Gustaf WINGREN, *Theology in Conflict: Nygren, Barth, Bultmann*. Eng. Oliver & Boyd, Edinburgh, 1958.

Walter WINK, *The Bible in Human Transformation. Toward a New Paradigm for Biblical Study*. Fortress Press, Philadelphia, 1973.

Ludwig WITTGENSTEIN, *Notebooks 1914-1916*. Eng. Blackwell, Oxford, 1961.

_____, *Tractatus Logico-Philosophicus*. Germ. and Eng. Routledge & Kegan Paul, London, 1961.

_____, "Some Remarks on Logical Form" in *P.A.S.S.* IX (1929), 162-71.

_____, "A Lecture on Ethics" (1929) in *Ph.R.* LXXIV (1965), 3-26.

_____, *Philosophische Bemerkungen* (1929-30). Blackwell, Oxford, 1964.

——————, "Wittgenstein's Lectures in 1930-33" in G. E. Moore, *Philosophical Papers* (cited above), pp. 252-324.

——————, *Philosophical Grammar* (1929-34). Blackwell, Oxford, 1974.

——————, *Letters to Russell, Keynes, and Moore.* Blackwell, Oxford, 1974.

——————, *The Blue and Brown Books: Preliminary Studies for the "Philosophical Investigations."* Blackwell, Oxford, 1958, [2]1969 (dictated 1933-35).

——————, "On Continuity: Wittgenstein's Ideas, 1938." Notes included in Rush Rhees, *Discussion of Wittgenstein* (cited above), pp. 104-57.

——————, *Remarks on the Foundations of Mathematics* (1937-44), Germ. and Eng. Blackwell, Oxford, 1956.

——————, *Philosophical Investigations* (1936-49). Germ. and Eng. Blackwell, Oxford, [3]1967.

——————, *Lectures and Conversations on Aesthetics, Psychology and Religious Belief* (1938 and 1942-46). Blackwell, Oxford, 1966.

——————, *Zettel* (mainly 1945-48). Germ. and Eng. Blackwell, Oxford, 1967.

——————, "Bemerkungen über Frazers *The Golden Bough*" in *Synthese* XVII (1967), 233-53 (probably after 1948).

——————, *On Certainty* (1950-51). Germ. and Eng. Blackwell, Oxford, 1969.

James D. WOOD, *The Interpretation of the Bible. A Historical Introduction.* Duckworth, London, 1958.

Norman J. YOUNG, *History and Existential Theology. The Role of History in the Thought of Rudolf Bultmann.* Westminster Press, Philadelphia, 1969.

J. A. ZIESLER, *The Meaning of Righteousness in Paul.* Cambridge University Press, 1972.

Indexes

Subjects

Presence-at-hand, 152–68, 176–81, 188
"Present" meaning, 10, 54, 60–63, 181–87, 205–12, 234–45, 252–92. See also hermeneutics, understanding, historical distance, horizon, fusion of horizons.
Pre-Socratic thinkers, 144, 150, 151, 337
Presuppositions, 9, 27–33, 54, 105, 108–10, 147, 163–68, 236–38, 297–99, 434–36, 439. See pre-understanding.
Pre-understanding, 16–19, 59–60, 103–14, 133–39, 194–97, 226, 231, 236–39, 283–84, 303–10, 315, 439, 442. See also hermeneutical circle.
Private language, 286–87, 379–85, 442, 444. See public criteria of meaning.
Process, interpretation as, 166, 305
Proclamation. See preaching.
Projection, 163, 184, 363–66
Propositions, 96–97, 166–68, 195, 196, 263–64, 313–14, 354, 359–70, 419–21, 433–37, 443
Psychology, 105, 192
Public criteria of meaning, 39–40, 233, 361, 379–85, 442, 444. See private language.
Public tradition, 40, 382. See public criteria of meaning.
Purist approach, 8
Puzzle picture, 417

Questions, questioning, 104–14, 133–34, 166–68, 226, 237–39, 242, 309–10, 313–14, 340, 370–71, 398–400. See also pre-understanding, hermeneutical circle.
Qumran, 19, 412

Rationality. See reason.
Rationalism, 183
Ready-to-hand (zuhanden), 152–68, 188
Reason, rationality, 65, 90–92, 199–200, 228–34, 294–300, 396–400
Recommendations, linguistic, 401–07
Redemption, 382
Reference, referential theory of meaning, 121–24

Reformation, reformers, 59, 100, 115, 214–16, 300, 316–19, 355. See Luther and Calvin.
Re-interpretation, 98–101, 298–99, 309. See hermeneutics.
Relativity. See historical relativism.
Repetition, 67, 98–101, 131, 150, 299, 307–10
Representations, representational form, 209, 365
Reproduction. See repetition.
Resurrection of Jesus Christ, 75, 271–75
Revelation, 175, 228, 240
"Reversal" in Heidegger, 187, 327–30
Righteousness, 406. See justification.
Rules of hermeneutics, 10, 11, 107
Rules of language, 379–83

Sachkritik, 266, 274, 290, 410, 442
Sacrifice, 270
Salvation-history, 56, 77, 120. See Geschichte, history.
Satire, 426
"Scaffolding of our thought," 74, 174, 361, 392, 395, 400
Science, sciences, 37, 158–60, 188, 207–11, 294–96, 312, 331–33, 360, 369, 372, 406
Scientific objectivity, 27, 158–61, 207–11. See objectivity.
Secularization, 435
Security, 178, 204. See authentic existence, justification.
Seeing as, 165–66, 402, 415–22
Self, 183, 203. See individual, Dasein, finitude, person.
Self-involvement, logic of, 40, 238, 269, 289, 292
Self-understanding, 176, 232, 237–38, 245, 292
Semantics, 8, 117–39, 440
Semiotics, 122
Sensations, 381–82
Sense and reference, 122–23
Sensus communis, 294–95
Sensus plenior, 20, 296–97
Septuagint, 100
Settings. See form criticism, context, language-game.
Showing (v. saying), 368–70, 399

161–69, 235–40, 294–314, 343–45, *368–70,* 388, 398, 399, 400
Universal. See topic-neutral.
Universal hermeneutics   313–14
Universal history,   66, 77, 83, 302. See history.
Use in language, use and meaning, 129, 133, 138, 310–12, *360–62, 374–78,* 381. See language-game.

Vagueness,   138. See ambiguity, propositions.
Value,   39, 64, 69, 75, 223, 247, 359–60, 368–70, 385, 419. See also ethics, dualism, Neo-Kantianism.
Verdict, verdictive logic,   419–21
Verstehen. See understanding.
Vienna Circle,   358
Vorhandenheit. See presence-at-hand.
Vorverständnis. See pre-understanding.

Western language-tradition,   327–35
Western philosophy,   148, 332–35. See philosophy.
Whorf hypothesis,   *133–39,* 440.
Wisdom literature,   397, 399
Wonder,   342, 369
Word,   128–29, 136–38, 312
Word-event. See language-event.
Word-magic,   337, 443
Word of God, *85–90,* 98–103, *223–26,* 316, 319, *432–38.* See also preaching, theology.
World, Worldhood,   30, 32, 44, 105, 145, 150, *154–61, 187–91, 297–99,* 312, 338, *343–47,* 366, 369–70, 378, 440–41
World-view,   133–39, 158–59, 230, *252–68,* 312. See science, myth, historical relativism.

Zen Buddhism,   341–42

Names

Principal discussions are in italics.

Achtemeier, P. J.   10, 41, 42, 346
Acton, Lord   71
Albright, W. F.   288
Allen, E. L.   146
Alston, W. P.   353
Amiot, F.   417
Anscombe, G. E. M.   364, 365, 366, 408
Apel, K. O.   34, 357–58, 361, 379
Aquinas, Thomas   261
Aristotle   154, 294, 312, 411
Assmann, H.   111
Ast, F.   103
Austin, J. L.   127, 135, 269, 337, 354, 355, 437
Ayer, A. J.   359, 369, 379, 401

Bambrough, R.   371
Barbour, I.   406
Barfield, O.   350

Barr, J.   8–9, 58, 97, 117, *124–29, 133–36,* 138, 311, 433, 440
Barrett, C. K.   143, 265, 389, 391, 394, 401, 419, 435
Barrett, W.   334
Barth, K.   20, 25, 32, 56, 66, *88–90,* 109, 130, 206, 208, 212, 214, 216, 224, 226, 233, 234, 272, *315–18,* 320, 322, 324,. 326
Bartok, B.   151
Bartsch, H.-W.   89
Baur, F. C.   279
Beasley-Murray, G. R.   288
Beintker, M.   207
Bell, R. H.   372
Benn, G.   334
Bergson, H.   192, 295, 303
Berkeley, G.   189
Betti, E.   28, 293, 308
Black, M.   129, 137, 353, 365, 370
Blackham, H. J.   143, 158, 188
Blackman, E. C.   10

Biblical References

Genesis		**Hosea**	
3:1–15, 23, 24	98, 224	6:3, 4	298
15:2–18	401		
15:6	389, 423	**Amos**	
42:16	411	2	298
		8:3	118
Exodus			
3:6	385	**Jonah**	
18:21	411	1:3, 9, 12	426
		2:1–9	426
Judges		4:3, 10, 11	426
3	298		
		Tobit	
2 Samuel		7:10	412
11:12	298		
19:44	14	**Wisdom**	
		12:12–18	394
2 Kings			
22:7	412	**Ecclesiasticus**	
		1:22	398
Psalms			
2	18	**1 Enoch**	
8:6	316	32:1, 3	98
25:10	412	61:1	98
37:24	106		
45:4	412	**1 QS**	
45:8	14	1:15	412
73	98	3:24	412
110	18	4:20, 21	412
		6:15	412
Proverbs		11:12	419
12:19	411		
14:24	398	**Matthew**	
18:2	397	5:14	132
23:23	412	5:15	316
		5:33, 38, 43	435
Isaiah		11:6	346
14	99	13:30	316
45:9	394	16:18	128
55:10, 11	101	20:1–16	191, 345, 351
		22:1–10	350, 352
Jeremiah		24:27	97
1:9, 10	101	25:1–13	351
5:14	101	25:10	97
18:1	394	25:14–30	6, 351
23:29	101	25:31–46	324
Daniel		**Mark**	
6:10	419	2:5	132

2:18, 19	222
14:62	263
Luke	
4:33–34	254
8:27–28	254
9:39–40	254
10:18, 23, 24	222
10:29–37	350, 351
11:20	254
13:11	131
14:7–11	352
14:16–24	350
15:11–32	6, 349, 351, 352
15:35–44	254
16:1–9	351
16:19–31	352
17:30	249
18:9–14	12–15, 352
22:3	131
22:42	132
24:25–27	17
24:39–43	272
John	
1:4–9	97
1:9	413
3:19	265
4:9	352
4:18	412
4:23, 24, 37	413
5:31, 32	413
6:32, 55	413
6:69	267
8:44, 45	413
9:5	97
10:33, 36	352
10:41	412
12:31	265
14:6, 16, 17	413
15:1	413
15:26	413
16:13	413
Acts	
2:22	268
17:31	264, 268, 272

Ancient Non-biblical References